Team Effectiveness in Complex Organizations

Cross-Disciplinary Perspectives and Approaches

Team Effectiveness in Complex Organizations

Cross-Disciplinary Perspectives and Approaches

Edited by

Eduardo Salas • Gerald F. Goodwin • C. Shawn Burke

Routledge
Taylor & Francis Group
New York   London

Routledge
Taylor & Francis Group
711 Third Avenue,
New York, NY 10017

Routledge
Taylor & Francis Group
27 Church Road
Hove, East Sussex BN3 2FA

© 2009 by Taylor & Francis Group, LLC
Routledge is an imprint of Taylor & Francis Group, an Informa business

Transferred to digital print 2012

First issued in paperback 2012

International Standard Book Number-13: 978-0-8058-5881-5 (Hardcover) 978-0-415-65435-7 (Paperback)

Except as permitted under U.S. Copyright Law, no part of this book may be reprinted, reproduced, transmitted, or utilized in any form by any electronic, mechanical, or other means, now known or hereafter
invented, including photocopying, microfilming, and recording, or in any information storage or retrieval
system, without written permission from the publishers.

Trademark Notice: Product or corporate names may be trademarks or registered trademarks, and are
used only for identification and explanation without intent to infringe.

Library of Congress Cataloging-in-Publication Data

Team effectiveness in complex organizations : cross-disciplinary perspectives and
    approaches / [edited by] Eduardo Salas, Gerald F. Goodwin, and C. Shawn Burke.
        p. cm.
    ISBN 978-0-8058-5881-5 (hbk.) -- ISBN 978-0-203-88931-2 (e-book)
    1. Teams in the workplace. 2. Organizational effectiveness. 3. Employees--Training
of. I. Salas, Eduardo. II. Goodwin, Gerald F. III. Burke, C. Shawn.

HD66.T4234 2008
658.4'022--dc22   2008019691

Visit the Taylor & Francis Web site at
http://www.taylorandfrancis.com

The Organizational Frontiers Series

The Organizational Frontiers Series is sponsored by The Society for Industrial and Organizational Psychology (SIOP). Launched in 1983 to make scientific contributions to the field, the series has attempted to publish books on cutting edge theory, research, and theory-driven practice in Industrial/Organizational psychology and related organizational science disciplines.

Our overall objective is to inform and to stimulate research for SIOP members (students, practitioners, and researchers) and people in related disciplines including the other subdisciplines of psychology, organizational behavior, human resource management, and labor and industrial relations. The volumes in the Organizational Frontiers Series have the following goals:

1) Focus on research and theory in organizational science, and the implications for practice.
2) Inform readers of significant advances in theory and research in psychology and related disciplines that are relevant to our research and practice.
3) Challenge the research and practice community to develop and adapt new ideas and to conduct research on these developments.
4) Promote the use of scientific knowledge in the solution of public policy issues and increased organizational effectiveness.

The volumes originated in the hope that they would facilitate continuous learning and a continuing research curiosity about organizational phenomena on the part of both scientists and practitioners.

The Organizational Frontiers Series

SERIES EDITOR

Robert D. Pritchard
University of Central Florida

EDITORIAL BOARD

Walter Borman
Personnel Decisions Research Institutes and University of South Florida

Adrienne Colella
Tulane University

Michele Gelfand
University of Maryland

Steve Kozlowski
Michigan State University

Eduardo Salas
University of Central Florida

Michael West
Aston University

SIOP Organizational Frontiers Series

Series Editor
ROBERT D. PRITCHARD
University of Central Florida

Salas/Goodwin/Burke: (2008) *Team Effectiveness in Complex Organizations: Cross-Disciplinary Perspectives and Approaches*

Kanfer/Chen/Pritchard: (2008) *Work Motivation: Past, Present and Future*

De Dreu/Gelfand: (2008) *The Psychology of Conflict and Conflict Management in Organizations*

Ostroff/Judge: (2007) *Perspectives on Organizational Fit*

Baum/Frese/Baron: (2007) *The Psychology of Entrepreneurship*

Weekley/Ployhart: (2006) *Situational Judgment Tests: Theory, Measurement and Application*

Dipboye/Colella: (2005) *Discrimination at Work: The Psychological and Organizational Bases.*

Griffin/O'Leary-Kelly: (2004) *The Dark Side of Organizational Behavior.*

Hofmann/Tetrick: (2003) *Health and Safety in Organizations.*

Jackson/Hitt/DeNisi: (2003) *Managing Knowledge for Sustained Competitive Knowledge.*

Barrick/Ryan: (2003) *Personality and Work.*

Lord/Klimoski/Kanfer: (2002) *Emotions in the Workplace.*

Drasgow/Schmitt: (2002) *Measuring and Analyzing Behavior in Organizations.*

Feldman: (2002) *Work Careers.*

Zaccaro/Klimoski: (2001) *The Nature of Organizational Leadership.*

Rynes/Gerhart: (2000) *Compensation in Organizations.*

Klein/Kozlowski: (2000) *Multilevel Theory, Research and Methods in Organizations.*

Ilgen/Pulakos: (1999) *The Changing Nature of Performance.*

Earley/Erez: (1997) *New Perspectives on International I-O Psychology.*

Murphy: (1996) *Individual Differences and Behavior in Organizations.*

Guzzo/Salas: (1995) *Team Effectiveness and Decision Making.*

Howard: (1995) *The Changing Nature of Work.*

Schmitt/Borman: (1993) *Personnel Selection in Organizations.*

Zedeck: (1991) *Work, Families and Organizations.*

Schneider: (1990) *Organizational Culture and Climate.*

Goldstein: (1989) *Training and Development in Organizations.*

Campbell/Campbell: (1988) *Productivity in Organizations.*

Hall: (1987) *Career Development in Organizations.*

Contents

Section I   Setting the Stage

Section II   Cross-Disciplinary Theoretical Approaches

Section III   Measurement Tools

Section IV   Methodological Tools and Developments

Section V   Commentaries and Summary: A Look Ahead

Series Foreword

This is the twenty-eighth book in the Organizational Frontiers Series of books. The overall purpose of the Series volumes is to promote the scientific status of the field. Ray Katzell first edited the series. He was followed by Irwin Goldstein, Sheldon Zedeck, and Neal Schmitt. The topics of the volumes and the volume editors are chosen by the editorial board or individuals propose volumes to the editorial board. The series editor and the editorial board then work with the volume editor(s) in planning the volume.

The success of the series is evident in the high number of sales (now over 50,000). Volumes have also received excellent reviews and individual chapters as well as volumes have been cited frequently.

This volume, edited by Eduardo Salas, Gerald F. Goodwin and C. Shawn Burke, is important because it presents current thinking and research on the effectiveness of teams. Teamwork has become an increasingly important part of work in all types of organizations both in the U.S. and internationally. At the same time, forming, developing, and supporting team effectiveness present unique challenges.

This volume is a major synthesis of the new research and thinking on teams and thus updates what is known in this important area. This is an update of the Frontier Series Guzzo & Salas (1995) volume. This new volume has a number of strengths. One is the multidisciplinary theme of the book. There are many theories, principles and tools that have been developed, so a science of team effectiveness is emerging. The editors and authors bring these broader perspectives to the attention of I/O Psychologists. Finally, the authors do a very nice job of identifying research needs that should have a significant impact on teams research for years to come. The editors and authors have indeed provided inspiration for researchers to explore beyond our self-set boundaries and have provided the impetus to engage in a broader set of challenges with a wider range of multi-disciplinary approaches.

The editors and chapter authors deserve our gratitude for clearly communicating the nature, application, and implications of the theory and research described in this book. Production of a volume such as this involves the hard work and cooperative effort of many individuals. The editors, the chapter authors, and the editorial board all played important roles in this endeavor. As all royalties from the series volumes are used to help support SIOP, none of the editors or authors received any remuneration. The editors and authors deserve our appreciation for engaging a difficult task for the sole purpose of furthering our understanding of

Team Effectiveness in Complex Organizations

organizational science. We also want to express our gratitude to Anne Duffy, our editor at LEA/Psychology Press, who has been a great help in the planning and production of the volume.

June 16, 2008

Robert D. Pritchard
University of Central Florida
Series Editor

Preface

Teams and work groups continue to be a significant asset to organizations. Industrial, military, and governmental organizations employ teams as a means to tackle difficult, interdependent, stressful, and complex tasks. Teams and work groups have become a way of life in organizations, and the science of team performance has kept up with the wide interest in these work forms. Many theories, principles, tips, methodologies, tools, and lessons have now been learned to help manage and develop teams and work groups. While we do not yet have all the answers about team and work group effectiveness, much progress has been made. However, as is often the case in such complex domains, much remains to be done.

The good news is that more disciplines are now involved in and contributing to understanding team effectiveness; the field is now multidisciplinary. That is, no single discipline in social science "owns" the field. For example, social, industrial/organizational, cognitive, military, human factors, and clinical psychologists are presently researching team effectiveness in organizations. The field has really evolved to a true multidisciplinary endeavor to include cognitive science, communications, computer science, mathematics, modeling, engineering, and medicine. While this multidisciplinarity is exciting, there tends to be lack of integration across disciplines, partly driven by the fact that each discipline tends to view the world from an ethnocentric manner focusing fairly narrowly on its piece of the "team effectiveness pie."

The goal of this book is to draw together the many disciplines to share perspectives and engage in a dialogue on how to better understand team effectiveness in organizations from their own perspectives and paradigms. We have sought to create a volume where many of the relevant disciplines are represented. In doing so, we hope to show industrial/organizational psychologists the research findings, theories, and methodologies from other related disciplines. Second, it is our hope that this will begin to bridge the gaps between disciplines, fostering intradisciplinary collaborations, and in turn making for a stronger science of team effectiveness. Finally, it has been over 10 years since the last SIOP Organizational Frontier volume on teams was put forth (see Guzzo & Salas, 1995). Since that time there have been substantial advances in the team research.

In gathering together contributors for this volume, two primary themes served to shape the chapters and the research agenda on team effectiveness in organizations. The first organizing theme centers on the cross and multidisciplinary nature of the work. The importance of this theme is seen in the chapters that compose Section 1 of the volume. Later sections expand on this theme by containing shared views, theories, methodologies, and research paradigms represented from social, human factors, military, and cognitive psychology, as well as industrial/organizational psychology. The volume also seeks to represent other disciplines studying teams and work groups such as cognitive engineering, computational modeling, simulation, organizational science, and social networking. In this fashion, we seek to represent (as much as possible) the diversity of team problems, types, and issues that organizations face.

The second organizing theme surrounding the volume concerns new issues, thinking or development in theories, methodologies or research paradigms—given the nature of team dynamics in organizations. For example, within Section 2, new, emerging, or extensions of theories and conceptual frameworks in work groups, teams, and multiteams are represented. Similarly, the chapters contained within Sections 3 and 4 represent new thinking or development in methodologies for assessing, capturing, recording, or interpreting the dynamic nature of team performance in organizations. Methodologies from social network analysis to dynamic assessment to computational modeling are represented within these sections.

Eduardo Salas
University of Central Florida

Gerald F. Goodwin
Army Research Institute

C. Shawn Burke
University of Central Florida

Acknowledgments

We would like to thank the Army Research Institute's Leader Development Research Unit, under the leadership of Stan Halpin, for its support in making much of what is in this volume. We are also grateful to Bob Pritchard, editor of the Organizational Frontier Series, for his encouragement and support in developing this volume. Finally, we thank all the authors for their contributions, ideas, and patience. We hope the book encourages more research and, in turn, causes the science of team performance to continue to evolve and mature.

Author Biographies

ALEXANDER ALONSO is senior research scientist at the American Institutes for Research. For more than 10 years his research interests have focused on the performance of multiteam systems in high-risk environments like the military and health care. Dr. Alonso has published or presented more than 40 papers on his work. Dr. Alonso is a member of the Human Factors and Ergonomics Society and the Society for Industrial and Organizational Psychology (SIOP) and also serves on the board of directors for the Society for Human Performance in Extreme Environments (HPEE). In 2007, he was part of a team awarded the M. Scott Myers Award for Applied Research in the Workplace by the SIOP for their work on training health-care teams. He holds a Ph.D. in industrial and organizational psychology from Florida International University.

DAVID P. BAKER is principal research scientist at the American Institutes for Research. He also holds a secondary appointment at the Carilion Clinic where he serves as director of the Center for Clinical Outcomes and Heath Service Research. For more than 15 years his research interests have focused on the performance of team in high-risk environments like aviation, the military, and health care. Dr. Baker has published or presented more than 75 papers on his work. Dr. Baker is a member of the American Psychological Association and the Human Factors and Ergonomics Society and serves on the editorial board of *Human Factors*. In 2007, he and his team were awarded the M. Scott Meyers Award for Applied Research in the Workplace by the Society for Industrial and Organizational Psychology for their work on training health-care teams. He holds a Ph.D. in industrial and organizational psychology from the University of South Florida.

JOSEPH V. BARANSKI is a defense scientist and head of the Collaborative Performance and Learning Section at Defence Research and Development Canada–Toronto. He received his Ph.D. in cognitive psychology in 1992 from Carleton University in Ottawa, Canada. His research interests include individual and team decision making and confidence with applications to military integrated operations, network enabled operations, and C2.

BENJAMIN BELL is interested in the application of artificial intelligence to simulation, training, and performance support environments. He has practiced in the field of artificial intelligence for more than 20 years, focusing on conceptualizing, designing, and directing research and tool development in applied settings, particularly for military applications. He holds a Ph.D. in artificial intelligence from Northwestern University, master's degrees from Embry Riddle and Drexel, and a B.S.E. from the University of Pennsylvania. Dr. Bell has extensive experience in developing computational models of learning and cognition, knowledge representation and abstraction, and software design and implementation. He has led academic and industry research teams in advanced training methodologies and technologies and has numerous refereed publications on scenario-based approaches to training, human decision making, and operator/crew performance modeling. Dr. Bell's interest in team modeling and team cognition has given rise to recent research efforts supported by the Defense Advanced Research Projects Agency (DARPA), the U.S. Air Force Research Laboratories (AFRL), and the Office of Naval Research (ONR), among others.

CAROL BLENDELL received a B.A. (Hons) degree in sociology with psychology from the University of Greenwich in London, in 1996 and a postgraduate diploma in psychology from Open University in Milton Keynes, England, in 2000. In 2007 she was awarded an M.Sc. with Merit in forensic psychology from London Metropolitan University. From 1997 to 2006, Ms. Blendell was senior consultant psychologist with QinetiQ Ltd. in Farnborough, England, and its forerunner Defence Evaluation Research Agency (DERA). Her main area of interest was team effectiveness, which included distributed and ad hoc teams and the design and evaluation of computer tools to support teamwork. From 2001 to 2005, she was the U.K. representative on a NATO team effectiveness panel. Carol is currently an analyst with the Defence Science and Technology Laboratory, an agency of the Ministry of Defence, and brings human factors to the operational analyst community.

ISABEL C. BOTERO is assistant professor in the School of Communication at Illinois State University. She received her Ph.D. in communications from Michigan State University in 2005. Her research interests include understanding dynamic functions and communication behaviors of leaders in teams, perceptions of justice in work teams and their effects on member communicative behaviors of team members, and voice and silence as information-sharing mechanisms in the organization.

C. SHAWN BURKE is research scientist at the Institute for Simulation and Training at the University of Central Florida. Her expertise includes teams and their leadership, team adaptability, team training, measurement, evaluation, and team effectiveness. Dr. Burke has published more than 60 journal articles and book chapters related to these topics and has presented or has had work accepted at more than 100 peer-reviewed conferences. She is currently investigating team adaptability and its corresponding measurement, issues related to multicultural team performance, leadership, and training of such teams. Dr. Burke earned her doctorate in industrial and organizational psychology from George Mason University. Dr. Burke serves as an ad hoc reviewer for *Human Factors, Leadership Quarterly, Human Resource Management, Journal of Occupational and Organizational Psychology,* and *Quality and Safety in Healthcare.* She has coedited a book on adaptability and is coediting a book on advances in team effectiveness research.

GWENDOLYN CAMPBELL is senior research psychologist at Naval Air Warfare Center Training Systems Division. She holds an M.S. and Ph.D. in experimental psychology from the University of South Florida and a B.A. in mathematics from Youngstown State University. Her research interests include the application of human performance modeling techniques within training systems and the development of a cognitively based science of instruction.

NANCY J. COOKE is professor of applied psychology at Arizona State University at the Polytechnic Campus and is science director of the Cognitive Engineering Research Institute and editor in chief of *Human Factors.* Dr. Cooke received a B.A. in psychology from George Mason University in 1981 and received her M.A. and Ph.D. in cognitive psychology from New Mexico State University in 1983 and 1987, respectively. Dr. Cooke specializes in the development, application, and evaluation of methodologies to elicit and assess individual and team cognition with applications in the design of remotely operated vehicles and emergency response systems. Her most recent work includes empirical and modeling efforts to understand the acquisition and retention of team skill and the measurement of team coordination and team situation awareness, especially through the analysis of communication. This work is funded primarily by the U.S. Air Force Research Laboratory and the Office of Naval Research.

MATTHEW A. CRONIN is assistant professor of management in the School of Management at George Mason University. He received his Ph.D. in the Tepper School of Business at Carnegie Mellon University. His research focuses on the cognitive and interpersonal processes that promote creativity, particularly in the context of teams. His research has been published in the *Academy of Management Review* and *Academy of Management Proceedings.*

RACHEL DAY is an industrial and organizational psychologist with more than six years of applied and research experience in the areas of training, evaluation, coaching, and test design. As a human capital consultant at ICF International, she currently manages leadership development and succession planning projects for federal government agencies. She also conducts research on career development and mentoring and has recently been involved with establishing formal mentoring programs for several of her clients. Dr. Day is an active member of the Society of Industrial and Organizational Psychology (SIOP) and is part of the team that received the prestigious 2007 SIOP M. Scott Myers award for Applied Research in the Workplace for work on medical team training. She has published and presented more than 18 scholarly articles in journals or professional conferences. She holds a Ph.D. in industrial and organizational psychology from the University of South Florida.

LESLIE A. DECHURCH is assistant professor of industrial and organizational psychology at the University of Central Florida. She received her Ph.D. degree in 2002 in industrial and organizational psychology from Florida International University. Dr. DeChurch leads the DELTA (Developing Effective Leaders, Teams, and Alliances) research laboratory at UCF, which is currently working on several laboratory- and case-based projects on multiteam systems in collaboration with the U.S. Army Research Institute for the Behavioral and Social Sciences. Her research has appeared in the *Journal of Applied Psychology, Leadership Quarterly, Journal of Applied Social Psychology, Group Dynamics: Theory, Research, and Practice, Small Group Research,* and the *International Journal of Conflict Management.* She is a member of the Society of Industrial and Organizational Psychology, the Academy of Management, and the American Psychological Association. Her current research interests include team and multiteam effectiveness, team leadership, and conflict management.

LISA A. DELISE is doctoral candidate and senior researcher of the Organizational Research Laboratory at The University of Tennessee in Knoxville. She earned her B.S. in psychology at Tulane University. Her research interests focus primarily on team processes, including development of cognitive congruence, information sharing, communication through distributed media, and exchange perceptions among team members.

DEBORAH DIAZGRANADOS is doctoral candidate in the industrial and organizational psychology program at the University of Central Florida and has been a graduate research assistant at the Institute for Simulation and Training since summer 2004. Ms. DiazGranados received a B.S. in psychology and management from the University of Houston and her M.S. in industrial and organizational psychology from the University of Central Florida. Her research interests include team processes and effectiveness, training, motivation, and leadership. Ms. DiazGranados has published and presented work related to these interests at national and international conferences. While at the University of Central Florida, Ms. DiazGranados has taught several undergraduate classes as adjunct professor. She has also has served as a consultant on projects for NAVAIR Orlando, the city of Winter Park, Florida, and other small business in the Orlando area.

DAVID DORSEY is vice president at Personnel Decisions Research Institutes (PDRI) in Washington, D.C. The work of Dr. Dorsey and his group ranges from studies of new quantitative research methods to approaches for optimizing individual, team, and organizational performance via assessment, performance measurement, and training and development interventions. His recent clients include the Office of the Director of National Intelligence, U.S. Army Special Forces, NAVAIR Orlando, the Defense Language Institute, the Government Accountability Office, several organizations in the U.S. Intelligence Community, and the Department of Labor. His applied research efforts have appeared in such journals as the *Journal of Applied Psychology*, *Human Performance*, *Personnel Psychology*, and *Human Factors*.

AMY C. EDMONDSON is the Novartis Professor of Leadership and Management at Harvard Business School. She received her A.M. in psychology and Ph.D. in organizational behavior from Harvard University. Her research has investigated how teams learn and how their learning affects the organizations in which they work. Her prior work has demonstrated the importance of a climate of psychological safety for enabling learning and innovation in teams in organizational contexts ranging from healthcare delivery to space exploration.

PETER J. M. D. ESSENS is chief scientist at TNO Human Factors for Command and Control and senior fellow at the Netherlands Defense Academy. He holds B.A. degrees in pedagogics and psychology, an M.Sc. in experimental psychology, and a Ph.D. in social sciences. As principal scientist he is leading studies of current and future command and control in the military and civil domain. His main interest is on innovation of organizations by optimizing the human role and use of cooperation technologies. His focus is on the integration of human, organizational, and technical perspectives to achieve high effectiveness, high flexibility, and high commitment with efficient manning. He chaired several North Atlantic Treaty Organization (NATO) study groups and is a member of the NATO Research and Technology Organization (RTO) Human Factors and Medicine (HFM) Panel and chair of a NATO Task Group on Team Effectiveness. In 2007, he and his task group team received the NATO RTO HFM Excellence Award for their command team effectiveness work.

PETER W. FOLTZ is vice president for Research at Pearson Knowledge Technologies Group and senior research associate at the University of Colorado Institute for Cognitive Science. His research has focused on computational modeling of knowledge, team research, and technologies for automated assessment. He has developed patented educational assessment technology, which is used by millions of students. He has published a range of articles on cognitive models of comprehension, team cognition, information retrieval, natural language processing, educational technology, and cognitive science.

GERALD F. GOODWIN is research psychologist at the U.S. Army Research Institute for Behavioral and Social Sciences. He received his M.S. and Ph.D. in industrial and organizational psychology from Pennsylvania State University. Dr. Goodwin's current research focus is on leadership, team effectiveness, and organizational issues in joint, interagency, and multinational contexts. He is also involved in structuring the research and development on cultural issues for the U.S. Army and the Department of Defense. He was previously employed at the American Institutes for Research, where his project work included test development, employment litigation support with an emphasis on statistical analysis, training evaluation, and performance modeling. He is a member of the Society for Industrial and Organizational Psychology, the American Psychological Association (APA), and APA Division 19 (Military Psychology). He currently serves as an ad hoc reviewer for the *Journal of Applied Psychology* and *Military Psychology and Human Performance* and is a member of the editorial board for *Human Factors*.

JAMIE C. GORMAN is postdoctoral research assistant at Arizona State University at the Polytechnic Campus and the Cognitive Engineering Research Institute in Mesa. Dr. Gorman received his B.A. in psychology from University of Texas–San Antonio in 2000 and M.A. and Ph.D. degrees in psychology from New Mexico State University in 2003 and 2006, respectively. Dr. Gorman's area of research specialization emphasizes team cognition, team coordination, and team communication. His research has focused on quantitatively representing team-level cognitive phenomena. He is also investigating team cognition using traditional cognitive laboratory methodologies including psychological refractory period.

STANLEY M. HALPIN has worked for the Department of the Army for 37 years. He is also adjunct instructor in the graduate school at Kansas State University. For the last 24 years he has served as the chief of the U.S. Army Research Institute's research group at Fort Leavenworth, Kansas. This group, until recently known as the Leader Development Research Unit, has conducted research on the U.S. Army's tactical decision-making processes, staff performance, and development of training techniques for decision makers and decision-making groups. Over the last few years the research unit has extended its research program to address leaders' interpersonal and team skills as well as cognitive skills. Dr. Halpin received a B.S. in industrial and labor relations from Cornell University in 1965 and an M.S. and Ph.D. in social psychology from Purdue University in 1970.

KATHERINE HAMILTON is doctoral candidate in industrial and organizational psychology at Pennsylvania State University. Her research interests focus on team effectiveness, particularly as it relates to team virtuality, intragroup conflict, and decision making.

BETH HEINEN is doctoral candidate in industrial and organizational psychology at George Mason University and associate at ICF International. Ms. Heinen's primary research interests include leadership, teamwork, training, and work–family issues. Specifically, Ms. Heinen has studied leadership's influence on task motivation, teamwork, work–family culture, and work–family conflict. Additionally, Ms. Heinen has examined how to train team adaptability and measurement issues in work–family constructs. As an associate for ICF International, Ms. Heinen provides organizational research and management consulting experience to clients such as the U.S. House of Representatives, the Department of Homeland Security, Monster Government Solutions, and the Minnesota Army National Guard. Ms. Heinen's primary work activities include job analysis, survey development and administration, leadership development, training development and evaluation, data analysis, and addressing other workforce issues, such as recruitment, retention, and motivation. Ms. Heinen has presented research at national conferences and published articles in peer-reviewed journals and book chapters.

SCOTT HUTCHISON is managing partner at the Organizational Research Group, LLC. He has extensive experience working in management and marketing in large corporations. His consulting experience includes conducting research primarily focused on team cognition and team performance in collaboration with military research laboratories.

JACLYN M. JENSEN is assistant professor of management in the School of Business at George Washington University. Dr. Jensen's research focuses on employee performance and organizational justice. She is interested in the antecedents to organizational citizenship behavior and counterproductive work behavior and the trade-offs and tensions between these forms of contextual performance. Her research has been published in *Organizational Behavior and Human Decision Processes* and *International Journal of Conflict Management* as well as in several book chapters. She received her Ph.D. and M.A. in industrial and organizational psychology from Michigan State University.

CHARLES KEIL received his doctorate in industrial and organizational psychology from George Mason University in 2001 and has more than 15 years of experience as an applied psychologist. He has engaged in numerous applied research and consulting projects in such diverse areas as cognitive and noncognitive assessment development, personnel selection, performance management, competency modeling, validation, usability testing, and employment litigation. He has also taught graduate-level multivariate statistics and psychometric theory. Dr. Keil is a member of the Society for Industrial and Organizational Psychology, National Council on Measurement in Education, and the American Psychological Association. He has authored or coauthored a number of journal articles, book chapters, or conference presentations concerning the measurement, prediction or development of human abilities, achievement, or performance.

BRIAN H. KIM is assistant professor of psychology at Occidental College. He received his M.A. in 2004 and Ph.D. in 2006 in industrial and organizational psychology from Michigan State University. In addition to work on the development of individuals within work teams, his research interests and published works cover topics in personnel selection and assessment issues involving expanded notions of job performance that may change across levels. He focuses on deception processes within and beyond selection, as well as quantitative methodologies.

LAURA M. KOEHLY is Investigator and Head of the Social Network Methods Section in the Social and Behavioral Research Branch of the National Human Genome Research Institute at the National Institutes of Health. She completed her Ph.D. in quantitative psychology at the University of Illinois–Urbana/Champaign, after which she completed postdoctoral training at the University of Texas M.D. Anderson Cancer Center. Her methodological research interests focus on the development of stochastic models for three-way social network data and incomplete social network data common to the study of family systems. She applies these methods to study the risk dissemination and cooperative adaptation processes of families coping with hereditary risk information. Eventually, she aims to develop effective evidence-based interventions that optimally utilize the structure of the family system to facilitate the dissemination of health information within the family and positive adaptation to family risk.

STEVE W. J. KOZLOWSKI is professor of organizational psychology at Michigan State University. His research program is focused on active learning and simulation-based training, enhancing team learning and effectiveness, and the active role of team leaders in the development of adaptive teams. The goal of this programmatic work is to generate actionable theory, research-based principles, and deployable tools to promote the development of adaptive individuals, teams, and organizations. Dr. Kozlowski is incoming editor (and former associate editor) of the *Journal of Applied Psychology*. He has served on the editorial boards of *Academy of Management Journal*, *Human Factors*, *Journal of Applied Psychology*, and *Organizational Behavior and Human Decision Processes*. He is a fellow of the American Psychological Association, the Association for Psychological Science, the International Association for Applied Psychology, and the Society for Industrial and Organizational Psychology. Dr. Kozlowski received his B.A. in psychology from the University of Rhode Island and his M.S. and Ph.D. degrees in organizational psychology from Pennsylvania State University.

KELLEY J. KROKOS is senior research scientist at the American Institutes for Research. She has been working in the field of industrial and organizational psychology since 1994. Her expertise and interests focus on defining, measuring, and evaluating individual and team job performance in high-risk work environments including aviation, health care, maritime, the military, and law enforcement. Her work products have been used as the basis for developing or improving a variety of systems including employee selection, certification, and training. In addition to numerous publications, reports, and presentations, Dr. Krokos recently coedited a special section in *Human Factors* on human error. She is currently a member of the American Psychological Association and the Society for Industrial and Organizational Psychology and serves as Vice President of the Society for Human Performance in Extreme Environments (HPEE). Dr. Krokos holds a Ph.D. in industrial and organizational psychology from North Carolina State University.

JOHN M. LEVINE did his undergraduate work at Northwestern University and received his Ph.D. in psychology from the University of Wisconsin–Madison. He is professor of psychology and senior scientist in the Learning, Research and Development Center at the University of Pittsburgh. His work focuses on small group processes, including innovation in work teams, reaction to deviance and disloyalty, temporal processes in groups, and majority and minority influence. He has published extensively on these and related topics. Dr. Levine is a fellow of the American Psychological Association and the American Psychological Society and has served as editor of the *Journal of Experimental Social Psychology*. He was recently appointed honorary professor of psychology at the University of Kent in Canterbury, England.

AUDREY LIM is doctoral candidate in industrial and organizational psychology at Pennsylvania State University. Her research focuses on teams as well as technology implementation in organizations.

MELANIE J. MARTIN is assistant professor of computer science at California State University–Stanislaus. She received her Ph.D. degree in 2005 in computer science from New Mexico State University. Her research interests include team communication and performance analysis, dialog modeling, natural language processing, information retrieval, machine learning, and health informatics.

JOHN E. MATHIEU is professor and the Cizik Chair of Management at the University of Connecticut. He received a Ph.D. in industrial and organizational psychology from Old Dominion University. He is a member of the Academy of Management and a fellow of the Society of Industrial Organizational Psychology and the American Psychological Association. His current research interests include models of team and multiteam processes and cross-level models of organizational behavior.

SUSAN MOHAMMED is associate professor of industrial and organizational psychology at Pennsylvania State University. She received her Ph.D. from Ohio State University. Her research focuses on teams and decision making, with a special emphasis on team mental models, team composition/diversity, and the role of time in team research.

RICHARD L. MORELAND received his B.A. degree from the University of Colorado in 1973 and his Ph.D. from the University of Michigan in 1978. Both degrees were in social psychology. In 1978, Dr. Moreland accepted a faculty position in the Department of Psychology at the University of Pittsburgh, where he is currently professor. He also has a secondary appointment there in the Joseph Katz School of Business. Dr. Moreland is a fellow of the American Psychological Society and a fellow of Division 8 (Personality & Social Psychology), Division 9 (Society for the Psychological Study of Social Issues), and Division 49 (Group Psychology & Group Psychotherapy) of the American Psychological Association. He has served as president of Division 49. Dr. Moreland is on the editorial boards of many journals and has been associate editor for *Group Processes and Intergroup Relations, Journal of Experimental Social Psychology, Management Science*, and *Personality and Social Psychology Bulletin*. He has also been a guest editor for special issues of the *British Journal of Social Psychology, Organizational Behavior and Human Decision Processes*, and *Small Group Research*. Dr. Moreland is interested in many aspects of groups and their members, including entitativity, reflexivity, and transactive memory. Most of his work, however, has focused on temporal changes in groups. Such changes include group formation and dissolution, group development, and group socialization.

JACQUES J. C. MYLLE started his career in 1964 as student at the Royal Military Academy. He served 13 years as Armoured Reconnaissance officer in the Belgian Forces in Germany and three as head of the Officers Armoured Reconnaissance Training Center for Officers and Non-Commissioned Officers. Designated for the Selection and Recruitment Centre in 1985, he studied psychology while being in charge of the officers' selection. Since 1990 he has served as head of the psychology department at the Royal Military Academy in Brussels. His responsibilities are teaching, research, and services to the military community. Particularly, he is a mathematical psychologist, using his competencies in various domains of application related to peace support operations. Dr. Mylle has a master's in social and military sciences, a master's in psychology, a special degree in education, a master's in quantitative methods in social sciences, and a Ph.D. in psychology.

CAROL PARIS currently serves as senior research psychologist for the Naval Air Warfare Center Training Systems Division. She has 11 years of Department of Defense (DoD) experience, conducting research in tactical decision making, team performance, human systems integration, and simulation training technologies. She currently serves as chair of the North Atlantic Treaty Organization (NATO) Human Factors and Medicine (HFM)-Task Group 156, "Measuring and Analyzing Command and Control Performance Effectiveness," and served on Task Group 023, "Team Effectiveness." In October 2000 Dr. Paris received the Dr. Arthur E. Bisson Prize for Naval Technology Achievement presented by the Office of Naval Research and in April 2001 received the M. Scott Myers Award for Applied Research in the Workplace presented by Society for Industrial and Organizational Psychology. She served three years with the U.S. Navy's Human Performance Center as supervisory psychologist. She holds a Ph.D. in human factors psychology from the University of Central Florida and is also certified by the International Society of Performance Improvement as a performance technologist.

HEATHER A. PRIEST is a Ph.D. candidate in human factors psychology at the University of Central Florida working at the Institute for Simulation and Training. She is currently doing research on teams and stress, leadership, culture, learning/collaborative technologies, and training effectiveness. Ms. Priest has presented at national and international conferences and been published in journals including *Ergonomics and Design* and *Human Factors and Ergonomics in Manufacturing.*

JOAN R. RENTSCH is professor of management, director of the industrial and organizational psychology program, and director of the Organizational Research Laboratory at The University of Tennessee. She earned her Ph.D. and M.A. in industrial and organizational psychology from the University of Maryland and her B.S. in psychology from The Ohio State University. Her research interests focus on psychological processes in organizations including cognition in teams and organizations and on the measurement of cognition. Her research appears in such journals as *Journal of Applied Psychology, Personnel Psychology, Journal of Organizational Behavior, Academy of Management Journal,* and *Organizational Research Methods.* She is also a founding partner of the Organizational Research Group, LLC. Dr. Rentsch's current research program includes examining team cognition, team processes, and team performance. Her research is aimed at providing scientific foundations for technological developments supporting collaborative decision making in situations characterized by such features as complex, dynamic, time sensitive, and multinational.

KATHRYN S. ROLOFF is a Ph.D. student in the social-organizational psychology program at Columbia University. She received her B.A. in psychology and administrative science from Colby College and her M.A. in psychology from Boston University. Prior to joining the program at Columbia, she worked as research associate at Harvard Business School and as research analyst at Boston University Medical School. Her research interests revolve around team processes such as learning, collaboration, and identity formation in diverse teams.

MICHAEL A. ROSEN is doctoral candidate in the applied experimental and human factors psychology program at the University of Central Florida and since fall 2004 has been a graduate research assistant at the Institute for Simulation and Training, where he won the student researcher of the year in 2006. He is currently a Multi-University Research Initative-Systems fsor Understanding and Measuring Macrocognition in Teams (MURI-SUMMIT) graduate research fellow and focuses on developing theory, methods, and tools for understanding and measuring cognitive and social processes in team problem solving. His research interests include individual and team decision making and problem solving, human–computer interaction, team performance, and training in high-stress high-stakes domains such as health care and the military. He has coauthored more than a dozen peer-reviewed journal articles and book chapters related to these interests as well as numerous proceedings papers and presentations at national and international conferences.

LEAH J. ROWE is research specialist at Arizona State University and research scientist at L-3 Communications. She received her M.S. in applied psychology at Arizona State University in 2007. Her research interests include knowledge acquisition, team cognition, team training, and performance measurement.

STEVEN RUSSELL is research scientist at Personnel Decisions Research Institutes in Arlington, Virginia. He holds a Ph.D. in industrial and organizational psychology from Bowling Green State University. His interests include the design and evaluation of training programs, criterion measurement, and test development and validation, including the use of item response theory (IRT) techniques.

JOAN M. RYDER is a cognitive engineering consultant for CHI Systems, Inc. She received an A.B. from Brown University and a Ph.D. from Brandeis University, both in psychology. Dr. Ryder has more than 25 years of experience in human factors engineering, training, and psychological research. She contributed to the development of the Cognition as a Network of Tasks (COGNET)/iGEN® framework and the ORGNET extensions for team modeling and led the effort to apply Organizational Cognition as a Network of Tasks (ORGNET) to design of an Air Defense Warfare (ADW) team. Her interests are in the areas of cognitive modeling, cognitive task analysis, and advanced instructional systems.

EDUARDO SALAS is trustee chair and professor of psychology at the University of Central Florida (UCF), where he also holds an appointment as program director for the Human Systems Integration Research Department at the Institute for Simulation and Training (IST). Previously, he was director of UCF's applied experimental and human factors Ph.D. program. Before joining IST, he was a senior research psychologist and head of the Training Technology Development Branch of NAWC-TSD for 15 years. During this period, Dr. Salas served as a principal investigator for numerous research and development programs—including Tactical Decision Making under Stress (TADMUS)—that focused on teamwork, team training, decision making under stress, and performance assessment. Dr. Salas has coauthored more than 300 journal articles and book chapters and has coedited 19 books. His expertise includes assisting organizations in how to foster teamwork, how to design and implement team training strategies, how to facilitate training effectiveness, how to manage decision making under stress, and how to develop performance measurement tools. Dr. Salas is a fellow of the American Psychological Association and the Human Factors and Ergonomics Society and is a recipient of the Meritorious Civil Service Award from the Department of the Navy.

PETER SCHUCK is research scientist with the U.S. Naval Research Lab in Washington, D.C. He holds a Ph.D. in applied physics from Cornell

University. His research interests include solar physics, image processing, and advanced statistical methods.

MARISSA SHUFFLER is an associate with ICF International, where she is involved in all aspects of organizational and management consulting. Ms. Shuffler has conducted research and analysis in a variety of areas, including leadership, social cognition, shared mental models, learning and development, adaptability, and motivation for military, private, and nonprofit organizations. Ms. Shuffler has performed these services for military, private, and nonprofit organizations. Her current areas of research include addressing workforce issues such as job satisfaction, leadership development and training, organizational communication, shared cognition, and multinational–multicultural distributed teams. Ms. Shuffler has presented research at national conferences and has published articles in scholarly journals and edited books on these and other topics. She holds a master's in industrial and organizational psychology from George Mason University.

ANDREW J. SLAUGHTER has a master's degree in psychology from Texas A&M University, where he is currently completing his Ph.D. His primary academic interests include the study of individual differences, job performance, social influence and leadership, and applications of social network analysis to organizational dynamics.

KIMBERLY A. SMITH-JENTSCH received her Ph.D. in industrial and organizational psychology from the University of South Florida in 1994. She worked as a research psychologist for the U.S. Navy from that time until 2003, when she joined the psychology department at the University of Central Florida. Her research interests include teams, training and development, simulation-based performance assessment, and mentoring. She has published articles on these topics in journals such as *Journal of Applied Psychology, Personnel Psychology, Journal of Organizational Behavior,* and *Journal of Vocational Behavior* and is currently a member of the editorial board for the *Journal of Applied Psychology.*

WENDI VAN BUSKIRK is research psychologist at the Naval Air Warfare Center, Training Systems Division. She is currently a doctoral candidate in the applied experimental and human factors psychology Ph.D. program at the University of Central Florida. Her research interests include human cognition and performance, instructional strategies, human performance modeling, and human–computer interaction.

AD L. W. VOGELAAR is a social psychologist who teaches psychology and leadership at the Netherlands Defence Academy. In 1990 he earned his Ph.D. at Leyden University in The Netherlands on the subject of job satisfaction. Presently, his main focus of research is military leadership.

DANIEL J. WATOLA is assistant professor of behavioral sciences and leadership at the U.S. Air Force Academy in Colorado Springs, Colorado. His research interests include training, teams, leadership, and the intersection of these domains. Currently, he is an Air Force officer and behavioral scientist serving as the Deputy Commander at the Air Force Research Laboratory in San Antonio, Texas. He received his B.S. in human factors engineering from the U.S. Air Force Academy and his Ph.D. in industrial and organizational psychology from Michigan State University.

LAURIE R. WEINGART is professor of organizational behavior and director of the Center for Interdisciplinary Research on Teams in the David A. Tepper School of Business at Carnegie Mellon University in Pittsburgh, Pennsylvania. She is cofounder of the Interdisciplinary Network for Group Research. Her research focuses on functional diversity, team cognition, and conflict in work groups and the tactical behavior and cognitive processes of negotiators in both dyads and groups. Her research has been published in the *Academy of Management Journal, Academy of Management Review, Journal of Applied Psychology, Journal of Personality and Social Psychology, Journal of Experimental Social Psychology, Cognitive Science, International Journal of Conflict Management,* and *Research in Organizational Behavior,* among others. She currently serves on the editorial boards of the *Journal of Personality and Social Psychology, Academy of Management Review, Organizational Behavior and Human Decision Processes, Group Dynamics,* and *Negotiation and Conflict Management Research.*

JESSICA L. WILDMAN is doctoral student in the industrial and organizational psychology program at the University of Central Florida, where she earned a B.S. in psychology in 2007. Ms. Wildman is a graduate research assistant at the Institute for Simulation and Training and her current research interests include team process and performance, team training, multicultural performance and multiteam systems. Ms. Wildman has been involved in an Army Research Laboratory grant regarding cultural influences on team adaptability among other projects.

SAMUEL R. WOOTEN II is master's student at University of Central Florida. He is a graduate research assistant at the Institute for Simulation and Training, where he is involved with multiteam system and culture-related projects. His research interests include multicultural teams, team processes, team adaptation (e.g., multicultural, environmental factors), and multiteam systems.

JANIE YU is doctoral student at Texas A&M University. Her primary research areas include impression management on noncognitive selection measures and the use of social network analysis to study organizational phenomena, such as the role of social influence on counterproductive work behaviors.

STEPHEN J. ZACCARO is professor of organizational psychology at George Mason University in Fairfax, Virginia. He is also a consultant on leadership development and assessment and an experienced executive coach. Previously, he served on the faculties of Virginia Polytechnic Institute and State University and the College of the Holy Cross. He received his Ph.D. in social psychology from the University of Connecticut. He has been studying, teaching, and consulting about leadership and teams for more than 25 years and has written more than 100 articles, book chapters, and technical reports on group dynamics, leadership, team performance, and work attitudes. He wrote a book titled *The Nature of Executive Leadership: A Conceptual and Empirical Analysis of Success* (American Psychological Association, 2001) and coedited three other books: *Occupational Stress and Organizational Effectiveness* (with Anne W. Riley, Praeger Publishers, 1987), *The Nature of Organizational Leadership: Understanding the Performance Imperatives Confronting Today's Leaders* (with Richard J. Klimoski, Pfeiffer, 2001), and *Leader Development for Transforming Organizations: Growing Leaders for Tomorrow* (with David V. Day and Stanley M. Halpin, Lawrence Erlbaum, 2004). He also coedited a special issue for *Group and Organization Management* (2002) on the interface between leadership and team dynamics, as well as special issues for *Leadership Quarterly* (1991–1992) on individual differences and leadership.

WAYNE ZACHARY is chief executive officer of CHI Systems, Inc., which he founded in 1985. He has been an active researcher in modeling and analysis of teams and organizations for 30 years. His multidisciplinary work in this area has explored issues in team training, team decision making, team design, and team and organizational conflict. He has developed a range of innovative methods for modeling these issues, including the Organizational Cognition as a Network of Tasks (ORGNET) model, which focuses on cognitive processes and work behavior, and the NETFLOW model, which represents information flow and conflict processes in teams using a social network framework. He has applied these models to numerous problems in military command and control and systems design. Dr. Zachary received a B.A. summa cum laude from Cleveland State University in anthropology and an M.A in anthropology, an M.S. in computer science, and a Ph.D. in cognitive anthropology from Temple University.

Section I

Setting the Stage

1

Team Effectiveness in Complex Organizations: An Overview

Gerald F. Goodwin, C. Shawn Burke,
Jessica L. Wildman, and Eduardo Salas

Over the last 40 years, there has a been a growing trend toward the utilization of teams for accomplishing work in organizations in private, public, and military sectors of the workplace (Kozlowski & Ilgen, 2006; Sundstrom, McIntyre, Halfhill, & Richards, 2000). Project teams, self-managed work teams, and top-management teams, among others, have become a regular element in the corporate lexicon. Within the military, there has been a parallel trend emphasizing teams and teamwork—recently codified in the formal Army doctrine on leadership (Department of the Army, 2006). Relatively concurrent with this trend has been an increasing focus of organizational research on the development of methods and theories for understanding team effectiveness (e.g., Campion, Medsker, & Higgs, 1993; Cannon-Bowers, Tannenbaum, Salas, & Volpe, 1995; Cooke, Salas, Kiekel, & Bell, 2004; Fleishman & Zaccaro, 1992; Fowlkes, Lane, Salas, Franz, & Oser, 1994; Ilgen et al., 2005; Marks, Mathieu, & Zaccaro, 2001). This volume is intended to provide an overview of the current state of the art in research on team effectiveness. In doing so, points of potential integration, gaps, and areas in need of further exploration are identified. It is hoped that this integration may provide some inspiration for researchers to explore beyond our self-set boundaries and give impetus to engage in a broader set of challenges with a wider range of multidisciplinary approaches.

From There to Here

Systematic study of early group phenomena began in the 1900s. Early studies were primarily motivated by organizational concerns; however, for the military World War II brought to the forefront recognition of the importance of teams. This small but growing interest in teams, particularly small units, grew through the 1970s. The body of research on team training throughout this period was summarized by Dyer (1984), who structured her review around several overarching questions regarding theories and models, tasks performed, measures, and training. Dyer concluded that some progress in understanding and influencing team performance had been made but that there remained substantial gaps in our understanding of teams. In summarizing the organizational team research, Bass (1982, p. 227) reached a similar conclusion, stating that "the most obvious long term research need is to learn much more about exactly what interaction processes result from properties of the team and the conditions, imposed on it, and what types of interaction processes are likely to be conducive to, or detrimental to, team productivity for members with certain capabilities."

In 1988, an incident in the Persian Gulf involving the *U.S.S. Vincennes* provided the momentum for a renewed focus on team effectiveness and team training, which gave rise to the Tactical Decision Making under Stress (TADMUS) research program, led by the U.S. Navy (Cannon-Bowers & Salas, 1998). The focus of this program was enhancing team decision making in combat environments and led to a substantial increase in the understanding of team processes and team training (Cannon-Bowers, Tannenbaum, et al., 1995; Smith-Jentsch, Zeisig, Acton, & McPherson, 1998; Tesluk, Mathieu, Zaccaro, & Marks, 1997). A decade of research exploring team processes identified a core set of processes: performance monitoring, back-up behavior, leadership, coordination, and communication (Salas, Sims, & Burke, 2005). In addition, significant advances were made in understanding and implementing team training programs—including advances in crew resource management (CRM) training (Salas, Burke, Bowers, & Wilson, 2001; Salas, Wilson, Burke, & Wightman, 2006), structured developmental feedback for teams (Smith-Jentsch et al., 1998), and a more advanced conceptualization of training evaluation (Cannon-Bowers, Salas, Tannenbaum, & Mathieu, 1995; Kraiger, Ford, & Salas, 1993).

Since the turn of the 21st century, technology, globalization, and the often distributed complex nature of work have led organizations to once again recognize the importance of understanding team effectiveness within such environments. This resurgence can be seen both in the military (e.g., needs for developing future battle concepts to match asymmetric warfare) as well as private and public organizational sectors (e.g., increased multinational organizations, cross-functional teams). This combination has spurred a great deal of exploration of topics supporting team effectiveness, particularly teams working in complex, dynamic, and often ill-structured environments (e.g., Cannon-Bowers & Salas, 1995, 2001; Cohen & Bailey, 1997; Edmondson, 1999; Gersick, 1988; Hackman & Wageman, 2005;

Kozlowski & Ilgen, 2006). The nature of much of this work is represented by the chapters in the current volume.

In 2003, the U.S. Army initiated a new line of research on team effectiveness, with a focus on understanding the factors underlying team effectiveness in multiservice, multinational organizations. Understanding and enhancing the effectiveness of these highly complex organizations are some of—if not the most—daunting research challenges currently facing the U.S. Department of Defense. As the Army began this new line of work, the significant challenges were to clearly establish what the field had learned in the preceding years, what areas the field was currently investigating, and what new directions should be engaged. The first of these challenges has culminated in a number of publications and presentations reviewing and summarizing the state of extant knowledge within the field (e.g., Burke et al., 2006; Salas, Rosen, Burke, Goodwin, & Fiore, 2006; Salas, Stagl, Burke, & Goodwin, 2007; Stagl, Salas, & Burke, 2006). These publications focus on theory development and empirical findings for a variety of topics and include a forthcoming authored book summarizing the body of research on team effectiveness in the period from Dyer's (1984) review to present.

The efforts to address the second challenge—current areas of investigation—are addressed with this volume. More specifically, this volume is intended to capture a cross-disciplinary examination of current research trends on team effectiveness, including theoretical, methodological, and empirical applications. In providing this view across the field, we have also invited commentary to assist in identifying strengths and weaknesses, insights and oversights, convergences and gaps. It is both our intent and our hope that this volume will provide additional inspiration to the body of researchers working within the team effectiveness domain and will spur new explorations that will substantially move the field forward.

Conceptualizing Team Performance

The search for a better, more complete understanding of team effectiveness has been enduring for decades. Numerous models have been developed and expanded, and recent research has attempted to bring the science together by integrating extant theories. In the following sections, we present a brief history outlining the development of the current conceptualization of team effectiveness. First, we describe the input-process-output (IPO) framework that served as the backbone for early team effectiveness models. Next, we describe the progression of team effectiveness research past the general IPO model into more specific areas of team performance.

Specifically, this includes delving deeper into team process, feedback loops, and team development. Finally, we conclude by describing a recent integrative framework of team effectiveness that brings together decades of research in one parsimonious model (Salas et al., 2007). The chapters within this volume address particular aspects of this framework individually in different ways. It is in the consideration of these chapters as aspects of the whole that will allow us to move forward with a richer understanding of the field and to identify potential gaps within the existing research base.

The IPO Framework

The IPO model has served as the foundation for the development of the majority of the early team effectiveness models. The IPO theory postulates that input factors, such as team and individual characteristics, function through mediators or moderators to influence outputs, such as team satisfaction and performance. Many of the most influential and well-known team effectiveness models follow this format (e.g., Hackman, 1983; Nieva, Fleishman, & Reick, 1978). For example, Gladstein (1984) presented a model of team effectiveness that suggested that individual-level input factors (i.e., group composition and group structure) influence group effectiveness through group processes. Hackman (1987) posited that input factors including organizational context and group design are connected to a set of team processes, which are related to team effectiveness. Later work has expanded the examination of the input factors that impact team process. For example, Campion et al. (1993) presented a metamodel of 19 input variables proposed to affect team effectiveness. These variables can be categorized into five groups: job design, interdependence, composition, context, and process. Technically, only the first four categories are considered input variables, whereas the last category represents the process term of the IPO model. Job design includes self-management, participation, task variety, task significance, and task identity. These input factors are based on the theory of motivational job design. Interdependence includes task interdependence, goal interdependence, and interdependent feedback and rewards. Campion and colleagues proposed that interdependence characteristics may increase the motivational properties of work and thus may be related to effectiveness. The composition theme is included based on its prevalence in other models of team effectiveness (e.g., Guzzo & Shea, 1992; Hackman, 1987) and includes heterogeneity, flexibility, relative size, and preference for group work. The next theme acknowledges the importance of organizational and situational context characteristics in team effectiveness. Context includes training, managerial support, and communication and cooperation between groups.

The strength of the IPO model was in its focus on the interaction among inputs, processes, and outputs, thereby originally making it a good match for the dynamic nature of team effectiveness. However, despite the widespread utilization of this framework, there has been some controversy surrounding the appropriateness of the IPO model in representing team effectiveness (e.g., Hackman, 2002; Ilgen et al., 2005; Sundstrom, de Meuse, & Futrell, 1990). As research has progressed in the realm of team effectiveness, theories have begun to move past the basic IPO model, further unpacking the processes and dynamicism that were lacking in early IPO models.

Parsing Team Processes

McIntyre and Salas (1995) emphasized the distinction between teamwork and taskwork processes. Taskwork can be defined as a team's interactions with tasks, tools, machines, and systems (Bowers, Braun, & Morgan, 1997, as cited in Marks, Mathieu, & Zaccaro, 2001), whereas teamwork refers to the set of interrelated thoughts, actions, and feelings that each team member engages in, that are needed to function as a team, and that combine to facilitate coordinated, adaptive performance (e.g., Marks et al., 2001; Morgan, Glickman, Woodard, Blaiwes, & Salas, 1986; Salas, Sims, & Klein, 2004). In the past decade, several researchers have attempted to explicitly describe what is included in this "set of thoughts, actions, and feelings." Numerous typologies describing a finite set of teamwork processes have been developed, each emphasizing different aspects of teamwork.

For example, Tannenbaum, Beard, and Salas (1992) proposed a relatively complex model of team effectiveness composed of a list of six team processes: coordination, communication, conflict resolution, decision making, problem solving, and boundary spanning. Fleishman and Zaccaro (1992) presented a taxonomy of team performance functions that categorized various processes into seven groups: orientation functions, resource distribution functions, timing functions, response coordination functions, motivational functions, system monitoring functions, and procedure maintenance. Cannon-Bowers, Tannenbaum, et al. (1995) built off the earlier work by Tannenbaum, Beard and Salas (1992) to define a set of teamwork skill dimensions including adaptability, shared situational awareness, performance monitoring and feedback, leadership and team management, interpersonal relations, coordination, communication, and decision making. McIntyre and Salas (1995) presented several principles describing the essential teamwork behaviors: performance monitoring, feedback, closed-loop communication, and backup behavior. Dickinson and McIntyre (1997) integrated team skill competencies and team attitude competencies into a model composed of team processes that interact in a complex web: communication, team orientation, team leadership, monitoring, feedback, backup behavior, and coordination. Finally, Marks and colleagues (2001) presented a temporally based taxonomy of teamwork processes outlining 10 critical teamwork processes that occur recursively over a series of IPO loops: mission analysis, goal specification, strategy formulation and planning, monitoring progress towards goals, systems monitoring, team monitoring and backup, coordination, conflict management, motivating and confidence building, and affect management.

Although each of these taxonomies lists different sets of teamwork processes, there is considerable overlap. Recent efforts have been made to integrate and consolidate these separate taxonomies. Specifically, Salas, Sims, and Burke (2005) described the "Big 5" of teamwork. This model examined past team process research and "boiled it down" to the five processes believed to be at the core of interdependent action: team leadership, team orientation, mutual performance monitoring, backup behavior, and adaptability.

Incorporation of Feedback Loops

As research continued to uncover the dynamic, complex nature of team effectiveness, the traditional IPO model began to fall out of favor. Based on the belief that the IPO model is insufficient for characterizing teams, Ilgen and colleagues (2005) suggested the input–mediation–output–input (IMOI) model as a better alternative. In this model, the mediation term represents a broader variety of variables that are important for explaining variability in team performance. Also, adding the extra input at the end of the model illustrates the cyclical feedback loop that occurs in teams. Basically, the outputs of team effectiveness cycles serve as inputs for the next performance episode, creating a recurring loop. Thus, Ilgen and colleagues contended that the IMOI model more accurately describes the complex, adaptive, and dynamic nature of teams.

Team Development

A growing focus on the dynamic nature of teams has also been reflected in increasing calls to concentrate on team development over time (Harrison, Mohammed, McGrath, Florey, & Vanderstoep, 2003). Perhaps most notable in this area is the work of Gersick (1988), who observed eight teams over their entire life spans and from this data developed the punctuated-equilibrium model of team effectiveness. This model suggests that teams determine an initial method of performance when they first come together and that they adhere to this method until the midpoint of the target objective. Upon reaching this midpoint, the team members become aware of the time left to completion, analyze their previous efforts, and adjust their strategy accordingly for the second half of the performance cycle. This theory of team development made a huge impact on team effectiveness research by further demonstrating the dynamic nature of team performance and the ability of teams to adapt their strategies in response to temporal conditions.

Although repeated calls for attention to aspects of time and team development have been made, only recently are we seeing a reemergence of this issue. Expanding on the findings from Gersick (1988), Waller, Zellmer-Bruhn, and Giambatista (2002) found that even though teams differentially focused on temporal factors dependent on the type of deadline imposed, the project midpoint remained a transition opportunity regardless of the stability of the team's deadline. Other efforts indicating the importance of time and team development have been seen in the area of team leadership. In this regard, Kozlowski, Gully, Nason, and Smith (1999) argued for the changing role of the leader as the team matures. Similarly, Hackman and Wageman (2005) claimed that the focus of coaching will differ depending on the developmental stage of the team.

A Consolidated View

The most recent work on team effectiveness has attempted to bring together the myriad extant theories to create one consolidated understanding. Salas et al. (2007) critically reviewed the literature and integrated 11 models and frameworks of team effectiveness into one multilevel, comprehensive framework (Figure 1.1). The framework highlights the role of team inputs in promoting teamwork and team performance. There are four categories of input factors: individual characteristics, team characteristics, task characteristics, and work structure. The framework also illustrates the moderating role of individual-level cognition between team inputs and throughputs. The processes constituting teamwork occur dynamically, simultaneously, and episodically over time, which leads to shared cognition (e.g., shared mental models, team situation awareness, psychological safety). This integrative framework draws on some of the most recent advancements in team literature and incorporates a focus on team cognition, team leadership, and the dynamic nature of performance. It is from this point of departure that we begin our journey into the very most recent advances in team effectiveness research. The following section provides a preview of the remainder of this volume.

Chapter Previews

The primary goal of this volume is to serve as a forum where multiple disciplines exchange and share perspectives on how to better understand team effectiveness. To further this goal, and for ease of reference, the

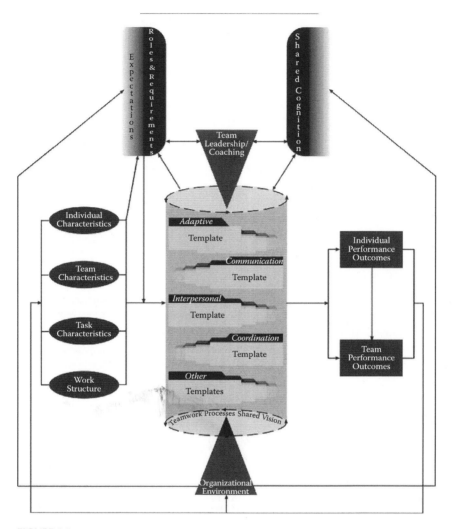

FIGURE 1.1
The conditions and processes of team performance. (From Salas, E., Stagl, K. C., Burke, C. S., & Goodwin, G. F., In J. W. Shuart, W. Spaulding, & J. Poland, (Eds.), *Modeling complex systems: Motivation, cognition and social processes, Nebraska Symposium on Motivation, 51*, pp. 185–243. Lincoln: University of Nebraska Press, 2007. With permission.)

volume is divided into five thematic sections. Section 1 focuses on team effectiveness from a more general, overhead point of view. Specifically, Richard Moreland and John Levine (Chapter 2) provide an integrative overview of small-group research and draw on this knowledge base to outline a set of overarching principles for improving theory and research on small groups. Eduardo Salas, Michael Rosen, Shawn Burke, and Gerald Goodwin (Chapter 3) provide another set of principles based on an integration of prior research—this time for achieving teamwork. They focus on the key behaviors, actions, cognitions, and attitudes that expert teams embody. By providing integrative overviews of small-group research and the composition of teamwork, these early chapters set the stage for the rest of the volume.

Theoretical Advances

Section 2 of this volume provides several of the most recent theoretical perspectives in team effectiveness research. This area of research has grown exponentially over recent years, and this section reflects the depth and breadth of that development. Within this section, the chapters can be subcategorized by their theoretical focus on one of four topics: leadership approaches, team learning, team cognition, and environmental factors. Several chapters describe differing approaches to effective team leadership. In Chapter 4, Stephen Zaccaro, Beth Heinen, and Marissa Shuffler outline a functional approach to team leadership that includes competencies required by team leaders and the role of team leadership in promoting team effectiveness. Steve Kozlowksi, Daniel Watola, Jaclyn Nowakowski, Brian Kim, and Isabel Botero (Chapter 5) also look at team leadership but shift the focus to adaptive teams and how team leaders react when faced with complex problems. In Chapter 6, Nancy Cooke, Jamie Gorman, and Leah Rowe take a cognitive engineering approach to the understanding and measurement of shared mental models within heterogeneous teams. Amy Edmondson and Kathryn Roloff (Chapter 7) examine the role of team leaders but also include the concepts of psychological safety and team learning in a medical context. In Chapter 8, Burke, Heather Priest, Samuel Wooten, Deborah DiazGranados, and Salas take a multidisciplinary perspective in understanding the cognitive processes in adaptive multicultural teams. In doing so a series of propositions are put forth regarding the cognitive knowledge and skills needed to facilitate adaptive performance within multicultural teams. Other chapters in this section provide theories of team cognition. In contrast to Cooke and colleagues (Chapter 6), Joan Rentsch, Lisa Delise, and Scott Hutchison (Chapter 9) take a different approach toward team cognition by applying the concept of schema theory in an attempt to define, understand, and measure this concept. The remaining chapters in the second section explore the impact of environmental context on team effectiveness. Leslie DeChurch and John Mathieu (Chapter 10) present the emerging concept of multiteam systems including core features and how they impact process, performance, and training requirements. Peter Essens, Ad Vogelaar, Jacques Mylle, Carol Blendell, Carol Paris, Stanley Halpin, and Joseph Baranski (Chapter 11) propose a theoretical framework of how teams function in complex military settings. Susan Mohammed, Katherine Hamilton, and Audrey Lim (Chapter 12) discuss the importance of time-related factors within team research. These theoretical developments represent some of the most influential developments in team effectiveness research and provide a myriad of opportunities for continued growth.

Methodological Advances

Measurement and methodological issues are of paramount importance to any field of research. Accordingly, Section 3 and Section 4 focus on recent efforts to improve the methodological aspects of team effectiveness research; specifically, they introduce recently developed measurement tools and methodological advancements, respectively. The first two chapters of the Section 3 examine the problem of assessing team performance in live environments. In Chapter 13, David Dorsey, Steven Russell, Charles Keil, Gwendolyn Campbell, Wendi Van Buskirk, and Peter Schuck document an approach to developing an automated measurement and feedback system within team simulations. Kelley Krokos, David Baker, Alexander Alonso, and Rachel Day (Chapter 14) describe a set of tools to aid in team assessment within dynamic environments. In Section 4, Peter Foltz and Melanie Martin (Chapter 15) present an approach for automated communication analysis of teams. Andrew Slaughter, Janie Yu, and Laura Koehly (Chapter 16) focus on the role of social network analysis in understanding and measuring social context and processes within teams. In Chapter 17, Wayne Zachary, Benjamin Bell, and Joan Ryder draw on cognitive engineering and modeling perspectives to present a framework and approach for computationally modeling teams and to provide research evidence in support of this approach. In short, the research described in the third and fourth sections provides new, innovative methods for measuring and analyzing team effectiveness.

Commentary and a Way Forward

Section 5 of this volume brings our dialogue of team effectiveness to a close by providing commentaries on the previously discussed topics along with a look into the future of team research. Kimberly Smith-Jentsch (Chapter 18) provides commentary regarding measurement issues, while Laurie Weingart and Matthew Cronin (Chapter 19) comment on the organizational aspects of team effectiveness. Finally, Salas and Jessica Wildman (Chapter 20) provide 10 unanswered research questions in need of deeper exploration that we hope, in addition to the rest of this volume, will inspire more and better team effectiveness research.

References

Bass, B. (1982). Individual capability, team performance, and team productivity. In M. D. Dunnette & E. A. Fleishman (Eds.), *Human performance and productivity, vol. 1: Human capability assessment* (pp. 179–232). Hillsdale, NJ: LEA.

Bowers, C. A., Braun, C. C., & Morgan, B. B. (1997). Team workload: Its meaning and measurement. In M. T. Brannick, E. Salas, & C. Prince (Eds.), *Team performance assessment and measurement: Theory, methods, and applications* (pp. 85–108). Mahwah, NJ: Lawrence Erlbaum Associates Publishers.

Burke, C. S., Stagl, K. C., Klein, C., Goodwin, G., Salas, E., & Halpin, S. M. (2006). What types of leadership behaviors are functional in teams? A meta-analysis. *Leadership Quarterly, 17,* 288–307.

Campion, M. A., Medsker, G. J., & Higgs, A. C. (1993). Relations between work group characteristics and effectiveness: Implications for designing work groups. *Personnel Psychology, 46,* 823–850.

Campion, M. A., Papper, E. M., & Medsker, G. J. (1996). Relations between work team characteristics and effectiveness: A replication and extension. *Personnel Psychology, 49,* 429–452.

Cannon-Bowers, J. A. & Salas, E. (1995). Military team research: 10 years of progress. *Military Psychology, 7,* 55–76.

Cannon-Bowers, J. A. & Salas, E. (Eds.). (1998). *Making decisions under stress: Implications for individual and team training.* Washington, DC: American Psychological Association.

Cannon-Bowers, J. A. & Salas, E. (2001). Reflections on shared cognition. *Journal of Organizational Behavior, 22,* 195–202.

Cannon-Bowers, J. A., Salas, E., Tannenbaum, S. I., & Mathieu, J. E. (1995). Toward theoretically based principles of training effectiveness: A model and initial empirical investigation. *Military Psychology, 7,* 141–165.

Cannon-Bowers, J. A., Tannenbaum, S. I., Salas, E., & Volpe, C. E. (1995). Defining team competencies and establishing team training requirements. In R. Guzzo, E. Salas, & Associates (Eds.), *Team effectiveness and decision making in organizations* (pp. 333–380). San Francisco, CA: Jossey-Bass.

Cohen, S. G. & Bailey, D. E. (1997). What makes teams work: Group effectiveness research from the shop floor to the executive suite. *Journal of Management, 23*(3), 239–290.

Cooke, N. J., Salas, E., Kiekel, P. A., & Bell, B. (2004) Advances in measuring team cognition. In E. Salas & S. M. Fiore (Eds.), *Team cognition* (pp. 83–106). Washington, DC: APA.

Department of the Army. (2006). Field Manual 6-22: Military Leadership. United States Department of Defense, Washington, D.C.

Dickinson, T. L. & McIntyre, R. M. (1997). A conceptual framework for teamwork measurement. In M. T. Brannick, E. Salas, & C. Prince (Eds.), *Team performance assessment and measurement: Theory, methods, and applications* (pp. 19–43). Mahwah, NJ: Lawrence Erlbaum Associates Publishers.

Dyer, J. L. (1984). Team research and team training: A state-of-the-art review. *Human Factors Review,* 285–323.

Edmondson, A. (1999). Psychological safety and learning behavior in work teams. *Administrative Science Quarterly, 44,* 350–383.

Fleishman, E. A. & Zaccaro, S. J. (1992). Toward a taxonomy of team performance functions. In R. W. Swezey & E. Salas (Eds.), *Teams: Their training and performance* (pp. 31–56). Westport, CT: Albex Publishing.

Fowlkes, J. E., Lane, N. E., Salas, E., Franz, T., & Oser, R. (1994). Improving the measurement of team performance: The TARGETs methodology. *Military Psychology, 6,* 47–61.

Gersick, C. J. G. (1988). Time and transition in work teams: Toward a new model of group development. *Academy of Management Journal, 31,* 9–41.

Gladstein, D. L. (1984). Groups in context: A model of task group effectiveness. *Administrative Science Quarterly, 29,* 499–517.

Guzzo, R. A. & Shea, G. P. (1992). Group performance and intergroup relations in organizations. In M. D. Dunnette & L. M. Hough (Eds.), *Handbook of industrial and organizational psychology* (2nd ed., pp. 269–313). Palo Alto, CA: Consulting Psychologists Press.

Hackman, J. R. (1983). *A normative model of work team effectiveness* (Technical Report No. 2). New Haven, CT: Yale School of Organization and Management.

Hackman, J. R. (1987). The design of work teams. In J. Lorsch (Ed.), *Handbook of organizational behavior* (pp. 315–342). Englewood Cliffs, NJ: Prentice-Hall.

Hackman, J. R. (2002). *Leading teams: Setting the stage for great performances.* Boston, MA: Harvard Business School.

Hackman, J. R. & Wageman R. (2005). A theory of team coaching. *Academy of Management Review, 30*(2), 269–287.

Harrison, D. A., Mohammed, S., McGrath, J. E., Florey, A. T., & Vanderstoep, S. W. (2003). Time matters in team performance: Effects of member familiarity, entrainment, and task discontinuity on speed and quality. *Personnel Psychology, 56*(3), 633–669.

Ilgen, D. R., Hollenbeck, J. R., Johnson, M., & Jundt, D. (2005). Teams in organizations: From input-process-output models to IMOI models. *Annual Review of Psychology, 56,* 517–543.

Kozlowski, S. W. J., Gully, S. M., Nason, E. R., & Smith, E. M. (1999). Developing adaptive teams: A theory of compilation and performance across levels and time. In D. R. Ilgen & E. D. Pulakos (Eds.), *The changing nature of work and performance: Implications for staffing, personnel actions, and development* (pp. 240–292). San Francisco, CA: Jossey-Bass.

Kozlowski, S. W. J. & Ilgen, D. R. (2006). Enhancing the effectiveness of work groups and teams. *Psychological Science in the Public Interest, 7*(3), 77–124.

Kraiger, K., Ford, J. K., & Salas, E. (1993). Application of cognitive, skill-based, and affective theories of learning outcomes to new methods of training evaluation. *Journal of Applied Psychology, 78*(2), 311–328.

Marks, M. A., Mathieu, J. E., & Zaccaro, S. J. (2001). A temporally based framework and taxonomy of team processes. *Academy of Management Review, 26,* 356–376.

McIntyre, R. M. & Salas, E. (1995). Measuring and managing for team performance: Emerging principles from complex environments. In R. Guzzo & E. Salas (Eds.), *Team effectiveness and decision making in organizations* (pp. 149–203). San Francisco, CA: Jossey-Bass.

Morgan, B. B., Jr., Glickman, A. S., Woodard, E. A., Blaiwes, A. S., & Salas, E. (1986). *Measurement of team behaviors in a Navy environment* (Technical Report Number 86-014). Orlando, FL: Naval Training Systems Center.

Nieva, V., Fleishman, E. A., & Reick, A. (1978). *Team dimensions: Their identity, their measurement, and their relationships* (Contract No. DARC 19-78-c-0001). Washington, DC: Response Analysis Corp.

Salas, E., Burke, C. S., Bowers, C. A., & Wilson, K. A. (2001). Team training in the Skies: Does crew resource management training work? *Human Factors, 43,* 641–674.

Salas, E., Rosen, M., Burke, C. S., Goodwin, G. F., & Fiore, S. M. (2006). The making of a dream team: What expert teams do best. In N. Charness, P. Feltovich, R. R. Hoffman, & K. A. Ericsson (Eds.), *The Cambridge handbook of expertise and expert performance* (pp. 439–453). Cambridge, England: Cambridge University Press.

Salas, E., Sims, D. E., & Burke, C. S. (2005). Is there "big five" in teamwork? *Small Group Research, 36*(5), 555–599.

Salas, E., Sims, D. E., & Klein, C. (2004). Cooperation at work. In C. D. Speilberger (Ed.), *Encyclopedia of applied psychology* (vol. 1, pp. 497–505). San Diego, CA: Academic Press.

Salas, E., Stagl, K. C., Burke, C. S., & Goodwin, G. F. (2007). Fostering team effectiveness in organizations: Toward an integrative theoretical framework of team performance. In J. W. Shuart, W. Spaulding, & J. Poland (Eds.), *Modeling complex systems: Motivation, cognition and social processes, Nebraska Symposium on Motivation, 51* (pp. 185–243). Lincoln: University of Nebraska Press.

Salas, E., Wilson, K. A., Burke, C. S., & Wightman, D. C. (2006). Does crew resource management training work? An update, an extension, and some critical needs. *Human Factors, 48,* 392–412.

Stagl, K. C., Salas, E., & Burke, C. S. (2006). Best practices in team leadership: What team leaders do to facilitate team effectiveness. In J. A. Conger & R. E. Riggio (Eds.), *The practice of leadership* (pp. 213–231). San Francisco, CA: Jossey-Bass.

Smith-Jentsch, K. A., Zeisig, R. L., Acton, B., & McPherson, J. A. (1998). Team dimensional training: A strategy for guided team self-correction. In J. A. Cannon-Bowers & E. Salas (Eds.), *Making decisions under stress: Implications for individual and team training* (pp. 271–298). Washington, DC: APA.

Sundstrom, E., McIntyre, M., Halfhill, T., & Richards, H. (2000). Work groups: From the Hawthorne studies to work teams of the 1990s and beyond. *Group Dynamics, Theory, Research, and Practice, 4*(1), 44–67.

Sundstrom, E., de Meuse, K. P., & Futrell, D. (1990). Work teams: Applications and effectiveness. *American Psychologist, 45,* 120–133.

Tannenbaum, S. I., Beard, R. L., & Salas, E. (1992). Team building and its influence on team effectiveness: An examination of conceptual and empirical developments. In K. Kelley (Ed.), *Issue, theory, and research in industrial/organizational psychology* (pp. 117–153). Amsterdam: Elsevier.

Tesluk, P., Mathieu, J. E., Zaccaro, S. J., & Marks, M. A. (1997). Task and aggregation issues in the analysis and assessment of team performance. In M. Brannick, E. Salas, & C. Prince (Eds.), *Team performance assessment and measurement: Theory, methods, and applications.* (pp.173–196). Mahwah, NJ: Lawrence Erlbaum Associates Publishers.

Waller, M . J., Zellmer-Bruhn, M. E., & Giambatista, R. C. (2002). Watching the
    clock: Group pacing behavior under dynamic deadlines. *Academy of Manage-
    ment Journal, 45*(5), 1046–1055.

2

Building Bridges to Improve Theory and Research on Small Groups

Richard L. Moreland and John M. Levine

These are exciting times for social scientists who study small groups and their members. For example, many conferences on topics related to groups have been held recently, both in the United States and abroad. Several of those conferences have led to intriguing books of readings (e.g., Paulus & Nijstad, 2003; Thompson, Levine, & Messick, 1999; Yzerbyt, Judd, & Corneille, 2004). Recent years have also witnessed the establishment of several journals devoted entirely to research on groups, such as *Group Dynamics: Theory, Research, and Practice* and *Group Processes and Intergroup Relations*. These (and other) journals have published some exciting findings. Such findings can be found in several recent handbooks (Frey, 1999; Hogg & Tindale, 2001; Poole & Hollingshead, 2005) that offer summaries of what is now known about groups. Finally, those who study groups have recently formed a new professional organization that brings together scientists from several branches of psychology (e.g., social, clinical, organizational, developmental) and from outside psychology (e.g., sociology, communications, political science, anthropology) to share their knowledge about groups and to work together to learn even more.

Given all this activity, it may be a good time to look ahead. If a new science of group behavior is indeed emerging, then what form should that science take? In the past, work on groups was often restricted by the number of people involved, the range of topics they studied, and their (limited) collaborations with one another. A broader and more integrated science is clearly preferable. The purpose of this chapter is to suggest several ways such a science might be created. Our suggestions involve building various bridges—bridges over time, among phenomena, across disciplines, and between academics and practitioners.

Bridges over Time

Reviews of scientific work on small groups show that it has a long history, one dating back at least to the 1930s (see Levine & Moreland, 1998). It should thus be possible for researchers to build bridges between past and current work by pursuing promising older theories (or avoiding unpromising ones) or by using new theories to reinterpret old findings. Several examples of such bridges can be found. Consider, for example, the work of Ringelmann (cited in Kravitz & Martin, 1986), from the late 1800s, which revealed a negative relationship between group size and performance. Why should larger groups perform less well? Latane, Williams, & Harkins (1979) argued and showed that both coordination and motivation problems (social loafing) might be responsible. Another example is a reinterpretation by Gaertner, Mann, Dovidio, Murrell, and Pomare (1990) of results from the classic Robbers' Cave experiment (Sherif, Harvey, White, Hood, & Sherif, 1961). In that experiment, conflict between groups was first strengthened and then weakened by encouraging those groups to compete with one another for scarce resources and then to cooperate to achieve shared goals. These results were interpreted by Sherif and colleagues (1961) as evidence for realistic group conflict theory (Campbell, 1965). Conversely, Gaertner and colleagues believed that cooperating to achieve shared goals may have been helpful in part because it led members of various groups to recategorize themselves as members of the same group. An experiment by Gaertner and colleagues supported this new interpretation, suggesting that social identity theory might provide a better explanation than realistic group conflict theory for the results of the Robbers' Cave experiment. Finally, Hamilton and Sherman (1996) built a bridge between Campbell's (1958) analysis of group entitativity and modern research on how people process information about groups versus individuals. They noted that as a group's entitativity increases (i.e., it seems more like a group rather than separate individuals), people are more likely to process information about its members as if they were a single person.

Other examples of building bridges over time could be cited; however, there are fewer of them than might be expected, and many counterexamples can be identified—older work on groups is often overlooked or ignored, even though it is relevant. Why does this happen? Several reasons can be identified. First, older work can be somewhat difficult to find. Many researchers now rely on keyword searches of computerized databases to find material relevant to their work, and those databases do not always go as far back in time as they should. Why not? There is an assumption (implicit or explicit) that scientific progress is always being made, so work that is "too old" must be outdated and therefore limited in value. That might be true in some fields, but not necessarily in small groups, where research areas can rise and fall rapidly in popularity and overall levels of research activity can be low. As a result, older work that is potentially important may not be included in a particular database.

Keyword searches are problematic in other ways as well. The databases that are searched, for example, are often discipline based. That makes it challenging to find relevant work in a field like small groups, which spans several disciplines. Also, keyword searches are most effective when everyone agrees about the terms by which work should be coded. But as time goes by, disagreements about terminology can arise, making it possible for older, yet relevant, work to be missed simply because it was coded using different terms. Finally, using computers to search databases, and then to print out whatever papers are found there, can substitute for making trips to the library. Yet such trips are a good way to uncover (sometimes serendipitously) older, relevant work.

Career pressures are another possible reason why bridges over time occur less often than they could. Although there are several paths to success for researchers in academia, one popular option is to identify a *new* phenomenon, one that no one else has noticed before. Studying a phenomenon already identified by others earns less respect (unless, of course, one can prove that the phenomenon does not really occur or that other people's explanations for it are incorrect). The desire to discover new phenomena may lead some researchers to ignore prior work that might be relevant, to misperceive their own work as different from prior work by others (even when that is not the case; see Wicklund, 1989), or in extreme cases, to make false or misleading claims about the originality of their work.

What can be done to build more bridges over time? First, as a field, we should reconsider the merits of discovering new phenomena versus developing better understandings of phenomena that have already been identified. Although the latter activity may seem less exciting, it can be just as worthwhile, sometimes even more so. Is it necessary, or even desirable, for everyone to discover and then "own" some group phenomenon? Aren't most phenomena large or complex enough to be "shared?" Second, "new" phenomena could be viewed much more skeptically. Suppose we assume that *no* phenomenon is likely to be new—every phenomenon has probably been observed and analyzed before by someone in or out of the social sciences. If so, then researchers who claim to have found something new should be challenged to justify their claim by reviewing carefully past work on similar phenomena and explaining exactly how their phenomena are different. Third, we should attempt to make access to past work easier. This might be accomplished in several ways. For example, past work that provides rich analyses of small groups—for example, Sherif and Sherif's (1964) book on adolescent groups—could be (re)introduced to researchers through an invited review in a journal or a conference presentation. Alternatively, a senior scholar could be asked to discuss older work that seemed valuable when it first appeared, but that was never adequately pursued.

Such a person could also be asked to identify linkages between current and older work that are not readily apparent and thus were overlooked. Finally, it might be worthwhile to develop a list of "lost classics"—older articles or books that contain interesting material on groups, but that are now unfamiliar to most people.

There are also things that individual researchers can do to help build bridges over time. A change in attitudes may be required in some cases. Rather than viewing past work as outdated (and thus useless) or threatening (because it undermines a claim to have discovered some new phenomenon), why not view it as an exciting chance to gain insight into that phenomenon? It can be gratifying to realize that somebody else, especially a researcher who worked long ago and under quite different circumstances, was thinking about similar issues in similar ways.

Bridges among Phenomena

Many people who study groups focus on a single phenomenon. This happens in part because group phenomena are complicated and thus cannot be understood quickly or easily. And as more time, energy, and other resources are spent, the need to justify all of that effort (Festinger, 1957) can lead a researcher to keep going, even if the results are disappointing (Staw & Ross, 1989). Self-perceptions can also change in ways that keep people focused on the same phenomenon. For example, they may review their past efforts to study a phenomenon and infer that they must be fascinated with that phenomenon (Bem, 1972), or may come to the same conclusion because so many colleagues seem to associate them with the phenomenon (Felson, 1993). Many people try to simplify their professional world by "assigning" every colleague a specialty and then resisting any changes in those assignments.

Attempts to build bridges by considering possible relationships among *different* group phenomena are uncommon, yet can be valuable. A personal example can be offered in this regard. When one of us arrived at the University of Pittsburgh, he was interested in groups and had already done some research on them, focusing on the assimilation of new members (Moreland, 1985). The other person was in the same department and was also interested in groups. He had done extensive research on groups, focusing on reactions toward marginal members (see Levine, 1980). We decided that our shared interest in groups was a good reason to collaborate, so we met to discuss what each of us knew. That discussion revealed some interesting similarities and differences between new and marginal group members. For example, both kinds of members are usually few in number, and although they belong to the group, they are not "full" members in the sense that they are not completely accepted. In other words, they are in the group, but not as far "in" as they could go. As for differences, full members' attitudes toward new members are usually more positive than their attitudes toward marginal members, and new members are often more committed than marginal members to the group.

The discussion raised issues that neither of us had considered before. How do new members become full members, for example, and how do full members become marginal members? Are the same psychological processes involved in both kinds of change? Are there people who are even further away from full membership, but still linked to the group, such as prospective members (who are thinking about entering the group, but have not done so yet) and ex-members (who once belonged to the group, but have now left it)? Later discussions regarding these and other issues led eventually to a complex model of group socialization (see Moreland & Levine, 1982, 2001) that both described and explained the passage of people through groups. It seems unlikely to us that this model could have been developed without bridge building.

An important feature of our model is the notion that social influence in groups flows not only from the group to the individual, but also from the individual to the group. This notion was derived from and then led to bridge building of a related kind, namely across various levels of analysis (see Kozlowski & Klein, 2000), from work on groups to work on individuals. Every part of our socialization model thus assumed parallel processes at both levels. We argued, for example, that a group evaluates its members to determine how much each one is contributing to the achievement of its goals, but that at the same time each member evaluates the group to determine how much it is contributing to the satisfaction of his or her personal needs. These evaluations produce feelings of commitment on both sides, from the group to the individual and from the individual to the group. Such feelings can rise and fall over time, and when they grow strong or weak enough a role transition will occur, but only if both parties are ready for it.

We are not the only theorists to have benefited from building bridges between work on groups and individuals. The individual has often been used as an implicit or explicit model for the group. Examples can be found in work on such phenomena as collective efficacy (Bandura, 1997), social identity (Tajfel & Turner, 1986), and moods (George, 1990). Although this practice has risks (see Kerr, Niedermeier, & Kaplan, 2000; Levine & Moreland, 1998), it can also be fruitful. Analogous bridge building is apparent in work relating groups to organizations and in work relating organizations to individuals (see, e.g., Staw, Sandelands, & Dutton, 1981).

Let us return for a moment to group socialization. After completing our model, we engaged in further bridge building among phenomena by considering whether an awareness of the group socialization process would provide insights into other group phenomena. In several papers that ana-lyzed such phenomena as minority influence (Levine & Moreland, 1985), group development (Moreland & Levine, 1988), workgroup culture (Levine & Moreland, 1991), intergroup relations (Levine, Moreland, & Ryan, 1998), and trust (Moreland & Levine, 2002), we built bridges between group socialization and those phenomena. In each case, this helped us to dis-cover things that others had overlooked. In our analysis of minority influ-ence, for instance, we considered some of the ways different types of group members produce intentional (and unintentional) changes in the groups to which they belong. For example, new members tend to be anxious, pas-sive, dependent, and conforming (Moreland & Levine, 1989), so they rarely attempt to change groups, and the attempts they do make seldom succeed. Yet there are a few tactics that can help newcomers to be more influential, such as arranging for respected old timers to "front" for them (see also Levine, Choi, & Moreland, 2003). And, ironically, the efforts of old timers to assimilate new members can sometimes allow such members to have unintended effects on groups, such as when newcomers ask old-timers to explain how and why things are done in certain ways, make comments that provoke social comparisons among groups, or belong to other groups that might cooperate or compete with the group they have just joined.

Other people who study small groups have also built bridges across phenomena and profited as a result. For example, Smith, Murphy, and Coats (1999) used attachment theory to analyze the commitment of mem-bers to groups. And Latane used his work with Darley on bystander inter-vention (Latane & Darley, 1970) to develop social impact theory (Latane, 1981) and dynamic social impact theory (Nowak, Szamrej, & Latane, 1990), both of which have been used to explain several other phenomena, such as social loafing. Yet bridges among phenomena, just like bridges over time, are less common than might be expected.

Journals devoted entirely to research on small groups are certainly helpful, in the sense that they help researchers discover what colleagues with potentially relevant research interests are doing. But at the same time, such journals may be harmful if they segment readers into nonover-lapping sets, each of which reads only the journals devoted to its favorite topics. Thus, researchers who study groups might become less likely to read articles on other topics, whereas researchers who study other topics might become less likely to read articles about groups. A similar prob-lem may arise as presentations on group research migrate out of general academic conferences into specialized conferences that focus exclusively on groups. So, although journals and conferences devoted to groups can certainly be valuable, we should be careful as a field to include our work in broader venues, where it can be seen by people who study other things (and where we can see their work as well).

But how does one actually build bridges among phenomena? Our experiences in developing the group socialization model offer some clues (e.g., take a serious interest in the work of another group researcher, acknowledge that his or her phenomenon and your own could be related, and then analyze that relationship carefully), but they may be too idiosyncratic to guide others. What else can be done?

Suppose we assume that all group phenomena are indeed related to one another at some level. How can those relations be identified and described? Theory can be helpful. One option is to develop a "grand" theory of groups, one that seems to explain almost everything. Consider, for example, the theory proposed by Arrow, McGrath, and Berdahl (2000) in their book on small groups as complex systems. Other examples include Robert Bales's System for Multiple Level Observation of Groups (SYM-LOG) theory (see Polley, Hare, & Stone, 1988), Von Cranach's theory of group action (Von Cranach, Ochsenbein, & Valach, 1986), and Simon's (1952) mathematical analyses of the interactions among group members. Such theories vary in their scope and quality, but it seems fair to say that none of them has ever "caught on" in terms of wide acceptance and influence. People may find it implausible that a single theory could explain so much, or maybe the theories themselves are too abstract to offer much insight into specific phenomena.

A second option is to develop a theory about some specific phenomenon and then to complicate that theory by including various moderators and mediators, considering further antecedents and consequences, and so on. This leads to the kinds of models that are found so often in articles and chapters—models illustrated by diagrams that contain numerous boxes and circles, with connecting arrows going in many directions. A well-known example is Janis's (1972) theory of groupthink. Other examples are Williams's (2001) work on the development of trust among group members; Salas, Sims, and Burke's (2005) work on the core components of teamwork; and Weldon and Weingart's (1993) work on how group goals affect group performance. This option is often more successful than the first—perhaps because the theories are narrower and have stronger empirical bases—yet their success (in terms of acceptance and influence) seems limited as well. As theories grow more complex, they can become confusing and difficult to test. In some cases, they may become (as complete theories) untestable and thus lose most of their value (see Park, 1990).

A third option, perhaps the most successful of all, is to develop a theory about some specific phenomenon and then to stretch that theory to explain as many other phenomena as possible. A good example is social identity/self-categorization theory, which was originally meant to explain *intergroup* relations but has since been extended to explain several forms of *intragroup* relations as well, including group formation (Turner, Sachdev, & Hogg, 1983), group cohesion (Hogg, 1992), group socialization

(Moreland, Levine, & McMinn, 2001), opinion polarization (Mackie, 1986), cooperation (Kramer & Brewer, 1984), and leadership (Hogg & van Knippenberg, 2003). This has impressed many people, who have begun to think about how the theory could be used to explain the phenomena they are studying themselves. In fact, a kind of "bandwagon" has emerged, as witnessed by the remarkable way social identity/self-categorization theory has spread not only throughout social psychology, but also to organizational psychology (see Ashforth & Mael, 1989). The only problem with all of this is that theoretical bandwagons eventually break down. How many people now use social exchange theory to analyze small groups, for example, despite its dominance in social psychology years ago? What causes such breakdowns? Sometimes there are inherent weaknesses in a theory that gradually become apparent as more people use it. Occasionally a theory is (over)extended to phenomena that it cannot explain well or that can be explained better by other theories. Finally, a theory can become overexposed, in the sense that people see it everywhere and become bored with it. This leads them to seek something new. There are signs that social identity/self-categorization theory may be developing some of these problems. For example, questions have been raised about several key issues in the theory, such as how group members come to agree about the specific outgroups with which their ingroup should be compared, and whether an outgroup is really important at all like the theory claims it to be (see Gaertner, Iuzzini, Guerrero, & Orina, 2006). What could be the next theoretical bandwagon for small-group researchers? A plausible guess is evolutionary theory, which has already been applied usefully to several group phenomena (see Kameda, Takezawa, & Hastie, 2003).

Bridges across Disciplines

Many social scientists advocate cross-disciplinary research (see Van Lange, 2006), which can indeed be quite valuable. De Dreu and Levine (2006) identified several possible benefits of such research: (1) stimulating people to develop innovative ideas; (2) offering opportunities for methodological triangulation; (3) helping people avoid "reinventing the wheel"; and (4) making apparent how a phenomenon can change across different settings. Cross-disciplinary research on groups may be *especially* valuable, because groups are studied by people from so many different disciplines. Persuasive evidence for this point can be found in the work of those researchers who have tried to analyze groups by bridging social psychology and other disciplines.

For example, consider Levine and Kaarbo's (2001) analysis of minority influence in political decision-making groups. By bridging social psychology and political science, they were able to develop many fresh ideas, including a new typology of minority influence and some insights into how actual minority and majority group members (as opposed to the hypothetical majorities and minorities studied by most social psychologists) interact with and influence each other. Another example is work by Kameda and colleagues on cognitive centrality (e.g., Kameda, Ohtsubo, & Takezawa, 1997). These researchers borrowed concepts and methods that sociologists use to study social networks, but rather than studying how people relate to one another (as sociologists do), they studied similarities and differences in the information that people possess. Kameda and colleagues predicted and found that people who are more central in a cognitive network (possess more of the knowledge that other group members also possess) are more influential during group decision making (cf. Wittenbaum & Park, 2001). Finally, Kerr's (1983) work on motivation losses in groups provided intriguing evidence of free riding (people take advantage of other members by working less hard at a group task), "sucker effects" (people who believe that other members are free riding work less hard at a group task), and even social compensation (people work harder at a group task if they believe that other members are doing their best, but cannot contribute enough for the group to succeed). Some of these phenomena were originally identified by economists.

Note that cross-disciplinary work can be done by a single person, because more than anything else (in our opinion) it involves integrating ideas from different disciplines. Although such integration may be easier to achieve when people from those disciplines collaborate, that is not always necessary.

Unfortunately, bridges across disciplines are rare in research on groups, even rarer than bridges over time or among phenomena. And this is not because opportunities for building such bridges are limited—many examples can be cited of group phenomena (e.g., power, cohesion, cooperation, decision making) that are studied by researchers from different disciplines. Yet these researchers often seem unaware of one another's work, or at least they never cite that work or incorporate it into their own research.

Why does this problem occur? One reason may be that researchers in one discipline often have limited access to the work of researchers from other disciplines. People tend to read only their own journals and attend their own conferences and thus hear far more about what other people in their own discipline are doing than about what people in other disciplines are doing. Another reason may be that when researchers do encounter relevant work from other disciplines, they can find it difficult to absorb. People from other disciplines often have special terms for group phenomena, use different methodologies to study those phenomena, and make implicit assumptions about groups that are confusing or (when made explicit) controversial.

But the main reason why bridges across disciplines are rare, in our opinion, is that researchers tend to be biased against scientific disciplines other than their own. There is much evidence that people favor (in both attitudes and behavior) members of their own group over members of other groups (Brewer, 1979; Mullen, Brown, & Smith, 1992), and disciplines can be viewed as groups. Psychologists thus believe they are "better" than sociologists; sociologists believe they are better than psychologists; and economists believe they are better than everyone else. What can be done to weaken these biases so that bridges across disciplines are more likely to be built? Answers to that question might be found in social psychological theory and research on intergroup relations. Much of that work focuses on how to improve the relationships between groups that dislike one another.

Consider, for example, research on the contact hypothesis, which was originally proposed by Allport (1954), who argued that part of the reason why people prefer their own group is that they are simply less familiar with other groups. To solve this problem, why not arrange for more contact between groups, so that people from different groups get to know one another better? A great deal of research has been done to test the contact hypothesis, and although some aspects of that research can be criticized (Dixon, Durrheim, & Tredoux, 2005), a clear result is that contact between groups often improves their relationships with one another (see Pettigrew & Tropp, 2005). Moreover, much has been learned about why and how such contact is helpful. A variety of factors, for example, can moderate the impact of contact on intergroup relations. Among the factors that make contact more helpful are equal status between the groups, conditions that encourage positive social interactions, and behavior that disconfirms stereotypes.

Given the apparent benefits of intergroup contact, how can people from different disciplines who study groups be brought together to weaken any "ingroup/outgroup" biases they might have? At a local level, one option may be to soften the boundaries that currently exist around different academic departments. In most universities, those boundaries are strong—people from different departments seldom interact with one another, and in many cases they even compete with one another for resources (e.g., money, students, faculty positions). It is difficult to work around these constraints, but not impossible. A few universities, for example, have created departments or schools that are explicitly cross-disciplinary in nature. Two examples are the Department of Social and Decision Sciences at Carnegie Mellon University and the School of Social Sciences at the University of California at Irvine. Researchers who study groups can be found at both places.

A more modest attempt to achieve similar goals is an informal research network that was formed in Pittsburgh by people from several departments (at both our own university and Carnegie Mellon University) who study groups and organizations. So far, the main activity of this network has been to sponsor external speakers who visit us to describe their work. Selecting these speakers (which involves extended discussions among network members), attending their talks (which may feature theories and methods unfamiliar to many audience members), and hearing questions from audience members (who represent a variety of disciplines) have been very educational. The network has helped us to view ourselves as social scientists who study groups, rather than as psychologists, sociologists, organizational scientists, and so on.

At a national level, of course, there are various scientific conferences where group researchers from different disciplines can meet and become more familiar with one another's work. Most of those conferences are sponsored by a single discipline, however, so people attending from other disciplines may feel anxious and self-conscious (see Kanter, 1977), even if they were invited to attend because of their special expertise. We remember, for example, a small, one-day conference on group research that we organized several years ago. We invited three or four people to speak during each of the two sessions (morning and afternoon). Most of the people at the conference were social psychologists, but some of the speakers were from other disciplines. The conference seemed to go very well, but afterward during informal discussions among the people who attended, two kinds of comments caught our attention. First, there were complaints from several of the social psychologists about having to listen to speakers from other disciplines. Second, the speakers in question said they were unusually anxious while giving their talks and worried about how their work was received.

Such problems might be ameliorated by making conferences explicitly cross-disciplinary and inviting a variety of participants, so that the proportions of people from different disciplines are more nearly equal. That, in fact, is the kind of conference that led to this book—a conference that was unusually successful. Conferences can also focus on specific topics, so that people are invited because of their interests and expertise and not their disciplinary affiliations. We have attended many such conferences, several of which were sponsored by the European Association of Experimental Social Psychology, and they were successful as well.

One reason contact between groups may improve relations is that it allows personal relationships to develop. If people from different groups become friends, then their biases against one another's groups should weaken. And as Wright, Aron, McLaughlin-Volpe, and Ropp (1987) showed, knowledge of that friendship can lead other group members to become less biased as well, in part because the friends provide examples of positive intergroup relations and in part because people come to view an outgroup friend of a fellow group member as someone who "belongs" to their own group. One implication of all this for scientific conferences is that they should be run in ways that foster friendships among people from different disciplines. A good example is a series of conferences on groups that Bibb Latane ran for several years at his beach home in Nags Head, North Carolina. These summer conferences were small in size and lasted for several days. Many of the participants were social psychologists, but people from other disciplines were often invited too. Conference participants certainly worked hard—several hour-long talks were given and discussed each day. But there was also considerable time for leisure activities, from which new friendships often developed. Some of those friendships, in turn, led later on to research projects that were cross-disciplinary in nature.

Finally, contact between groups may also improve their relations with one another because it fosters a common ingroup identity (Gaertner et al., 2000). Rather than viewing themselves as members of one group or the other, people come to view themselves as members of a new group, one that is larger and more inclusive. Biases are likely to weaken as a result, because people who once were only outgroup members are now ingroup members as well. An interesting issue that has generated much debate among social psychologists who study intergroup relations is whether it is better to suppress the original group identities that people bring to an intergroup contact situation, so that they can be replaced by the new, shared group identity or to let both the original group identities and the shared group identity coexist (see Barreto & Ellemers, 2003). Coexistence may be the better option, because efforts to suppress a social identity can sometimes strengthen it instead, and even if such efforts succeed they can create conflicts between someone who has abandoned an old group identity and others who belong to that group, but still identify strongly with it.

In terms of scientific conferences, all of this suggests that relationships among people from different disciplines could be improved by downplaying disciplinary backgrounds and emphasizing instead a larger social category to which everyone already belongs or could belong. Consider people who study small groups, for example. Rather than inviting them to a "psychology conference" or a "sociology conference," why not invite them to a conference of "social scientists," or better yet, a "small-groups" conference? The latter tactic is exemplified by a conference held in summer 2006 in Pittsburgh. The conference was sponsored by a new organization called INGRoup, the Interdisciplinary Network for Group Research. Attendance at the conference was open to everyone (regardless of discipline) interested in small groups, and people from several disciplines spoke about their work. A major goal of the conference organizers was to encourage more cross-disciplinary research on groups. They also hoped to make the conference an annual event and to attract as many new members to their organization as possible, so that it would become a successful professional association. People who joined that association would presumably come to share a common in-group identity, namely, "group researchers." Disciplinary backgrounds are likely to become less salient as a result, but they need not be abandoned. In fact, as noted earlier, it might be better if they were not.

Bridges between Academics and Practioners

The rarest bridges of all may be those that link academics who study groups with practitioners who use groups in their professions. Examples of such professionals include lawyers, who want to create and influence juries that will return favorable verdicts; coaches, who want their teams to win more games; teachers, who want students to learn more in the classroom; military officers, who want their units to be more victorious; and group psychotherapists, who want to improve their patients' personal adjustment. As a result of their extensive experiences with groups, these (and other) practitioners may have valuable insights into group dynamics, insights that might benefit academics. As a side note, another potential source of information about groups is the media (e.g., books, television, films), where portrayals of groups often provide rich descriptions of phenomena and sometimes suggest theories about why they occur. Examples include Buford's (1991) book *Among the Thugs*, which focused on violent behavior among the fans of professional soccer teams, and Simmons's (2002) book *Odd Girl Out*, which focused on the vagaries of friendships in groups of young girls.

Academics, with their skills at designing research and testing hypotheses about groups, could benefit practitioners by helping them to identify the most effective procedures for achieving their goals. As an example, consider the widespread enthusiasm among practitioners (e.g., managers, coaches, officers) for using group reflection (asking group members to review their past performance and to discuss what they did well and poorly) to improve future performance. Do groups that reflect really perform better, and if so, then why? Surprisingly little research in this area has been done (West, 1996), so the answers to these questions are not known. The fact that practitioners believe something helps groups does not guarantee that what they believe is true, as research on brainstorming has dramatically revealed (cf. Paulus, Dzindolet, Poletes, & Camacho, 1993). And even if research showed that group reflection was helpful, it might still be possible through further research to identify ways group reflection could be improved, making it, for example, more efficient or effective.

Collaborations between academics and practitioners are susceptible to misunderstandings and conflicts (see Moreland, 1996), which may help to explain why they are rare. Some of these problems occur because academics and practitioners have different values and interests. While planning collaborative research on groups, for example, academics put their faith in theory, whereas practitioners trust their experience or intuition. And while conducting that research, academics prefer working in simple and controlled settings, tend to distance themselves from participants, and are willing (in principle) to accept any outcome. In contrast, practitioners tolerate (and sometimes even enjoy) complex and uncontrolled settings, develop close relationships with members of the groups they manage, and may refuse to accept negative outcomes. Finally, after completing collaborative research, academics are more likely than practitioners to worry about the internal validity of any findings. When external validity is considered, academics are also more likely than practitioners to worry about the generalizability of their findings to other groups.

Of course, academics and practitioners *can* collaborate successfully, despite these difficulties, and the results are often impressive. When it comes to small groups, for example, consider work by Hastie and colleagues on jury decision making (see Pennington & Hastie, 1990; Penrod & Hastie, 1979). Among their many discoveries was the distinction between verdict-driven and evidence-driven deliberation. The former focuses on whether the defendant is guilty or innocent, whereas the latter focuses on analyzing all of the evidence presented during the trial. A verdict-driven deliberation often takes less time, but suffers from stronger conformity pressures and thus can leave some jury members feeling dissatisfied with the group's decision. Another example is work by Sutton and Hargadon (1996) on group brainstorming in organizational settings. IDEO, the organization they studied, develops new products for other companies, and brainstorming is an important part of that process. Sutton and Hargadon noted that brainstorming served a variety of purposes for IDEO, beyond just generating lots of ideas (the outcome that laboratory research on brainstorming has emphasized). For example, group brainstorming provided an opportunity for "status auctions," where IDEO workers competed informally with each other to gain or to maintain status within the organization. Finally, consider work by Ross and Staw (1993) on the escalation of commitment that occurred while the Shoreham nuclear power plant was built on Long Island, New York. Previous research on escalation, done mostly in the laboratory, emphasized the role of psychological factors that lead people to devote more and more resources to support unwise decisions. Shoreham, however, led Ross and Staw to focus on social and political factors as well.

Note that the practitioners who must have collaborated on these research projects (e.g., judges and lawyers, managers and workers, builders and politicians) apparently contributed in ways that did not warrant their inclusion as authors on the resulting articles and books. At most, they were simply thanked for their help in a footnote or forward. We could not identify any examples of collaborative research on groups in which academics and practitioners had comparable status, at least judging by the publications that resulted. This raises some interesting issues, such as what "collaboration" really means and how the contributions of practitioners to collaborative research projects are evaluated by academics.

What can be done to build more (and better) bridges between academics and practitioners? One option is to improve communication between their two worlds. Some of the group work done by practitioners (e.g., in business, military, or psychotherapy settings) is classified or confidential, so academics seldom hear about it. And although most of the work on groups that academics do is available to practitioners, because it appears in journals or books that they are free to read, it can be inaccessible if written in ways that they find difficult to understand. Some efforts to solve the latter problem have been made. For example, Division 49 (Group Psychology and Group Psychotherapy) of the American Psychological Association (APA) publishes *Group Dynamics: Theory, Research, and Practice*, a journal meant to reach an audience of both academics and practitioners. The original plan for that journal (one that is seldom followed today, maybe because it was too ambitious) was for each article to be accompanied by a commentary written by someone from a world other than the authors'. Thus, an article written by academics would be accompanied by a commentary from practitioners and vice versa. Another example is the *Academy of Management Executive*, a journal meant for business executives that contains brief, clear summaries of research findings from academia that are potentially relevant to management issues. The content of that journal often includes work on teams. Finally, Division 9 (the Society for the Psychological Study of Social Issues) of the APA maintains an office and staff in Washington, D.C. whose purpose is to keep politicians informed about the latest work by academics that is relevant to social issues. Many politicians are concerned about particular societal groups, and the briefings and position papers offered to them by Division 9 sometimes focus on issues involving those groups (e.g., family violence, prejudice, terrorism).

Another option for building bridges between academics and practitioners is to provide more opportunities for contact between them. Contact would improve communication, of course, but it might also allow personal relationships to develop between academics and practitioners, or to promote a shared group identity ("group experts"). Some of the suggestions we offered earlier for building bridges across disciplines may be relevant again here. Practitioners can be viewed as a "discipline" of their own. As a discipline, they could be included in conferences designed to promote cross-disciplinary research on groups. An example is the annual conference sponsored by Division 14 (the Society for Industrial and Organizational Psychology) of the APA. Both academics and practitioners attend this conference (in roughly equal numbers) and speak about their work. And much of that work, especially in recent years, focuses on groups.

There may be other ways to arrange for greater contact between academics and practitioners. For example, academics could spend time in professional settings where groups are used so that they can meet practitioners and become more familiar with their problems and insights. Some academics who have done this include Rick Guzzo, who visited a Wall Street investment firm to analyze the relative merits of group versus individual portfolio management, and Gary Stasser, who visited the Center for Creative Leadership to share ideas about how business executives seek and use information to make group decisions. There is no reason practitioners should not spend time in academia as well. Consider the executive education programs offered by most business schools, for example, which allow business people to attend courses and workshops on such topics as leadership and negotiation. Longer visits to academia could be also arranged if organizations and government agencies provided fellowships to sponsor such visits, as the military has sometimes done.

There are, of course, risks as well as benefits associated with visits to professional settings by academics, or visits to academia by practitioners. Visitors to new settings may feel anxious and confused, and unless they develop broader, more complex self-images (see Linville, 1982), they might begin to wonder who they really are (academics or practitioners). Long-term visitors could even "go native," abandoning a former identity and embracing a new one, which might create problems when they return home. And it would be naïve to expect visitors' hosts to welcome all of their ideas, or for any new ideas that visitors acquire to be welcomed by colleagues when they return home. In fact, research by Gruenfeld and colleagues (e.g., Gruenfeld, Martorana, & Fan, 2000) suggests that most of the intellectual influence that occurs in either direction is indirect rather than direct (see also Nemeth & Staw, 1989) and that visitors may receive a chilly reception when they return.

Conclusions

The field of small groups is healthy and seems poised to grow even bigger and stronger. Some gentle guidance at this critical stage might thus have a large impact on the development of that field. We believe that fragmentation of the field is one of its most serious problems, and to deal with that fragmentation we have suggested building several types of bridges: bridges over time, among phenomena, across disciplines, and between academics and practitioners. As noted earlier, some bridges of each type have already been built; however, many more are possible, and they are needed to create a truly integrated field. Although the diverse types of bridges may seem unrelated, they do have features in common. At all of their foundations, for example, are two important values. The first is curiosity—a desire to learn everything that can be learned about small groups. In several reviews of theory and research on groups (Levine & Moreland, 1990, 1998, 2006), we have identified a set of five major topic areas: group composition, group structure, conflict in groups, group performance, and the ecology of groups. None of these areas is understood completely, and some of them are hardly understood at all. It thus seems foolish to overlook, ignore, or reject any potentially useful ideas about groups that can be found. A second value at the foundations of all the bridges is respect for anyone who (like us) is intrigued by groups and wants to learn more about them. Does it really matter if that person is a dim voice from the past, a colleague studying some phenomenon other than the one(s) that we prefer to study, a social scientist working in another discipline, or a practitioner who is not a scientist at all? Ideas ought to be evaluated on the basis of their merits, not their sources. These two values—curiosity and a respect for others—seem important for any scientific discipline, and they will surely benefit the emerging field of small groups as well.

References

Allport, G. W. (1954). *The nature of prejudice*. Oxford: Addison-Wesley.

Arrow, H., McGrath, J. A., & Berdahl, J. L. (2000). *Small groups as complex systems: Formation, coordination, development, and adaptation*. Newbury Park, CA: Sage.

Ashforth, B. E. & Mael, F. (1989). Social identity theory and the organization. *Academy of Management Review, 14*, 20–39.

Bandura, A. (1997). *Self-efficacy: The exercise of control*. New York: Freeman.

Barreto, M. & Ellemers, N. (2003). The effects of being categorized: The interplay between internal and external social identities. *European Review of Social Psychology, 14*, 139–179.

Bem, D. J. (1972). Self-perception theory. In L. Berkowitz (Ed.), *Advances in experimental social psychology* (Vol. 6, pp. 1–62). New York: Academic Press.

Brewer, M. B. (1979). Ingroup bias in the minimal intergroup situation: A cognitive-motivational analysis. *Psychological Bulletin, 86*, 307–324.

Buford, B. (1991). *Among the thugs: The experience, and seduction, of crowd violence*. New York: W.W. Norton.

Campbell, D. T. (1965). Ethnocentric and other altruistic motives. In D. Levine (Ed.), *Nebraska symposium on motivation* (Vol. 13, pp. 283–311). Lincoln: University of Nebraska Press.

Campbell, D. T. (1958). Common fate, similarity, and other indices of the status of aggregates as social entities. *Behavioral Science, 3,* 14–25.

De Dreu, C. K. W. & Levine, J. M. (2006). Bridging social psychology and the organizational sciences. In P A. M. Van Lange (Ed.), *Bridging social psychology: Benefits of transdisciplinary approaches* (pp. 347–352). Mahwah, NJ: Erlbaum.

Dixon, J., Durrheim, K., & Tredoux, C. (2005). Beyond the optimal contact strategy: A reality check for the contact hypothesis. *American Psychologist, 60,* 697–711.

Felson, R. B. (1993). The (somewhat) social self: How others affect self-appraisals. In J. M. Suls (Ed.), *The self in social perspective* (pp. 1–26). Hillsdale, NJ: Erlbaum.

Festinger, L. (1957). *A theory of cognitive dissonance.* Stanford, CA: Stanford University Press.

Frey, L. R. (Ed.). (1999). *The handbook of group communication theory and research.* Thousand Oaks, CA: Sage.

Gaertner, L., Iuzzini, J., Guerrero, W. M., & Orina, M. M. (2006). Us without them: Evidence for an intragroup origin of positive ingroup regard. *Journal of Personality and Social Psychology, 90,* 526–439.

Gaertner, S. L., Dovidio, J. F., Nier, J. A., Banker, B. S., Ward, C. M., Houlette, M., et al. (2000). The common ingroup identity model for reducing intergroup bias: Progress and challenges. In R. Brown & D. Capozza (Eds.), *Social identity processes: Trends in theory and research* (pp. 133–148). London: Sage.

Gaertner, S. L., Mann, G. A., Dovidio, J. F., Murrell, A. J., & Pomare, M. (1990). How does cooperation reduce intergroup bias? *Journal of Personality and Social Psychology, 59,* 692–704.

George, J. M. (1990). Personality, affect, and behavior in groups. *Journal of Applied Psychology, 75,* 107–116.

Gruenfeld, D. H., Martorana, P. V., & Fan, E. T. (2000). What do groups learn from their worldliest members? Direct and indirect influence in dynamic teams. *Organizational Behavior and Human Decision Processes, 82,* 45–59.

Hamilton, D. L. & Sherman, S. J. (1996). Perceiving persons and groups. *Psychological Review, 103,* 336–355.

Hogg, M. A. (1992). *The social psychology of group cohesiveness: From attraction to social identity.* New York: New York University Press.

Hogg, M. A. & Tindale, S. T. (Eds.). (2001). *Blackwell handbook of social psychology: Group processes.* Malden, MA: Blackwell.

Hogg, M. A. & van Knippenberg, D. (2003). Social identity and leadership processes in groups. In M. Zanna (Ed.), *Advances in experimental social psychology* (Vol. 35, pp. 1–52). New York: Elsevier.

Janis, I. (1972). *Victims of groupthink: A psychological study of foreign-policy decisions and fiascoes.* Boston: Houghton-Mifflin.

Kameda, T., Ohtsubo, Y., & Takezawa, M. (1997). Centrality in sociocognitive networks and social influence: An illustration in a group decision-making context. *Journal of Personality and Social Psychology, 73,* 296–309.

Kameda, T., Takezawa, M., & Hastie, R. (2003). The logic of social sharing: An evolutionary game analysis of adaptive norm development. *Personality and Social Psychology Review, 7,* 2–19.

Kanter, R. M. (1977). Some effects of proportions on group life: Skewed sex ratios and responses to token women. *American Journal of Sociology, 82*, 965–990.

Kerr, N. L. (1983). Motivation losses in small groups: A social dilemma analysis. *Journal of Personality and Social Psychology, 45*, 819–828.

Kerr, N. L., Niedermeier, K. E., & Kaplan, M. F. (2000). On the virtues of assuming minimal differences in information processing in individuals and groups. *Group Processes and Intergroup Relations, 3*, 203–217.

Kozlowski, S. W. J. & Klein, K. J. (2000). A multilevel approach to theory and research in organizations: Contextual, temporal, and emergent processes. In K. J. Klein & S. W. J. Kozlowski (Eds.), *Multilevel theory, research, and methods in organizations; Foundations, extensions, and new directions* (pp. 3–90). San Francisco, CA: Jossey-Bass.

Kramer, R. M. & Brewer, M. B. (1984). Effects of group identity on resource use in a simulated commons dilemma. *Journal of Personality & Social Psychology, 46*, 1044–1057.

Kravitz, D. A. & Martin, B. (1986). Ringelmann rediscovered: The original article. *Journal of Personality and Social Psychology, 50*, 936–941.

Latane, B. (1981). The psychology of social impact. *American Psychologist, 36*, 343–356.

Latane, B. & Darley, J. M. (1970). *The unresponsive bystander—Why doesn't he help?* New York: Appleton-Century-Crofts.

Latane, B., Williams, K., & Harkins, S. (1979). Many hands make light the work: The causes and consequences of social loafing. *Journal of Personality and Social Psychology, 37*, 822–832.

Levine, J. M. (1980). Reaction to opinion deviance in groups. In P. Paulus (Ed.), *Psychology of group influence* (2nd ed., pp. 375–429). Hillsdale, NJ: Erlbaum.

Levine, J. M., Choi, H. S., & Moreland, R. L. (2003). Newcomer innovation in work teams. In P. Paulus & B. Nijstad (Eds.), *Group creativity: Innovation through collaboration* (pp. 202–224). New York: Oxford University Press.

Levine, J. M. & Kaarbo, J. (2001). Minority influence in political decision-making groups. In C. K. W. De Dreu & N. K. De Vries (Eds.), *Group consensus and minority influence: Implications for innovation* (pp. 229–257). Malden, MA: Blackwell.

Levine, J. M. & Moreland, R. L. (1985). Innovation and socialization in small groups. In S. Moscovici, G. Mugny, & E. Van Avermaet (Eds.), *Perspectives on minority influence* (pp. 143–169). Cambridge, England: Cambridge University Press.

Levine, J. M. & Moreland, R. L. (1990). Progress in small group research. *Annual Review of Psychology, 41*, 585–634.

Levine, J. M. & Moreland, R. L. (1991). Culture and socialization in work groups. In L. Resnick, J. M. Levine, & S. D. Teasdale (Eds.), *Perspectives on socially shared cognition* (pp. 257–279). Washington, DC: APA Press.

Levine, J. M. & Moreland, R. L. (1998). Small groups. In D. Gilbert, S. Fiske, & G. Lindzey (Eds.), *The handbook of social psychology* (4th ed., Vol. 2, pp. 415–469). Boston: McGraw-Hill.

Levine, J. M. & Moreland, R. L. (Eds.). (2006). *Small groups*. Philadelphia, PA: Psychology Press.

Levine, J. M., Moreland, R. L., & Ryan, C. S. (1998). Groups socialization and intergroup relations. In C. Sedikides, J. Schopler, & C. A. Insko (Eds.), *Intergroup cognition and intergroup behavior* (pp. 283–308). Mahwah, NJ: Erlbaum.

Linville, P. W. (1982). Affective consequences of complexity regarding the self and others. In M. S. Clark & S. T. Fiske (Eds.), *Affect and cognition: The 17th Annual Carnegie Symposium on Cognition* (pp. 79–109). Hillsdale, NJ: Erlbaum.

Mackie, D. M. (1986). Social identification effects in group polarization. *Journal of Personality and Social Psychology, 50,* 720–728.

Moreland, R. L. (1985). Social categorization and the assimilation of "new" group members. *Journal of Personality and Social Psychology, 48,* 1173–1190.

Moreland, R. L. (1996). Lewin's legacy for small groups research. *Systems Practice, 9,* 7–26.

Moreland, R. L. & Levine, J. M. (1982). Socialization in small groups: Temporal changes in individual-group relations. In L. Berkowitz (Ed.), *Advances in experimental social psychology* (Vol. 15, pp. 137–192). New York: Academic Press.

Moreland, R. L. & Levine, J. M. (1988). Group dynamics over time: Development and socialization in small groups. In J. McGrath (Ed.), *The social psychology of time: New perspectives* (pp. 151–181). Newbury Park, CA: Sage.

Moreland, R. L. & Levine, J. M. (1989). Newcomers and oldtimers in small groups. In P. Paulus (Ed.), *Psychology of group influence* (2nd ed., pp. 143–186). Hillsdale, NJ: Erlbaum.

Moreland, R. L. & Levine, J. M. (2001). Socialization in organizations and work groups. In M. Turner (Ed.), *Groups at work: Theory and research* (pp. 69–112). Mahwah, N.J.: Erlbaum.

Moreland, R. L. & Levine, J. M. (2002). Socialization and trust in work groups. *Group Processes and Intergroup Relations, 5,* 185–201.

Moreland, R. L., Levine, J. M., & McMinn, J. G. (2001). Self-categorization and work group socialization. In M. Hogg & D. Terry (Eds.), *Social identity processes in organizational contexts* (pp. 87–100). Philadelphia, PA: Psychology Press.

Mullen, B., Brown, R., & Smith, C. (1992). Ingroup bias as a function of salience, relevance, and status: An integration. *European Journal of Social Psychology, 22,* 103–122.

Nemeth, C. J. & Staw, B. M. (1989). The tradeoffs of social control and innovation within groups and organizations. In L. Berkowitz (Ed.), *Advances in experimental social psychology* (Vol. 22, pp. 175–210). New York: Academic Press.

Nowak, A., Szamrej, J., & Latane, B. (1990). From private attitude to public opinion: A dynamic theory of social impact. *Psychological Review, 97,* 362–376.

Park, W. -W. (1990). A review of research on groupthink. *Journal of Behavioral Decision Making, 3,* 229–245.

Paulus, P. B., Dzindolet, M. T., Poletes, G., & Camacho, L. M. (1993). Perception of performance in group brainstorming: The illusion of group productivity. *Personality and Social Psychology Bulletin, 19,* 78–89.

Paulus, P. B. & Nijstad, B. A. (2003). *Group creativity: Innovation through collaboration.* Oxford: Oxford University Press.

Pennington, N. & Hastie, R. (1990). Practical implications of psychological research on juror and jury decision making. *Personality and Social Psychology Bulletin, 16,* 90–105.

Penrod, S. & Hastie, R. (1979). Models of jury decision making: A critical review. *Psychological Bulletin, 86,* 462–492.

Pettigrew, T. F. & Tropp, L. R. (2005). Allport's intergroup contact hypothesis: Its history and influence. In J. F. Dovidio, P. Glick, & L. A. Rudman (Eds.), *On the nature of prejudice: Fifty years after Allport* (pp. 262–277). Malden, MA: Blackwell.

Polley, R. B., Hare, A. P., & Stone, P. J. (1988). *The SYMLOG practitioner: Applications of small group research*. New York: Praeger.

Poole, M. S. & Hollingshead, A. B. (Eds.). (2005). *Theories of small groups: Interdisciplinary perspectives*. Thousand Oaks, CA: Sage.

Ross, J. & Staw, B. M. (1993). Organizational escalation and exit: Lessons from the Shoreham Nuclear Power Plant. *Academy of Management Journal, 36,* 701–732.

Salas, E., Sims, D. E., & Burke, C. S. (2005). Is there a "Big Five" in teamwork? *Small Group Research, 36,* 555–599.

Sherif, M., Harvey, O. J., White, J., Hood, W. R., & Sherif, C. W. (1961*). Intergroup conflict and cooperation: The Robbers' Cave Eexperiment*. Norman, OK: Institute of Group Relations.

Sherif, M. & Sherif, C. W. (1964). *Reference groups: Exploration into conformity and deviation of adolescents*. New York: Harper & Row.

Simmons, R. (2002). *Odd girl out: The hidden culture of aggression in girls*. New York: Harcourt.

Simon, H. A. (1952). A formal theory of interaction in social groups. *American Sociological Review, 17,* 202–211.

Smith, E., Murphy, J., & Coats, S. (1999). Attachment to groups: Theory and management. *Journal of Personality and Social Psychology, 77,* 94–110.

Staw, B. M. & Ross, J. (1989). Understanding behavior in escalation situations. *Science, 246,* 216–220.

Staw, B. M., Sandelands, L. E., & Dutton, J. E. (1981). Threat-rigidity effects in organizational behavior: A multilevel analysis. *Administrative Science Quarterly, 26,* 501–524.

Sutton, R. I. & Hargadon, A. (1996). Brainstorming groups in context: Effectiveness in a product design firm. *Administrative Science Quarterly, 41,* 685–718.

Tajfel, H. & Turner, J. C. (1986). The social identity theory of intergroup behaviour. In S. G. Worchel & W. Austin (Eds.), *Psychology of intergroup relations* (2nd ed., pp. 7–24). Chicago, IL: Nelson-Hall.

Thompson, L. L., Levine, J. M., & Messick, D. M. (Eds.) (1999). *Shared cognition in organizations: The management of knowledge*. Mahwah, NJ: Erlbaum.

Turner, J. C., Sachdev, L., & Hogg, M. A. (1983). Social categorization, interpersonal attraction, and group formation. *British Journal of Social Psychology, 22,* 227–239.

Van Lange, P. A. M. (Ed.). (2006). *Bridging social psychology: Benefits of transdisciplinary approaches*. Mahwah, NJ: Erlbaum.

Von Cranach, M., Ochsenbein, G., & Valach, L. (1986). The group as a self-active system: Outline of a theory of group action. *European Journal of Social Psychology, 16,* 193–229.

Weldon, E. & Weingart, L. R. (1993). Group goals and group performance. *British Journal of Social Psychology, 32,* 307–334.

West, M. A. (1996). Reflexivity and work group effectiveness: A conceptual integration. In M. A. West (Ed.), *Handbook of work group psychology* (pp. 555–579). Chichester, England: Wiley.

Wicklund, R. A. (1989). The appropriation of ideas. In P. B. Paulus (Ed.), *Psychology of group influence* (2nd ed., pp. 393–423). Hillsdale, NJ: Erlbaum.

Williams, M. (2001). In whom we trust: Group membership as an affective context for trust development. *Academy of Management Review, 26,* 377–396.

Wittenbaum, G. M. & Park, E. S. (2001). The collective preference for shared information. *Current Directions in Psychological Science, 10,* 70–73.

Wright, S. C., Aron, A., McLaughlin-Volpe, T., & Ropp, S. A. (1997). The extended contact effect: Knowledge of cross-group friendships and prejudice. *Journal of Personality and Social Psychology, 73,* 73–90.

Yzerbyt, V., Judd, C. M., & Corneille, O. (Eds.). (2004). *The psychology of group perception: Perceived variability, entitativity, and essentialism.* New York: Psychology Press.

3

The Wisdom of Collectives in Organizations: An Update of the Teamwork Competencies

Eduardo Salas, Michael A. Rosen,
C. Shawn Burke, and Gerald F. Goodwin

Introduction

What do we mean by the *wisdom of collectives*? This is best illustrated by examining the trend toward discussing emergence within teams (Kozlowski & Klein, 2000) and other social systems (Chu, Strand, & Fjelland, 2003; Streufert, 1997). Emergence is characterized by the creation of "novel and coherent structures, patterns and properties during the process of self-organization in complex systems" (Goldstein, 1999, p. 49). Emergent properties are the result of the interaction of the components of the system from which these emergent properties arise but cannot be reduced to or described wholly in terms of the elementary components of the system considered in isolation. The whole truly is greater than (or at least different from) the sum of its parts. In this way some teams are able to synergistically combine the attributes of its members to produce outcomes well beyond the capacity of any one individual member or of the pooled or summated output of all its members (Cannon-Bowers, Salas, & Converse, 1993; Salas, Cannon-Bowers, & Johnston, 1997; Salas, Rosen, Burke, Goodwin, & Fiore, 2006). This is what we refer to with the phrase the *wisdom of collectives*: the increased capacity for performance of various types afforded by the interactions of team members.

It is the purpose of this chapter to document what is known about the mechanisms of teamwork interaction that enable the development of the wisdom of collectives. Surely all collectives are not equal. Not all teams are able to leverage their team member expertise effectively (e.g., Hirschfeld, Jordan, Feild, Giles, & Armenakis, 2006). So what separates exceptional from average and poorer performing teams? Understanding the processes of teamwork is key to understanding the wisdom of collectives, the means by which teams successfully interact to produce superior team outcomes. This issue has been studied from many different vantage points, and a complete review of these efforts is well beyond the scope of any one chapter. Therefore, the intent of this chapter is to both retrospectively and prospectively chart the course of the study of teams by demarcating where we've been, where we are, and where we should be headed as a field of inquiry. To this end, we set out to meet the following goals. First, we provide an overview of teamwork by reviewing the current scientific understanding of teams and recent developments in the field. Second, we further delineate teamwork by updating the teamwork competencies—the knowledge, skills, and attitudes (KSAs) necessary for effective teamwork—proposed more than a decade ago by Cannon-Bowers, Tannenbaum, Salas, and Volpe (1995). Third, we present a research agenda for furthering our understanding of the wisdom of collectives in organizations.

What Are the Mechanisms of Teamwork?

In this section we provide an up-to-date global view of teamwork by reviewing recent developments in the science of teams. To discuss teamwork appropriately requires the definition of a small constellation of related terms. The interdisciplinary nature of team research has led to great theoretical and practical advances in knowledge, but the ontological drift of terminology between research communities continues to be an issue that impedes understanding and further advancement. Therefore, we begin our discussion of teamwork with a set of definitions on which we anchor the remainder of our discussion.

Definitions

First, a *team* is defined as a set of two or more individuals that adaptively and dynamically interacts through specified roles as they work toward shared and valued goals (Dyer, 1984; Salas, Dickinson, Converse, & Tannenbaum, 1992). Team member interdependency is a critical feature of defining the essence of a team (Saavedra, Earley, & Van Dyne, 1993). In addition to this, teams can often be characterized as having heterogeneous and distributed expertise (Salas, Stagl, Burke, & Goodwin, 2007); that is, team members often have different specializations in knowledge and skills. In fact, it is this diversity of expertise that creates the potential for teams to complete work outside the scope of any one individual's capabilities. The social dynamics of effective teamwork are necessary to realize this potential.

Teamwork is the "dynamic, simultaneous and recursive enactment of process mechanisms which inhibit or contribute to team performance and performance outcomes" (Salas, Stagl, Burke & Goodwin, 2007, p. 190). To clarify this definition, it is useful to think of competencies within a team as belonging to one of two types: teamwork and taskwork (McIntyre & Salas, 1998; Morgan, Glickman, Woodard, Blaiwes, & Salas, 1986). Taskwork competencies are the knowledge, skills, attitudes, and other characteristics (KSAOs) used to accomplish individual task performance; the application of these skills does not require interdependent interaction within the team. Teamwork competencies are the KSAOs necessary for members to function within an interdependent team. Therefore, team members must possess not only individual-level expertise relevant to the technical performance of their own individual tasks but also expertise in the social dynamics of teamwork (Salas et al., 2006). Teamwork is the *process* of enacting these teamwork competencies. Much of the remainder of this chapter is devoted to the description of these teamwork processes.

Team performance is a multilevel process arising as team members enact both their individual taskwork performance processes and individual- and team-level teamwork processes (Kozlowski & Klein, 2000; Salas et al., 2007). This can be contrasted with the definition of teamwork already provided, which focuses on the enactment of teamwork processes alone. Therefore, teamwork is nested within team performance in that team performance is the combination of both individual performance and teamwork processes. This definition is consistent with the conceptualization of performance as a process and not an outcome (Campbell, 1990).

Team effectiveness is an evaluation of the outcomes of team performance processes relative to some set of criteria. It is a judgment of how well the results of performance meet some set of relatively objective (e.g., metrics of productivity) or subjective (e.g., supervisor or observer ratings) standards. These standards are ideally aligned with the goals of the team and organization. Hackman (1987) proposed three dimensions of team effectiveness. First, the relevant stakeholders judge whether the team is meeting standards of quality and quantity. Second, group members evaluate whether they are satisfied with their team participation. Third, the degree to which the team's interaction has maintained, weakened, or strengthened the work group's capacity to continue to work together should be assessed.

The increasing interest in teams has led to a proliferation of theoretical models and frameworks of teamwork, team performance, and team effectiveness. A recent review identified 138 attempts from various disciplines that model or frame aspects of team performance or team effectiveness (Salas et al., 2007). This abundance of theories, models, and frameworks is indicative of a "golden age" of interest in teams. Unfortunately, this large number of models, which are often context or domain specific in nature, also complicates the process of translating the current understanding of teams into actionable and practical guidance for organizations. However, there have been several recent and notable efforts in the area of integrating these models and frameworks of teamwork, team performance, and team effectiveness. The following section discusses several of these efforts.

What Is Teamwork?

Teamwork is the means by which individual task expertise is translated, magnified, and synergistically combined to yield superior performance outcomes, the wisdom of the collectives. This section briefly summarizes the current state of the science regarding teamwork. Our review here is necessarily selective and focuses primarily on work seeking to characterize teamwork in a global and generalizable manner. First, we review a recently advanced model of teamwork (Salas, Sims, & Burke, 2005) because it represents a broad cross-section of the literature. Second, we turn toward other recently advanced frameworks for organizing and understanding teamwork behaviors. Third, we discuss some of the newly developed extensions to the traditional Input–Process–Output (IPO) method of describing teamwork.

A Model of Teamwork

Salas and colleagues (2005) proposed the idea that there might be a "big five" in teamwork; that is, across, for example, domains, team goals, and tasks, there are five core components of teamwork: (1) team leadership; (2) adaptability; (3) mutual performance monitoring; (4) backup behavior; and (5) team orientation. The importance of each component may vary in degree across contexts, but each of the five teamwork components in some form is essential for any type of teamwork. In addition to the five components of teamwork, three coordinating mechanisms are identified: (1) shared mental models; (2) closed-loop communication; and (3) mutual trust. These coordinating mechanisms facilitate the enactment of the five factors of teamwork. Each of the coordinating mechanisms and core components of teamwork are briefly discussed in the following sections.

The Five Core Components of Teamwork

Team leadership has substantial ramifications for the effectiveness of teams and organizations at large. The functional approach to leadership, which has emerged as a dominant perspective (e.g., Fleishman et al., 1991; Hackman, 2002; Zaccaro, Rittman, & Marks, 2001), characterizes leadership as "social problem solving that promotes coordinated, adaptive team performance by facilitating goal definition and attainment" (Salas, Burke, & Stagl, 2004, p. 343). Leaders solve social problems through four general types of actions: (1) the search for and structuring of information; (2) the use of information in problem solving; (3) the management of personnel resources; and (4) the management of material resources.

To meet the demands of increasingly dynamic task environments, the concept of shared leadership has been explored. Shared leadership is the "transference of the leadership function among team members to take advantage of member strengths (e.g., knowledge, skills, attitudes, perspectives, contacts, and time available) as dictated by either environmental demands or the development stage of the team" (Burke, Fiore, & Salas, 2004, p. 105). This can allow the team to be more responsive to changing environmental conditions and to more optimally leverage the heterogeneous individual level expertise of team members. There is preliminary research showing that shared leadership is more effective than traditional leadership structures (Pearce & Sims, 2002).

Adaptability within teams underlies many team functions and behaviors (Burke, Stagl, Salas, Pierce, & Kendall, 2006) and can be characterized as the team's ability to change team performance processes in response to cues from the environment in a manner that results in functional team outcomes (Burke et al., 2006; Entin & Serfaty, 1999). Adaptability is an essential component of teamwork, especially for teams operating under dynamic conditions. Until recently, there has been only a small amount of research dealing with temporal aspects of team processes and performance (Dyer, 1984). This void is beginning to be addressed (e.g., Gersick, 1988; Morgan, Salas, & Glickman, 2001). For example, Burke and colleagues (2006) proposed a model of team adaptation. At the center of this model is adaptive team performance, defined as "an emergent phenomenon which compiles over time from the unfolding of a recursive cycle whereby one or more team members utilize their resources to functionally change current cognitive or behavioral goal directed action or structures to meet expected or unexpected demands" (ibid., p. 1192). Adaptive team performance is achieved as the team passes through four phases. The first phase consists of situation assessment, a process by which team members recognize cue patterns in the environment and build a coherent understanding of their present circumstances. The second phase is plan formulation, where the team generates and decides on a course of action appropriate for the current situation. The third phase is plan execution, which is achieved via team coordination mechanisms. The fourth and final phase is team learning, wherein the team evaluates the effectiveness of its performance. The results of this evaluation will feed into future performance episodes (i.e., passes through the adaptive cycle) as emergent affective and cognitive states developed in previous performance episodes influence performance in future episodes. Adaptability has been framed in other ways as well, such as the self-regulation of processes relative to individual and team goals (Deshon, Kozlowski, Schmidt, Milner, & Wiechmann, 2004) and temporal entrainment (Harrison, Mohammed, McGrath, Florey, & Vanderstoep, 2003).

Mutual performance monitoring is the ability to "keep track of fellow team member's work while carrying out their own … to ensure that everything is running as expected and … to ensure that they are following procedures correctly" (McIntyre & Salas, 1995, p. 23). This is an essential component of teamwork, but it can also have negative effects on performance depending on the perceptions of performance monitoring by team members. That is, if mutual performance monitoring is thought of as team members attempting to "keep tabs" on one another for the purposes of avoiding personal responsibility for errors, the negative affect generated by this practice will likely outweigh its potential benefits. Therefore, a team must develop an accepting culture of this practice and attitudes toward mutual performance monitoring that frame it as a valuable means of elevating levels of performance. Additionally, teams must develop shared mental models for mutual performance monitoring to be successful. Team members must understand normative aspects of the team, task, and equipment to detect deviations from normal or expected conditions. Knowing *what should be* happening is a necessary condition to obtaining useful information from observations of *what is* happening at any one point in time.

Backup behavior (or supporting behavior) is "the discretionary provision of resources and task-related effort to another … [when] there is recognition by potential backup providers that there is a workload distribution problem in their team" (Porter et al., 2003, pp. 391–392). As implied already, mutual performance monitoring is a necessary prerequisite for backup behavior, and backup behavior is necessary to leverage mutual performance monitoring into performance gains. Backup behavior can be either physical or verbal (or other communicative) assistance. This supports effective team performance in three key ways (Marks, Mathieu, & Zaccaro, 2001). First, this assistance allows team members to provide timely feedback to one another so that performance processes can be adjusted. Second, backup behavior allows team members to provide assistance during task performance. Third, backup behavior allows teams to dynamically readjust their performance strategies and processes when a detrimental imbalance in the workload distribution is detected. This affords the team an adaptive capacity. Expert command and control teams exhibit two specific backup behaviors that enable consistently high levels of performance (Smith-Jentsch, Johnston, & Payne, 1998; Smith-Jentsch, Zeisig, Acton, & McPherson, 1998). First, team members correct the errors of other team members, a process that reduces the number of errors in the team's performance and helps to develop the skill levels of team members as they receive feedback on poor performance. Second, team members provide and request assistance and backup when it is needed.

Team orientation is more than an individual's preference for working within a team versus working in isolation as an individual. It is the propensity to coordinate, evaluate, and use the task inputs of fellow teammates (Driskell & Salas, 1992). These preferences and patterns of behavior are essential for effective teamwork. For example, when teams experience increasing levels of stress (e.g., time pressure), empirical studies show that team members can succumb to attentional narrowing, in that they shift their focus away from the team and focus on their individual taskwork (Driskell & Salas, 1991; Kleinman & Serfaty, 1989). Team members under stress become less likely to accept input or feedback from others on their team. This loss of team perspective is associated with poor team performance (Driskell, Salas, & Johnston, 1999).

Coordinating Mechanisms

These five core components of teamwork are made possible by three core coordination mechanisms: shared mental models, closed-loop communication, and mutual trust. These coordination mechanisms facilitate the enactment of the five teamwork components by ensuring that information is distributed in an appropriate and timely manner. Each of these mechanisms is discussed in more detail in this section.

Shared mental models are organized knowledge structures that facilitate execution of interdependent team processes (Klimoski & Mohammed, 1994). An individual-level mental model is a knowledge structure involved in the process of integrating information and comprehending a phenomenon of interest (Johnson-Laird, 1983). Expanded to the team level, a mental model that is shared is a knowledge structure or mental representation that is partially shared and partially distributed throughout a team. This "sharedness" or distribution allows team members to interpret incoming information in a similar or compatible manner and thereby facilitates effective coordination. Team members that share mental representations are better able to develop similar causal explanations of the environment as well as inferences about possible states of the environment in the near future. This results in more effective and adaptive team performance and higher-quality decision making in teams (Cannon-Bowers et al., 1993; Mathieu, Heffner, Goodwin, Salas, & Cannon-Bowers, 2000; Stout, Cannon-Bowers, & Salas, 1996). Similarly, shared mental models enable the implicit communication that is characteristic of highly effective teams (Mohammed & Dumville, 2001). However, the accuracy of mental models is more important to team performance than sharedness (Edwards,

Day, Arthur, & Bell, 2006). Accuracy can be thought of as a prerequisite to obtaining benefits from shared mental models since there is no performance gain to be had from sharing inaccurate mental models.

Closed-loop communication is a specific pattern of communication that enables effective teamwork. In general, communication is the "exchange of information between a sender and a receiver" (McIntyre & Salas, 1995, p. 25). The importance of communication as control and guidance in social systems has been understood for many years (e.g., Wiener, 1954). This point has been emphasized within team research by the information-processing perspective of teams (Hinsz, Tindale, & Vollrath, 1997), where teams must acquire information about the environment and distribute that information internally to perform actions (MacMillan, Entin, & Serfaty, 2004). Communication is the means by which teams translate individual-level understanding into the team-level dynamic representations that guide coordinated action (Cooke, Salas, Kiekel, & Bell, 2004). Effective teams are able to shift between implicit and explicit communication in response to changing environmental demands and task constraints (Entin & Serfaty, 1999; Espinosa, Lerch, & Kraut, 2004). When effective teams engage in explicit communication, they use closed-loop communication (Bowers, Jentsch, Salas, & Braun, 1998). Three characteristics defined closed-loop communication: (1) a message being initiated by the sender; (2) that message being received, interpreted, and acknowledged by the intended receiver; and (3) a follow-up by the sender ensuring that the message was received and appropriately interpreted (McIntyre & Salas, 1995). This pattern of communication helps to ensure that all team members are operating under the same goals, plans, and understanding of the situation (Orasanu, 1990, 1994).

Additionally, Smith-Jentsch and colleagues (Smith-Jentsch, Zeisig, et al. 1998; Smith-Jentsch, Johnston, et al., 1998) identified four specific teamwork behaviors contributing to good team communication. First, team members should use the proper "phraseology." Teams that speak with a specialized communication terminology are able to pass large amounts of information very quickly (Klein, Feltovich, Bradshaw, & Woods, 2005). Second, team members should provide complete internal and external reports. Third, team members should minimize unnecessary communications (e.g., chatter). This minimizes the workload inherent in team communication and coordination by focusing only on the essentials of interaction necessary for team performance. Fourth, team members should make sure that their communications are clear and audible. This minimizes the chance of misinterpretations of communications.

Mutual trust in the context of teams has been defined as "the shared perception ... that individuals in the team will perform particular actions important to its members and ... will recognize and protect the rights and interests of all the team members engaged in their joint endeavor" (Webber,

2002, p. 205). As discussed, trust is essential to effective teamwork factors such as mutual performance monitoring and backup behavior. Without mutual trust, resources of the team (e.g., attention, communication) may be squandered on unnecessary checking up on team members to ensure that they are performing adequately (Cooper & Sawaf, 1996). Mutual trust also underlies team processes and outcomes such as the degree of team member contributions and participation, outcome quality and retention (Bandow, 2001; Jones & George, 1998).

The model of teamwork is a synthesis of theoretical models of teamwork and illustrates an important point about teamwork that is best described through a comparison of teamwork with the research literature concerning individual expertise. The global view of individual expertise has come to be understood as a "prototype" of various mechanisms (e.g., metacognition, skilled memory, conceptual organization of knowledge; Hoffman, Feltovich, & Ford, 1997; Holyoak, 1991; Sternberg, 1997). However, the relative importance of these mechanisms for expert performance in any one task will be dictated by the constraints of that task. Therefore, expertise is a process of psychological and physiological adaptation to the task (Ericsson & Lehmann, 1996). We argue that the same holds true for teams. Teamwork can be delineated in a global sense as a prototype of what generally constitutes teamwork, but the importance of these teamwork processes to superior performance will differ depending on the nature of the specific team task. The following sections explore specific aspects of this prototype of teamwork in more detail.

Other Organizations of Teamwork Behaviors

The model of teamwork presented in the previous sections is an attempt to generate a parsimonious model, one that captures the essence of teamwork over as broad a range of teams, tasks, and contexts as possible, with as few constructs as possible. The five components and three coordinating mechanisms, however, are not the only aspects of teamwork identified in the literature, and other synthesized models of teamwork have been proposed for teamwork in general (e.g., Militello, Kyne, Klein, Getchell, & Thordsen, 1999; Rasmussen & Jeppesen, 2006) as well as for specific aspects of teamwork—such as distributed planning (Klein & Miller, 1999) and team coaching (Hackman & Wageman, 2005). Instead of moving toward a parsimonious model of teamwork (i.e., capturing the most explanatory power of teamwork behaviors over the broadest spectrum of contexts with the smallest number of explanatory mechanisms), some researchers have attempted to organize the bulk of the literature concerning teamwork behaviors, with the aim of inclusiveness and comprehensiveness instead of parsimony.

Notably, Rousseau, Aube, and Savoie (2006) organized a significant portion of the teamwork behavior literature (integrating 29 of the more than 100 extant frameworks of teamwork; for a complete listing of published team related frameworks, see Salas et al., 2007) around the action regulation theory of Frese and Zapf (1994). Action regulation theory asserts that high performance is attained by individuals that engage in the sequential application of regulation functions to task accomplishment. To successfully complete a task, individuals must do the following:

1. Orient themselves to the task and criteria for gauging success (i.e., an orientation phase)
2. Perform and carry out tasks (i.e., an execution phase)
3. Monitor their progress toward their goals (i.e., an evaluation phase)
4. Make adjustments as needed based on the results of performance evaluation (i.e., an adjustment phase)

Within this action regulation theory framework, Rousseau and colleagues (2006) hierarchically organized teamwork behaviors. They began with two macrolevel categories: (1) regulation of team performance; and (2) management of team maintenance. There are two categories of teamwork subsumed under management of team maintenance: (1) psychological support; and (2) integrative conflict management. There are four categories within the regulation of team performance category: (1) preparation of work accomplishment (i.e., team mission analysis, goal specification, and planning); (2) work assessment behaviors (i.e., performance monitoring, and systems monitoring); (3) task-related collaborative behaviors (i.e., coordination, cooperation, and information exchange); and (4) team adjustment behaviors (i.e., backing up behaviors, intrateam coaching, collaborative problem solving, and team practice innovation). By organizing teamwork behaviors with a framework of regulation processes, Roussea and colleagues introduced the element of time into their conceptual structure of teamwork behaviors. Different teamwork behaviors are more likely to occur during different phases of activity (e.g., mission analysis will likely occur in a team's preparation phase). This organization parallels the temporal framework of team processes (Marks et al., 2001). The next section discusses temporal issues in teamwork more directly. In doing so, we shift from discussing the components to the structure of various models of teamwork.

Evolution of the IPO Model: A Focus on Time in Teamwork

Teamwork is most often conceptualized using the IPO model structure (e.g., Hackman, 1987; Salas et al., 1992). IPO models describe teamwork through relationships between input variables (e.g., individual and team characteristics, task characteristics), process variables (e.g., mutual performance monitoring, communication, coordination, leadership), and outcome variables (e.g., performance outcomes, productivity, and satisfaction). Although this has been a widely adopted perspective, it has come to be criticized for representing teamwork as relatively "static" in nature (e.g., Marks et al., 2001). This general criticism comes in two specific varieties, each focused on a different time scale in the life of a team. These issues, and research targeted at remedying the shortcomings of teamwork research in relation to time, are discussed next.

First, IPO models are criticized for condensing and oversimplifying how teams function during task performance. For instance, Marks et al. (2001) provided a temporally based framework for team processes that defines the level of analysis or interest in terms of performance episodes: "distinguishable periods of time over which performance accrues and feedback is given" (p. 359). These performance episodes are distinguished in relation to goals and the team's progress toward accomplishing them. Because teams often pursue multiple goals concurrently (e.g., Deshon et al., 2004), different performance episodes can co-occur and overlap, something not explicitly accounted for in the traditional IPO models. Additionally, although most IPO models do incorporate a feedback loop, which indicates that the team outcomes of performance are "recycled" as team inputs for future performance episodes, IPOs have been criticized for focusing on too broad of a time slice, such that the cycle of the IPO indicates a large portion of the team's development. Marks and colleagues (2001) proposed that the IPO cycle should be associated with the performance episode, indicating that team performance outcomes are recycled into inputs frequently as teams accomplish goals and subgoals of their tasks. When teamwork processes are collapsed or aggregated across multiple performance episodes, the picture of team performance becomes static and summary in nature.

The second variety of criticism holds that IPO models tend to deemphasize the long-term development of teams. This is essentially the first criticism extended in the opposite direction; instead of deemphasizing short-term performance, IPOs are criticized for not addressing longer-term team development. In the real world, teams learn, develop, and mature over their lifetimes (Edmondson, 2002; Gersick, 1988, 1989; Morgan et al., 2001). Kozlowski and colleagues (1999) addressed this concern by proposing a theory of incremental and continuous learning in teams (a theory of compilation and performance across levels and time). Central to this theory is the idea that teams continuously learn and adapt as they engage in performance. This process is repeated as nested IPO cycles build team knowledge and skills while team processes and outcomes are progressively and incrementally enhanced.

Ilgen and colleagues (2005) proposed a shift from the IPO framework to what they describe as an Input–Mediator–Output–Input (IMOI) framework. The exchange of the P (i.e., process) for M (i.e., mediator) indicates that there are more factors than team processes that influence team outcomes (e.g., emergent states). The addition of the extra I indicates an increased emphasis on the cyclical nature of team performance wherein outputs of one performance episode are translated into inputs for future performance. This IMOI framework is consistent with the conceptualization of team performance as nested IPO cycles (e.g., Burke et al., 2006; Kozlowski et al., 1999; Marks et al., 2001; Salas et al., in press). This focus on time is expanded by researchers that take a dynamical systems perspective on teams and small groups (e.g., Arrow, McGrath, & Berdahl, 2000; Cooke, Gorman, & Rowe, Chapter 6 in this volume). Although this perspective holds great promise for developing more robust understanding of how teams function, it is in its infancy and represents a radical departure from the current IPO frameworks of teams (as well as from some fundamental notions in the behavioral sciences such as the nature of causation).

In sum, team researchers have made great progress on many fronts in recent years. Although criticized to some degree, the IPO framework has proven highly robust and adaptable. It has been scaled both up and down in terms of temporal frames to better explain team performance. Models and frameworks have been proposed that have great parsimony as well as great inclusiveness. What is clear from this brief review is the importance of time in the study of teams. This recent growth in understanding of teams and teamwork has led to a more robust understanding of the building blocks of superior team performance, the competencies that team members must possess to engage in effective teamwork. The following section updates a previously proposed set of teamwork competencies in light of the recent empirical and theoretical findings regarding teams.

The ABCs of Teamwork: The Competencies

The ABCs of teamwork refer to the attitudes, behaviors, and cognitions (i.e., KSAOs) that constitute team competencies. In this context, attitudes are the affective attributes necessary for effective team performance; behaviors are the skills and procedures needed for teamwork; and cognitions are the necessary elements of knowledge and experience necessary for effective teamwork. An understanding of the ABCs of teamwork is essential for designing tasks and equipment, for conducting training, for evaluating performance, and for defining selection criteria. For the purposes of training teams, it is necessary to diagnose differences between individual and team performance (i.e., between the presence or absence of teamwork and taskwork competencies) to provide remediation and corrective feedback of the appropriate type and at the appropriate level. Feedback on individual level KSAOs can be useful in building individual-level expertise, but feedback on teamwork is necessary to leverage that expertise in expert teams by developing teamwork competencies.

Cannon-Bowers and colleagues (1995; Cannon-Bowers & Salas, 1997) proposed a set of teamwork competencies more than a decade ago. Due to the state of the literature at the time, the proposed competencies were primarily based on theory; however, the building interest in team research allows for a review and update of these proposed competencies with respect to the substantial amount of empirical literature now available. Table 3.1 provides an updated and revised list of team competencies, definitions, example markers of the presence or absence of these competencies, as well as representative sources and a rating of the degree to which the competency is supported by empirical evidence. These competencies are briefly discussed in the following sections.

Attitudes

An attitude is taken to be "an internal state that influences an individual's choices or decisions to act in a certain way under particular circumstances" (Cannon-Bowers et al., 1995, p. 352) and in the team context is taken to be the internal states that are associated with the team and that affect the team's interaction processes. In their presentation of the original proposed teamwork competencies, Cannon-Bowers and colleagues (1995) commented on the lack of work linking team attitudes or affect to team effectiveness and performance. Much has changed in the last decade. Team affect and attitude have received much theoretical and empirical attention. The original proposed team attitude competencies included team orientation, collective efficacy, team cohesion, interpersonal relations, mutual trust, and the belief in the importance of teamwork (ibid.). As can be seen in Table 3.1, most of these constructs have born out more extensive empirical investigation. Team/collective efficacy (e.g., Eby & Dobbins, 1997; Jackson, Colquitt, Wesson, & Zapata-Phelan, 2006; Tasa, Taggar, & Seijts, 2007), team/collective orientation (e.g., Gibson, 2003; Katz-Navon & Erez, 2005; Watson, Chemers, & Preiser, 2001), team cohesion (e.g., Beal, Cohen, Burke, & McLendon, 2003; Carless & De Paola, 2000), and mutual trust (e.g., Aubert & Kelsey, 2003; Bandow, 2001; Webber, 2002) are original team attitude competencies that have received extensive empirical support. In addition to these, the increased focus on continuous development, learning and adaptation in teams over time has illuminated the importance of several other team-level affects. Specifically, psychological safety (e.g., Edmondson, 1999), team-learning orientation (e.g., Bunderson & Sutcliffe,

TABLE 3.1

Summary of the ABCs of Teamwork

Proposed KSAs	Description	Example Behavioral Markers	Representative Sources	Empirical Evidence
Attitudes				
Team/collective orientation	"A preference for working with others and the tendency to enhance individual performance through the coordination, evaluation, and utilization of task inputs from other group members while performing group tasks" (Salas, Guthrie, Wilson, Priest, & Burke, 2005, p. 200).	Team members are accepting of input from other teammates; input is evaluated based on quality, not source. Team members have high levels of task involvement, information sharing, participatory goal setting, and strategizing. Team members value team goals over individual goals.	Alavi & McCormick (2004) Driskell & Salas (1992) Eby & Dobbins (1997) Jackson, Colquitt, Wesson, & Zapata-Phelan (2006) Mohammed & Angell (2004) Salas, Sims, & Burke (2005)	+
Team/collective efficacy	"A sense of collective competence shared among individuals when allocating, coordinating, and integrating their resources in a successful concerted response to specific situational demands" (Zaccaro, Blair, Peterson, & Zazanis, 1995, p. 309).	Team members have positive evaluations of their leader's ability. Team members share positive evaluations about the team's ability to accomplish its goals.	Bandura (1986) Gibson (2003) Katz-Navon & Erez (2005) Watson, Chemers, & Preiser (2001) Zaccaro, Blair, Peterson, & Zazanis (1995)	+

Construct	Definition	Indicators	References	
Psychological safety	"A shared belief that the team is safe for interpersonal risk taking" (Edmondson, 1999, p. 354).	Team members believe other members have positive intentions. Team members aren't rejected for being themselves. Team members respect each other's abilities. Team members are interested in each other as people. Team members have high team efficacy.	Edmondson (1999)	~
Team learning orientation	"A shared perception of team goals related to learning and competence development; goals that guide the extent, scope, and magnitude of learning behaviors pursued within a team" (Bunderson & Sutcliffe, 2003, p. 553).	Team members seek and give feedback. Team members discuss errors. Team members experiment with processes and procedures. Team members make changes and improvements in processes. Team members seek information and feedback from outside the team. Team members manage conflict constructively.	Bunderson & Sutcliffe (2003) Yazici (2005)	~
Team cohesion	The degree to which team members exhibit interpersonal attraction, group pride, and commitment to the task.	Team members have a shared a task focus and commitment to attaining the goals of the team. Team members have a desire to remain a member of the team. Team members express pride associated with team membership.	Beal, Cohen, Burke, & McLendon (2003) Carless & De Paola (2000) Zaccaro, Gualtieri, & Minionis (1995)	+

TABLE 3.1

Summary of the ABCs of Teamwork (Continued)

Proposed KSAs	Description	Example Behavioral Markers	Representative Sources	Empirical Evidence
Mutual trust	"The shared belief that team members will perform their roles and protect the interests of their teammates" (Salas, Sims, & Burke, 2005, p. 561).	Team members share a belief that team members will perform their tasks and roles. Team members share a belief that fellow team members will work to protect the interests of the team. Team members are willing to admit mistakes; they are not fearful of reprisal. Team members share information openly.	Aubert & Kelsey (2003) Bandow (2001) Webber (2002) Salas, Sims, & Burke (2005)	+
Team empowerment	"Team members' collective belief that they have the authority to control their proximal work environment and are responsible for their team's functioning" (Mathieu, Gilson, & Ruddy, 2006, p. 98).	Team members decide which team processes to engage in and how to execute those processes.	Mathieu, Gilson, & Ruddy (2006) Kirkman, Rosen, Tesluk, & Gibson (2004)	?
Team reward attitude	"An individual's general evaluation of receiving rewards based on the performance of the team" (Shaw, Duffy, & Stark, 2001, p. 904).	Team members have positive evaluations of rewarding team (versus individual) performance. Team members value teamwork.	Haines & Taggar (2006) Shaw, Duffy, & Stark (2001)	?
Team goal commitment/ team conscientiousness	The degree to which team members feel an attachment to the team level goal and the degree to which they are determined to reach this goal.	Team members have common and valued goals. Team members monitor the team's progress toward its goals. Team members engage in supportive behaviors when necessary.	Aubé & Rousseau (2005) English, Griffith, & Steelman (2004) Weldon & Weingart (1993)	?

Behaviors

	Definition	Behavioral markers	References	
Mutual performance monitoring	The ability of team members to "keep track of fellow team members' work while carrying out their own ... to ensure that everything is running as expected" (McIntyre & Salas, 1995, p. 23).	Team members recognize errors in their teammates' performance. Team members recognize superior performance in their teammates. Team members offer relevant information/resources before requested. Team members have an accurate understanding of their teammates' workload. Team members offer feedback to their fellow teammates to facilitate self-correction.	Dickinson & McIntyre (1997) Marks & Panzer (2004) McIntyre & Salas (1995) Salas, Sims, & Burke (2005)	+
Adaptability	"Ability to adjust strategies based on information gathered from the environment through the use of backup behavior and reallocation of intrateam resources. Altering a course of action or team repertoire in response to changing conditions (internal or external)" (Salas, Sims, & Burke, 2005, p. 560).	Team members modify or replace routine performance strategies when characteristics of the environment and task change. Team members detect changes in the internal team and external environments. Team members make accurate assessments about underlying causes of environmental changes.	Burke, Stagl, Salas, Pierce, & Kendall (2006) Entin & Serfaty (1999) Kozlowski, Gully, Nason, & Smith (1999) LePine (2003, 2005) Salas, Sims, & Burke (2005)	+
Backup/supportive behavior	"Ability to anticipate other team member's needs through accurate knowledge about their responsibilities. This includes the ability to shift workload among members to achieve balance during high periods of workload or pressure" (Salas, Sims, & Burke, 2005, p. 560).	Team members proactively step in to assist fellow team members when needed. Team members communicate the need for assistance. Team members can identify unbalanced workload distributions. Team members redistribute workload to underutilized team members.	Marks, Mathieu, & Zaccaro (2000) McIntyre & Salas (1995) Porter et al. (2003) Salas, Sims, & Burke (2005)	+

TABLE 3.1

Summary of the ABCs of Teamwork (Continued)

Proposed KSAs	Description	Example Behavioral Markers	Representative Sources	Empirical Evidence
Implicit coordination strategies	"Synchronization of member actions based on unspoken assumptions about what others in the group are likely to do" (Wittenbaum & Strasser, 1996, p. 23).	Team members compensate for increasing workload conditions by reducing the "communication overhead" (i.e., explicit communication). Team members sequence interdependent taskwork without overt communication.	Adelman, Miller, Henderson, & Schoelles (2003) Entin & Serfaty (1999) Espinosa, Lerch, & Kraut (2004) MacMillan, Entin, & Serfaty (2004) Rico, Sanchez-Manzanares, Gill & Gibson (2008)	+
Shared/ distributed leadership	"The transference of the leadership function among team members in order to take advantage of member strengths (e.g., knowledge, skills, attitudes, perspectives, contacts, and time available) as dictated by either environmental demands or the development stage of the team" (Burke, Fiore, & Salas, 2004, p. 105).	Team members accurately recognize and identify the member with the highest levels of relevant knowledge and skill for a particular situation/problem. Team members shift leadership functions in response to changing task/environmental conditions.	Pearce & Sims (2002) Hiller, Day, & Vance (2006) Day, Gronn, & Salas (2004)	~

Mission analysis	"The interpretation and evaluation of the team's mission, including identification of its main tasks as well as the operative environmental conditions and team resources available for mission execution" (Marks, Mathieu, & Zaccaro, 2001, p. 365).	Team members explicitly articulate the team's objectives. Team members discuss the purpose of the team in the context of the present performance environment. Team members discuss how the available team resources can be applied to meeting the team goals.	Marks, Mathieu, & Zaccaro (2001) Mathieu & Schulze (2006)	~
Problem detection	An initial sensing that a problem requiring attention exists or will soon exist.	Team members rapidly detect problems or potential problems in their environment. Team members work to determine underlying causes in conflicting knowledge. Team members quickly recognize a need for action when it arises. Team members clearly communicate problem definitions.	Larson & Christensen (1993) Moreland & Levine (1992)	~
Conflict resolution/ management	"Preemptive conflict management involves establishing conditions to prevent, control, or guide team conflict before it occurs. Reactive conflict management involves working through task and interpersonal disagreements among team members" (Marks, Mathieu, & Zaccaro, 2001, p. 363).	Team members seek solutions that have mutual gains for all interests. Team members openly discuss task related conflict. Team members (find it acceptable to) change their minds and express their doubts.	De Dreu & Weingart (2003) Gladstein, 1984 Jehn (1995) Jordan & Troth (2004) Simons & Peterson (2000)	+

TABLE 3.1

Summary of the ABCs of Teamwork (Continued)

Proposed KSAs	Description	Example Behavioral Markers	Representative Sources	Empirical Evidence
Motivation of others	Generating and maintaining goal directed effort toward completion of the team's mission.	Team members encourage each other to perform better or to continue performing well. Team members provide feedback regarding team successes. Team members communicate beliefs of the teams' ability to succeed.	Fleishman & Zaccaro (1992) Marks, Mathieu, & Zaccaro (2001)	~
Intrateam feedback	The provision of information about team or individual performance either before, during, or after a performance episode.	Team members engage in a cycle of prebrief, performance, debrief. Team members provide preperformance information (feed forward). Team members develop and integrate lessons learned from past performance. Team members provide information to correct deficient performance during a performance episode. Team members provide constructive and specific comments to other team members.	Inzana, Driskell, Salas, & Johnston (1996) Smith-Jentsch, Johnston, & Payne (1998) Smith-Jentsch, Zeisig, Acton, & McPherson (1998)	+
Task-related assertiveness	"The capacity to effectively communicate in interpersonal encounters by sharing ideas clearly and directly" (Pearsall & Ellis, 2006, p. 577).	Team members communicate task-relevant information without hesitation. Team members share their opinions with others in a persuasive manner.	Marks, Mathieu, & Zaccaro (2001) Pearsall & Ellis (2006) Smith-Jentsch, Salas, & Baker (1996)	+

Process	Definition	Behaviors	Citations	+
Planning	The generation of a proposed sequence of actions intended to accomplish a set goal.	Team members explicitly articulate expectations for how a proposed course of action should unfold. Team members explicitly define desired outcomes. Team members collectively visualize how a planned course of action will be carried out and where it can go wrong. Team members seek out information and feed it to fellow team members. Team members share unique information.	Klein & Miller (1999) Mathieu & Schulze (2006) Militello, Kyne, Klein, Getchell, & Thordsen (1999) Stout, Cannon-Bowers, Salas, & Milanovich (1999)	+
Coordination	"The process of orchestrating the sequence and timing of interdependent actions" (Marks, Mathieu, & Zaccaro, 2001, pp. 367–368).	Team taskwork behaviors are sequenced so that "down time" for team members is minimized (e.g., team members don't have to wait for other team members' input to do their taskwork). Team members communicate information about their status, needs, and objectives as often as necessary (and not more). Team members synchronize teamwork behaviors without overt communication in high-workload conditions. Team members pass information to one another relevant to the task in a timely and efficient manner.	Brannick, Prince, Prince, & Salas (1992) Fleishman & Zaccaro (1992) Malone & Crowston (1994) Marks, Mathieu, & Zaccaro (2001) Smith-Jentsch, Johnston, & Payne (1998)	+

TABLE 3.1

Summary of the ABCs of Teamwork (Continued)

Proposed KSAs	Description	Example Behavioral Markers	Representative Sources	Empirical Evidence
Team leadership	"Ability to direct and coordinate the activities of other team members, assess team performance, assign tasks, develop team knowledge, skills, and abilities, motivate team members, plan and organize, and establish a positive atmosphere" (Salas, Sims, & Burke, 2005, p. 560).	Team leaders instill shared affects and motivation and define team goals with prebriefs. Team leaders promote team learning through two-way interactions in debriefs to generate lessons learned from performance episodes. Team leaders create team interdependencies. Team leaders communicate a clear mission and vision for the team. Team leaders gather and provide performance relevant information to team members. Team leaders work to keep teams intact.	Burke, Stagl, Klein, et al. (2006) Day, Gronn, & Salas (2004) Salas, Sims, & Burke (2005) Stagl, Salas, & Burke (2006) Zaccaro, Rittman, & Marks (2001)	+
Problem solving	The process of (1) identifying and representing a discrepancy between the present and desired state of the environment and (2) discovering a means to close this "gap."	Team members rapidly knowledge information when needed. Teams engage in contingency planning. Teams accurately recognize the internal expertise in the team and weights input accordingly. Team members accurately prioritize problem features. Team members dynamically assess and adjust their problem solution.	Bonner (2004) Jordan & Troth (2004) Oser, Gualtieri, Cannon-Bowers, & Salas (1999)	+

	Definition	Behavioral markers	References	
Closed-loop communication/ information exchange	A pattern of communication characterized by (1) a message being initiated by the sender, (2) the message being received, interpreted, and acknowledged by the intended receiver, and (3) a follow-up by the sender ensuring that the message was received and appropriately interpreted.	Team members follow up to ensure that messages are received and understood. Team members acknowledge messages when they are sent. Team members cross check information with the sender to ensure that the message's meaning is understood. Team members seek information from all available sources. Team members provide "big picture" updates to one another as appropriate. Team members proactively pass information without being asked.	Bowers, Jentsch, Salas, & Braun (1998) McIntyre & Salas (1995) Salas, Sims, & Burke (2005) Smith-Jentsch, Johnston, & Payne (1998) Smith-Jentsch, Zeisig, Acton, & McPherson (1998)	+
Cognitions				
Rules for matching a situation with an appropriate action (cue–strategy associations)	Team members have a repertoire of performance strategies and courses of action associated with frequently occurring situations and problems.	Team members are able to rapidly recall an appropriate course of action when presented with a common situation and collectively decide on its fit with that situation. Team members shift strategies in response to changes in the task, team, and environment as appropriate.	Cannon-Bowers & Salas (1997) Kline (2005) Stout, Cannon-Bowers, Salas, & Milanovich (1999)	+

TABLE 3.1

Summary of the ABCs of Teamwork (Continued)

Proposed KSAs	Description	Example Behavioral Markers	Representative Sources	Empirical Evidence
Accurate problem models	"Shared understanding of the situation, the nature of the problem, the cause of the problem, the meaning of available cues, what is likely to happen in the future, with or without action by the team members, shared understanding of the goal or desired outcome, and a shared understanding of the solution strategy" (Orasanu, 1994, p. 259).	Team members make compatible predictions about the consequences of proposed courses of action. Team members recognize the need for action and adjustments to planned courses of action when these solutions don't go as planned. Team members make similar judgments about the causes of successful and ineffectual plans. Team members engage in closed-loop communication to build this shared mental representation.	Fiore & Schooler (2004) Orasanu (1990, 1994) Orasanu & Salas (1993) Salas, Rosen, Burke, Nicholson, & Howse (2007)	+
Accurate and shared mental models (transactive memory and team situational awareness)	"An organized knowledge structure of the relationships among the task the team is engaged in and how the team members will interact" (Salas, Sims, & Burke, 2005, p. 561).	Team members are able to recognize when other team members need information they have. Team members anticipate and predict the needs of their fellow team members. Team members implicitly adjust performance strategies to changing conditions in the team, task, and environment as needed. Team members use standardized terminology ("phraseology").	Artman (2000) Cannon-Bowers & Salas (1997) Cannon-Bowers, Tannenbaum, Salas, & Volpe (1995) Endsley (1995) Klein, Feltovich, Bradshaw, & Woods (2005) Klimoski & Mohammed (1994)	+

	Definition	References	Support
	Team members use concise communication. Team members have compatible explanations of task cues. Team members attempt to determine the underlying causes of conflicts information. Team members actively seek information relevant to the task. Problems are explicitly defined. Team members engage in confirming and cross-checking information. Team members rapidly identify problems or potential problems.	Mathieu, Heffner, Goodwin, Salas, & Cannon-Bowers (2000); Salas, Cannon-Bowers, Fiore, & Stout (2001); Salas, Prince, Baker, & Shrestha (1995); Salas, Sims, & Burke (2005); Stout, Cannon-Bowers, & Salas, (1996)	+
Team mission, objectives, norms, resources	An understanding of the purpose, vision, and means available to the team for reaching the team objectives and completing the mission as well as the "shared expectations that constrain and drive the action of group members" (Graham, 2003, p. 323).	Cannon-Bowers & Salas (1997); Cannon-Bowers, Tannenbaum, Salas, & Volpe (1995); Marks, Mathieu, & Zaccaro (2001)	~
Understanding of multiteam system (MTS) couplings	An understanding in the team of how their performance (inputs, processes, and outcomes) is tied to the larger organizational structure, including other teams. Team members (especially leaders) understand the goal hierarchies in the larger organizational unit and work to meet these goals. Team members (especially leaders) engage in appropriate levels of effective conflict management with other team leaders in the MTS when different aspects of the goal hierarchy conflict.	Hoegl, Weinkauf, & Gemueden (2004); Marks, DeChurch, Mathieu, Panzer, & Alonso (2005); Williams & Mahan (2006)	

Note: + indicates substantial empirical support; ~ indicates moderate empirical support; x indicates no empirical support.

2003; Yazici, 2005), and team-goal commitment (e.g., Aubé & Rousseau, 2005; English, Griffith, & Steelman, 2004; Weldon & Weingart, 1993) are necessary for teams to effectively learn and develop. Additionally, a team reward attitude (e.g., Haines & Taggar, 2006; Shaw, Duffy, & Stark, 2001) and team empowerment (e.g., Kirkman, Rosen, Tesluk, & Gibson, 2004; Mathieu, Gilson, & Ruddy, 2006) have been linked to team effectiveness.

Behaviors

Cannon-Bowers and colleagues (1995) provided an extensive list of team-work behaviors (or skills) including task organization, mutual performance monitoring, shared problem-model development, flexibility, compensatory behavior, information exchange, dynamic reallocation of functions, and mission analysis, among many others. They noted that there had been much more theoretical and empirical work devoted to delineating the skills (or behaviors) of teamwork than either team attitudes or cognitions. This is likely true today as well for the simple reason that team behaviors are much more amenable to measurement than are team attitudes or cognitions. Many of the original team behavior competencies remain, with increased empirical support; however, some have been dropped or subsumed within others. For example, task organization—"sequencing and integrating task inputs according to team and task demands" (Cannon-Bowers & Salas, 1997)—has not been attended to empirically, most likely do to its similarity to coordination. As discussed in the big five model of teamwork, mutual performance monitoring, adaptability, backup/supportive behavior, and team leadership (in both the traditional hierarchical sense and in shared or distributed configurations) are critical for effective teamwork. Additionally, closed-loop communication and information exchange (e.g., Bowers et al., 1998; Orasanu, 1990; Smith-Jentsch et al., 1998) help to ensure that everyone on the team is operating under the most up-to-date and accurate information. This, in turn, enables coordination within the team (e.g., Brannick, Prince, Prince, & Salas, 1992; Marks et al., 2001; Smith-Jentsch et al., 1998); however, effective teams are able to coordinate implicitly without this overt communication during high workload performance episodes (e.g., Adelman, Miller, Henderson, & Schoelles, 2003; Entin & Serfaty, 1999; MacMillan et al., 2004). Problem detection and solving skills (e.g., Larson & Christensen, 1993; Moreland & Levine, 1992) remain highly important, as well as task related assertiveness (e.g., Pearsall & Ellis, 2006; Smith-Jentsch, Salas, & Baker, 1996). Related to communication skills enacted during a performance episode, intra-team feedback (e.g., Inzana, Driskell, Salas, & Johnston, 1996; Smith-Jentsch, Zeisig, et al., 1998) concerning performance as well as conflict resolution and management skills (e.g., De Dreu & Weingart, 2003; Jordan & Troth, 2004; Simons & Peterson, 2000) are essential to increase a team's performance levels. Additionally, there are several team behaviors that generally occur before task performance such as mission analysis (e.g., Marks et al., 2001; Mathieu & Schulze, 2006), planning (e.g., Klein & Miller, 1999; Mathieu & Schulze, 2006; Stout, Cannon-Bowers, Salas, & Milanovich, 1999), and the motivation of fellow team members (e.g., Fleishman & Zaccaro, 1992; Marks et al., 2001).

Cognitions

Shared mental model theory was the impetus behind many of the original knowledge competencies for teams (Cannon-Bowers et al., 1995). As is apparent by the team cognition competencies listed in Table 3.1, this remains an influential perspective. Team members must have accurate and shared knowledge of the team's mission, objectives, norms, and resources (Graham, 2003; Marks et al., 2001). Additionally, team members must share mental models about the task as well as team members' roles, specialized knowledge, and skill (i.e., transactive memory; Austin, 2003; Lewis, 2004). As team members engage in performance, this shared knowledge helps them to build accurate problem models, a critical step in dynamic team performance. The team (or shared) problem model consists of a "shared understanding of the situation, the nature of the problem, the cause of the problem, the meaning of available cues, what is likely to happen in the future, with or without action by the team members, shared understanding of the goal or desired outcome, and a shared understanding of the solution strategy" (Orasanu, 1994, p. 259). These problem models are emergent cognitive states in that they are formed dynamically as the team members interact with the task environment and their fellow team members. In fact, problem models can be thought of as a specific instance of team situation awareness (SA; Artman, 2000; Salas, Prince, Baker, & Shrestha, 1995) that is considered to be "built on a combination of the degree of shared understanding within the team (i.e., shared mental models) and each individual member's SA (based on preexisting knowledge bases and cue/pattern assessments)" (Salas, Cannon-Bowers, Fiore, & Stout, 2001, p. 173). Problem models and team situation awareness more generally form the basis of a team's ability to apply cue-strategy associations or matching rules for applying specific team strategies to different situations. This requires that team members have a repertoire of strategies and associated cues (Stout, Cannon-Bowers, Salas, & Milanovich, 1999). In addition to these knowledge competencies that do not differ much from the originally proposed competencies, team members (especially team leaders) must have knowledge of their relationship to the larger organizational system (i.e., multiteam systems; MTS). Teams must understand the interdependencies between multiple teams to effectively function in larger units (Marks et al., 2005).

As with all types of performance, reaching high levels of team performance requires fitting the appropriate skills and strategies to the task constrains. Characteristics of the work to be done will determine the effectiveness of various teamwork and team performance processes. Table 3.2 provides a list of mechanisms of expert team performance. These mechanisms are adaptations that mediate performance and allow teams to exhibit reliably and consistently superior levels of performance outcomes.

Where Do We Go from Here?

There is no question that collective (whether teams, groups, units, or networks) wisdom has contributed to the welfare of industries, agencies, and organizations at large. Recent reviews have clearly demonstrated this and more. From this, a robust science of team performance and team effectiveness has emerged. To paraphrase Levine and Moreland (1990), this science is alive, well, energized, and multidisciplinary. But, of course, more remains to be done. This section highlights three premises that will evolve (we hope) our understanding of the wisdom of collectives.

First, we believe that shared cognition in teams needs a deeper look. Though some progress has been made, the precise meaning and nature of shared cognition remains elusive. There are a plethora of labels for this construct, and we continue to struggle with the measurement of shared cognition. So, no science will emerge here until we develop precise, reliable, valid, and diagnostic metrics of shared cognition. In the absence of metrics, confusion on what share cognition is will remain. We need operational and measurable definitions of what shared cognition is and what elements contribute to it. Recent work in this area (e.g., Burke, Burke, Lazzara, Smith-Jentsch, & Salas, 2007; Cooke et al., 2004; Gorman, Cooke, & Winner, 2006; Letsky, Warner, Fiore, Rosen & Salas, 2007; Smith-Jentsch & Scielzo, 2007) may shed some light on this issue.

Second, the wisdom of the collectives is dynamic. It comprises processes that unfold over time and that operate on different time scales. And so we cannot ignore the effect of time in teams. It seems that as a science we continue to have theories, methods, studies, and findings that ignore the dynamic nature of team performance. We must move toward making time and its effects part of our routine team studies. While this is difficult, it is not impossible. So, the call for more longitudinal or time-based studies goes out again.

Finally, wisdom cannot be solely extracted by looking at self-report data or ratings of overall performance—the predominate methods used to collect data in team research. Of course, we need better, richer, deeper, and

TABLE 3.2

Mechanisms of Expert Team Performance

Expert Teams...

Hold Shared Mental Models

They have members who anticipate each other.

They can communicate without the need to communicate overtly.

They interpret environmental cues in a compatible or complementary manner.

They can reach an intuitive consensus on problem definition and course of action selection.

They use concise communication and standardized terminology.

Optimize Resources by Learning and Adapting

They are self-correcting.

They compensate for each other.

They reallocate functions.

They engage in a deliberate process of maintaining and building expertise.

They adjust performance processes to meet changes in the task/environment.

They seek feedback from within and outside the team.

They discuss errors.

Have Clear Roles and Responsibilities

They manage expectations.

They have members who understand each others' roles and how they fit together.

They ensure team member roles are clear but not overly rigid.

Have a Clear, Valued, and Shared Vision

They have a clear and common purpose.

They are guided by common values.

Engage in a Cycle or Discipline of Pre-brief → Performance → Debrief

They regularly provide feedback to each other, both individually and as a team.

They establish and revise team goals and plans.

They differentiate between higher and lower priorities.

They have mechanisms for anticipating and reviewing issues or problems of members.

They periodically diagnose team "effectiveness," including its results, its processes, and its vitality (morale, retention, energy).

They generate lessons learned from performance episodes.

They plan for performance by discussing performance strategies.

Have Strong Team Leadership

They are led by someone with good leadership skills and not just technical competence.

They have team members who believe the leaders care about them.

They have leaders that provide situation updates.

TABLE 3.2

Mechanisms of Expert Team Performance (Continued)

They have leaders that foster teamwork, coordination, and cooperation.

They have leaders that self-correct first.

They have leaders that provide guidance for making improvements.

They have leaders that set team and individual priorities.

They share leadership functions as needed.

Develop a Strong Sense of "Collective," Trust, Teamness, and Confidence

They manage conflict well; team members confront each other effectively.

They have a strong sense of team orientation.

They trust other team members' "intentions."

They strongly believe in the team's collective ability to succeed.

They develop collective efficacy.

They create an atmosphere that encourages learning and development.

They feel the team is safe for taking interpersonal risks.

Manage and Optimize Performance Outcomes

They make fewer errors.

They communicate often "enough"; they ensure that fellow team members have the information they need to be able to contribute.

They make better decisions.

The have a greater chance of mission success.

They adjust performance processes as needed to maintain high levels of performance.

Cooperate and Coordinate

They identify teamwork and task work requirements.

They ensure that, through staffing or development, the team possesses the right mix of competencies.

They consciously integrate new team members.

They distribute and assign work thoughtfully.

They examine and adjust the team's physical workplace to optimize communication and coordination.

They manage team interdependencies in a timely manner.

They ensure team members have all of the information they need when they need it.

They effectively manage conflict.

Source: Adapted from Salas, E., Rosen, M. A., Burke, C. S., Goodwin, G. F., & Fiore, S., In K. A. Ericsson, N. Charness, P. J. Feltovich, & R. R. Hoffman, (Eds.), *The Cambridge handbook of expertise and expert performance* (pp. 439–453). New York: Cambridge University Press, 2006 (With permission).

more meaningful methodologies to study teams. We need more "anthropological" studies of team studying, more rigorous qualitative studies, more observational studies, and more studies of teams in context performing in stressful and meaningful environments. So our view needs to balance its methodological portfolio with studies "in the wild." Some work in this area is emerging in the naturalistic decision making movement (see Hoffman, 2007). We hope that more will appear in the literature.

Concluding Remarks

Progress continues to be made in understanding how teams, groups, units, or networks function: how and when they perform well; how they derail; how they think, do, and feel; how they communicate; how the shared cognition emerges; and how they posses the unique wisdom to adapt. Indeed, we know a fair amount about team functioning. We hope that this chapter adds to our wisdom and motivates scholars in several disciplines to continue the pursuit of understanding the wisdom of collectives.

Acknowledgments

The views herein are those of the authors and do not necessarily reflect those of the organizations with which they are affiliated or their sponsoring agencies. Writing this paper was partially supported by the U.S. Army Research Institute for the Behavioral and Social Sciences Contract W74V8H-04-C-0025 and the Office of Naval Research Collaboration and Knowledge Interoperability (CKI) Program and ONR MURI Grant #N000140610446 (Dr. Michael Letsky, Program Manager).

References

Adelman, L., Miller, S. L., Henderson, D., & Schoelles, M. (2003). Using Brunswikian theory and a longitudinal design to study how hierarchical teams adapt to increasing levels of time pressure. *Acta Psychologica, 112*(2), 81–206.

Alavi, S. B., & McCormick, J. (2004). Theoretical and Measurement Issues for Studies of Collective Orientation in Team Contexts. *Small Group Research, 35*(2), 111–127.

Arrow, H., McGrath, J. E., & Berdahl, J. L. (2000). *Small groups as complex systems: Formation, coordination, development, and adaptation.* Thousand Oaks, CA: Sage.

Artman, H. (2000) Team situation assessment and information distribution. *Ergonomics, 43*(8), 1111–1129.

Aubé, C., & Rousseau, V. (2005). Team Goal Commitment and Team Effectiveness: The Role of Task Interdependence and Supportive Behaviors. *Group Dynamics: Theory, Research, and Practice, 9*(3), 189–204.

Aubert, B. A., & Kelsey, B. L. (2003). Further Understanding of Trust and Performance in Virtual Teams. *Small Group Research, 34*(5), 575–618.

Austin, J. R. (2003). Transactive memory in organizational groups: The effects of content, consensus, specialization, and accuracy on group performance. *Journal of Applied Psychology, 88*(5), 866–878.

Bandow, D. (2001). Time to create sound teamwork. *Journal for Quality and Participation, 24,* 41–47.

Bandura, A. (1986). *Social foundations of thought and action: A social cognitive theory.* Engelwood Cliffs, NY: Prentice-Hall.

Beal, D. J., Cohen, R. R., Burke, M. J., & McLendon, C. L. (2003). Cohesion and performance in groups: A meta-analytic clarification of construct relations. *Journal of Applied Psychology, 88*(6), 989–1004.

Boas, S., Zakay, E., Esther, B., & Popper, M. (2000). Leadership and social identification in military units: Direct and indirect relationships. *Journal of Applied Social Psychology, 30*(3), 612–640.

Bonner, B. L. (2004). Expertise in group problem solving: Recognition, social combination, and performance. *Group Dynamics: Theory, Research, and Practice, 8*(4), 277–290.

Bowers, C. A., Jentsch, F., Salas, E., & Braun, C.C. (1998). Analyzing communication sequences for team training needs assessment. *Human Factors, 40*(4), 672–679.

Brannick, M. T., Prince, A., Prince, C. & Salas, E. (1995). The measurement of team process. *Human Factors, 37*(3), 641–651.

Bunderson, J. S. & Sutcliffe, K.M. (2003). Management team learning orientation and business unit performance. *Journal of Applied Psychology, 88*(3), 552–560.

Burke, C. S., Fiore, S. M., & Salas, E. (2004). The role of shared cognition in enabling shared leadership and team adaptability. In C. L. Pearce & J. A. Conger, (Eds.), *Shared leadership: Reframing the hows and whys of leadership* (pp. 103–121). Thousand Oaks, CA: Sage.

Burke, C. S., Stagl, K. C., Salas, E., Pierce, L., & Kendall, D. (2006). Understanding team adaptation: A conceptual analysis and model. *Journal of Applied Psychology, 91,* 1180–1207.

Campbell, J. P. (1990). Modeling the performance prediction problem in Industrial and Organizational Psychology. In M. D. Dunette & L. M. Hough, (Eds.), *Handbook of industrial and organizational psychology.* Palo Alto, CA: Consulting Psychologists Press.

Campion, M. A., Medsker, G.J. & Higgs, A.C. (1993). Relations between work group characteristics and effectiveness: Implications for designing effective work groups. *Personnel Psychology, 46,* 823–847.

Cannon-Bowers, J. A. & Salas, E. (1997). Teamwork Competencies: The interaction of team member knowledge, skills, and attitudes. In H. F. O'Neil, Jr. (Ed.), *Workforce readiness: Competencies and assessment* (pp. 151–174). Mahwah, NJ: Erlbaum.

Cannon-Bowers, J. A., Salas, E., & Converse, S. (1993). Shared mental models in expert team decision making. In N. J. J. Castellan (Ed.), *Individual and group decision making* (pp. 221–246). Hillsdale, NJ: Erlbaum.

Cannon-Bowers, J. A., Tannenbaum, S. I., Salas, E., & Volpe, C. E. (1995). Defining competencies and establishing team training requirements. In R. Guzzo & E. Salas (Eds.), *Team effectiveness and decision making in organizations* (pp. 333–380). San Francisco, CA: Jossey-Bass.

Carless, S. A. & DePaola, C. (2000). The measurement of cohesion in work teams. *Small Group Research, 31*(1), 71–88.

Castka, P., Bamber, C., Sharp, J., & Belohoubek, P. (2001). Factors affecting successful implementation of high performance teams. *Team Performance Management, 7*(7–8), 123–134.

Chidester, T. R., Helmreich, R. L., Gregorich, S. E., & Geis, C. E. (1991). Pilot personality and crew coordination: Implications for training and selection. *International Journal of Aviation Psychology, 1*(1), 25–44.

Chu, D., Strand, R., & Fjelland, R. (2003). Theories of complexity: Common denominators of complex systems. *Complexity, 8*(2), 19–30.

Cooke, N. J., Salas, E., Kiekel, P. A., & Bell, B. (2004). Advances in measuring team cognition. In E. Salas & S. M. Fiore, (Eds.), *Team cognition: Understanding the factors that drive process and performance* (pp. 83–106). Washington, DC: American Psychological Association.

Cooper, R. & Sawaf, A. (1996). *Executive EQ: Emotional intelligence in leadership and organizations*. New York: Grosset/Putnam.

Day, D. V., Gronn, P., & Salas, E. (2004). Leadership capacity in teams. *Leadership Quarterly, 15*(6), 857–880.

De Dreu, C. K., & Weingart, L. R. (2003). Task versus relationship conflict, team performance, and team member satisfaction: a meta-analysis. *Journal of Applied Psychology, 88*(4), 741–749.

Dekker, S. (2003). Failure to adapt or adaptations that fail: contrasting models on procedures and safety. *Applied Ergonomics, 34*, 233–238.

DeShon, R. P., Kozlowski, W. J., Schmidt, A. M., Milner, K. R., & Wiechmann, D. (2004). A multiple-goal, multilevel model of feedback effects on the regulation of individual and team performance. *Journal of Applied Psychology, 89*(6), 1035–1056.

Dickinson, T. L. & McIntyre, R. M. (1997). A Conceptual framework for team measurement. In M. T. Brannick, Salas, E., & Prince, C. (Ed.), *Team performance measurement: Theory, methods, and applications* (pp. 19–43). Mahwah, NJ: Erlbaum.

Driskell, J. E. & Salas, E. (1991). Group decision making under stress. *Journal of Applied Psychology, 76*(3), 473–478.

Driskell, J. E. & Salas, E. (1992). Collective behavior and team performance. *Human Factors, 34*, 277–288.

Driskell, J. E., Salas, E., & Johnston, J. (1999). Does stress lead to a loss of team perspective? *Group Dynamics: Theory, Research, and Practice, 3*(4), 291–302.

Dyer, J. L. (1984). Team research and team training: A state of the art review. In F. A. Muckler (Ed.), *Human factors review* (pp. 285–323). Santa Monica, CA: Human Factors Society.

Eby, L. T. & Dobbins, G. H. (1997). Collectivistic orientation in teams: an individual and group-level analysis. *Journal of Organizational Behavior, 18,* 275–295.

Edmondson, A. C.(1999). Psychological safety and learning behavior in work teams. *Administrative Science Quarterly, 44,* 350–383.

Edmondson, A. C. (2002). The local and variegated nature of learning in organizations: A group-level perspective. *Organization Science, 13*(2), 128–146.

Edmondson, A. C. (2003). Speaking up in the operating room: How team leaders promote learning in interdisciplinary action teams. *Journal of Management Studies, 40*(6), 1419–1452.

Edmondson, A. C., Bohmer, R. M., & Pisano, G. P. (2001). Disrupted routines: team learning and new technology implementation in hospitals. *Administrative Science Quarterly, 46*(4), 685–716.

Edwards, B. D., Day, E. A., Arthur, W., & Bell, S. T. (2006). Relationships among team ability composition, team mental models, and team performance. *Journal of Applied Psychology, 91*(3), 727–736.

Eisenstat, R. A. & Cohen, S.G. (1990). Summary: Top management groups. In J. R. Hackman (Ed.), *Groups that work (and those that don't): Creating conditions for effective teamwork* (pp. 78–86). San Francisco, CA: Jossey-Bass.

Endsley, M. R. (1995). Toward a theory of situation awareness in dynamic systems. *Human Factors, 37*(1), 32–64.

English, A., Griffith, R. L. & Steelman, L. A. (2004). Team Performance: The Effect of Team Conscientiousness and Task Type. *Small Group Research, 35*(6), 643–665.

Entin, E. E. & Serfaty, D. (1999). Adaptive team coordination. *Human Factors, 41*(2), 312–325.

Ericsson, K. A. & Lehmann, A. C. (1996). Expert and exceptional performance: Evidence of maximal adaptation to task constraints. *Annual Review of Psychology, 47,* 273–305.

Espinosa, J. A., Lerch, F. J., & Kraut, R. E. (2004). Explicit versus implicit coordination mechanisms and task dependencies: One size does not fit all. In E. Salas & S. M. Fiore, (Eds.), *Team cognition: Understanding the factors that drive process and performance* (pp. 107–129). Washington, DC: American Psychological Association.

Fiore, S. M. & Schooler, W. J. (2004). Process mapping and shared cognition: Teamwork and the development of shared problem models. In E. Salas & S. M. Fiore (Eds.). *Team cognition: Understanding the factors that drive process and performance* (pp. 133–152). Washington, D.C.: American Psychological Association.

Fleishman, E. A. & Zaccaro, S. J. (1992). Toward a taxonomy of team performance functions. In. R. Swezey & E. Salas (Eds.), *Teams: Their Training and Performance* (pp. 31–56). Norwood, NJ: Ablex.

Fleishman, E. A., Mumford, M. D., Zaccaro, S. J., Levin, K. Y., Korotkin, A. L., & Hein, M. B. (1991). Taxonomic efforts in the description of leader behavior: A synthesis and functional interpretation. *Leadership Quarterly, 4,* 245–287.

Frese, M. & Zapf, D. (1994). Action as the core of work psychology: A German approach. In M. D. Dunnette & L. M. Hough (Eds.), *Handbook of Industrial and Organizational Psychology* (2nd ed., Vol. 4, pp. 271–340). Palo Alto, CA: Consulting Psychologists.

Gersick, C. J. (1988). Time and transition in work teams: Toward a new model of group development. *Academy of Management Journal, 31*(1), 9–41.

Gersick, C. J. (1989). Marking time: Predictable transitions in task groups. *Academy of Management Journal. 32*(2), 274–309.

Gibson, C. B. (2003). The Efficacy Advantage: Factors Related to the Formation of Group Efficacy. *Journal of Applied Social Psychology, 33*(10), 2153–2186.

Ginnett, R. C. (1990). Airline cockpit crew. In J. R. Hackman (Ed.), *Groups that work (and those that don't): Creating conditions for effective teamwork* (pp. 427–448). San Francisco, CA: Jossey-Bass.

Gladstein, D. L. (1984). Groups in Context: A Model of Task Group Effectiveness. *Administrative Science Quarterly, 29*(4), 499–517.

Goldstein, J. (1999). Emergence as a construct: History and issues. *Emergence, 1*(1), 49–72.

Gorman, J. C., Cooke, N. J., & Winner, J. L. (2006). Measuring team situation awareness in decentralized command and control environments. *Ergonomics, 49*(12–13), 1312–1325.

Graham, C. R. (2003). A model of norm development for computer-mediated teamwork. *Small Group Research, 34*(3), 322–352.

Hackman, J. R. (1987). The design of work teams. In J. Lorsch (Ed.), *Handbook of organizational behavior* (pp. 315–342). New York: Prentice Hall.

Hackman, J. R. (2002). *Leading teams: setting the stage for great performances*. Boston, MA: Harvard Business School Press.

Hackman, J. R. & Wagemen, R. (2005). A theory of team coaching. *Academy of Manaagement Review, 30*(2), 269–287.

Haines, V. Y. & Taggar, S. (2006). Antecedents of team reward attitude. *Journal of Management Review, 30*(2), 194–205.

Harrison, D. A., Mohammed, S., McGrath, J. E., Florey, A. T., & Vanderstoep, S. W. (2003). Time matters in team performance: effects of member familiarity, entrainment, and task discontinuity on speed and quality. *Personnel Psychology, 56*(3), 633–669.

Hiller, N. J., Day, D. V. & Vance, R. J. (2006). Collective enactment of leadership roles and team effectiveness: A field study. *The Leadership Quarterly, 17*, 387–397.

Hinsz, V. B., Tindale, R. S., & Vollrath, D. A. (1997). The emerging conceptualization of groups as information processors. *Psychological Bulletin, 121*(1), 43–64.

Hirschfeld, R. R., Jordan, M. H., Feild, H. S., Giles, W. F., & Armenakis, A. A. (2006). Becoming team players: Team members' mastery of teamwork knowledge as a predictor of team task proficiency and observed teamwork effectiveness. *Journal of Applied Psychology, 91*(2), 467–474.

Hoegl, M., Weinkauf, K., & Gemuenden, H. G. (2004). Interteam Coordination, Project Committee, and Teamwork in Multiteam R&D Projects: A Longitudinal Study. *Organizational Science, 15*(1), 38–55.

Hoffman, R. R. (Ed.). (2007). *Expertise out of context*. Mahwah, NJ: Erlbaum.

Hoffman, R. R., Feltovich, P. J., & Ford, K.M. (1997). A general conceptual framework for conceiving of expertise and expert systems. In P. J. Feltovich, K. M. Ford, & R. R. Hoffman, (Eds.), *Expertise in context* (pp. 543–580). Menlo Park, CA: AAAI Press/MIT Press.

Holyoak, K. J. (1991). Symbolic connectionism: toward third-generation theories of expertise. In K.A. Ericsson & J. Smith, (Eds.), *Toward a general theory of expertise: Prospects and limits* (pp. 301–335). Cambridge, England: Cambridge University Press.

Ilgen, D. R. Hollenbeck, J. R., Johnson, M., & Jundt, D. (2005). Teams in organizations: From input-process-output models to IMOI models. *Annual Review of Psychology, 56*, 517–543.

Inzana, C. M., Driskell, J. E., Salas, E., & Johnston, J. H. (1996). Effects of preparatory information on enhancing performance under stress. *Journal of Applied Psychology, 81*(4), 429–435.

Jackson, C. L. Colquitt, J. A., Wesson, M. J., & Zapata-Phelan, C.P. (2006). Psychological Collectivism: A Measurement Validation and Linkage to Group Member Performance. *Journal of Applied Psychology, 91*(4), 884–899.

Jehn, K. A. (1995). A Multimethod Examination of the Benefits and Detriments of Intragroup Conflict. *Administrative Science Quarterly. 40*(2), 256–282.

Johnson-Laird, P. N. (1983). *Mental Models: Towards a cognitive science of language, inference, and consciousness.* Cambridge, MA: Harvard University Press.

Johnston, J. H., Smith-Jentsch, K. A., & Cannon-Bowers, J. A. (1997). Performance measurement tools for enhancing team decision-making training. In M. T. Brannick, E. Salas, & C. Prince (Eds.), *Team performance assessment and measurement: Theory, methods, and applications* (pp. 311–327). Mahwah, NJ: Erlbaum.

Jones, G. & George, J. (1998). The experience and evolution of trust: Implications for cooperation and teamwork. *Academy of Management Review, 23*, 531–546.

Jordan, P. J., & Troth, A. C. (2004). Managing emotions during team problem solving: Emotional intelligence and conflict resolution. *Human Performance, 17*(2), 195–218.

Katz-Navon, T. Y., & Erez, M. (2005). When collective- and self-efficacy affect team performance: The role of task interdependence. *Small Group Research, 36*(4), 437–465.

Kirkman, B. L., Rosen, B., Tesluk, T., & Gibson, C. (2004). The impack of team empowerment on virtual team performance: The moderating role of face-to-face interaction. *Academy of Management Journal, 47*, 175–192.

Klein, G., Feltovich, P. J., Bradshaw, J. M., & Woods, D. D. (2005). Common ground and coordination in joint activity. In W. B. Rouse & K. R. Boff, (Eds.), *Organizational simulation* (pp. 139–184). Hoboken, NJ: Wiley-Interscience.

Klein, G. & Miller, T. E. (1999). Distributed planning teams. *International Journal of Cognitive Ergonomics, 3*(3), 203–222.

Kleinman, D. L. & Serfaty, D. (1989). *Team performance assessment in distributed decision-making.* Paper presented at the Symposium on Interactive Networked Simulation for Training, Orlando, FL.

Klimoski, R. & Mohammed, S. (1994). Team mental model: Construct or metaphor? *Journal of Management, 20*(2), 403–437.

Kline, D. A. (2005). Intuitive team decision making. In H. Montgomery, R. Lipshitz, & B. Brehmer (Ed.), *How professionals make decisions* (pp. 171–182). Mahwah, NJ: Erlbaum.

Kozlowski, S. W. J., Gully, S. M., Nason, E. R., & Smith, E. M. (1999). Developing adaptative teams: A theory of compilation and performance acsross levels and time. In D. R. Ilgen & E. D. Pulakos (Eds.), *The Changing Nature of Work and Performance: Implications for Staffing, Personnel Actions, and Development.* San Francisco, CA: Jossey-Bass.

Kozlowski, S. W. J. & Klein, K. J. (2000). A multilevel approach to theory and research in organizations: Contextual, temporal, and emergent processes. In K. J. Klein & S. W. J. Kozlowski (Eds.), *Multilevel theory, research, and methods in organizations: Foundations, extensions, and new directions* (pp. 3–90). San Francisco, CA: Jossey-Bass.

Larson, J. R. & Christensen, C. (1993). Groups as problem-solving units: Toward a new meaning of social cognition. *Br. J. Soc. Psychol., 32*, 5–30.

LaPorte, T. R. & Consolini, P. M. (1991). Working in practice but not in theory: Theoretical challenges of high reliability organizations. *Journal of Public Administration Research and Theory, 1*(1), 19–48.

Letsky, M., Warner, N., Fiore, S. M., Rosen, M. A., & Salas, E. (2007). *Macrocognition in complex team problem solving.* Paper presented at the 11th International Command and Control Research and Technology Symposium (ICCRTS), Cambridge, England.

LePine, J. A. (2003). Team adaptation and post change performance: Effects of team composition in terms of members' cognitive ability and personality. *Journal of Applied Psychology, 88*, 27–39.

LePine, J. (2005). Adaptation of teams in response to unforeseen change: effects of goal difficulty and team composition in terms of cognitive ability and goal orientation. *Journal of Applied Psychology, 90*(6), 1153–1167.

Levine, J. M. & Moreland, R. L. (1990). Progress in small group research. *Annual Review of Psychology, 41*, 585–634.

Lewis, K. (2004). Knowledge and performance in knowledge-worker teams: A longitudinal study of transactive memory systems. *Management Science, 50*(11), 1519–1533.

MacMillan, J., Entin, E. E., & Serfaty, D. (2004). Communication overhead: The hidden cost of team cognition. In E. Salas & S. M. Fiore (Eds.), *Team cognition: Understanding the factors that drive process and performance* (pp. 61–82). Washington, DC: American Psychological Association.

Malone, T. W. & Crowston, K. (1994). The interdisciplinary study of coordination. *ACM Computing Surveys, 26*(1), 87–119.

Marks, M. A., DeChurch, L. A., Mathieu, J. E., Panzer, F. J., & Alonso, A. (2005). Teamwork in multiteam systems. *Journal of Applied Psychology, 90*(5), 964–971.

Marks, M. A., Mathieu, J. E., & Zaccaro, S. J. (2001). A temporally based framework and taxonomy of team processes. *Academy of Management Review, 26*, 356–376.

Marks, M. A. & Panzer, F. J. (2004). The influence of tean monitoring on team processes and performance. *Human Performance, 17*(1), 25–41.

Mathieu, J. E., Gilson, L. L. & Ruddy, T. M. (2006). Empowerment and team effectiveness: An empirical test of an integrated model. *Journal of Applied Psychology, 91*(1), 97–108.

Mathieu, J. E., Heffner, T. S., Goodwin, G. F., Salas, E., & Cannon-Bowers, J. (2000). The influence of shared mental models on team process and performance. *Journal of Applied Psychology, 85*(2), 273–283.

Mathieu, J. E. & Schulze, W. (2006). The influence of team knowledge and formal plans on episodic team process-performance relationships. *Academy of Management Journal, 49*(3), 605–619.

Militello, L. G., Kyne, M. M., Klein, G., Getchell, K., & Thordsen, M. (1999). A synthesized model of team performance. *International Journal of Cognitive Ergonomics, 3*(2), 131–158.

McIntyre, R. M. & Salas, E. (1995). Measuring and managing for team performance: Emerging principles from complex environments. In R. A. Guzzo & E. Salas (Eds.), *Team effectiveness and decision making in organizations* (pp. 9–45). San Francisco, CA: Jossey Bass.

Mohammed, S. & Angell, L. C. (2004). Surface- and deep-level divesity in workgroups: examining the moderating effects of team orientation and team process on relationship conflict. *Journal of Organizational Behavior, 25*(8), 1015–1039.

Mohammed, S. & Dumville, B. C. (2001). Team mental models in a team knowledge framework: Expanding theory and measure across disciplinary boundaries. *Journal of Organizational Behavior, 22*(2), 89–103.

Moreland, R. L. & Levine, J. M. (1992). Problem identification by groups. In S. W. Worchel, W. Wood, & J. A. Simpson (Eds.), *Group processes and productivity* (pp. 17–47). Newbury Park, CA: Sage.

Morgan, B. B., Jr., Glickman, A. S., Woodward, E. A., Blaiwes, A. S., & Salas, E. (1986). *Measurement of team behaviors in a Navy environment* (No. 86-014). Orlando, FL: Naval Training Systems Center.

Morgan, B. B., Jr., Salas, E., & Glickman, A. S. (2001). An analysis of team evolution and maturation. *Journal of General Psychology, 120*(3), 277–291.

Orasanu, J. (1990). *Shared mental models and crew decision making* (No. 46). Princeton, NJ: Princeton University, Cognitive Science Laboratory.

Orasanu, J. (1994). Shared problem models and flight crew performance. In N. Johnston, N. McDonald, & R. Fuller (Eds.), *Aviation psychology in practice* (pp. 255–285). Brookfield, VT: Ashgate.

Orasanu, J. & Salas, E. (1993). Team decision making in complex environments. In G. Klein, J. Orasanu, R. Calderwood & C. E. Zsambok (Eds.), *Decision making in action: Models and methods* (pp. 327–345). Norwood, NJ; Albex.

Oser, R. L., Gualtieri, J. W., Cannon-Bowers, J. A., & Salas, E. (1999). Training team problem solving skills: an event-based approach. *Computers in human behavior, 15*, 441–462.

Patel, V. L. & Arocha, J. F. (2001). The nature of constraints on collaborative decision making in health care settings. In E. Salas & G. Klein (Eds.), *Linking expertise and naturalistic decision making* (pp. 383–405). Mahwah, NJ: Lawrence Erlbaum Associates.

Pearce, C. L. & Ensley, M. D. (2004). A reciprocal and longitudinal investigation of the innovation process: the central role of shared vision in product and process innovation teams. *Journal of Organizational Behavior, 25*, 259–278.

Pearce, C. L. & Sims, H. P. (2002). Vertical versus shared leadership as predictors of the effectiveness of change management teams: An examination of aversive, directive, transactional, transformational and empowering leader behaviors. *Group Dynamics: Theory, Research, and Practice, 6*(2), 172–197.

Pearsall, M. J. & Ellis, A. P. J. (2006). The effects of critical team member assertiveness on team performance and satisfaction. *Journal of Management, 32*(4), 575–594.

Perkins, A. L., Shaw, R. B., & Sutton, R. I. (1990). Summary: Human service teams. In J. R. Hackman (Ed.), *Groups that work (and those that don't): Creating conditions for effective teamwork* (pp. 349–360). San Francisco: Josey-Bass.

Porter, C. O., Hollenbeck, J. R., Ilgen, D. R., Ellis, A. P., West, B. J., & Moon, H. (2003). Backing up behaviors in teams: the role of personality and legitimacy of need. *Journal of Applied Psychology, 88*(3), 391–403.

Rasmussen, T. H. & Jeppesen, H. J. (2006). Teamwork and associated psychological factors: A review. *Work & Stress, 20*(2), 105–128.

Rico, R., Sánchez-Manzanares, M., Gil, F., & Gibson, C. (2008). Team Implicit Coordination Processes: A Team Knowledge-Based Approach. *The Academy of Management Review, 33*(1), 163–184.

Rousseau, V., Aubé, C., & Savoie, A. (2006). Teamwork behaviors: A review and an integration of frameworks. *Small Group Research, 37*(5), 540–570.

Saavedra, R., Earley, P. C., & Van Dyne, L. (1993). Complex interdependence in task-performing groups. *Journal of Applied Psychology, 78*(1), 61–72.

Salas, E., Burke, C. S., & Stagl, K. C. (2004). Developing teams and team leaders: Strategies and principles. In D. Day, S. J. Zaccaro, & S. M. Halpin (Eds.), *Leader development for transforming organizations: Growing leaders for tomorrow* (pp. 325–355). Mahwah, NJ: Lawrence Erlbaum Associates, Inc.

Salas, E., Cannon-Bowers, J. A., Church-Payne, S., & Smith-Jentsch, K. A. (1998). Teams and teamwork in the military. In C. Cronin (Ed.), *Military psychology: An introduction* (pp. 71–87). Upper Saddle River, NJ: Pearson.

Salas, E., Cannon-Bowers, J. A., Fiore, S. M., & Sout, R. J. (2001). Cue-recognition training to enhance team situation awareness. In M. McNeese, E. Salas, & M. Endsley (Eds.), *New trends in collaborative activities: Understanding system dynamics in complex environments* (pp. 169–190). Santa Monica, CA: Human Factors and Ergonomics Society.

Salas, E., Cannon-Bowers, J. A., & Johnston, J. H. (1997). How can you turn a team of experts into an expert team?: Emerging training strategies. In C. E. Zsambok & G. Klein (Eds.), *Naturalistic decision making* (pp. 359–370). Mahwah, NJ: Erlbaum.

Salas, E., Dickinson, T., Converse, S., & Tannenbaum, S. (1992). Toward an understanding of team performance and training. In R. Swezey & E. Salas (Eds.), *Teams: Their training and performance.* Norwood, NJ: Ablex Publishing.

Salas, E., Prince, C., Baker, D. P. & Shrestha, L. (1995). Situation awareness in team performance: Implications for measurement and training. *Human Factors, 37*(1), 123–136.

Salas, E., Rosen, M. A., Burke, C. S., Goodwin, G. F., & Fiore, S. (2006). The making of a dream team: when expert teams do best. In K. A. Ericsson, N. Charness, P. J. Feltovich, & R. R. Hoffman, (Eds.), *The Cambridge handbook of expertise and expert performance* (pp. 439–453). New York: Cambridge University Press.

Salas, E., Rosen, M. A., Burke, C. S., Nicholson, D., & Howse, W. R. (2007). Markers for enhancing team cognition in complex environments: The power of team performance diagnosis. *Aviation, Space, and Environmental Medicine Special Supplement on Operational Applications of Cognitive Performance Enhancement Technologies, 78*(5), B77–85.

Salas, E., Sims, D. E., & Burke, C. S. (2005). Is there a big five in teamwork? *Small Group Research, 36*(5), 555–599.

Salas, E., Stagl, K. C., Burke, C. S., & Goodwin, G. F. (2007). Fostering team effectiveness in organizations: Toward an integrative theoretical framework of team performance. In J. W. Shuart, W. Spaulding, and J. Poland (Eds.), *Modeling complex systems: Motivation, cognition and social processes, Nebraska Symposium on Motivation* (Vol. 51). Lincoln: University of Nebraska Press.

Shaw, J. D., Duffy, M. K., & Stark, E. M. (2001). Team reward attitude: Construct development and initial validation. *Journal of Organizational Behavior, 22,* 903–917.

Simons, T. L. & Peterson, R. S. (2000). Task conflict and relationship conflict in top management teams: The pivotal role of intragroup trust. *Journal of Applied Psychology, 85*(1), 102–111.

Smith-Jentsch, K. A. (1995). *Measurement and debriefing tools refined and validated as SWOS.* Presentation at the meeting of the TADMUS Technical Advisory Board, Moorestown, NJ.

Smith-Jentsch, K. A., Johnston, J. A., & Payne, S. C. (1998). Measuring team-related expertise in complex environments. In J. A. Cannon-Bowers & E. Salas (Eds.), *Making decisions under stress: Implications for individual and team training* (pp. 61–87). Washington, DC: American Psychological Association.

Smith-Jentsch, K. A., Salas, E., & Baker, D. P. (1996). Training team performance-related assertiveness. *Personnel Psychology, 49*(909–36).

Smith-Jentsch, K. A. & Scielzo, S. (2007). *An empirically-tested approach for measuring team-related cognition and behavior to support training and development.* Paper presented at the Second Annual Conference of the Interdisciplinary Network for Group Research, Lansing, MI.

Smith-Jentsch, K. A., Zeisig, R. L., Acton, B., & McPherson, J. A. (1998). Team dimensional training: A strategy for guided team self-correction. In J. A. Cannon-Bowers & E. Salas (Eds.), *Making decisions under stress: Implications for individual and team training* (pp. 271–297). Washington, DC: American Psychological Association.

Stagl, K. C., Salas, E., & Burke, C. S. (2006). Best practices in team leadership: What team leaders do to facilitate team effectiveness. In J. A. Conger, & R.E. Riggio, (Eds.), *The practice of leadership: Developing the next generation of leaders* (pp. 172–198). Hoboken, NJ: John Wiley & Sons.

Sternberg, R. J. (1997). Cognitive conceptions of expertise. In P. J. Fletovich, K. M. Ford, & R. R. Hoffman, (Eds.), *Expertise in context* (pp. 149–162). Menlo Park, CA: AAAI Press/MIT Press.

Stout, R. J., Cannon-Bowers, J. A., & Salas, E. (1996). The role of shared mental models in developing team situational awareness: Implications for training. *Training Research Journal, 2,* 85–116.

Stout, R. J., Cannon-Bowers, J. A., Salas, E., & Milanovich, D. M. (1999). Planning, shared mental models, and coordinated performance: An empirical link is established. *Human Factors, 41*(1), 61–71.

Streufert, S. (1997). Complexity: An integration of theories. *Journal of Applied Social Psychology, 27*(23), 2068–2095.

Tasa, K., Taggar, S., & Seijts, G. H. (2007). The development of collective efficacy in teams: A multilevel and longitudinal perspective. *Journal of Applied Psychology, 92*(1), 17–27.

Watson, C. B., Chemers, M. M., & Preiser, N. (2001). Collective efficacy: A multi-level analysis. *Personality and social psychology bulletin, 27*(8), 1057–1068.

Webber, S. S. (2002). Leadership and trust facilitating cross-functional team success. *Journal of Management Development, 21,* 201–214.

Weldon, E., & Weingart, L. R. (1993). Group goals and group performance. *British Journal of Social Psychology, 32*(4), 307–328.

Wiener, N. (1954). *The human use of human beings: Cybernetics and society.* Boston, MA: Houghton Mifflin.

Williams, C. C. & Mahan, R. P. (2006). Understanding multiteam system functioning. In W. Bennett, Jr., C. E. Lance & D. J. Woehr (Eds.), *Performance measurement: Current perspectives and future challenges* (pp. 205–224). Mahwah, NJ: Erlbaum.

Yazici, H. J. (2005). A study of collaborative learning style and team learning performance. *Education and Training, 47*(3), 216–229.

Zaccaro, S. J. Blair, V., Peterson, C., & Zazanis, M. (1995). Collective Efficacy. In J. E. Maddux (Ed.), *Self-Efficacy, Adaptation, and Adjustment: Theory, Research, and Application.* New York, NY: Plenum.

Zaccaro, S. J. Gualtieri, J., & Minionis, D. (1995). Task Cohesion as a Facilitator of Team Decision Making Under Temperal Urgency. *Military Psychology, 7*(2), 77–93.

Zaccaro, S. J., Rittman, A. L., & Marks, M. A. (2001). Team leadership. *Leadership Quarterly, 12,* 451–483.

Section II

Cross-Disciplinary Theoretical Approaches

4

Team Leadership and Team Effectiveness*

Stephen J. Zaccaro, Beth Heinen, and Marissa Shuffler

Team leadership is essential for team effectiveness. The contribution of leadership to effective team performance rests on the extent to which team leaders help members achieve a *synergistic threshold*, where collective effort accomplishes more than the sum of individual abilities or efforts. Collins and Guetzkow (1964) defined such a threshold in decision-making groups as reflecting an "assembly bonus," where decisions emerging from group interaction are superior in quality to those made by the group's most capable member (see also Michaelson, Watson, & Black, 1989). Groups and teams rarely achieve a synergistic threshold, or the assembly bonus (Hill, 1982), primarily because of process loss (Steiner, 1972). Process losses can be attributed to the failure of team members to develop the best means of combining their individual capabilities in a concerted direction or to the unwillingness or inability of members to exert sufficient levels of individual effort (ibid.). The activities of effective team leadership, therefore, need to center on providing the direction for collective action and on helping teams reach and maintain a state of minimal process loss (cf. Gardner & Schermerhorn, 1992; Jacobs & Jaques, 1990).

Despite the importance of leadership for team effectiveness, literatures on leadership and team dynamics have not offered an abundance of conceptual frames to explain how leadership contributes to team effectiveness. For example, Hackman and Walton (1986) noted, "we have not found among existing leadership theories, one that deals to our satisfaction with the leadership of *task performing groups in organizations*" (p. 73, italics in original). Fifteen years later, even with some important contributions in the interim (e.g., Beyerlein, Johnson, & Beyerlein, 1996; Kozlowski, Gully, McHugh, Salas, & Cannon-Bowers, 1996; Kozlowski, Gully, Salas, & Cannon-Bowers, 1996), Zaccaro, Rittman, and Marks (2001, p. 452) noted, "We

* This research was supported by the United States Army Research Institute for the Behavioral and Social Sciences (W74V8H-05-K-0004). The views expressed in this chapter are those of the authors and do not necessarily reflect the views of the U.S. Department of the Army or any other organization.

know surprisingly little about how leaders create and manage effective teams." Salas, Burke, and Stagl (2004, p. 342) stated similarly, "One area that has been relatively neglected in the team literature is the role of the team leader."

This relative lack of conceptual frames and models in the face of huge separate literatures on leadership and team dynamics, respectively, has resulted primarily from the tendency of traditional leadership theories not to make the distinction between leader–*subordinate* interactions and leader–*team* interactions (Burke et al., 2006; Salas et al., 2004). Leadership models such as path goal theory (House, 1971; House & Dessler, 1974), leader member exchange theory (Dansereau, Graen, & Haga, 1975), and inspirational leadership theories (Bass, 1985; Bass & Avolio, 1993; Conger & Kanungo, 1987; House, 1977) provide excellent treatments of how leadership behaviors influence subordinate attitudes, beliefs, motives, effort, and performance. Other frameworks, such as contingency theory (Fiedler, 1964, 1971), normative decision models (Vroom & Yetton, 1973), and leader substitutes theory (Kerr & Jermier, 1978) describe how group properties and variables moderate the display or effectiveness of particularly leadership activities. Though these approaches make substantial contributions to the understanding of organizational leadership, they do not define precisely how leadership contributes to *team* effectiveness (see House's [1996] revision of path goal theory as an exception). Such definitions need to focus not on dyadic or individual consequences of leadership activities but rather on how team leaders and team leadership processes foster more *interconnectivity, integration,* and *coherence* among team members. Accordingly, the prime unit of analysis for criteria in studies of team leadership should reside at the team or group level, not at the individual level. Predictor units of analysis can be at both the individual (e.g., leader) and team level.

Perhaps in response to the relative paucity of truly team-based leadership research, the recent literature in this domain has experienced a significant surge in conceptual frameworks, models, and empirical studies (e.g., Basadur, 2004; Burke et al., 2006; Day, Gronn, & Salas, 2004, 2006; Ellemers, De Gilder, & Haslam, 2004; Hackman & Wageman, 2005; Marta, Leritz, & Mumford, 2005; Morgeson, 2005; Peterson, Smith, Martorana, & Owens, 2003; Zaccaro & Klimoski, 2002). The present chapter reviews and integrates this body of theoretical and empirical research to develop a somewhat comprehensive model describing how leaders and team leadership processes contribute to team effectiveness or to the minimization of process loss and the achievement of the team synergy.

Leader-Centric versus Team-Centric Leadership

At this point we need to highlight a distinction in the extant literature between two perspectives on leadership and team dynamics. One perspective emphasizes the importance of individuals who occupy the leader role in the team and who have primary responsibility for shaping the conditions of team effectiveness. Thus, researchers have labeled such leader-centered approaches as "traditional" (Day et al., 2004), "heroic" (Manz & Sims, 1991; Yukl, 2006), "vertical" (Conger & Pearce, 2003; Pearce & Sims, 2002), "top-down" (Locke, 2003), and "hierarchical" (Jaques, 1990). Researchers in this perspective generally direct their focus of inquiry on the attributes of individual leaders and the processes they use to influence team dynamics. Thus, leaders and leadership processes are defined within Input–Process–Output (IPO) models of team dynamics (Hackman & Morris, 1975; McGrath, 1964) as key inputs to team processes (Day et al., 2004). Followers are treated as mostly passive recipients of the leader's influence, or their primary role is to grant legitimacy to the leader's exercise of power and influence (Hollander & Julian, 1970). Leadership development interventions within such perspectives target growth in individual leadership skills (Day, 2000).

A more recent perspective emphasizes principles of collective leadership, where the responsibility for directing and managing collective efforts becomes shared among team members (Manz & Sims, 1980). This perspective, referred to as involving "shared leadership" (Pearce & Conger, 2003b), "self-managed teams" (Manz & Sims, 1987), or "distributed leadership" (Day et al., 2004) has roots in early writings on situational leadership (e.g., Gibb, 1954), in models of followership and leader emergence (Hollander & Julian, 1970), in leadership substitutes models (Kerr & Jermier, 1978), and in theories of transformational leadership that center on the empowerment of subordinates (Bass, 1985; Burns, 1978). Self-managing teams are typically defined as not having a formal or appointed leader (Day et al., 2004). One individual may often emerge as a leader by virtue of his or her performance within the team and subsequently adopts the responsibilities of a formal leader role incumbent, or across tasks the leadership responsibilities may rotate to different individuals who possess the skills and expertise to lead in particular situations (Gibb, 1947, 1954). Both processes reflect either emergent or distributed leadership, but, at the task level, leadership influence still remains within an individual. Another version of this perspective defines leadership not as an input to team process but rather as a quality that "emerges or is drawn from teams as a function of working on and accomplishing shared work" (Day et al., 2004, p. 859). Here, leadership is truly shared within a single task or project, with different members contributing leadership influence (Pearce & Conger, 2003a). Leadership development interventions within this perspective take a more systems approach, focusing on the team or organization in addition to individuals (Day & Zaccaro, 2004; Day et al., 2004).

Perhaps because of the ubiquity of leader-entered perspectives in the literature, models of team-centered leadership tend to be framed in "oppositional" terms relative to leader-centered models (Conger & Pearce, 2003; Day et al., 2004; Locke, 2003; Pearce & Sims, 2002). Dumaine (1990, p. 52), for example, questioned, "Who needs a boss?" However, several theorists have acknowledged, or argued, that both leader-centered and team-centered processes contribute to team effectiveness (Conger & Pearce, 2003; Cox, Pearce, & Perry, 2003; Druskat & Wheeler, 2003; Pearce, 2004). Indeed, regarding one type of organizational team that often utilizes self-management procedures, Cox et al. (2003, p. 58) noted:

> Shared leadership supplements but does not replace vertical leadership in new product development teams (e.g., Pearce & Sims, 2000, 2002). Indeed, the vertical leader, often the formally designated project or program manager, retains a range of important responsibilities even in shared leadership contexts. These responsibilities include forming the team, managing boundaries, providing as-needed leadership support, and maintaining the shared leadership system in the team. We position vertical leadership as an antecedent variable that may affect the extent to which shared leadership emerges in an NPD [new product development] team.

Roles of Leaders in Shared Leadership Systems

The role of individual leaders in team-centered leadership systems can be conceptualized in three ways: as *internal leaders, external leaders,* or *executive coordinators.* Many organizational teams may have formal internal leaders even when, in some or all instances, leadership functions are distributed among team members. These internal team leaders serve as active and frequent participants in team interactions. However, they have the responsibility for deciding when and how much team members participate in leadership influence. Several situational leadership models describe how team factors such as member maturity and expertise (Hersey & Blanchard, 1988) and cohesion (Kerr & Jermier, 1978) foster more participative leadership. Vroom and Yetton's (1973) leader decision model described such variables as the distribution of unique information within the team, the likelihood of decision acceptance or cooperation by team members, and the importance and structure of the team problem that determine when participative leadership will be more fruitful than directive leadership.

The functions of an internal team leader include designing and developing the team so that members can subsequently practice effective self-management (Pearce, 2004). These functions include staffing the team with members who have sufficient levels and diversity of requisite task, teamwork, and leadership skills; specifying a clear purpose and direction for the team's collective action; specifying expectations for team interaction; and coaching team members in their individual and collective practice of shared team leadership (Pearce, 2004; Wageman, 2001). Internal leaders also have some responsibility for managing the team's boundaries and its relationships with external constituencies. Boundary management includes (1) making sure team goals and processes are aligned with organizational strategy, policies, and structures, and (2) building social capital outside of the team to support team activities and to ensure team resources (Ancona & Caldwell, 1988; Kline, 2003).

Whereas internal leaders of self-managed teams interject frequently in team interactions and dynamics, external leaders have more distant connections to the team. They still have the formal role and responsibility of leading and managing team action. However, team members are likely to have more responsibility for defining specific member roles and structuring team processes. Accordingly, the functions of the external leader become oriented more toward setting the overall direction and parameters for team action and supporting and facilitating the teams' efforts in self-management. External leaders may also staff the team (Klimoski & Jones, 1995; Klimoski & Koles, 2001; Klimoski & Zukin, 1999), ideally selecting members who can work effectively together in sharing leadership functions. The responsibility of such leaders is to foster the internal and external conditions for effective team self-management. Manz & Sims (1987) defined several leader "encouraging behaviors" that help establish the appropriate atmosphere for self-governance. These behaviors resemble those linked to team self-regulation (Kane, Zaccaro, Tremble, & Masuda, 2002) and include encouraging team self-observations, self-analysis, self-criticism or reinforcement, collective goal setting, performance goal monitoring, and adjustments of collective action when the team is off course. The role of the external leader is to model and foster these team conditions. As they become more established, the external leader plays a diminished role in routine team functioning. Thus, the external leader may exert direct influence most frequently early in the tenure of a self-managing team (cf. Kozlowski, Gully, Salas, et al., 1996).

External leaders focus significant resources on the management of the team's boundary (Druskat & Wheeler, 2003). Because they operate mostly outside of the team, such leaders are better positioned to develop networks and social capital to assist team functioning. Druskat and Wheeler described several boundary functions of external team leaders, including seeking information from outside managers, peers, and specialists; developing an understanding of the power dynamics in the organization; and obtaining support from external constituencies. Morgeson (2005) also noted another key role of external leaders: to help teams deal with unexpected or novel events that arise in the organization's environments. Taken together, these functions illustrate the external leader as a resource for the team to improve its position within the organization and to smooth over rough waters created by turbulence in the operating environment. The external leader intervenes in team internal functioning primarily to foster team self-leadership.

Several researchers have identified organizational teams with no formal leadership roles, either internal or external. For example, Day et al. (2004) described the advent and increasing popularity of fast-forming project teams having members operating at the same position level. Sundstrom, McIntyre, Halfhill, and Richards (2000) defined such teams as being cross-functional, where managers or personnel come from different organizational units and are time limited in their tenure. Citing Gordon (1992), Day et al. noted that such teams comprise more than one third of all organizational teams. Sundstrom et al. (2000) also defined another form of temporary team, called advisory teams, in which members come together to consider and resolve production problems. Citing ongoing surveys by Lawler, Mohrman, and Ledford (1998), they noted that 78% of Fortune 1000 companies report the use of self-managing teams. Day et al. summarized this phenomenon by stating that "it is an increasingly common expectation for employees to be able to work effectively in teams and often where there is no formally appointed leader (or where team members are all at the same level)" (p. 859).

Although we agree that the incidence of self-managing teams in organizations has risen dramatically over the last 20 years, we would argue that researchers need to consider the systems-level characteristics of such teams as they are embedded within organizations (Katz & Kahn, 1978). Temporary project teams do not form in an organizational vacuum—they are established within a strategic framework constructed by top- or mid-level (depending on the level of the project team) managers. Members of such teams typically have more responsibility than teams with internal or close external leaders for team direction setting and operational management. They also need to carry out many of the external boundary spanning described earlier, again as a team. They may be composed of other managers or personnel with similar ranks and position authority and no formal internal or close external leader. However, the broad parameters of their work, and the conditions of team success, are still set by other superordinate leaders. We label these leaders as *executive coordinators*.

Executive coordinators establish project or work teams in line with broad strategic directives but give team members considerable latitude in how such directives are to be translated into more specific organizational goals and objectives. Such leaders have little input into how the teams structure member roles, divide task responsibilities, or allocate team resources. However, they do facilitate the supportiveness of the overall intraorganizational and interorganizational networks within which such teams need to operate. Many middle- and top-management teams operate within such leadership arrangements (Ensley, Pearson, & Pearce, 2003).

Perhaps the most significant responsibility of executive coordinators is to ensure that the team has the strength, skills, and resources to operate success-fully as self-leaders and managers (cf. Kozlowski, Gully, Salas et al., 1996). This responsibility involves staffing the team with members having sufficient and diverse expertise in appropriate functional areas as well as the social capital within the organization to effectively self-manage team boundary processes. Because these members are likely to be middle- to upper-level managers with their own consistencies, their *behavioral integration* (Hambrick, 1994) may be difficult to accomplish. According to Hambrick (pp. 188–189):

> Behavioral integration is the degree to which the group engages in mutual and collective interaction. In the context of top management groups, behavioral integration has three major elements: (1) quantity and quality (richness, timeliness, accuracy) of information exchange, (2) collaborative behavior, and (3) joint decision making. Thus, behavioral integration is a "meta-construct" for describing various elements of group process.

In the context of self-managing teams, we would expand behavioral integration to include processes such as direction setting and boundary management. Accordingly, the coaching support of the executive coordinator may apply most effectively to these aspects of self-managing teams.

The three forms of leaders in team-centered leadership arrangements—internal, external, and executive coordinator—vary mostly on the amount of discretion team members have in team direction setting and operational management. They also vary on the proportion of time and social resources devoted to boundary management. Internal leaders have the most input on team direction and internal processes, whereas executive coordina-tors have the least. External leaders and especially executive coordinators spend proportionately more time than internal leaders on managing the team's connections to the larger organization and operating environment.

Shared Leadership Expertise

The three types of leaders share the function of providing support and encouragement to the efforts of team members toward managing their own internal and external leadership processes. The literature on self-managing and self-leading team defines coaching as a primary role for leaders of such teams (Hackman & Wageman, 2005). We would extend this perspective even to more traditional leader-centered teams and would argue that team leaders can operate most effectively, and indeed can help facilitate team adaptation to change, when a significant proportion of leadership functions are distributed among team members. The task of the leader, particularly early in the team tenure, becomes developing the ability of team members to do collective leadership (cf. Kozlowski, Gully, Salas, et al., 1996). Day et al. (2004) defined this collective ability within the team as "leadership capacity," in which basic leadership functions such as the alignment of individual goals and the formation of shared social identity emerge from the interrelationships and interactions of team members.

We recognize the importance of leadership capacity within the team but expand the conceptualization of this construct in two ways. First, this shared leadership ability encompasses not only leadership behaviors but also knowledge systems and expertise that form the foundation of leader direction setting and operational management. For this reason, we label this capacity of the team as *leadership expertise*. Second, we argue that although such leadership expertise can arise out of team interactions, team leaders have significant responsibility for establishing the conditions that afford the emergence of such expertise (cf. Kozlowski, Gully, McHugh et al., 1996). They can have direct influences on the processes that promote such emergence (Zaccaro, Ely, & Shuffler, 2007).

Leadership expertise at the team level reflects in part the team members' collective capacity to routinely display leadership skills associated with direction setting and team operations management. Direction-setting skills include environmental scanning and sense making, planning and goal setting, and sense giving that supports action plans (Zaccaro, 2001; Zaccaro et al., 2001). Operational management skills include team building, norm development, communication of task and role requirements, development of team members' human and social capital, the ability to align specific member capabilities with task requirements, and conflict management (ibid.). When team members can collectively and effectively conduct these leadership processes, then the team can be defined as possessing high leadership expertise.

Our consideration of shared leadership expertise also derives in part from the work of Lord and Hall (2005). Lord and Hall rooted the development and acquisition of leadership skills by an individual in the growth of cognitive systems and knowledge structures from novice levels of understanding to expert levels. They defined leadership skill in terms of "how leaders *access* and *use* information as well as the *content* of their underlying knowledge of the tasks, and social issues related to leadership" (p. 593). Accordingly, they conceptualized leader skill development in terms of changes toward more complex and principled-based knowledge structures as well as in terms of changes in how leaders utilize such information.

At the novice level, leadership skills reflect surface structures, which are "the immediately observable components of leadership processes" (Lord & Hall, 2005, p. 598). These refer to generic activities of leadership in direction setting and managing unit operations. For example, Hirst, Mann, Bain, Pirola-Merlo, and Richver (2004, p. 312) noted that leaders "learning to lead" reported greater learning and skill acquisition in facilitative leadership, which refers to leadership acts that "promote respect and positive relationships between team members, productive conflict resolution, and open expression of ideas and opinions." They also reported gains in leadership skills that foster team reflexivity, or the ability of team members to exchange information, and to reflect about team actions and events. Skill development at the novice level centers on the acquisition of these generic behavior patterns, which novices perceive as generalizing across most leadership situations and as crucial to their self-definition as leaders (Lord & Hall, 2005).

According to Lord and Hall (2005), leadership skill at the intermediate level reflects more proceduralized knowledge of leadership behavior and more principle-based understanding of what behaviors apply, and how they apply, in specific problem domains. Lord and Hall noted that, with intermediate skill, leadership behavior becomes more automatized, and leaders can devote more cognitive resources than novices to the "metamonitoring" of their leadership activities and to the generation of solutions to less familiar organizational problems. Intermediate leadership skills foster more context-driven problem responses rather than the more generic responses typical of novice-level leaders. The intermediate level of skill attainment is crucial for the leader to effectively facilitate high levels of team performance and, indeed, to later coach and encourage team self-management.

Expert levels of leadership skills entail "deeper, more principled definitions of problems, which may involve a greater understanding of the factors defining the situational contingencies that influence *both* leaders and subordinates" (Lord & Hall, 2005, p. 602, italics in original). According to Lord and Hall, expert leaders possess deep knowledge structures that integrate elements of leadership self-identity, core leadership values, task, social and emotion regulation skills, and principle-based or more abstract classification of organizational problems. High-level leadership expertise also entails a transition from an individual-level leadership identity to a more collective identity that defines the leader self "in terms of specific collectives such as groups and organizations" (ibid., p. 596). Such shift in identification contributes to the leader's ability to foster shared and distributed leadership in followers.

Lord and Hall (2005) defined their framework as explicitly about skill acquisition and development in individual leaders. However, a team's ability to effectively and collectively enact leadership would require attaining similar levels of expertise among its members, especially if the team, such as a top-management team, is expected to have a long or permanent tenure. Novice levels of leadership skills among team members would result in more generic and less context-driven problem responses. Likewise, the content of their leadership expertise would be lower. To be truly effective at distributed leadership, members of the team need to share deeper, broader, and more principle-based social knowledge structures around the practice of such leadership. They also need to be able to access and use information in ways that reflect situational understanding and that allow for greater metamonitoring of members' self- and team leadership activities.

Formal team leaders have significant responsibility in fostering the development of shared and distributed leadership expertise. Lord and Hall (2005) noted that the acquisition of leadership expertise occurs over an extended period of time. Thus, we would not expect a leader to take a team of inexperienced individuals and turn them quickly into expert leaders. Instead, the leader may need to focus on moving the team from no understanding of leadership to perhaps some level of surface understanding. If the team is to exist for a long enough time, then perhaps team members can begin to acquire the deeper, more situation-specific elements of intermediate levels of leadership skill. Note that the challenge for the team leader lies not only in developing the leadership expertise of individual members but also in developing team work skills that improve how well they integrate and that collectively engage their expertise (cf. Kozlowski, Gully, Salas, et al., 1996). This means that when growing distributed leadership skills within the team, leaders need to focus on facilitating team processes that promote collective direction setting, collective management of team operations, and a collective awareness at a principled level of how these leadership activities are driven by contextual exigencies.

Lord and Hall (2005, p. 603) suggested that leaders with expert-level leadership skills possess a greater orientation toward creating shared expertise:

> Another important aspect of deeper leadership structures is that they may involve an increased focused on *changing others* rather than on changes within leaders. Thus, while the development of surface leadership skills may involve more leader-relevant changes, expert level leadership may involve knowledge and principles pertaining to developing behavioral and self-regulatory skills in others. We suspect that leaders must have proceduralized behavioral and self-regulatory skills in addition to strong social and emotional skills in order to develop other-focused principled leadership knowledge. We also believe that such expert level knowledge is required for developing effective systems level leadership rather than leader focused leadership.

We noted earlier three types of leader roles in a team-centered leadership arrangement—internal, external, and executive coordinator. Though the responsibilities for team directing setting and operations management vary across these roles, the responsibility for developing shared and distributed leadership expertise remains the same. Two important questions for further consideration (although not here) are as follows:

1. What are the processes and the developmental interventions that are best suited to developing shared leadership expertise (cf. Day et al., 2004; O'Connor & Quinn, 2004)?
2. How do these processes change in focus, content, and weight across the team coaching and development activities of internal leaders, external leaders, and executive coordinators?

An Integrative Model of Team Leadership and Team Effectiveness

In the previous section of this chapter we began to describe a model of leader–team effectiveness that emphasizes the responsibility of the team leader to develop the store of leadership expertise and capacity residing among team members. In this section, we expand these ideas and integrate existing frameworks into an overarching model of leadership and team dynamics. We build specifically on previous models (Zaccaro, 2001; Zaccaro et al., 2001) but integrate ideas and postulates from several other theories and models.

This model, shown in Figure 4.1, rests on two central assumptions. First, the impact of effective team leadership lies in fostering greater interconnectivity, integration, and coherence among team members. Team leadership establishes the direct and indirect conditions that help team members work well together. It contributes to the reduction of process loss. It also promotes the team's ability to be adaptive to changing environmental circumstances (Marks, Zaccaro, & Mathieu, 2000). The focus of analysis resides at the *nexuses* of team members' actions, not on how team leadership influences individual attitudes, beliefs, motives, or behaviors.

The second assumption of the model extends the first one by arguing that the influence of leadership on team performance and effectiveness is mediated mostly by its effects on team interaction dynamics (Zaccaro et al., 2001). Internal leaders as team members can perhaps influence team performance directly on certain kinds of tasks, such as disjunctive or single solution tasks, where the performance of the most capable member determines the level of group productivity (Steiner, 1972). However,

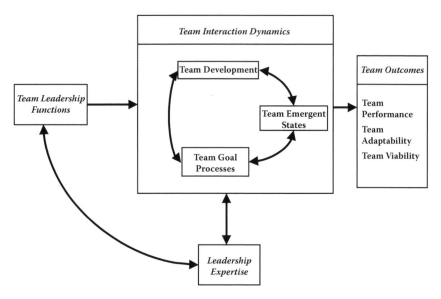

FIGURE 4.1
An integrative model of team leadership and team effectiveness.

leaders may still need to persuade group members to adopt the answer even on such tasks when they have derived the correct solution, and group interaction processes will subsequently determine group success (Davis, 1973; Zaccaro & McCoy, 1988). External leaders and executive coordinators can also directly influence team performance when they fail to procure the appropriate amount of resources needed by the team to do its work. Then no matter how much ability members have, how effectively they interact together, and how much they reduce process loss, they will still not be able to succeed. However, we suspect that these instances represent a relatively smaller proportion of the variance in team situations and that the impact of leadership on team performance will occur mostly through the direct influences of leaders on team interaction dynamics.

The derivation of the leadership–team effectiveness model in Figure 4.1 has its roots in functional perspectives of leadership (Fleishman et al., 1991; Hackman & Wageman, 2005; Hackman & Walton, 1986; Lord, 1977; Mumford, Zaccaro, Harding, Jacobs, & Fleishman, 2000; Zaccaro et al., 2001). This approach defines team leadership in terms of social problem-solving processes that advance the team's attainment of its performance goals. These processes include interpreting and diagnosing team problems, generating and evaluating team solutions, and implementing selected solutions (Mumford et al., 2000; Zaccaro et al., 2001).

Zaccaro et al. (2001) noted several distinctions regarding the functional leadership perspective. First, team leadership includes significant boundary-spanning and boundary-management activities. Team problems that need to be addressed by the leader will likely have their origination in shifting environmental dynamics. Second, leaders have discretion and choice in their decisions about team directions in problem solving: "Team actions that are completely specified or fully elicited by the situation do not require the intervention of team leaders (ibid., p. 454). Third, the functional leadership perspective does not attempt to specify specific leadership behaviors but, rather, general behavioral sets that vary considerably across team situations. As Hackman and Wageman (2005, p. 273) noted, "A functional approach to leadership leaves room for an indefinite number of ways to get key group functions accomplished, and avoids the necessity of delineating all the specific behaviors or styles a leader should exhibit in given circumstances—a trap into which it is easy for leadership theorists to fall." Thus, functional leadership models rest on the generic social problem-solving functions of leadership, without specifying particular stylistic ways of leading to solving team problems; leaders can use a range of styles, behavioral patterns, and solutions to address team problems (Zaccaro, 1999, 2002).

While the foundation of the functional leadership perspective dates back to McGrath (1962, cited in Hackman & Walton, 1986) and Roby (1961), Hackman and Walton provided the first full elaboration of leadership influences in team processes. Their perspective has been reflected in a number of other more recent research studies (e.g., Burke et al., 2006; DeChurch & Marks, 2006; Morgeson, 2005; Zaccaro et al., 2001; Zeigert, 2004). We build on this work in Table 4.1 to elaborate the team leadership processes and team interaction dynamics that define the components of our leader–team effectiveness model.

Leadership Functions

The extant conceptual and empirical literature suggest three core team leadership functions: (1) setting the direction for team action; (2) managing team operations; and (3) developing the team's capacity to manage their own problem-solving processes (Burke et al., 2006; Cohen, Ledford, & Spreitzer, 1996; Cox et al., 2003; Fleishman et al., 1991; Hackman & Walton, 1986; Kozlowski, Gully, McHugh, et al., 1996; Kozlowski, Gully, Salas, et al., 1996; Nygren & Levine, 1996; Zaccaro, 2001; Zaccaro et al., 2001; Zeigert, 2004). Team direction-setting processes include scanning and appraisal of the team's operating environment, as well as information acquisition regarding the resource capabilities and existing state of the team (Fleishman et al., 1991; Zaccaro, 2001). Team leaders need to establish a conceptual frame of the team's operating environment, one that models the nature of problems confronting the team and encodes contingencies that would influence the derivation and evaluation of solutions (cf. Jacobs & Jaques, 1987; Jacobs & McGee, 2001). This process of sense making, in

TABLE 4.1

Team Leadership Functions and Team Interaction Dynamics

Team Leadership Functions	Team Interaction Dynamics
Direction setting	Team goal processes
• Environmental scanning	• Transition
• Sense making	• Mission analysis
• Planning	• Goal specification
• Sense giving	• Strategy formulation
Managing team operations	• Action
• Staffing the team	• Monitoring progress toward goals
• Calibrating member roles to task requirements	• Systems monitoring
	• Backup behaviors
• Facilitating the development of team communication structures, norms, roles, and performance expectations	• Coordination
	• Interpersonal
	• Conflict management
• Monitoring team actions and providing feedback	• Motivation and confidence building
	• Affect management
• Aligning team actions with environmental contingencies	Team emergent states
	• Cognitive
• Procuring team resources	• Shared mental models
• Communicating information about the team to external constituencies	• Motivational
	• Cohesion
• Acting as a communication buffer between external constituencies and team members	• Trust
	• Collective efficacy
	• Affective
Developing team's leadership capacity	Team development
• Developing member leader expertise	• Emergence of collective identity
• Coaching shared direction setting	• Norm development
• Coaching team planning and role assignment	• Member skill acquisition
• Coaching collective information processing	• Growth in self-management skills and leader expertise

turn, provides the basis for leader and team planning and team goal setting. Likewise, sense making should lead to a sense-giving process where leaders provide to team members a version of the conceptual frame they have formed of environmental dynamics that helps members understand the rationale and context for their collective actions. Marks et al. (2000; see also Burke, 1999) found that such leader briefings contributed significantly to the team's development of shared mental models and, in turn, to the ability of the team to adapt to environmental novelty.

As described, then, the direction-setting role of team leaders requires considerable boundary management and interplay within the team's environment. To promote team effectiveness, the leader's proffered direction for the team needs to facilitate alignment between team actions and environmental demands/contingencies. This requirement places a premium on the leader's ability to acquire information from the operating environment. Ancona and Caldwell (1988) defined several similar boundary-management functions in team, such as *scout* activities and *sentry* activities. Scout activities involve environmental scanning, gathering information and resources modeling or mapping the environment, and feedback seeking. Sentry activities entail filtering and translating environmental information for team members. In most teams, these functions become the province of team leaders; in fully self-managing teams, they become some of the key elements of collective leadership expertise.

Managing team operations represents the second major component of effective team leadership. The leader's influence on team operations often begins with the staffing of the team and assignment of members having particular knowledge, skills, and abilities to specific team roles (Klimoski & Jones, 1995). Team staffing can range from the complete start of a new team, where leaders choose the entire team, to the replacement of one to significant numbers of team members. Team start-up and team member replacement present various challenges and issues to the team leader (Klimoski & Zukin, 1999). Choosing all new members of the team requires attention to both individual member skills and how well members are likely to work together (Klimoski & Koles, 2001). For team member replacement, leaders need to consider not only member capabilities but also how well the new potential member can be aligned with team structures, roles, expectations, and norms (ibid.). The amount of discretion leaders have for staffing is likely to increase as they ascend organizational levels.

Staffing requires selecting and fitting members to the team and its purpose. However, the general fit of member capabilities will need to be calibrated to shifting requirements as teams cycle through different tasks and different stages of performance episodes. Thus, team leadership requires an acute awareness of the strengths and weaknesses of particular members and how these capabilities, or lack thereof, intersect with team task requirements. Part of team operational management also entails developing and modeling task competencies in team members to enhance the human capital in the team (Fleishman et al., 1991).

Effective team coordination requires members to understand and accept behavioral expectations regarding expected and necessary actions at different cycles of team performance. Accordingly, another aspect of team operations management for leaders concerns the development and maintenance of norms, role expectations, and communication structures among team members. This development is especially crucial early in a team's development. Kozlowski, Gully, McHugh et al. (1996) argued that leaders are principally important at early stages in a team's tenure, because newly formed teams are particularly receptive to the structuring actions of high status individuals. They proposed (pp. 270–273) that team leaders who explicitly define social structures, team functions, goals, and performance expectations as well as who promote open communications, model self-disclosure, and coach individual performance are more likely to foster teams with high levels of coherence. We would extend these behaviors to include team structure maintenance and monitoring behaviors.

Team leadership processes also entail enhancing the levels of effort members willingly apply toward collective action (Hackman & Walton, 1986). Recent models of transformational leadership point to the role of leaders in motivating and empowering teams. Sivasubramaniam, Murry, Avolio, and Jung (2002) found that transformational leadership behaviors enhance group potency or beliefs about the team's ability to perform well—such beliefs are important precursors to team member motivation (Zaccaro, Blair, Peterson, & Zazanis, 1995). Transformational leaders highlight the importance of transcendent group and organizational goals and appeal to members' higher-order-need strengths (Bass, 1985; Gillespie & Mann, 2004). Özaralli (2003) reported that transformational leadership increased work meaningfulness, impact, and autonomy. Gillespie and Mann found that this form of leadership was associated with higher feelings of trust among team members. Trust and perceived work meaningfulness are also critical precursors of team member motivation.

Just as with team direction setting, team operational management requires not only a team internal focus but also a focus on events and activities beyond the team's boundary. Work teams operate within larger organizational systems, sometimes as part of special multiteam systems (Mathieu, Marks, & Zaccaro, 2001). Team leaders in such systems need to ensure that their team operations and activities are synchronized, sequentially and simultaneously, with the operations and activities of other work teams (DeChurch & Marks, 2006).

Team operations management also requires that leaders represent their team to outside constituencies and to procure the resources needed for team action. Earlier, we cited Ancona and Caldwell's (1988) scout and sentry group roles as key components of the team leader's direction-setting responsibilities. Their descriptions of *ambassador* and *guard* activities correspond to functions of team operations management. Ambassador activities involve informing outsiders of team states, actions, and progress. These activities also include the aforementioned coordination functions, negotiation of interteam relationships and resource exchanges, and molding of the environment, where possible, to make it more compatible to the team's agenda. Guard activities include determining the external requests and information that warrant team attention and buffering team members from unreasonable or illegitimate external demands. A number of conceptual frames posit these activities as important functions of team leadership (e.g., Cox et al., 2003; Druskat & Wheeler, 2003; House, 1996; Zaccaro et al., 2001; Zeigert, 2004).

Developing Team's Leadership Capacity

Earlier in this chapter, we argued that team leaders have an important responsibility to develop the shared leadership capacity and expertise in the team. When members can distribute and enact major leadership functions, the team leader can devote more resources to external networking and respond more quickly to unexpected or novel environment demands on the team. This aspect of team leadership entails coaching team members on shared activities related to team direction setting and operations management. Hackman and Wageman (2005, p. 273) identified three forms of team coaching:

- *Motivational coaching*: "Its functions are to minimize free-riding effects or 'social loafing' and to build shared commitment to the group and its work."
- *Consultative coaching*: "Its functions are to minimize mindless adoption or execution of task routines in uncertain or changing task environments and to foster the invention of ways of proceeding with the work that are especially well aligned with task requirements."
- *Educational coaching*: "Its functions are to minimize suboptimal weighing of member's contributions (i.e., when the weight given to the individuals' members contributions are at variance with their actual talents) and to foster the development of members' knowledge and skill."

Note how these three forms of coaching are intended to foster the teams' accomplishment of several leadership functions, mostly those mentioned earlier under team operations management. To this list, we would add *leadership coaching,* which helps team members (1) set or reset team directions and goals; (2) establish and maintain the alignment between team actions and environmental dynamics, including alignment with the actions of other work teams in the system; and (3) engage in a variety of environmental scanning and external team boundary functions (cf. Kozlowski, Gully, McHugh et al., 1996).

The development of leadership capacity in the team also requires the leader to foster growth in members' cognitive representations of team problem situations and solution principles. Recall Lord and Hall's (2005) exposition of leader expertise as an increasingly principled and context-based representation of organizational problem domains. To fully maximize the potential leadership capacity of team members, team leaders need to focus part of their coaching on activities that promote the development of such shared cognitive representations.

Team Interaction Dynamics

Our model of leadership and team effectiveness argues that team leadership functions influence team effectiveness through their impact on team interaction dynamics. We have posited three intersecting components of team dynamics that receive leadership influence: *team performance goal processes, team emergent states,* and *team development.* Later, we describe how these components can reciprocally influence team leadership through growth and utilization of shared leadership expertise.

Zaccaro et al. (2001) specified that team leadership influenced team effectiveness through four sets of team interaction processes: cognitive, motivational, affective, and coordination. Their exposition, however, did not clearly separate interaction dynamics (e.g., collective information exchanges) from subsequent changes in team "states" (e.g., shared mental models) that result from these dynamics. Marks, Mathieu, and Zaccaro (2001) labeled such first-order outcomes of team processes as "emergent states" and defined them as "properties of the team that are typically dynamic in nature and vary as a function of team context, inputs, processes, and outcomes" (p. 357). These emergent states include cognitive, motivational, and affective properties that emerge from team interaction. Marks et al. also specified three core types of team interaction processes: transition, action, and interpersonal. These sets of processes incorporate many of the processes Zaccaro et al. (2001) included in their categories.

Because the team processes defined by Marks et al. (2001) center on team interaction in performance episodes, they have been labeled in our model as team goal processes. They also reflect the team-level goal-generation and goal-striving processes specified by Chen and Kanfer (2006). However, our review of recent models such as Cox et al. (2003), Hackman and Wageman (2005), and Burke et al. (2006) as well as earlier studies by Kozlowski, Gully, McHugh, et al. (1996) and Kozlowski, Gully, Salas, et al. (1996) suggest that the development processes of the team needed to be separated from team goal processes and team emergent states as a different component of team interaction dynamics. Thus, our model of leadership and team effectiveness posits three sets of mediators, each reciprocally influencing the other, to explain how team leaders and leadership processes influence team effectiveness.

The transition processes defined by Marks et al. (2001) include mission analysis, formulation, and planning, goal specification, and strategy formulation. These entail the collective information-processing activities of the team as members interpret mission requirements in the context of environmental dynamics and develop a collective action plan. Leadership actions in boundary spanning, direction setting, development of member capabilities, and establishment of performance and role expectations influence the team transition processes. Action processes defined by Marks et al. include monitoring progress toward goals, systems monitoring, backup behaviors, and member coordination. These processes include the synchronization and integration of member activities, as well as self- and team regulation of performance episodes (Fleishman & Zaccaro, 1992; Zaccaro et al., 2001). Leadership actions in direction setting, calibrating of members roles, monitoring team actions, and prompting metacognitive processes within the team are likely to contribute to more effective action processes.

Marks et al. (2001) specified interpersonal processes in team performance episodes as including conflict management, motivation and confidence building, and affect management. These processes are intended to ensure that minimal process loss occurs during team performance. Recall that process loss results from faulty coordination and lessened effort from team members. Conflict management helps reduce the likelihood of coordination losses, whereas affect management, motivation, and confidence-building activities curtail effort losses. Leadership processes related to staffing the team, to developing team members, to providing feedback, and to facilitating role and performance expectations will likely influence these processes.

The leader's interactions with the team, as well as team interaction dynamics, establish shared psychological states within the team. Zaccaro et al. (2001) defined different collective states resulting from team cognitive, motivational, and affective processes. Information exchanges among team members as well as collective information processing and metacognitive activities should foster greater agreement among members' cognitive representations of team problem situations. Such shared agreement, or team mental models (Klimoski & Mohammed, 1994), "represent knowledge and understanding about the purpose of the team and its characteristics, the connections and linkages among team purposes, characteristics, and collective actions, and the various roles/behavior patterns required of individual members to successful enact collective action" (Zaccaro et al., 2001, p. 459). Leader sense-giving processes and role-structuring activities contribute directly to the development of team mental models (Burke, 1999; Marks et al., 2000).

Group cohesion, collective efficacy, and shared trust represent emergent states that derive from a pattern of successful interactions and goal accomplishment by the team (Zaccaro et al., 2001). Leadership processes that contribute to these motivational emergent states include modeling appropriate task strategies and encouraging and empowering team members (ibid.). Leaders can also help set emotion control norms that prevent a state of emotional contagion in teams. Such states can occur when some members react emotionally to team events and when their affect is imitated by other team members (Barsade & Gibson, 1988; Zaccaro et al., 2001). Also, negative affective states can result from team conflict that focuses on "personal incompatibilities" among members (Amason, 1996, p. 129) or from time-urgent tasks and deadlines. Leadership processes that (1) set norms for effective communication and resolution of conflict and that (2) produce clear performance goals and performance strategies, with consistent monitoring of member progress will likely help modulate the affective states of the team in ways that minimize emotional contagion and process loss due to stress (Pirola-Merlo, Härtel, Mann, & Hirst, 2002; Zaccaro et al., 2001).

When teams form, they go through phases that, if passed through successfully, entail an integration of individual motives, goals, and attitudes relative to the team's overall mission and performance processes (Kozlowski, Gully, McHugh, et al., 1996). Individual goals and preferences give way to shared understandings about members' responsibilities and about corresponding collective gains in the group, common behavioral expectations or norms, and shared overall performance goals (Tuckman, 1965). The results of this process include greater member attachment to the team, team trust, cohesion, and coherence (Kozlowski, Gully, McHugh, et al., 1996)—emergent states that contribute significantly to subsequent team goal processes. Ongoing team performance interactions and emerging collective states in turn influence the pace and outcomes of team developmental processes.

Kozlowski, Gully, Salas, et al. (1996) defined four separate team leadership roles: mentor, instructor, coach, and facilitator.* They argued that leaders influence team development processes by engaging in these roles at different phases of team growth. Mentoring processes intended to nurture a collective mission and performance goals as well as to promote shared affect and attitudes become instrumental in the early formation stages of the team. As the team evolves, the leader's instructor role becomes more important in building skill proficiencies among team members and in fostering more individual expert knowledge structures and self-efficacy beliefs. The fully mature team, defined as an "expert team" by Kozlowski, Gully, Salas, et al., emerges from iterative coaching and facilitating processes, as the leader fosters more collective capabilities, team efficacy, shared mental models, and collective information processing. According to Kozlowski, Gully, Salas, et al., the results of leadership efforts at different stages of team development are growth and maintenance of team coherence, with corresponding benefits for team coordination and adaptability.

Leadership Expertise

Kozlowski, Gully, Salas, et al. (1996) defined the leader's role in facilitating the emergence of an expert team. This returns us to our earlier theme

---

* The discussion in this chapter on how leaders help new teams develop taskwork, teamwork, and shared leaderhsip skills was informed in part by research from Kozlowski and his colleagues (e.g., Kozlowski, Gully, McHugh, et al., 1996; Kozlowski, Gully, Salas, et al., 1996). Please see Kozlowski, Watula, Jensen, Kim, & Botero, (this volume) for an update and extension of their work. Their notion of adaptive capacity would be a significant component of shared leadership expertise as defind in this chapter.

on developing leadership expertise. Teams develop high levels of expertise when their "members have developed the meta-cognitive and self-regulatory capabilities that enable them to learn and to refine their shared cognition as a team without explicit direction" (ibid., p. 264). These are the capabilities that foster effective self-management. Team leadership processes are instrumental in their development. However, Kozlowski, Gully, Salas, et al. (p. 264) also noted that, even with high team expertise:

> The leader's role is to facilitate effective team performance by helping the team to make the best use of its shared affect, cognition and behavior. The leader facilitates team performance by assessing the task situation, clarifying team objectives and priorities, and monitoring the team's performance. The team self-manages as it adapts to changing task and situational conditions, with the leader lending a hand to maintain coherence.

We would extend their notions further by suggesting that the leader's role in the development of leadership capacity and leadership expertise within the team means the leader helps team members acquire the skills and expertise to *collectively* assess situations, *collectively* clarify direction, *collectively* monitor performance processes, and *collectively* maintain team coherence. Thus, we have specified a direct link in our model between leadership processes and team leadership expertise. We also expect that as leadership expertise grows within the team, functional leadership processes necessary for team success will change (cf. Kozlowski, Gully, McHugh, et al., 1996); accordingly, we have defined the link between leadership and team leadership expertise as a reciprocal one. Finally, we note in our model that effective team interaction dynamics over a series of varying performance episodes will also give rise to leadership expertise within the team. Such experiences help team members begin to develop the more principle-based and context-specific shared knowledge structures that Lord and Hall (2005) defined as key elements of such expertise. These shared leadership knowledge structures should in turn influence subsequent team interaction dynamics; hence, our model also contains a reciprocal link between leadership expertise and team interaction dynamics.

Conclusions and Implications

Research on team leadership has advanced significantly over the last 10 to 12 years. One key to this advancement has been a focus on how team leaders foster more effective team integration and coordination. This distinction marks team leadership as separate from other forms of leadership. In this chapter we have seconded the notion that the primary function of team leadership is to promote an effective synergistic combination of individual member resources. Accordingly, the analysis of team leadership needs to reside at the group level. We have cited a number of recent studies in this chapter that have examined team processes, emergent states in teams, and team performance outcomes as the proposed consequences of different leadership processes. Such research is facilitating a greater understanding about how team leadership fosters collective effectiveness.

Several researchers have called for a greater focus on how leadership functions emerge and become shared among team members (Day et al., 2004, 2006). Given the primary focus in past research on individual-centric perspectives of leadership, we also agree with the increased need for such a focus. However, we caution researchers not to lose sight of the importance of the individuals who do occupy formal leader roles in such teams. We have noted, as have others (Conger & Pearce, 2003; Cox et al., 2003; Pearce, 2004), that shared leadership does not preclude vertical leadership. In this chapter we have articulated three roles for leaders in team-centric leadership systems—as internal leaders, external leaders, and executive coordinators. The particular role adopted by the leader will likely depend on the leadership capacity and expertise already shared by group members. The arguments by Day et al. (2004) and Kozlowski, Gully, McHugh, et al. (1996) have been particularly instrumental in describing the interchange between leadership requirements and team maturation. In this chapter we have also emphasized the important role team leaders have to develop the collective capacity and expertise of other team members to effectively display leadership. Although these ideas have applied to dyadic relationships between leaders and subordinates (Manz & Sims, 1987), we have applied them within the context of understanding team leadership as operating at the nexuses of member interactions to influence team interconnectivity. Research on team leadership needs to articulate more clearly how self-managing teams gain shared leadership expertise, and in particular how team leader roles change as members acquire such expertise. For example, recent research by Morgeson (2005) suggests that the leader's role in self-managing teams may be to monitor and help the team respond to unexpected, novel, or crisis events. Other studies along this line can help broaden further our understanding of team leadership in different types of teams.

We have noted several models of team leadership that have appeared in the literature, and we have summarized several of these contributions into an integrative model. This model retains the IPO framework (Hackman & Morris, 1975; McGrath, 1964) that characterizes almost all other models of team leadership. This reflects our basic assumption that the fundamental role of team leadership processes is to promote team interconnectivity and synergy. Therefore, our model proposes that the effects of leadership on team outcomes are mediated entirely by its influences on team interaction dynamics. However, the model does not define these dynamics in strictly linear terms. Instead, based upon the arguments by Marks et al. (2001), team goal processes (goal generation and goal striving; Chen & Kanfer, 2006) exhibit reciprocating influences with team emergent states, reflecting recurrent "I-P-O-type cycles that run sequentially and simultaneously" (Marks et al., 2001, p. 359). Performance feedback, particularly by team leaders, becomes crucial in these performance episodes for team learning and the development of more effective synergy (Bell & Kozlowski, 2002; Edmondson, 2003; Zaccaro et al., 2007). Our model, however, adds team development dynamics to the interplay between team goal processes and team emergent states. We suspect that this interplay will vary in quality and form across different stages of team maturation and that team leaders have an important role in monitoring and shaping these shifting influences (Kozlowski, Gully, McHugh, et al., 1996).

Research on team leadership has grown significantly in recent years, enough to begin to address Hackman and Walton's (1986) observations of paucity in this domain. These empirical and conceptual contributions have also grown in sophistication, promising new advancements and some exciting growth in our understanding of team leadership. We hope the model offered in this chapter provides another impetus to this growth.

References

Amason, A. C. (1996). Distinguishing the effects of functional and dysfunctional conflict on strategic decision making: Resolving a paradox for top management teams. *Academy of Management Journal, 39*, 123–148.

Ancona, D. G. & Caldwell, D. F. (1988). Beyond task and maintenance: Defining external functions in groups. *Group and Organization Studies, 13*, 468–494.

Barsade, S. G. & Gibson, D. E. (1998). Group emotion: A view from top and bottom. In D. Gruenfeld (Ed.), *Composition* (81–102). Stamford, CT: JAI Press.

Basadur, M. (2004). Leading others to think innovatively together: Creative leadership. *Leadership Quarterly, 15*, 103–121.

Bass, B. M. (1985). *Leadership and performance beyond expectations.* New York: Free Press.

Bass, B. M. & Avolio, B. J. (1993). Transformational leadership: A response to critiques. In M. M. Chemers & R. Ayman (Eds.), *Leadership theory and research* (pp. 49–80). San Diego, CA: Academic Press.

Bell, B. S. & Kozlowski, S. W. J. (2002). Adaptive guidance: Enhancing self-regulation, knowledge, and performance in technology-based training. *Personnel Psychology, 55*, 267–306.

Beyerlein, M. M., Johnson, D. A., & Beyerlein, S. T. (1996) (Eds.). *Interdisciplinary studies of work teams (Vol. 3: Team Leadership).* Greenwich, CT: JAI Press.

Burke, C. S. (1999). *Examination of the cognitive mechanisms through which team leaders promote effective team processes and adaptive performance.* Unpublished dissertation, George Mason University.

Burke, C. S., Stagl, K. C., Klein, C., Goodwin, G. F., Salas, E., & Halpin, S. (2006). What types of leadership behaviors are functional in team? A meta-analysis. *Leadership Quarterly, 17,* 288–307.

Burns, J. M. (1978). *Leadership.* New York: Harper & Row.

Chen, G. & Kanfer, R. (2006). Towards a systems theory of motivated behavior in work teams. *Research in Organizational Behavior, 27,* 223–267.

Cohen, S. G., Ledford, Jr. G. E., & Spreitzer, G. M. (1996). A predictive model of self-managing work team effectiveness. *Human Relations, 49*(5), 643–676.

Collins, E. G. & Guetzkow, H. (1964). *A social psychology of group processes for decision making.* New York: Wiley.

Conger, J. A. & Kanungo, R. N. (1987). Toward a behavioral theory of charismatic leadership in organizational settings. *Academy of Management Review, 12,* 637–647.

Conger, J. A. & Pearce, C. L. (2003). A landscape of opportunities: Future research on shared leadership. In C. L. Pearce & J. A. Conger (Eds.), *Shared leadership: Reframing the hows and whys of leadership* (pp. 285–303). Thousand Oaks, CA: Sage.

Cox, J. F., Pearce, C. L., & Perry, M. (2003). Toward a model of shared leadership and distributed influence in the innovation process: How shared leadership can influence new product development team dynamics and effectiveness. In C. L. Pearce & J. A. Conger (Eds.), *Shared leadership: Reframing the hows and whys of leadership* (pp. 48–76). Thousand Oaks, CA: Sage.

Dansereau, F., Jr., Graen, G., & Haga, W. J. (1975). A vertical dyad linkage approach to leadership within formal organizations: A longitudinal investigation of the role making process. *Organizational Behavior and Human Performance, 13,* 46–78.

Davis, J. H. (1973). Group decision and social interaction: A theory of social decision schemes. *Psychological Review, 80,* 97–125.

Day, D. V. (2000). Leadership development: A review in context. *Leadership Quarterly, 11,* 581–613.

Day, D. V., Gronn, P., & Salas, E. (2004). Leadership capacity in teams. *Leadership Quarterly, 15,* 857–880.

Day, D. V., Gronn, P., & Salas, E. (2006). Leadership in team-based organizations: On the threshold of a new era. *Leadership Quarterly, 17,* 211–216.

Day, D. V. & Zaccaro, S. J. (2004). Toward a science of leader development. In D. V. Day, S. J. Zaccaro, & S. M. Halpin (Eds.), *Leader development for transforming organizations: Growing leaders for tomorrow* (pp. 383–399). Mahwah, NJ: Lawrence Erlbaum Associates.

DeChurch, L. & Marks, M. A. (2006). Leadership in multiteam systems. *Journal of Applied Psychology, 91,* 311–329.

Druskat, V. & Wheeler, J. V. (2003). Managing from the boundary: The effective leadership of self-managing work teams. *Academy of Management Review, 46,* 435–457.

Dumaine, B. (1990, May 7). Who needs a boss? *Fortune,* 52–60.

Edmondson, A. C. (2003). Speaking up in the operating room: How team leaders promote learning in interdisciplinary action teams. *Journal of Management Studies, 40,* 1419–1452.

Ellemers, N., De Gilder, D. D., & Haslam, S. A. (2004). Motivating individuals and groups at work: A social identity perspective on leadership and group performance. *Academy of Management Review, 29*, 459–478.

Ensley, M. D., Pearson, A., & Pearce, C. L. (2003). Top management team process, shared leadership, and new venture performance: A theoretical model and research agenda. *Human Resource Management Review, 13*, 329–346.

Fiedler, F. E. (1964). A contingency model of leadership effectiveness. In L. Berkowitz (Ed.), *Advances in experimental social psychology* (Vol. 1, pp. 149–190). New York: Academic Press.

Fiedler, F. E. (1971). Validation and extension of the contingency model of leadership effectiveness. A review of the empirical findings. *Psychological Bulletin, 76*, 128–148.

Fleishman, E. A., Mumford, M. D., Zaccaro, S. J., Levin, K. Y., Korotkin, A. L., & Hein, M. B. (1991). Taxonomic efforts in the description of leader behavior: A synthesis and functional interpretation. *Leadership Quarterly, 2*(4), 245–287.

Fleishman, E. A. & Zaccaro, S. J. (1992). Toward a taxonomy of team performance functions. In R. W. Swezey & E. Salas (Eds.), *Teams: Their training and performance*. Norwood, NJ: ABLEX.

Gardner, W. L. III & Schermerhorn, J. R. Jr. (1992). Strategic operational leadership and the management of supportive work environments. In R. L. & J. G. Hunt (Eds.), *Strategic leadership: A multiorganizational-level perspective*. In Westport, CT: Quorum Books.

Gibb, C. A. (1947). The principles and traits of leadership. *Journal of Abnormal & Social Psychology, 42*, 267–284.

Gibb, C. A. (1954). Leadership. In G. Lindzey (Ed.), *Handbook of social psychology*. Cambridge, MA: Addison-Wesley.

Gillespie, N. A. & Mann, L. (2004). Transformational leadership and shared values: The building blocks of trust. *Journal of Managerial Psychology, 19*, 588–607.

Gordon, J. (1992). Work teams: How far have they come? *Training, 29*, 59–62.

Hackman, J. R. & Morris, C. G. (1975). Group tasks, group interaction processes, and group performance effectiveness: A review and proposed integration. In L. Berkowitz (Ed.), *Advances in experimental social psychology* (Vol. 8). New York: Academic Press.

Hackman J. R. & Wageman, R. (2005). A theory of team coaching. *Academy of Management Review, 30*, 269–287.

Hackman, J. R. & Walton, R. E. (1986). Leading groups in organizations. In P. S. Goodman & Associates (Eds.), *Designing effective work groups*. San Francisco, CA: Jossey-Bass.

Hambrick, D. C. (1994). Top management groups: A conceptual integration and reconsideration of the "team" label. *Research in Organizational Behavior, 16*, 171–213.

Hersey, P. & Blanchard, K. H. (1988). *Management of organizational behavior: Utilizing human resources* (5th ed.). Englewood Cliffs, NJ: Prentice Hall.

Hill, M. (1982). Group versus individual performance: Are N + 1 heads better than one? *Psychological Bulletin, 91*, 517–539.

Hirst, G., Mann, L., Bain, P., Pirola-Merlo, A., & Richver, A. (2004). Learning to lead: The development and testing of a model of leadership learning. *Leadership Quarterly, 15*, 311–327.

Hollander, E. P. & Julian, J. W. (1970). Studies in leader legitimacy, influence, and motivation. In L. Berkowitz (Ed.), *Advances in experimental social psychology* (Vol. 5.). New York: Academic Press.

House, R. J. (1971). A path goal theory of leader effectiveness. *Administrative Science Quarterly, 16,* 321–339.

House, R. J. (1977). A 1976 theory of charismatic leadership. In J. G. Hunt & L. Larson (Eds.), *Leadership: The cutting edge.* Carbondale: Southern Illinois University Press.

House R. J. (1996). Path goal theory of leadership: Lessons, legacy, and a reformulated theory. *Leadership Quarterly, 7,* 323–352.

House, R. J. & Dessler, G. (1974). The path-goal theory of leadership: Some post hoc and a priori tests. In J. G. Hunt & L. L. Larson (Eds.), *Contingency approaches to leadership.* Carbondale: Southern Illinois University Press.

Jacobs, T. O. & Jaques, E. (1990). Military executive leadership. In K. E. Clark & M. B. Clark (Eds.), *Measures of leadership.* Greensboro, NC: Center for Creative Leadership.

Jacobs, T. O. & Jaques, E. (1987). Leadership in complex systems. In J. Zeidner (Ed.), *Human productivity enhancement.* New York: Praeger.

Jacobs, T. O. & McGee, M. L. (2001). Competitive advantage: Conceptual imperatives for executives. In S. J. Zaccaro & R. Klimoski (Eds.), *The nature of organizational leadership: Understanding the performance imperatives confronting today's leaders* (pp. 42–78). San Francisco, CA: Jossey-Bass.

Jaques, E. (1990). In praise of hierarchy. *Harvard Business Review* (Jan.–Feb.), 127–133.

Kane, T. D., Zaccaro, S. J., Tremble, T., & Masuda, A. D. (2002). An examination of the leader's regulation of groups. *Small Group Research, 33,* 65–120.

Katz, D. & Kahn, R. L. (1978). *The social psychology of organizations.* New York: Wiley.

Kerr, S. & Jermier, J. M. (1978). Substitutes for leadership: Their meaning and measurement. *Organizational Behavior and Human Performance, 22,* 375–403.

Klimoski, R. & Jones, R. G. (1995). Staffing for effective group decision making: key issue in matching people and teams. In R.A. Guzzo & E. Salas (Eds.), *Team effectiveness and decision making in organizations* (pp. 291–332). San Francisco, CA: Jossey-Bass.

Klimoski, R. & Koles, K. L. K. (2001). The chief executive officer and top management team interface. In S. J. Zaccaro & R. Klimoski (Eds.), *The nature of organizational leadership: Understanding the performance imperatives confronting today's leaders* (pp. 219–269). San Francisco, CA: Jossey-Bass.

Klimoski, R. & Mohammed, S. (1994). Team mental model: Construct or metaphor? *Journal of Management, 20,* 403–437.

Klimoski, R. J. & Zukin, L. B. (1999). Selection and staffing for team effectiveness. In E. Sundstrom & Associates (Eds.), *Supporting work team effectiveness: Best management practices for fostering high performance.* San Francisco, CA: Jossey-Bass.

Kline, T. J. B. (2003). *Teams that lead: A matter of market strategy, leadership skills, and executive strength.* Mahwah, NJ: Lawrence Erlbaum Associates.

Kozlowski, S. W. J., Gully, S. M., McHugh, P. P., Salas, E., & Cannon-Bowers, J. A. (1996). A dynamic theory of leadership and team effectiveness: Developmental and task contingent leader roles. *Research in Personnel and Human Resources Management, 14,* 253–305.

Kozlowski, S. W. J., Gully, S. M., Salas, E., & Cannon-Bowers, J. A. (1996). Team leadership and development: Theory, principles, and guidelines for training leaders and teams. In M. M. Beyerlein, D. Johnson, & S. T. Beyerlein (Eds.), *Interdisciplinary studies of work teams (Vol. 3: Team Leadership)*. Greenwich, CT: JAI Press.

Lawler, E. E., Mohrman, S. A., & Ledford, G. E. (1998). *Strategies for high performance organizations: Employee involvement, TQM, and reengineering programs in Fortune 1,000 corporations.* San Francisco, CA: Jossey-Bass.

Locke, E. A. (2003). Leadership: Starting at the top. In C. L. Pearce & J. A. Conger (Eds.), *Shared leadership: Reframing the hows and whys of leadership* (pp. 271–284). Thousand Oaks, CA: Sage.

Lord, R. G. (1977). Functional leadership behavior: Measurement and relation to social power and leadership perceptions. *Administrative Science Quarterly, 22,* 114–133.

Lord, R. G. & Hall, R. J. (2005). Identity, deep structure, and the development of leadership skill. *Leadership Quarterly, 15,* 591–615.

Manz, C. C. & Sims, H. P. Jr. (1980). Self management as a substitute for leadership: A social learning perspective. *Academy of Management Review, 5,* 361–367.

Manz, C. C. & Sims, H. P. Jr. (1987). Leading workers to lead themselves: The external leadership of self-managing work teams. *Administrative Science Quarterly, 32*(1), 106–129.

Manz, C. C. & Sims, H. P. Jr. (1991). Superleadership: Beyond the myth of heroic leadership. *Organizational Dynamics, 19,* 18–35.

Marks, M. A., Mathieu, J., & Zaccaro, S. J. (2001). A temporally based framework and taxonomy of team processes. *Academy of Management Review, 26,* 356–376.

Marks, M., Zaccaro, S. J., & Mathieu, J. (2000). Performance implications of leader briefings and team interaction training for team adaptation to novel environments. *Journal of Applied Psychology, 85,* 971–986.

Marta, S., Leritz, L. E., & Mumford, M. D. (2005). Leadership skills and the group performance: Situational demands, behavioral requirements, and planning. *Leadership Quarterly, 16,* 97–120.

Mathieu, M., Marks, M. A., & Zaccaro, S. J. (2001). Multi-team systems theory. In N. Anderson, D. Oniz, & C. Viswesvaran (Eds.), *The international handbook of work and organizational psychology.* London: Sage Publications.

McGrath, J. E. (1964). *Social psychology: A brief introduction.* New York: Holt.

Michaelson, L. K., Watson, W. E., & Black, R. H. (1989). A realistic test of individual versus group consensus decision making. *Journal of Applied Psychology, 74,* 834–839.

Morgeson, F. P. (2005). The external leadership of self managing teams: Intervening in the context of novel and disruptive events. *Journal of Applied Psychology, 90,* 497–508.

Mumford, M. D., Zaccaro, S. J., Harding, F. D., Jacobs, T. O., & Fleishman, E. A. (2000). Leadership skills for a changing world: Solving complex social problems. *Leadership Quarterly, 11,* 11–35.

Nygren, R. & Levine, E. L. (1996). Leadership of work teams: Factors influencing team outcomes. In M. M. Beyerlein, D. Johnson, & S. T. Beyerlein (Eds.), *Interdisciplinary studies of work teams (Vol. 3: Team Leadership)*. Greenwich, CT: JAI Press.

O'Connor, P. M. G., & Quinn, L. (2004). Organizational capacity for leadership. In C. D. McCauley & E. Van Velsor (Eds.), *The Center for Creative Leadership handbook of leadership development* (2nd ed.) (pp. 417–437). San Francisco, CA: Jossey-Bass.

Özaralli, N. (2003). Effects of transformational leadership on empowerment and team effectiveness. *Leadership and Organization Development Journal, 24,* 335–344.

Pearce, C. L. (2004). The future of leadership: Combining vertical and shared leadership to transform knowledge work. *Academy of Management Executive, 18,* 47–57.

Pearce, C. L. & Conger, J. A. (2003a). All those years ago: The historical underpinnings of shared leadership. In C. L. Pearce & J. A. Conger (Eds.), *Shared leadership: Reframing the hows and whys of leadership* (pp. 1–18). Thousand Oaks, CA: Sage.

Pearce, C. L. & Conger, J. A. (2003b). *Shared leadership: Reframing the hows and whys of leadership.* Thousand Oaks, CA: Sage.

Pearce, C. L. & Sims, H. P. (2000). Shared leadership: Toward a multi-level theory of leadership. In M. M. Beyerlein, D. A. Johnson, & S. T. Beyerlein (Eds.), *Advances in interdisciplinary studies of work teams: Team leadership* (Vol. 7, pp. 115–139). Greenwich, CT: JAI Press.

Pearce, C. L. & Sims, H. P. (2002). Vertical versus shared leadership as predictors of the effectiveness of change management teams: An examination of aversive, directive, transactional, transformational and empowering leader behaviors. *Group dynamics: Theory, Research, and Practice, 6,* 172–197.

Peterson, R. S., Smith, D. B., Martorana, P. V., & Owens, P. D. (2003). The impact of chief executive officer personality on top management team dynamics: One mechanism by which leadership affects organizational performance. *Journal of Applied Psychology, 88,* 795–808.

Pirola-Merlo, A., Härtel, C., Mann, L., & Hirst, G. (2002). How leaders influence the impact of affective effects on team climate and performance in R&D teams. *Leadership Quarterly, 13,* 561–581.

Roby, T. B. (1961). The executive function in small groups. In L. Petrullo & B. Bass (Eds.), *Leadership and interpersonal behavior.* New York: Holt, Reinhardt, & Winston.

Salas, E., Burke, C. S., & Stagl, K. C. (2004). Developing teams and team leaders: Strategies and principles. In D. Day, S. J. Zaccaro, & S. M. Halpin (Eds.), *Leader development for transforming organizations: Growing leaders for tomorrow* (pp. 325–355). Mahwah, NJ: Lawrence Erlbaum Associates, Inc.

Steiner, I. (1972). *Group process and productivity.* New York: Academic Press.

Sundstrom, E., McIntyre, M., Halfhill, T., & Richards, H. (2000). Work groups: From the Hawthorne Studies to work teams of the 1990s and beyond. *Group Dynamics: Theory Research and Practice, 4,* 44–67.

Sivasubramaniam, N., Murry, W. D., Avolio, B. J., & Jung, D. I. (2002). A longitudinal model of the effects of team leadership and group potency on group performance. *Group & Organization Management, 27*(1), 66–96.

Tuckman, B. W. (1965). Developmental sequences in small groups. *Psychological Bulletin, 63,* 384–399.

Vroom, V. H. & Yetton, P. W. (1973). *Leadership and decision-making.* Pittsburgh, PA: University of Pittsburgh Press.

Wageman, R. (2001). How leaders foster self-managing team effectiveness: Design choices versus hands-on coaching. *Organization Science, 12*(5), 559–577.

Yukl, G. (2006). *Leadership in organizations.* Upper Saddle River, NJ: Pearson Prentice Hall.

Zaccaro, S. J. (1999). Social complexity and the competencies required for effective military leadership. In J. G. Hunt, G. E. Dodge, & L. Wong (Eds.), *Out-of-the-box leadership: Transforming the twenty-first century Army and other top performing organizations* (pp. 131–151). Stamford, CT: JAI Press, Inc.

Zaccaro, S. J. (2001). *The nature of executive leadership: A conceptual and empirical analysis of success.* Washington, DC: APA Books.

Zaccaro, S. J. (2002). Organizational leadership and social intelligence. In R. Riggio (Ed.), *Multiple intelligences and leadership* (pp. 29–54). Mahwah, NJ: Erlbaum.

Zaccaro, S. J., Blair, V., Peterson, C., & Zazanis, M. (1995). Collective efficacy. In J. Maddux (Ed.), *Self-efficacy, adaptation, and adjustment.* New York: Plenum.

Zaccaro, S. J., Ely, K., & Shuffler, M. (2007). The leader's role in group learning. In V. Sessa, & M. London (Eds.), *Work group learning: Understanding, improving and assessing how groups learn in organizations* (pp. 193–214). Mahwah, NJ: Lawrence Erlbaum Associates.

Zaccaro, S. J. & Klimoski, R. (2002). The interface of leadership and team processes. *Group and Organization Management, 27,* 4–13.

Zaccaro, S. J. & McCoy, M. C. (1988). The effects of task and interpersonal cohesiveness on performance of a disjunctive group task. *Journal of Applied Social Psychology, 18,* 837–851.

Zaccaro S. J., Rittman A. L., & Marks, M. A. (2001). Team leadership. *Leadership Quarterly, 12*(4), 451–483.

Ziegert, J. C. (2004). *A unified theory of team leadership: Towards a comprehensive understanding of leading teams.* Paper presented at the 19th Annual Conference of the Society for Industrial and Organizational Psychology, Chicago, IL.

5

Developing Adaptive Teams: A Theory of Dynamic Team Leadership

Steve W. J. Kozlowski, Daniel J. Watola,
Jaclyn M. Jensen, Brian H. Kim, and Isabel C. Botero

As we engage the new millennium, accelerating technological, cultural, political, and financial turbulence buffets organizations—often unpredictably so. Responding to an uncertain and unpredictable future is not so much an issue of advanced strategy and planning but rather one of organizational innovation, agility, and adaptability (Terreberry, 1968). Organizations that can adapt quickly will survive and may even exploit hidden opportunities in the unexpected. Those that are slow to adapt face decline and dissolution. These environmental trends have been evident for some three decades. Many organizations have responded by creating leaner and more agile structures, by shifting to team-based work organizations (Lawler, Mohrman, & Ledford, 1995), and by building the capabilities of their members.

The dramatic shift to team-based work systems and the emphasis on building member capabilities place a spotlight on the critical role of team leaders. Team leaders are arguably the key linchpin for developing team member capabilities (Likert, 1961)—that is, the processes and emergent states that underlie team effectiveness. Yet, with very few exceptions, leading *teams*, focusing on *process dynamics*, and building *adaptive capabilities* have not been foci of popular leadership theories: "The role of leaders in the development of the coordinated, adaptive, and coherent behavior of effective teams is not well articulated. Although there is a substantial literature on leadership in organizations … it is difficult to apply the prescriptions from this research directly to teams" (Kozlowski, Gully, McHugh, Salas, & Cannon-Bowers, 1996, p. 255).

This comment is not intended to imply that marshalling subordinates to deal with the uncertainties and challenges of change is not of interest to mainstream leadership theories. Certainly, it is very much of interest to the currently dominant model—transformational leadership—which focuses on leader behavior dimensions that inspire subordinates to transcend

TABLE 5.1

Leadership in General and Team Leadership: Distinguishing Features

Features	Leadership in General	Team Leadership
Approach	Structure of leadership	Process of leadership
Contingencies	If considered, fixed to leadership situation May vary across situations	Dynamic task and developmental contingencies Varies within situation
Level of focus and member role linkages	Ambiguous, primarily individual level Roles not distinguished, loosely connected; additive contributions	Individual and team levels Distinctive roles, tightly coupled; coordination requirements
Emphases	Universal ideal Or, if contingencies, fitting leader to, for example, situation, task, or subordinates	Regulating team processes to build skills; fit to shifting internal and external demands Transitioning focus of development as skills compile
Distinctive features and conclusion	Focus on structure of leadership Focus on individuals Context free or fixed Universal and static	Focus on process of leadership Focus on individuals and teams Contingent on context dynamics Leadership and team processes as dynamic, fluid, and emergent

Source: ©S. W. J. Kozlowski, 2006. All rights reserved worldwide. (Used with permission.)

self-interest and to strive for challenging goals (Bass, 1985). However, transformational leadership, like many other popular approaches, is not very specific as to how this happens. As highlighted concisely in Table 5.1, many *general* leadership theories focus on the *structure* of leadership—identifying dimensions that are intended to be universally applicable across people, contexts, tasks, and time. Some structural approaches acknowledge contingencies that should modify leader action to fit contextual demands, although even these approaches are largely *static*. Once the leader fits, that is it. What is missing from universalistic approaches is an articulation of *how* leaders build and shape team development. A focus on *team* leadership necessitates attention to the *process* by which teams develop critical capabilities. Contingencies that necessitate shifts in leader action are linked to task and team development *dynamics* that vary within teams and over time.

The purpose of this chapter is to posit a prescriptive metatheory—an overarching framework and set of fundamental principles—of team leadership that fills this gap in the literature. The theoretical emphasis is on articulating the process of how leaders should build team capabilities, which are the underlying aspects of team effectiveness and adaptability, by leveraging contingencies that arise from the dynamics of team tasks and the progression of team skill development. We integrate, update, and refine prior work addressing team leadership, team development, and team processes. We begin by drawing on theories that focus on *leadership functions* in the team context (e.g., Hackman & Walton, 1986). To sculpt the theoretical core, we integrate the functions with theories that focus on team leadership dynamics (e.g., Kozlowski, Gully, McHugh, et al., 1996). *Task dynamics* are derived from attention to the episodic nature of team tasks (Marks, Mathieu, & Zaccaro, 2001), learning cycles that integrate with task episodes (Kozlowski, Gully, Salas, & Cannon-Bowers, 1996), and dynamic goal-regulation processes that underlie individual and team performance (DeShon, Kozlowski, Schmidt, Milner, & Wiechmann, 2004). *Developmental dynamics* are derived from models of team development (Tuckman, 1965), transition (Gersick, 1988), and compilation across levels—individual to team—as team members gain experience (Kozlowski, Gully, Nason, & Smith, 1999). We then integrate these task and developmental dynamics and explicate them in detail, highlighting the key capabilities that team leaders should target for development, how they can instill them, and how leader actions shift to fit these dynamic contingencies. We close with a concise discussion of implications for team leadership research and practice.

Team Leadership: Theoretical Underpinnings and Integration

A Functional Perspective

A team is composed of a set of members who interact dynamically, interdependently, and adaptively toward a common and valued goal, with each member having a specific role to fulfill within the team (Salas, Dickinson, Converse, & Tannenbaum, 1992). Although most leadership theories are not grounded in a team (or any) context, one stream of work has centered on delineating the *functions* that leaders serve in the maintenance, development, and effectiveness of teams (e.g., Hackman & Walton, 1986; McGrath, 1962). According to McGrath (1962, p. 5), "... The primary purpose of leadership is to insure that the group fulfills all critical functions necessary to its own maintenance and the accomplishment of its task." As shown in Table 5.2, an examination across this literature for consistencies yields four linked executive leadership functions—*planning* and *organizing, monitoring* and *acting*—that are directed *internally* or *externally* toward team *task* or *social* domains. Note that while the planning/organizing and monitoring/acting functions are nearly universal—Schutz (1961) is an exception for monitoring/acting—there is less consistency across the foci. Indeed, only McGrath encompasses all functions and foci. We follow

TABLE 5.2

Team Leadership Functions and Foci

Functions		Foci	
Plan–Organize	Monitor–Act	Internal–External	Task–Social Domains
Schutz (1961)	N/A	Schutz (1961)	Schutz (1961)
Roby (1961)	Roby (1961)	N/A	Roby (1961)
Roby (as cited in McGrath, 1962)[a]	Roby (1962)[a]	Roby (1962)[a]	N/A
McGrath (1962)	McGrath (1962)[b]	McGrath (1962)[b]	McGrath (1962)
Lord (1977)	Lord (1977)	N/A	Lord (1977)
Hackman & Walton (1986)	Hackman & Walton (1986)	N/A	N/A
Komaki, Desselles, & Bowman (1989)	Komaki, Desselles, & Bowman (1989)	N/A	N/A
Fleishman et al. (1991)	Fleishman et al. (1991)	N/A	Fleishman et al. (1991)

Note: Citations organized in chronological order. N/A, not applicable.
[a] Roby is drawn from an unpublished manuscript reported by McGrath (1962).
[b] McGrath's (1962) leadership functions cross the internal–external and monitor–act dimensions.
Source: © S. W. J. Kozlowski, 2006. All rights reserved worldwide. (Used with permission.)

McGrath for comprehensiveness and use the functions and their foci to form the core structure of our theoretical approach.

One thing to note, however, is that although the team leader functions summarized in Table 5.2 are process-like, they are static in nature. The leadership functions are intended to be applied flexibly to enable group maintenance, development, and effectiveness, but the theories do not address the specifics of when and why particular functions should be applied. In other words, dynamic contingencies that should influence the application of leadership functions and their foci are not specified. To fill this gap, we turn our attention to theories that take a more dynamic perspective on team leadership, development, and effectiveness. Two dynamic processes run through this literature. One centers on the cyclical and episodic nature of team tasks, and the other centers on team member skill compilation and development.

Task Dynamics

Team tasks are not fixed. Rather, they cycle episodically in the load they place on team member resources—cognitive, behavioral, and attitudinal/motivational—that are engaged as the team strives to learn and accomplish its goals (Kozlowski, Gully, McHugh, et al., 1996; Kozlowski, Gully, Salas, et al., 1996; Marks et al., 2001). Marks, Zaccaro, and Mathieu (2000) suggested that the episodic nature of team tasks emphasized the importance of different team processes. During the *transition phase* that occurs between task engagements, team processes center on evaluating prior performance and planning for future activities. This is followed by an *action phase* during which members coordinate activities and strive for goal accomplishment, with subsequent transition–action episodes. Prior theoretical work by Kozlowski and colleagues (Kozlowski, Gully, McHugh, et al., 1996; Kozlowski, Gully, Salas, et al., 1996) posited that the cyclic and iterative nature of team tasks provided an opportunity for leaders to explicitly shape team regulatory processes underlying learning, skill development, and performance. In their framework, the leader prompted the setting of developmental goals during low load, monitored team performance and intervened as necessary during high load, and diagnosed errors and provided feedback as the task cycled back to low load.

Integrating across these frameworks, we conceptualize a task engagement cycle as an iterative three-phase process: (1) preparation; (2) action engagement; and (3) reflection. The dynamics of the task cycle provide an opportunity for the leader to explicitly prompt individual and team regulatory processes designed to build targeted individual and team skills. Recent research has demonstrated that parallel goal–action regulation processes at the individual and team levels account for both individual and team performance (DeShon et al., 2004). As illustrated in the bottom portion of Figure 5.1, the load on team member resources is low prior to an engagement episode. During *preparation,* team leaders should set *developmental goals* designed to build *task* and *social* capabilities appropriate for the team's current developmental phase that will direct member resources as they engage the task. Leaders should also brief the team with strategies commensurate with their current capabilities to aid goal accomplishment. These developmental goals will shape team learning as members work toward goal accomplishment. As the team transitions to *action,* the load on member resources increases as they fully engage the task. The leader *monitors* and actively *develops* targeted *attitudes, behaviors,* and *cognitions.* Because team tasks can place loads on member resources that exceed their current capabilities—particularly early in team development—leaders are also prepared to directly *intervene* as necessary by *prompting coordination, adjusting strategy, updating situation assessments,* and *maintaining performance.* As the task engagement cycle concludes, the load on member resources is reduced, and the team transitions to *reflection.* Leaders should then *facilitate process feedback,* helping team members to *diagnose deficiencies* and to identify capabilities that need further development in subsequent engagements. The task cycles are iterative, providing multiple opportunities for leaders to harness the regulatory process to build targeted and

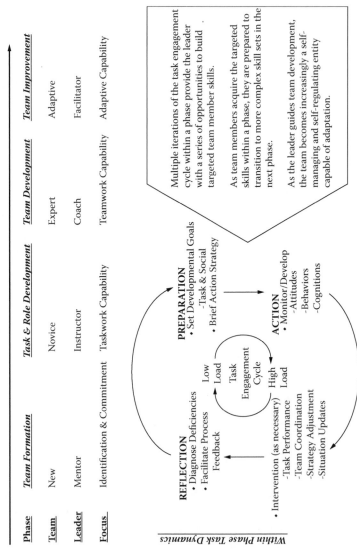

FIGURE 5.1
Task engagement cycles and developmental phase transitions. © S. W. J. Kozlowski, 2006. All rights reserved worldwide. (Used with permission.)

successively more complex skills. Task cycles are not fixed in duration but are variable depending on the nature of the task. This conceptualization of task dynamics maps the contingencies that should drive the *process* of leader skill building. The next aspect of the theory is to articulate developmental dynamics (contingencies) that dictate which targeted skills are appropriate at different phases of team development.

Developmental Dynamics

There are two dominant perspectives on the process of team development. Stage models propose a successive series of dominant activities that capture team members' attention. Although there are many, many stage models, they are well typified by the classic model of team forming, storming, norming, and performing (Tuckman, 1965; see Kozlowski et al., 1999 for a summary of stage models). As teams *form*, members are uncertain about their roles and the team. They begin to *storm* as members vie with one another to set direction and establish roles. They *norm* as conflicts get resolved and the team forms a social structure. Finally, the team is able to *perform* as members devote attention to the task at hand. Because Tuckman's model was derived from a literature review centered on clinical, therapy, and training groups (T-groups), it tends to emphasize the uncertainty members face as the endeavor to create a social structure in the absence of a well-defined task structure (Kozlowski et al., 1999).

The punctuated equilibrium model (PEM; Gersick, 1988) proposes that teams initially establish a set of roles and pattern of interaction that persist until the midpoint of their life cycle. At that point, there is a major reorganization and investment of energy—the punctuated equilibrium—as the team strives to meet its deadline. Note that the PEM was developed from observations of project teams with a fixed timeline, which may have had some influence on the temporal dynamics (Kozlowski & Bell, 2003). Although the stage and PEM approaches are often characterized as being in opposition, research suggests that they are complementary. Linear development is more evident when the focus is on group process and structure and the timing is more micro, whereas the punctuated shift is more evident when the focus is on the group's approach to its task and macrotiming (Chang, Bordia, & Duck, 2003).

Kozlowski and colleagues (1999) synthesized the team development literature and integrated these two approaches, viewing team development as a process of compiling successively more complex skills that enabled flexible, coordinated, and adaptive team performance behaviors. The overall process of compilation is one of linear progression, punctuated by transitions as skills crystallize within a phase and the team shifts attention to the development of more complex knowledge and skills. In addition, they also viewed the phase transitions as shifting across focal levels—individual, dyadic, and team—such that members first focus on their own task and social needs, then shift to immediate role connections, and finally meld together into an adaptive team network. Unlike most previous team development models, their approach asserted the primacy of the team task—that is, the patterns of interdependence dictated by the workflow of the team task and its implications for member coordination and synchronicity. Consistent with previous models, they acknowledged that a supportive social structure was a necessary condition for team development but that it was not sufficient. Their model asserted the primary importance of compiling team capabilities to fit the team task structure, with social structure in a supporting role.

Our theory builds on these team development models and integrates them with the cyclical nature of team tasks. We posit that leader efforts to build targeted skills within phases yields team capabilities that in turn provide a basis for developmental transitions (cf. Hackman & Wageman, 2005; Kozlowski, Gully, Salas, et al., 1996). Thus, leaders use the task cycles to guide teams to acquire successively more complex skill sets as they make developmental transitions: new, novice, expert, and adaptive. This set of developmental contingencies is illustrated in the top portion of Figure 5.1. Team development is conceptualized as a linear process punctuated by phase transitions as members acquire skills and transition to the acquisition of more complex skills—guided by the leader.

Figure 5.2 maps the broader team development process in more specific detail by crossing task and skill development dynamics. The left-hand portion of the figure incorporates the key aspects of the previously described task engagement cycle relating to preparation, action, and reflection that apply to each of the developmental phases. The developmental phases and their foci are arrayed along the top of the figure moving from left to right. The body of the figure specifies the skill-building targets that team leaders address within each phase. The phases are intended to capture "ideal" developmental targets and modal activities of team members. In that sense, phase transitions are "soft" rather than "hard" boundaries. The function of the team leader is to map an explicit regulatory process to the naturally occurring task engagement cycle, using the process to guide the compilation of increasingly more complex skills as the team progresses developmentally.

During preparation, leaders target specific task and social developmental goals and provide action strategies. Across phases, the goals shift from an individual focus to a team focus, and the strategies become increasingly more sophisticated and team determined. During action, team leaders target specific attitudinal/motivational, behavioral, and cognitive capabilities for monitoring and development. They intervene as necessary, with internal intervention more likely early in team development and external

Phase:	Team Formation	Task & Role Development	Team Development	Team Improvement
Focus:	Team Identification & Commitment	Individual Taskwork Capability	Teamwork Capability	Adaptive Capability
PREPARATION				
Developmental Goals				
Task-Related	*Team Orientation* - Mission - Objectives	*Taskwork* - Individual Task Mastery - Self-Efficacy	*Teamwork* - Task Role Interactions - Task Role Revision	*Adaptation* - Team Self-Management - Continuous Improvement
Social	*Team Socialization* - Norms - Social Integration	*Role Socialization* - Acceptance - Attachment	*Cooperation* - Role Interaction - Mutual Trust	*Social Cohesion* - Synergistic Interaction - Conflict Management
Action Strategy	- Provide Action Strategy	- Provide Rationale for Action Strategy	- Facilitate Action Strategy Selection	- Facilitate Development of New Action Strategies
ACTION				
Monitor	Member Interaction	Individual Performance	Team Performance	Adaptive Performance
Develop				
Attitudes	*Commitment* - Team Mission - Other Members	*Self-Efficacy* - Individuals' Task Focus - Social Self-Efficacy	*Team Efficacy* - Team Task Focus - Mutual Trust & Respect	*Team Potency* - Novel Team Task Focus - New Team Contexts
Behaviors	*Interaction* - Bonding - Reciprocal Commitment	*Taskwork* - Self-Regulation - Individual Help-Seeking	*Teamwork* - Coordination - Backup Behaviors	*Adaptation* - Shared Leadership - Exploration & Risk-Taking
Cognitions	*Team Identity* - Boundaries - Shared Responsibility	*Individual Mental Models* - Task Mental Model - Interpersonal Mental Model	*Shared Mental Model* - Members' Task Interactions	*Compatible Mental Model* - Knowledge Specialization - Transactive Memory
Intervene	- Individual Task Assistance - Team Coordination	- Individual Task Assistance - Team Coordination	- Team Coordination - Task, Strategy, & Goal Revisions	- Situation Updates - Final Decisions
REFLECTION	- Diagnose Deficiencies - Provide Individual-Level Developmental Feedback	- Facilitate Member Reflection - Provide Individual-Level Developmental Feedback	- Facilitate Team Reflection - Provide Team-Level Developmental Feedback	- Monitor Team Reflection & Developmental Feedback

FIGURE 5.2

Team developmental phases, targeted knowledge and skills, and phase transitions. © S. W. J. Kozlowski, 2006. All rights reserved worldwide. (Used with permission.)

boundary spanning more likely later in development. Similarly, reflection shifts from more of a leader-directed individual focus early on to more of a team-directed regulatory process as team skills compile. We now turn attention to explicating this process in detail, integrating supporting literature, and illustrating the theoretical processes and outcomes with a common example.

Leadership, Team Development, and Adaptation

Phase 1: Team Formation

As teams first form, the new members must identify and commit to the team. Team identification occurs when members associate themselves with the qualities, characteristics, and views of the team (Christ, van Dick, Wagner, & Stellmacher, 2003); team commitment occurs when members accept and support the team's mission, values, and goals (Ellemers, VanRijswijk, Bruins, & DeGilder, 1998). To build identification and commitment, the leader orients members to the team's mission, norms, and values to help them understand its purpose, to facilitate future performance, and to promote satisfaction (Bishop & Scott, 2000; Gabarro, 1987; Katz, 1978; Schein, 1968). Additionally, the leader socializes members by clarifying norms for social interaction and by facilitating member integration (Kozlowski et al., 1999). During orientation and socialization, the leader adopts the role of a mentor, facilitating each member's understanding of key features of the team, its mission, and its members (Ostroff & Kozlowski, 1993).

Preparation

Team Orientation

The leader's task developmental goal is to orient new members. In new teams, members seek to reduce ambiguity regarding the team's purpose and their role in fulfilling its mission (Levine & Moreland, 1998; Tuckman, 1965). They seek information about the team's mission, objectives, and goals so they can learn more about their team, can perform more effectively, and can feel more satisfied with their performance (Mitchell & Silver, 1990; Morrison, 1993). By focusing on task and interpersonal relations, members are more satisfied, committed, identified, and adjusted (Ellemers et al., 1998; Ostroff & Kozlowski, 1992). Increased interpersonal familiarity is also related to the speed and quality of team performance (Harrison, Mohammed, McGrath, Florey & Vanderstoep, 2003). The leader should communicate the mission, its supporting goals, and how the team mission fits in the broader organization.

Team Socialization

Social developmental goals concern team socialization, or informing members of the behaviors and attitudes necessary for them to assume their role in the team (Schein, 1968). Leaders should inculcate team norms (i.e., patterns of behaviors characteristic of the group) and expectations for interpersonal interactions. In addition, they should clarify the consequences maladaptive working relationships can have on team performance. Forsyth (1999) stated that norms are critical to teams as they provide direction and motivation, organize social interactions, and make team members' responses predictable and meaningful to each other. By explaining and modeling team norms, the leader specifies standards of behavior that facilitate team functioning (Adkins, 1995; Katz & Kahn, 1978). By explaining expectations for interpersonal interaction, the leader provides characteristics and expectations for member social roles (Ilgen & Hollenbeck, 1991), emphasizes the benefits of working together (Lewicki & Bunker, 1996), and facilitates future team functioning (Saks & Ashforth, 1997).

Morrison (1993) and Chao, O'Leary-Kelly, Wolf, Klein, and Gardner (1994) suggested that one important outcome of socialization is social integration, or developing successful working relationships with others. To become an effective team member, newcomers need to be oriented in social time and space relative to other members (Katz, 1978). Social integration affects members' social skills because it provides new members with support to facilitate learning while reducing stress associated with adjusting to a new environment (Jablin, 2001). Thus, it aids team assimilation by transforming newcomers to contributing members.

Action Strategy

As members become oriented and socialized, they are expected to accomplish the team's assigned tasks. However, at this point members possess limited task proficiency, rudimentary coordinative capability, and almost no team task experience. Therefore, prior to engagement the leader should provide them with an action strategy based on his or her assessment of the task, the team's capabilities, and environmental conditions. By providing the action strategy, the leader allows individual members to focus on what they need to do, when they need to do it, and who they need to work with to accomplish their tasks. Over time, members will use this experience to develop task mental models and will understand the merits of different action strategies.

Action

Develop and Monitor

When tasks are more routine and within the range of the team's current capabilities, the leader can take advantage of this opportunity and orient task activities toward team socialization: building commitment, encouraging social interaction, and creating a team identity. The leader builds members' *commitment*, or identification with the team, by promoting acceptance of the team's goals and values as well as a desire to exert effort on behalf of the team (Bishop & Scott, 2000). More specifically, leaders develop affective commitment, which represents the extent to which members become identified with, emotionally attached to, and involved with the team and other members (Meyer & Allen, 1984). Commitment has been shown to be positively related to extra-role behaviors (Becker & Billings, 1993) and team performance (Bishop & Scott, 1997; Scott & Townsend, 1994). As commitment develops, members identify with each other more and begin to lay a foundation for group cohesion (Festinger, 1950; Gross & Martin, 1952; Gully, Devine, & Whitney, 1995) that is beneficial for several outcomes, including greater likelihood of accepting group goals, decisions, and norms (Forsyth, 1999); greater satisfaction with the team (Hackman, 1992; Roy, 1973); and greater responsibility for group outcomes (Widmeyer, Brawley, & Carron, 1992). Thus, the leader's developmental focus should center on building team commitment by creating positive affect toward the team task, its goals, and its members.

Behaviorally, the leader should create opportunities for social *interaction* to promote member bonding and a feeling of "groupness" (Moreland, 1987). Before members attend to their individual tasks and roles within the team, they must first learn about each other and build interpersonal relationships (Katz, 1978; Kozlowski & Hults, 1986). Similar to team identification, which involves commitment to team goals and values, bonding refers to integration with and commitment to fellow team members (Reade, 2003). Over time, successful social bonding may lead to reciprocal commitment, such that members are willing to exert extra effort on behalf of the team (ibid.) and the team is accepting of individual needs and the importance of satisfying them (Moreland & Levine, 2001). Furthermore, these interactions are also the mechanism by which members can learn other members' knowledge, skills, and abilities (KSAs) and how they might contribute to task performance (Edmondson, Bohmer, & Pisano, 2001). Thus, leaders should encourage members to interact and bond to begin laying the foundation for coordination in more complex task environments.

Finally, the leader seeks to create a *team identity*, a set of behaviors and characteristics by which an individual is recognized as a team member (Jones & George, 1998). Whereas commitment to the team refers to acceptance of goals and values, team identity addresses the notion that team members are not simply individuals but are also members of a larger grouping of people with its own set of boundaries and expectations. Team identity arises simply from members defining themselves as such, and teams with stronger in-unit identity demonstrate a belief that they can be effective, have more positive social interactions, and feel more comfortable performing other members' tasks when needed (Campion, Papper, & Medsker, 1996). Thus, team identity enables members to recognize the importance of their participation for achieving team outcomes and is valuable for the existence of the team as an identifiable entity (Edmondson et al., 2001).

Intervention

In the team formation phase, members generally lack the task expertise and team skills required to contend with even moderately complex tasks. As a result, the leader must endeavor to buffer the new team from high complexity as much as possible. One proactive means of buffering involves establishing formal structures (e.g., rules, procedures, routines) to simplify tasks such that members' capabilities are not overwhelmed. If team member capabilities are overwhelmed, the leader may have to rely on reactive buffering, such as providing individual task assistance and coordination between members. These interventions also assist the leader in diagnosing deficiencies in individual and team capabilities and serve as foci for development under subsequent low-complexity task conditions.

Reflection

As the task engagement cycle concludes, the leader reflects on individual and team performance to identify skill deficits and to offer developmental feedback regarding members' violations of team norms, expectations, or values. This provides the leader with an opportunity to reinforce members' orientation and socialization. However, as members grow increasingly comfortable with each other and committed to the team over time, the leader should also provide them with developmental feedback with respect to task skills. This feedback should be provided at the individual level as members are not prepared to attend to issues involving team coordination (Klaus & Glaser, 1970). Finally, leaders should use this reflection to influence the developmental efforts of subsequent task engagement cycles by amending task and social developmental goals and action strategies during task preparation and task developmental activities.

Illustration: The New Emergency Room Team

Consider a newly formed emergency room (ER) team nominally consisting of residents, interns, medical students, physicians' assistants, nurses, and technicians and led by an attending physician or chief resident. To develop a new team, the attending reviews the developmental goals. Task developmental goals are focused on providing team orientation and might involve generating member commitment toward the hospital's mission (e.g., providing quality health care to an economically disadvantaged community). Social developmental goals center on team socialization and involve communicating norms and expectations for interns' interactions with physician assistants and nurses. Given adequate warning of assignments, the attending will brief members on the anticipated task and will define an appropriate strategy.

When the team is engaged in routine tasks such as attending an orientation course or social activities designed to introduce members to one another, the attending is able to focus on developing the team rather than intervening on its behalf. For example, he or she can support team orientation by reviewing hospital policies with interns and can foster team socialization by observing pairs of medical students working together while taking a patient's history. However, when a critical care patient arrives, interns may be faced with injuries that are beyond their "book" knowledge and limited skills. Therefore, the attending may have to intervene by guiding them through new procedures, by choreographing their interactions, or potentially by taking over critical procedures to save the patient. Thus, novel tasks may necessitate active intervention by the leader, although this is expected to diminish as team capabilities compile with development.

Once the patient is stable, the attending guides reflection on team performance, assesses members' progress toward achieving developmental goals, and provides appropriate feedback to individual members. For example, the attending might ask a resident to review ER policies regarding patient triage or admonish an intern for violating team norms. Over repeated task engagement cycles, members commit to the team, bond with one another, and develop a team identity. They are no longer a new ER team but a novice ER team, with members prepared to focus on improving their individual task capabilities.

Phase 2: Task and Role Development

Members are now ready to improve their individual taskwork capabilities and their respective roles on the team (Ostroff & Kozlowski, 1992). To improve proficiency, members build individual task mastery by establishing routines, priorities, and strategies (Bandura, 1977; Ford, Quiñones, Sego, & Sorra, 1992) that will lead to effective team performance in later phases (Klaus & Glaser, 1970; Morgan, Glickman, Woodard, Blaiwes, & Salas, 1986). They also improve coordination by negotiating social roles to establish expectations and by developing role attachment and acceptance (Seers, 1996). To facilitate the novice team's development, the leader adopts the role of an instructor to develop members' abilities, to assist in negotiating roles, and to build individual efficacy by providing task information, modeling task behavior, and offering opportunities for members to practice (Bandura, 1977; Ford et al., 1992).

Preparation

Taskwork

During preparation, the leader frames the team's task developmental goals in terms of achieving individual task proficiency. Taskwork behaviors are related to task execution and require members to develop task-specific knowledge, skills, and attitudes, whereas teamwork behaviors require members to develop the ability to communicate and coordinate their actions with others (Cannon-Bowers, Salas, & Converse, 1993). In this phase, the leader focuses on developing taskwork competencies as a foundation for the development of teamwork competence in the next phase. Team members achieve task mastery, including declarative knowledge, self-regulatory skills, and individual performance strategies, through practice and experimentation (Gist & Mitchell, 1992; Morrison, 1993). Task proficiency is critical to the development of self-efficacy and resilience in face of challenges (Bandura, 1998). As task routines evolve, members make fewer errors (Anderson, 1987), resolve task ambiguities, and learn the task-based responsibilities of other members (Volpe, Cannon-Bowers, Salas, & Spector, 1996). By developing taskwork proficiency, leaders ensure that members have the essential knowledge and skills required to contribute to the team.

Role Socialization

The leader frames social developmental goals in terms of building social role acceptance and attachment. Drawing on the commitment literature, social role acceptance and attachment are akin to normative commitment, whereby individuals believe they "ought" to fulfill their social role as a team member (Allen & Meyer, 1990). After socialization, members realize the team depends on their unique contributions, and a sense of obligation builds as members feel a responsibility to take on the role they have been given. Normative commitment, role acceptance, and role attachment will contribute to effective task interactions (Gabarro, 1987), as task relationships build upon the socioemotional relationships established in the team formation phase (Seers, 1996). Furthermore, they are expected to reinforce earlier socialization (Moreland & Levine, 1982), to provide members with knowledge of how social skills and efforts contribute to team success (Edmondson et al., 2001), and to help develop role-based behavior that complements the behaviors of other members and contributes to team effectiveness (Seers, 1996). By understanding what others expect of them and what they can expect from others, members begin to develop loyalty and commitment to each other and to the team (Adler & Adler, 1988).

Action Strategy

The leader prepares the team for an upcoming task by using his or her experience to select an appropriate action strategy. However, because the leader is dealing with a novice team rather than a new team, he or she should discuss the rationale for selecting the particular strategy. Specifically, he or she can reveal salient characteristics of the task or environment, can provide "war stories" to justify the selected strategy, and can present alternative strategies and the reasons for their rejection. By providing a rationale, the leader makes explicit the strategy selection process and prepares members for later phases when the team will be expected to select an action strategy on its own (Kozlowski, Gully, McHugh, et al., 1996).

Action

Develop and Monitor

When tasks fall within the team's capabilities, the leader develops members' *self-efficacy*, an individually held belief about one's capabilities on a specific task or set of specific tasks (Bandura, 1997). Task self-efficacy is an essential element of successful performance, as higher efficacy leads to individuals overcoming challenges, approaching difficulty with a positive outlook, and more effectively setting new goals (Bandura & Cervone, 1986). Success builds self-efficacy. Thus, leaders should set increasingly difficult goals, should provide mastery experiences, and should assign members to tasks of increasing complexity to strengthen their task efficacy over time (Bandura, 1982).

Self-efficacy toward individual social roles, or the way members relate to others interpersonally, also underlies team task interaction. Empirically, individuals with clear social roles report higher self-efficacy for job performance (Chen & Bliese, 2002). Thus, leaders should instill a belief in members that they can fulfill their social roles in the team and should promote positive social relationships by providing opportunities for members to turn knowledge about their social role into action (Anderson & Betz, 2001). Self-efficacy is also positively related to performance adaptability (Kozlowski, Toney, et al., 2001). By developing members' self-efficacy for task performance and social roles, leaders can create a team composed of efficacious members eager to learn, to stretch their capabilities, and to master the complexity of the task domain.

In addition to member attitudes, leaders need to develop members' self-regulatory and help-seeking behaviors. *Self-regulatory behaviors* refer to the behavioral and cognitive processes that occur when individuals pursue goals (Bandura, 1997) and include strategies for learners to plan, monitor, and modify their cognition and effort (Corno & Mandinach, 1985; Zimmerman & Pons, 1986, 1988). Self-regulation relates to metacognition, an individual's knowledge of and control over his or her cognition (Flavell, 1979). Schmidt and Ford (2003) found that self-regulation has a positive effect on monitoring (i.e., metacognitive) activity, self-efficacy, and performance on a complex task. In a reciprocal fashion, self-efficacy affects the aspects of performance that members monitor, the goals they set for themselves, and their goal commitment (Locke, Frederick, Lee, & Bobko, 1984). Therefore, leaders should enhance both self-efficacy and self-regulation by encouraging active reflection and performance monitoring.

Individual help seeking, or members seeking assistance from the leader, is also vital for successful task performance. Leaders should ensure that members understand that seeking help is acceptable and desirable as it can improve their task performance as well as strengthen their social roles (Edmondson et al., 2001). Ostroff and Kozlowski (1992) reported new members who increased help seeking behavior also increased task knowledge, team adjustment, and team commitment over time. Thus, leaders can serve as instructors when clarifying goals and roles, when establishing performance expectations, and when offering performance feedback (Gabarro, 1987; Katz, 1980). Individuals who feel comfortable asking for help will likely be cooperative (Seers, 1996) and open to personal development, change, and growth, which are necessary for a team to succeed in the next phase of development.

Finally, leaders should help members construct a *mental model* to organize their cognitions. Mental models are "... mechanisms whereby humans generate descriptions of system purpose and form, explanations of system functioning and observed system states, and predictions of future system states" (Rouse & Morris, 1986, p. 351). Leaders should encourage members to develop an individual task mental model incorporating knowledge of task procedures, strategies, likely scenarios, and contingencies they might encounter during task performance and the relationship between components of their task and task responsibilities (Cannon-Bowers et al., 1993). The purpose of this mental model is to help members cognitively describe and explain task-related events. For example, Park and Gittelman (1995) studied the characteristics of mental models and their influence on dynamic performance and found that individuals with more developed mental models had a greater understanding of system features and functions and improved task performance relative to those with less developed models. Kozlowski, Gully, et al. (2001) showed that individuals with more coherent mental models were better able to adapt their performance when confronted with a more complex and dynamic task environment.

Leaders can also encourage members to develop an interpersonal mental model or network, which encompasses a social understanding of how an individual fits into the team, how his or her role fits into the team's social structure, and how his or her contributions are essential for team effectiveness. This type of mental model is derived from the work of Edmondson et al. (2001) and Lewicki and Bunker (1996), who discuss knowledge relevant to interpersonal situations. An interpersonal mental model is expected to help individuals understand, describe, and explain their personal social interactions in the team environment (Mathieu, Heffner, Goodwin, Salas, & Cannon-Bowers, 2000). Both a task and interpersonal mental model are beneficial when integrating individual understanding into a shared team understanding, with the ultimate goal of building a team representation of task and social responsibilities.

Intervention

Whenever possible, the leader should exercise the team in situations that fit its current degree of proficiency. As members of a novice team are still learning their tasks and are not yet fully focused on their interactions, they are likely to require the leader's assistance in both the taskwork and teamwork domains when faced with an overly challenging task. When task demands overwhelm members' task capabilities, the leader can set proximal subgoals to limit difficulty, to provide direct support to affected members, and to intervene to ensure members do not fail in their assigned tasks. Because coordination among members is necessary for effective performance (Hage, 1980), leaders can intervene by encouraging members to work together, by orienting lost members, and by providing assistance where needed if the team is faced with task demands that overwhelm its coordinative capabilities (Seers, 1996).

Reflection

At the conclusion of a task cycle, the leader should work closely with individual members to help them diagnose skill deficiencies and should provide developmental feedback regarding task competence and role expectations (Miller & Jablin, 1991). It is important that members receive individual-level feedback so they can work to maximize their individual performance before they focus (later) on team performance (Klaus & Glaser, 1970). As positive feedback increases task self-efficacy (Tuckman & Sexton, 1991), leaders should discuss what members did correctly and should address their deficiencies.

Illustration: The Novice Emergency Room Team

The attending prepares the novice team for this phase by reinforcing the task and social developmental goals of building members' taskwork skills and socializing members to their roles, respectively. Relevant subgoals might include fostering members' self-efficacy for basic medical procedures or generating commitment toward fulfilling social roles within the team. When a task is anticipated, the attending defines a task strategy and explains why it is appropriate to consider salient situational or task characteristics when evaluating alternative strategies and to prepare the team for a time when it will be expected to select an appropriate strategy on its own.

During routine tasks, such as when interns make rounds or see walk-in patients, the attending supports taskwork skill development by assigning cases that moderately challenge members' existing capabilities and then by monitoring their performance. As members successfully accomplish routine procedures (e.g., providing intravenous fluids, suturing shallow lacerations), they build self-efficacy and enrich their task mental models. Similarly, the attending can support role socialization by encouraging appropriate social behavior. For example, if a medical student elects to chat with a nurse rather than to pay attention to the chief resident's demonstration of a new procedure, the attending might remark how the student's inattention could lead to poor team performance. By reminding members that there is a time for work and a time for play, the attending instills in members a sense of responsibility to fulfill their given roles. When confronted by more challenging tasks that exceed the team's current capabilities (e.g., an emergent case arrives), the attending observes members as they provide care consistent with their individual abilities. If the patient's needs exceed members' skills, the attending intervenes by providing direct instruction or performing a procedure. Since members are focused on developing their task rather than team skills, the attending continues to orchestrate member interactions as needed by, for example, directing a resident to ready a defibrillator while an intern performs cardiopulmonary resuscitation (CPR) or asking a student to find a chest tube when an intern anticipates the collapse of a patient's lung.

As the task cycle concludes, the attending reflects on the team's performance, encourages members to reflect on their own performance, and offers appropriate feedback at the individual level. For example, the attending might ask a resident to practice suturing or might encourage an intern to ask for a second opinion when unsure of a diagnosis. Over time, members develop self-efficacy, taskwork competence, and task mental models. These outcomes signal a novice team that is ready to transition to an expert team where members are prepared to develop their teamwork capability.

Phase 3: Team Development

The leader shifts developmental focus from the individual to the team level to improve teamwork, the set of behaviors, cognitions, and attitudes that interact to influence group performance (Weaver, Bowers, Salas, & Cannon-Bowers, 1997). Since members have achieved basic taskwork proficiency in the preceding phase, the leader now provides them with opportunities to learn how their task contributions fit within the team context. This promotes coordination and builds trust. Developing effective team skills can minimize process loss due to coordination failures among members, can allow the team to handle increasingly complex tasks, and can evolve an expert team (Fleishman & Zaccaro, 1992).

Preparation

Teamwork

During preparation, the leader offers task developmental goals that focus on teamwork skills and processes. Specifically, members must learn who to interact with, what they are expected to provide, and when to provide it (Kozlowski et al., 1999). As members interact, they discover inefficiencies or conflicts to resolve through task role negotiation and revision processes (Jackson & LePine, 2003; Marks et al., 2001). Task role exploration and knowledge acquisition are critical to the team's ability to efficiently and effectively accomplish tasks (Cannon-Bowers et al., 1993) and can be accomplished using group goals and goal-relevant feedback, which are related to team performance (e.g., DeShon et al., 2004; Weldon, Jehn, & Pradhan, 1991).

Cooperation

To enhance members' task interactions, the leader also focuses on the social developmental goal of promoting cooperation. Cooperative acts create positive feelings and stimulate interactions that reinforce shared values and attitudes (Jones & George, 1998). Cooperation is fostered through role interactions that build trust (Gambetta, 1988). Trust allows team processes to occur more smoothly and predictably, despite unexpected conflict or task requirements, by creating reliable and positive interdependencies among members that lead to openness, confidence, and team identification (Sheppard & Sherman, 1998). Developmental experiences for enhancing cooperation may include fostering an understanding of others' personality and needs (Cannon-Bowers et al., 1993), a sense of dependability among members (Mayer, Davis, & Schoorman, 1995; McAllister, 1995), and mutual respect (Tyler, 1999). These characteristics are critical for team performance in this phase and also provide a foundation for adaptive processes in the next phase.

Action Strategy

The leader now facilitates, rather than dictates, the selection of an appropriate action strategy. Based in part on Roby's (1961) work regarding executive functioning, Hackman and Walton (1986) asserted that leaders should provide expert coaching and assistance to help the team develop its processes, including the choice of a task-appropriate performance strategy.

Moreover, there is some support for the idea that teams become more receptive to strategy as they become oriented to the team, establish their proficiency, and gain experience (Hackman & Wageman, 2005; Woolley, 1988). The process of developing an action strategy in collaboration with members may also increase similarity and accuracy of members' mental models regarding the upcoming task (Marks et al., 2000).

Action

Develop and Monitor

When tasks are routine, the leader can promote processes that lead individuals to cooperate, to feel solidarity, and to act as a combined entity for attaining shared goals (Turner, Hogg, Oakes, Reicher, & Wetherell, 1987). These outcomes result from cognitive and affective processes as well as from task-relevant behaviors. Although self-efficacy was relevant during the prior phase, the team's collective efficacy is of interest during this phase. *Team efficacy* is the shared belief that the team will perform effectively on a particular task (Gully, Incalcaterra, Joshi, & Beaubien, 2002). It has been shown to affect team performance by increasing the effort and resources applied to a task (Shea & Guzzo, 1987), persistence and strategy selection (May & Schwoerer, 1994), goal setting (Durham, Knight, & Locke, 1998), sharing of mental models (Peterson, Mitchell, Thompson, & Burr, 2000), and coordination (Marks, 1999). Furthermore, meta-analytic findings support a relationship between team efficacy and team effectiveness. This relationship is moderated by interdependence after controlling for the individual and team levels of analysis, with the relationship being somewhat stronger for high interdependence ($\rho = .45$) relative to low interdependence teams ($\rho = .34$; Gully et al., 2002). Team efficacy is also presumed to improve group cohesion (Zaccaro, Blair, Peterson, & Zazanis, 1995), satisfaction, and organizational commitment (Riggs & Knight, 1994) and is influenced by past experiences, social modeling, and feedback (Bandura, 1986). Thus, the leader should provide opportunities for members to perform well as a team and should foster team efficacy via encouragement and modeling.

Attitudinal and affective factors such as mutual trust and respect can also increase coordination among members (Weaver et al., 1997), especially when the team is placed in risky situations and members must rely on each other to do what is expected (LePine, Hollenbeck, Ilgen, & Hedlund, 1997). Generally, *trust* is the confidence in expectations that another's motives will be positive toward oneself in situations entailing risk (Sheppard & Sherman, 1998). Some research has found trust to be initially low in action teams because members are functionally diverse (Jackson, May, & Whitney, 1995). Thus, the leader should foster a climate for trust and a shared perception that members will perform particular actions and will recognize and protect each others' rights and interests (Webber, 2002).

The leader should also provide learning opportunities for teamwork skills and coordination (Fleishman & Zaccaro, 1992; Hackman, 1987), communication (Dickinson & McIntyre, 1997), and mutual performance monitoring (i.e., backup behaviors; Blickensderfer, Cannon-Bowers, & Salas, 1997). *Team coordination* activities comprise "... the process of orchestrating the sequence and timing of interdependent actions" (Mathieu et al., 2000, p. 367) and involves exchanges of information and mutual adjustments (Marks, Sabella, Burke, & Zaccaro, 2002). When members coordinate their actions, they anticipate needs and "push" information or actions to other members rather than waiting for members to "pull" information from each other (Entin & Serfaty, 1999). Effective communication allows members to monitor each others' performance, to share the workload when help is needed, to explicitly coordinate tasks in real time, to adjust team strategy, and to develop and enhance shared mental models. For example, Komaki, Desselles, and Bowman (1989) showed that leadership behaviors aimed at providing feedback about team coordination during a regatta race were strongly related to performance. Salas, Fowlkes, Stout, Milanovich, and Prince (1999) demonstrated that teamwork behaviors of assertiveness, communication, mission analysis, and situational awareness increased through training and improved team performance for naval aircrews. *Backup behaviors*, or actions performed to assist other members (Fleishman & Zaccaro, 1992) have also been shown to influence team performance. Nieva, Fleishman, and Rieck (1978) described mutual performance monitoring, error correction, and compensatory performance (i.e., assisting another member when they experience overload or failure) as key adaptive team functions. Such behaviors have been found to be important for team effectiveness (Morgan, Salas, & Glickman, 1993) and linked to a willingness to accept and provide help (Denson, 1981; Dyer, 1984).

Finally, a leader should create opportunities for members to learn task and role interrelationships and to develop a common cognitive framework for understanding team processes. A team's *shared mental model* refers to the procedural knowledge about how and when members should interact within a given task domain (Cannon-Bowers et al., 1993). It enables coordination when members possess common assumptions and expectations regarding others' roles and responsibilities and understand effective ways to perform their roles in the team context, which can lead to improved team performance (Peterson et al., 2000). Mathieu et al. (2000) found that convergence in shared team and task mental models influenced team performance through increased coordination, cooperation, and communication. Furthermore, Marks et al. (2002) found that cross-training develops shared mental models, with mental model similarity related to coordination processes, backup behaviors, and team performance.

Intervention

Although members in this phase are able to perform their taskwork, the team is still likely to encounter demanding tasks that are beyond its current capabilities, that disrupt team processes, and that prevent effective functioning (Hackman, 1987; Marks et al., 2001). Task demands that overwhelm members can be dealt with via adjustments or corrections to the team task, strategy, or goals. At times, the leader can serve as a buffer between the team and the environment by mitigating (or facilitating) factors that hinder (or enhance) team functioning (cf. McGrath, 1964). Under high-workload conditions, members may also become overly focused on their individual taskwork rather than teamwork, resulting in communication breakdowns and related problems (Bowers, Braun, & Morgan, 1997; Salas et al., 1999). In such cases, the leader should intervene to assist coordination and communication (e.g., encouraging team members to work together, redirecting lost team members) to maintain team performance.

Reflection

During reflection, the leader facilitates the team's assessment of individual and team performance and provides appropriate developmental feedback at the team level. At this point, the expert team has acquired greater task and teamwork skills with each task cycle and is now capable of diagnosing its own performance and providing feedback with the leader's guidance. In this phase, team-level feedback is critical, as DeShon et al. (2004) showed that team feedback was important for helping develop calibrated team goals (i.e., difficult but attainable) and focus effort on coordination to enhance team performance.

Illustration: The Expert Emergency Room Team

In the team development phase, the attending focuses on the task developmental goal of building teamwork capability and the social developmental goal of promoting cooperative behaviors to increase team task performance. Task-related subgoals might include recognizing other members' preferences for receiving inputs from others, whereas social subgoals might include fostering a high degree of trust among members. As members have developed their task capabilities in the preceding phase, the attending facilitates their selection of an appropriate action strategy when tasks assignments are anticipated.

When tasks are routine, interns, residents, nurses, and technicians are working together to clear nonemergency patients without direct supervision of the attending physician. Members rely on each others' respective expertise and interact to interview, diagnose, and treat patients. Their repeated interactions allow them to support one another, to build trust, and to generate a shared mental model of team processes. When emergency patients stretch their skills, members perform their specialized tasks and coordinate their activities as best they can. However, the attending observes their performance to ensure their task or teamwork capabilities are not overwhelmed. Should the former occur, the attending might redefine the task or strategy (e.g., refer the patient to a specialist in another department). In the event of the latter, he or she would intervene by providing the coordination that members are unable to muster.

At the end of the task cycle, the attending facilitates the team's reflection of its performance and provides team-level feedback with respect to teamwork capability. For example, the attending might remind members to attend to each others' activities (i.e., mutual performance monitoring) to provide proactive rather than reactive assistance. After multiple iterations of the task engagement cycle, the team builds teamwork capability, team efficacy, and a shared mental model. Given these tools, the expert team is prepared to transition to a self-regulating adaptive team.

Phase 4: Team Improvement

The team now focuses on developing adaptability, or the ability to incrementally improve and rapidly respond to novel and changing task demands (Kozlowski et al., 1999). Given the dynamic nature of modern work environments, adaptability has become an increasingly desirable and essential characteristic of individuals and teams (Smith, Ford, & Kozlowski, 1997), and this recognition has spurred research on the nature of adaptive performance (e.g., Pulakos, Arad, Donovan, & Plamondon, 2000). To develop adaptability, the leader adopts the role of a facilitator, allowing the team to apply its existing task and team capabilities to accomplish assigned tasks while intervening only when necessary to recover team coherence (Kozlowski, Gully, McHugh, et al., 1996). As the team grows increasingly adept at responding to a dynamic task environment, it becomes an adaptive team and works to continuously improve its responsiveness, efficiency, and effectiveness (Kozlowski et al., 1999).

Preparation

Adaptability

During preparation, the leader frames the team's task developmental goals in terms of achieving adaptability, that is, on developing the team's ability to self-manage and continuously improve. At this point, members have acquired and demonstrated the taskwork and teamwork capabilities necessary to perform routine tasks effectively. Thus, the leader is able to spend less time intervening within the team and more time attending to critical functions external to the team, such as scanning the environment (Hackman

& Walton, 1986) or obtaining information and resources (Fleishman et al., 1991). Ancona and Caldwell (1988, 1992) suggested that this "external perspective" was appropriate for understanding team behavior, especially in uncertain and complex task environments. In her study of consulting teams, Ancona (1990) found external activities to be better predictors of team performance than internal processes when teams were externally dependent. The leader's external orientation affords the team the opportunity to self-manage via shared leadership, a group process whereby leadership behaviors are distributed among team members (Pearce & Sims, 2002). However, shared leadership alone does not make an adaptive team; it must also continuously improve. Avolio, Jung, Murry, and Sivasubramaniam (1996) suggested that highly developed teams are more willing to restructure or even abandon inadequate assumptions to adapt to new challenges, and such teams are also more likely to continuously develop themselves by confronting new challenges over time. Thus, when teams explore alternative solutions, they learn more efficient ways of accomplishing tasks and are better able to address novel problems by quickly modifying existing solutions or proposing new ones (Kozlowski et al., 1999).

Social Cohesion

The leader frames social developmental goals in terms of achieving group cohesion, or "the resultant of all forces acting on members to remain in the group" (Festinger, 1950, p. 274). Barrick, Stewart, Neubert, and Mount (1998) referred to Festinger's construct as social cohesion and in a field study of work teams found it was significantly related to both team viability and team performance ($r = .40$ and $r = .27$, respectively). With the leader increasingly focused on external functions, the team must build on its foundation of commitment and trust to self-manage while simultaneously maintaining social cohesion, the "… synergistic interactions between team members" that include workload balancing, effective communication, and conflict management (Barrick et al., 1998, p. 382). Team conflict management is critical to an adaptive team and is related to group cohesion. For example, Sullivan and Feltz (2001) found that integrative conflict-resolution tactics (e.g., mutual disclosure, inclusive efforts) were related to team cohesion. Thus, as social cohesion increases, members are expected to manage conflict more effectively in the leader's absence and to engage in more risky, exploratory behaviors designed to develop new task strategies and to increase team adaptability.

Action Strategy

Unlike preceding phases, the leader in the team improvement phase neither provides the action strategy nor helps the team select an existing strategy. Rather, the leader develops the team's adaptive capability by facilitating its creation of new action strategies in preparation for anticipated tasks. At this point, the team has learned and applied a number of successful task strategies and is capable of identifying appropriate courses of action. For example, by proposing a series of "what if" scenarios for members to address, the leader can encourage the team to explore and create new and increasingly effective strategies for dealing with both routine and novel tasks. This degree of risk taking and exploration is essential to the team's acquisition of an adaptive capability.

Action

Develop and Monitor

When tasks are routine, the leader cultivates adaptive capability by developing or encouraging favorable attitudes, behaviors, and cognitions such as team potency, shared leadership, and compatible mental models, respectively. Unlike team efficacy, which refers to a team's shared perception that it can be effective at specific tasks, *team potency* refers to a team's shared perception that it can be effective in general across tasks and contexts (Shea & Guzzo, 1987). Gully et al. (2002) reported a corrected mean correlation of .37 between team-level potency and team-level performance. Leaders should seek to develop team potency not only because of its relationship to team performance but also because such perceptions are likely to affect how teams frame and address novel situations. That is, a high-potency team would be more likely to develop adaptability by engaging in continuous improvement behaviors such as taking risks and exploring alternative solutions to problems. Guzzo, Yost, Campbell, and Shea (1993) suggested that leaders can enhance team potency by providing KSAs to members, by creating successful mastery experiences, and by providing positive feedback.

The leader should also develop *shared leadership* within the team. Under shared leadership, leader responsibilities, functions, or behaviors are broadly distributed across members rather than concentrated in a single, appointed leader (Pearce & Sims, 2000, 2002). Burke, Fiore, and Salas (2003) suggested that shared leadership enables a more adaptive team by preventing the appointed leader from being cognitively overloaded or overwhelmed by responsibilities. In their study of leadership in selling teams, Perry, Pearce, and Sims (1999) concluded that shared leadership—rather than vertical (i.e., traditional) leadership—was most appropriate for highly interdependent teams performing complex functions. Furthermore, Pearce and Sims (2000) proposed a model of shared leadership that includes several antecedents that are salient in the team improvement phase—including a leader that actively supports shared leadership, a mature team comprised of skilled and familiar members, and a task environment characterized by task interdependence, criticality, and urgency. In their study of change management teams, Pearce and Sims (2002) found empirical evidence that shared leadership explained more variance in team effectiveness than vertical leadership (i.e., leadership exercised by an appointed leader) and that high-performing teams exhibited more leadership behaviors overall and more shared leadership in particular compared with low-performing teams.

When members possess the authority, skills, and motivation to lead, they must then determine who should lead, when they should lead, and when they should relinquish leadership. Shared cognition enables the smooth transference of shared leadership, which is critical for team adaptability (Burke et al., 2003). The concept of a *compatible mental model* is one form of shared cognition that enables this process. As team members enter the team improvement phase, they possess a shared mental model of how they should interact to accomplish assigned tasks. However, as they begin to explore alternate strategies, their mental models diverge when they learn how their unique expertise can be applied in novel ways to new problems. Despite this deviation from sharedness, members' mental models remain compatible, such that any given member knows who has the knowledge, skills, or abilities required to address a given problem. The idea of a compatible mental model is similar to the concept of transactive memory as a shared system for encoding, storing, and retrieving information in groups (Wegner, 1986, 1995). In essence, a team's transactive memory system consists of the knowledge possessed by individual members and a shared awareness of which members know what. Hollingshead (2001) suggested that such systems are adaptive for teams because they reduce the encoding and storage demands made on individuals, reduce the memory overlap across individuals, and provide individuals with wider access to information stored in other members. Empirically, transactive memory has predicted team performance on technical assembly (Liang, Moreland, & Argote, 1995) and clerical memorization tasks (Hollingshead, 2000). By developing compatible mental models and a transactive memory in team members, the leader provides the team with an increased ability to deal with the cognitive demands of a dynamic task environment.

Intervention

The team will self-regulate while the leader scans the external environment to identify factors that might affect the team's task performance. This external, future-oriented perspective is expected to place the leader in a position of having superior knowledge of the task environment relative to the team (Endsley, 1995). Consequently, during taskwork it is possible for the team's shared task mental model to diverge over time from reality as depicted by the leader's task mental model. Such divergence is especially likely in dynamic task environments characterized by stress and high workloads, which might distract members or distort their perceptions of the task environment (Serfaty, Entin, & Johnston, 1998). To maintain task coherence, the leader should provide periodic *situation updates* to the team to revise their shared task mental model (Kozlowski, Gully, McHugh, et al., 1996). Leader situation updates not only provide the team with a more accurate understanding of the task environment but also indicate to members which cues are important to attend to in the environment (Entin & Serfaty, 1999).

However, an external orientation should not entirely detach the leader from that team, as one of the most fundamental functions of a leader is to make decisions (Roby, 1961). Although an adaptive team is highly capable, self-regulating, and cohesive, there will be times when members have legitimate disagreements that cannot be settled quickly or easily without disrupting team performance. Such a situation may require that the leader make a *final decision* based on superior knowledge of both the team's internal and external environments. Such decisions will recover team coherence by focusing the team on the complex task at hand rather than on continued conflict (Entin & Serfaty, 1999).

Reflection

At the conclusion of each task cycle, the leader will monitor the team's review of individual and team performance and progress toward task and social developmental goals. However, the leader is not expected to manage its efforts, as the team is self-diagnosing and capable of providing effective feedback to members. Instead, the leader will focus on more global developmental activities such as member performance evaluations, career development, and long-term team planning. By attending to these higher-order functions, the leader promotes team adaptability by encouraging the team to self-manage the analysis of its risk taking, exploration, and continuous improvement strategies.

Illustration: The Adaptive Emergency Room Team

The attending prepares the team by focusing on the task and social developmental goals of improving the team's adaptive capability and building social cohesion, respectively. A task-related subgoal might include engendering a continuous improvement orientation in members, whereas a social subgoal might involve resolving member conflicts at the lowest level possible. When an assigned task is anticipated, the attending facilitates the team's integration of past learning to develop new action strategies that are more effective, reduce service times, and conserve resources.

Members are applying their task expertise in coordination with others to effectively accomplish routine cases with little difficulty or supervision. To develop an adaptive capability, the attending encourages member risk taking and exploration of alternative means of accomplishing tasks. Thus, residents may modify procedures if they find them to be more effective or efficient. The attending might also develop adaptive capability by encouraging the team to self-manage tasks, resource allocation, and interpersonal problems. For example, residents with specialized expertise are expected to voluntarily take patients that would benefit from their experience; interns have developed a sufficient degree of mutual respect such that potential conflicts can be resolved satisfactorily without the intervention of the chief resident or attending. Such experiences groom members for future leadership roles and free the attending to focus on external concerns such as requisitioning equipment or lobbying for additional funding. When emergent cases increase task complexity, members are able to respond rapidly and appropriately based on their shared memory of past similar experiences, smooth interactions, and adaptive responses to novel stimuli. Despite members' diverse skills and capabilities, they may still require the attending's advice or decision when, for example, ambiguous symptoms result in differential diagnoses or interpersonal problems are so severe as to be irresolvable by the affected parties. Furthermore, the attending's increased monitoring of the external environment may yield important information. For example, if residents know that hospital's sole computed tomography (CT) scan will be soon be unavailable due to planned maintenance, they can devise alternatives or negotiate resource sharing with neighboring medical facilities.

At the close of each task cycle, the team reflects on its performance and provides appropriate team-level developmental feedback. During reflection, members share the results of their continuous improvement explorations so the entire team can benefit from their experiences. Members also address and resolve interpersonal conflicts before they begin to fracture team cohesion. Developmental feedback might focus on identifying opportunities for future exploration (e.g., interfacing with top researchers or practitioners, inefficient processes) and self-management (e.g., stimulating initiative in junior residents). After multiple successful iterations the team develops adaptive capabilities, specialized yet compatible mental models, and team potency, which allow it to grow increasingly effective over time.

Discussion and Conclusion

We began this chapter by highlighting what we regard as a significant gap in leadership theory. By and large, most popular theories of leadership in organizations focus on its *structure*—the "what" of leadership. The theories are for the most part context free, intended to be universally applicable across people, settings, tasks, and time. And the theories are largely static; the nature of effective leadership does not change. Certainly, we acknowledge that some structural theories incorporate contingency factors that determine which dimensions of leadership best fit the situation, but the contingencies are not dynamic. They are tied to the situation. Thus, most popular approaches to leadership adopt a static, structure-oriented, between-unit perspective. Our theory is focused on the leadership *process*—the "how" of leadership. It is a "middle-range" theory grounded in the team context to make dynamic contingencies that arise from our process focus more salient and to allow us to make the resulting implications for effective leadership more specific. Our approach is a dynamic, process-oriented, within-unit perspective.

It is important to recognize that these perspectives are complementary rather than in opposition because they deal with critical aspects of leadership—structure and process—at differing points of a team life cycle. Transformational leadership, arguably the current dominant model based on popularity and support (Judge & Piccolo, 2004), assumes that subordinates have the underlying capabilities needed to respond positively to the leader's vision, to transcend self-interest, and to work toward challenging collective goals. How do these capabilities arise? Our theory posits that early in the team life cycle a process of team development guided by the leader builds these essential team capabilities. Structural theories that assume such skills are in place have more relevance later in the team life cycle. In that sense, our theory addresses an important gap in the literature yet is compatible with structural theories.

Research Implications

Our metatheory is broadly integrative, synthesizing diverse literatures that address functional leadership, team task and developmental process dynamics, and a wide range of member capabilities that underlie team effectiveness. The dynamic process perspective we adopt, which enhances our conceptualization of leadership, also makes a comprehensive evaluation of the theory in any one study impossible—it is too big, complex, and dynamic for current methods to encompass in a single design. To some extent this challenge is mitigated by the fact that there is broad support in the literature for the basic prescriptions of the theory. However, just because the theory is complex does not mean that it cannot be evaluated. Rather, it means that any given evaluation has to be focused on a more specific *model* (i.e., specific focal constructs and functional relationships) derived from the broader theoretical framework that evaluates a particular key aspect of the theory. Moreover, the complexity of the theory suggests that triangulation via the use of multiple methods—both quantitative and qualitative—is likely necessary.

For example, one key aspect of the theory centers on the leader using the task cycle to prompt a regulatory process that builds targeted skills. This aspect of the theory can be examined by fixing a developmental phase and by investigating whether leader functions that prompt the quality of self-regulation yield better learning and skill development. Given the depth of support for self-regulatory processes as an effective account for individual and team learning and performance (e.g., DeShon et al., 2004; Karoly, 1993) one would expect so, but it should be subject to empirical test. The *quantitative* precision necessary to evaluate dynamic regulation processes suggests that an evaluation of this aspect of the theory would likely need to be conducted in a laboratory or simulation design. Indeed, simulation-based research on action teams in emergency medicine is progressing in that direction (Fernandez et al., in press). However, a *qualitative* evaluation of the process could be conducted in a team-based setting where tasks are episodic and involve novices striving to improve their skills. A setting like the ER in a teaching hospital—like the illustration used in the prior section—could serve as an ideal setting for such an evaluation. One line of research that takes such an approach is in progress (Klein, Ziegert, & Xiao, 2002; Klein, Ziegert, Knight, & Xiao, 2006). Similarly, another key aspect of the theory centers on developmental transitions and progression. There is some limited experimental work showing that developmental progression can be prompted by manipulating the focus of regulatory activity, shifting from individual to team as incorporated in our theory (DeShon, Kozlowski, Schmidt, Wiechmann, & Milner, 2001). However, an evaluation of the full range of developmental progression would likely necessitate a quantitative and qualitative evaluation in a field setting of multiple teams progressing across a meaningful developmental process. Here we note that the volume of good field research—quantitative or qualitative—on team development is extraordinarily sparse given the importance of the process to team effectiveness (Kozlowski & Bell, 2003). If our theory prompts any rigorous and systematic field research on team development, it would be an important contribution. The bottom line is that accumulative evidence on key aspects of the theory would provide support and elaboration. Disconfirming evidence would necessitate revision (e.g., to key capabilities or their sequencing) or outright rejection if sufficiently severe (e.g., the regulatory cycle does not improve skill acquisition or there is no reasonably systematic order to developmental progression).

Practical Implications

Given the support for our approach provided by the incorporated literature (and also assuming confirmation of key aspects of the theory in more focused empirical evaluations), what implications does it have for enhancing team leadership? First, it means that there is more to effective leadership than emulating fixed behavioral targets. The prescriptions of our theory presume a highly experienced, socially sensitive leader with a sophisticated set of skills. The leader needs to be able to gauge the capabilities of the team and its members, to create or leverage calibrated opportunities to build skills, and to shift task or development processes in response to dynamic contingencies. Thus, it means that organizational designs predicated on adaptive teams will need to invest in leader development as a long-term process. Second, as a long-term process leader development is in part predicated on a diverse yet systematic set of developmental experiences (Halpin, 2004). However, given the environmental forces impinging on organizations, there is a clear need to compress the process of compiling necessary expertise. Ongoing evolution in the use of computer simulation to provide "synthetic experiences" offers the promise of building the necessary leader competencies more rapidly. Finally, our theory provides a point of departure for specifying competencies that leaders of adaptive teams should possess. As sketched in this chapter, the competencies are molar. Watola and Kozlowski (2005) made an initial effort to specify finer-grained leader competencies and, in particular, the cues that should signal the application of different competencies within a phase of development. Extension across the phases would yield a comprehensive set of team leader competencies that could serve as training specifications. The specifications in turn would provide a basis for mapping a systematic set of leader development experiences, for designing synthetic experiences, and for creating guidelines for application of the theory by leaders.

We also recognize that the progression of the team from novice to adaptive will not always be a forward-moving process (Kozlowski et al., 1999). In any team environment, members may come and go as their assignments change and as the organization requires their expertise in another area (or as members are fired for poor performance). As team members depart and are replaced, the team may regress somewhat until the new member is brought up to speed. This is well documented as a process of newcomer socialization and is easily incorporated in the model; rather than the team as a whole needing to be socialized (as in our model description), the new member is assimilated to the team (Chen, 2005; Chen & Klimoski, 2003). The presence of a new team member may also require the leader to reexamine the team's task and social goals to ensure that the team is operating at its best, given the new member's expertise and work preferences. Although the leader should always be pushing the team to move forward, some regression movement may be a necessary part of the team's life cycle. The life cycle of the team may be most strongly affected when the leader is the target of change. A new leader, however, should not signal the demise of any team. As teams develop, the institutional knowledge of the team rests not only with the leader but also with the team members in their shared and compatible mental models. The success of the leader–team relationship may rest on the team's ability to orient the leader to the group in much the same way a more experienced leader would socialize a novice team to its new environment.

Conclusion

Organizational adaptability is increasingly desirable, but it is not fundamentally a property of organizations per se; rather, it is an emergent property. Adaptability is based on the capabilities of the members of an organization and, in particular, how well team leaders are able to build and leverage those capabilities. This theory of *dynamic team leadership* extends our continuing efforts to develop an understanding of this complex and critical process.

Acknowledgments

This chapter is based on research sponsored by the Army Research Institute for the Behavioral and Social Sciences (Grant No. 1435-04-03-CT-71272), with Klein, Kozlowski, and Xiao as principal investigators. The U.S. Government is authorized to reproduce and distribute reprints for governmental purposes notwithstanding any copyright notation thereon.

The views and conclusions contained herein are those of the authors and should not be interpreted as necessarily representing the official policies or endorsements, either expressed or implied, of the Air Force Research Laboratory, the Army Research Institute, or the U.S. government.

References

Adkins, C. L. (1995). Previous work experience and organizational socialization: A longitudinal examination. *Academy of Management Journal, 38*(3), 839–862.

Adler, P. A. & Adler, P. (1988). Intense loyalty in organizations: A case study of college athletics. *Administrative Science Quarterly, 33*(3), 401–417.

Allen, N. J. & Meyer, J. P. (1990). The measurement and antecedents of affective, continuance and normative commitment to the organization. *Journal of Occupational Psychology, 63*(1), 1–18.

Ancona, D. G. (1990). Outward bound: Strategies for team survival in the organization. *Academy of Management Journal, 33*, 334–365.

Ancona, D. G. & Caldwell, D. F. (1988). Beyond task and maintenance: Defining external functions in groups. *Group & Organization Studies, 13*(4), 468–494.

Ancona, D. G. & Caldwell, D. F. (1992). Bridging the boundary: External activity and performance in organizational teams. *Administrative Science Quarterly, 37*(4), 634–665.

Anderson, J. R. (1987). Skill acquisition: Compilation of weak-method problem situations. *Psychological Review, 94*(2), 192–210.

Anderson, S. L. & Betz, N. E. (2001). Sources of social self-efficacy expectations: Their measurement and relation to career development. *Journal of Vocational Behavior, 58*(1), 98–117.

Avolio, B. J., Jung, D. I., Murry, W., & Sivasbramaniam, N. (1996). Building highly developed teams: Focusing on shared leadership process, efficacy, trust, and performance. In M. M. Beyerlein & D. A. Johnson (Eds.), *Advances in interdisciplinary studies of work teams: Team leadership* (Vol. 3, pp. 173–209). Stamford, CT: JAI Press, Inc.

Bandura, A. (1977). Self-efficacy: Toward a unifying theory of behavioral change. *Psychological Review, 84*(2), 191–215.

Bandura, A. (1982). Self-efficacy mechanism in human agency. *American Psychologist, 37*(2), 122–147.

Bandura, A. (1986). *Social foundations of thought and action.* Englewood Cliffs, NJ: Prentice Hall.

Bandura, A. (1997). *Self-efficacy: The exercise of control.* New York: Freeman.

Bandura, A. (1998). Personal and collective efficacy in human adaptation and change. In J. G. Adair & D. Belanger (Eds.), *Advances in psychological science* (Vol. 1, pp. 51–71). Hove, England: Psychology Press/Erlbaum (UK) Taylor & Francis.

Bandura, A. & Cervone, D. (1986). Differential engagement of self-reactive influences in cognitive motivation. *Organizational Behavior and Human Decision Processes, 38*(1), 92–113.

Barrick, M. R., Stewart, G. L., Neubert, J. M., & Mount, M. K. (1998). Relating member ability and personality to work-team processes and team effectiveness. *Journal of Applied Psychology, 82,* 377–391.

Bass, B. M. (1985). *Leadership and performance beyond expectations.* New York: Free Press.

Becker, T. E. & Billings, R. S. (1993). Profiles of commitment: An empirical test. *Journal of Organizational Behavior, 14*(2), 177–190.

Bishop, J. W. & Scott, K. D. (1997). Employee commitment and work team productivity. *HRMagazine, 11,* 107–111.

Bishop, J. W. & Scott, K. D. (2000). An examination of organizational and team commitment in a self-directed team environment. *Journal of Applied Psychology, 85*(3), 439–450.

Blickensderfer, E., Cannon-Bowers, J. A., & Salas, E. (1997). Theoretical bases for team self-corrections: Fostering shared mental models. In M. M. Beyerlein & D. A. Johnson (Eds.), *Advances in interdisciplinary studies of work teams* (Vol. 4, pp. 249–279). Greenwich, CT: JAI Press.

Bowers, C. A., Braun, C. C., & Morgan, B. B. Jr. (1997). Team workload: Its meaning and measurement. In M. T. Brannick & E. Salas (Eds.), *Team performance assessment and measurement: Theory, methods, and applications* (pp. 85–108). Mahwah, NJ: Lawrence Erlbaum Associates.

Burke, C. S., Fiore, S., & Salas, E. (2003). The role of shared cognition in enabling shared leadership and team adaptability. In J. A. Conger & C. L. Pearce (Eds.), *Shared leadership: Reframing the how's and why's of leadership* (pp. 103–122). Thousand Oaks, CA: Sage Publications.

Campion, M. A., Papper, E. M., & Medsker, G. J. (1996). Relations between work team characteristics and effectiveness: A replication and extension. *Personnel Psychology, 49*(2), 429–452.

Cannon-Bowers, J. A., Salas, E., & Converse, S. A. (1993). Shared mental models in expert team decision making. In N. J. Castellan (Ed.), *Individual and group decision making: Current issues* (pp. 221–246). Hillsdale, NJ: LEA.

Chang, A., Bordia, P., & Duck, J. (2003). Punctuated equilibrium and linear progression: Toward a new understanding of group development. *Academy of Management Journal, 46*(1), 106–117.

Chao, G. T., O'Leary-Kelly, A. M., Wolf, S., Klein, H. J., & Gardner, P. D. (1994). Organizational socialization: Its content and consequences. *Journal of Applied Psychology, 79,* 730–743.

Chen, G. (2005). Newcomer adaptation in teams: Multilevel antecedents and outcomes. *Academy of Management Journal, 48,* 101–116.

Chen, G. & Bliese, P. D. (2002). The role of different levels of leadership in predicting self- and collective efficacy: Evidence for discontinuity. *Journal of Applied Psychology, 87*(3), 549–556.

Chen, G. & Klimoski, R. J. (2003). The impact of expectations on newcomer performance in teams as mediated by work characteristics, social exchanges, and empowerment. *Academy of Management Journal, 46,* 591–607.

Christ, O., van Dick, R., Wagner, U., & Stellmacher, J. (2003). When teachers go the extra mile: Foci of organisational identification as determinants of different forms of organisational citizenship behaviour among schoolteachers. *British Journal of Educational Psychology, 73*(3), 329–341.

Corno, L. & Mandinach, E. B. (1985). Using existing classroom data to explore relationships in a theoretical model of academic motivation. *Journal of Educational Research, 77*(1), 33–42.

Denson, R. W. (1981). *Team training: Literature review and annotated bibliography.* U.S. Air Force Human Resources Lab, Logistics & Technical Training Div, Wright-Patterson Air Force Base, OH.

DeShon, R. P., Kozlowski, S. W. J., Schmidt, A. M., Milner, K. A., & Wiechmann, D. (2004). A multiple-goal, multilevel model of feedback effects on the regulation of individual and team performance. *Journal of Applied Psychology, 89*(6), 1035–1056.

DeShon, R. P., Kozlowski, S. W. J., Schmidt, A. M., Wiechmann, D., & Milner, K. A. (2001, April). *Developing team adaptability: Shifting regulatory focus across levels.* Paper presented at the 15th Annual Conference of the Society for Industrial and Organizational Psychology, New Orleans, LA.

Dickinson, T. L. & McIntyre, R. M. (1997). A conceptual framework for teamwork measurement. In M. T. Brannick & E. Salas (Eds.), *Team performance assessment and measurement: Theory, methods, and applications* (pp. 19–43). Mahwah, NJ: Lawrence Erlbaum Associates.

Durham, C. C., Knight, D., & Locke, E. A. (1998). Effects of leader role, team-set goal difficulty, efficacy, and tactics on team effectiveness. *Organizational Behavior and Human Decision Processes, 72*(2), 203–231.

Dyer, J. C. (1984). Team research and team training: State-of-the-art review. In F. A. Muckler (Ed.), *Human factors review* (pp. 285–323). Santa Monica, CA: Human Factors Society.

Edmondson, A. C., Bohmer, R. M., & Pisano, G. P. (2001). Disrupted routines: Team learning and new technology implementation in hospitals. *Administrative Science Quarterly, 46*(4), 685–716.

Ellemers, N., Van Rijswijk, W., Bruins, J., & De Gilder, D. (1998). Group commitment as a moderator of attributional and behavioural responses to power use. *European Journal of Social Psychology, 28*(4), 555–573.

Endsley, M. R. (1995). Toward a theory of situational awareness in dynamic systems. *Human Factors, 37*(1), 32–64.

Entin, E. E. & Serfaty, D. (1999). Adaptive team coordination. *Human Factors, 41*(2), 312–325.

Fernandez, R., Vozenilek, J., Hegarty, C., Motola, I., Reznek, M., Phrampus, P., & Kozlowski, S. W. J. (in press). Developing expert medical teams: Toward an evidence-based approach. *Academic Emergency Medicine.*

Festinger, L. (1950). Informal social communication. *Psychological Review, 57,* 271–282.

Flavell, J. H. (1979). Metacognition and cognitive monitoring: A new area of cognitive-developmental inquiry. *American Psychologist, 34*(10), 906–911.

Fleishman, E. A., Mumford, M. D., Zaccaro, S. J., Levin, K. Y., Korotkin, A. L., & Hein, M. B. (1991). Taxonomic efforts in the description of leader behavior: A synthesis and functional interpretation. *Leadership Quarterly Special Issue: Individual Differences and Leadership, 2*(4), 245–287.

Fleishman, E. A. & Zaccaro, S. J. (1992). Toward a taxonomy of team performance functions. In R. W. Swezey & E. Salas (Eds.), *Teams: Their training and performance* (pp. 31–56). Norwood, NJ: Ablex.

Ford, J. K., Quiñones, M. A., Sego, D. J., & Sorra, J. S. (1992). Factors affecting the opportunity to perform trained tasks on the job. *Personnel Psychology, 45*(3), 511–527.

Forsyth, D. R. (1999). *Group dynamics* (3rd ed.). Belmont, CA: Brooks/Cole.

Gabarro, J. J. (1987). The development of working relationships. In J. W. Lorsch (Ed.), *Handbook of organizational behavior* (pp. 171–189). Englewood Cliffs, NJ: Prentice Hall.

Gambetta, D. (1988). Can we trust trust? In D. Gambetta (Ed.), *Trust: Making and breaking cooperative relations* (pp. 213–237). New York: Blackwell.

Gersick, C. J. (1988). Time and transition in work teams: Toward a new model of group development. *Academy of Management Journal, 31*(1), 9–41.

Gist, M. E. & Mitchell, T. R. (1992). Self-efficacy: A theoretical analysis of its determinants and malleability. *Academy of Management Review, 17*(2), 183–211.

Gross, N. & Martin, W. E. (1952). On group cohesiveness. *American Journal of Sociology, 57,* 546–554.

Gully, S. M., Devine, D. J., & Whitney, D. J. (1995). A meta-analysis of cohesion and performance: Effects of levels of analysis and task interdependence. *Small Group Research, 26,* 497–520.

Gully, S. M., Incalcaterra, K. A., Joshi, A., & Beaubien, J. M. (2002). A meta-analysis of team-efficacy, potency, and performance: Interdependence and level of analysis as moderators of observed relationships. *Journal of Applied Psychology, 87*(5), 819–832.

Guzzo, R. A., Yost, P. R., Campbell, R. J., & Shea, G. P. (1993). Potency in groups: Articulating a construct. *British Journal of Social Psychology, 32,* 87–106.

Hackman, J. R. (1987). The design of work teams. In J. Lorsch (Ed.), *Handbook of organizational behavior* (pp. 315–342). New York: Prentice Hall.

Hackman, J. R. (1992). Group influences on individuals in organizations. In M. D. Dunnette & L. M. Hough (Eds.), *Handbook of industrial and organizational psychology* (Vol. 3, pp. 199–267). Palo Alto, CA: Consulting Psychologist Press.

Hackman, J. R. & Wageman, R. (2005). A theory of team coaching. *Academy of Management Review, 30,* 269–287.

Hackman, J. R. & Walton, R. E. (1986). Leading groups in organizations. In P. S. Goodman & Associates (Eds.), *Designing effective work groups.* San Francisco, CA: Jossey-Bass.

Hage, J. (1980). *Theories of organizations.* New York: Wiley & Sons.

Halpin, S. (2004, April). *Accelerating leader development.* Paper presented at the U. S. Army Research Institute for the Behavioral and Social Sciences STO Review Program, Fort Leavenworth, KS.

Harrison, D. A., Mohammed, S., McGrath, J. E., Florey, A. T., & Vanderstoep, S. W. (2003). Time matters in team performance: Effects of member familiarity, entrainment, and task discontinuity on speed and quality. *Personnel Psychology, 56*(3), 633–669.

Hollingshead, A. B. (2000). Perceptions of expertise and transactive memory in work relationships. *Group Processes & Intergroup Relations, 3*(3), 257–267.

Hollingshead, A. B. (2001). Cognitive interdependence and convergent expectations in transactive memory. *Journal of Personality and Social Psychology, 81,* 1080–1089.

Ilgen, D. R. & Hollenbeck, J. R. (1991). The structure of work: Job design and roles. In M. D. Dunnette & L. M. Hough (Eds.), *Handbook of industrial and organizational psychology* (Vol. 2, pp. 165–207). Palo Alto, CA: Consulting Psychologists Press.

Jablin, F. M. (2001). Organizational entry, assimilation, and disengagement/exit. In F. M. Jablin & L. L. Putnam (Eds.), *The new handbook of organizational communication* (pp. 732–818). Thousand Oaks, CA: Sage Publications, Inc.

Jackson, C. L. & LePine, J. A. (2003). Peer responses to a team's weakest link: A test and extension of Lepine and van Dyne's model. *Journal of Applied Psychology, 88*(3), 459–475.

Jackson, S. E., May, K. E., & Whitney, K. (1995). Understanding the dynamics of diversity in decision-making teams. In R. A. Guzzo, E. Salas, & Associates (Eds.), *Team effectiveness and decision making in organizations.* San Francisco, CA: Jossey-Bass.

Jones, G. R. & George, J. M. (1998). The experience and evolution of trust: Implications for cooperation and teamwork. *Academy of Management Review, 23*(3), 531–546.

Judge, T. A. & Piccolo, R. F. (2004). Transformational and transactional leadership: A meta-analytic test of their relative validity. *Journal of Applied Psychology, 89*(5), 755–768.

Karoly, P. (1993). Mechanisms of self-regulation: A systems view. *Annual Review of Psychology, 44,* 23–52.

Katz, D. & Kahn, R. L. (1978). *The social psychology of organizations* (2nd ed.). New York: John Wiley.

Katz, R. (1978). Job longevity as a situational factor in job satisfaction. *Administrative Science Quarterly, 23*(2), 204–223.

Katz, R. (1980). Time and work: Toward an integrative perspective. *Research in Organizational Behavior, 2,* 81–127.

Klaus, D. J. & Glaser, R. (1970). Reinforcement determinants of team proficiency. *Organizational Behavior & Human Decision Processes, 5*(1), 33–67.

Klein, K. J., Ziegert, J. C., Knight, A. R., & Xiao, Y. (2006). Dynamic delegation: Hierarchical, shared and deindividualized leadership in extreme action teams. *Administrative Science Quarterly, 51,* 590–621.

Klein, K. J., Ziegert, J. C., & Xiao, Y. (2002). *Action team leadership: A multimethod examination of emergency medical teams.* Paper presented at the SIOP Annual Conference, Toronto, Canada.

Komaki, J. L., Desselles, M. L., & Bowman, E. D. (1989). Definitely not a breeze: Extending an operant model of effective supervision to teams. *Journal of Applied Psychology, 74,* 522–529.

Kozlowski, S. W. J. & Bell, B. S. (2003). Work groups and teams in organizations. In W. C. Borman, D. R. Ilgen, & E. J. Klimoski (Eds.), *Handbook of psychology: Industrial and organizational psychology* (Vol. 12, pp. 333–375). London, England: Wiley.

Kozlowski, S. W. J., Gully, S. M., Brown, K. G., Salas, E., Smith, E. M., & Nason, E. R. (2001). Effects of training goals and goal orientation traits on multidimensional training outcomes and performance adaptability. *Organizational Behavior & Human Decision Processes, 85*(1), 1–31.

Kozlowski, S. W. J., Gully, S. M., McHugh, P. P., Salas, E., & Cannon-Bowers, J. A. (1996). A dynamic theory of leadership and team effectiveness: Developmental and task contingent leader roles. In G. R. Ferris (Ed.), *Research in personnel and human resource management* (Vol. 14, pp. 253–305). Greenwich, CT: JAI Press.

Kozlowski, S. W. J., Gully, S. M., Nason, E. R., & Smith, E. M. (1999). Developing adaptive teams: A theory of compilation and performance across levels and time. In D. R. Ilgen & E. D. Pulakos (Eds.), *The changing nature of work performance: Implications for staffing, personnel actions, and development* (pp. 240–292). San Francisco, CA: Jossey-Bass.

Kozlowski, S. W. J., Gully, S. M., Salas, E., & Cannon-Bowers, J. A. (1996). Team leadership and development: Theory principles, and guidelines for training leaders and teams. In M. Beyerlein, D. Johnson, & S. Beyerlein (Eds.), *Advances in interdisciplinary studies of work teams: Team leadership* (Vol. 3, pp. 251–289). Greenwich, CT: JAI Press.

Kozlowski, S. W. J. & Hults, B. M. (1986). Joint moderation of the relation between task complexity and job performance for engineers. *Journal of Applied Psychology, 71*(2), 196–202.

Kozlowski, S. W. J., Toney, R. J., Mullins, M. E., Weissbein, D. A., Brown, K. G., & Bell, B. S. (2001). Developing adaptability: A theory for the design of integrated-embedded training systems. In E. Salas (Ed.), *Advances in human performance and cognitive engineering research* (Vol. 1, pp. 59–123). Amsterdam: JAI/Elsevier Science.

Lawler, E. E., Mohrman, S. A., & Ledford, G. E. (1995). *Creating high performance organizations: Practices and results of employee involvement and total quality management in Fortune 1000 companies.* San Francisco, CA: Jossey-Bass.

LePine, J. A., Hollenbeck, J. R., Ilgen, D. R., & Hedlund, J. (1997). Effects of individual differences on the performance of hierarchical decision-making teams: Much more than G. *Journal of Applied Psychology, 82*(5), 803–811.

Levine, J. M. & Moreland, R. L. (1998). Small groups. In D. T. Gilbert, S. T. Fiske, & G. Lindzey (Eds.), *Handbook of social psychology* (4th ed., pp. 415–469). Boston, MA: McGraw Hill.

Lewicki, R. J. & Bunker, B. B. (1996). Developing and maintaining trust in work relationships. In R. M. Kramer & T. R. Tyler (Eds.), *Trust in organizations: Frontiers of theory and research* (pp. 114–139). Thousand Oaks, CA: Sage Publications, Inc.

Liang, D. W., Moreland, R., & Argote, L. (1995). Group versus individual training and group performance: The mediating factor of transactive memory. *Personality & Social Psychology Bulletin, 21*(4), 385–393.

Likert, R. (1961). *New patterns of management.* New York: McGraw-Hill.

Locke, E. A., Frederick, E., Lee, C., & Bobko, P. (1984). Effect of self-efficacy, goals, and task strategies on task performance. *Journal of Applied Psychology, 69*(2), 241–251.

Lord, R. G. (1977). Functional leadership behavior: Measurement and relation to social power and leadership perceptions. *Administrative Science Quarterly, 22*(1), 114–133.

Marks, M. A. (1999). A test of the impact of collective efficacy in routine and novel performance environments. *Human Performance, 12*(3–4), 295–309.

Marks, M. A., Mathieu, J. E., & Zaccaro, S. J. (2001). A temporally based framework and taxonomy of team processes. *Academy of Management Review, 26*(3), 356–376.

Marks, M. A., Sabella, M. J., Burke, C. S., & Zaccaro, S. J. (2002). The impact of cross-training on team effectiveness. *Journal of Applied Psychology, 87*(1), 3–13.

Marks, M. A., Zaccaro, S. J., & Mathieu, J. E. (2000). Performance implications of leader briefings and team-interaction training for team adaptation to novel environments. *Journal of Applied Psychology, 85*(6), 971–986.

Mathieu, J. E., Heffner, T. S., Goodwin, G. F., Salas, E., & Cannon-Bowers, J. A. (2000). The influence of shared mental models on team process and performance. *Journal of Applied Psychology, 85*(2), 273–283.

May, D. R. & Schwoerer, C. E. (1994). Employee health by design: Using employee involvement teams in ergonomic job redesign. *Personnel Psychology, 47,* 861–876.

Mayer, R. C., Davis, J. H., & Schoorman, F. D. (1995). An integrative model of organizational trust. *Academy of Management Review, 20*(3), 709–734.

McAllister, D. J. (1995). Affect- and cognition-based trust as foundations for interpersonal cooperation in organizations. *Academy of Management Journal Special Issue: Intra- and Interorganizational Cooperation, 38*(1), 24–59.

McGrath, J. E. (1962). *Leadership behavior: Some requirements for leadership training.* Washington, DC: U.S. Civil Service Commission, Office of Career Development.

McGrath, J. E. (1964). *Social psychology: A brief introduction.* New York: Holt, Rinehart, & Winston.

Meyer, J. P. & Allen, N. J. (1984). Testing the "side-bet theory" of organizational commitment: Some methodological considerations. *Journal of Applied Psychology, 69*(3), 372–378.

Miller, V. D. & Jablin, F. M. (1991). Information seeking during organizational entry: Influences, tactics, and a model of the process. *Academy of Management Review, 16*(1), 92–120.

Mitchell, T. R. & Silver, W. S. (1990). Individual and group goals when workers are interdependent: Effects on task strategies and performance. *Journal of Applied Psychology, 75*, 185–193.

Moreland, R. L. (1987). The formation of small groups. In C. Hendrick (Ed.), *Group processes* (Vol. 8, pp. 80–110). Thousand Oaks, CA: Sage Publications, Inc.

Moreland, R. L. & Levine, J. M. (1982). Socialization in small groups: Temporal changes in individual-group relations. In L. Berkowitz (Ed.), *Advances in experimental social psychology* (pp. 143–186). New York: Academic Press.

Moreland, R. L. & Levine, J. M. (2001). Socialization in organizations and work groups. In M. E. Turner (Ed.), *Groups at work: Theory and research* (pp. 69–112). Mahwah, NJ: Lawrence Erlbaum Associates.

Morgan, B. B., Salas, E., & Glickman, A. S. (1993). An analysis of team evolution and maturation. *Journal of General Psychology, 120*, 277–291.

Morgan, B. B. Jr., Glickman, A. S., Woodard, E. A., Blaiwes, A. S., & Salas, E. (1986). *Measurement of team behavior in a navy environment* (No. NTSC TR-86-014). Orlando, FL: Naval Training Systems Center.

Morrison, E. W. (1993). Newcomer information seeking: Exploring types, modes, sources, and outcomes. *Academy of Management Journal, 36*(3), 557–589.

Mullen, B. & Copper, C. (1994). The relation between group cohesiveness and performance: An integration. *Psychological Bulletin, 115*(2), 210–227.

Nieva, V. F., Fleishman, E. A., & Rieck, A. M. (1978). *Team dimensions: Their identity, their measurement, and their relationships* (Technical Report). Washington, DC: ARRO.

Ostroff, C. & Kozlowski, S. W. J. (1992). Organizational socialization as a learning process: The role of information acquisition. *Personnel Psychology, 45*, 849–874.

Ostroff, C. & Kozlowski, S. W. J. (1993). The role of mentoring in information gathering processes of newcomers during early organizational socialization. *Journal of Vocational Behavior, 42*, 170–183.

Park, O. -C. & Gittelman, S. S. (1995). Dynamic characteristics of mental models and dynamic visual displays. *Instructional Science, 23*(5–6), 303–320.

Pearce, C. L. & Sims, H. P., Jr. (2000). Shared leadership: Toward a multilevel theory of leadership. In *Team development* (Vol. 7, pp. 115–139). Amsterdam: Elsevier Science Inc.

Pearce, C. L. & Sims, H. P., Jr. (2002). Vertical versus shared leadership as predictors of the effectiveness of change management teams: An examination of aversive, directive, transactional, transformational, and empowering leader behaviors. *Group Dynamics: Theory, Research, and Practice, 6*(2), 172–197.

Perry, M. L., Pearce, C. L., & Sims, H. P. J. (1999). Empowered selling teams: How shared leadership can contribute to selling team outcomes. *Journal of Personal Selling & Sales Management, 19*(3), 35–51.

Peterson, E., Mitchell, T. R., Thompson, L., & Burr, R. (2000). Collective efficacy and aspects of shared mental models as predictors of performance over time in work groups. *Group Processes & Intergroup Relations, 3*(3), 296–316.

Pulakos, E. D., Arad, S., Donovan, M. A., & Plamondon, K. E. (2000). Adaptability in the workplace: Development of a taxonomy of adaptive performance. *Journal of Applied Psychology, 85*(4), 612–624.

Reade, C. (2003). Going the extra mile: Local managers and global effort. *Journal of Managerial Psychology, 18*(3), 208–228.

Riggs, M. L. & Knight, P. A. (1994). The impact of perceived group success-failure on motivational beliefs and attitudes: A causal model. *Journal of Applied Psychology, 79*(5), 755–766.

Roby, T. B. (1961). The executive function in small groups. In L. Petrullo & B. M. Bass (Eds.), *Leadership and interpersonal behavior* (pp. 48–65). New York: Holt, Rinehart, & Winston.

Rouse, W. B. & Morris, N. M. (1986). On looking into the black box: Prospects and limits in the search for mental models. *Psychological Bulletin, 100*(3), 349–363.

Roy, D. F. (1973). "Banana time"—job satisfaction and informal interaction. In W. G. Bennis, D. E. Berlew, E. H. Schein, & F. I. Steele (Eds.), *Interpersonal dynamics* (pp. 403–417). Homewood, IL: Dorsey.

Saks, A. M. & Ashforth, B. E. (1997). Organizational socialization: Making sense of the past and present as a prologue for the future. *Journal of Vocational Behavior, 51*(2), 234–279.

Salas, E., Dickinson, T. L., Converse, S. A., & Tannenbaum, S. I. (1992). Toward an understanding of team performance and training. In R. W. Swezey & E. Salas (Eds.), *Teams: Their training and performance* (pp. 3–29). Norwood, NJ: Ablex.

Salas, E., Fowlkes, J. E., Stout, R. J., Milanovich, D. M., & Prince, C. (1999). Does CRM training improve teamwork skills in the cockpit? Two evaluation studies. *Human Factors, 41*(2), 326–343.

Schein, E. H. (1968). Organizational socialization and the profession of management. *Industrial Management Review, 9*, 1–16.

Schmidt, A. M. & Ford, J. K. (2003). Learning within a learner control training environment: The interactive effects of goal orientation and metacognitive instruction on learning outcomes. *Personnel Psychology, 56*(2), 405–429.

Schutz, W. C. (1961). The ego, FIRO theory and the leader as completer. In L. Petrullo & B. M. Bass (Eds.), *Leadership and interpersonal behavior* (pp. 48–65). New York: Holt, Rinehart and Winston, Inc.

Scott, K. D. & Townsend, A. M. (1994). Teams: Why some perform and other do not. *HRMagazine, 8*, 62–67.

Seers, A. (1996). Better leadership through chemistry: Toward a model of emergent shared team leadership. In M. M. Beyerlein & D. A. Johnson (Eds.), *Advances in interdisciplinary studies of work teams: Team leadership* (Vol. 3, pp. 145–172). Stamford, CT: JAI Press, Inc.

Serfaty, D., Entin, E. E., & Johnston, J. H. (1998). Team coordination training. In J. A. Cannon-Bowers & E. Salas (Eds.), *Making decisions under stress: Implications for individual and team training* (pp. 221–245). Washington, DC: American Psychological Association.

Shea, G. P. & Guzzo, R. A. (1987). Groups as human resources. In K. M. Rowland & G. R. Ferris (Eds.), *Research in personnel and human resource management* (Vol. 5, pp. 323–356). Greenwich, CT: JAI Press.

Sheppard, B. H. & Sherman, D. M. (1998). The grammars of trust: A model and general implications. *Academy of Management Review, 23*(3), 422–437.

Smith, E. M., Ford, J. K., & Kozlowski, S. W. J. (1997). Building adaptive expertise: Implications for training design strategies. In M. A. Quiñones & A. Dudda (Eds.), *Training for a rapidly changing workplace: Applications of psychological research* (pp. 89–118). Washington, DC: American Psychological Association.

Sullivan, P. J. & Feltz, D. L. (2001). The relationship between intrateam conflict and cohesion within hockey teams. *Small Group Research, 32*(3), 342–355.

Terreberry, S. (1968). The evolution of organizational environments. *Administrative Science Quarterly, 12*(4), 590–613.

Tuckman, B. W. (1965). Developmental sequence in small groups. *Psychological Bulletin, 63*, 384–399.

Tuckman, B. W. & Sexton, T. L. (1991). The effect of teacher encouragement on student self-efficacy and motivation for self-regulated performance. *Journal of Social Behavior and Personality, 6*(1), 137–146.

Turner, J. C., Hogg, M. A., Oakes, P. J., Reicher, S. D., & Wetherell, M. S. (1987). *Rediscovering the social group: A self-categorization theory.* Cambridge, MA: Basil Blackwell.

Tyler, T. R. (1999). Why people cooperate with organizations: An identity-based perspective. In R. I. Sutton & B. M. Staw (Eds.), *Research in organizational behavior* (Vol. 21, pp. 201–246). Stamford, CT: JAI Press, Inc.

Volpe, C. E., Cannon-Bowers, J. A., Salas, E., & Spector, P. E. (1996). The impact of cross-training on team functioning: An empirical investigation. *Human Factors, 38*(1), 87–100.

Watola, D. J. & Kozlowski, S. W. J. (2005, April). Leader competencies for developing adaptive teams. In D. V. Day & S. M. Halpin (chairs), *Leader development theory and research in the United States Army.* Symposium presented at the 20th Annual Conference of the Society for Industrial and Organizational Psychology, Los Angeles, CA.

Weaver, J. L., Bowers, C. A., Salas, E., & Cannon-Bowers, J. A. (1997). Motivation in teams. In M. M. Beyerlein & D. A. Johnson (Eds.), *Advances in interdisciplinary studies of work teams* (Vol. 4, pp. 167–191). Greenwich, CT: JAI Press.

Webber, S. S. (2002). Leadership and trust facilitating cross-functional team success. *Journal of Management Development, 21*(3), 201–214.

Wegner, D. M. (1986). Transactive memory: A contemporary analysis of the group mind. In B. Mullen & G. R. Goethals (Eds.), *Theories of group behavior* (pp. 185–205). New York: Springer-Verlag.

Wegner, D. M. (1995). A computer network model of human transactive memory. *Social Cognition, 13*, 319–339.

Weldon, E., Jehn, K. A., & Pradhan, P. (1991). Processes that mediate the relationship between a group goal and improved group performance. *Journal of Personality & Social Psychology, 61*(4), 555–569.

Widmeyer, W. N., Brawley, L. R., & Carron, A. V. (1992). Group dynamics in sport. In T. S. Horn (Ed.), *Advances in sport psychology* (pp. 163–180). Champaign, IL: Human Kinetics Publishers.

Woolley, A. W. (1988). Effects of intervention content and timing on group task performance. *Journal of Applied Behavioral Science, 34*, 30–49.

Zaccaro, S. J., Blair, V., Peterson, C., & Zazanis, M. (1995). Collective efficacy. In J. Maddux (Ed.), *Self-efficacy, adaptation, and adjustment* (pp. 305–328). New York: Plenum.

Zimmerman, B. J. & Pons, M. M. (1986). Development of a structured interview for assessing student use of self-regulated learning strategies. *American Educational Research Journal, 23*(4), 614–628.

Zimmerman, B. J. & Pons, M. M. (1988). Construct validation of a strategy model of student self-regulated learning. *Journal of Educational Psychology, 80*(3), 284–290.

6

An Ecological Perspective on Team Cognition

Nancy J. Cooke, Jamie C. Gorman, and Leah J. Rowe

Why Team Cognition?

Technology has complicated the role of the human in most complex systems. Manual or motor tasks carried out by a single individual have been supplanted by multiple-person tasks that are highly cognitive in nature. Assembly lines have been replaced by teams of designers, troubleshooters, and process controllers. Teams plan, decide, remember, make decisions, design, troubleshoot, solve problems, and generally think as an integrated unit. These activities are examples of team cognition, a construct that has arisen with the growing need to understand, explain, and predict these cognitive activities of teams. But does *team cognition* mean that teams think, or is it that the individuals within the teams think, relegating team cognition to a collection of individual thinkers? Questions like these are important prerequisites to understanding team cognition.

But why focus on team cognition? Just as applied psychologists have linked individual cognition to individual performance (Durso et al., 1999), team cognition has been linked to team performance. The idea is that a great number of team performance deficiencies or errors in complex cognitive systems can be attributed to problems with team cognition. There are many notable examples supporting this claim. Team decision making and coordination failures are at least partially tied to the Vincennes–Iranian airbus incident of 1988 (Collyer & Malecki, 1998), the Space Shuttle *Challenger* disaster in 1986 (Vaughan, 1996), and recent failures in organizational response to Hurricane Katrina (CNN, 2005). A better understanding of team cognition and its relationship to team performance should enable us to measure and assess it and to intervene through training and design as needed.

Team Cognition: Definitions

This chapter focuses on *team*, rather than *group*, cognition. We define a team as a special type or subset of group—one in which the members have different, though interdependent, roles. This definition is compatible with Salas, Dickinson, Converse, and Tannenbaum's (1992), in which a team is defined as "a distinguishable set of two or more people who interact dynamically, interdependently, and adaptively toward a common and valued goal/object/mission, who have each been assigned specific roles or functions to perform, and who have a limited life span of membership" (p. 4). Though much of what is being learned about team cognition should also apply to group cognition, some interesting issues arise when groups with heterogeneous or specialized team members are considered.

We define *team cognition* as the cognitive activity that occurs at a team level. Thus, if more than one individual is involved in planning and these individuals depend on each other for different aspects of planning, there is team cognition. The presence of team cognition does not imply the absence of individual cognition. Both occur simultaneously. In fact, one level (individual) is nested within the other (team). The focus of this chapter, however, is on team-level cognition. A number of theoretical perspectives, which are parallel to theories of individual cognition, can be taken on team cognition. This chapter describes an ecological perspective on team cognition and contrasts it with more traditional perspectives. The ecological perspective stems from the early work of William James, James Gibson, and Roger Barker (Heft, 2001) and is not a mainstream perspective on either individual or team cognition. Mainstream perspectives on team cognition have been largely inspired by cognitive psychology and the information-processing approach to cognition. Before proceeding with a detailed analysis of how the two perspectives explain team cognition, some background on ecological psychology as contrasted with the more traditional information processing perspective is provided.

Information-Processing versus Ecological Psychology

Whereas the information-processing approach focuses on the "analogy between the mind and the digital computer" (Eysenck & Keane, 2000, p. 1), ecological psychology focuses on the changing relationships, or dynamics, between people and their environment (which includes other people). Some defining characteristics of each of the two approaches are listed in Table 6.1. To summarize, major differences between the two approaches can be found

TABLE 6.1

Basic Characteristics of Information-Processing and Ecological Psychology

Information-Processing Theory
A. Computer metaphor: Perception and thought are inherently computational.
B. Mind–environment dualism.
C. The locus of cognitive processing is "within" the individual.
Ecological Theory
A. Dynamical systems metaphor: Perception and thought are inherently dynamic.
B. Mind–environment mutuality.
C. The locus of cognitive processing is "between" individuals and their environment.

in the general metaphor for formulating psychological questions, the philosophical tradition of each theory, and the locus of cognitive processing.

The information-processing perspective has been inspired by the computer metaphor (Lachman, Lachman, & Butterfield, 1979). Information flow diagrams are commonly used to convey stages of input, output, processing, and feedback loops along the way. Cognitive structure or representation is central to much theorizing. Computational systems operate on this database or "knowledge base." In this tradition, the processes that operate on this database (cognitive processing) are also a form of knowledge, "hence the program that governs the behavior of a symbol system can be stored, along with other symbol [knowledge] structures, in the system's own memory, and executed when activated" (Simon, 1981, p. 22). The strong view of information-processing holds that all perception and thought are inherently computational, with a program tapping into memory to construct a meaningful representation from meaningless stimulus inputs.

In contrast, ecological psychology has been associated with a dynamical systems metaphor and holds that perception and thought are inherently dynamic. According to this view, perception and action are the basis for perceptual systems (Gibson, 1966) and further that the intersection of actor and environment is the basis of the conscious mind (James, 1904). The dynamical systems metaphor for addressing psychological questions characterizes psychological phenomena using equations of motion, interactions, or general activity and models how the system evolves qualitatively in time, including stable states, bifurcations (e.g., symmetry breaking), and coordinative states (e.g., self-organization).

The information-processing perspective is also one of constructivism and mind–environment dualism. Stimulation is imbued with meaning by cognitive processes, secondary qualities are inferred from primary qualities (e.g., color from wavelength), and "psychological" quantities are scaled to "physical" dimensions (e.g., psychophysics). In contrast, the ecological perspective is one of direct perception of mind–environment mutuality. For example, perceivers or actors directly perceive change and nonchange (i.e., not stimulation per se) in their relationship to the ambient environment (these invariants are stimulus information, but not stimuli; Gibson, 1979) where potential relationships are just as meaningful as realized relationships to the extent they can alter our opportunities for action.

Finally, the locus of cognition according to the information-processing approach is "within" the individual, whereas for ecological psychology the locus of cognitive processing is "between" individuals and their environment. Thus, individuals are the starting point for information processing, whereas for ecological psychology it is the coupling between individuals and their environment.

An Information-Processing Perspective on Team Cognition

The traditional view of team cognition portrays a team as an information processor, consisting of a collection of individual information processors. Thus, most often the information-processing metaphor is applied to individual team members, cognition is measured at the individual level, and then results are aggregated to reflect the team level. In addition, the target of most measurement efforts is cognitive structure (e.g., mental models, situation models) as opposed to the process of aggregation itself. However, there are some exceptions in which the information processing is applied at the team level and measures reflect team process as well as structure (e.g., Hinsz, 1999).

Interestingly, the input–process–output (IPO) framework, the generic model for early conceptualizations of team performance, was inspired by theories from the social psychology of small groups and industrial organizational psychology. This framework was originally oriented toward team process more than structure. It was suggested that team interaction processes be studied as mediators of the effects of individual, group, and environmental factors on team output and cohesiveness (Hackman, 1987). A generic version of the IPO framework is presented in Figure 6.1.

In the course of applying the IPO framework to team cognition, the locus of team cognition has been credited differentially to each of the three components of the framework. For instance, Mathieu, Goodwin, Heffner, Salas, and Cannon-Bowers (2000) conceptualized team cognition as an outcome, whereas others have considered collective cognition as an input in the IPO framework (e.g., Mohammed & Dumville, 2001). Others have viewed team cognition in terms of process behaviors such as leadership, assertiveness, adaptability, communications, planning, and decision

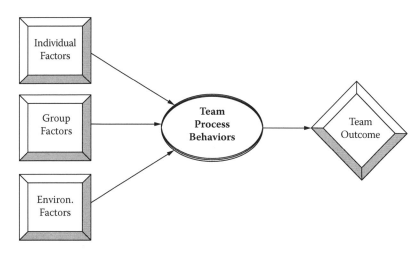

FIGURE 6.1
A generic input–process–output (IPO) framework.

making (Brannick, Prince, Prince, & Salas, 1995) that are thought to transform individual inputs into effective team outcomes. Most importantly for this discussion, there has been an increasing tendency to locate team cognition at the input portion of the IPO model. Accordingly, team cognition is often conceived as the collection of knowledge about the task and team held by individual team members (Figure 6.2).

Shared Mental Models

Theories of shared mental models are exemplary of input-oriented theories of team cognition that focus on knowledge or cognitive structure and rely heavily on individual measurement and aggregation. Researchers have demonstrated that team mental models greatly influence several aspects of the team including team process and team performance (Mathieu et al., 2000; Stout, Cannon-Bowers, Salas, & Milanovich, 1999). For instance, the shared mental model literature indicates that a high similarity of mental

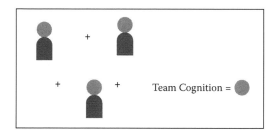

FIGURE 6.2
Team cognition as aggregate of team member knowledge.

models within a team should lead to effective team performance (Blick-ensderfer, Cannon-Bowers, & Salas, 1997; Converse, Cannon-Bowers, & Salas, 1991; Mathieu et al., 2000; Stout, 1995). Furthermore, high knowledge similarity within a team should lead to anticipatory process behaviors (Entin & Serfaty, 1999).

On the other hand, results stemming from shared mental model research have been inconsistent (see Cooke et al., 2003; Levesque, Wilson, & Wholey, 2001; Mathieu et al., 2000; Rentsch & Klimoski, 2001; Smith-Jentsch, Campbell, Milanovich, & Reynolds, 2001). Team member mental models are assumed to converge over time because of increased intrateam interaction (Clark & Brennan, 1991; Levesque et al., 2001; Liang, Moreland, & Argote, 1995; Moreland, 1999; Rentsch & Hall, 1994). Whereas some studies indicate that mental models converge with sheer experience and that this convergence predicts team performance (Rentsch & Klimoski, 2001; Smith-Jentsch et al. 2001), other studies do not find a relationship between convergence and team performance (Levesque et al., 2001). Some differences can be explained in terms of task or domain dependencies, whereas others may be linked to choice of measurement methods.

At the most basic level, the degree to which a mental model is shared by team members can be estimated through a comparison of the knowledge structures of team members. One way that shared mental models have been assessed in this manner is through comparisons of conceptual representations derived using Pathfinder (e.g., Stout et al., 1999). The similarity between two Pathfinder networks can be quantified in terms of proportion of shared links. Accuracy of a conceptual representation like Pathfinder can similarly be estimated through comparison with an expert or other referent representation. Other methods utilized to measure mental models are think aloud protocols, interviews, diagramming, and verbal troubleshooting (Rowe, 1994; Rowe & Cooke, 1995). When these methods have been applied to the measurement of team mental models, measurement tends to occur at the individual level, and individual team member results are aggregated for team-level measurement.

Although it has been central in the team cognition literature, the term *shared mental model* is somewhat ambiguous (Cooke, Salas, Cannon-Bowers, & Stout, 2000). First, the target of the mental model is not always clear (e.g., knowledge of the task, knowledge of team roles, understanding of equipment, and team member beliefs). The term *sharing* is equally vague. To share can mean to have or use the same entity (e.g., share the beliefs), but it can also mean to distribute (e.g., share the dessert) (Figure 6.3). In the context of team cognition and shared mental models, sharing can imply either knowledge similarity or common knowledge that is held among team members (i.e., everyone knows the same thing) or knowledge distribution in which knowledge is shared by apportioning it to team members according to expertise or role (Figure 6.4). In this sense knowledge

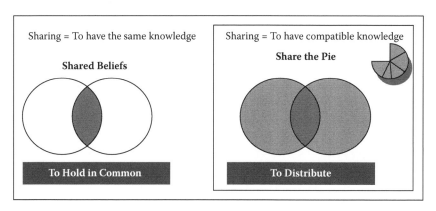

FIGURE 6.3
Two connotations of sharing.

is complementary, not common with respect to the team. It has been suggested that realistically, team knowledge is not likely completely common or distributed but rather overlapping with portions that are distributed or common (Cooke et al., 2000; Klimoski & Mohammed, 1994).

Team Situation Awareness

Another input-oriented and traditionally individual-knowledge-focused construct is team situation awareness (TSA). Shared mental models and TSA are theoretically linked in that a shared mental model—or a long-term understanding of the task, team, or equipment on the part of the team—is thought to be an important factor in TSA, and specifically in the construction

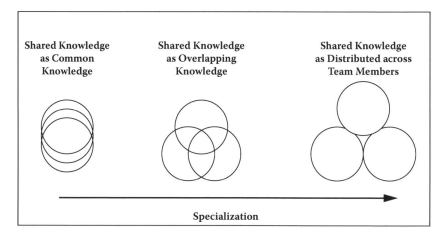

FIGURE 6.4
Varieties of shared knowledge (circles represent knowledge or mental models held by individual team members).

of a team situation model (Cooke, Stout, & Salas, 2001). A situation model is a representation of a state of the world or system that reflects a snapshot of a typically dynamic target. Like shared mental models, much theorizing on TSA has been adopted from theories of individual situation awareness.

The aviation industry has made situation awareness (SA) at the individual level a topic of much interest (Durso & Gronlund, 1999; Endsley, 1995; Fracker, 1989; Orasanu, 1995; Wellens, 1993). Endsley (1988) defined SA as "the perception of the elements in the environment within a volume of time and space, the comprehension of their meaning, and the projection of their status in the near future" (p. 97). Situation Awareness Global Assessment Technique (SAGAT) is a tool that has been utilized to measure TSA in a manner aligned with this definition (Endsley, 1995). SAGAT is administered using a freeze technique, where in the midst of an activity the activity is stopped and specific situation awareness probes, or queries, are answered by the participant. It is challenging to measure SA at the individual level in this manner because, among other reasons, the situation often changes more rapidly than individuals can be queried.

TSA has been defined as the collection of the SA (shared or unique) of individual team members (Bolstad & Endsley, 2003). To achieve a TSA score utilizing SAGAT, Bolstad and Endsley averaged each of the team member's scores. They reported results for a study involving U.S. Army officers participating in a simulation exercise. SAGAT, administered using the freeze technique, was used to measure each individual's situation awareness. Composite scores were then created by averaging the individual query score for each SAGAT query. Results indicated that accuracy on queries varied across the roles in the task and was not shared to the degree expected within the group; however, no information on performance was provided, and it is not clear whether these teams required a common understanding of the knowledge tested to do their jobs.

In the same way, Cooke et al. (2004) measured TSA in an unmanned air vehicle (UAV) ground control task using individual SAGAT-like queries. During UAV missions, questions were given that asked specific mission-related SA questions of each team member. In addition, a consensus measure was used in which the team as a whole was asked to respond after coming to consensus. This consensus procedure was an attempt to avoid aggregation. Unfortunately, the consensus process may have been unrepresentative of team process in the actual task, making the team result of questionable relevance to the real task. Although the aggregate-team SA correlated positively with team performance, there was concern that the measure was not as pertinent to the team's awareness of the situation as much as the awareness of the experimental procedure (e.g., anticipating upcoming queries).

Not all investigations of TSA have focused on knowledge. Other research in this arena has indicated that process factors such as early collection and exchange of information, coupled with planning, are linked with high levels of SA (Orasanu, 1995) and, furthermore, that high levels of SA are linked with high levels of performance.

Summary

Shared mental models and team situation awareness are two key constructs relevant to team cognition from an information-processing perspective. Both constructs are input oriented with regard to the IPO framework. That is, the knowledge involved in shared mental models and team situation awareness knowledge requirements are taken as the starting point in decision making or planning and other cognitive activity, leading to a final outcome. Thus, the measures tend to capture and represent knowledge of individuals and not the cognitive process across individuals. Finally, both constructs focus on the individual as the unit of analysis, not the team. This focus is also reflected in the individually oriented metrics and the aggregation process that transforms multiple individual results into a team result.

Not only are information-processing theories of team cognition intimately tied to the utilized measures, but they also have implications for the types of research questions asked and the kinds of interventions suggested by the results. For instance, the shared mental models and TSA constructs and surrounding theories tend to lead to research questions that center on team member knowledge similarity and the relationship between that similarity and performance. Findings that speak to this similarity may suggest applications for increasing knowledge similarity among team members such as shared displays or cross-training, but it is not clear that such applications would be beneficial for highly specialized teams.

Limitations of the Information-Processing View Applied to Team Cognition

The application of information processing to team cognition has generated numerous concepts, theories, metrics, and research findings. Like any perspective, it has its limitations; this section identifies some of them.

Heterogeneous Teams and Division of Labor

The information-processing perspective typically takes the individual as its unit of measurement and then aggregates across individuals on the same team to approximate the team level. Sometimes aggregation schemes can be quite complex and are based on hypotheses regarding team process

behavior (Hinsz, 1995, 1999). However, in most cases the aggregation procedure involves averaging or summation (e.g., Langan-Fox, Code, & Langfield-
Smith, 2000). Two assumptions lie behind these basic forms of aggregation.

First, underlying the most simple aggregation schemes (i.e., sum, average) is the assumption that all team members are equivalent when it
comes to their contribution (i.e., knowledge, skills, and abilities) to specific
team outcomes. Although this may be true for homogeneous groups that
one would find on juries or perhaps in business meetings or in classroom
experiments, it is not the case for heterogeneous teams. For instance,
emergency response teams bring together individuals with very different
skills and backgrounds to comprehensively address the emergency (e.g.,
weather, terrorism, aviation, HAZMAT, fire safety, and others depending
on the event). Examples of heterogeneous teams can be found in many
settings including operating rooms, nuclear power plants, military command and control, and commercial aviation. In fact, Salas et al.'s (1992)
definition of *team* stressed the fact that members are interdependent with
specific roles or functions to perform. Heterogeneity is also consistent
with the division of labor that becomes increasingly necessary with the
growing complexity of a task. It is not clear that averaging is appropriate
for a team that consists of highly differentiated team members.

Whereas one aspect of this limitation has to do with heterogeneity of
team member background, another has to do with the condition that even
for homogeneous teams with very similar backgrounds, participation in a
decision or problem solution may not be equivalent across team members.
Some team members may be more confident or vocal than others. Some
may have leadership qualities. Others may simply be having a bad day.
Averaging or summing scores across team members assumes that team
member inputs are all combined in the same manner. This limitation is
thus not one of heterogeneous structure, as is the first limitation, but rather
heterogeneous process. Heterogeneous process may be a natural byproduct of heterogeneous background (e.g., an expert in a particular area may
contribute more to a decision in that area than another nonexpert team
member). On the other hand, heterogeneous process may also be a factor
on homogeneous teams simply because there are individual differences
in participation style. To summarize, basic aggregation schemes are not
appropriate for teams that are heterogeneous in regard either to structure
(i.e., knowledge) or process.

In general, however, the most basic limitation is that the (linear) aggregate is treated as the whole. This is not appropriate for coupled processes,
such as team member interactions, which are usually nonlinear, involving
many interactions. For example, taking 12 individuals and telling them
each one word of a meaningful 12-word sentence, having them individually think about each word, and then adding together their reports of
these thoughts (not necessarily in the order of the original sentence) does

not faithfully reproduce the meaning of the sentence (cf. James, 1890/1950, p. 160). To accomplish this, the 12 must interact. A lack of incorporating interaction similarly limits the aggregation model for studying complex systems such as those in team environments.

Scalability Issues

As previously mentioned, the information-processing approach tends to evaluate team cognition in terms of knowledge similarity. Teams with members who are on the same page regarding taskwork and teamwork knowledge or who hold common mental models or a shared understanding of the situation are predicted to be more effective. However, the "common knowledge" criterion seems to break down as teams grow to sizes not typically reflected in the experimental work on team cognition. The "common knowledge" notion not only loses its meaning for heterogeneous teams but also becomes questionable as teams grow from three-person teams to the hundreds found in some military command-and-control environments. For these very large teams, is "common knowledge" still a reasonable objective? Pushed to its extreme we see decision-making biases such as "group think" (Janis, 1972) that result when too much is shared. It may also be that too much common knowledge on a very large team might lead to a type of "cognitive loafing" that parallels "social loafing" (Karau & Williams, 2001). In this latter case, several individuals may relinquish their participation in decision making because they perceive that their input is redundant and unneeded.

Admittedly exclusive reliance on the "common knowledge" criterion creates a straw man of the information-processing perspective. However, the concepts of similarity or sharedness are the basis of most current research on team cognition, including shared mental models and team situation awareness, even if the "common knowledge" criterion makes little sense as teams grow in size.

Decentralized/Self-Organizing Teams

The sheer volume of cognitive activity in modern work systems has tended to make centralized and hierarchical teams slow and unresponsive to rapid change. These considerations are linked to the elimination of a single dominant centralized or executive controlling mechanism in teams, which oversees all aspects of operations, and a growing need for decentralized and self-organized teams. A limitation of the information-processing view on team cognition is rooted in the emergence of decentralized and self-organized teams in military, business, and other sociotechnical environments (Appelbaum, 1997; Franz, 2004). Specifically, this type of team structure exhibits a high degree of functional, and dynamical, organization rather than assigned sets of routines. Team cognition in decentralized and self-organized teams leads to limitations for the information-processing view that can be described as two related computational problems when dealing with complex systems: (1) the problem of reduced degrees of freedom and (2) the problem of the delegating action in a highly complex environment.

As a computational problem delegating actions in a many-element system by a central controlling device (e.g., a shared mental model) can quickly become infeasible. In terms of computational complexity, tracking such a state space grows as nk^2, where n are subsystems and k are system elements—in this case, team members and their tasks. Clearly, this state space grows exponentially with the number of elements in the system and proportional to the number of subsystems controlling them. The second computational problem is how to achieve a reduction in the number of variables to be tracked and controlled. The degrees of freedom problem introduced by Bernstein (1967) involves a reduction in the number of variables (degrees of freedom) that need to be controlled to perform coordinated action. A functional or ecological description accomplishes this by defining systems (and subsystems) by the functions they serve. For our purposes, a team consisting of n team members, each responsible for k elements, can be reduced to a low dimensional parameter if we typify the supposed computational problem as one of mutual *adjustment* rather than of executive *control*. In other words, integration is central rather than differentiation. A parameter relevant to team cognition, for example, might be a variable that captures higher-order coordination as opposed to tracking the nk^2 elements individually.

Statics versus Dynamics in Team Cognition

Essentially a static (or static equilibrium) is a balance of forces, such that all forces are in a constant relation to one another and there is no dynamic component. Psychology does not deal with physical forces, however, but rather with information. In terms of team cognition then, by narrowing in on knowledge structure as opposed to process, information processing (IP) has become preoccupied with the acquisition of a static (knowledge) distribution of information across team members. In other words, what should be the constant and unchanging relations among team member knowledge for enhancing process and performance (Figure 6.5)?

However, in practice, teams must often go beyond a static model of the task to complete the task. For example, a UAV team can photograph targets even when one of several lines of crucial communication is cut (Gorman, Cooke, Pedersen, Connor, & DeJoode, 2005). Thus, the function can be identical even when the circumstances of the task are far from ordinary; that is, it can be *adaptive*. In light of this, team cognition may involve more than just a static distribution of knowledge; namely, novel (or self-organized)

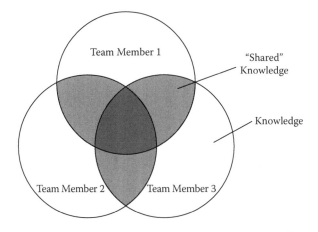

FIGURE 6.5
A static distribution of knowledge—in this case, situation awareness requirements.
(Adapted from Endsley, M. R. and Jones, W. M. (1997). Situation awareness, information
dominance and information warfare. *Technical Report 97–01*, US Air Force Armstrong Laboratory. With permission.)

interaction dynamics that are specific to novel task conditions. Though
a focus on team process over structure is a step in the right direction, IP
theory does not readily provide us with the analytical tools to proactively
address this sort of adaptive behavior on the part of the team. The issue of
team adaptation to novel task conditions will be revisited in our discussion of measuring TSA from an ecological perspective.

Empirical Evidence

Finally, based on the information-processing perspective, predictions that
can be made regarding the relationship between team cognition and team
performance appear to vary greatly with the task. In particular, the accuracy and intrateam similarity of knowledge is thought to be predictive of
team performance. In addition, as teams gain experience it has been proposed that degree of overlap among shared mental models increases.

However, some researchers failed to find convergence among mental
models over time despite finding general support for the relationship
between knowledge and performance (Mathieu et al., 2000), whereas others (Levesque et al., 2001) found that there is divergence among team members in terms of knowledge over time. This pattern might be expected for
teams with a high division of labor, whereas the former would not.

Numerous studies have reported correlations between team cognition
and team performance (Hinsz, Tindale, & Vollrath, 1997; Mathieu et al.,
2000; Stout et al., 1999), but others have found no relation. For instance,
manipulations affecting the process of knowledge sharing impacted the

knowledge or mental model but did not impact team performance (Cooke et al., 2003, 2004).

These mixed results are not surprising given the complexities involved in team research. Null results could arise for any number of reasons (e.g., low statistical power, and insensitive measures), and results in the unexpected direction often arise from task differences. However, it is also possible that the input-oriented constructs, central to the information-processing view of team cognition, only account for a small portion of variance in team cognition.

An Ecological Perspective

This section extends the ecological perspective described earlier to team cognition. It is proposed that the ecological approach to team cognition addresses many of the limitations of the information-processing approach. This discussion of the ecological perspective on team cognition focuses on team coordination and team situation awareness.

Whereas the information-processing perspective considers the locus of team cognition to be within the individual team member, the ecological approach views team cognition as an emergent feature that results from a history of interactions between team members. Thus, according to this view, measuring any aspect of the team independent of the team in action does not directly address team cognition. Operational definitions, therefore, need to be developed at the level of team activity, and specifically team member interaction. For example, how do we measure team members' communication, and how do we measure changes in patterns of interaction over time? Additionally, how do team members act as sources of information for other team members? Thus, the ecological perspective puts the focus on team activity and interaction dynamics rather than on individual knowledge and, as a result, raises a different set of research questions with different implications for theory and practice.

Team Coordination

What does it mean to consider team interaction as the fundamental unit of team cognition? Consider a general problem solver with the relatively simple goal of reaching a destination (Simon, 1981). Consider, as Simon did, an ant traversing a beach to reach a destination. The complexity of the ant's path is not the result of complex cognition on the ant's part but rather is rooted in the complexity of the task environment to which the ant is coupled (i.e., the undulations of the beach). Thus, the complexity of the ant's behavior lies at the intersection between the ant and the beach. We might say that the ant's behavior is coordinated with the layout of the beach. If we consider only the ant's "knowledge" independent of its coupling with the structure of the beach, we are left with an incomplete description of its behavior. A similar problem arises when we do not take team member–team member couplings to be the irreducible elements of team cognition. This is precisely where an ecological approach becomes most useful.

It is a relatively simple matter to demonstrate the utility of focusing on interaction dynamics in the examination of team cognition. Cooke et al. (2004) conducted a series of experiments on simulated unmanned aerial vehicle operations. Consider, for example, a sequence of observations made on the transcribed utterances of a single team member, without reference to the utterances of the other team members:

1. Okay, I am headed back on course now.
2. 2.5.
3. Yeah, we have now changed course to S-STE.
4. Go ahead.
5. Roger that.

This apparently incoherent sequence of utterances is similar to listening to one side of a telephone conversation. However, by embedding this sequence in the utterances from the other team members this sequence becomes meaningful and goal directed; that is, the amount of "randomness" in this conversation can be reduced by viewing it in light of surrounding constraints. In this case, the utterances are coordinated with the structure of the conversation:

1. Okay, I am headed back on course now.

   What's the radius for PRK?

2. 2.5.

   OK. Your altitude seems really low.

3. Yeah, we have now changed course to S-STE.

   AVO I have some more information … . Would you let me know when you are ready for that information?

4. Go ahead.

   Immediately after S-STE, you will need to dive down to max. 1000 altitude. Does that make sense?

5. Roger that.

Whereas the explanatory utility of embedding action in context may seem obvious, we have found it seldom used in team cognition applications. As noted already, this is not surprising given the computational complexity involved in studying the embedded behavior of teams from an information-processing perspective. Thus, we have made efforts to develop low-dimensional (relative to the number of team members) ecological measures of team cognition—that is, measures taken at the team member–team member and team member–environment level of analysis.

In our most recent round of UAV experiments, we measured the "pushing and pulling" of information elements specific to the timing of navigation and photographing of ground targets by a team of three UAV team members: a pilot, navigator, and photographer. Three information elements were identified for this purpose: t_I, navigator provides pilot information; t_N, back-and-forth negotiation between photographer and pilot and t_F, feedback from photographer to all. Essentially, these three elements are interrelated over time; that is, they may overlap reconnaissance targets. However, a more general question is whether these elements serve as mutual informational constraints on team cognition over time; in other words, can they be integrated into a measure of coordination?

We developed a local optimal model (LOM) that relates each of the information elements to each other (Figure 6.6). In the model, the onset of navigator to pilot information, I, is ideally the first element in the sequence, followed by pilot and photographer negotiation, N, which culminates with feedback, F, from the photographer. The slope of the line relating the onset times $F - I$ to the times $F - N$ gives a measure with two qualitative states separated by a transition point at

$$F - I / F - N = 1$$

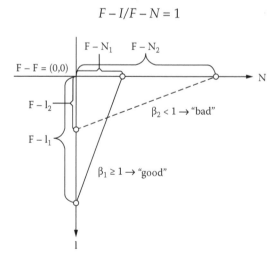

FIGURE 6.6
The slope relating the onset of elements I, N, and F as a measure of coordination.

Deviations less than 1 indicate poor coordination relative to the LOM, whereas deviations greater than 1 indicate good coordination relative to the LOM. Specifically, high scores (> 1) indicate a high degree of frontloading in terms of route planning, whereas low scores (< 1) indicate the absence of any such frontloading. These scores can be further modeled using time-scaling techniques (Gorman, 2005) to gauge the amount of randomness versus development of constraint in terms of deviations from the nominal strategic process embodied in the LOM. These models also provide more detailed information concerning various "styles" of coordination by teams treated differently in an experiment. For example, these models can tell us if teams in one condition should develop stricter, mean-reverting coordination "boundaries" compared with teams in another condition.

Team Situation Awareness

In general system-theoretic terminology (Von Bertalanffy, 1969), the perturbation of an element of a system will have an effect on other elements of the system. In terms of coordination dynamics this means that perturbation of a team member, or team members, can push the trajectory of the team as a whole off its course. In contrast to the more traditional information-processing knowledge elicitation methods, we have been exploring these concepts as a way to measure TSA relative to experimental perturbation (or "roadblock"), which pushes coordination dynamics away from its mean state. A well-placed (or from a team's perspective, badly placed) roadblock can displace the trajectory of team coordination, such that teams will require some time before reacquiring their stable trajectory (Figure 6.7). In this case, the timing of three information elements—information, negotiation, and feedback—that normally approximate a line when plotted against each other is pushed away from this trajectory by a TSA roadblock; recovery time is an index of team coordination stability.

Rooted in ecological psychology, firsthand perception (Reed, 1996) is the notion that given a division of labor, each team member will experience the roadblock in a different way. For example, a pilot and a photographer will perceive a sudden drop in altitude in different ways, depending on their role in the team. In the first case, this can alter the pilot's experience of control and in the second the photographer's judgment of camera zoom settings. If these two share their unique perspectives of the roadblock with each other, then each now has an additional perception of the road-block, albeit secondhand, and may facilitate a coordinated perception of the unwanted perturbation. Likewise, assuming that the various unique perspectives are coordinated, a team may be able to enact a solution that overcomes a roadblock by responding as a coordinated whole. It is crucial, however, to point out that this sort of team-level awareness is not purely introspective or knowledge based; it is predicated on adaptation via team

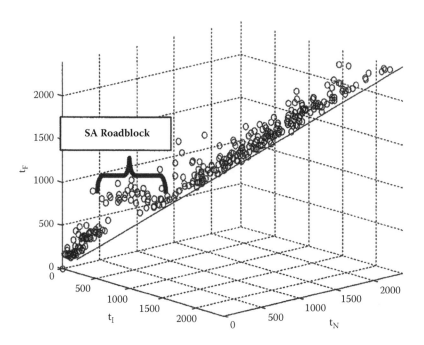

FIGURE 6.7
Team coordination dynamics in response to a situation awareness "roadblock."

member interaction. Further, situational roadblocks, whether experimentally introduced or observed in reports of events (e.g., report of events of September 11, 2001), should be embodied in situational exigencies that are extrinsic to the normal course of team operations. Thus, any sort of unusual event that impacts the functional synergy of a team may be ripe for measuring team SA.

In our most recent set of experiments we began introducing three types of roadblocks to teams (Cooke et al., 2007): (1) unusual changes to the task environment (e.g., ad hoc targets); (2) unforeseen UAV route constraints (e.g., enemy activity); and (3) unpredictable cutting of communication links (e.g., navigator to pilot). These were introduced to see if teams noticed and, if so, what they did about it. These roadblocks were also designed so that if not successfully addressed, teams' performance would be impaired; that is, they would not be able to take a photo of their target. The Coordinated Assessment of Situation by Teams (CAST; Gorman et al., 2005) measure was taken by monitoring team communication and action during exposure to the roadblock at three levels: (1) independent/firsthand perception; (2) secondhand/coordinated perception; and (3) coordinated action (Figure 6.8).

For analysis, each roadblock event was characterized as a signal detection trial. Specifically, some subset of check boxes (or "links"; Figure 6.8)

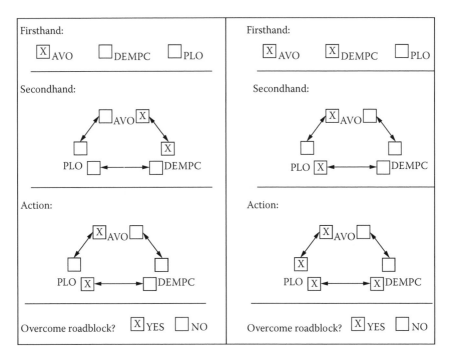

FIGURE 6.8
The CAST TSA instrument.

was necessary (signal) and some boxes were not (noise) to accurately identify and deal with specific roadblocks. These formed a set of "normative
vectors" that corresponded to the optimal solutions of the various roadblocks. Hits and false alarms—proportions of necessary links versus
unnecessary links, respectively—were computed for each roadblock
against the normative vectors. Here we present results calculated across
all three components of the CAST instrument.

Figure 6.9 shows the average sensitivity to roadblocks (up and left
diagonal distance from the dashed line) of teams before and after an
experimental manipulation. The experimental manipulation was a retention interval (3 to 11 weeks) crossed with the familiarity of team members
on returning from the retention interval (either they returned with the
same team members or a new set of team members). Our results suggest
that teams had similar sensitivity to the roadblocks prior to the experimental manipulation. Postmanipulation however, there were differences
in team TSA involving both accuracy of response and inefficiency, or oversharing, during the response. Gorman et al. (2005) argued that this sort of
oversharing of information is inefficient (especially for larger teams) and
could be considered maladaptive. However, this oversharing is implied
as necessary to generate a shared mental model in which the team holds

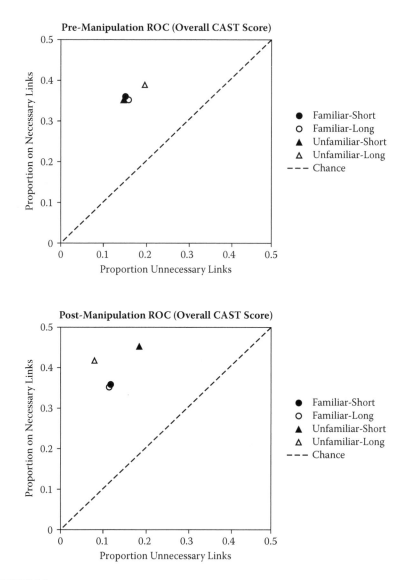

FIGURE 6.9
Mean premanipulation TSA (top); mean postmanipulation TSA (bottom); team sensitivity to roadblock manipulation can be interpreted as proximity to the upper left corner of the graphs.

all information in common. Specifically, high hit rate coupled with low false-alarm rate is indicative of the right information getting to the right person at the right time—and no more than this—in light of an unusual situation. This was most common in the unfamiliar, long retention interval teams. This result may lend itself to further hypotheses, including the need for team member turnover, especially over longer retention intervals, to facilitate good team TSA processes rather than to attempt to instill a shared mental model.

Conclusions

The framework within which we conceptualize team cognition has important implications for theory building, measurement, training and assessment, and design relevant to team cognition. We conclude with examples of such implications.

For theory, the implications should be quite clear, yet a simple analogy is made. The questions and analysis of information-processing and ecological theories of team cognition can resemble, say, the analysis of water, which may take two levels, respectively. Should we analyze H_2O or the flow of this substance H_2O? On one level we would analyze the combining of the parts H and O and on another how the flow (parts not withstanding) pervades over various strata. In a like manner, the study of team cognition can be reduced to an analysis of parts or, alternatively, how it flows over various surfaces, or situations. In our research we have found the latter to be more beneficial to understanding the cognitive abilities of teams (Cooke et al., 2007). Notwithstanding this result, these two perspectives formulate entirely different questions (not to mention levels of analysis) of team cognition. Two are discussed next. The first is the information-processing perspective; namely, questions are addressed at the level of the individual, and then these are summed to the team level. The second is the ecological view, in which questions are addressed to the interaction and the level of the individual does not come into play. Each approach may be capable of good or harm; nevertheless, between these alternatives the scientist must choose, and theories (and thus measures) will obtain at a like scaling. In short, the scientist must choose between analyzing the elements (information processing) or the flow (ecological perspective).

We have also provided some examples of measures that have been inspired by ecological views of team cognition. In general, the ecological focus is on measuring communication and interaction as opposed to static and situational knowledge. As always the perspective prescribes the measure. For instance, under the ecological perspective we have been inspired to measure coordination, a team phenomenon that has received minimal attention under the information-processing perspective. The perspective also prescribes how to measure. The example of team situation awareness measures is relevant here in that query-based measures such as SAGAT

(Bolstad & Endsley, 2003) are much different than Gorman et al.'s (2005) interaction-based measure, CAST.

The perspective taken on team cognition also has interesting implications for training and design. How should we train or design for teams to enhance team cognition and, therefore, team performance? A shared mental model view advocates training or design that facilitates the convergence of knowledge. For instance, cross-training in which team members are indoctrinated into the tasks and roles of other team members has been thought to induce shared mental models (Cannon-Bowers, Salas, Blickensderfer, & Bowers, 1998). Likewise, shared or common displays in which team members can view information used primarily by other team members might also promote knowledge sharing (Endsley, 1988). Alternatively, an ecological perspective would focus more on the interaction. Team performance would be improved according to this perspective by focusing on communication, interaction, or coordination variation in situ. In addition, perturbations to coordination may positively affect training, so instead of cross-training each team member, members assume the same team role but are mixed with new team members or perturbed with roadblocks for some variety in coordination.

In summary, the ecological approach to team cognition offers an alternative way of thinking about team cognition that has unique implications for theory, measurement, training, and design. These ecological ideas open up new possibilities for research and development and are open to revision. Even in this early stage, however, the ecological perspective on team cognition illustrates the practical benefits of having one or even more good theories to guide improvements in team performance.

References

Appelbaum, S. H. (1997). Socio-technical systems theory: An intervention strategy for organizational development. *Management Decision*, 35, 452–463.

Bernstein, N. A. (1967). *The co-ordination and regulation of movements*. Oxford: Pergamon Press.

Blickensderfer, E., Cannon-Bowers, J. A., & Salas, E. (1997). *Training teams to self-correct: An empirical evaluation*. Paper presented at the Meeting of the Society for Industrial and Organizational Psychology, St. Louis, MO (April 10–13).

Bolstad, C. A. & Endsley, M. R. (2003). Measuring shared and team situational awareness in the Army's future objective force. In *Proceedings of the Human Factors And Ergonomics Society 47th annual meeting* (pp. 369–373). Santa Monica, CA: Human Factors and Ergonomics Society.

Brannick, M. T., Prince, A., Prince, C., & Salas, E. (1995). The measurement of team process. *Human Factors, 37*, 641–651.

Cannon-Bowers, J. A., Salas, E., Blickensderfer, E., & Bowers, C. A. (1998). The impact of cross-training and workload on team functioning: A replication and extension of initial findings. *Human Factors, 40,* 92–101.

Clark, H. & Brennan, S. E. (1991). Grounding in communication. In L. B. Resnick, J. Levine, & Teasley (Eds.), *Socially shared cognition.* Washington, DC: American Psychology Association.

CNN (2005). *Hurricane Katrina: CNN Reports: State of Emergency.* Kansas City, KS: Andrew McMeel Publishing.

Collyer, S. C. & Malecki, G. S. (1998). Tactical decision making under stress: History and overview. In J. A. Cannon-Bowers & E. Salas (Eds.), *Decision making under stress: Implications for individual and team training* (pp. 3–15). Washington, DC: American Psychological Association.

Converse, S., Cannon-Bowers, J. A., & Salas, E. (1991). Team member shared mental models. *Proceedings of the 35th Human Factors Society annual meeting,* (pp.1417–21). Santa Monica, CA: Human Factors and Ergonomics Society.

Cooke, N. J., DeJoode, J. A., Pedersen, H. K., Gorman, J. C., Connor, O. O., & Kiekel, P. A. (2004). *The role of individual and team cognition in uninhabited Air Vehicle Command-and-Control.* Technical Report for AFOSR Grants F49620-01-1-0261 and F49620-03-1-0024.

Cooke, N. J., Gorman, J. C., Pedersen, H. K., Winner, J. L., Duran, J., Taylor, A., Amazeen, P. G., & Andrews, D. (2007). *Acquisition and retention of team coordination in command-and-control.* Technical Report for AFOSR Grant FA9550-04-1-0234 and AFRL Award No. FA8650-04-6442.

Cooke, N. J., Kiekel, P.A., Salas, E., Stout, R. J., Bowers, C., & Cannon-Bowers, J. (2003). Measuring team knowledge: A window to the cognitive underpinnings of team performance. *Group dynamics: Theory, research and practice, 7,* 179–199.

Cooke, N. J., Salas, E., Cannon-Bowers, J. A., & Stout, R. (2000). Measuring team knowledge. *Human Factors, 42,* 151–173.

Cooke, N. J., Stout, R., & Salas, E. (2001). A knowledge elicitation approach to the measurement of team situation awareness. In M. McNeese, E. Salas, & M. R. Endsley (Eds.), *New trends in cooperative activities: Understanding system dynamics in complex environments* (pp. 114–139). Santa Monica, CA: Human Factors and Ergonomics Society.

Durso, F. D. & Gronlund, S. D. (1999). Situation awareness. In F. T. Durso, R. Nickerson, R. Schvaneveldt, S. Dumais, M. Chi, & S. Lindsay (Eds.), *The handbook of applied cognition* (pp. 283–314). London: Wiley.

Durso, F. T., Nickerson, R., Schvaneveldt, R., Dumais, S., Chi, M., & Lindsay, S. (Eds., 1999). *The handbook of applied cognition.* London: Wiley.

Endsley, M. R. (1988). Design and evaluation for situation awareness. In *Proceedings of the Human Factors Society 32nd annual meeting* (pp. 97–101). Santa Monica, CA: The Human Factors and Ergonomics Society.

Endsley, M. R. (1995). Measurement of situation awareness in dynamic systems. *Human Factors, 37,* 65–84.

Endsley, M. R. and Jones, W. M. (1997). Situation awareness, information dominance and information warfare. *Technical Report 97–01,* US Air Force Armstrong Laboratory.

Entin, E. E. & Serfaty, D. (1999). Adaptive team coordination. *Human Factors, 41,* 312–325.

Eysenck, M. W. & Keane, M. T. (2000). *Cognitive psychology: A student's handbook.* Philadelphia: Taylor & Francis Inc.

Fracker, M. L. (1989). Attention allocation in situation awareness. In *Proceedings of the Human Factors Society 33rd annual meeting* (pp. 1396–1400). Santa Monica, CA: The Human Factors and Ergonomics Society.

Franz, G. F. (2004). *Decentralized command and control of high-tech forces: Aligning practice with doctrine at the operational level.* Newport, RI: Naval War College.

Gibson, J. J. (1966). *The senses considered as perceptual systems.* Boston: Houghton-Mifflin.

Gibson, J. J. (1979). *The ecological approach to visual perception.* Boston: Houghton-Mifflin.

Gorman, J. C. (2005). The concept of long memory for assessing the global effects of augmented team cognition. *Proceedings of the 11th International Conference on Human-Computer Interaction,* July 22–27, Las Vegas, NV.

Gorman, J. C., Cooke, N. J., Pedersen, H. K., Connor, O. O., & DeJoode, J. A. (2005). Coordinated awareness of situation by teams (CAST): Measuring team situation awareness of a communication glitch. *Proceedings of the Human Factors and Ergonomics Society 49th Annual Meeting,* Orlando, FL, 274–277 Santa Monica, CA: Human Factors and Ergonomics Society.

Hackman, J. R. (1987). The design of work teams. In J. W. Lorsch (Ed.), *Handbook of organizational behavior* (pp. 315–342). Englewood Cliffs, NJ: Prentice Hall.

Heft, H. (2001). *Ecological psychology in context.* Mahwah, NJ: Erlbaum.

Hinsz, V., Tindale, R. S., & Vollrath, D. A. (1997). The emerging conceptualization of groups as information processors. *Psychological Bulletin, 121,* 43–64.

Hinsz, V. B. (1995). Group and individual decision making for task performance goals: Processes in the establishment of goals in groups. *Journal of Applied Social Psychology, 25,* 353–370.

Hinsz, V. B. (1999). Group decision making with responses of a quantitative nature: The theory of social decision schemes for quantities. *Organizational Behavior and Human Decision Processes, 80,* 28–49.

James, W. (1904). Does "consciousness" exist? *Journal of Philosophy, Psychology, and Scientific Methods, 1,* 477–491.

James, W. (1950). *The principles of psychology* (vol. 1). Mineola, NY: Dover. (Original work published 1890.)

Janis, I. L. (1972). *Victims of groupthink: A psychological study of foreign-policy decisions and fiascoes.* Boston: Houghton Mifflin.

Karau, S. J. & Williams, K. D. (2001). Understanding individual motivation in groups: The collective effort model. In M. E. Turner (Ed.), *Groups at work: Theory and research* (pp. 113–141). Mahwah, NJ: Erlbaum.

Klimoski, R. & Mohammed, S. (1994). Team mental model: Construct or metaphor? *Journal of Management, 20,* 403–437.

Lachman, R., Lachman, J. L., & Butterfield, E. C. (1979). *Cognitive psychology and information processing: An introduction.* Hillsdale, NJ: Erlbaum.

Langan-Fox, J., Code, S., & Langfield-Smith, K. (2000). Team mental models: Techniques, methods, and analytic approaches. *Human Factors, 42,* 242–271.

Levesque, L. L., Wilson, J. M., & Wholey, D. R. (2001). Cognitive divergence and shared mental models in software development project teams. *Journal of Organization Behavior, 22,* 135–144.

Liang, D. W., Moreland, R. L., & Argote, L. (1995). Group versus individual training and group performance: The mediating role of transactive memory. *Personality and Social Psychology Bulletin, 21,* 384–393.

Mathieu, J. E., Goodwin, G. F., Heffner, T. S., Salas, E., & Cannon-Bowers, J. A. (2000). The influence of shared mental models on team process and performance. *Journal of Applied Psychology, 85,* 273–283.

Mohammed, S. & Dumville, B. C. (2001). Team mental models in a team knowledge framework: Expanding theory and measurement across discipline boundaries. *Journal of Organizational Behavior, 22,* 89–106.

Moreland, R. L. (1999). Transactive memory: Learning who knows what in work groups and organizations. In L. Thompson, J. Levine, & D. Messick (Eds.), *Shared cognition in organizations: The management of knowledge* (pp. 3–31). Mahwah, NJ: Lawrence Erlbaum Associates.

Orasanu, J. M. (1995). Evaluating team situation awareness through communication. In D. J. Garland & M. R. Endsley (Eds.), *Proceedings of an International Conference on Experiment Analysis and Measurement of Situation Awareness* (pp. 283–288). Daytona Beach, FL: Embry–Riddle Aeronautical University Press.

Reed, E. S. (1996). *The necessity of experience.* London: Yale University Press.

Rentsch, J. R. & Hall, R. J. (1994). Members of great teams think alike: A model of team effectiveness and schema similarity among team members. In M. M. Beyerlein & D. A. Johnson (Eds.), *Advances in interdisciplinary studies of work teams: Theories of self-managing work teams* (Vol. 1, pp. 223–262). Greenwich, CT: JAI Press.

Rentsch, J. R. & Klimoski, R. J. (2001). Why do "great minds" think alike?: Antecedents of team member schema agreement. *Journal of Organizational Behavior, 22,* 107–120.

Rowe, A. L. (1994). *Mental models of physical systems. Examining the relationship between knowing and doing.* Unpublished doctoral dissertation, Rice University, Houston.

Rowe, A. L. & Cooke, N.J. (1995, Fall). Measuring mental models: Choosing the right tools for the right job. *Human Resource Quarterly, 6*(3), 243–255.

Salas, E., Dickinson, T. L., Converse, S. A., & Tannenbaum, S. I. (1992). Toward an understanding of team performance and training. In R. W. Swezey & E. Salas (Eds.), *Teams: Their training and performance* (pp. 3–29). Norwood, NJ: Ablex.

Simon, H. A. (1981). *The sciences of the artificial.* Cambridge, MA: MIT Press.

Smith-Jentsch, K. A., Campbell, G. E., Milanovich, D. M., & Reynolds, A. M. (2001). Measuring teamwork mental models to support training needs assessment, development, and evaluation: Two empirical studies. *Journal of Organizational Behavior, 22,* 179–194.

Stout, R. J., (1995). Planning effects on communication strategies: A shared mental models perspective. *Proceedings of the Human Factors and Ergonomics Society 39th Annual Meeting,* (pp. 1278–1282). Santa Monica, CA: Human Factors and Ergonomics Society.

Stout, R. J., Cannon-Bowers, J. A., Salas, E., & Milanovich, D. M. (1999). Planning, shared mental models, and coordinated performance: An empirical link is established. *Human Factors, 41,* 61–71.

Vaughan, D. (1996). *The challenger launch decision: Risky technology, culture, and deviance at NASA.* Chicago: University of Chicago Press.

Von Bertalanffy, L. (1969). *General system theory.* New York: George Braziller.

Wellens, A. R. (1993). Group situation awareness and distributed decision mak-
    ing: From Military to civilian applications. In N. J. Castellan, Jr., *Individual
    and Group Decision Making* (pp. 267–291). Hillsdale, NJ: Lawrence Erlbaum.

7

Overcoming Barriers to Collaboration: Psychological Safety and Learning in Diverse Teams

Amy C. Edmondson and Kathryn S. Roloff

Introduction

A nurse working the night shift in a busy urban hospital makes her evening rounds—reviewing patients' treatment plans, taking temperatures, and administering medications. She notices that the dosage for one of the patient's meds seems a bit high. Fleetingly, she considers calling the doctor at home to check the order. Just as fleetingly, she recalls the doctor's disparaging comments about her abilities the last time she called. All but certain the dose is in fact fine (the patient has an unusual condition and is on an experimental protocol, justifying the high dose), she pulls the drug from the supply cabinet and heads for the patient's bed.

In the nurse's hesitation and almost imperceptible decision not to call the physician, she has implicitly considered—and effectively discounted—the possibility that a patient may be harmed. The discount is not caused by a lack of caring about human life; quite the contrary, she has devoted her career to caring for and helping to heal the sick. Instead, in that subtle moment of opportunity to voice rather than suppress a concern, her brain has exaggerated the importance of the doctor's scorn and minimized to near zero the chance of future harm to the patient.

Far from the urban hospital, a young pilot in a military training flight notices that the senior pilot, a captain, may have made a crucial misjudgment but lets the moment go by without pointing out the error. The young pilot not only is of lower rank and status but also is formally evaluated on every flight. The prospect of speaking up to the superior officer brings significant emotional costs, even though the pilots are intended as interdependent members of a cockpit team. Unlike the nurse, the pilot chooses silence possibly over preservation of his own life. Here again, he discounts the chances that not speaking up will lead to a fatal crash and possibly exaggerating the anticipated discomfort of being chastised or ignored.

A senior executive, recently hired by a successful consumer products company, has grave reservations about a planned takeover. New to the top-management team, and conscious of his own status as an outsider, he remains silent because other executives seem uniformly enthusiastic. Many months later, when it is clear the takeover has failed badly, the team gathers to review what happened. Aided by a consultant, each executive muses on what he or she might have done to contribute to, or fail to avoid, the failure. The newest member, a relative outsider, reveals his prior concerns, openly apologetic about his past silence, explaining—with palpable emotion—that the others' enthusiasm left him afraid to be "the skunk at the picnic."

A research scientist located in the United Kingdom and working on a new product development team with eight members in five countries and three continents concludes that a Japanese manufacturing engineer is obstructing progress. Unfamiliar with business norms in Japan, the British scientist assumes that the information she wanted existed and was frustrated when it was not forthcoming from the distant team member. Later she would learn that the desired information represented a genuine gap in the engineer's knowledge of his customer and that the engineer had not understood the significance of certain veiled criticisms coming from other team members.

Why Collaboration Is Hard

Collaboration is "the coming together of diverse interests and people to achieve a common purpose via interactions, information sharing, and coordination of activities" (Jassawalla & Sashittal, 1998, p. 239). The vignettes at the outset of the chapter—based on real data, shortened and deidentified, but gathered during extensive field research in hospitals, the military, and large corporations—capture moments of failed collaboration. Moments like these—some but not all with the potential for severely negative consequences—happen countless times throughout the day in almost every workplace, usually without much conscious attention.

When uncertainty clouds our tentative thoughts and views, which seem at odds with those of others', we take the path of reduced interpersonal resistance; it feels natural to do so in all but the most familiar settings. It happens when a lot is at stake (e.g., a patient's health, an aircraft's safety, a costly takeover) and when not much is at stake (e.g., a small improvement idea not communicated to the individual or team who could act on it). Either way, the silence, along with the incomplete thoughts that lie behind the silence, inhibits team learning in organizations that depend on such learning for their ongoing viability and survival. What explains these lapses of team communication?

An underlying premise in this chapter is that effective communication across disciplinary, status, geographic, or other boundaries is particularly challenging under conditions of uncertainty, as illustrated in all four of the previous vignettes. It is proposed that psychological safety may mitigate the communication challenges such differences may pose. Psychological safety describes a climate in which people feel free to express work-relevant thoughts and feelings. Seemingly simple, expressing work-relevant thoughts and feelings can be unexpectedly challenging when those thoughts stand a chance to oppose or disagree with the views of others and when uncertainty makes it hard to know for sure that one is right or how one might be received. Yet this is what is required of teams and team members to realize the promise of collaboration across differences.

The Popularity of Teams

Among the benefits of teams is their ability to integrate diverse expertise as needed to accomplish complex, uncertain work that is difficult to plan, structure, and subdivide in advance. Although historically the focus of team studies was on reorganizing production processes, increasingly team studies extend far beyond the factory floor. Top-management teams develop corporate strategies; sales teams sell sophisticated products and services to complex organizational customers; product development teams (often geographically dispersed) develop sophisticated new technologies; and project teams design and implement organizational change initiatives. Each of these examples involves people, often with very different backgrounds or expertise, working interdependently to accomplish challenging goals. Their tasks may vary in terms of the degree of interdependence and the amount of collaboration that is required, but they have in common the need for individuals to communicate across boundaries to get the job done. This chapter examines team cognitions and processes that affect collaboration.

The use of teams is increasingly popular in organizations. According to Manufacturing Performance Institute's Census of Manufacturers for 2004, 80% of respondents report using teams to accomplish their business goals compared with about 70% in 2003. As Glenn Parker (2003) noted, generalism has replaced specialization, collaboration has replaced autonomy, empowerment has replaced power, and teamwork has replaced individualism (p. 1).

Despite the fact that team use is steadily increasing, team effectiveness is not keeping up at the same pace. In the same report, only about 14% of organizations surveyed rated their teaming efforts as "highly effective" whereas just over half (50.4%) rated their teams as "somewhat effective." In short, although utilizing teams can be efficient and effective, it is difficult to achieve the maximum potential teams have to offer.

The need to communicate across differences in culture, expertise, status, or location is one reason for this difficulty. To begin with, teams at work are likely to be increasingly diverse. According to a report by the U.S. Equal Employment Opportunity Commission (2003), minority group representation in management positions has substantially increased over the past decade. Although increasing diversity in the workforce is a potential asset, the ability of organizations to use the benefits of cultural diversity varies. Further, teams often encompass differences in disciplinary training accompanied by different assumptions, jargon, and other barriers to communication. Some teams also face geographic dispersion (i.e., differences in location), clearly a barrier to easy communication. Finally, status differences can inhibit open communication as they did in the first two vignettes that opened this chapter.

Chapter Overview

This chapter focuses on the construct of psychological safety and how it might moderate the effects of diversity on collaboration, learning, and performance in teams. In the pages that follow, we examine what has been learned in a growing body of research on psychological safety and team learning. We then review and illustrate three types of team diversity and consider the implications of these differences for collaboration. Finally, we present a conceptual model depicting the relationship between psychological safety and diversity-based barriers to collaboration and learning (Figure 7.1).

Research on Psychological Safety and Learning in Teams

Psychological safety has been defined as a belief that one is not at risk of embarrassment or rejection in a particular setting or role (Edmondson, 1999b). The term captures the degree to which people perceive their

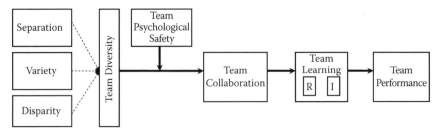

FIGURE 7.1
Conceptual model.

work environment as conducive to taking the kinds of interpersonal risks previously described. In psychologically safe work environments, people believe that if they make a well-intentioned mistake others will not think less of them for it and that those others will not resent or penalize them for asking for help, information, or feedback. This usually tacit, or taken for granted, belief fosters the confidence to take interpersonal risks, allowing oneself and one's colleagues to learn.

History of Psychological Safety Research

More than 40 years ago, Schein and Bennis (1965) noted that psychological safety was important for enabling organizational change, because employees had to feel secure and capable of changing their behavior for larger-scale change to occur. Since that time, several researchers have explored psychological safety in work settings. Schein (1985, pp. 298–299) argued that psychological safety helps people overcome the defensiveness, or "learning anxiety"—which occurs when people are faced with change, ambiguity, and uncertainty in their work environment—by creating an environment that is not threatening. With psychological safety, individuals are free to focus on collective goals and problem prevention rather than on self-protection.

Kahn (1990) argued that psychological safety enables personal engagement at work. His richly described settings included an architectural firm and a summer camp. He studied how psychological safety affects individuals' willingness to *engage* (i.e., to "employ or express themselves physically, cognitively and emotionally during role performances") rather than to *disengage* (i.e., to "withdraw and defend their personal selves") (p. 694). Kahn suggested that psychological safety was one of three psychological conditions that influenced the behavior of the team members studied. Support and trust were seen as important components of interpersonal relationships that promote psychological safety. Further, Kahn argued that individuals would be more likely to believe they would be given the benefit of the doubt—a defining characteristic of psychological safety—when relationships within a given group were characterized by trust and respect.

West (1990), researching teams in hospitals and other organizations in the United Kingdom, discussed a similar construct, *participative safety*, and related it to learning and innovation, drawing from qualitative and quantitative field research. West defined participative safety as "a construct in which the contingencies are such that involvement in decision-making is motivated and reinforced while occurring in an environment which is perceived as interpersonally non-threatening" (p. 311).

Edmondson (1999b) introduced *team psychological safety* as a group-level construct, meaning that it characterizes the team as a unit rather than as individual team members. Consistent with this, her empirical research found that perceptions of psychological safety tend to be highly similar among people who work closely together (e.g., members of an intact team) both because team members are subject to the same set of contextual influences and because these perceptions develop out of salient shared experiences (e.g., Edmondson, 1999b, 2003a; Nembhard and Edmondson, 2006). For example, members of a team will conclude that making a mistake does not lead to rejection when they have had team experiences in which appreciation and interest are expressed in response to discussion of their own or others' mistakes.

Team psychological safety suggests neither a careless sense of permissiveness nor an unrelentingly positive affect in a team but rather members' confidence that their team will not embarrass, reject, or punish someone for speaking up. This confidence stems from mutual respect and trust among team members. Team psychological safety thus involves but goes beyond interpersonal trust; it describes a team climate characterized by interpersonal trust and mutual respect in which people are comfortable being themselves (Edmondson, 1999b).

Team psychological safety is not the same as *group cohesiveness*. Notably, research on *groupthink* suggested that cohesiveness could reduce— rather than enhance—willingness to disagree and to challenge others' views (Janis, 1982), thereby limiting rather than enabling interpersonal risk taking in a group. Similarly, creating psychological safety is not a matter of "being nice," nor does the term suggest an absence of pressure or problems. Rather, it describes a climate in which the focus can be on productive—if difficult—discussion that enables early prevention of problems and accomplishment of shared goals, because people are less likely to focus on self-protection. Conversation in environments high in psychological safety may be unusually direct and even confrontational, because people are less focused on self-protection and are thus less likely to choose their words overly cautiously. For this reason, particular attention has been paid to psychological safety in the clinical psychology literature as an important element of the therapeutic context (Rappoport, 1997; Swift & Copeland, 1996).

Psychological Safety Research across Levels of Analysis

Recent research on psychological safety includes individual and organizational levels of analysis, in addition to the group level (Table 7.1). At the organizational level, Baer and Frese (2003) noted a significant relationship between psychological safety and overall firm performance in a study of 47 firms. The researchers collected survey data on the psychological climate of organizations in midsized industrial and service sector firms and

TABLE 7.1

Illustrative Research on Psychological Safety at Three Levels of Analysis

Level	Relationship	Outcome	Researchers
Individual	Supervisor–subordinate	Information sharing	Tynan (2005)
Group	Individual–team	Team learning	Edmondson (1999b)
Organization	Team–firm	Firm performance	Baer & Frese (2003)

found that firms with greater overall levels of psychological safety outperformed other firms.

Another recent study by Tynan (2005) applied the construct of team psychological safety to the individual level. Studying the relationship between supervisors and employees in a laboratory setting, Tynan defined individual psychological safety as having two dynamic components: self and other. *Self* psychological safety was defined as how safe an individual feels in relation to a specific target person, and *other* psychological safety was defined as an individual's perception of how safe a specific other person feels.

Against this background of prior research, the focus of this chapter is on the group-level construct of team psychological safety. Following Edmondson (2002), we note that much of the essential learning that takes place in organizations happens in teams. In particular, production teams are positioned to continuously improve operational performance, product development teams to innovate in ways that can ensure the future success of the organization, and senior management teams to develop new strategy. All three of these team-based activities constitute essential organizational learning. Further, research links team learning to team performance, which also promotes overall firm performance (Edmondson, 2002; Edmondson and Smith, 2006; Senge, 1990).

Team Psychological Safety

In recent models of team psychological safety (e.g., Edmondson, 2004; Edmondson & Mogelof, 2006), several antecedents of psychological safety have been proposed, including leader behavior—notably leadership inclusiveness (Nembhard & Edmondson, 2006), trusting and respectful interpersonal relationships, the use of "practice fields" (Senge, 1990), and individual differences in personality. Leadership behavior is an especially critical antecedent. Field research on teams consistently finds that team leaders play an important role in creating a climate of psychological safety (e.g., Edmondson, 1999b, 2003b). Team leaders promote psychological safety by explicitly inviting input and feedback, especially while modeling openness and fallibility themselves (Edmondson, 2003a, 2003b; Nembhard and Edmondson, 2006). Through coaching, team leaders can release exclusive knowledge from individuals, thus overcoming the natural tendency of teams to rely on shared knowledge (Edmondson, 1999b, 2003b).

Proposed consequences included help seeking, feedback seeking, speaking up about errors and concerns, innovative behavior and innovation, and boundary spanning (Edmondson, 1999a, 2004; Baer & Frese, 2003). Although some of these proposed relationships have not yet been tested empirically, a few have the benefit of initial empirical support—notably the relationships between psychological safety and speaking up, learning behavior, boundary spanning, and innovation, as well as the relationship between leader behavior and psychological safety (Edmondson, 1996, 1999a, 1999b, 2003a, 2003b).

Speaking Up

In a study of operating room teams, speaking up was paramount to the success of team outcomes, specifically in implementing a new technology. In hospital settings, the interpersonal climate can be particularly daunting when it comes to taking risks by speaking up due to the salient power hierarchies that exists within medical teams. Team leaders are usually high-status senior physicians who, in some cases, can be intimidating to lower-status team members. This visibility characterizes military settings as well; status (rank) is literally worn on the uniform, and less visible elements of status are also extremely clear and salient to others. In this surgical study, team leaders played a critical role in mitigating self-censorship by inviting team members to speak, motivating team members toward goals, and minimizing the effect of status differences, in some cases, by explicitly stating that all team members' roles are important (Edmondson, 2003b).

Recently, Detert and Edmondson (2006) explored the intrapersonal experience of considering whether or not to speak up at work. This qualitative research found that individual voice decisions are influenced by individual differences and organizational context, as previously assumed, but also by very specific features about the situation, such as who is present and the topic of the latent voice episode. This study also examined the costs of this silence to both individuals and their organizations. When individuals decide not to speak, organizations lose the opportunity to learn from the observations, knowledge, or suggestions of these individuals who concluded that the cost of speaking outweighs the potential benefit.

Learning from Failure

The role of psychological safety in error reporting and quality improvement efforts in health-care settings has received much attention (e.g., Carroll & Quijada, 2004; Michie & West, 2004; Edmondson, 1996; Nembhard & Edmondson, in press; Tucker & Edmondson, 2003; Wakefield et al., 2001).

Recent research investigated the relationship between professional status and psychological safety in hospitals and its effect on improvement efforts. Notably, although psychological safety increased, on average, with professional status, in some work groups inclusive leadership mitigated the status differences. These groups had greater engagement in quality improvement (Nembhard & Edmondson, 2006) and more extensive team-learning activity (Tucker, Nembhard, & Edmondson, 2006).

Beyond error reporting, team members have shared beliefs about the interpersonal consequences of failure—specifically, insidious social influences about tolerance (or lack thereof) for failure to prevent team members from speaking up (Cannon & Edmondson, 2001). Meanwhile, failure can serve as a valuable learning experience for teams and organizations. Team leaders who reduce the interpersonal threat associated with failure by promoting psychological safety are more likely not only to find out about the failure but also to proactively engage in team learning. Team learning is a broader construct that encompasses some of the specific proactive behaviors previously discussed, such as speaking up and error reporting.

Team Learning

Individual learning is conceptualized by Argyris and Schon (1978) as a process of detecting and correcting errors. In this iterative process, actions are taken, reflected on, and modified in an ongoing way (Kolb, 1984; Schon, 1983). Organizational learning has been conceptualized as the encoding of inferences from history into routines that guide behavior (Levitt & March, 1988). It is a process through which organizations modify their behavior by sharing knowledge, insights, and mental models and by building on past knowledge and experience (Stata, 1989). Thus, organizational learning is a change process of some sort (Schein, 1985). Likewise, team learning has been defined as a "process of reflection and action, characterized by asking questions, seeking feedback, experimenting, reflecting on results, and discussing errors or unexpected outcomes of action" (Edmondson, 1999b, p. 353), which results in "a relatively permanent change in the team's collective level of knowledge and skill" (Ellis et al., 2003, p. 882). Note that, as defined, team learning should be enabled by collaboration, which includes information sharing and coordination of activities. Under conditions of even modest uncertainty or change, team learning is likely to result in improved team performance (Edmondson, 1999b). As organizations rely more heavily on teams to accomplish work, team learning is essential for organizational learning and change (Edmondson, 2002; Senge, 1990).

Team learning does not happen automatically (Edmondson, Bohmer, & Pisano, 2001; West, 2000) but instead requires coordination and some degree of structure to ensure that insights are gained from members' collective experience and are also used to guide subsequent action (Edmondson, 2003a). Some of the critical structural factors that support psychological safety and hence impact learning are team leader behavior, clear learning goals, and a team-learning orientation.

Team leaders play a critical role in team learning (Edmondson, 1999b) as well as in psychological safety. One study found that learning increases as team leaders involve team members more in the decision-making process (Sarin & McDermott, 2003). Team leaders must provide the structure necessary for learning while mediating the interpersonal climate enough so that team members feel safe taking risks.

Additionally, shared goals are considered a prerequisite for team effectiveness (Hackman, 1987), and goals also can motivate the collective learning process. In a study of new product development teams Lynn, Akgun, and Keskin (2003) discussed *vision clarity*, or having a clear team goal, as a central motivating factor to team learning. The degree to which team leaders provide structure by outlining goals and expectations increases learning (Sarin & McDermott, 2003). Collective identification, the emotional significance that the members of a given group attach to their membership in that group, can mediate team learning and performance, generally the higher the collective team identification is, the better the performance outcomes (Van Der Vegt & Bunderson, 2005).

Goals and structures are important for learning in other ways. Tjosvold, Yu, and Hui (2004) found that having cooperative team goals—rather than engaging in efforts to escape responsibility for mistakes—promotes a problem-solving orientation. This orientation puts mistakes to good use by reducing blaming and promoting learning. Similarly, Bunderson and Sutcliffe (2003) recognized that encouraging, emphasizing, and rewarding collective team-learning goals fosters more effective team learning. A learning-goal orientation stresses an emphasis on development of skill, knowledge, and competence as opposed to a performance goal orientation, which emphasizes demonstrating competence and avoiding failure (ibid.). Cannon and Edmondson (2001) showed that shared beliefs about failure are a group-level construct and that they affect a team's ability to learn from mistakes.

In addition to emphasizing a learning or problem-solving orientation, learning can be induced in more direct ways. Notably, Zellmer-Bruhn (2003) studied three large firms from the pharmaceutical industry to see how interruptions in team routines affected learning. She found that interruptions in team processes could spur knowledge-transfer efforts and hence could increase the acquisition of new team routines.

Finally, teams engage in different kinds of learning depending on their structure and purpose. For example, new product development teams might be expected to exhibit more learning behavior than production teams because of the nature of their task (Edmondson, 1999b). Different team types engage in different learning processes, which can be categorized into *radical* learning and *incremental* learning: The former invents and explores new possibilities, and the latter improves existing processes (Edmondson, 2002). Most product development teams can be classified as engaging in radical learning that requires creating new combinations of knowledge and dramatically new products and processes. In contrast, most production teams are positioned to engage in incremental learning—improving the efficiency and quality of current organizational products and processes. Most organizations require both types of learning for continued success in a changing and competitive market environment.

This review is concluded by noting that team learning should not only promote a team's performance but, when conducted widely and with some level of coordination in an organization (Edmondson, 2002), should also be related to the organization's performance.

> *Proposition 1:* Team learning directly promotes team performance and indirectly promotes organizational performance.

The next section proposes a set of theoretical relationships antecedent to Proposition 1. Specifically, the effects of diversity on collaboration among members—viewed as necessary for team-learning behavior—are explored, and a moderating effect of psychological safety is proposed. Our focus is on collaboration because of its emphasis on integrating diverse interests or people to achieve a common purpose, a central aim of teams in today's organizations.

Diversity, Psychological Safety, and Collaboration in Teams

Today's organizations employ individuals with diverse skills and experiences, often requiring them to work together to accomplish challenging interdisciplinary projects. As organizations continue to push the front of technology and become more global in their orientation, the need for diverse teams is likely to increase. Despite the benefit diversity holds for teams, harnessing the payoff associated with diversity is difficult (Chatman & Flynn, 2001; Ely & Thomas, 2001; Foldy, 2004; Lau & Murnighan, 2005).

At the same time, the challenge of collaborating across differences (e.g., gender, expertise, or status) is also substantial. In this section, examples of diversity that might affect team process are described. We draw from Harrison and Klein (2007) to organize these examples of diversity into three conceptual types. It is posited that these three types capture the essential differences faced by members of organizational work teams. The likely impact of these differences on collaboration and team learning are then summarized, and the role that psychological safety plays in ensuring that differences are harnessed and put to good use in teams is described.

Three Types of Diversity

Diversity is a topic of central importance in organizational research on teams. However, researchers have lacked consensus on a clear definition of diversity, diluting the interpretability of different findings. Within-team diversity has been defined as "the distribution of differences among the members of a unit with respect to a common attribute X" (Harrison & Klein, 2007, p. 4). Common attributes include gender, ethnicity, professional status, or educational degree. A team is considered diverse if its members differ in respect to at least one attribute.

Beyond its definition, the theoretical construct of diversity lacks clarity in the literature. Recently, therefore, Harrison and Klein (2007) posited that diversity can be conceptualized in three ways: *separation, variety,* and *disparity*. Diversity manifested as separation occurs when group differences in a particular attribute take different values along a horizontal continuum. For example, differences in opinion with respect to a particular issue represent a form of separation diversity, as do differences in time zone or physical location. For diversity manifested as variety, group differences are classified categorically. For example, differences in educational degrees categorize individual members into groups like "psychologists" or "engineers" constituting variety diversity. Lastly, for diversity manifested as disparity, group differences fall along a vertical continuum ranked according to the social value of a particular attribute. For example, differences in professional status among team members present a form of disparity diversity.

In what follows, we examine examples of each of the three types of diversity and their impact on collaboration. First we examine location differences within teams as a form of separation diversity. Second, we discuss the impact of differences in team member expertise, a form of variety diversity. Third, we discuss professional status differences in team members as an example of disparity diversity. In addition, we briefly consider demographic diversity, which includes both variety diversity—differences in demographic features—and disparity diversity, when demographic attributes are associated with differences in social power.

Separation

Psychologically, individuals have a strong preference for perceived in-groups and a bias against perceived out-groups (Tajfel, 1970). From this understanding, it is clear that when salient horizontal differences exist between members of a team, individuals will categorize members into their in-group or out-group depending on similarity to or distance from them. In terms of teams, individuals have been found to prefer homogeneity over heterogeneity due to a preference for the perceived similarity in values, attitudes, and beliefs between members of a homogenous in-group (Herriot & Pemberton, 1995). Team homogeneity has also been found to enhance trust and communication among members (Pfeffer, 1983; Schneider, 1987); however, the quality of the communication is likely to be narrow in scope and less useful for accomplishing team goals.

Despite deeply entrenched cognitive biases toward similarity, it is well established that group conformity leads to groupthink and interferes with the creative processes of teams (Janis, 1982). Many researchers have noted that positive conflict arises from disagreement and stimulates learning and collaboration in teams (Gibson & Vermeulen, 2003). However, achieving the learning that can come from conflict is difficult when disagreements arise because differences in values, attitudes, or belief are deeply personal (Edmondson & Smith, 2006).

Another form of separation diversity is literal separation. A growing number of teams work across different locations. Noted David Arnold (2004, p. 1), "Companies are globalizing." In many global companies, work teams in geographically dispersed locations all over the world are used to integrate expertise. Oftentimes teams at specific locations develop *situated knowledge,* or site-specific work practices and understanding (Sole & Edmondson, 2002). Sole and Edmondson found that situated-knowledge functions are a form of tacit team knowledge, as illustrated in the final anecdote with which this chapter opened. Such location-specific knowledge can be a source of useful input for geographically dispersed work teams, yet it can go ignored and underutilized much the same way tacit-individual knowledge is underutilized without team psychological safety.

An additional issue posed by geographically distributed work teams is balancing local needs with global efficiency. Global companies tend to emphasize global integration as opposed to emphasizing responsiveness and knowledge management, which ultimately decreases learning in teams (Zellmer-Bruhn & Gibson, 2006). Two challenges arise: First, global companies must seek to actively access situated knowledge; second, global companies must effectively balance global integration with unique local needs.

Teams are unlikely to be totally homogenous in terms of beliefs, attitudes, or opinions. Similarly, it is likely that effective collaborations across borders will be challenging.

Proposition 2a: Separation diversity in a team inhibits collaboration.

Variety

There are many potential categorical differences among team members. Team members may vary in terms of gender, ethnicity, educational degree, and countless other ways. One of the major sources of variety diversity in organizational work teams stems from differences in expertise. Strategically, organizations choose to combine individuals with various sources of experience and education to add to the pool of team knowledge; however, teams often have difficulty adequately accessing and managing this unique knowledge.

Teams with high levels of expertise differences are often called cross-functional teams. Such teams with multidisciplinary integration are on the rise in organizations, especially for innovation projects. Under the right conditions, expertise differences can stimulate learning behaviors in teams (Van Der Vegt & Bunderson, 2005).

Cross-functional teams are useful in organizations for multiple reasons. These teams serve as a mechanism for combining different sets of highly specialized skills into one cohesive group. The obvious benefit of this form of collaboration is the qualified, high-level information that can be brought to the table by each team member. On the other hand, specialized team members can become spokespersons for their discipline, resulting in reduced flexibility and increased conflict (Lovelace, Shapiro, & Weingart, 2001). When the team's learning goal is relinquished for political agendas and ego associated with discipline identity, teamwork is reduced and consensus becomes difficult. However, the conflict that arises in groups with expertise differences can improve team learning because it is caused in part by the sharing of multiple perspectives and scenarios while preventing the threats of groupthink.

In addition to expertise differences, demographic differences serve as a major source of variety diversity in work teams. Stemming from the increases in travel and immigration aided by the technological advances of the 20th century, the United States is becoming home to increasingly more cultures. At the same time, mobility within the United States has led to an increase in other demographic differences such as age, gender, and regional origin in the workplace. Organizations recognize this trend and often create diverse teams to access unique cultural perspectives. Yet merely having members of various cultures on a team is not enough to realize the associated benefits (Foldy, 2004). Lau and Murnighan (2005) found that when significant cultural differences are apparent in groups, oftentimes individuals will identify stronger with their cultural subgroup rather than with the group.

Individuals identify with cultural subgroups for many reasons. First, team members that belong to team cultural minorities are often unique by virtue of number. Being in the cultural minority is often an obvious part of an individual's identity, and these individuals perceive their evaluation as a team member as tied to their cultural identity.

In short, teams with variety diversity combine individuals who come from a wide range of backgrounds, thus maximizing the range of experience, knowledge, and information available to a team. Yet it is clear that the collaboration necessary to access these resources is difficult to achieve. Team members must be willing to share their unique knowledge with the team. We thus posit a negative main effect of variety diversity on collaboration.

Proposition 2b: Variety diversity in a team inhibits collaboration.

Disparity

Disparity diversity may be the most challenging source of diversity for ensuring collaboration. When differences between members fall on a vertical scale where those at the top have the most power and those at the bottom have the least, lower-power individuals may find it hard to speak up, as illustrated in our opening vignettes from the hospital and cockpit. Considerable research has shown that speaking "up" in a hierarchical setting is challenging and has documented the silencing effects of status differences (see, e.g., Detert & Edmondson, 2006 for a review). Although work teams face many differences in power, there are two major sources that most team must deal with: ethnicity and professional status.

Although demographic differences are categorical, they sometimes also fall along a power hierarchy due to the nature of social power hierarchies in the United States; for example, power differences in organizations have been documented for gender and race (e.g., Ely & Thomas, 2001). Individuals cognizant of the threat of negative stereotypes associated with cultural identity may become hindered by self-fulfilling prophecies (Steele & Aronson, 1995) or a perceived need to "overcome" negative stereotypes before being valued on equal turf with the other members of the team. Similarly, unconscious negative stereotypes significantly hinder the team's performance by virtue of team members "dancing around the issue," which allows negative stereotypes to arise in other, more subtle ways (Gaertner & Dovidio, 2005).

Teams and organizations that work to actively acknowledge and utilize unique cultural knowledge, ipso facto, support many of the same factors associated with increased psychological safety, notably respect for different points of view and norms of openness in communication. Thus, in culturally diverse teams, members' perspectives on cultural diversity can serve to increase or decrease team psychological safety and team learning. When teams are initially formed, cultural diversity can promote team learning by including a wide range of perspectives that increase the amount of team knowledge; however, over time if these power hierarchies associated with ethnic differences persist, then these differences can limit the effectiveness of communication and hence collaboration (Schippers, Den Hartog, Koopman, & Wienk, 2003). Thus, over time, without an active attempt to reduce power differences, ethnic diversity is likely to limit the effectiveness of communication by silencing less powerful team members and hence reducing collaboration in a team. This is in part because members of different identity groups—whether based on age, race, gender, or cultural background—come to the team with different taken for granted assumptions that, when left unexplored and unchallenged, can give rise to misunderstandings.

Teams can also encompass differences in professional status, another form of disparity diversity. Professional status has been found to significantly impact team beliefs about psychological safety (Nembhard & Edmondson, 2006). Team members are well aware of the benefits that come with professional status. Yet even team members with identical professional identities can have status differences (consider resident-level and senior attending physicians working together to care for patients, or the pilots with whom this chapter opened). When teams include one or more members of different status, the stakes for taking interpersonal risks increase for the lower-status members. Lower-status team members are particularly fearful of the negative consequences associated with perceived incompetence such as decreased chances of promotion or salary raise. Such fears can prohibit a candid flow of discourse that is replaced instead by politeness and indirectness, abstract conversation, and feigned reflective discussion (Edmondson, 2002).

The insidiousness of fear provoked in individuals on teams where hierarchical status differences are particularly salient can lead to disaster. In the case of the Space Shuttle *Columbia* disaster in February 2003, status differences between aerospace engineers and top-management leaders precluded the engineers from speaking up in a crucial mission management team meeting with concerns about foam strikes, contributing to the ultimate tragedy of the failed mission and loss of eight astronauts' lives (Edmondson, Roberto, Bohmer, Ferlins, & Feldman, 2005).

In summary, social hierarchies in teams can significantly hinder collaboration by rendering team members fearful and lacking in power. Although sometimes these effects are unintentional, the potential withdrawal and silence of affected team members poses a significant threat to collaboration.

Proposition 2c: Disparity diversity in a team inhibits collaboration.

TABLE 7.2

Examples of Team Diversity

	Demographic	Expertise	Location	Status
Type of diversity	Variety or disparity	Variety	Separation	Disparity
Composition of team	Multiple identity groups based on demographic origins	Multiple sets of skills and expertise based on education and work experience	Geographically dispersed team members	More than one status level
Team challenges	Tacit knowledge based on culture, gender, race, age or other salient identity	Team members who identify with expertise-related subgroups over team identity	Creating a team goal adapted to multiple local needs	Social norms of deference to authority
Collaboration enabled by	Sharing individual perspectives Creating an orientation toward valuing cultural differences	Sharing expertise-based knowledge as possible Fostering a collective group identity	Periodic visits to other sites Attention to unique local knowledge and focus on shared goal	Leadership inclusiveness to minimize experienced status gaps

When Diversity Types Co-Occur

Diversity in a team—as separation, variety, or disparity—creates the potential for integration of different perspectives, whether in management, product development, military operations, or health-care delivery (Table 7.2 presents examples of team diversity). Yet, as argued already, this integration, which is accomplished by collaboration across differences, may not always happen. Further, the three types of diversity are not mutually exclusive; teams are likely to contain combinations of them. Harrison and Klein (2007) cautioned that the effects of each type of diversity behave very differently in groups depending on the distribution of differences. For example, an emergency room (ER) team composed of nurses, residents, and physicians faces issues of status, expertise, and often demographic differences as well. Teams with more than one kind of diversity will face even more serious barriers to collaboration, particularly if the areas of diversity overlap, creating deeper fissures, or "fault lines" (Lau & Murnighan, 2005). Fault lines occur when two or more identity groups in a team show a high degree of overlap (e.g., gender and function, or status and expertise), increasing the chances of conflict. Recent empirical work shows that such fault lines in teams increase the chances of conflict, which also suggests that collaboration will be harmed.

Proposition 2d: Multiple types of diversity in a team will further inhibit collaboration.

As exemplified in Table 7.2, various types of diversity create potential barriers to collaboration, but each can be overcome on its own through careful attention to group process. For demographic differences, it is helpful to ensure that the unique perspectives that come with age, gender, race, or cultural background are discussable, which can help people value these differences and see them as resources for the group's task. This approach—integration and learning perspective (Ely & Thomas, 2001)—has been shown to help diverse teams in a law firm work together. Similarly, expertise diversity can be mitigated by skillful sharing of relevant knowledge and by a strong collective group identity (Van Der Vegt & Bunderson, 2005). Field research on dispersed teams showed that visiting each others' sites was a powerful way to build trust and understanding and to facilitate collaboration long after the visits were over (Sole & Edmondson, 2002). When teams were able to discover and leverage site-specific knowledge, the teams were better able to take advantage of their rich sources of diversity. Finally, the communication inhibiting effects of status differences (Lee, Edmondson, Thomke, & Worline, 2004) are mitigated by leadership inclusiveness, in which higher-status individuals in a group actively invite and express appreciation for the views of others (Nembhard & Edmondson, 2006).

Mitigating Diversity-Based Barriers to Collaboration and Team Learning

In this section, we develop a model in which psychological safety moderates the negative main effects of diversity on collaboration proposed in the previous section. First, we discuss the relationship between collaboration and learning in teams and then argue that psychological safety can help team members overcome diversity-based barriers to the open communication and integration of perspectives that are critical to effective collaboration.

Collaboration and Team Learning

Candid communication between team members is a mechanism by which teams tap into tacit, closely held individual knowledge. Releasing individually held knowledge is critical for achieving team learning and thus successful team performance (Edmondson, 1999b, 2002, 2004). Further, team learning has been defined as a group process that includes sharing information, discussing errors and problems, and seeking feedback

—activities that are inherently collaborative, and so we propose that collaboration in teams enables team learning.

Proposition 3: Collaboration promotes team learning.

As discussed earlier in this chapter, team learning is a critical component of team performance (Edmondson, 1999b). Likewise, effective collaboration is a necessary component of team learning. Despite the barriers to collaboration discussed already, research has shown that diversity within teams can stimulate team-learning behavior when the organization context supports open communication (Gibson & Vermeulen, 2003). We posit that psychological safety is a critical component of the organizational context that moderates a team's ability to overcome barriers to collaboration, improving team learning and thus team performance.

Psychological Safety as a Moderator

Research on diverse groups has suggested that specific organizational context variables (e.g., empowerment and knowledge management systems) are highly influential in stimulating learning in diverse teams (Gibson & Vermeulen, 2003). Likewise, we suggest that psychological safety is another such variable that facilitates the appropriate conditions to release individual knowledge, ultimately stimulating learning behavior.

Prior work has shown that psychological safety is associated with team learning. Here we argue that, particularly for diverse teams, psychological safety moderates the relationship between diversity and collaboration and learning. Psychological safety helps create a forum where differences can be brought to the surface and discussed without fear of consequences. Similarly, Lau and Murnighan (2005) suggested that psychological safety would reduce the harmful effects of fault lines on conflict, and Van Der Vegt and Bunderson (2005) showed that collective identification, defined in such a way that psychological safety would surely be simultaneously present, moderated the negative effects of expertise diversity on team learning. When the team climate fostered an emotional connection to membership in that group, likely enabling psychological safety, moderate levels of expertise diversity positively influenced team learning and performance. In contrast, when emotional connection to membership was low, expertise differences were less likely to be utilized well, reducing the potential for team learning and performance (Van Der Vegt & Bunderson, 2005). In short, without psychological safety, expertise differences are more likely to lead to communication difficulties than when psychological safety is present (Edmondson, 1999b; Lau & Murnighan, 2005).

For each of the three barriers to collaboration and team learning presented herein, a key issue is a lack of effective communication between team members. Therefore, fostering a climate of psychological safety in such diverse teams may stimulate collaboration and learning.

> *Proposition 4:* Psychological safety moderates the negative relationship between team diversity and collaboration, allowing diverse teams to collaborate and learn and thereby achieving challenging team and organizational goals.

Furthermore, if teams facing more than one collaboration barrier experience significantly greater obstacles to collaboration than teams without such barriers then, as argued already, psychological safety may be progressively more important for teams with multiple types of diversity.

> *Proposition 5:* The need for psychological safety for collaboration and learning increases as the number of types of differences increases.

Conclusion

This chapter argues that team diversity poses barriers to collaboration in teams, largely through impeding effective communication. At the same time, we suggest that effective collaboration among diverse individuals—integration of differences toward shared goals—is essential for both team learning and team performance in complex and uncertain contexts. Superficial or ingenuous conversation may soothe in the short run but is likely to block progress in the longer run. This is especially true for teams engaged in innovation and involved in other work activities that call for behavioral and organizational change.

Building on prior work that shows a relationship between psychological safety and team learning, we proposed a new set of relationships in which psychological safety is conceptualized as a moderator of a theoretical negative relationship between team diversity and collaboration. Specifically, we argued that psychological safety enables team diversity to be better accessed and leveraged—reaping the benefits associated with a diverse set of skills, experiences, knowledge, or backgrounds—in ways that would not be possible if team members are unwilling to take the interpersonal risks associated with speaking up and listening carefully to each other. We also offered a brief review of research suggesting that team-learning behavior has positive effects on team and organizational outcomes. Teams are essential learning units in organizations, so when teams are learning organizations are learning, generally with positive effects for organizational performance (Edmondson, 2002; Senge, 1990).

Team diversity—a complicated theoretical construct as well as a complex real-world phenomenon—has been the topic of considerable research to date. Much of this research has been lab based rather than occurring in real organizations. In part, this may be because of the messiness or complexity of diversity in real teams—which rarely encompass only one type of difference—so it can be difficult to separate effects of different kinds of diversity in the field. At the same time, field research offers the opportunity for surprises that lead to new insights. Each of the vignettes that opened this chapter qualified, at the time of their discovery, as such a surprise. Together, they remind us that human beings can fail to act in their own or in their organization's best interest when small interpersonal risks loom large in the moment and that communication with colleagues can be thwarted in mundane ways, despite shared aims and considerable motivation to achieve them. We therefore propose that including the construct of psychological safety in future research on team diversity, collaboration, and learning would be valuable.

In sum, team learning is essential for organizations in dynamic and uncertain environments but is difficult to accomplish, especially when teams are composed of diverse members. Creating psychologically safe environments in diverse teams is a way to overcome implicit assumptions that limit collaboration and learning and to unlock the enormous potential of team collaboration.

References

Abraham, R. (2004). Emotional competence as an antecedent to performance: A contingency framework. *Genetic, Social, and General Psychology Monographs, 130*(2), 117–143.

Akgun, A. E., Lynn, G. S., & Reilly, R. (2002). Multi-dimensionality of learning in new product development teams. *European Journal of Innovation Management, 5*(2), 57–72.

Alderfer, C. P. (1987). An intergroup perspective on organizational behavior. In J. W. Lorsch (Ed.), *Handbook of organizational behavior* (pp. 190–222). Englewood Cliffs, NJ: Prentice Hall.

Argyris, C. & Schon, D. (1978). *Organizational learning: A theory of action perspective.* Reading, MA: Addison-Wesley.

Arnold, D. (2004). *The mirage of global markets: How globalizing companies can succeed as markets localize.* Upper Saddle River, NJ: Pearson Education, Inc.

Ashford, S. J. & Cummings, L. L. (1983). Feedback as an individual resource: Personal strategies of creating information. *Organizational Behavior and Human Performance, 32*(3), 370–399.

Baer, M. & Frese, M. (2003). Innovation is not enough: Climates for initiative and psychological safety, process innovations, and firm performance. *Journal of Organizational Behavior, 24*(1), 45–68.

Barrick, M. R., Stewart, G. L., Neubert, M. J., & Mount, M. K. (1998). Relating member ability and personality to work processes and team effectiveness. *Journal of Applied Psychology, 83*(3), 377–391.

Bunderson, J. S. & Sutcliffe, K. M. (2003). Management team learning orientation and business unit performance. *Journal of Applied Psychology, 88*(3), 552–560.

Cannon, M. D. & Edmondson, A. C. (2001). Confronting failure: Antecedents and consequences of shared beliefs about failure in organizational work groups. *Journal of Organizational Behavior, 22*, 161–177.

Cannon, M. D. & Edmondson, A. C. (2005). Failing to learn and learning to fail (intelligently): How great organizations put failure to work to innovate and improve. *Long Range Planning, 38*, 299–319.

Carroll, J. S. (1998). Organizational learning activities in high-hazard industries: The logics underlying self-analysis. *Journal of Management Studies, 35*(6), 699–717.

Carroll, J. S. & Quijada, M. A. (2004). Redirecting traditional professional values to support safety: Changing organizational culture in health care. *Quality & Safety in Health Care, 13s*, 16–21.

Chatman, J. A. & Flynn, F. J. (2001). The influence of demographic heterogeneity on the emergence and consequences of cooperative norms in work teams. *Academy of Management Journal, 44*(5), 956–974.

Creed, D. W. E. & Miles, R. E. (1995). Trust in organizations: A conceptual framework linking organizational forms, managerial philosophies, and the opportunity cost of controls. In R. M. Kramer & T. R. Tyler (Eds.), *Trust in organizations: Frontiers in theory and research* (pp. 16–38). Thousand Oaks, CA: Sage Publications.

DeCremer, D., Snyder, M., & DeWitte, S. (2001). The less I trust, the less I contribute (or not)? The effects of trust, accountability, and self-monitoring in social dilemmas. *European Journal of Social Psychology, 31*, 93–107.

Detert, J. R. & Edmondson, A. C. (2006). *Latent voice episodes: The situation-specific nature of speaking up at work.* Harvard Business School Working Paper 06-024, Boston, MA.

Edmondson, A. C. (1996). Learning from mistakes is easier said than done: Group and organizational influences on the detection and correction of human error. *Journal of Applied Behavioral Science, 32*(1), 5–28.

Edmondson, A. C. (1999a). A safe harbor: Social psychological factors affecting boundary spanning in work teams. In Mannix, B., Neale, M. & R. Wageman (Eds.), *Research on Groups and Teams* (pp. 179-200). Greenwich, CT: Jai Press, Inc.

Edmondson, A. C. (1999b). Psychological safety and learning behavior in work teams. *Administrative Science Quarterly, 44*(2), 350–383.

Edmondson, A. C. (2002). The local and variegated nature of learning in organizations: A group-level perspective. *Organization Science, 13*(2), S17–S34.

Edmondson, A. C. (2003a). Managing the risk of learning: Psychological safety in work teams. In M. West (Ed.), *International handbook of organizational teamwork and cooperative working* (pp. 255–276). London: Blackwell.

Edmondson, A. C. (2003b). Speaking up in the operating room: How team leaders promote learning in interdisciplinary action teams. *Journal of Management Studies, 40*(6), 1419–1452.

Edmondson, A. C. (2004). Psychological safety, trust and learning: A group-level lens. In R. Kramer & K. Cook (Eds.), *Trust and distrust in organizations: Dilemmas and approaches* (pp. 239–272). New York: Russell Sage.

Edmondson, A. C., Bohmer, R. M., & Pisano, G. P. (2001). Disrupted routines: Team learning and new technology implementation in hospitals. *Administrative Science Quarterly, 46*(4), 685–716.

Edmondson, A. C. & Mogelof, J. P. (2006). Examining psychological safety in innovations teams. In L. Thompson & H. Choi (Eds.), *Creativity and innovation in organizations* (pp. 109–136). Mahwah, NJ: Lawrence Erlbaum Associates Press.

Edmondson, A. C., Roberto, M. R., Bohmer, R. M. J., Ferlins, E. M., & Feldman, L. R. (2005). The recovery window: Organizational learning following ambiguous threats. In M. Farjoun & W. Starbuck (Eds.), *Organization at the limits: NASA and the* Columbia *disaster* (pp. 220–245). London: Blackwell.

Edmondson, A. C. & Smith, D. M. (2006). *Too hot to handle? Engaging hot conflict to make better decisions and build resilient management teams.* Harvard Business School Working Paper 06-030, Boston, MA.

Ellis, A. P. J., Hollenbeck, J. R., Ilgen, D. R., Porter, C. O., West, B. J., & Moon, H. (2003). Team learning: Collectively connecting the dots. *Journal of Applied Psychology, 88*(5), 821–835.

Ely, R. J. & Thomas, D. A. (2001). Cultural diversity at work: The effects of diversity perspectives on work group processes and outcomes. *Administrative Science Quarterly, 46*(2), 229–273.

Foldy, E. G. (2004). Learning from diversity: A theoretical explanation. *Public Administration Review, 64*(5), 529–538.

Gaertner, S. L. & Dovidio, J. F. (2005). Understanding and addressing contemporary racism: From adversion racism to the common ingroup identity model. *Journal of Social Issues, 61*(3), 615–639.

Gibson, C. & Vermeulen, F. (2003). A healthy divide: subgroups as a stimulus for team learning behavior. *Administrative Science Quarterly, 48*, 202–239.

Hackman, J. R. (1987). The design of work teams. In J. W. Lorsch (Ed.), *Handbook of organizational behavior* (pp. 315–342). Englewood Cliffs, NJ: Prentice Hall.

Harrison, D. A. & Klein, K. J. (2007). What's the difference? Diversity constructs as separation, variety, or disparity in organizations, 32(4), 1199–1228. *Academy of Management Review.*

Herriot, P. & Pemberton, C. (1995). *Competitive advantage through diversity.* London: Sage.

Industry Week/Manufacturing Performance Institute (2004). *Census of manufacturers 2004 executive summary.* Retrieved January 3, 2006, from http://www.mpi-group.net/ thoughtleadership/MPI_2004_executive_summary.pdf

Janis, I. L. (1982). *Victims of groupthink* (2d ed.). Boston, MA: Houghton Mifflin.

Jassawalla, A. R. & Sashittal, H. C. (1998). An examination of collaboration in high-technology new product development processes. *Journal of Product Innovation Management, 15*, 237–254.

Kahn, W. A. (1990). Psychological conditions of personal engagement and disengagement at work. *Academy of Management Journal, 33*(4), 692–724.

Kolb, D. A. (1984). *Experiential learning.* Englewood Cliffs, NJ: Prentice-Hall.

Kramer, R. M. (1999). Trust and distrust in organizations: Emerging perspectives, enduring questions. *Annual Review of Psychology, 50,* 569–598.

Lau, D. C. & Murnighan, J. K. (2005). Interactions within groups and subgroups: The effects of demographic faultlines. *Academy of Management Journal, 48*(4), 645–659.

Leape, L. L., Brennan, T. A., Laird, N., Lawthers, A. G., Localio, A. R., Barnes, B. A., et al. (1991). The nature of adverse events in hospitalized patients: Results of the Harvard Medical Practice Study II. *New England Journal of Medicine, 324*(6), 377–384.

Lee, F., Edmondson, A. C., Thomke, S., & Worline, M. (2004). The mixed effects of inconsistency on experimentation in organizations. *Organization Science, 15*(3), 310–326.

Levitt, B. & March, J. G. (1988). Organizational learning. *Annual Review of Sociology, 14,* 319–340.

Lovelace, K., Shapiro, D. L., & Weingart, L. R. (2001). Maximizing cross-functional new product teams' innovativeness and constraint adherence: A conflict communications perspective. *Academy of Management Journal, 44*(4), 779–793.

Lynn, G. S., Akgun, A. E., & Keskin, H. (2003). Accelerated learning in new product development teams. *European Journal of Innovation Management, 6*(4), 201–212.

Mayer, R. C., Davis, J. H., & Schoorman, F. D. (1995). An integrative model of organizational trust. *Academy of Management Review, 20*(3), 709–734.

Michie, S. & West, M. A. (2004). Managing people and performance: An evidence based framework applied to health service organizations. *International Journal of Management Reviews, 5–6*(2), 91–11.

Nembhard, I. & Edmondson, A. C. (2006). Making it safe: The effects of leader inclusiveness and professional status on psychological safety and improvement efforts in health care teams. *Journal of Organizational Behavior, 37*(7), 941–966.

Neuman, G. A. & Wright, J. (1999). Team effectiveness: Beyond skills and cognitive ability. *Journal of Applied Psychology, 84*(3), 376–389.

Parker, G. M. (2003). *Cross-functional teams: Working with allies, enemies, and other strangers.* San Francisco, CA: Jossey-Bass.

Pfeffer, J. (1983). Organizational demography. *Research in Organizational Behavior, 5,* 299–357.

Rappoport, A. (1997). The patient's search for safety: The organizing principle in psychotherapy. *Psychotherapy, 34*(3), 250–261.

Sarin, S. & McDermott, C. (2003). The effect of team leader characteristics on learning, knowledge application, and performance of cross-functional new product development teams. *Decision Sciences, 34*(4), 707–739.

Schein, E. & Bennis, W. (1965). *Personal and organizational change through group methods.* New York: Wiley.

Schein, E. H. (1985). *Organizational culture and leadership.* San Francisco, CA: Jossey-Bass.

Schneider, B. (1987). The people make the place. *Personnel Psychology, 40,* 437–454.

Schon, D. (1983). *The reflective practitioner: How professionals think in action.* New York: Basic Books.

Schippers, M. C., Den Hartog, D. N., Koopman, P. L., & Wienk, J. A. (2003). Diversity and team outcomes: The moderating effects of outcome interdependence and group longevity and the mediating effects of reflexivity. *Journal of Organizational Behavior, 24*(6), 779–802.

Senge, P. M. (1990). *The fifth discipline: the art and practice of the learning organization.* New York: Doubleday.

Snyder, M. (1974). Self-monitoring of expressive behavior. *Journal of Personality and Social Psychology, 30*(4), 526–537.

Sole, D. & Edmondson, A. (2002). Situated knowledge and learning in dispersed teams. *British Journal of Management, 13*(S), S17–S34.

Stasser, G. (1999). The uncertain role of unshared information in collective choice. In L. Thompson, J. Levine, & D. Messick (Eds.), *Shared cognition in organizations* (pp. 49–69). Mahwah, NJ: Lawrence Erlbaum Associates.

Stata, R. (1989). Organizational learning: The key to management innovation. *Sloan Management Review, 12*(1), 63–74.

Steele, C. M. & Aronson, J. (1995). Stereotype threat and the intellectual test performance of African Americans. *Journal of Personality and Social Psychology, 69*(5), 797–811.

Swift, W. & Copeland, J. (1996). Treatment needs and experiences of Australian women with alcohol and drug problems. *Drug & Alcohol Dependence, 40*(3), 211–219.

Tajfel, H. (1970). Experiments in intergroup discrimination. *Scientific American, 223,* 96–102.

Tjosvold, D., Yu, Z., & Hui, C. (2004). Team learning from mistakes: The contribution of cooperative goals and problem solving. *Journal of Management Studies, 41*(7), 1223–1245.

Tucker, A. L. & Edmondson, A. C. (2003). Why hospitals don't learn from failures: Organizational and psychological dynamics that inhibit system change. *California Management Review, 45*(2), 55–72.

Tucker, A., Nembhard, I., & Edmondson, A.C. (2006). *Learning on the front lines: A multi-method investigation of organizational learning in hospitals.* Manuscript submitted for publication.

Turnley, W. H. & Bolino, M. C. (2001). Achieving desired images while avoiding undesired images: Exploring the role of self-monitoring in impression management. *Journal of Applied Psychology, 86*(2), 351–360.

Tynan, R. (2005). The effects of threat sensitivity and face giving on dyadic psychological safety and upward communication. *Journal of Applied Social Psychology, 35*(2), 223–247.

U.S. Equal Employment Opportunity Commission (2003). Characteristics of Private Sector Employment. Washington, D.C.

Van Der Vegt, G. S. & Bunderson, J. S. (2005). Learning and performance in multidisciplinary teams: The importance of collective team identification. *Academy of Management Journal, 48*(3), 532–547.

Wakefield, B. J., Blegen, M. A., Uden-Holman, T., Vaughn, T., Chrischilles, E., & Wakefield, D. S. (2001). Organizational culture, continuous quality improvement, and medication administration error reporting. *American Journal of Medical Quality, 16*(4), 128–34.

Weick, K. E. & Roberts, K. H. (1993). Collective mind in organizations: Heedful interrelating on Flight Decks. *Administrative Science Quarterly, 38*(3), 357–382.

West, M. A. (1990). The social psychology of innovation in groups. In M. A. West & J. L. Farr (Eds.), *Innovation and creativity at work: Psychological and organizational strategies* (pp. 309–333). Chichester, England: John Wiley & Sons.

West, M. A. (2000). Reflexivity, revolution and innovation in work teams. In M. M. Beyerslein, D. A. Johnson & S. T. Beyerlein (Eds.), *Product development teams* (pp. 1–29). Stanford, CT: JAI Press.

Zellmer-Bruhn, M. E. (2003). Interruptive events and team knowledge acquisition. *Management Science, 49*(4), 514–528.

Zellmer-Bruhn, M. E. & Gibson, C. (2006). *Multinational organization context: Implications for team learning and performance. Academy of Management Journal, 49*(3), 401–518.

8

Understanding the Cognitive Processes in Adaptive Multicultural Teams: A Framework

**C. Shawn Burke, Heather A. Priest, Samuel R. Wooten II,
Deborah DiazGranados, and Eduardo Salas**

> To exist is to change, to change is to mature, to mature is to go on creating oneself endlessly.
>
> **Henri Bergson**

Organizations in the twenty-first century are couched within environments that are increasingly dynamic, ambiguous, and competitive. Within such environments, it has been argued that the only constant is change (Drucker, 1992; Schmid, 2006). Success within such dynamic environments requires that organizations be adaptive both within and across organizational levels. Although much is known about individual adaptation, less is known about how teams and collectives adapt. As many organizations have increasingly moved to team-based structures, there is a need to examine the conditions, processes, and emergent states that lead to adaptive teams. In recognition of this need, research has begun to examine team adaptation and the corresponding processes that promote it (Burke, Stagl, Salas, Pierce, & Kendall, 2006; Fleming, Wood, Dudley, Bader, & Zaccaro, 2003; LePine, 2003; Pulakos, Dorsey, & White, 2006). However, few of these efforts have explicitly examined team composition with relation to cultural diversity and its impact on team adaptation.

As globalization has become a business strategy indicative of organizations that are able to remain competitive within large and evolving markets, cultural diversity's impact on team adaptation needs to be better understood. Navigation of the complexity inherent within global organizations, whereby coordination and resource mobilization happens both within and across geographic and cultural boundaries, is not easy. Moreover, our lack of knowledge about the factors that contribute to team adaptation within multicultural teams makes it difficult to successfully develop and maintain such teams. Evidence for this can be seen in the fact that although the United States has acknowledged the importance of stability, security, transition, and reconstruction, there have been repeated arguments that soldiers are not being properly prepared to operate within such environments (Crowley et al., 2006; Pierce, 2002). A similar state of affairs exists within nonmilitary organizations as indicated by high early return rates (16% to 40%) for expatriates (see Employee Benefit Plan Review, 2001; Shaffer, Harrison, & Gilley, 1999). Although these return rates do not indicate whether the expatriates were working as individuals or within a team, given the increasing prevalence of team-based forms of work it is reasonable to expect that a good proportion of expatriates are working within such structures.

Globalization, competition, and dynamic environments are not expected to be a passing "fad," suggesting that it is imperative not only to understand team adaptation but also such phenomena within multicultural teams. In this vein, the current chapter has three primary purposes. First, we seek to build a model of multicultural team adaptation by extending the model of team adaptation presented by Burke et al. (2006) to include an examination of the impact of within-team cultural diversity. In doing so, existing literature in the areas of team adaptation, multicultural and cross-cultural teams, negotiation, perspective taking, and sensemaking are leveraged and integrated. These areas are utilized to delineate the cognitive and behavioral processes that serve to assist members in navigating the challenges inherent within multicultural teams so that the team remains adaptive and productive. Second, using the refined model, propositions are developed that can be used to guide research. Finally, a few practical implications are delineated within the concluding comments.

We begin the chapter by briefly describing team adaptation and the distal outcome of interest and by identifying a few of the prominent challenges within multicultural teams to set the context.

Team Adaptation

Though few would argue against the importance of team adaptation within today's business environment, researchers have only recently begun to examine the antecedents, processes, and emergent states that comprise adaptive team performance, ultimately leading to team adaptation (Fleming et al., 2003; Klein & Pierce, 2001; Kozlowski, Gully, Nason, & Smith, 1999; Kozlowski et al., 2001; LePine, 2003). Although work on team adaptation has increased over the last several years, Burke et al. (2006) noted that there was not yet an integrated model that depicted the multilevel, dynamic nature of team adaptation. In this vein, a model of the antecedents, dynamic processes, and emergent states that comprise adaptive team performance, ultimately leading to team adaptation, was proposed (Figure 8.1). Within the model, Burke et al. conceptualized team adaptation as "a change in team performance, in response to a salient cue or cue stream, that leads to a functional outcome for the entire team and is manifested in the innovation of new or modification of existing structures, capacities, and/or behavioral or cognitive goal-directed actions" (p. 1190).

Serving as a direct input to the distal outcome of team adaptation is adaptive team performance, "the process by which team members use the available resources to functionally change current cognitive or behavioral goal-directed action or structures to meet expected or unexpected demands" (Burke et al., 2006, p. 1192). Adaptive team performance is continuously evolving and compiles bottom up across levels and time. The processes and emergent states that characterize adaptive team performance are conceptualized as belonging to one of four phases: situation assessment, plan formulation, plan execution, and team learning. Phase 1 (situation assessment) is composed of searching cues, recognition processes, meaning ascription, and communication of meaning to team members. The processes enacted within this phase result in emergent states, such as shared mental models and team situation awareness. In turn, these emergent states serve as inputs to the next phase: plan formulation.

Though Burke et al. (2006) briefly described the plan formulation phase, the specific processes that comprise it were not delineated. As such, Rosen et al. (2008) expanded on the conceptualization by delineating the following processes plan formulation: (1) mission analysis; (2) goal specification; (3) strategy formulation; (4) role differentiation; and (5) preemptive conflict management. The resulting emergent states (Figure 8.1) give the commands and information meaning as well as create shared mental models that are critical to the success of phase 3.

The next phase, plan execution, again uses the preceding phase's emergent processes as input variables. The processes here include individual-level processes of mutual monitoring, communication, backup behavior, and leadership, whereas coordination appears as a team-level behavior. To the original set of processes, Rosen et al. (2008) added individual-level behaviors such as systems monitoring and affect management, as well as the team-level behaviors of reactive conflict management and strategy formulation. Shared mental models, team situation awareness, and psychological safety are states that emerge from this phase and influence the final phase of the model.

The final phase of adaptive team performance is team learning. Similar to the plan formulation phase, the specific processes involved in team

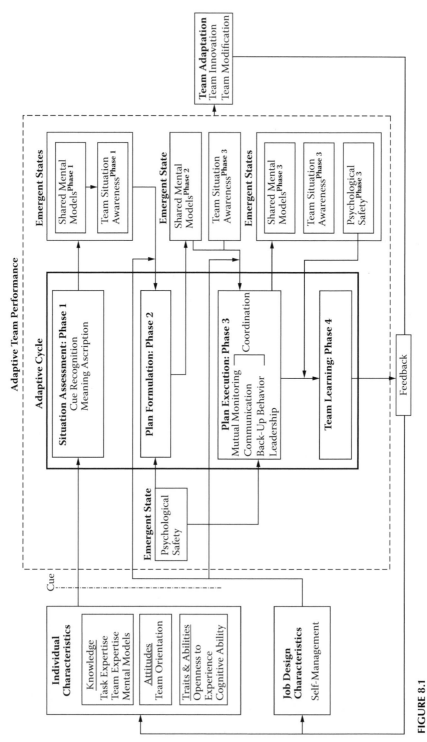

FIGURE 8.1

ITO model of team adaptation. (From Burke et al., 2006. With permission.)

learning were not delineated within the original model proposed by Burke et al. (2006). Burke, Salas, and DiazGranados (2008) as well as Rosen et al. (2008) extended the team-learning component of the original model. Most recently, Rosen et al. decomposed team learning into the following processes: (1) information search and structuring; (2) event review; (3) reflection and critique; and (4) summarizing lessons learned.

Although the primary focus within Burke et al. (2006) is the delineation of adaptive team performance, a few variables that serve as primary inputs into the adaptive team performance cycle were also identified. The initial characteristics proposed include knowledge (task and team expertise, mental models), attitudes (team orientation), and traits and abilities (openness to experience and cognitive ability). While the recent work by Rosen et al. (2008) further delineated aspects of the original model proposed by Burke et al., noticeably missing within both conceptualizations—especially in light of the current discussion on multicultural teams—is the recognition of the impact of culture or more specifically within team cultural diversity on team adaptation. Even though we contend that the basic model proposed by Burke et al. and refined by Rosen et al. holds within multicultural teams, it is important to examine how cultural diversity may impact the adaptive cycle and the components contained within. To begin the initial examination and to further set the context, a brief description of multicultural teams and their inherent challenges are presented next.

Multicultural Teams

At the most general level, *multicultural teams* is a term that has been used to define a team composed of members from varying cultures, where culture is not limited to nationality but can represent a myriad of variables. Multicultural teams have been defined as those teams "diverse in demographic attributes, including functional, occupational, hierarchical, and national backgrounds of members" (Salk & Arya, 2005, p. 190). Multicultural teams have also been defined as "teams in which the members represent different occupational, organizational, national, ethnic, or political backgrounds" (Jelinek & Wilson, 2005, p. 210). However, the definition that most closely aligns to our thinking is the one proposed by Gibson and Grubb (2005), who viewed multicultural teams as "a collection of individuals, small in number, who have representatives from more than one national background among them, who are interdependent and mutually accountable for accomplishing a set of objectives, and who recognize themselves as a team" (p. 70).

While the multiple perspectives present within multicultural teams may offer many advantages to organizations by offering the potential for greater access to diverse information and thereby serving as a facilitating mechanism for team adaptation, such teams often fail to capitalize on such synergy. Evidence exists that often the diversity present within multicultural teams serves to decrease social integration, trust, communication and produces conflict (Mannix & Neale, 2005). In line with acknowledging both its importance and complexity, a recent report by Wunderle (2006) stated that "cultural interpretation, competence, and adaptation are prerequisites for achieving a win-win relationship..." and that culture is "dangerous ground that, if not breached, must be navigated with caution, understanding and respect" (p. 3).

So how do members of culturally diverse teams effectively navigate the challenges present within such teams? We would argue that fundamental to many of the challenges is the notion of sensemaking. Sensemaking serves as the foundational layer to team adaptation within multicultural teams as it is the process whereby members assign meaning to member action. It is especially difficult within multicultural teams where the possibility exists for the cognitive frames that drive sensemaking to be different among team members. Within this view, the actions that individuals are attempting to make sense of are the behavioral actions that comprise adaptive team performance (Figure 8.1).

A Conceptual Framework of Multicultural Team Adaptation

One of the greatest challenges within complex situations is to make sense of the situation, assigning meaning to situational cues such that correct action can be taken. Nowhere is this more true than within multicultural teams where members have different cultural backgrounds, which in turn, guide their preferences, values, and behaviors. Many of the processes that comprise sensemaking align with those that appear within the situation assessment phase of the adaptive team performance cycle (Figure 8.1). Thereby, the literature on sensemaking integrated with that on culture, team cognition, team adaptation, negotiation, and perspective taking serves to form the basis of the framework developed in Figure 8.2. The framework represents a multilevel conceptualization of the factors that impact team adaptation within multicultural teams, with a specific focus on examining the initial cognitive processes and on underlying cognitive content that facilitates the sensemaking process, a precursor to a team's ability to be adaptive within multicultural environments.

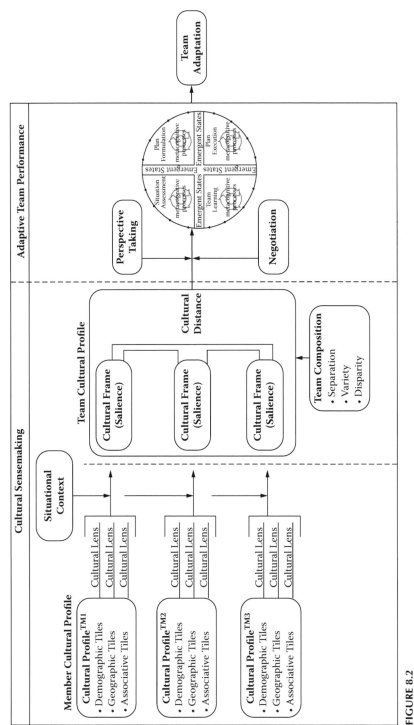

FIGURE 8.2
Explicating the sensemaking process needed for multicultural team adaptation.

The conceptual framework in Figure 8.2 incorporates seven primary components, representing a mix of cognitive and behavioral constructs. The cognitive components are primarily emphasized in the left-hand side of the framework and depict the cognitive knowledge needed for sensemaking within multicultural teams. Examination of the left-hand side of the framework illustrates that sensemaking within multicultural teams relies on three primary types of knowledge: (1) cultural profile at the individual and team level; (2) situational context; and (3) cultural identity salience. This knowledge is used to determine the cultural distance among team members, where cultural distance has been defined as "the sum of factors creating, on the one hand, a need for knowledge, and on the other hand, barriers to knowledge flow and hence also for other flows between the home and the target countries" (Barkema, Oded, Freek, & Bell, 1997, p. 427). Low cultural distance implies that existing knowledge structures are likely to be more compatible and therefore that the implicit information used to make sense of team member interaction and the broader social environments is more similar; in contrast, the opposite is true when cultural distance is high. As depicted in Figure 8.2, cultural distance will determine the degree of cognitive (i.e., perspective taking) and behavioral (i.e., negotiation) adaptation needed to facilitate the components of the adaptive team performance cycle and, ultimately, team adaptation. The next few sections of the chapter go into more detail in terms of the framework components and corresponding propositions (Table 8.1).

Unpacking Sensemaking: Delineating Knowledge Components

The left-hand side of Figure 8.2 can be conceptualized as the knowledge that underlies the sensemaking process within adaptive multicultural teams. While rarely being applied specifically to multicultural teams, the construct of sensemaking has a long history within the broader literature base. Despite its long history, its description as a process has remained fairly abstract, offering little guidance to practitioners. For example, sensemaking has been defined in the following ways:

1. "A process in which individuals develop cognitive maps of their environment" (Ring & Rands, 1989, p. 342).
2. "The reciprocal interaction of information seeking, meaning ascription, and action" (Thomas, Clark, & Gioia, 1993, p. 240).

Most widely known is the description provided by Weick (1995), "sensemaking is about such things as placement of items into frameworks, comprehending, redressing surprise, constructing meaning, interacting in the pursuit of mutual understanding, and patterning" (p. 6). Weick further argued that the process of sensemaking is grounded in identity

TABLE 8.1

Summary of Propositions Derived from Conceptual Framework

Proposition	Summary
Proposition 1	Members who understand that culture is multifaceted such that it produces a series of lenses through which each team member will view fellow member actions and the environment will be better able to assign meaning to action within the team (i.e., facilitate sensemaking).
Proposition 2	Members who have an understanding of the range of cultural lenses available to fellow members will be better able to assign meaning to action within the team (i.e., facilitate sensemaking).
Proposition 3	Members who possess knowledge regarding how the situational context interacts with available cultural lenses to determine the salience of any particular lens will be better able to predict and assign meaning to member action.
Proposition 4	Contextual cues that highlight team member similarity will increase the likelihood that members adopt a cognitive frame more similar to fellow/targeted team members (i.e., social identity).
Proposition 5	Contextual cues that highlight team member differences will increase the likelihood that members adopt a unique cognitive frame compared with fellow or targeted team members (i.e., personal identity).Leaders can increase the tendency for a social identity to become salient within the team by highlighting situational cues that illustrate member similarity in terms of experiences, values, or common bonds.
Proposition 6	Members of adaptive teams use their knowledge of the interaction between context and identity salience to mitigate perceptions of cultural differences.
Proposition 6a	Members who highlight cues that illustrate member similarity in terms of experience, values, or common bonds can decrease perceptions of the cultural distance within the team by increasing the tendency for social identity to become salient.
Proposition 6b	Members who highlight cues that illustrate member uniqueness in terms of experiences, values, or common bonds can increase the tendency for a personal identity to become salient, thereby decreasing stereotypes.
Proposition 7	The specific nature of the cultural distance will have an effect on the need for adaptive action within the later stages of sensemaking and early stages of adaptive team performance. Specifically, higher levels of adaptive action will be required when high levels of cultural distance are representative of separation or disparity as compared to variety.
Proposition 8	As the cultural distance between interdependent members increases, sensemaking and adaptive team performance become more difficult due to a lack of compatible mental models.

TABLE 8.1

Summary of Propositions Derived from Conceptual Framework (Continued)

Proposition	Summary
Proposition 9	Members who use perspective taking to mitigate the negative relationship between cultural distance and adaptive team performance will have a larger impact when cultural distance among interdependent team members is high.
Proposition 10	Members who use principled negotiation to mitigate the negative relationship between cultural distance and adaptive team performance will have a larger impact when cultural distance among interdependent team members is high.

construction. It is retrospective, social, and ongoing; it is focused on and by extracted cues; and it is driven by plausibility (ibid.).

The sensemaking process has been argued to happen primarily on a tacit level, until individuals are confronted by an unexpected or discrepant cue that then serves to make the process salient to members. Perhaps most dangerous within the context of multicultural teams are the times when the sensemaking process remains latent due to deep-level diversity versus the salient surface-level diversity. For example, with regards to deep-level diversity, Gibson and Zellmer-Bruhn (2002) found that cultures differ in the metaphors that are used to describe teams and, correspondingly, teamwork (e.g., sports, military, family groups, community groups, or a circle of associates). Though not often recognized, these metaphors can be used to understand expectations regarding member roles, activity scope, interaction, degree of ambiguity, and objectives.

The definitions previously provided offer an indication of what the purpose and characteristics of sensemaking are, but they do little to ground the process in terms of the mechanisms through which it occurs. However, due to its grounding in identity construction, sensemaking possibly is influenced by the cognitive frames that individuals hold. With this in mind, we argue that the first component that must exist to make sense of discrepant cues within multicultural teams is the determination of individual team members' culture profile—in particular, the salience of a particular identity or identities. Within the context of the developed framework a cultural profile can be thought of as the various layers of culture that exist within each individual team member (Figure 8.2). When aggregated the pattern of individual member identities form to create a team identity. To better understand this knowledge component, we briefly review the literature to describe the individual components of a cultural profile, how this translates into each member having a series of cultural lenses through which actions are perceived, and, finally, how the lenses combine with contextual factors to prime a specific identity or frame for each team member.

Team Member Cultural Profile

The study of culture is not a new phenomenon, as such multiple definitions of culture have been provided. Culture has been defined as "what a group learns over a period of time as that group solves its problems of survival in an external environment and its problems of internal integration" (Schein, 1992, p. 17). It has also been defined as a "taken-for-granted system of values, beliefs, and attitudes that shape and influences perception and behavior" (Jelinek & Wilson, 2005, p. 210) and "patterned ways of thinking, feeling, and reacting ... the essential core of culture consists of traditional ... ideas and especially their attached values" (Kluckhohn, 1951, p. 6). Most recent definitions of culture acknowledge its complexity and dynamism based on ecological and sociopolitical events (see Berry, Poortinga, Segall, & Dasen, 1992), as well as its multidimensionality within and across levels (Chao & Moon, 2005; Erez & Gati, 2004).

Although many have begun to recognize the complexity of culture, few researchers have gone so far as to develop conceptualizations of culture that reflect its multilevel, dynamic nature. Two recent exceptions are Erez and Gati (2004) and Chao and Moon (2005). Erez and Gati described a framework that illustrates the structural and dynamic features of culture. The structural dimension portrays a hierarchy of nested levels beginning with the representation of culture at an individual level nested within groups, organizations, nations, and, finally, global culture. It is argued not only that culture as a shared meaning system exists at each level but also that interrelationships among the levels exist (ibid.).

While recognizing the interaction of culture across levels and detailing the dominant cultural dimensions within each level, the focus of the framework is more attuned to differences across levels than to how different cultures may reside within a single individual. The former perspective is important; however, we argue that to facilitate the assignment of correct meaning to actions an understanding of the various cultural forms that may reside within an individual team member must first be understood. Therefore, we turn to the work of Chao and Moon (2005).

Chao and Moon (2005) conceptualized culture as a mosaic (Figure 8.2), "a pattern of cultural identities within individuals that has implications for the conceptualization and assessment of culture at multiple levels of analysis" (p. 1128). Accordingly, within each person dwells a mosaic composed of demographic, geographic, and associative factors (i.e., tiles; ibid.). Demographic tiles are generally physical in nature or inherited (e.g., age, ethnicity, gender, race), and geographic tiles reflect the physical features of the region within which one resides (e.g., climate, temperature, coastal/

inland, urban/rural, regional/country). Finally, associative factors represent all groups with whom an individual chooses to identify (e.g., family, religion, employer, profession, politics). Chao and Moon said that to truly understand culture, individual identities must be examined within the context of the underlying structures. This approach is in many ways similar to views of culture in anthropology that recognize both the intrapersonal and extrapersonal aspects of culture (D'Andrade, 1995; Hannerz, 1992; Shore, 1991; Strauss & Quinn, 1997), albeit it more detailed.

Chao and Moon (2005) made the case that examining culture in this manner can assist in identifying and predicting behavior patterns. In turn, this provides a basis for their inclusion in our framework. Specifically, team members must understand that latent within each team member is a mosaic or layering of cultures, which serve both to interact with one another and drive member actions. The demographic, geographic, and associative tiles that comprise an individual's mosaic serve to act as multiple lenses through which the world is perceived and acted on. The purpose of these lenses is not only to filter and organize information but also to focus sensemaking, structure planning, and to frame team member interactions (Klein, 2004).

> *Proposition 1:* Team members who understand that culture is multifaceted such that it produces a series of lenses through which each team member will view fellow members' actions and the environment will be better able to correctly assign meaning to action within the team (i.e., to facilitate sensemaking).

> *Proposition 2:* Team members who have an understanding of the range of cultural lenses available to fellow members will be better able to assign meaning to action within the team (i.e., to facilitate sensemaking).

Understanding culture as a multilevel, multilayered phenomenon is vital to effective sensemaking because it provides the foundation for deciphering the cultural profiles that act to guide member action and serves as the first, necessary, but not sufficient step in effective sensemaking. Within multicultural teams the challenge is to determine which cultural identity within the mosaic individual team members are operating from. This in and of itself is a complicated process as an individual's cultural identity is not a static phenomenon but can be structured in a variety of ways depending on the situational context and prior experience (Figure 8.2). For example, Roccas and Brewer (2002) contended that cultural identities may be structured in one of four ways: unified, dominant, merger, or compartmentalization. Unified identities refer to situations in which two identities are combined, resulting in a hybrid culture. It has been disputed that the creation of a hybrid culture is one method by which the challenges often present within multicultural teams can be decreased (see Earley

& Mosakowski, 2000). Dominant cultural identities refer to situations in which one primary identity exists to the exclusion of other identities. Mergers represent the presence of multiple identities across situations, thereby arguing that an individual can simultaneously hold two identities at once (ibid.). Conversely, compartmentalization refers to the idea that an individual can hold two nonconvergent cultural identities that operate independently based on different situational cues.

Situational Context

Even though knowledge of the cultural factors that reside within individual team members will assist in the sensemaking process, it is not enough. As the multiple layers of culture can combine in various ways (Roccas & Brewer, 2002), even coexisting, successful teams are able to, first, determine which cultural identity is salient, and, second, how this manifests itself (i.e., what does this mean in terms of adaptive, coordinated action). Without such recognition it will be difficult to build and maintain the shared cognition, affect, and behavior needed for adaptive team performance. We, along with others (e.g., Chao & Moon, 2005), maintain that the situational context plays a large role in determining which identity is salient within a specific setting. To better understand how the situation moderates the link between an individual member's cultural profile (the various mosaic of tiles inherently residing within individuals) and the saliency of a specific cultural identity, we turn to the literatures on social identity and self-categorization. In addition, the literature based on social identity theory can provide insight into the heuristics (i.e., perceived and actual identity) used by members to assign meaning, especially early in the team's life cycle.

Social identity theory states that individuals use one of three mechanisms to determine their identity within particular groups (i.e., categorization, identification, and comparison), thereby offering insight into how an identity may become salient. Categorization refers to the case in which we and others are placed in categories based on perceived similarities; it is used most frequently within ambiguous situations. Identification occurs when individuals identify with a group to which they perceive they belong. This process serves to create in- and out-groups and is best illustrated through the concept of social and personal identity. While both represent an individual's concept of self, social identity is the notion that individuals feel as though they belong to a group, whereas personal identity is the notion that they think of themselves as unique individuals. Within this context, individuals can identify with many groups and can switch between social and personal identities as well as varying group membership depending on the context of the situation. This is in line with the more complex structural forms of identity (e.g., mergers, compartmentalization). For example, consider an individual within a multicultural team; the composition of the team and environmental cues may activate different identities to be salient. Imagine a military team composed of Americans and several North Atlantic Trade Organization (NATO) partner nations. If the cues in the environment highlight that members are all part of a military collective, then the Americans may assume a social identity associated with the military; otherwise, the Americans may perceive themselves as being unique, and a personal identity of being American may become salient in this situation.

Social comparison is the final mechanism used to determine choice and salience of identity. Social comparison states that we learn about our own attitudes and abilities by comparing ourselves with others to whom we are similar. People are motivated to positively differentiate the in-group from similar out-groups on pertinent dimensions of comparison so that they maintain distinctiveness and social identity. For example, if a team is operating within a professional environment (e.g., a board room), team members may identify more closely with the norms that govern their role as a professional (e.g., engineer, psychologist). However, if the situation is rooted in a casual environment, like a cocktail party, the norms that guide their behavior may be associated more with their personal identity. The cues in the environment (e.g., tables and presentation projector versus an open bar and hors d'oeuvres) cause one identity to be more salient.

Self-categorization theory is another literature base that can be leveraged to provide insight into how the situational context may influence the salience of cultural identities. Self-categorization is an elaboration of social identity theory and is based on the hypothesis that individuals' perception of themselves is variable and their identity is multiple (Turner, Hogg, Oakes, Reicher, & Whetherell, 1987). Turner and colleagues proposed that the sense of self is influenced by those social groups with which we can compare ourselves. We and others are then categorized so that differences are maximized between categories and minimized within categories (i.e., metacontrast principle, in-group/outgroup formation). The magnitude of the difference between in-groups and out-groups relies on the strength to which the members identify with their social identity (i.e., belonging to a group) compared with personal identity (i.e., seen as a unique individual). Verkuyten and DeWolf (2002) found that when social identity is salient, perceptions and corresponding explanations contain more stereotypes. Those being categorized are no longer depicted as individuals but as representatives of the relevant prototype. It is important to differentiate from social identity theory and to consider that prototypes form according to the metacontrast principle (e.g., Hogg & Terry, 2000). Prototypes are stored in an individual's memory; however, they can be modified or created by a person's environment (e.g., Fiske & Taylor, 1991). Crucial to this idea is that individuals have many prototypes stored in their memory and that the determination of which prototype emerges is highly context dependent and influenced by what out-group is contextually salient.

The present discussion of these theories allows for the integration of information from social identity and self-categorization theories to delineate how the social context can shape which identity is chosen (Hogg & Terry, 2000). The cognitive systems used, as described by social identity and self-categorization theories (Figure 8.3), are governed by two processes: uncertainty reduction and self-enhancement. Both of these processes match social categories to properties of the social context, which,

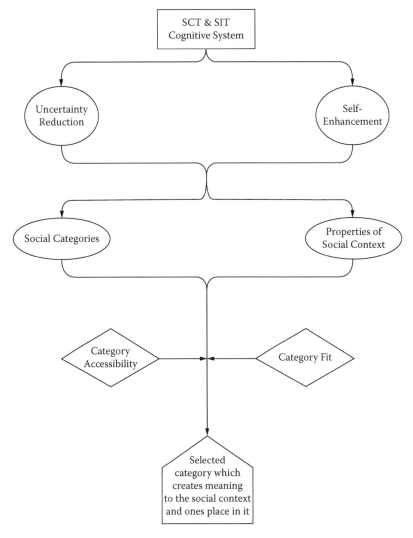

FIGURE 8.3
Categorization process leading to identity salience.

in turn, activate a category and create an understanding of the situation and meaning to ones place within it. Category accessibility and category fit thus create an interaction effect that allows an individual to draw from available categories and then to investigate which one provides the best fit. Although the previous argument is made with respect to identity in general, the same would be expected regarding the salience of a specific cultural identity.

> *Proposition 3:* Team members who possess knowledge regarding how the situational context interacts with available cultural lenses to determine the salience of any particular lens will be better able to predict and assign meaning to member action.

Individuals do what they do because of who they believe they are (Korte, 2006). Therefore, when people select a group to belong to there are constraints. History, personality, status, and opportunity are all factors that individuals consider during the group/identity selection process. Once the group is selected, people adopt the norms (behaviors) of the group that will guide performance. People will modify their behavior to adopt the group norms and values while striving for consensus within the group. In other words, a personal identity is altered through depersonalization, and the outcome is the social identity. The more individuals identify themselves with a social group, the greater is the tendency to show intergroup differentiation (Oaker & Brown, 1986). If two groups' goals are perceived to be similar to one another, it is less likely that people will change their identity from a social to a personal one. The social identity becomes more salient. Therefore, one way to increase the salience of the social identity—and, correspondingly, the cultural identity that is predominant within the group— is to emphasize the similarity among team members.

> *Proposition 4:* Contextual cues that highlight team member similarity will increase the likelihood that members adopt a cognitive frame more similar to fellow/targeted team members (i.e., social identity).

If depersonalization is the process by which individuals go from a personal identity to a social identity (becoming a group member), then it may be fair to assume that personalization is the process by which personal identity can be made salient. If team members know that individuals are using their social identity, this will increase intergroup differentiation (i.e., social identity is generally more powerful), thus making negotiation with the out-group more difficult than if personal identity can be made salient. One method to personalize individuals is to highlight their characteristics, goals, ideas, or behaviors that may run counter to the group. For example, for an American within a multicultural team primarily composed of members with a collectivist orientation, highlighting the individualistic nature of the American would serve as one manner by which personalization would occur. In the same way, highlighting the characteristics of one discipline that is significantly different from the other members of a multidisciplinary project team would also personalize that member (e.g., engineer vs. psychologist). Validating these features in a culturally intelligent way may provide a level of understanding where the in-group members are able to see themselves and the out-group on a personal level, thus facilitating negotiations.

> *Proposition 5:* Contextual cues that highlight team member differences will increase the likelihood that members adopt a unique cognitive frame compared with fellow/targeted team members (i.e., personal identity).

Certainty provides meaning and confers confidence in how to behave and what to expect from our world (Hogg & Terry, 2000). If we join a group whose prototype (i.e., perceptions, attitudes, feelings, and behaviors) is aligned with ours, it creates confidence and reduces uncertainty. Uncertainty reduction theory states that when individuals are uncertain about their self-concept and their group entitivity is high the outcome is strong identification with the group (ibid.). Categorization lightens a person's cognitive load by reducing uncertainty, thus creating stability. However, there are negative outcomes of this process. Rigidity to outside ideas and prejudices toward out-group members can create conflict. Pride, involvement, stability, and meaning are some reasons a person chooses to identify with a group, which leads to social identity as a possible driver of competition and a struggle between groups for (1) power, (2) status, (3) superiority, and (4) material advantage. During times of uncertainty, contextually or highly uncertain individuals are attracted to prototypes that are characterized by being (1) simple, (2) clear, (3) highly focused, and (4) consensual to reduce uncertainty. Prototypes such as these produce a pronounced entitativity, are very cohesive, and provide a powerful social identity.

> *Proposition 6:* Members of adaptive teams use their knowledge of the interaction between context and identity salience to mitigate perceptions of cultural differences.
>
> *Proposition 6a:* Team members who highlight cues that illustrate member similarity in terms of experience, values, or common bonds can decrease perceptions of the cultural distance within the team by increasing the tendency for social identity to become salient.
>
> *Proposition 6b:* Team members who highlight cues that illustrate member uniqueness in terms of experiences, values, or common bonds can increase the tendency for a personal identity to become salient, thereby decreasing stereotypes.

Team Cultural Profile

Once the cultural identity of each team member is determined, the next action within the sensemaking process is to determine how individuals' identities manifest themselves at the team level, thus producing varying degrees of cultural distance within the team (Figure 8.2). Cultural distance is defined as "perceiving one's two cultural identities as separate and dissociated versus hyphenated or fused" (Benet-Martínez & Haritatos, 2005, p. 1026) and reflects the dissimilarities between culture with regards to various characteristics like language, religion, values, attitudes toward authority, treatment of women versus men, legal systems, and forms of government (Chirkov, Lynch, & Niwa, 2005).

To better understand how members' individual cultural profiles may manifest at the team level and may impact the type and degree of adaptive action (i.e., functional change in cognitive or behavioral goal-directed actions or team structure) required, we turn to the work of Harrison and Klein (2007). These authors developed a taxonomy that describes three different types of diversity: separation, variety, and disparity. It is argued that the three types differ both in terms of the specific nature of the diversity as well as the collective distribution of the differences. Within Harrison and Klein's taxonomy, separation can be defined as "composition of differences in position or opinion among unit members, primarily of value, belief, or attitude; disagreement or opposition" (p. 1203). This is most indicative of the types of diversity that would be expected to be seen with a specific focus on multicultural teams. Regarding separation, high levels of cultural distance would be witnessed by a bimodal distribution, producing interpersonal conflict, reduced cohesion, and trust. Although variety is also a concern within multicultural teams, it is less of a focus within the current chapter. Specifically, variety is defined as "composition of differences in kind, source, or category of relevant knowledge or experience among unit members; unique or distinctive information" (ibid.). Harrison and Klein argued that with respect to variety, high levels of cultural distance are actually functional and lead to higher decision quality and levels of creativity. High levels of cultural distance here would be represented by a uniform distribution. Once again, while this is seen within multicultural teams, due to different training philosophies, country resources, and member experience it is not the primary focus within the current chapter. Finally, disparity can be defined as "composition of differences in proportion of socially valued assets or resources held among unit members; inequality or relative concentration" (ibid.). Disparity is often a characteristic of multicultural teams since it is tied to differences in values and norms for social interaction. Within this conceptualization of diversity, high levels of cultural distance would be indicated by a positively skewed distribution (ibid.).

Proposition 7: The specific nature of the cultural distance will have an effect on the need for adaptive action within the later stages of sense-making and early stages of adaptive team performance. Specifically, higher levels of adaptive action will be required when high levels of cultural distance are representative of separation or disparity as compared to variety.

While the various manners in which the cultural identities combine within a team (i.e., separation, variety, or disparity) will impact how cultural distance is operationalized within the team as well as its functionality, in most cases (i.e., separation, disparity) research contends that the greater the gap between cultures (i.e., the larger the cultural distance), the more difficult multicultural interactions will be (Berry et al., 1992; Ward, Bocher, & Furnham, 2001). While the increase in difficulty that comes from cultural distance is almost universal, different lines of research identify different difficulties (Slangen, 2006). For example, when looking at the international management literature, challenges between individuals who have a high cultural distance include problems based on different organizational practices like management and strategic decision-making styles, conflict-resolution strategies, human-resource management practices, and codes of ethics (Child, Faulkner, & Pitkethly, 2001; Cushman & King, 1985; Kogut & Singh, 1988; Langlois & Schlegelmilch, 1990; Ngo, Turban, Lau, & Lui, 1998; Ralston, Gustafson, Mainiero, & Umstot, 1993; Schneider & De Meyer, 1991). Ultimately, management research holds that greater cultural distance (i.e., the more divergent) will result in more incompatible practices and, in turn, more complicated transfers and handoffs that are costly to manage (Geringer, Beamish, & daCosta, 1989; Kogut & Singh, 1988).

Conversely, the organizational literature blames problems in intercultural interactions on large cultural distances that result in misunderstandings and misattributions due to individual team members being so strongly embedded in their own culture (Buono & Bowditch, 1989). The fact that individuals are so embedded within their own culture makes interactions problematic and leads to negative feelings toward the outgroup, further fueling misunderstandings, confusion, stress, discomfort, and hostility (Elsass & Veiga, 1994; Hofstede, 2001; Olie, 1996; Slangen, 2006). These negative feelings, termed *acculturative stress,* lead to decreases in commitment, loyalty, cooperation, satisfaction, and productivity (Buono & Bowditch, 1989; Very, Lubatkin, & Calori, 1998).

Whether looking at the management, culture, or organizational literature, one thing becomes clear: As the cultural distance between team members increases, the coordinated actions comprising adaptive team performance become more difficult. As the discrepancy in cultural distance among team members becomes larger, it is reflective of discrepant cognitions regarding values, beliefs, and expected actions. In turn, unless recognized and communicated, this makes it difficult—if not impossible—

to form the compatible mental models repeatedly shown as precursors to adaptive team performance. Drawing from the literature on shared mental models, it becomes apparent that the identification of factors to mitigate cultural distance will become more important as the degree of task interdependence increases and as member actions are more tightly coupled.

> *Proposition 8:* As the cultural distance between interdependent team members increases, sensemaking and adaptive team performance become more difficult due to a lack of compatible mental models.

Adaptive Action—Individual Level

The ultimate goal of the sensemaking process within multicultural teams is to gain an understanding of the cultural lens that is salient for individual team members as well as the broader individual cultural profile such that the team's profile—and more specifically cultural distance among members—can be determined. The team's cultural composition, and as a result the cultural distance between members, will be a determinant of the amount of adaptation the team will need to engage in. When the cultural distance within the team is high, there is a lack of compatible mental models within the team, which in turn guide the interpretation and display of behaviors. So what are the skills needed to mitigate the cultural distance among team members? We make a case that perspective taking and negotiation are two essential primary skills for adaptive team performance within multicultural teams (Figure 8.2). These skills are the ones that facilitate members being able to "see" the situation through alternate "cultural lenses." Though perspective taking may also impact early sensemaking processes, the primary focus of perspective taking within the framework, put forth in Figure 8.2, is its use to mitigate existing cultural differences within the team.

Perspective Taking

Perspective taking is an individual-level cognitive skill defined as "the ability to hold two or more potentially conflicting points of view in mind" (Sanchez, Olson-Buchanan, Schmidtke, & Rechner, 2006, p. 3). Similarly, Galinksy, Ku, and Wang (2005) defined perspective taking as "the process of imagining the world from another's vantage point or imagining oneself in another's shoes" (p. 110). Although perspective taking has been primarily conceptualized at the individual level, it may emerge to the team level through the process of compilation (Kozlowski & Klein, 2000). Specifically, within multicultural teams, perspective taking at the individual and team level is functionally equivalent, but variability in the manner in which individual members engage in perspective taking is expected due to members having different cognitive frames with regard to culture.

While the description of perspective taking may sound similar to the notions of empathy, the two constructs have been theoretically and empirically distinguished (see Davis, 1980). Perspective taking is the adaptation of the psychological point of view of others (Davis, 1983). Its relevance to multicultural teams lies in its facilitation of social coordination and social bonds (Galinksy et al., 2005). It has also recently been cited as a critical mechanism in coordination in that taking the perspective of others, especially members of out-groups, increases the overlap between mental representations (e.g., cultural factors) and decreases stereotyping.

Along this same line, research has found other positive benefits of perspective taking. Aberson and Haag (2007) found that when individuals had improved perspective taking, they reported reduced intergroup anxiety, which led to less stereotype endorsement and reduced negative attitudes toward others. This, in turn, may facilitate early sensemaking processes as members attempt to understand actions of culturally diverse members. Other studies have found a benefit in perspective taking in that it increases the positive feeling toward out-group members and eliminates in-group biases (Cadinu & Rothbart, 1996; Galinsky & Moskowitz, 2000; Jones & Nisbett, 1971; Smith & Henry, 1996). All of this also increases overlap in cognition between the self and others as discussed in other studies of perspective taking (Galinsky & Moskowitz, 2000). Finally, Distefano and Maznevski (2000) argued that decentering, a key skill in bridging differences within multicultural teams, relies heavily on perspective taking. Specifically, decentering is defined as "the process of sending and receiving communication with the other person's perspective in mind" (Gibson & Zellmer-Bruhn, 2002, p. 114).

> *Proposition 9:* Team members who use perspective taking to mitigate the negative relationship between cultural distance and adaptive team performance will have a larger impact when the cultural distance among interdependent team members is high.

The means by which perspective taking is facilitated is not entirely clear beyond references to increased contact with others. Specifically, research has found that individuals who have more experience with diversity (through interaction or training) often exhibit more effective perspective taking (Aberson & Haag, 2007; Gurin, Nagda, & Lopez, 2004). The literature on cultural frame switching (CFS) also offers some possible answers as to the facilitation of behaviors similar to perspective taking. CFS refers to the ability to have access to and to apply different cultural systems (e.g., values, meaning) in response to cultural cues (Hong, Morris, Chiu, & Benet-Martínez, 2000). Research has explained that "cultural frame switching occurs in response to contextual cues that make different cultural identities salient .... When a given cultural identity is salient, beliefs, theories, and standards that define the salient identity govern people's thinking and acting" (Verkuyten et al., 2005, p. 597). This constructionist view of culture is based on two key premises. First, culture is not an internal, integrated, and highly general structure, but rather culture is internalized as a "loose network of domain-specific knowledge structures, such as categories and implicit theories" (Bruner, 1990; D'Andrade, 1984; Hong et al., 2000, p. 710; Shore, 1996; Strauss, 1992). Second, individuals have the ability to acquire more than one cultural system that may influence their behaviors, even if these systems contain conflicting views, values, or perspectives (Hong et al., 2000). This perspective holds that although conflicting cultural systems can be possessed by a single individual, it is not possible for both systems to guide cognition simultaneously. Therefore, individuals who hold multiple cultural reference systems must switch between their cultural frames.

CFS allows individuals to switch the lenses they use to view the world at that specific time. One mechanism to do this identified in the literature is to internalize culture as networked discrete constructs that guide cognition when they are accessible, primed, and, therefore, brought to the forefront of individuals' focus. The cultural frames are said to be primed (i.e., brought to the forefront of an individuals' mind by cues that "remind" individuals of culturally consistent content) and thus become accessible. Then each cultural frame can be evaluated against these situational cues; as a result, based on a combination of factors individuals can switch to the primed frames, whichever will meet their needs and is consistent with situational factors. For example, Hong and colleagues (2000) found that cultural icons are potent and distinctive, priming frames and spreading activation for a network of cultural constructs within an individual.

While CFS is a constructionist view of acculturation almost exclusively applied to bicultural individuals, the process can offer a great deal of knowledge that can be applied to teams. To that end, research (Benet-Martínez, Lee, & Leu, 2006) has provided evidence that bicultural individuals possess more complex cultural representations that allow for high cultural empathy (i.e., the ability to both detect and understand another's cultural preferences) and cultural flexibility (i.e., the ability to switch between cultural frameworks or strategies). Furthermore, although the relationship still needs further exploration, research has also implied that biculturalism and CFS may inhibit stereotyping and prejudice (Van der Zee & Van der Gang, 2005). We contend that bicultural individuals are experts at CFS and can be used as leverage to inform how team members may apply this process.

For example, Hong and colleagues (2000) identified cultural cues that informed CFS from case studies taken from interviews with bicultural individuals. They suggested that, for one, CFS may occur in response to contexts and symbols within the environment that may be more associated with one of their cultures over the other. Another study (Verkuyten & Pouliasi, 2002) found that in addition to contextual or situational cues, the use of language, cultural icons, and individuals' willingness to adopt the most salient culture given a particular set of circumstances may also influence CFS. Situational cues like language or icons may cause a specific culture to be more salient and persons to adopt that frame in their interactions. However, some consequences could cause the CFS to become more or less desirable to individuals, suppressing or facilitating the switch to the other frame. In essence, just because a frame is primed does not mean it will be utilized. One suggestion as to what determines the adoption of a frame is group identification or social identification, whereas other suggestions include individual motives, needs, goals, and experiences. Specifically, people's identification (see earlier section on social identity) and individual needs, motives, and goals are used to make sense of the situation and to determine the most beneficial frame to use.

Negotiation

Negotiation is a second vital skill within multicultural teams. This behavioral skill refers to the "process by which two or more parties multilaterally bargain resources for mutual intended gain" (Beam & Segev, 1997, p. 268). It has also been defined by Lomuscio, Wooldridge, and Jennings (2001) as "the process by which a group of agents communicate with one another and try to come to a mutually acceptable agreement on some matter" (p. 4). This skill becomes increasingly important within teams as cultural distance increases. Specifically, the greater the cultural distance within the team the more members must negotiate disparate cognitions, behaviors, and attitudes. In these cases members may use a form of negotiation to develop the shared coherence that leads to the creation of a hybrid culture that allows the processes within adaptive team performance to occur.

Several researchers have said that one way the differences among members within multicultural teams can be mitigated is through the formation of a third hybrid culture (see Earley & Mosakowski, 2000; Graen & Wakabayashi, 1994). This hybrid culture does not reflect any one cultural frame but represents an integration or *negotiated compromise* among the various frames and identities that are present within the team. Negotiation is one strategy by which latent conflict as well as manifested conflict, which often appears as the cultural distance among team members increases, can be resolved. It is a two-way dialogue where the end goal is to reach some type of agreement, which, though often not perfect to either side, allows both sides to move forward cooperatively toward an overarching common goal.

There are several types of negotiation; however, perhaps the one most relevant to the current goal of creating shared cognition concerning the requisite task and teamwork strategies that the team will use is that of principled negotiation (see Fisher, Ury, & Patton, 1991). Principled negotiation falls within the midpoint of using soft techniques whereby one party is not satisfied at all but is afraid of producing more conflict and hard techniques where each instance is seen as a contest and often hard feelings are produced among parties involved in the negotiation. Principled negotiation is a technique in which compromise is reached based on merit rather than through haggling (ibid.). Within this approach to negotiation, mutual gains are sought when possible, and on those issues where this is not possible true compromise is often reached.

While we acknowledge that the manner in which negotiation is proposed within the current framework may not be the typical use of negotiation since members are not bargaining for hard objective products, we do think it is applicable because members are often coming into multicultural teams with strong ties to their cultural identities and the requisite values (producing a mixed-motive situation). To produce a third hybrid culture where the beliefs, values, and preferences among team members become not shared but compatible requires negotiation such that a superordinate culture can be created that is not the result of any one single cultural identity. This is especially important as it has been argued that different cultural identities also bring different ideologies and metaphors concerning how teams should be thought of and function (e.g., Earley & Gibson, 2002; Gibson & Zellmer-Bruhn, 2002). Finally, it is also important to acknowledge that although we maintain that negotiation is a vital skill that must be present for adaptive team performance to occur, others have argued that the specific strategies used within this process will vary across cultures (Adair & Brett, 2005; Gelfand, Erez, & Aycan 2007). For example, Gelfand, Leslie, and Keller (in press) proposed a typology of conflict cultures by crossing two dimensions that describe norms for handling conflict (i.e., negotiation strategies): (1) active or passive; and (2) agreeable or disagreeable. Within this typology actively handled conflict is characterized by behaviors promoting open engagement and low levels of situational constraint, whereas conflict that is passively managed has the opposite characterization. Looking at the second dimension (i.e., agreeableness/disagreeableness), norms promoting agreeableness promote behavior aimed toward collective interests and moving toward others in seeking a negotiated solution; the converse is true of norms for disagreeable conflict management. Ultimately Gelfand et al. (in press) stated that crossing the two axes results in four types of conflict cultures: (1) dominating (active, disagreeable); (2) collaborative (active, agreeable); (3) avoidant (passive, agreeable); and (4) passive aggressive (passive, disagreeable). They hypothesized the various conflict cultures will differentially be used based on several factors, one of which is the cultural composition of the organization. Specifically, dominating conflict cultures are most common in environments characterized by vertical individualism, masculinity, and looseness, whereas collaborative conflict cultures most often appear in cultures characterized by horizontal collectivism, looseness, and femininity. Additionally, conflict-avoidant conflict cultures will coincide with preferences for vertical collectivism, uncertainty avoidance, and tightness, and passive aggressive cultures will coincide with preferences for high-power distance and tightness (ibid.). Here we extend this thought to the team's composition. The implication is that certain negotiation strategies are likely to be differentially expected or accepted based on the team's composition.

> *Proposition 10*: Team members who use principled negotiation to mitigate the negative relationship between cultural distance and adaptive team performance will have a larger impact when cultural distance among interdependent team members is high.

Concluding Comments

Multicultural teams are increasingly common within the organizational landscape. Perhaps more importantly, they are not expected to disappear anytime soon. When used successfully, they can promote great rewards not only in terms of team adaptation but in some cases may also provide increased goodwill among partnering nations. However, time and time again it has been shown that the diversity present within multicultural teams can act as a double-edged sword posing coordination and communication difficulties in already complex environments.

While research on multicultural teams has increased over the last several years, there have been few integrated frameworks that serve to examine the interaction of cultural diversity and team adaptation. The present chapter has provided some initial ideas regarding such a framework. At this early stage, we have focused on delineating the impact of a team's cultural diversity on the front-end processes and states needed to facilitate adaptive team performance and team adaptation. Specifically, we have made a case for the fact that much of the confusion and process loss within multicultural teams arises from a lack of understanding the multilayered nature of culture and the situational, contextual variables that serve to moderate the specific structure and content of the emerging cultural identity. The ability to recognize or predict the cultural identity in which team members are operating allows members to judge what adaptive action is necessary to begin to form the initial compatible knowledge structures needed for adaptive team performance to occur. We further outlined that when the cultural distance or discrepancy between cognitive schemas is high, perspective taking and negotiation skills are needed to assist in forming compatible knowledge structures. However, when the cultural distance is not great, cultural diversity may not negatively impact adaptive team performance in that knowledge structures, albeit slightly different, are compatible.

The presented framework is only an initial step toward organizing thoughts about multicultural teams and team adaptation; we recognize that many other factors besides the situational context may moderate many of the underlying relationships. However, due to our primary focus on the front end of this process we chose to begin our examination with how situational factors might impact the cultural identity that is primed. The initial framework has only begun to scratch the surface in delineating the knowledge components and processes involved in the initial sensemaking activities that are needed for adaptive multicultural teams. However, due to the complex nature of this process we are able to extract several areas in need of further research. First and foremost, although many of the propositions set forth leverage against more established work, others are in need of empirical validation within the context of multicultural teams. Second, an area we think has much potential in terms of preparing team members to work within such teams is the focus on how the situational context can be used to prime a specific cultural identity. Not only does a better understanding of how context impacts the salience of a particular cultural identity provide a manner in which members can better interpret verbal and nonverbal actions of team members, but this understanding also can be used as an influence to encourage collaboration. Specifically, to the extent that leaders understand these complex dynamics, they can be used to frame communications such that maximum cooperation and collaboration is promoted. It is our hope that this chapter stimulates dialogue, thought, and expansion of the ideas presented and focuses attention on the important topic of how cultural diversity may impact the adaptive cycle as well as the distal outcome of team adaptation.

Acknowledgments

The views expressed in this work are those of the authors and do not necessarily reflect official Army policy. This work was supported in part by funding from the Army Research Laboratory's Advanced Decision Architecture Collaborative Technology Alliance (Cooperative Agreement DAAD19-01-2-0009).

We would like to thank Linda Pierce and Michele Gelfand for their comments on earlier versions of the chapter.

References

Aberson, C. L. & Haag, S. C. (2007). Contact, perspective taking, and anxiety as predictors of stereotype endorsement, explicit attitudes, and implicit attitudes. *Group Processes and Intergroup Relations, 10*(2), 179–201.

Adair, W. L. & Brett, J. M. (2005). The negotiation dance: Time, culture, and behavioral sequences in negotiation. *Organization Science, 16*(1), 33–51.

Barkema, H. G., Oded, S., Freek, V., & Bell, J. H. J. (1997). Working abroad, working with others: How firms learn to operate international joint ventures. *Academy of Management Journal, 40*, 426–442.

Beam, C. & Segev, A. (1997). Automates negotiations: A survey of the state of the art. *Wirtschaftsinformatik, 39*(3), 268.

Benet-Martínez, V. & Haritatos, J. (2005). Bicultural identity integration (BII): Components and psychosocial antecedents. *Journal of Personality, 73*(4), 1015–1050.

Benet- Martínez, V., Lee, F., & Leu, J. (2006). Biculturalism and cognitive complexity: Expertise in cultural representations.*Journal of Cross-Cultural Psychology, 37*(4), 386–407.

Bergson, H. (1911). *Creative evolution* (A. Mitchell). New York: Henry Holt. (Original work published 1907.)

Berry, J. W., Poortinga, Y. H., Segall, M. H., & Dasen, P. R. (1992). *Cross-cultural psychology: Research and application.* New York: Cambridge University Press.

Bruner, J. S. (1990). *Acts of meaning.* Cambridge, MA: Harvard University Press.

Buono, A. F. & Bowditch, J. L. (1989). *The human side of mergers and acquisitions.* San Francisco, CA: Jossey-Bass.

Burke, C. S., Priest, H. A., Upshaw, C., Salas, E., & Pierce, L. (2007). A sensemaking approach to understanding multicultural teams: An initial framework. To appear in D. I. Stone & E. F. Stone-Romero (Eds.), *Cultural diversity and human resource practices* (pp. 269–306). Mahwah, NJ: LEA.

Burke, C. S., Salas, E., & DiazGranados, D. (2008). The role of team learning in facilitating team adaptation within complex environments: Tools and strategies. In V. I. Sessa & M. London (Eds.), *Group learning* (pp. 217–241). Mahwah, NJ: Lawrence Erlbaum Associates.

Burke, C. S., Stagl, K. C., Salas, E., Pierce, L., & Kendall, D. L. (2006). Understanding team adaptation: A conceptual analysis and model. *Journal of Applied Psychology, 91*(6), 1189–1207.

Cadinu, M. R. & Rothbart, M. (1996). Self-anchoring and differentiation processes in the minimal group setting. *Journal of Personality and Social Psychology, 70*, 661–677.

Chao, G. T. & Moon, H. (2005). The cultural mosaic: A metatheory for understanding the complexity of culture. *Journal of Applied Psychology, 90*(6), 1128–1140.

Child, J., Faulkner, D., & Pitkethly, R. (2001). *The management of international acquisitions.* Oxford, England: Oxford University Press.

Chirkov, V. I., Lynch, M., & Niwa, S. (2005). Application of the scenario questionnaire of horizontal and vertical individualism and collectivism to the assessment of cultural distance and cultural fit. *International Journal of Intercultural Relations, 29*(4), 469–490.

Crowley, J., Currion, P., Frost, E., Graham, J., Griffiths, P., Hanchard, D., et al. (2006). *Stability, security, transition, and reconstruction: Observations and recommendations from the field*. Retrieved March 3, 2007, from http://www.strongangel3.net/files/sstr_20061107_web.pdf.

Cushman, D. P. & King, S. S. (1985). National and organizational cultures in conflict resolution: Japan, the United States, and Yugoslavia. In W. G. Gudykunst, L. P. Stewart, & S. Ting-Toomey (Eds.), *Communication, culture, and organizational processes* (pp. 114–133). Beverly Hills, CA: Sage Publications.

D'Andrade, R. (1984). Cultural meaning systems. In R. A. Shweder, & R.A. LeVine (Eds.), *Culture theory: Essays on mind, self, and emotion*. Cambridge University Press, Cambridge, UK, pp. 88–119.

D'Andrade, R. (1995). *The development of cognitive anthropology*. Cambridge: Cambridge University Press.

Davis, M. H. (1980). A multidimensional approach to individual differences in empathy. *JSAS Catalog of Selected Documents in Psychology, 10(4)*, 85.

Davis, M. H. (1983). Measuring individual differences in empathy: Evidence for a multidimensional approach. *Journal of Personality, 44*, 113-126.

Distefano, J. J. & Maznevski, M. L. (2000). Creating value with diverse teams in global management. *Organizational Dynamics, 29*(1), 45–63.

Drucker, P. F. (1992). The new society of organizations. *Harvard Business Review, 70*(5), 95–104.

Earley, P. C. & Gibson, C. B. (2002). *Multiactional work teams: A new perspective*. Mahwah, NJ: Lawrence Erlbaum Associates.

Earley, P. C. & Mosakowski, E. (2000). Creating hybrid team cultures: An empirical test of transnational team functioning. *Academy of Management Journal, 43*, 26–49.

Elsass, P. M. & Veiga, J. F. (1994) Acculturation in acquired organizations: A force-field perspective.*Human Relations, 47*(4), 431–453.

Employee Benefit Plan Review (2001). Survey of expatriates shows differing employer-employee perceptions. *Employee Benefit Plan Review, 55*(12), 40–41.

Erez, M. & Gati, E. (2004). A dynamic, multi-level model of culture: From the micro level of the individual to the macro level of a global culture. *Applied Psychology: An International Review, 53*(4), 583–598.

Fisher, R., Ury, W., & Patton, B. (1991) *Getting to yes: Negotiating agreement without giving in*. Boston, MA: Houghton Mifflin Company.

Fiske, S. T. & Taylor, S. E. (1991). *Social cognition* (2d ed.). New York: McGraw-Hill.

Fleming, P. J., Wood, G. M., Dudley, N. M., Bader, P. K., & Zaccaro, S. J. (2003, April). An adaptation training program for military leaders and teams. In E. D. Pulakos (Chair), *Mission critical: Developing adaptive performance in U. S. Army Special Forces*. Symposium conducted at the 18th annual meeting for the Society of Industrial and Organizational Psychology, Orlando, FL.

Galinsky, A. D. & Moskowitz, G. B. (2000). Perspective-taking: Decreasing stereotype expression, stereotype accessibility, and in-group favoritism. *Journal of Personality and Social Psychology, 78*(4), 708–724.

Galinsky, A. D., Ku, G., & Wang, C. S. (2005). Perspective-taking and self-other overlap: Fostering social bonds and facilitating social coordination. *Group Process and Intergroup Relations, 8*(2), 109–124.

Gelfand, M. J., Erez, M., & Aycan, Z. (2007). Cross-cultural organizational behavior. *Annual Review of Psychology, 58*, 479–514.

Gelfand, M. J., Leslie, L. M., & Keller, K. (in press). On the etiology of conflict cultures. *Review of Organizational Behavior.*

Geringer, J. M., Beamish, P. W., & daCosta, R. C. (1989). Diversification strategy and internationalization: Implications for MNE performance. *Strategic Management Journal, 10*(2), 109–119.

Gibson, C. B. & Grubb, A. R. (2005). Turning the tide in multinational teams. In D. L. Shapiro, M. A. Von Glinow, & J. Cheng, (Vol. Eds.), *Managing multinational teams: Global perspectives* (Vol. 18, pp. 69–95). Amsterdam, The Netherlands: Elsevier.

Gibson, C. B. & Zellmer-Bruhn, M. E. (2002). Minding your metaphors: Applying the concept of teamwork metaphors to the management of teams in multicultural contexts. *Organizational Dynamics, 31*(2), 101–116.

Graen, G. B. & Wakabayashi, M. (1994). Cross-cultural leadership-making: Bridging American and Japanese diversity for team advantage. In: H.C. Triandis, M. D. Dunnette, & L. M. Hough (Eds.), *Handbook of industrial and organizational psychology: Volume 4* (pp. 415–446). New York: Consulting Psychologist Press.

Gurin, P., Nagda, B. A., & Lopez, G. E. (2004). The benefits of diversity in education for democratic citizenship. *Journal of Social Issues, 60* (1), 17–34.

Hannerz, U. (1992). *Cultural complexity: Studies in the social organization of meaning.* New York: Columbia University Press.

Harrison, D. A., & Klein, K. J. (2007). What's the difference? Diversity constructs as separation, variety, or disparity in organizations. *The Academy of Management Review, 32*(4), 1199–1228.

Hofstede, G. (2001). *Culture's consequences comparing values, behaviors, institutions, and organizations across nations.* Thousand Oaks, CA: Sage Publications.

Hogg, M. A. & Terry, D. J. (2000). Social identity and self-categorization processes in organizational contexts. *Academy of Management Review, 25,* 121–140.

Hong, Y., Morris, M., Chiu, C., & Benet-Martínez, V. (2000). Multicultural minds: A dynamic constructivist approach to culture and cognition. *American Psychologist, 55,* 709–720.

Jelinek, M. & Wilson, J. (2005). Macro influences on multicultural teams: A multilevel view. In D. L. Shapiro, M. A. Von Glinow, & J. L. C. Cheng (Eds.), *Managing multinational teams: Global perspectives* (pp. 209–233). Amsterdam, Netherlands: Elsevier.

Jones, E. E., Kannouse, D. E., Kelley, H. H., Nisbett, R. E., Valins, S., & Weiner, B. (1972). *Attribution: Perceiving the causes of behavior.* Morristown, NJ: General Learning Press.

Jones, E. E. & Nisbett, R. E. (1971). *The actor and the observer: Divergent perceptions of the causes of behavior.* Morristown, NJ: General Learning Press.

Klein, G. & Pierce, L. G. (2001, June). Adaptive teams. In *Proceedings of the 2001 6th International Command and Control Research and Technology Symposium,* Annapolis, MD: Department of Defense Cooperative Research Program.

Klein, H. A. (2004). Cognition in natural settings: The cultural lens model. In M. Kaplan (Ed.), *Cultural ergonomics. Advances in human performance and cognitive engineering research* (Vol. 4, 249–280). Elsevier.

Kluckhohn, C. (1951). The study of culture. In D. Lerner & H. D. Lasswell (Eds.), *The policy sciences.* Stanford, CA: Stanford University Press.

Kogut, B. & Singh, H. (1988). The effect of national culture on the choice of entry mode. *Journal of International Business Studies, 19*(3), 411–432.

Korte, R. F. (2006). A review of social identity theory with implications for training and development. *Journal of European Industrial Training, 31*(3), 166–180.

Kozlowski, S. W. J., Gully, S. M., Nason, E. R., & Smith, E. M. (1999). Developing adaptive teams: A theory of compilation and performance across levels and time. In D. R. Ilgen & E. D. Pulakos (Eds.), *The changing nature of work and performance: Implications for staffing, personnel actions, and development.* San Francisco, CA: Jossey-Bass.

Kozlowski, S. W. J. & Klein, K. J. (2000). A multilevel approach to theory and research in organizations: Contextual, temporal, and emergent processes. In K. J. Klein & S. W. J. Kozlowski (Eds.), *Multilevel theory, research and methods in organizations: Foundations, extensions, and new directions* (pp. 3–90). San Francisco, CA: Jossey-Bass.

Kozlowski, S. W. J., Toney, R. J., Mullins, M. E., Weissbein, D. A., Brown, K. G., & Bell, B. S. (2001). Developing adaptation: A theory for the design of integrated-embedded training systems. *Advances in Human Performance and Cognitive Engineering Research, 1,* 59–122.

Langlois, C, C. & Schlegelmilch, B. B. (1990). Do Corporate Codes Of Ethics Reflect National Character? Evidence from Europe and the United States. *Journal of International Business Studies, 21*(4), 519–539.

LePine, J. A. (2003). Team adaptation and postchange performance: Effects of team composition in terms of members' cognitive ability and personality. *Journal of Applied Psychology, 88,* 27–39.

Lomuscio, A., Wooldridge, M., & Jennings, N. R. (2001). A classification scheme for negotiation in electronic commerce. In F. Dignum & C. Sierra (Eds.), *Agent-mediated electronic commerce: A European agentlink perspective.* Springer-Verlag Lecture Notes in AI Volume 1991.

Mannix, E. & Neale, M. A. (2005). What differences make a difference? The promise and reality of diverse teams in organizations. *Psychological Science in the Public Interest, 6*(2), 31–55.

Ngo, H. Y., Turban, D., Lau, C. M., & Lui, S. Y. (1998). Human resource practices and firm performance of multinational corporations: Influences of country origin. *International Journal of Human Resource Management, 9*(4), 632–652.

Oaker, G. & Brown, R. (1986). Intergroup relations in a hospital setting: A further test of social identity theory. *Human Relations, 39*(8), 767–778.

Olie, R. L. (1996). *European transnational mergers.* Unpublished doctoral dissertation. University of Maastricht, Maastricht, The Netherlands.

Pierce, L. G. (2002). *Preparing and supporting adaptable leaders and teams for support and stability operations.* Paper presented at Defense Analysis Seminar XI, Seoul, Korea. 11th ROK-US Defense Analysis Seminar Proceedings (Manpower Policy, Session 4), pp. 97–129.

Pulakos, E., Dorsey, D., & White, S. (2006). Adaptability in the workplace: Selecting an adaptive workforce. In C. S. Burke, L. G. Pierce, & E. Salas (Eds.), *Understanding adaptability: A prerequisite for effective performance within complex environments. Advances in human performance and cognitive engineering research* (pp. 41–71). Amsterdam, The Netherlands: Elsevier.

Ralston, D. A., Gustafson, D. J., Mainiero, L., & Umstot, D. (1993). Strategies of upward influence: A cross-national comparison of Hong Kong and American managers. *Asia Pacific Journal of Management, 10*(2), 157–175.

Ring, P. S. & Rands, G. P. (1989). Sensemaking, understanding, and committing: Emergent interpersonal transaction processes in the evolution of 3M's microgravity research program. In A. H. Van den Ven, H. L. Angle, & M. S. Poole (Eds.), *Research on the management of innovation. The Minnesota studies* (pp. 337–366). New York: Ballinger.

Roccas, S. & Brewer, M. B. (2002). Social identity complexity. *Personality & Social Psychology Review, 6,* 88–106.

Rosen, M. A., Bedwell, W. L., Wildman, J., Fritzsche, B. A., Salas, E., & Burke, C. S. (2008). So you want to measure team adaptation?: Some guiding principles. Manuscript submitted for publication.

Salk, J. E. & Arya, B. (2005). Social performance learning in multinational corporations: Multicultural teams, their social capital and use of cross-sector alliances. In D. L. Shapiro, M. A. Von Glinow, & J. L. C. Cheng (Eds.), *Managing multinational teams: Global perspectives* (pp. 189–207). Amsterdam, The Netherlands: Elsevier.

Sanchez, R. J., Olson-Buchanan, J. B., Schmidtke, J. M., & Rechner, P. L. (2006, May). *Multiple perspective taking in team member exchange in a virual environment.* Paper presented at the 21st annual meeting of the Society for Industrial and Organizational Psychology, Dallas, TX.

Schein, E. (1992). *Organizational culture and leadership.* San Francisco, CA: Jossey-Bass.

Schneider, S. C. & De Meyer, A. (1991). Interpreting and responding to strategic issues: the role of national culture. Strategic Management Journal, *12,* 307–320.

Schmid, H. (2006). Leadership styles and leadership change in human and community service organizations. *Nonprofit Management and Leadership, 17*(2), 179–194.

Shaffer, M., Harrison, D., & Gilley, K. (1999). Dimensions, determinants, and differences in the expatriate adjustment process. *Journal of International Business Studies, 30*(3), 557–581.

Shore, B. (1991). Twice-born, once conceived: Meaning construction and cultural cognition. *American Anthropologist, 93*(1), 9–27.

Shore, B. (1996). *Culture in mind: Cognition, culture, and the problem of meaning.* New York: Oxford University Press.

Smith, E. R. & Henry, S. (1996). An in-group becomes part of the self: Response time evidence. *Personality and Social Psychology Bulletin, 22,* 635–642.

Slangen, A. H. L. (2006). National cultural distance and initial foreign acquisition performance: The moderating effect of integration, *Journal of World Business, 4*(1–2), 161–170.

Stagl, K. C., Burke, C. S., Salas, E., & Pierce, L. (2006). Team adaptation: The realization of team synergy. In C. S. Burke, L. Pierce, & E. Salas (Eds.), *Advances in human performance and cognitive engineering research* (pp. 117–142). Oxford, England: Elsevier Science.

Starbuck, W. & Milliken, F. (1988). Executive perceptual filters: What they notice and how they make sense. In D. Hambrick (Ed.), *The executive effect: Concepts and methods for studying top managers* (pp. 35–65). Greenwich, CT: JAI Press.

Strauss, C. (1992). Models and motives. In R. G. D'Andrade & C. Strauss (Eds.), *Humans motives and cultural models* (pp. 1–20). New York: Cambridge University Press.

Strauss, C. & Quinn, N. (1997). *A cognitive theory of cultural meaning*. Cambridge, England: Cambridge University Press.

Thomas, J. B., Clark, S. M., & Gioia, D. A. (1993). Strategic sensemaking and organizational performance: Linkages among scanning, interpretation, action, and outcomes. *Academy of Management Journal, 36*(2), 239–270.

Turner, J. C., Hogg, M. A., Oakes, P. J., Reicher, S. D., & Whetherell, M. S. (1987). Rediscovering the social group: A self-categorization theory. Oxford: Blackwell.

Van Kleef, G. A., Steinel, W., Knippenberg, D. V., Hogg, M. A., & Svensson, A. (2007). Group member prototypicality and intergroup negotiation: How one's standing in the group affects negotiation behaviour. *British Journal of Social Psychology, 46*, 129–152.

Van der Zee, K. & Van der Gang, I. (2005). *Individual differences in reactions to cultural diversity under threat: The generalizability of the anxiety buffer hypothesis.* Poster presented at the 6th annual convention of the Society for Personality and Social Psychology, New Orleans, LA.

Verkuyten, M. & DeWolf, A. (2002). Ethnic minority identity and group context: Self-descriptions, acculturation attitudes and group evaluations in an intra- and intergroup situation. *European Journal of Social Psychology, 32*, 781–800.

Verkuyten, M., & Pouliasi, K. (2002). Biculturalism among older children: Cultural fram switching, attributions, self-identification, and attitudes. *Journal of Cross-Cultural Psychology, 33*(6), 596–609.

Very, P., Lubatkin, M., & Calori, R. (1998). A cross national assessment of acculturative stress in recent European mergers. In M. C. Gertsen, A. M. Soderberg, & J. E. Torp (Eds.), *Cultural dimensions of international mergers and acquisitions* (pp. 85–110). New Yor: Walter de Gruyter.

Ward, C., Bocher, S., & Furnham, A. (2001). *The psychology of culture shock* (2d ed.). Hove, East Sussex: Routledge.

Weick, K. E. (1995). *Sensemaking in organizations*. London: Sage Publications, Inc.

Wunderle, W. D. (2006). *Through the lens of cultural awareness: A primer for U.S. Armed Forces deploying to Arab and Middle Eastern countries*. Fort Leavenworth, KS: Combat Studies Institute Press.

9

Cognitive Similarity Configurations in Teams: In Search of the Team MindMeld™

Joan R. Rentsch, Lisa A. Delise, and Scott Hutchison

Teams today must make decisions requiring integration of large amounts of difficult, intricate, and distributed information. Increasingly, teams are tackling these complicated decision-making tasks in complex environments (e.g., time compressed, multicultural, virtual, networked), with complex compositions (e.g., multicultural members, diverse expertise), and with complex structures (e.g., ad hoc, distributed, shared leadership, rotating membership), all of which make efficient, high-quality information processing critical to team success. Information sharing, an initial phase of information processing within teams, is challenging for teams composed of homogeneous team members working face to face (e.g., Stasser, 1991; Stasser & Titus, 1985, 1987). Therefore, it is intensely demanding for today's teams, particularly those composed of heterogeneous members who fulfill unique roles, who possess unique knowledge, and who must collaborate asynchronously through technology. Understanding the cognitive processes required to collaborate under these conditions is essential to promoting wise team decision making and high team performance. These cognitive processes include similar understandings among team members regarding many aspects of the team, its task, and its context. There exists a need for team members to develop functional and similar understandings of each other, their task, their process, and so on to be effective, particularly in dynamic situations requiring adaptation. That is, team members must experience a "mind meld" that will produce cognitive similarity among them.

The purpose of the present chapter is to articulate and elaborate various forms of Team MindMeld, or cognitive similarity, that may exist among team members. First, the functions of cognitive similarity in teams are described. Next, a framework is presented that defines cognitive similarity and includes forms of cognition, forms of similarity, and cognitive content domains. Types and configurations of cognitive similarity are presented in that framework. Then, configurations of cognitive similarity in teams are illustrated with examples that target information sharing in teams and team adaptability. The examples highlight the variety of possible relationships that may exist among types of cognitive similarity and team processes and outcomes. Lastly, training and technology are offered as two methods for inducing a Team MindMeld.

Cognitive Similarity in Teams

Cognitive similarity among individuals has intrigued psychologists, anthropologists, and sociologists. For example, within industrial/organizational psychology, cognitive similarity among members of organizations has been represented in the organizational socialization, climate, and culture literatures (James, Hater, Gent, & Bruni, 1978; Louis, 1980; Moreland & Levine, 1989; Rentsch, 1990; Schneider & Reichers, 1983). More recently, organizational researchers have studied cognitive similarity among team members in the forms of perception (e.g., team climates, group cultures, shared beliefs, shared expectations), structured cognition (e.g., mental models, schemas), and interpretative convergence (e.g., sensemaking, cognitive consensus) using a variety of measurement techniques including questionnaires, structural assessments, and ethnographic techniques (Rentsch, Small, & Hanges, 2008).

Members of teams develop similar cognitions that enable them to understand ambiguous stimuli and events to make sense of what is happening around them. A key period for the development of similar cognitions within a team occurs when team members are socialized into a new team and are faced with novel events. Within the team context, encountering novel situations activates interpretation efforts that involve social construction processes. As new team members are socialized into existing teams (Levine & Moreland, 1991), they learn from their teammates how to interpret team-related events. In newly formed teams, members negotiate common interpretations of events, and these interpretations will serve as a basis for sensemaking with regard to future events (Walsh, Henderson, & Deighton, 1988). Team members make sense of their situation by drawing on their past experiences and on their interactions with others. The social construction process that occurs when team members interact directly or indirectly with one another, particularly when they are solving novel problems (e.g., Berger & Luckmann, 1966; Schneider & Reichers, 1983), produces cognitive similarity among the team members. Training, selection, socialization, similar past experiences, and technology are forces that can be managed to assist the social construction process and to communicate schema content (Rentsch & Hall, 1994).

Cognitive similarity among team members has the potential to enhance or to inhibit team performance. Theoretical perspectives, based on assumptions of functional cognitive content and of an optimal level of similarity, emphasize the positive effects of cognitive similarity within teams. Given these assumptions, cognitive similarity among team members will facilitate performance, in part, by affording the team efficiencies (Cannon-Bowers, Salas, & Converse, 1993; Kraiger & Wenzel, 1997; Rentsch & Hall, 1994). For example, cognitive similarity benefits teams by promoting smooth interactions among team members due to increasing team members' ability to predict and understand teammates' behaviors. Furthermore, team members understand how to behave in manners that their teammates will accept. Cognitive similarity among team members influences the kinds of environmental information attended to and the interpretations of that information (Levy, 2005). Thus, cognitive similarity among team members enhances such team processes as communication (Weick, 1993), the experience and interpretation of conflict (Rentsch & Zelno, 2003), and the teamwork behaviors of team members (Greenberg, 1995; Naumann & Bennett, 2000; Xie & Johns, 2000; Zohar, 2000). Furthermore, cognitive similarity among team members has been found to be positively associated, either directly or indirectly through team processes (e.g., Marks, Sabella, Burke, & Zaccaro, 2002; Marks, Zaccaro, & Mathieu, 2000), with team performance (e.g., Gibson, 2001; Kirkman, Tesluk, & Rosen, 2001; Levy, 2005; Naumann & Bennett, 2002; Rentsch & Klimoski, 2001; Smith-Jentsch, Mathieu, & Kraiger, 2005), and team member satisfaction (Mason & Griffin, 2003; Mohammed & Ringseis, 2001).

The research evidence to date clearly indicates that advanced understanding of cognitive similarity among team members will be associated with effective teams. Furthermore, researchers have approached the study of cognitive similarity from several perspectives (e.g., perceptual, structural, and interpretive), and each perspective has produced promising results. The following section presents a framework for integrating these perspectives.

Framework for Cognitive Similarity

Cognitive similarity is an overarching concept that is relevant to dyads, teams, and organizations. Rentsch et al. (2008) defined cognitive similarity as forms of related meanings or understandings attributed to and utilized to make sense of and interpret internal and external events including affect, behavior, and thoughts of self and others that exist among individuals. They deliberately elected to refer to "similar" rather than "shared" cognition to distinguish between shared or identical cognitions and nonidentical or *similar* cognitions. Cognition is assumed to exist exclusively within individuals. Personal experiences, including direct and indirect interactions with others, will influence an individual's cognitions, and, through social construction processes, these cognitions become similar to those of the others with whom they interact. Multiple types of cognitive similarity exist and are defined by the intersection of three features: (1) the form of the cognition; (2) the form of similarity; and (3) the cognitive content domain. Types of cognitive similarity in combination produce configurations of cognitive similarity (ibid.).

Forms of Cognition

Research on teams in organizations has examined at least three forms of cognition in the study of cognitive similarity (Rentsch et al., 2008). Perceptual cognition addresses meaning reflected in descriptions and expectations constructed to alleviate uncertainty and to facilitate prediction. Perceptual cognition is developed based on patterns identified from accumulated observations. One form of perceptual cognition is team-level climate, which researchers have referred to as *shared perceptions.* For example, climate for innovation, climate for creativity, climate for safety, and procedural justice team climate have been examined in teams (e.g., Anderson & West, 1998; Bain, Mann, & Pirola-Merlo, 2001; Colquitt, Noe, & Jackson, 2002; Naumann & Bennett, 2000, 2002; Pirola-Merlo & Mann, 2004; Zohar, 2000; Zohar & Luria, 2005). Researchers have studied other forms of perceptual cognition in teams including shared beliefs (e.g., Gibson, 2003) and shared expectations (e.g., Xie & Johns, 2000). Although these researchers use the term *shared,* their methods (e.g., evaluations of agreement and interrater reliability) indicate that they acknowledge nonidentical cognitions. Perceptual cognition, as it is assessed, does not provide deep understanding of causal, relational, or explanatory links. Therefore, it is more closely associated with the description of cognitive content (i.e., cognitive nodes containing the contents of beliefs, attitudes, values, perceptions, prototypes, and expectations) than with the description of underlying cognitive structure.

Structured cognition refers to the organization (structure) of knowledge and incorporates causal, relational, and explanatory connections among nodes of cognitive content. Underlying characteristics of structured cognition include integration, differentiation, centrality, density, and content and directionality of linkages. For example, a very dense structure would consist of many connections among all or most content nodes, reflecting a high degree of integration among concepts in the content domain. Such features have not been the subject of much investigation in team research but present avenues for future work on cognitive similarity. Researchers have studied overlap among team members' cognitive structures in the forms of shared mental models (e.g., Marks et al., 2000, 2002; Mathieu, Heffner, Goodwin, Cannon-Bowers, & Salas, 2005) and similar schemas (e.g., Rentsch & Klimoski, 2001; Rentsch & Zelno, 2003). Cognitive structures are the basis of interpretive meaning.

Interpretive cognition involves value-laden explanations or frames for describing events and therefore ascribing meaning to events. Perceptual cognition, as it has been studied, provides the cognitive contents (i.e., nodes) that are linked to form structured cognition, which in turn produces interpretive cognition. Interpretive cognition, which is reflected in frames, underlying dimensions, and interpretive categories, has been studied in teams (e.g., Baba, Gluesing, Ratner, & Wagner, 2004; Fiol, 1994; Gioia & Thomas, 1996; Mohammed & Ringseis, 2001).

These are just three forms of cognition that may be similar among team members. Research on all of these forms has yielded fruitful results that promote understanding of team functioning. Although these three forms of cognition are the primary forms studied in team research, other forms of cognition may exist. Regardless of the form of cognition under investigation, team members appear to develop some form of similarity with respect to the cognition. Several forms of similarity may exist.

Forms of Similarity

Typically, in the team literature, cognition held in common among individuals is referred to as shared or consensual. However, referring to cognition as similar—that is, having imperfect or nonidentical overlap—more accurately describes the degree of commonness that will exist among individuals' cognitions. Many forms of similarity exist, including congruence, accuracy, complementarity, and forms of similarity based on the social relations model. Researchers have only scratched the surface of the complexity of similarity. Next, three commonly examined forms of cognitive similarity are identified.

Cognitive congruence is the form of cognitive similarity defined by the degree of match in cognition among individuals where there is no target or "correct" value for individual cognitions to match. This is the most typically studied form of cognitive similarity. Cognitive accuracy, another form of cognitive similarity, is defined as the degree of match in cases where a "true score" or target value exists. Team members' characteristics, task characteristics, and contextual features are examples of targets. Training effectiveness, for example, may be evaluated by examining the degree to which trainees' cognitions match the instructor's cognitions (i.e., the target value; Smith-Jentsch et al., 2005). In addition to congruent and accurate forms, similarity may also take a complementary form. For example, team members' cognitions may be complementary in structure or content, fitting together like puzzle pieces. Complementary cognitions among individuals are those that balance or compensate for the cognitions of others. Although complementary cognition implies differences in cognition, obviously not all differences are complementary. To be complementary, individuals' cognitions must fit together to compensate for gaps in others' understandings of a knowledge domain. Cognitive convergence/divergence and integration/differentiation are possible example forms of cognitive complementarity.

Recently, additional forms of similarity, derived from the application of the social relations model to cognitions among team members, were introduced (Rentsch & Woehr, 2004). The social relations model (SRM) differentiates influences of person perceptions as due to the perceiver, the target, or the idiosyncratic interaction of the perceiver and the target (Kenny, 1994). The model enables generation of interesting questions that instigate additional forms of similarity likely to be related to team functioning and performance (e.g., Do Chris and Pat view each other similarly? Do Chris and Pat view Jamie similarly but view Terry differently?). For example, cognitive similarity within a team might be described using team meta-accuracy, which is the degree to which all team members are accurate in understanding how their teammates view them.

Similarity can be evaluated in terms of the degree to which similarity is apprehended and the degree to which is it reciprocal. Most likely, team members will not be aware of the way in which or the extent to which their cognitions are similar. Indeed, the extent to which cognitive similarity is apprehended serves as another variable for investigation in this research stream. Reciprocity, another dimension, may be relevant for some forms of similarity. For example, parents know how their child construes the world (i.e., they know how the child cognitively organizes information and know how the child thinks). The parents' cognitions (e.g., schemas) of their child's cognitions (e.g., schemas) are quite accurate, because they teach the child how to organize information and how to create meaning (i.e., the parents aid the child's cognitive development). However, the degree of cognitive accuracy in this case is not reciprocal, because the child's cognitions of how the parents think will not be highly accurate.

Underlying dimensions associated with forms of similarity include level, variability, stability, and, when examining multiple forms of similarity, profile shape. One note about similarity level is warranted. Typically, similarity assessments involve a comparison of members' cognitions. Level of cognitive similarity is determined by the average of these. A very high level of similarity, particularly in the form of congruence, is sometimes associated with groupthink. Groupthink refers to members of a group conforming to a strong leader's opinion. Although too much similarity may create stagnation, the extent to which similarity may be detrimental will depend to some degree on the content of the cognition. Groupthink may result from similar cognitions regarding the need to conform to the leader and the group but will not result from similar cognitions about speaking one's mind and openly discussing alternate opposing viewpoints in a decision-making group. Generally, researchers agree that some optimal level of similarity exists that will vary depending on the form of cognition and the cognitive content domain.

It should be noted that, in general, the underlying dimensions of similarity have not been addressed in detail in the research and offer avenues for future research. Regardless of the form (or features) of similarity of interest, similarity may be assessed with respect to any specific feature (e.g., complexity, integration, coherence) of any specific form of cognition (e.g., perceptual, structural, or interpretive). In addition, all forms of similarity may be related to various cognitive content domains.

Cognitive Content Domains

Individuals have the potential to develop cognitions with respect to any content domain. That is, the possible cognitive content domains are infinite. Content domains relevant to teams include self, team members, team leadership, and the team task. Researchers of cognition in teams recognize the need to specify the content or domain of the cognition (e.g., Mohammed, Klimoski, & Rentsch, 2000). For example, Cannon-Bowers et al. (1993) pointed out that team members may develop cognitions for understanding the equipment, the task, team interactions, and team models. The domain of relevant team content should be elaborated and specified depending on the research question and the outcomes of interest. For example, with respect to differential content of congruent cognitions, Mathieu, Heffner, Goodwin, Salas, and Cannon-Bowers (2001) found that congruent team mental models were related to team performance and team process but that congruent task mental models were related to team process only.

Underlying dimensions that describe content domains include degree of abstraction, level of articulation (depth), breadth, functionality, and stability (Rentsch et al., 2008). For example, Mathieu et al. (2005) recently described the importance of the functionality of the cognitive content. In addition, there may be variance in the stability of cognitive content (e.g., equipment content may be more stable than team interaction content; Cannon-Bowers et al., 1993).

Types and Configurations of Cognitive Similarity

Types of cognitive similarity are determined by the intersection of (1) the form of the cognition; (2) the form of similarity; and (3) the cognitive content domain (Figure 9.1). The underlying dimensions of these features (e.g., level or variability of similarity, stability or abstractness of content domain) further define the specific type of cognitive similarity of interest.

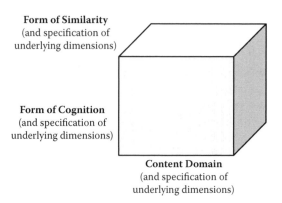

Form of Similarity
(and specification of
underlying dimensions)

Form of Cognition
(and specification of
underlying dimensions)

Content Domain
(and specification of
underlying dimensions)

FIGURE 9.1
Components of types of cognitive similarity.

Clearly, defining types of cognitive similarity and delineating their roles in nomological networks will advance the theoretical and practical usefulness of cognitive similarity in teams. For example, if team members have accurate (form of similarity) beliefs (form of cognition) about each other's competence (content domain), then they should be better able to assign tasks appropriately to team members. Sample types of cognitive similarity are shown in Table 9.1.

Combinations of cognitive similarity types form cognitive similarity configurations. For example, on a product development team, a cognitive similarity configuration consisting of (1) complementary perceptions of the environment, (2) accurate beliefs about customer needs, and (3) congruent expectations about meeting team goals may be highly related to team effectiveness. The complementarity of environmental perceptions enables the team to identify environmental elements such as market stability and

TABLE 9.1

Sample Types of Cognitive Similarity

Content Domain	Form of Cognition	Form of Similarity
Team members' cognition	Schema	Accuracy
Task	Schema	Complementary
Teamwork	Mental model	Congruence
Competence	Beliefs	Accuracy
Leadership	Expectations	Complementary
Innovation	Climate perceptions	Congruence
Customers	Defining dimensions	Accuracy
Product development	Frames	Complementary
Strategic vision	Frames	Congruence

market segmentation areas. The accurate beliefs about customers may aid the team in identifying the product features potential buyers desire and in understanding how these desired features may differ in each type of environment. The congruent expectations of the goals to be met—based on incorporating the customer and environment information into manageable, agreed on goals—can guide the team in working toward and ultimately achieving appropriate levels of team performance.

Next, configurations of cognitive similarity potentially related to information sharing in teams and team adaptability are illustrated. In doing so, several specific types of cognitive similarity are described.

Illustrative Examples of Cognitive Similarity Configurations

Our examples of cognitive similarity configurations contain several types of cognitive similarity based on schemas as the form of cognition. Of course, more than one form of cognition could comprise a configuration. However, schemas are versatile forms of structured cognition that underlie perceptual and interpretative cognition and are highly relevant to the study of cognitive similarity in teams. The presentation of examples therefore begins with an overview of schemas.

Sample Form of Cognition: Schemas

Lord and Maher (1991) noted that researchers in industrial/organizational psychology have used schemas in research investigating performance appraisal, leadership, organizational culture, goal setting, and decision-making research. Recently, schemas have become of interest to team researchers (e.g., Rentsch & Klimoski, 2001).

A schema is defined as "a mental codification of experience that includes a particular organized way of perceiving cognitively and responding to a complex situation or set of stimuli" (Merriam-Webster Online, 2008). One outcome of gaining experience in a given domain is the organization of information into aggregated and interconnected structures or "packages of knowledge" (Lord & Maher, 1991). These "packages," referred to as schemas, enable individuals to perceive, understand, interpret, and give meaning to stimuli (Rumelhart, 1980). Furthermore, they influence inferences, expectations, attention, and memory (Bartlett, 1932). As internal representations of the external world, schemas are dynamic and adaptable, which makes them particularly useful for interpreting ambiguous and novel stimuli (Rumelhart, 1980).

Schemas enable flexible information processing, because they form complex interconnected knowledge structures. They develop with respect to general or specific content (information) and represent knowledge at all levels of abstraction (Rumelhart, 1980). Furthermore, they may become embedded in other schemas or become otherwise interrelated with other schemas. The interconnectedness of schemas is highly beneficial and is a characteristic of expertise. As individuals gain expertise, they become progressively able to access and utilize the interconnectedness of their schemas, thereby increasing their cognitive flexibility and information processing capabilities while concurrently decreasing their cognitive load and conscious processing. The interconnectedness of organized knowledge also supports sensemaking and interpretation (Lord & Maher, 1991).

Schemas are implicit. Therefore, individuals (e.g., team members) may find it difficult, if even possible, to communicate their schema content and structure to one another (Lord & Maher, 1991). Schemas are active. Their formation and utilization involve activation of a knowledge unit by a recognized stimulus that sets off a chain reaction that activates other related schemas while inhibiting unrelated schemas. Together, these interconnected schemas form interpretive cognitive structures that provide meaning (Rumelhart, Smolensky, McClelland, & Hinton, 1988). Schemas are emergent and learned through experience. Opportunities for elaborating existing schemas or for developing new schemas are presented when existing schemas are revealed as inadequate for understanding an extraordinary situation or an exceptional experience.

Several features including coherence, integration, differentiation, elaboration, interconnectedness, size, rigidity, sensitivity to activation, and the nature of the linkages among content nodes (e.g., strength, or causal/temporal association) characterize schemas. Many of these features are related to expertise. It should be noted that the research on cognitive similarity has not addressed most of these features; therefore, they provide avenues for future research.

Because schemas affect the attention, encoding, and recall stages of information processing, they also influence behavior. For example, differential understanding of goals (reflective of a goal schema) has been shown to influence how individuals approach tasks (Dweck, 1986; Lord & Maher, 1991). Obviously, the effects of schemas may be functional or dysfunctional. One dysfunctional effect is their force as a constraint on, for example, perception, information processing, and action. Indeed, they may serve to clutch individuals in a cognitive rut, thus limiting their perceptual and interpretive flexibility.

Sample Types of Cognitive Similarity Based on Schemas, Sample Forms of Similarity, and Sample Cognitive Domains

Several examples of types of cognitive similarity are provided based on the intersection of schema (form of cognition) with various forms of similarity and several cognitive content domains. In all examples, functional schema content and an optimal level of similarity is assumed.

As noted already, team-relevant domains are many and vary in terms of specificity (Cannon-Bowers et al., 1993). For example, team members may develop a core teamwork schema that organizes information about how to operate as a contributing team member. A core teamwork schema will generalize across teams. Therefore, as team members' core teamwork schemas become increasingly expert, they are likely to be able to transition smoothly into new teams (Rentsch, Heffner, & Duffy, 1994). When schema congruence exists among team members regarding core teamwork, team members are likely to experience good interpersonal interactions and efficient teamwork. In addition to developing such general schemas, team members will likely develop specific schemas. They may develop teamwork schemas that are unique to any particular team, thereby enabling them to act effectively within the context of the idiosyncrasies of the given team. For example, members of a basketball team might develop a type of cognitive similarity for playing basketball. Specifically, they might develop basketball teamwork (content) schema (cognitive form) congruence (form of similarity). This type of cognitive similarity will prescribe teamwork on the court that involves moving the ball around until a member has an open shot, thereby increasing the chances that one of its players will take a high percentage shot and the team will score more baskets. However, this specific teamwork schema for scoring may not be applicable when one of these team members plays a pickup game with a different group of players.

Another type of cognitive similarity is based on schemas (cognitive form) and accuracy (form of similarity). Team members' may develop schemas of a target (e.g., teammate, leader, enemy, expert, task constraints) that match the target. On decision-making teams, for example, the team's decision-making process may be more effective when team members have accurate schemas about their teammates than if they have inaccurate schemas. If team members understand each other's task constraints and expertise (content domain), then the team will engage in an effective decision-making process. Specifically, accurate schemas regarding teammates' task constraints, expertise, and frames of reference will be related to low levels of socioemotional conflict on teams (Rentsch & Zelno, 2003). Accurate (form of similarity) schemas (form of cognition) of teammates' schemas of teamwork (content) have been shown to be related to team effectiveness (Jenkins & Rentsch, 1995).

It should be noted that schema accuracy is similar to, but different from, transactive memory. Transactive memory is the "combination of knowledge possessed by each individual and a collective awareness of who knows what" (Austin, 2003, p. 866). Transactive memory refers to team members knowing what others know, being accurate about that knowledge, and agreeing about knowledge sources and team member expertise. Typically, transactive memory is conceptualized as knowing the source of task-oriented expert knowledge within the team (e.g., Mohammed & Dumville, 2001; Moreland, 1999; Wegner, 1986). Schema accuracy is broader than transactive memory. Schema accuracy may exist with respect to knowing who knows what, but it may also exist with respect to processes, perceptions, relationships, and so on. Furthermore, schema accuracy may exist with respect to the degree to which individuals are accurate in their understanding of others' schemas (i.e., others' understanding). Knowing how teammates organize information and therefore knowing how they think (schema accuracy) is very different from knowing which teammate knows what (transactive memory). This type of cognitive similarity (schema accuracy of teammates' schemas) has many interesting implications for team processes.

Another type of cognitive similarity is based on a complementary form of schema similarity. For example, two campers comprise a team when setting up camp in the Great Smoky Mountain National Forest, and they may be most effective when their type of cognitive similarity is complementary (form of similarity) schemas (form of cognition) for setting up camp (content). This will occur when one camper has a schema for setting up camp that includes knowledge about building fires for cooking, using ashes to clean cooking utensils, and the desired proximity of the camp to a water source. Although this camper knows quite a bit about setting up camp, he may know nothing about camping in forests where black bears live. The other camper's schema for setting up camp includes this knowledge. She knows that at night food must be kept away from the bears by hanging it between trees and that if a bear approaches the camp, the campers can scare it off by standing close together, raising their hands, and making loud noises so as to create the perception of a large threatening creature. However, this camper does not understand anything about campfires or water sources. Thus, as a team, each camper's schema for setting up camp complements or fills the knowledge gaps in the other's schema, thereby augmenting the team's capability for setting up camp.

Sample Cognitive Similarity Configurations and Information Sharing in Teams

Decision making in teams is complicated by inefficient information-sharing tendencies and by inclinations to experience negative affect. In unstructured face-to-face discussions, team members tend to share a disproportionate amount of common information and fail to share critical unique information (Stasser & Titus, 1985, 1987). This tendency is particularly detrimental to teams in which each member possesses unique, expert information that the team must extract and integrate to achieve high-quality solutions. In addition, team members tend not to discuss shared information sufficiently due to team members experiencing negative affect or socioemotional conflict. Socioemotional conflict involves interpersonal incompatibilities among team members (e.g., Amason & Sapienza, 1997; De Dreu, 1997) and has been associated with decreased team performance. Furthermore, there appears to be an association between actively debating information in an effort to identify a best solution to a problem and the experience of negative emotional reactions. A cognitive similarity configuration approach offers insights and solutions for reducing ineffective information sharing and negative affect in team decision-making processes.

Team members may experience negative emotional reactions when debating issues, because they misinterpret teammates' behaviors (Baron, 1997; Ensley & Pearce, 2001). Behaviors such as pointing out the weaknesses of arguments, offering dissenting opinions, disagreeing, and presenting alternatives must necessarily occur to generate and evaluate integrative solutions. However, although team members engaging in these behaviors may interpret them as methods that contribute productively to collaboration, other members toward whom the behaviors are directed may interpret them as threats or personal attacks and may withdraw from the discussion (Baron, 1988; Ensley & Pearce, 2001). Clearly, these team members have different schemas regarding how to contribute to team decision making.

Congruent teamwork schemas, in combination with accurate team member schemas, may alleviate misinterpretations and facilitate team effectiveness in decision-making teams (Rentsch & Zelno, 2003). If team members possess highly congruent teamwork schemas—containing knowledge about, for example, debate, cooperative goal interdependence, openness, and sensitivity to others—then they will interpret such behaviors as disagreeing and deliberating as efforts to support collaboration, and their experience of negative affect will be minimized. In addition, if team members develop accurate schemas about their teammates, then they will predict and understand their teammates' actions and reactions, which will enable them to avoid provoking negative affect from others and to modulate their own emotional reactions to others. Accurate schemas regarding team members' expertise, task-related constraints, and frames of reference will aid team members in making charitable attributions for ambiguous behavior exhibited by teammates (i.e., behaviors that they could interpret as negative).

This illustrative cognitive similarity configuration offers two types of cognitive similarity, each of which is expected to exert differential pressure on team members' behaviors and affective responses, thereby simultaneously promoting active information sharing, idea generation, debate and discussion, and evaluation of potential problem solutions while minimizing or eliminating negative emotional reactions and subsequent withdrawal from the team task. One type of cognitive similarity without the other is unlikely to be as effective as the cognitive similarity configuration that includes both.

Sample Cognitive Similarity Configurations and Team Adaptability

Adaptation is defined as the capability to adjust knowledge and skills for performance in novel settings or in situations with changing requirements (Kozlowski, 1998). These new situations can be internal to the team or external in the team's environment. Internal events to which teams must adapt might include a training episode, member rotation, task change, new leadership, or change in team members' physical proximity to one another. External events requiring adaptation include organizational restructuring, change in policy or culture, change in the physical environment, or change in the timeframe allotted for task completion.

Communication and coordination are keys to team adaptability. Members must be able to communicate information about changes to which they must adapt, to develop plans for operating within the changed system, and to implement those plans in a coordinated manner to adapt successfully. Blickensderfer, Cannon-Bowers, and Salas (1998) indicated that implicit coordination is the method through which teams adapt in complex environments and that effective teams achieve implicit coordination through cognitive similarity. After team members develop cognitive similarity, effective teams can use information gathered from the environment to adjust their strategies and to adapt readily to the environment (e.g., Entin & Serfaty, 1999; Marks et al., 2000).

The role of cognitive similarity in team adaptability has received some attention in the research on team training. For example, teams in which members were cross-trained to gain interpositional knowledge about other team members' tasks were able to anticipate the needs of their teammates (e.g., Blickensderfer et al., 1998). The ability to anticipate teammates' needs assists team members in moving the team's task toward completion, because they can identify and perform backup or compensatory actions when another teammate is struggling. In terms of cognitive similarity configurations, Serfaty, Entin, and Johnston (1998) found that shared task mental models were important for high performance in situations requiring adaptation but that for teams to maximize adaptive performance, they also required training on team processes, which would create shared mental models of team process in addition to the team task.

Environment monitoring, efficacy development, need anticipation, and backup are processes that may be important for team adaptability. These processes may be affected by types of cognitive similarity that have differential relationships with each team process associated with effective adaptability and with the outcomes expected from a team's ability to adapt. Table 9.2 presents sample configurations of cognitive similarity based on schema accuracy and congruence and various contents hypothesized to be related to team adaptability.

The role of cognitive similarity configurations deserves study with respect to fostering a team's ability to adapt. For example, a restaurant kitchen staff at a large restaurant forms a team that must maintain a high level of environmental monitoring to adapt to daily customer demands. After the lunch rush and before the dinner crowd, fewer team members will be working, and they will work at a slower, more leisurely pace than they did at the lunch rush or at other busy serving times. However, if a busload of seniors arrives suddenly and unexpectedly in the middle of the afternoon, creating an "understaffed rush" condition, the team must adapt. Suddenly, the kitchen staff must adapt to the large number of customers. They must prepare orders quickly while working with fewer team members than they typically have during expected busy times. These conditions will likely increase the workload stress level, but the team must produce the same quality output that their customers and their managers expect. In this case, it is probable that cognitive similarity configurations will be important in maintaining high performance and that those types of cognitive similarity comprising the configurations may differentially affect the team processes required for adapting to the unexpected change in task demands. In this scenario, accurate schemas with regard to the environment and to teammates will promote functional adaptation. Team members will be able to monitor the developing situation and, therefore, will be able to determine how the team should adapt when they possess accurate schemas. For example, accurate schemas of the environment (e.g., they can predict the number of meals needed) and accurate schemas of how their teammates understand the environment (e.g., knowing the head chef finds an unexpected crowd to present an exhilarating challenge) will smooth the adaptation process. Members must be able to survey the environment and to assess where changes are occurring (e.g., additional waitstaff in the kitchen, orders being placed more frequently, the chef getting a little too generous with the portions) and also to understand the impact those changes will have on the team. Accurate environment schemas will increase the ability of the team members to monitor the environment in similar ways and to identify the changes that the team needs to make to adapt to

TABLE 9.2

Example Cognitive Similarity Configuration Related to Team Adaptability

Schema Form	Schema Content					
	Task	Teamwork	Team Members	Technology	Environment	Other Teams
Congruence	Similar understanding of task attributes enables members to anticipate teammates' needs and to perform backup behaviors	Similar understanding of teamwork processes enables members to focus on performing adaptation behaviors through effective processes	Similar understanding of team members promotes assessment of which members have KSAs needed to perform novel adaptation	Similar understanding of technology aids the team to utilize technology features to alter task or teamwork processes effectively	Similar understanding of environment promotes agreement on the features forcing adaptation and which resources must be exchanged	Similar understanding of other teams enables agreement on the duties of each team and how they should be performed in relation to one another
Accuracy	Task schema accuracy aids in understanding how others view the task, signaling differences to incorporate or remove to adapt	Teamwork schema accuracy enhances understanding of member behaviors, reducing conflict through enabling smooth teamwork processes	Team member schema accuracy enables behavior interpretation and attribution, signaling training needs for new duties in response to adaptation	Technology schema accuracy highlights potential training issues and may reveal new ways to utilize technology to aid team adaptation	Environment schema accuracy assists members to monitor changes in environment and impact of changes on team and to determine best adaptation method	Other team schema accuracy promotes behavior interpretation in terms of team constraints, allowing expectations to develop and adaptation to occur

Note: Based on the cognitive form of schema and similarity forms of congruence and accuracy.

that environment. When all team members have accurate schemas of the environment and the way others interpret the environment, it is likely that they will identify the same changes for the team to address. If they identify different aspects of change (possibly due to complementary task schemas, which could be beneficial), then members will be able to understand why teammates suggest different changes based on what they know about their teammates' interpretations of the situation (accurate schemas of team members). Effective monitoring resulting from accurate environment and team member schemas should lead to the team identifying and implementing appropriate adjustments. Therefore, the team will be able to maintain the speed and quality of its outputs.

In addition, complementary schemas about team members' abilities and skills in the kitchen will also promote the team's ability to adapt due to the effects of these schemas on team efficacy development. Team members may have well-developed schemas about different team members, presumably the ones with whom they work most closely (e.g., a dishwasher may have more well-formed schemas about the abilities of a bus person than about the head chef, and a sous chef may have more well-formed schemas about the head chef than about the dishwasher). Although each team member may not have fully developed schemas about every other teammate, all members will likely develop accurate schemas about a few teammates. They will be able to predict those teammates' performance in the unexpected "understaffed rush" condition, and they will understand the expertise of these teammates and how it will aid them in adapting to stressful situations in the kitchen. The set of accurate schemas about teammates that exists among the team members will be complementary, because although each member may not have the same schemas about everyone, the complete set of schemas present among the team members will comprise knowledge about the expertise and abilities of all the members on the team. In this way, no gaps will exist with regard to schemas about team members, but not every member will need to have an accurate schema about every other member. This configuration of complementary schemas will form the conditions for all members of the team to develop a sense of team efficacy. When members believe that their team has the necessary skills and motivation to adapt, efficacy will increase, and perceptions of efficacy have been linked to increased performance in adaptation situations (Chen, Thomas, & Wallace, 2005). Members will, in turn, develop efficacy about their team's ability to adapt based on the schemas they have of those with whom they work closely.

Congruent task schemas can also help a team to implement the need anticipation and backup processes important for adaptation. In a restaurant kitchen, several team members (particularly those in the same job categories) should have an understanding of each portion of the food preparation and serving tasks (usually achieved through cross-training to increase the interpositional knowledge). When teammates have congruent understandings of the task, they are better able to anticipate the needs of their teammates. Although this is important in typical teamwork situations, the ability to anticipate needs is essential in an adaptation situation. When adaptation is necessary, team members must use not only their environment schema accuracy to identify where adaptation needs to occur but also their task schema congruence to identify which tasks can be modified, which need to be performed at a different pace, and which may present overwhelming stress for their teammates. Task schema congruence would aid members in anticipating needs and can increase the likelihood that members can perform backup behaviors during change periods to help the team maintain its performance level.

In summary, these examples illustrate the usefulness of cognitive similarity configurations in a team's ability to increase performance and to adapt to novel situations. Specifically, they show that different types of schema similarity configurations can differentially affect the enactment of team processes. Increasing the effectiveness of each of the processes (e.g., environment monitoring, efficacy development, need anticipation, backup) ultimately has the effect of increasing team performance. Although the team may be able to improve its performance by increasing one type of similarity configuration, its performance may be improved threefold by developing a cognitive similarity configuration that includes cognitive congruence, accuracy, and complementarity with respect to diverse content domains.

Future Research

Next, avenues for future research are described by focusing on additional elements related to conceptualizing and assessing cognitive similarity configurations. Training and technology are also highlighted as mechanisms for influencing cognitive similarity configurations.

Conceptualizing and Assessing Cognitive Similarity Configurations

The cognitive similarity configuration approach is applicable to dyads, teams, units, and organizations. The challenge for researchers is to articulate clearly the theoretical underpinnings of which types of cognitive similarity comprise relevant configurations to address the criterion variable of interest. Within team research, the most predictive or explanatory configurations may vary depending on such moderator variables as the nature of task, the team, the leadership, and contextual features. Thus, the study of cognition in teams requires the further development of theory regarding cognitive similarity in teams.

The illustrative examples provided with respect to teams centered on schema as the form of cognition. The capacity of schemas to stimulate activation of other schemas makes schemas particularly useful forms of cognition within the framework of cognitive similarity configurations. Similar kinds of schema activation among individuals on a team are particularly relevant to configurations of cognitive similarity (and may serve as another form of similarity). The examples also highlighted congruence and accuracy as forms of similarity within various content domains. Clearly, configurations may be composed of various forms of cognition (e.g., mental models and perceptions) in combination with forms of similarity other than those illustrated here.

The complexity of cognitive similarity configurations may be articulated by considering the role of the features of the cognitive forms, similarity forms (e.g., level, variability, stability), and content domains (e.g., stability, level, abstraction, integration). This specificity may enhance prediction of affective reactions, effective processes, and outcomes for teams.

In addition, articulating the relationships between the types of cognitive similarity comprising a configuration will sometimes involve recognizing that low similarity in some domains may be desirable when high similarity exists in other domains. For example, expert knowledge will be differentially distributed among team members; therefore, cognitive similarity among team members with respect to expert knowledge will (and probably should) be low. However, the team's use of this distributed expertise will be possible to the extent that they possess cognitive congruence with respect to the teamwork processes of constructively eliciting and sharing information. In addition, cognitive accuracy with respect to how other team members understand one's area of expertise will aid team members in expressing their expert knowledge to each other in a way that assures its usefulness within the team.

Implicit in the above example is that various types of cognitive similarity comprising the configurations may have differential relationships with criterion variables and with each other. Relationships among variables taking forms other than linear should also be considered. For example, exposing optimal levels of similarity may require testing for curvilinear relationships.

Mechanisms for Achieving Cognitive Similarity: Training and Technology

Efforts should continue with respect to influencing cognitive similarity configurations. Training and technology are two forces for achieving cognitive similarity (Rentsch & Zelno, 2003). Training is an effective mechanism for modifying cognition and has been shown to alter such forms of cognition as interpositional knowledge (Cannon-Bowers, Salas, Blickensderfer, & Bowers, 1998), shared mental models and understanding of others' responsibilities (Marks et al., 2002), and procedural recall and memory differentiation (Liang, Moreland, & Argote, 1995) in expected ways. In addition, training has been effective in increasing cognitive similarity among team members. For example, Smith-Jentsch, Campbell, Milanovich, and Reynolds (2001) demonstrated that computer-based training increased team members' teamwork mental model congruence and accuracy with respect to an expert model.

One implication of the cognitive configuration perspective for training is that form of cognition, form of similarity, and content domain must be clearly specified given the team and its task. For example, with respect to information sharing in teams, training designed to increase team member schema congruence should focus on defining and recognizing behaviors that support information sharing and interpreting them as functional rather than as attacks. Additional training designed to support information sharing should be aimed at increasing schema accuracy regarding teammates and should focus on teammates' task constraints and expertise.

A second potent mechanism for influencing cognitive similarity in teams is technology. Technology is most relevant to distributed team members working virtually. This technology can be designed to facilitate schema-related communications that can increase cognitive similarity. The Organizational Research Group has introduced The Advanced Cognitive Engineered Intervention Technologies approach (ACE-IT; Rentsch & Hutchison, 1999). This approach involves conducting a collaborative task analysis to identify the required cognition (i.e., cognitive form, similarity form, and cognitive content) for completing the task. This cognition information is integrated with the team members' existing cognition in the development of technology designed to aid team members to acquire the required cognition as they are working together to complete the team task. Software mediators, intelligent agents, and technological interventions embedded in the technology can guide team members to acquire the required cognitive similarity configurations as they work with the technology (ibid.). Virtual reality technology also provides the opportunity for team members to experience their teammates' experiences and thereby to increase cognitive similarity. For example, while the team completes a task, each team member's sensory experience and behaviors could be recorded. The recordings could be replayed so each team member could experience the activity from his or her teammates' perspectives. This approach combines training and technology to be used in conjunction to assist teams in building the most appropriate cognitive configurations for their particular tasks.

Conclusion

As teams continue to be utilized to make decisions while working in dynamic environments with complex compositions and team structures, the study of similar cognitions in teams must continue. The team members must experience a "mind meld" that will produce cognitive similarity among team members. New types of cognitive similarity and new means for achieving a Team MindMeld™ must be identified and pursued. The cognitive similarity configuration approach provides several avenues for future research on information sharing and adaptability (among other variables) in teams.

Acknowledgment

The authors' work on this chapter was funded in part by a grant to Joan Rentsch from the Office of Naval Research (Award N00014-05-1-0624).

References

Amason, A. C. & Sapienza, H. J. (1997). The effects of top management team size and interaction norms on cognitive and affective conflict. *Journal of Management, 23*(4), 495–516.

Anderson, N. R. & West, M. A. (1998). Measuring climate for work group innovation: development and validation of the team climate inventory. *Journal of Organizational Behavior, 19*, 235–258.

Austin, J. R. (2003). Transactive memory in organizational groups: The effects of content, consensus, specialization, and accuracy on group performance. *Journal of Applied Psychology, 88*(5), 866–878.

Baba, M. L., Gluesing, J., Ratner, H., & Wagner, K. H. (2004). The contexts of knowing: Natural history of a globally distributed team. *Journal of Organizational Behavior, 25*, 547–587.

Bain, P. G., Mann, L., & Pirola-Merlo, A. (2001). The innovation imperative: The relationships between team climate, innovation, and performance in R&D teams. *Small Group Research, 32*, 55–73.

Baron, R. A. (1988). Attributions and organizational conflict: The mediating role of apparent sincerity. *Organizational Behavior and Human Decision Processes, 41*, 111–127.

Baron, R. A. (1997). Positive effects of conflict: Insights from social cognition. In C. K. W. De Dreu & E. Van de Vliert (Eds.), *Using conflict in organizations* (pp. 177–191). London: Sage Publications.

Bartlett, F. C. (1932). *Remembering*. London: Cambridge University Press.

Berger, P. L. & Luckmann, T. (1966). *The social construction of reality*. New York: Doubleday.

Blickensderfer, E., Cannon-Bowers, J. A., & Salas, E. (1998). Cross-training and team performance. In J. A. Cannon-Bowers & E. Salas (Eds.), *Making decisions under stress: Implications for individual and team training* (pp. 299–311). Washington, DC: American Psychological Association.

Cannon-Bowers, J. A., Salas, E., Blickensderfer, E., & Bowers, C. (1998). The impact of cross-training and workload on team functioning: A replication and extension of initial findings. *Human Factors, 40*(1), 92–101.

Cannon-Bowers, J. A., Salas, E., & Converse, S. (1993). Shared mental models in expert team decision making. In N. J. Castellan (Ed.), *Individual and group decision making* (pp. 221–246). Hillsdale, NJ: Lawrence Erlbaum Associates.

Chen, G., Thomas, B., & Wallace, J. C. (2005). A multilevel examination of the relationships among training outcomes, mediating regulatory processes, and adaptive performance. *Journal of Applied Psychology, 90*(5), 827–841.

Colquitt, J. A., Noe, R. A., & Jackson, C. L. (2002). Justice in teams: Antecedents and consequences of procedural justice climate. *Personnel Psychology, 55*, 83–109.

De Dreu, C. K. W. (1997). Productive conflict: The importance of conflict management and conflict issue. In C. K. W. De Dreu & E. Van de Vliert (Eds.), *Using conflict in organizations* (pp. 9–22). London: Sage Publications.

Dweck, C. S. (1986). Motivational processes affecting learning. *American Psychologist, 41*(10), 1040–1048.

Ensley, M. D. & Pearce, C. L. (2001). Shared cognition in top management teams: Implications for new venture performance. *Journal of Organizational Behavior, 22*, 145–160.

Entin, E. & Serfaty, D. (1999). Adaptive team coordination. *Human Factors, 41*(2), 312–325.

Fiol, C. M. (1994). Consensus, diversity, and learning in organizations. *Organizational Science, 5*, 403–420.

Gibson, C. B. (2001). Me and us: Differential relationships among goal-setting training, efficacy and effectiveness at the individual and team level. *Journal of Organizational Behavior, 22*, 789–808.

Gibson, C. B. (2003). The efficacy advantage: Factors related to the formation of group efficacy. *Journal of Applied Social Psychology, 33*, 2153–2186.

Gioia, D. A. & Thomas, J. B (1996). Institutional identity, image, and issue interpretation: Sensemaking during strategic change in academia. *Administrative Science Quarterly, 41*, 370–403.

Greenberg, D. N. (1995). Blue versus gray: A metaphor constraining sensemaking around a restructuring. *Group and Organization Management, 20*, 183–209.

James, L. R., Hater, J. J., Gent, M. J., & Bruni, J. R. (1978). Psychological climate: Implications from cognitive social learning theory and interactional psychology. *Personnel Psychology, 31*, 783–813.

Jenkins, N. M. & Rentsch, J. R. (1995, May). The effects of teamwork schema similarity on team performance and fairness perceptions. In J. Mathieu (Chair), *Mental models and team effectiveness: Three empirical tests.* Symposium presented to the 10th Annual Conference of the Society for Industrial and Organizational Psychology, Orlando, FL.

Kenny, D. A. (1994). *Interpersonal perception: A social relations analysis.* New York: Guilford Press.

Kirkman, B. L., Tesluk, P. E., & Rosen, B. (2001). Assessing the incremental validity of team consensus ratings over aggregation of individual-level data in predicting team effectiveness. *Personnel Psychology, 54,* 645–667.

Kozlowski, S. W. J. (1998). Training and developing adaptive teams: Theory, principles, and research. In J. A. Cannon-Bowers & E. Salas (Eds.), *Making decisions under stress: Implications for individual and team training* (pp. 115–153). Washington, DC: American Psychological Association.

Kraiger, K. & Wenzel, L. H. (1997). Conceptual development and empirical evaluation of measures of shared mental models as indicators of team effectiveness. In M. T. Brannick, E. Salas, & C. Prince (Eds.), *Team performance assessment and measurement: Theory, methods, and applications* (pp. 63–84). Mahwah, NJ: Lawrence Erlbaum Associates.

Levine, J. M. & Moreland, R. L. (1991). Culture and socialization in work groups. In L. B. Resnick, J. M. Levine, & S. D. Teasley (Eds.), *Perspectives on socially shared cognition.* Washington, DC: American Psychological Association.

Levy, O. (2005). The influence of top management team attention patterns on global strategic posture of firms. *Journal of Organizational Behavior, 26,* 797–819.

Liang, D. W., Moreland, R., & Argote, L. (1995). Group versus individual training and group performance: The mediating factor of transactive memory. *Personality and Social Psychology Bulletin, 21*(4), 384–393.

Lord, R. G. & Maher, K. J. (1991). Cognitive theory in industrial and organizational psychology. In M. D. Dunnette & L. M. Hough (Eds.), *Handbook of industrial and organizational psychology* (Vol. 2, pp. 1–62). Palo Alto, CA: Consulting Psychologists Press.

Louis, M. R. (1980). Surprise and sense making: What newcomers experience in unfamiliar organizational settings. *Administrative Science Quarterly, 25,* 226–251.

Marks, M. A., Sabella, M. J., Burke, C. S., & Zaccaro, S. J. (2002). The impact of cross-training on team effectiveness. *Journal of Applied Psychology, 87*(1), 3–13.

Marks, M. A., Zaccaro, S. J., & Mathieu, J. E. (2000). Performance implications of leader briefings and team-interaction training for team adaptation to novel environments. *Journal of Applied Psychology, 85*(6), 971–986.

Mason, C. M. & Griffin, M. A. (2003). Identifying group task satisfaction at work. *Small Group Research, 34,* 413–442.

Mathieu, J. E., Heffner, T. S., Goodwin, G. F., Cannon-Bowers, J. A., & Salas, E. (2005). Scaling the quality of teammates' mental models: Equifinality and normative comparisons. *Journal of Organizational Behavior, 26*(1), 37–56.

Mathieu, J. E., Heffner, T. S., Goodwin, G. F., Salas, E., & Cannon-Bowers, J. A. (2001). The influence of shared mental models on team process and performance. *Journal of Applied Psychology, 85,* 27.3–282.

Merriam-Webster Online (2008). Retrieved from http://www.merriam-webster.com/dictionary/schema.

Mohammed, S. & Dumville, B. C. (2001). Team mental models in a team knowledge framework: Expanding theory and measurement across disciplinary boundaries. *Journal of Organizational Behavior, 22*(2), 89–106.

Mohammed, S., Klimoski, R., & Rentsch, J. R. (2000). The measurement of team mental models: We have no shared schema. *Organizational Research Methods, 3*, 123–165.

Mohammed, S. & Ringseis, E. (2001). Cognitive diversity and consensus in group decision making: The role of inputs, processes, and outcomes. *Organizational Behavior and Human Decision Processes, 85*, 310–335.

Moreland, R. L. (1999). Transactive memory: Learning who knows what in work groups and organizations. In L. L. Thompson, J. M. Levine, & D. M. Messick (Eds.), *Shared cognition in organizations: The management of knowledge* (pp. 3–31). Mahwah, NJ: Erlbaum.

Moreland, R. L. & Levine, J. M. (1989). Newcomers and oldtimers in small groups. In P. B. Paulus (Ed.), *Psychology of group influence* (2d ed.). Hillsdale, NJ: Lawrence Erlbaum.

Naumann, S. E. & Bennett, N. (2000). A case for procedural justice climate: Development and test of a multilevel model. *Academy of Management Journal, 43*, 881–889.

Naumann, S. E. & Bennett, N. (2002). The effects of procedural justice climate on work group performance. *Small Group Research, 33*, 361–377.

Pirola-Merlo, A. & Mann, L. (2004). The relationship between individual creativity and team creativity: Aggregating across people and across time. *Journal of Organizational Behavior, 25*, 235–257.

Rentsch, J. R. (1990). Climate and culture: Interaction and qualitative differences in organizational meanings. *Journal of Applied Psychology, 75*, 668–681.

Rentsch, J. R. & Hall, R. J. (1994). Members of great teams think alike: A model of team effectiveness and schema similarity among team members. In M. M. Beyerlein, D. A. Johnson, & S. T. Beyerlein (Eds.), *Advances in interdisciplinary studies of work teams: Theories of self-managing work teams* (Vol. 1, pp. 223–261). Greenwich, CT: JAI Press.

Rentsch, J. R., Heffner, T. S., & Duffy, L. T. (1994). What you know is what you get from experience: Team experience related to teamwork schemas. *Group & Organization Management, 19*(4), 450–474.

Rentsch, J. R. & Hutchison, A. S. (1999). *Advanced cognitive engineered intervention technologies (ACE-IT)*. Knoxville, TN: Organizational Research Group.

Rentsch, J. R. & Klimoski, R. J. (2001). Why do "great minds" think alike?: Antecedents of team member schema agreement. *Journal of Organizational Behavior, 22*, 107–120.

Rentsch, J. R., Small, E. E., & Hanges, P. J. (2008). Cognitions in organizations and teams: What is the *meaning* of cognitive similarity? In B. Smith (Ed.), *The people make the place: Exploring dynamic linkages between individuals and organizations* (pp. 127–156). London: Routledge.

Rentsch, J. R. & Woehr, D. J. (2004). Quantifying congruence in cognition: Social relations modeling and team member schema similarity. In E. Salas, & S. M. Fiore (Eds.), *Team cognition: Understanding the factors that drive process and performance* (pp. 11–31). Washington, DC: American Psychological Association.

Rentsch, J. R. & Zelno, J. A. (2003). The role of cognition in managing conflict to maximize team effectiveness: a team member schema similarity approach. In M. A. West, D. Tjosvold, & K. Smith (Eds.), *International handbook of organizational teamwork and cooperative teamworking* (pp. 131–150). West Sussex, England: John Wiley & Sons, Ltd.

Rumelhart, D. E. (1980). On evaluating story grammars. *Cognitive Science, 4*(3), 313–316.

Rumelhart, D. E., Smolensky, P., McClelland, J. L., & Hinton, G. E. (1988). Schemata and sequential thought processes in PDP models. In A. M. Collins & E. Smith (Eds.), *Readings in cognitive science: A perspective from psychology and artificial intelligence* (pp. 224–249). San Mateo, CA: Morgan Kaufmann, Inc.

Schneider, B. & Reichers, A. (1983). On the etiology of climates. *Personnel Psychology, 36,* 19–39.

Serfaty, D., Entin, E. E., & Johnston, J. H. (1998). Team coordination training. In J. A. Cannon-Bowers & E. Salas (Eds.), *Making decisions under stress: Implications for individual and team training* (pp. 221–245). Washington, DC: American Psychologica Association.

Smith-Jentsch, K. A., Campbell, G. E., Milanovich, D. M., & Reynolds, A. M. (2001). Measuring teamwork mental models to support training needs assessment, development, and evaluation: Two empirical studies. *Journal of Organizational Behavior, 22,* 179–194.

Smith-Jentsch, K. A., Mathieu, J. E., & Kraiger, K. (2005). Investigating linear and interactive effects of shared mental models on safety and efficiency in a field setting. *Journal of Applied Psychology, 90,* 523–535.

Stasser, G. (1991). Pooling of unshared information during group discussion. In S. Worchel, W. Wood, & J. A. Simpson (Eds.), *Group process and productivity* (pp. 48–67). Thousand Oaks, CA: Sage Publications, Inc.

Stasser, G. & Titus, W. (1985). Pooling of unshared information in group decision making: Biased information sampling during discussion. *Journal of Personality and Social Psychology, 48*(6), 1467–1478.

Stasser, G. & Titus, W. (1987). Effects of information load and percentage of shared information on the dissemination of unshared information during group discussion. *Journal of Personality and Social Psychology, 53*(1), 81–93.

Walsh J. P., Henderson, C. M., & Deighton, J. (1988). Negotiated belief structures and decision performance: An empirical investigation. *Organizational Behavior and Human Decision Processes, 42,* 194–216.

Wegner, D. M. (1986). Transactive memory: A contemporary unit analysis of the group mind. In B. Mullen & G. R. Goethals (Eds.), *Theories of group behavior* (pp. 185–205). New York: Springer-Verlag.

Weick, K. E. (1993). The collapse of sensemaking in organizations: The Mann Gulch disaster. *Administrative Science Quarterly 38,* 628–652.

Xie, J. L. & Johns, G. (2000). Interactive effects of absence culture salience and group cohesiveness: A multi-level and cross-level analysis of work absenteeism in the Chinese context. *Journal of Occupational and Organizational Psychology, 73,* 31–52.

Zohar, D. (2000). A group-level model of safety climate: Testing the effect of group climate on microaccidents in manufacturing jobs. *Journal of Applied Psychology, 85,* 587–596.

Zohar, D. & Luria, G. (2005). A multi-level model of safety climate: Cross-level relationships between organization and group-level climates. *Journal of Applied Psychology, 90,* 661–628.

10

Thinking in Terms of Multiteam Systems

Leslie A. DeChurch and John E. Mathieu

On August 29, 2005, Hurricane Katrina made landfall along the Gulf Coast of the United States. With storm surges ranging from 12 to 27 feet in Alabama, Mississippi, and Louisiana, Katrina took more than 1,300 lives, displaced hundreds of thousands more, and inflicted well more than $25 billion in damages. But it was not just the winds and storm surge that led to such damage. The select bipartisan committee charged with investigating the disaster concluded the following:

> We are left scratching our heads at the range of inefficiency and ineffectiveness that characterized government behavior right before and after this storm. But passivity did the most damage. The failure of initiative cost lives, prolonged suffering, and left all Americans justifiably concerned our government is no better prepared to protect its people than it was before 9/11, even if we are. (Select Bipartisan Committee 2006, p. 359)

Soon after the disaster, analysts blamed the problems on "a colossal failure of leadership" (Clift, 2005) and pervasive management problems throughout the system: "At every turn, political leaders failed Katrina's victims …. There's plenty of blame to go around—the White House, Congress, federal agencies, local governments, police and even residents of the Gulf Coast who refused orders to evacuate" (Moss Kanter, 2005). Whereas such conclusions may well be warranted, it has since become clear that pervasive problems could be found throughout the entire system, which was designed to deal with such events. Again, from the congressional committee:

> Leadership requires decisions to be made even when based on flawed and incomplete information. Too often during the immediate response to Katrina, sparse or conflicting information was used as an excuse for inaction rather than an imperative to step in and fill an obvious vacuum. Information passed through the maze of departmental operations centers and ironically named "coordinating" committees,

losing timeliness and relevance as it was massaged and interpreted for internal audiences." (Select Bipartisan Committee, 2006, p. 359)

The take-away message is that the system designed to deal with natural disasters (e.g., Katrina) represents a complex web of relationships among (1) local, city, state, and federal governments; (2) public, private, and military organizations; (3) paid and volunteer workers; (4) emergency planners and first responders; and (5) myriad other constituencies. The system that was designed to anticipate such disasters, to minimize their consequences, and to help people respond efficiently and effectively after they occur failed—and failed miserably. Moreover, although hundreds of recommendations for improvement have been proffered, few clear-cut remedies to prevent similar circumstances in the future have been forthcoming.

What we are dealing with in the case of the Katrina disaster is a complex system that is unlike traditional organizational forms. It represents a network of organizations, subunits, and teams whose efforts need to be orchestrated. Notably, while less encompassing than the Katrina system, public, private, and military organizations have rapidly been transforming to more complex, team-based work designs in the past couple of decades. Applied organizational research has paralleled such a shift and has demonstrated an increased emphasis on the actions and effectiveness of teams. In short, teams have become the critical building block of modern organizations (Sundstrom, 1999). This chapter expands on the traditional emphasis of what makes a team of people effective and considers the defining characteristics and drivers of the effectiveness of networks of teams, or what we refer to as a *multiteam system* (MTS). We begin by outlining some of the driving forces moving organizations to adopt more complex and diffuse work arrangements such as MTSs. In so doing we identify the defining features of MTSs and differentiate them from other organizational forms. We then consider some emerging research evidence concerning the effectiveness of MTSs, focusing on some of the key drivers of their success. We conclude with an agenda for future research and application focused on MTSs.

Evolution of Organizational Forms

The basic structure of the modern organization is evolving in two primary directions. First, organizations are becoming largely team based (Sundstrom, 1999). Rather than relying on individual jobs as the focal unit, organizations are reaping the benefits of collectives such as project teams, task forces, quality circles, and emergency response teams. Assigning tasks to work units has the advantage of bringing together individuals with a broad range of expertise and experience. As work becomes more complex and specialized, there is a greater need for individuals and teams to interface with others. Teams are efficient in this regard; they capitalize on the benefits of specialization of labor while making explicit the need to coordinate effort toward the attainment of common goals.

The second major trend is a move toward empowerment (Argyris, 1998; Spreitzer, 1995). In particular, empowered or self-managing work teams are becoming a common organizational form (Kirkman & Rosen, 1999; Mathieu, Gilson, & Ruddy, 2006). In such designs, management identifies the overall scope of teams' work, but team members are responsible for setting up their own role structures and operational norms. In short, many of the activities traditionally performed by middle management are driven down in the organization and become the province of team members. The logic is that the people who are best positioned to know what to do, and when to execute actions in a dynamic environment, should have the authority and responsibility to make such calls. Empowering workers has been credited with improving key job attitudes and with enhancing team processes and effectiveness (ibid.). Furthermore, with the advent of digitization, the Internet, and globalization, team membership can now easily span across companies, countries, time zones, and cultures. The diversity of team forms and membership only adds to the complexity of coordination demands, both within teams and across teams in an MTS. The result is a flatter and more complex organizational structure thought to enable increased responsiveness and adaptive capability than the more bureaucratic designs of the past.

Operating in organizations that are structured around both team arrangements and principles of empowerment creates segments of tightly coupled systems of teams that need to operate in sync to attain collective goals. As organizations continue to increase their reliance on work teams, both the range of potential opportunities and scope of complexities arising from the use of team structures come into focus. As a result, there is a pressing need for theory and research to guide the management of these new collectives.

Defining Multiteam Systems

Defining the nature and boundaries of an organized collective is a difficult enterprise and is subject to debate. Moreover, we acknowledge that demarcating where the boundaries are and rules for membership of a collective is somewhat arbitrary. These challenges, however, are no less true when researchers and scholars have sought to define *teams* or *organizations*.

Mathieu, Marks, and Zaccaro (2001, p. 290) first introduced the notion of MTSs, defining them as follows:

> [An MTS is] two or more teams that interface directly and interdependently in response to environmental contingencies toward the accomplishment of collective goals. MTS boundaries are defined by virtue of the fact that all teams within the system, while pursuing different proximal goals, share at least one common distal goal; and in so doing exhibit input, process, and outcome interdependence with at least one other team in the system.

Notably, this conception of an MTS as a unique entity encompasses five distinguishing characteristics. First, an MTS is composed of two or more teams. Minimally, an MTS is composed of two teams and is maximally composed of N teams interacting with each other. Teams that make up an MTS, which we refer to as *component teams*, are nonreducible and distinguishable wholes with interdependent members and proximal goals.

Second, an MTS is a unique entity that is larger than a team yet is typically smaller than the larger organization within which it is embedded. Some MTSs may even cross traditional organizational boundaries. They differ from teams, organizations, and other collective forms such as departments and subsystems in their architecture and functioning. Third, all component teams exhibit input, process, and outcome interdependence with at least one other team in the system. This important concept represents the "glue" that defines and holds together an MTS. Fourth, an MTS is an open system whose particular configuration stems from the performance requirements of the environment that it confronts and the technologies that it adopts. The performance requirements, in turn, serve to articulate a goal hierarchy that guides the actions of an MTS. And fifth, although MTS component teams may not share proximal goals, they share one or more distal goals.

The building blocks of an MTS are the *component teams*. For example, consider a computer systems company whereby projects are identified by *business teams*, are passed along to a *solution definition team* and then to *solution development and delivery teams,* then onto a *release management team*, and then are supported by *customer service teams*. Whereas much of this activity unfolds in a sequential mode, other aspects must simultaneously evolve in concert with one another. Some individuals may simultaneously be members of multiple teams; others may change team membership as a project evolves; and still others may remain on a given team and work on multiple projects at the same time. The Input–Process–Outcome (IPO) relationships so often the subject of inquiry in teams research play out in each of these component teams. However, it is possible for each of the teams to be individually successful and yet for the system to fail. Collective success depends on joint effort at multiple levels. Individuals within teams must work together internally to perform their team's function (i.e., intrateam coordination), and entire teams must be in sync so that their efforts combine in a way that will ultimately lead to the success of the entire system (i.e., interteam coordination). Research on large-scale organizational projects has identified a similar distinction, noting that individual teams differ in the extent to which their focus is on the team or the project (Hoegl & Weinkauf, 2005).

The MTS concept basically describes the functioning of a tightly coupled network of teams. Recent team-focused research has emphasized the point that teams need to well manage interfaces with their external environments if they are to be effective (Ancona & Caldwell, 1992; Choi, 2002; Tesluk & Mathieu, 1999). Yet the focus of even those studies remains the individual team. We submit that an examination of the joint interactions between tightly coupled teams will yield additional insights regarding the effectiveness of the larger system—namely, the MTS. We make the assumption that MTS performance is more than the sum of individual team efforts. Moreover, we argue that an effective MTS is one where members can shift attention from within-team activities to cross-team activities as warranted by changes in the performance environment.

MTSs versus Teams

Mathieu et al. (2001) argued that MTSs are larger entities than individual teams yet are generally not full-scale organizations. They are perhaps best conceptualized as tightly coupled networks of teams. Arguably, one could characterize an MTS as simply a large team with subunits. However, we do not believe that accurately portrays its unique nature. Naturally, the boundary between when a large team versus an MTS, unit, network, organization, or some other collective is somewhat arbitrary and blurry. Indeed, Gully (2000, p. 32) argued that organizational "teams are coupled to one another and to the organization as a whole, but their boundaries are distinct enough to give them a separate identity. This is similar to the notion of loose coupling, or partial inclusion. In this sense, boundaries of teams both separate and link the work done by teams."

Mathieu et al.'s (2001) MTS concept simultaneously emphasizes both the system as a whole as well as the component teams. Both Hackman (2003) and Arrow and McGrath (1995) discussed "bracketing" types of theoretical approaches and research designs. Each proclaimed the benefits of studying team phenomenon by considering not only the team level of analysis but also the individuals who make up the teams, as well as the larger context within which teams operate. Arrow and McGrath described such arrangements as individuals nested in teams, which, in turn, are nested in larger systems. The boundary between adjacent systems constitutes a two-way interface or interchange where the higher level provides support for a lower level whereas the lower level serves in a production function for the larger system (ibid., p. 380).

We submit that the distinction between teams and MTSs lies in the nature of the interdependencies within and across that boundary. Members of component teams are highly interdependent and consider themselves as a team. In other words, although individual team members cannot operate alone, component teams can execute independent actions and operate without necessarily being in concert with other teams in the system. In contrast, the interdependencies across teams are less immediate and required. Individual members are well aware that they are part of the larger collective, yet their primary identities are derived from their team. Mathieu et al. (2001) described how MTS component teams may be responsible for markedly different functions, may pursue different proximal goals, and may operate in substantially different temporal cycles. Yet the success of the collective whole (i.e., MTS) will depend in large part on how well members orchestrate actions that require collaborations across teams. What makes the MTS unit of inquiry unique from other collectives such as organizations, however, is that the larger system is identified not by formal organizational structures (e.g., strategic business units) or even by organizational membership but rather in terms of the network of input, process, and outcome interdependencies between teams and the goals they pursue. For example, Mathieu et al. described the functioning of an emergency response MTS that was composed of teams that spanned multiple public and private organizations. Our opening example concerning the Katrina situation illustrates just how complex such systems can be.

MTS Interdependence

A critical feature of an MTS is the functional interdependence that exists throughout the system. In a global economy, one could argue that all organizational entities are interdependent to some extent. Thus, we introduce the notion of *functional interdependence* which stems directly from the activities that each of the component teams perform. Functional interdependence is a state by which entities have mutual reliance, determination, influence, and shared vested interest in processes they use to accomplish work activities. The purpose of this section is to illustrate the importance of functional interdependence to an MTS.

Following from the definition of teams that we adopted, all MTS component teams exhibit interdependence among their members (Salas et al., 1992; Sundstrom, DeMeuse, & Futrell, 1990). Here, we focus our attention on the interdependence that exists between teams that comprise an MTS. To do so, we have adopted a tripartite framework to explain the role of functional interdependence in an MTS. This framework depicts three forms of functional interdependence: inputs, processes, and outcomes associated with the operations of an MTS. Each team within the MTS is functionally interdependent (i.e., input, process, and outcome) with at least one other team. The rules for interdependence among teams within an MTS are delineated specifically because this serves as one way to elucidate the differences between an MTS and an organization. This also helps to articulate the boundaries of MTS membership.

Outcome interdependence is the extent to which personal benefits, rewards, costs, or other outcomes received by team members depend on the performance or successful goal attainment of others (Alper, Tjosvold, & Law, 1998; Guzzo & Shea, 1992; Wageman, 1995). Everyone in the MTS shares a vested interest in the accomplishment of superordinate goals. However, by *functional outcome interdependence*, we are also describing the accomplishment of subgoals that require the joint activities of two or more teams. At least at the superordinate level, all teams are working toward common objectives that require their synthesized efforts. However, MTS functional outcome interdependence also resides at lower levels in the goal hierarchy, where component teams coordinate activities to achieve more proximal goals. Superordinate goal accomplishment requires the compilation of different sets of functional activities, each with different sets of subgoals. Highly interdependent component teams share in more proximal outcomes that emerge from collective subgoal accomplishment, such as satisfaction, development, quality of work life, and perhaps financial benefits. Thus, functional outcome interdependence flows in large part from the collective goal hierarchy of the MTS.

Process interdependence is defined as the amount of *interteam* interaction required for goal accomplishment and refers to the degree to which teams depend on each other to perform the tasks at hand. Process interdependence is similar to the concept of task interdependence in teams (Van de Ven, Delbecq & Koening, 1976), yet we have chosen the term *process interdependence* because component teams are not simply working together on a single task but rather on a collective mission. Teams work collaboratively to carry out processes such as boundary spanning, communication, and integration of actions, efforts, and timing.

The literature on teams has further depicted the nature of task interdependence by describing different forms of interdependent working arrangements to delineate more specifically the spectrum of teamwork arrangements (Saavedra et al., 1993; Tesluk, Mathieu, Zaccaro, & Marks,

1997; Van de Ven, 1980). These forms include pooled, sequential, reciprocal, and intensive interdependence and are summarized in Tesluk et al. (1997). Goal hierarchies within an MTS give rise to multiple kinds of functional process interdependencies that may encompass one of these forms of inter-dependence, or may involve various combinations of these arrangements.

Input interdependence identifies the extent to which component teams must share inputs such as people, facilities, environmental constraints, equipment, and information related to collective goal accomplishment. By *functional input interdependence*, we mean that the inputs teams share are used for the attainment of more proximal goals. This notion is parallel to the concept of resource interdependence that has been defined at the team level (Wageman, 1995).

In sum, functional interdependence is a defining characteristic of an MTS, whereby each component team must have input, process, and out-put interdependence with at least one other component team. This yields a complex system; a tightly coupled network of teams bounded by their functional interdependencies. Whereas interdependent work arrange-ments can take different forms (e.g., sequential, reciprocal, intensive), our critical point is that no one individual team can single-handedly accom-plish an MTS superordinate goal. This also means that other teams that have limited interaction with component teams would not fulfill MTS membership criteria.

Firefighting MTS

Consider the example of a firefighting MTS presented in Exhibit A at the end of this chapter. Whereas this example is nowhere near as complex as the Katrina system, it does exemplify many of the key attributes of an MTS. First, the firefighting MTS includes multiple diverse types of teams. In particular, there are fire suppression, ventilation, and search and rescue teams—and in a large multialarm instance such as the one we describe, there would be numerous versions of each active simultane-ously. Figure 10.1 displays the nature of the interdependencies among key firefighting component teams.

Second, teams at the scene may well represent only a subset of those available from any particular company. Simultaneously, in a multial-arm fire there are teams from different companies involved, as well as the possibility of a blend of paid and volunteer firefighting teams. Third, teams need to share resources (e.g., information, water), to coordinate their efforts, and literally will live and die on the basis of how well they work together. Fourth, the firefighting An MTS is an open system that

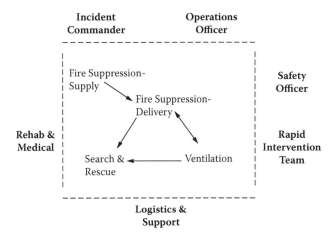

FIGURE 10.1
Functional interdependencies in the firefighting MTS.

must adapt as environmental circumstances warrant (e.g., wind shifts, the discovery of potentially explosive stored materials) and must confront entities that are outside of its membership yet that are involved in the situation (e.g., crowd and traffic control). MTS is also an open system in the sense that additional firefighters and teams will need to be rotated into the MTS over time as people tire and as other demands present themselves. Finally, although different teams are clearly performing different activities, everyone involved shares the common goals of protecting lives and property.

MTS Research Investigations

Much of what we know about MTSs resides at the level of the component team. The voluminous literature on team effectiveness tells us a great deal about the functioning of individual teams. However, research on single teams tells little of the dynamics of teams interacting with each other and with their respective environments. Toward this aim, a number of recent research efforts have examined multiteam systems. The first initiative was a multiuniversity laboratory-based program of research: Air Combat Effectiveness Simulation (ACES). The ACES program capitalized on the control afforded in laboratory simulations to investigate three substantive issues surrounding MTSs: training, interdependencies, and leadership. Additionally, a number of related field investigations have begun to explore the complexities of real-world MTSs.

The ACES Program of Research

The Air Combat Effectiveness Simulation (Mathieu, Cobb, Marks, Zaccaro, & Marsh, 2004) multiteam research program was undertaken by a team of researchers spanning four universities. Three laboratories were equipped with the ACES test bed and conducted multiple investigations of MTS research questions. We first provide a brief overview of the generic methodology used in these studies and then present the major highlights of findings stemming from this research.

ACES Methodology

All studies used the ACES multiteam simulation, where different configurations of individuals nested within teams performed an F-22 battle task (Mathieu et al., 2004). All studies employed a minimum of two live teams, each consisting of two individuals (a pilot and a weapons specialist). Some studies added in artificial intelligence (AI)-controlled MTS member teams, whereas others integrated a two-person command team.

The basic structure of the ACES simulation is depicted in Figure 10.2. Each MTS (ranging from four to six participants) was brought into an ACES lab at either George Mason University, Florida International University, or Pennsylvania State University and tested in a separate session. Participants completed an extensive series of background measures, were

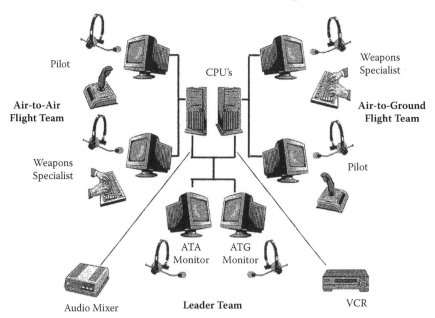

FIGURE 10.2
ACES diagram.

assigned to roles on the MTS simulation, and were trained in their individual roles. Next the MTSs performed a series of missions where data was collected via several methods including videotape, direct observation, voice recording, and Air Combat Maneuvering Instrumentation (ACMI) data file on a variety of teamwork process and performance constructs. Both between- and within-subjects manipulations of focal constructs were incorporated in most of the studies, and measures of focal process and performance variables were targeted at both the within- and between-team levels of measurement.

A primary aim of the ACES research was to examine and test one of the most basic propositions about MTSs: that both within- and between-team processes are critical to collective success. Multiple studies examined this issue. In each, the quality of work processes both (1) among members of a team and (2) between distinct teams were assessed, as was an indicator of network-level (MTS) performance. That is, performance was measured directly at the MTS level and operationalized as the degree to which the entire system achieved its assigned goals. So far, two different studies have examined the relative impact of within- versus between-team process on collective (MTS) performance (DeChurch & Marks, 2006; Marks, DeChurch, Mathieu, Panzer, & Alonso, 2005). Both found that between-team processes explained significant incremental variance in MTS performance after accounting for within-team process. Essentially, how effectively teams synchronize effort with other teams is a potent predictor of MTS success, even after the extent to which each team worked together well was taken into account. This is a powerful testament to the idea that individual team success is not the ultimate criteria. Teams can be individually successful and still fail to realize their ultimate goals.

This basic finding has important implications for the study of teams in organizations. Notably, it suggests a need to first identify the goal of interest and then to identify which units are interdependent, or need one another, to attain the goal. Research limited at examining individuals nested within teams will not capture the important role of teamwork processes that arise at levels higher than the individual team. These processes are an example of emergent bottom-up processes (Klein & Kozlowski, 2000) in that they originate in the cognition, affect, and behavior of the individuals comprising component teams. However, they are complex in that emergence is played out both at the level of the component team and at the level of the multiteam system.

Training for Multiteamwork

Cobb, Mathieu, and Marks (2003) examined the influence of team training on the effectiveness of ACES component teams and the MTS as a whole. They hypothesized and found support for a positive influence of MTS transition processes (e.g., mission analysis, planning) on both team and MTS action processes (e.g., within-team and MTS coordination during missions), which in turn related positively to MTS performance. Whereas traditional training in teamwork skills enhanced within team action processes, it did not influence MTS (i.e., cross-team) action processes. Their results highlight the fact that simply enhancing the effectiveness of component teams does not ensure that they will be more effective as a collective.

Goal Hierarchies and Multiteamwork

The goal hierarchy is a critical notion in describing MTSs. Its delineation of component teams and the nature of interdependencies among them really capture the essence of the MTS perspective. The goal hierarchy implies that a certain array of teams is needed to perform a superordinate goal. These teams must work toward their individual team goals and also collaborate, to a greater or lesser extent, toward the accomplishment of more distal collective goals. The extent and nature of requisite interactions among teams derive from their relation in the goal hierarchy. Drawing on our firefighting MTS, the ultimate goal of the MTS is saving lives. This requires the joint efforts of various teams, some of whom are working together near the fire to extinguish the fire and locate and extract victims. Concurrently, other teams, like the rehabilitation/medical team, are setting up away from the fire in a location that is safe for emergency medical technicians (EMTs) to begin stabilizing victims; this provides an easy exit route to transport victims to the hospital. Here the water supply and delivery teams are extremely proximal in the goal hierarchy, whereas the supply team and the medical team are more loosely coupled. Thus, the coordination demands ought to be more intense for teams that are more closely tied in by the goal hierarchy and less intense the more removed teams are from one another in the goal hierarchy.

The ACES simulation was used to examine the impact of MTS goal hierarchies on optimal work processes (Marks et al., 2005). The goal hierarchy describes the basic structure of an MTS. In general, *structure* describes the set of roles and responsibilities that comprise a system and specifies the nature of interrelationships among those roles. In our earlier discussion of functional interdependence, it was noted that the structure of an MTS is largely defined by the functional interdependencies that exist across teams. Teams—who share inputs, who need to coordinate to complete their work, or whose rewards are dependent on one another—are said to be functionally interdependent.

Marks et al. (2005) examined the relative influence of between- and within-team processes as a function of the level of interdependence among teams in an MTS. The study employed a repeated measures design where each MTS operated in a low- and a high-interdependence task environment. Interestingly, the structure of the MTS in terms of interdependence largely dictated the level of teamwork process that was most predictive of success. Between-team processes were more important when MTSs performed highly interdependent tasks as opposed to less interdependent tasks. Conversely, within-team processes were more critical to performance on less, as opposed to more, interdependent tasks.

Leadership in Multiteam Systems

Working in an MTS is extremely complex, and leadership is both critical and challenging. Some of the essential issues related to leading an MTS concern the (1) balance between managing the dynamics of component teams versus managing the team-to-team interfaces and (2) structure of the leadership function. In an MTS leaders need to balance efforts aimed at aligning individuals within teams with those aimed at aligning units. Leaders play a critical role in the success of individual teams as well as of the MTS. Since MTSs are teams composed of both individual members and intact component teams, different skills and behaviors are needed for effective intrateam and interteam leadership.

The ACES program examined the impact of leadership aimed at within-versus between-team interaction. DeChurch and Marks (2006) created a training manipulation that primed leaders to focus their actions on leading their individual teams (control conditions) versus leading at the interface between teams (experimental conditions). Two leadership functions were examined that correspond to the two Marks, Mathieu, and Zaccaro (2001) team task phases: strategy development (i.e. transition phase) and coordination facilitation (i.e. action phase). Findings showed that leader actions aimed at cross-team integration had a significant impact on between-team teamwork and overall MTS performance. These findings illustrate the need for MTS leaders to maintain a dual focus on within- and between-team actions.

Related Field Investigations

Field investigations of MTS phenomena are beginning to appear in the literature. To our knowledge, no research has yet to examine the effectiveness of MTSs as the focal unit of analysis. There is, however, an evolving body of research that has considered organizational contextual influences on team effectiveness. Generally, organizational contextual influences can be defined as factors that are external to the team yet that emanate from within the larger organizational system in which teams are nested. For example, Gladstein (1984) found that organizational reward systems have strong influences on team functioning. Campion and colleagues

(Campion, Medsker, & Higgs, 1993; Campion, Papper, & Medsker, 1996) and Hyatt and Ruddy (1997) provided evidence that organizational factors such as recognition and rewards, training systems, and information sharing had both direct and indirect effects on group effectiveness.

In the current context, our attention is focused on organizational contextual factors that link different teams to one another and thereby influence on the effectiveness of component teams. For example, Kirkman and Rosen (1999) argued that the presence of an organizational climate of openness can provide teams with a well-developed social structure and sociopolitical support and thereby can enhance team processes and performance. Additionally, Tesluk, Vance, and Mathieu (1999) found several significant relationships between the organizational district-level participative climate and lower-level unit and individual-level outcomes. They concluded "that the extent to which the climate within a work unit [team] encourages participation is, in part, a function of the practices and policies that support employee involvement in the broader organizational context" (p. 293). Similarly, Mathieu, Maynard, Taylor, Gilson, and Ruddy (2007) found a significant relationship between the openness of organizational district climates and component team performance, as mediated by team processes.

It has also been suggested that teams function more effectively as self-contained units when they have strong information networks along with communication and cooperation channels both within and between teams (Beer, Eisenstat, & Spector, 1990; Cummings, 1978; Kirkman & Rosen, 1999). In other words, when teams receive information and support from other teams in a system, they are better able to execute team processes and thereby to perform more effectively. Indeed, Mohrman, Cohen, and Mohrman (1995) argued that between-team integration processes "are central to the ability of the organization to create teams that are able to make a difference in the attainment of goals through the interaction of team members with one another and with other teams" (p. 171). Indeed, field investigations by Kirkman and Rosen (1999) and Mathieu et al. (2006) found significant correlations between effective cross-team (i.e., MTS) coordination and team outcomes. Moreover, Mathieu et al. (2007) found a significant direct positive effect of MTS coordination processes on the performance of component teams.

In summary, field studies have begun to consider the influence of MTS processes on the functioning and effectiveness of component teams. Initial work has been encouraging and numerous significant relationships have been found. However, work needs to expand and to consider MTSs as the focal unit of analysis and to examine how different arrangements, coordinating mechanisms, leadership processes, and so forth influence not only the effectiveness of the component team but also the effectiveness of the overall collective.

Themes for Future Thinking in Terms of Multiteam Systems

MTSs are a new structure already in widespread use in modern organizations. These networks of teams form when a collective goal requires a set of skills and expertise not available from any one team or any collection of teams working independently. They are used in a wide variety of settings ranging from military operations to new product development, and their tasks are not easily distinguished using existing taxonomies (i.e., project, action, decision making), since most MTSs contain teams performing a wide variety of tasks. As such, MTSs are a new breed, and understanding them will require us to address new challenges and to think in different terms. The following section presents some of the new terms as a starting point for future research.

Time and Team Development

The inherent complexity and size of an MTS makes temporal considerations even more prominent. As opposed to thinking about the role of time in the development of a single team, we must now consider the development of multiple teams, likely to be in distinct task cycles and stages of development—a real coordination challenge. A particularly helpful view of time in MTSs is tied to the notion of performance episodes (Marks et al., 2001). This view posits that teams cycle through transition and action phases as they work toward collective goals. These transition and action phases can and often do recur, in the sense that teams typically work toward multiple goals over time. Transition periods are analogous to planning stages and require teams to engage in processes like goal setting, mission analysis, and strategy development. These processes prepare the team for the action phase, when it is engaged in goal-directed behavior utilizing processes like coordination and systems monitoring. Performance episodes are a promising way to conceptualize the role of time in MTSs because they are tied directly to the goals of each team and of the MTS.

There are several tenets of the recurring phase model with implications for considering the role of time in MTSs. First, component teams need to engage in different processes depending on their task phase. Thus, in a given phase within-team process will require team members to collectively enact goals and strategies. Depending on the nature of the team's linkages with other teams as dictated by the goal hierarchy, teams will also need to operate in a way that is compatible with other teams. Using the example of planning processes, this may mean that teams consider other teams' needs in developing their plans or even explicitly in planning for interaction with other teams during subsequent action phases.

One open issue concerns the coordination of effort between teams simultaneously engaged in different task cycles requiring different processes.

Second, the recurring phase model depicts the unit of time as the performance episode as opposed to the clock or calendar. Thus, although an MTS requires multiple teams to work together, it does not necessarily yoke teams whose tasks are in parallel performance episodes. How do teams align their efforts when their episode lengths vary greatly? This is also likely to be a source of breakdowns.

MTS Design: Size, Heterogeneity, and Distribution

The architecture of an MTS is substantially more complex than that of a single team. Traditional features like size, heterogeneity, and distribution play out both among members of each component team as well as between distinct functionally interdependent component teams.

Size

In research on teams, size typically refers to the number of individuals comprising a team. It is generally acknowledged that as team size increases, there are greater coordination challenges and the likelihood of noncooperative coalitions forming increases. Conversely, smaller teams may not have the cognitive, behavioral, and creative resources necessary for a given task. In MTSs, size is an even greater issue because it describes the number of teams and the number of individuals within each team. Thus, the coordination challenges are now multiplicatively greater and span hierarchical levels. We are not suggesting that future work on MTSs focus on how size affects functioning but rather that the size of MTSs might be a critical contingency variable in the study of other variables. For example, coordinating mechanisms, use of technology, and leadership structures will all differ depending on the complexity of the MTS.

Heterogeneity

Another challenge facing MTSs is their degree of heterogeneity. Since MTSs often consist of teams spanning multiple functionalities, organizations, national cultures, and even primary languages, the complexity of creating coherence will be far greater than in a single team. Furthermore, heterogeneity will play out both within and across component teams.

Mathieu et al. (2001) distinguished between internal and cross-boundary MTSs. An internal MTS is composed of teams from a single organization. Here, all component teams are embedded in the same organization, thereby experiencing many of the same cultural and contextual forces. In contrast, cross-boundary MTSs contain component teams that span at least two organizations. Thus, component teams share interdependencies with a team or teams who are themselves embedded in a distinct organizational culture. Heterogeneity is likely to increase significantly as the number of embedding organizations increases.

Considering the role of heterogeneity in MTSs is complex, and a promising concept is that of the fault line (Lau & Murnighan, 1998). The notion of fault lines has been used in social psychological contexts to describe situations where group members differ in terms of demographic attributes and are therefore more likely to experience discord in the course of interacting (ibid.). Fault lines have been found to be particularly important in factional groups, where individuals hold memberships on and therefore identify with multiple groups simultaneously (Li & Hambrick, 2005). The structure of an MTS implies that individuals simultaneously hold memberships in their component team and in the MTS. To the extent that component teams' goals or work processes are incongruent, there are likely to be fault lines present at the boundaries of component teams.

Distribution

When we speak of distribution in teams, there is an acknowledgment that some teams work face to face while others work more virtually. The underlying dimension of interest might distinguish things like the percent of the time spent working virtually or the degree of geographic separation. With MTSs there is the almost certainty of virtuality. Thus, the relevant comparisons are not between face-to-face and virtual MTSs but rather between systems that vary on the percentage of collocated and virtual interactions.

Furthermore, multiple aspects of the MTS operating environment need to be considered. Kirkman and Mathieu (2005) identified three dimensions that describe the degree of virtuality of a team: synchronicity, informational value, and extent of use of virtual tools. *Synchronicity* describes the extent to which communications among members incur a time lag. Synchronous communication occurs in real time, whereas asynchronous communication involves some degree of delay in the transmission of information from one party and the reception of information by another. *Informational value* describes the richness of information that is transmitted among members. When informational value is low, many of the nonverbal cues discernable in face-to-face interaction are stripped away. The *extent of reliance on virtual tools* describes the utilization of communication technology such as video conferencing and collaborative software applications.

In MTSs, the degree of virtuality varies both within and across teams and has important implications for the functioning of the MTS. Kirkman and

Mathieu (2005) advanced the idea that the optimality of these dimensions of virtuality depends on the team performance environment. For example, asynchronous communication slows coordination but enables additional time for a deeper possession of information. Depending on the type of MTS task, this might be an asset or a detriment to effectiveness. In the Katrina example introduced earlier, the urgency of the situation elevated the importance of immediate information exchange across teams.

Coordinating Mechanisms

A primary challenge facing any MTS concerns how to maintain alignment across units. We use the term *coordinating mechanism* to describe different methods for attaining system integration. March and Simon (1958) and later Thompson (1967) described three basic means for achieving coordination in an organization: standardization, coordination by plan, and coordination by mutual adjustment. Standardization uses rules or set operating procedures to regulate behavior. MTSs might use standardization to align the efforts of teams whose interdependence is pooled or that operate in more routine environments. Coordination by plan will be more appropriate when interdependence and environmental dynamicism are intermediate. Coordination by mutual adjustment occurs in real time as interdependent units provide continuous feedback to regulate and adjust their actions in response to the environment to maintain alignment with one another. Coordination by mutual adjustment is likely to be key in MTSs, and future work is needed detailing the drivers of this form of coordination. This type of coordination seems particularly well suited for highly interdependent teams and for MTS operating in dynamic contexts with changing team memberships. Technology and leadership seem especially important as coordinating mechanisms in MTSs, as both enable and regulate the flow of information.

Coordination by Leadership

Researchers have largely characterized the responsibilities of team leaders as providing functional leadership, which defines a leader's primary responsibility as "to do, or get done, whatever is not being adequately handled for group needs" (McGrath, 1962, p. 5). From this broad perspective, the team leader's role is to intervene in the team as necessitated by demands of the environment, task, and team members (Zaccaro, Rittman, & Marks, 2001) and by doing so to ensure that "all functions critical to both task accomplishment and group maintenance are adequately taken care of" (Hackman & Walton, 1986, p. 75). Zaccaro et al. further characterized team leadership as social problem solving and outlined three primary responsibilities: (1) boundary spanning to determine obstacles to goal attainment; (2) identifying appropriate plans and solutions that enable goal attainment; and (3) within the confines of a larger social system, implementing solutions that provide direction. Zaccaro et al. went on to link team leadership to team processes, contending that team leaders affect team performance by enhancing important intrateam processes. To explain the alignment between team leadership and team processes, they suggested that core leadership processes enhance four categories of team processes critical to team success: (1) cognitive processes; (2) motivational processes; (3) affective processes; and (4) coordination processes. These processes enable members of a team or MTS to synchronize their efforts toward attainment of a collective objective.

Thus, we submit that MTS leaders serve essentially the same roles in leading MTSs but that they are responsible for a dual focus on within- and between-team functioning, which increases the complexity of the leader's role (Mathieu et al., 2001). Within the component or operational teams in a system, leaders must facilitate synchronization of team member contributions toward proximal team goals. At the same time, leaders must also focus on between-team functions involving monitoring and maintaining the alignment of various teams. These functions enable the teams to work in concert to attain their higher-level collective outcomes. Therefore, the success of an MTS hinges on leaders' ensuring component team effectiveness while successfully aligning operations between teams.

Coordination by Technology

Maintaining alignment requires feedback. The component teams of an MTS need to continuously inform one another of their progress to facilitate appropriate timing and sequencing of interdependent actions. In a four-person team interacting face to face, this is easily done through verbal or visual cues. However, in large complex collectives like MTSs, verbal and visual cues will typically be completely overwhelmed with information aimed at maintaining alignment with members of the same team. Thus, additional stimulus modalities will be necessary to transmit information about team progress to tightly coupled teams. Information technology is ideally suited for this purpose.

The firefighting MTS introduced in Exhibit A contains an excellent example of how leaders and technology facilitate coordination across distinct teams. Many firefighting units are implementing complex global positioning systems (GPSs) that display exactly where each firefighter is located at the scene. Firefighters wear a locating device on their backpacks that emits a constant radio signal. Meanwhile, the operations officer monitors a three-dimensional computerized display to track the progress and status of each firefighter.

Future Directions

Research on team effectiveness has traditionally taken a prescriptive approach, with an eye toward developing practicable knowledge on how individual effort can be channeled toward collective goals (Kozlowski & Bell, 2002). However, the continuing evolution of collective work structures into complex networks of teams presents those interested in studying and using teams with a new challenge. The problem is complex; nonetheless, it is imperative that future work on teams begin to think in terms of multiteam systems. We now conclude with some promising next steps in this process.

First and foremost, research is needed that explicitly examines and tests propositions at the MTS level of analysis. There are excellent investigations of the role of contextual forces on single team effectiveness (Mathieu et al., 2007) and on the need for teams to "boundary span" (Ancona & Caldwell, 1992) to be effective, but the outcomes of those studies remain at the team level. Very few empirical studies have predicted outcomes residing at levels higher than the team. To do this, investigators need to begin by defining the particular MTS structure under investigation. This involves specifying the MTS goal, the teams that are interdependent with regard to that goal, and the nature of the interdependencies that exist across teams. In addition, outcome variables need to capture the degree of MTS goal attainment, as distinct from simply the sum of component team goal attainment levels. While the size of MTSs will make data collection cumbersome and sample sizes modest, this research is sorely needed if we are to develop evidence-based prescriptions regarding multiteam effectiveness.

In addition to the need for more traditional empirical work on MTSs, a second avenue for future investigations is to utilize nontraditional designs. Illustrative case studies (cf. Cook, Sutton, & Useem, 2005), multisource ethnography, and mathematical modeling applications may all prove useful in contributing to our understanding of multiteam dynamics. Finally, how do we leverage MTS success? Though a substantial amount of conceptual and empirical work is needed to build the basic science behind understanding multiteam systems, we need to keep our sights on ways to translate findings into organizational practices. In pursuing the directions previously outlined, we need to consider the ways personnel selection, training, and other systems can be designed to maximize MTS effectiveness. Basically, new organizational forms will require new ways to think about traditional human resources and design challenges.

References

Alper, S., Tjosvold, D., & Law, K. S. (1998) Interdependence and controversy in group decision making: Antecedents to effective self-managing teams, *Organizational Behavior and Human Decision Processes, 74*(1), 33–52.

Ancona, D. G. & Caldwell, D. F. (1988). Beyond task and maintenance: Defining external functions in groups. *Group & Organizational Studies, 13,* 468–494.

Ancona, D. G. & Caldwell, D. F. (1992). Bridging the boundary: External activity and performance in organizational teams. *Administrative Science Quarterly, 37,* 634–665.

Argyris, C. (1998). Empowerment: The emperor's new clothes. *Harvard Business Review, 76*(3), 98.

Arrow, H. & McGrath, J. E. (1995). Membership dynamics in groups at work: A theoretical framework. In B. M. Staw & L. L. Cummings (Eds.), *Research in Organizational Behavior, 17,* 373–411. Greenwich, CT: JAI Press.

Beer, M., Eisenstat, R. A., & Spector, B. (1990) Why change programs don't produce change. *Harvard Business Review, 68*(6), 158–166.

Campion, M. A., Medsker, G. J., & Higgs, A. C. (1993). Relations between work group characteristics and effectiveness: Implications for designing effective work groups. *Personnel Psychology, 46,* 823–847.

Campion, M. A., Papper, E. M., & Medsker, G. J. (1996). Relations between work team characteristics and effectiveness: A replication and extension. *Personnel Psychology, 49,* 429–452.

Choi, J. N. (2002). External activities and team effectiveness—Review and theoretical development. *Small Group Research, 33*(2), 181–208.

Clift, E. (2005, September 2). A colossal failure of leadership. *Newsweek.* Retrieved December 5, 2005, from http://www.msnbc.msn.com/id/9174806/site/newsweek

Cobb, M. A., Mathieu, J. E., & Marks, M. A. (2003, April). The impact of training and environmental complexity on the effectiveness of multiteam systems. In J. E. Mathieu (chair), *Investigations of Multi-team systems,* Symposium conducted at annual meeting of the Society for Industrial & Organizational Psychology, Orlando, FL.

Cook, J., Sutton, L., & Useem, M. (2005). Developing leaders for decision making under stress: Wildland firefighters in the south canyon fire and its aftermath. *Academy of Management Learning & Education, 4,* 461–485.

Cummings, T. G. (1978). Self-regulating work groups: A socio-technical synthesis. *The Academy of Management Review, 3*(3), 625–634.

DeChurch, L. A. & Marks, M. A. (2006). Leadership in multi-team systems. *Journal of Applied Psychology, 91,* 311–329.

Gladstein, D. L. (1984). Groups in context: A model of task group effectiveness. *Administrative Science Quarterly, 29,* 499–517.

Gully, S. M. (2000). Work teams research: Recent findings and future trends. In M. M. Beyerlein (Ed.), *Work teams: Past, present and future* (pp. 25–44). Amsterdam, The Netherlands: Kluwer Academic Publishers.

Guzzo, R. A. & Shea, G. P. (1992). Group performance and intergroup relations in organizations. In M. D. Dunnette, & L. M. Hough, *Handbook of Industrial and Organizational Psycholoigy,* pp. 269–313. Palo Alto, CA: Consulting Psychologists Press, Inc.

Hackman, J. R. (2003). Learning more by crossing levels: evidence from airplanes, hospitals, and orchestras. *Journal of Organizational Behavior, 24*(8), 905–922.

Hackman, J. R., & Walton, R. E. (1986). Leading groups in organizations. In P. S. Goodman (Eds.), *Designing effective work groups* (pp. 72–119). San Francisco, CA: Jossey-Bass.

Hoegl, M. & Weinkauf, K. (2005). Managing task interdependencies in multi-team projects: A longitudinal study. *Journal of Management Studies, 42*(6), 1287–1308.

Hyatt, D. E. & Ruddy, T. M. (1997). An examination of the relationship between work group characteristics and performance: Once more into the breech. *Personnel Psychology, 50,* 533–585.

Kirkman, B. L. & Malthieu, J. E. (2005). The deminsions and antecedents of team virtuality. *Journal of Management, 31*(5), 700–718.

Kirkman, B. L. & Rosen, B. (1999). Beyond self-management: Antecedents and consequences of team empowerment. *Academy of Management Journal, 42,* 58–74.

Klein, K. & Kozlowski, S. W. J. (2000). *Multilevel theory, research and methods in organization.* San Francisco, CA: Jossey-Bass.

Kozlowski, S. W. J. & Bell, B. S. (2002). Work groups and teams in organizations. In W. Borman, D. Ilgen, & R. Klimoski (Eds.), *Comprehensive handbook of psychology: Industrial and organizational psychology* (Vol. 12, pp. 333–375): New York: Wiley.

Lau, D. C. & Murnighan, J. K. (1998). Demographic diversity and faultlines: The compositional dynamics of organizational groups. *Academy of Management Review, 23*(2), 325–340.

Li, J. T. & Hambrick, D. C. (2005). Factional groups: A new vantage on demographic faultlines, conflict, and disintegration in work teams. *Academy of Management Journal, 48*(5), 794–813.

March, J. G. S. & Simon, H. A. (1958). *Organizations.* New York: Wiley.

Marks, M. A., DeChurch, L. A., Mathieu, J. E., Panzer, F. J., & Alonso, A. A. (2005). Teamwork in multi-team systems. *Journal of Applied Psychology, 90*(5), 964–971.

Marks, M. A., Mathieu, J. E., & Zaccaro, S. J. (2001). A temporally based framework and taxonomy of team processes. *Academy of Management Review, 26*(3), 356–376.

Mathieu, J. E., Cobb, M. A., Marks, M. A., Zaccaro, S. J., & Marsh, S. (2004). Multi-team ACES: A research platform for studying multi-team systems. In S. G. Schiflett, L. R. Elliott, E. Salas, & M. Coovert (Eds.), *Scaled worlds: Development, validation and applications* (pp. 297–315). Burlington, VT: Ashgate.

Mathieu, J. E., Gilson, L. L., & Ruddy, T. M. (2006). Empowerment and team effectiveness: An empirical test of an integrated model. *Journal of Applied Psychology, 91,* 97–108.

Mathieu, J. E., Marks, M. A., & Zaccaro, S. J. (2001). Multi-team systems. In N. Anderson, D. Ones, H. K. Sinangil, & C. Viswesvaran (Eds.), *International handbook of work and organizational psychology* (pp. 289–313). London: Sage Publications.

Mathieu, J. E., Maynard, M. T., Taylor, S. R. Gilson, L. L., & Ruddy, T. M. (2007). An examination of the effects of organizational district and team contexts on team processes and performance: A meso-mediational model. *Journal of Organizational Behavior, 28,* 891–910.

McGrath, J. E. (1962). Leadership behavior: Some requirements for leadership training. Washington, DC: U.S. Civil Service Commission [Mimeographed].

Mohrman, S. A., Cohen, S. G., & Mohrman, A. M., Jr. (1995). Designing team-based organizations: New forms for knowledge work. San Francisco: Josey-Bass.

Moss Kanter, R. (2005, September 8). Katrina's failure of leadership. *Miami Herald.*

Saavedra, R., Earley, P. C., & Van Dyne, L. (1993). Complex interdependence in task-performing groups. *Journal of Applied Psychology, 78,* 61–72.

Salas, E., Dickinson, T. L., Converse, S. A., Tannenbaum, S. I. (1992). Toward an understanding of team performance and training. In R. W. Swezey & E. Salas (Eds), *Teams: Their Training and Performance,* pp. 3–29. Ablex Publishing Corporation, Westport, CT.

Select Bipartisan Committee to Investigate the Preparation for and Response to Hurricane Katrina. (2006, February 15). *A Failure of Initiative.* Retrieved July 22, 2008, from http://www.gpoacess.gov/congress/index.html

Spreitzer, G. M. (1995). Psychological empowerment in the workplace: Dimensions, measurement, and validation. *Academy of Management Journal, 38*(5), 1442–1465.

Sundstrom, E. (1999). The challenges of supporting work team effectiveness. In E. Sundstrom (Ed.), *Supporting work team effectiveness* (pp. 3–23). San Francisco, CA: Jossey-Bass.

Sundstrom, E., DeMeuse, K., & Futrell, D. (1990). Work teams: Applications and effectiveness. *American Psychologist, 45*(2), 120–133.

Tesluk, P. & Mathieu, J. E. (1999). Overcoming roadblocks to effectiveness: Incorporating management of performance barriers into models of work group effectiveness. *Journal of Applied Psychology, 84,* 200–217.

Tesluk, P., Mathieu, J. E., Zaccaro, S. J., & Marks, M. A. (1997). Task and aggregation issues in analysis and assessment of team performance. In M. T. Brannick, E. Salas, & C. Prince (Eds.), *Team performance assessment and measurement: Theory, methods, and applications.* Mahwah, NJ: Lawrence Erlbaum Associates.

Tesluk, P., Vance, R. J., Mathieu, J. E. (1999). Examining employee involvement in the context of participative work environments. *Group & Organization Management, 24,* 271–299.

Thompson, J. D. (1967). *Organizations in Action.* New York: McGraw-Hill.

Van de Ven, A. H., Delbecq, A. L., & Koening, R. Jr., (1976). Determinants of coordination modes within organizations. *American Sociological Review, 41*(2), 322–338.

Van de Ven, A. H. & Ferry, D. L. (1980). *Measuring and assessing organizations.* New York: Wiley-Interscience.

Wageman, R. (1995). Interdependence and group effectiveness. *Administrative Science Quarterly, 40,* 145–180.

Zaccaro, S. J., Rittmen, A. L., & Marks, M. A. (2001). Team leadership. *Leadership Quarterly, 12,* 451–483.

Exhibit A

A Firefighting MTS

At 10:17 AM the call comes in to the 911 center and is simultaneously routed to Fire Station Q via the computerized tracking and dispatch computer network. A resident reports that she sees fire coming from a house across the street, and the trucks from Station Q begin to roll. The default complement of vehicles dispatched includes three engines of varying capacity: a multipurpose rescue vehicle, a general utility vehicle, and an ambulance. Minutes later the force arrives at the scene, and the captain from Station Q, as the highest-ranking officer on location, assumes command (i.e., incident commander). He immediately realizes that the initial call was mistaken: It is not a resident fire; it is a neighboring multiunit apartment complex that is ablaze, so he calls for a backup complement of vehicles and crews from two neighboring districts. The ultimate goals for the firefighters are well understood and straightforward. First and foremost is the preservation of lives—not only the occupants' but also of firefighters'. Second is the protection of property, whereas third is actually extinguishing the fire. Finally, throughout the engagement, firefighters will be wary of hazardous materials and will do everything within their control to minimize environmental damage.

At this point, a collective has been configured in direct response to the needs of this particular situation. The overall goal is large in scope and requires a complex configuration of teams working together. This system is larger than a team because the goal requires diverse specialized units. Also notable is that though some consistency exists in the types of teams comprising the MTS, the exact set of teams changes from situation to situation. MTS composition is fluid and dynamic in a way that is functional to adaptive capability.

Upon arrival the incident commander assigns an operations officer and a safety officer to oversee this large system of response teams. The operations officer works as the hub of action coordination, whereas the safety officer works in a parallel function serving to provide a quality control function, backup, and safety monitor. Simultaneously, a rehabilitation/medical team prepares to deal with injured occupants and spent or injured firefighters, while a logistics and support team establishes itself and prepares to facilitate resources and to liaison with external representatives (e.g., crowd control, media relations). A staging area is set up where firefighters are placed into teams—particularly if the department is a volunteer one (most assignments are predetermined in full-time departments).

The operations officer manages the primary firefighting force that is differentiated into three types of teams. First, the *fire suppression team* is responsible for getting water on the fire. They are further broken down into supply teams that work to get water to the scene (e.g., from hydrants, ponds, or even residents' swimming pools) and delivery teams that actually administer the water onto the fire. Also reporting to the operations officer are members of the *search and rescue team*. These are the firefighters who look for survivors and trapped individuals. The rescue teams are tasked with extricating known surviving occupants, whereas the search team members go throughout the structure looking for others. The *ventilation team* is the third one reporting to the operations officer and is responsible for managing airflow in the fire. Notably, yet another team is formed: the *rapid intervention team*. This team is essentially a mini reserve force that has all of the aforementioned teams represented and is used by the incident commander and operating officer should an unexpected need arise.

Functionally, the fire suppression teams (delivery and supply), search and rescue teams, and ventilation teams work very closely together. The latter two are yoked to the fire suppression team, since until water is available at the fire no entry activities can be performed safely. Accordingly, the delivery team depends on the supply team to maintain water flow—although how much water is dispensed has implications for future supplies. Once sufficient water becomes available, the delivery, search and rescue, and ventilation teams work closely together in an interdependent way to manage the fire and to protect lives.

Search and rescue team members will scowl the site in a systematic fashion looking for survivors and assessing the structural integrity of the building along the way. Their passage must be protected by, and synchronized with, the combined efforts of the ventilation and fire suppression delivery teams. Fire and smoke follow airflows, and spraying water on flames generates heat and steam. All of these elements can be life threatening and must be managed. For example, should the ventilation team send air flow toward the fire suppression delivery team, which is spraying water on the flames, if the latter will be exposed to excessive heat and steam? This will limit their fire-extinguishing capabilities and will take a large toll on the firefighters as well. Naturally where the search and rescue team members are during this process places them at risk or relative safety.

Although the component teams in this MTS are all performing markedly different operations, their efforts are tied together by a goal hierarchy demanding quality transitions from one to the other, all in pursuit of the ultimate goal of saving lives and property. There are two important points to make. First, at any given time, the MTS goal hierarchy specifies the nature of the interdependence among teams. When the teams first arrive on the scene, the fire suppression and search and rescue teams' goals are linked *sequentially*; the fire suppression teams must get water on the fire before search and rescue operations can commence. Second, the nature of the goal hierarchy shifts as the task cycles unfold over time. Once the teams are in place and begin operations, the fire suppression and search and rescue teams become more *reciprocally* interdependent. The outcome of the efforts of the fire suppression team determines where the search and rescue teams begin conducting their operations. However, as search and rescue teams learn more about the situation and search different locations they provide feedback to the fire suppression team members to alter the location of their operations. The fire suppression and search and rescue teams are performing markedly different tasks, though their ability to synchronize effectively over time will be a critical factor in determining the success of the entire operation. If the fire suppression team does an outstanding job of soaking the parts of the structure where there are no victims, they might be successful in attaining a team goal, but by not enabling the search and rescue teams to reach victims their team efforts do not enable MTS success.

Orchestrating the efforts of the wide variety of teams in what looks like chaos to the untrained observer is the critical challenge facing the incident commander and operations officer once they have begun to execute their strategies. Breakdowns in coordination have potentially dire consequences and must be minimized. Some of the most likely, and dangerous, breakdowns stem from firefighters getting out of position. For example, if search and rescue members fail to clear an area as fast as anticipated and fail to check in, they run the risk of getting trapped should ventilation decide to redirect the fire. Equally dangerous might be fire suppression teams that are making great headway and advance beyond their zone of discretion and into dangerous situations. In short, maintaining interteam coordination is vital for the ultimate effectiveness of the firefighting MTS.

11

Team Effectiveness in Complex Settings: A Framework*

Peter J. M. D. Essens, Ad L. W. Vogelaar, Jacques J. C. Mylle,
Carol Blendell, Carol Paris, Stanley M. Halpin, and
Joseph V. Baranski

Military teams share many characteristics with teams in other application areas. They differ, however, in critically important ways, such as the
life-and-death nature of their work, the high levels of uncertainty, the far-
reaching consequences of their decisions and actions, and the complexity
and dynamics of the military context. Crisis response operations, anti-
terrorism operations, peace support operations, humanitarian aid operations, and warfare are so diverse in nature that they require a range of
qualities and skills of the military involved. Mission effectiveness has
become multifaceted and is defined differently by various stakeholders.
Operations with multiservice, with multinational military forces, and
with ad hoc teams even at lower command levels have brought forward
issues such as cultural diversity, communication, and leadership (Essens,
Vogelaar, Tanercan, & Winslow, 2001). Effective teamwork is a critical mission success factor. In our interactions with the military, we identified the
need of commanders to gain and maintain better insight into the effectiveness of their teams. Commanders need to assess, control, and adjust
the qualities of their teams before and during the mission to achieve intermediate and end goals and to learn from the experience after the mission
for future missions. To meet this need, a North Atlantic Trade Organization (NATO) research panel was formed under the auspices of the NATO
Research & Technology Organization for the purpose of developing a
theoretically grounded diagnostic instrument for commanders to assess
the effectiveness of their command teams. The primary development of

* This chapter is based on a North Atlantic Trade Organization (NATO) study (NATO/
RTO/HFM Task Group 023 on Team Effectiveness) and report (HFM-087 TP/59) written
by the authors (published by NATO RTO, April, 2005).

this instrument was completed in 2005 (Essens et al., 2005), with further refinement and validation progressing under the auspices of a follow-on NATO research panel. This chapter describes the theoretical basis for this diagnostic instrument that was developed and provides insights into the unique aspects and considerations of teamwork in modern military command environments.

A team is said to be effective if it achieves its goals. But what are the factors that enable and facilitate the achievement of those goals? Our premise is that to be potentially effective, commanders must understand (1) what conditions they start with, particularly mission demands and individual and team capabilities; (2) what the end goals, intermediate goals, and criteria are; and (3) what they can direct and control in task and team processes. Effective commanders regularly review the task and team processes against intermediate outcomes and adjust these or even seek to adjust condition factors if possible. We developed a team effectiveness model tuned to the military context: the Command Team Effectiveness (CTEF) model (Essens et al., 2005). This model is intended to provide the basis for support for commanders to assess and direct their teams. In this chapter, we start with a short review of team effectiveness models and then describe the components of the CTEF model and self-diagnostic instrument in more detail. Throughout this description, we note the unique aspects of the military command environment where teamwork is essential.

Team Effectiveness Models

For more than 50 years, scientists have attempted to understand and measure command team effectiveness. Yet today, there exists no single, universally accepted model of team effectiveness (Henderson & Walkinshaw, 2002). One obstacle in developing such a model is the ambiguity of the concepts used, characteristic for science in development. Teams are often evaluated in terms of their performance or effectiveness—but with little explanation as to what is meant by either of these terms. Yet it is critical that performance and effectiveness be clearly distinguished from each other (ibid.). Performance pertains to how well the work processes are being carried out. This includes activities that are directly related to the operational tasks, such as planning and decision making done individually and as a team as well as those activities required to work together as a team, such as coordinating, providing feedback, and maintaining cohesion. Effectiveness pertains specifically to the accomplishment of the objectives, milestones, and goals as defined by the requirements of the context or the stakeholders. As Hackman (1987, p. 323) suggested, only looking at the productive or task output is not sufficient as effectiveness criterion, social and personal criteria should also be included, in terms of how positive they end up. Team effectiveness criteria should cover task and team related outcomes. However, there is more to a team's effectiveness then its outcome. In a dynamic, open system similar results may be achieved with different initial conditions and in many different ways. A lucky shot is obviously not indicative of a team's effectiveness. Besides the criteria on task and team outcomes, additional criteria include how well the initial conditions were dealt with, how well the processes were carried out (performance), and how well the team adjusted its processes and learned from its progress (feedback). This model of team effectiveness also includes the possible operational situation that if the conditions are so bad that the expected outcomes cannot be achieved an effective team identifies that in time and adjusts the conditions or the expected outcomes.

Only those models believed to have most relevance and application to command team effectiveness are reviewed here. In a command context, situational demands (e.g., mission) and human capabilities are critical. As such, theoretical viewpoints that account for input factors both external and internal to the team were identified as highly relevant. The complexity of modern military missions and their stakes require high-quality information and decision-making processes. Additionally, this mission complexity is often reflected in a highly dynamic and changing performance environment. These complexities and dynamics have often been represented in theoretical models by feedback loops. Additionally, the differentiation between task-related processes (e.g., decision making) and teamwork-related processes (e.g., coordination) was deemed an important aspect of the military command environment. A mix of generalists and specialists are often involved in the process, sometimes distributed geographically across the operational area. These conditions require a strong sense of a common cause and shared intent with clear goal statements. As such, theories that deal with shared cognitions and affect were identified as having relevance to this environment.

The Input–Process–Outcome (IPO) framework is pervasive in the research literature related to teams (Driskell, Salas, & Hogan, 1987; Hackman, 1983). The input factors reflect the team's "potential" for productivity. However, potential for productivity does not equal effectiveness. Instead, the difference between potential and actual effectiveness is a function of team processes; that is, factors that members do not bring to the group but that emerge out of group interaction (e.g., communication structures, task performance strategies). Driskell et al. (1987) argued that the interaction of the group-input factors and group processes may lead either to process gain or process loss. Furthermore, this model suggests that some input conditions can promote process gain, referred to as *assembly bonus effects* (Collins & Guetzkow, 1964).

Building on the basic IPO framework, Salas, Dickinson, Converse, and Tannenbaum (1992) proposed a normative model of team effectiveness. Hackman (1983) suggested that for a team to be successful it must have a clear, engaging direction, an enabling performance situation, good team design with clear task structure, core team norms, supportive organizational context, and expert coaching and process assistance. Salas et al. (1992) further suggested that organizational context and group design affect the member interaction process, which in turn affects the quality of team performance. As in Hackman, team effectiveness is denoted by the capability of team members to work together over time, the satisfaction of member needs, and the acceptability of task outcomes by those individuals who demand or receive them. Team effectiveness is dependent on the level of effort exerted by the team members, the amount of knowledge and skills they can apply to the task, and the appropriateness of task performance strategies. In addition, Salas et al. (1992) contended that the resources allocated to the team also influence effectiveness—appropriate tools and equipment, for example, are factors that enhance a team's performance.

Tannenbaum, Beard, and Salas (1992) further included variables relevant to team building. Building on the IPO structure, these authors acknowledged the importance of the situational context throughout the process and incorporated feedback loops to indicate the often cyclic nature of team performance. Tannenbaum et al. further defined the team's context with an emphasis on organizational characteristics and structures. For example, an organization's reward structure may influence the team's behavior. The reward may be individual or team based and therefore may incite competition or cooperation, which may influence team effectiveness (Hackman, 1983; Steiner, 1972). Tannenbaum et al. also incorporated team interventions into the process (or throughput) phase. Team interventions, such as team training and team building, are included as moderating techniques to improve goal setting and to enhance team characteristics and interpersonal relationships, thus improving the team processes and, therefore, team performance. Tannenbaum et al. also suggested that ongoing evaluation (i.e., feedback) of team performance may affect team processes and, therefore, team performance.

Klimoski and Jones (1995) introduced team members' mixture of knowledge, skills and attitudes (KSAs) as well as leadership into the defined set of input constructs and emphasized that team effectiveness does not emerge from individual effort alone. The interpersonal dynamics of the team, the level of hostility or distrust in the team, and levels of compatibility among team members are all factors that can shape the effectiveness of a team. Shanahan (2001) also identified leadership as a critical factor for team effectiveness, differentiating taskwork, team-work, and leadership. It is the primary function of taskwork to turn inputs into outputs. How well the taskwork is carried out is influenced by teamwork and by how well the team is led. Leadership, therefore, is considered here as a function that must be performed. This function may be uniquely identified with the formal team leader, although in higher-performing teams it is more likely to be taken up by the team members who consider themselves to be best placed to exercise this function at the current time. Shanahan also noted that the overall process is influenced by a variety of given structural factors, such as physical resources, selection, training, and career planning.

Rasker, van Vliet, van den Broek, and Essens (2001) provided a comprehensive review of the team effectiveness literature and developed a model, with some empirical evidence, based on five categories of factors: situational, organizational, team, individual, and task. The team and individual factors make up the human elements of the model both at the team (e.g., size, structure, cohesion, leadership, composition) and at the individual level (i.e., knowledge, skills, and attitudes to enable good teamwork). All of these factors, taken together, are mediated by teamwork, which ultimately determines team effectiveness. Here team effectiveness is composed of observable, predefined objectives such as accuracy, timeliness, and the extent to which those goals were satisfied. Other team-related criteria, such as motivation and satisfaction, are noted as playing a more critical role when the team must operate together for long periods of time or on diverse problems.

Most models reviewed did not contain adequate feedback loops or a sufficient representation of the development of the team. Continuous assessment and adjustment within a team is critical to its effectiveness—throughout the process, at intermediate review, and after the mission. Recently Ilgen, Hollenbeck, Johnson, and Jundt (2005) proposed an input-mediator-output-input (IMOI) framework, in which the processes are replace by mediational (M) variables to reflect the broader range of variables that influence effectiveness. An extra input category at the end was added to emphasize the notion of cyclical causal feedback. They also proposed a new terminology for the stages of team effectiveness to capture development of the team: the forming stage (IM), the functioning stage (MO), and the finishing stage (OI). In the forming stage, affective variables (e.g., trust and psychological safety) and task-related variables (e.g., planning and shared mental models) are used. In the functioning phase, bonding, adapting to novel and dynamic situations, and learning each other's standpoints and behaviors are used. The finishing phase, which addresses factors that team members discover from having worked within the context of a team, has received little attention in the literature thus far.

The CTEF model described here (Essens et al., 2005) builds on these prior efforts (for a brief review of variables in the aforementioned team effectiveness models see Table 11.1) but identifies different factors to have priority in terms of influencing team effectiveness. It places more importance on specific military context, and it takes taskwork and teamwork as integral components of team effectiveness.

A Team Effectiveness Model for Command Teams

In the CTEF model, an emphasis is placed on factors that best fit the command teams' environment, that have been demonstrated to have a significant contribution to team effectiveness, and that have minimal conceptual overlap with each other. The CTEF model has three building blocks—conditions, processes, and outcomes—each with a number of components that are characterized by a number of aspects. Additionally there are three conditional feedback loops (Figure 11.1). The majority of the models reviewed adopted a three-stage input-process-output (IPO) architecture. To emphasize the dynamic nature of the "input," and to avoid the idea of a closed loop input-output, the CTEF model uses the term conditions, a key component in complex environments of military command. Also CTEF uses outcome, instead of output which has the connotation of product or quantity, to focus on the results or effects of the team.

The conditions set specifies components that address the context and the people. Context versus people can be interpreted as "demands versus capabilities." Conditions represent a cluster of factors that determine how effective the team can be under the given circumstances. If the demands largely exceed the capabilities of the team members, then the chances are high that the team will be unable to reach its goal; if demands and capabilities are more or less in balance, then the team will be more likely to reach its goals. Finally, if the capabilities clearly exceed the demands, then it may be relatively easy for the team to accomplish its mission. The context is denoted by the mission framework, the (assigned) task, and the organization to which the team belongs; the people are denoted by the leader of the team, the individual team members, and aspects of the team as a whole. Processes are the second primary building block of the CTEF model, and they include two key components: task-focused behaviors and team-focused behaviors. These behaviors capitalize on the strengths inherent in certain conditions (e.g., motivating highly skilled team members by delegating tasks to them) as well as serve to compensate for the limitations inherent in other conditions (e.g., reducing situational uncertainty through an active search for information). Outcomes are defined as the

TABLE 11.1

Overview of Variables in the Reviewed Team Effectiveness Models

Inputs or Conditions

Essens et al. (2005)	Driskell, Salas, & Hogan (1987)	Salas, Dickinson, Converse, & Tannenbaum (1992)	Tannenbaum, Beard, & Salas (1992)	Klimoski & Jones (1995)	Rasker, van Vliet, van den Broek, & Essens (2001)	Blendell, Henderson, Molloy, Pascual (2001)
Mission framework	Environmental stress		Level of stress Uncertainty		Time stress Uncertainty Dynamism	
Organization	Reward structure	Reward structure Education system Information system Material resources	Reward system Management control Resource scarcity Competition Intergroup relations Climate		Reward system Mission, objectives, and goals Social support	
Task	Structure	Structure	Organization Type Complexity		Structure Complexity Interdependency Load	Procedures
Leader/Team member	Personality Skills Status		Personality Task KSAs Mental models General abilities Motivation Attitudes		Knowledge, skills, and attitudes Teamwork skills	Aptitude/personality

TABLE 11.1

Overview of Variables in the Reviewed Team Effectiveness Models (Continued)

Essens et al. (2005)	Driskell, Salas, & Hogan (1987)	Salas, Dickinson, Converse, & Tannenbaum (1992)	Tannenbaum, Beard, & Salas (1992)	Klimoski & Jones (1995)	Rasker, van Vliet, van den Broek, & Essens (2001)	Blendell, Henderson, Molloy, Pascual (2001)
Team	Norms Structure Size	Norms Composition	Norms Work assignment Communication structure Power distribution Homogeneity Team resources Climate Cohesiveness	Norms Composition Size Organization Leadership	Structure Composition Size Cohesion Leadership	Composition Leadership style Experience Level of distribution
Processes						
Task behaviors		Level of effort Level of KS applied Strategies	Decision making Problem solving	Level of effort Use of skills Strategies	Decision making Shared situational awareness	Situation awareness
Teamwork	Group interaction Reduce process losses Create process gains	Reduce process losses Create process gains	Coordination Communication Conflict resolve Boundary spanning Training interventions	Coordination Potency Compatibility	Coordination Communication Adaptability Performance monitoring Self-correction Backing up Collective behavior	Providing guidance Stating priorities Communication Monitoring Feedback Backing up Motivation Climate Identity

Outcomes

Task outcomes	Output to stakeholder criteria	Quality, quantity, time, errors, costs	Task accomplishment Quality	Output to stakeholder criteria Quality, quantity, time, errors, costs	Accuracy Timeliness Error rate
Team outcomes	Working together Satisfaction	Team norms Roles Communication patterns Individual KSAs Mental models Motivation Attitudes	Satisfaction and emotional tone Turnover	Satisfaction	Satisfaction

Feedback (from outcomes)

Conditions adjustment			Team interventions Feedback		
Process adjustment Organizational learning			Team interventions		

Note: The variables coordination, communication and boundary spanning in the reviewed team effectiveness models are considered to be task focused behaviors in the CTEF model.

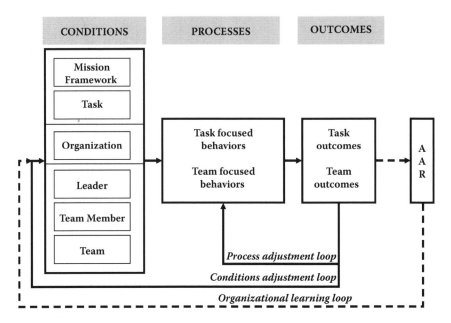

FIGURE 11.1
The CTEF model with its basic components. (From Essens, P. J. M. D., Vogelaar, A. L. W., Mylle, J. J. C., Blendell, C., Paris, C., Halpin, S. M., et al., *Military command team effectiveness: Model and instrument for assessment and improvement*, NATO RTO HFM-087 TP/59, Paris, France, 2005. With permission.)

results of the processes. Two foci are important: (1) To what extent did the team reach its assigned goals (i.e., task outcomes)?; and (2) to what extent did the team develop itself (i.e., team outcomes)? Feedback loops represent the dynamic and adaptive characteristics of a command team. The feedback loops are distinguished.

Conditions

Mission Framework

The mission framework component attempts to capture some of the critical aspects that collectively provide a global description of the operational environment in which the team is performing. Indeed, numerous factors can potentially comprise this component. However, extensive discussions with high-level military commanders from several nations converged on four aspects that seemed most relevant for command team effectiveness

TABLE 11.2

Detailed Layout of the CTEF Model

Conditions			
Mission framework	Situation uncertainty Stress potential Constraints Stakes	Leader	Skills Knowledge Match personal to organizational goals
Task	Complexity Workload Goal characteristics	Team member	Skills Knowledge Match personal to organizational goals
Organization	Goal congruity Command structure Autonomy Organizational support	Team	Composition Size Architecture Maturity Goals
Processes			

Task-focused behaviors	Managing information
	Assessing the situation
	Making decisions
	Planning
	Directing and controlling
	Liaising with other teams
		Team-focused behaviors	Providing and
			  maintaining vision
			Maintaining common
			  intent
			Interacting within the
			  team
			Motivating
			Adapting to changes
			Providing team
			  maintenance

Outcomes (for intermediate or end goals)			

Task outcomes	Goal achievement
	Stakeholders criteria met
	Other stakeholders'
	  satisfaction
	Staying
	  within limits/intentions
		Team outcomes	Mutual trust
			Morale
			Cohesion
			Collective confidence in
			  success
			Shared vision
			Mutual respect

Feedback (from outcomes)	Conditions adjustment
	  loop
	Process adjustment loop
	Organizational learning
	  loop		

in contemporary operations: situational uncertainty, stress potential, constraints, and stakes.

Situational uncertainty refers to the lack of information or understanding of objects and their properties in an operational environment. It is a principle impediment to effective command team planning and decision making. Situational uncertainty can be further broken down into uncertainty about intelligence, adversary intent, logistics or required resources, and utilization of resources. Uncertainty about intelligence and adversary intent reflects a lack of information on the external task environment and generally affects decision-making processes related to selection of a particular course of action. Uncertainty about logistics and resource utilization reflects a lack of information on the organizational capabilities in executing a particular course of action.

Military operations, by their very nature, have high stress potential. Three main forms of stress potential are included here due to their operational relevance and thus potential for affecting command team effectiveness: physical danger, operational intensity, and psychological stressors. Physical danger refers more specifically to risks for physical harm such as enemy threat, mines, force protection issues, and overall risk. Operational intensity reflects factors deriving from the pace or breadth of operations and includes time pressure, sleep deprivation, and information overload. Psychological stressors include the perceived impact of the mission and interpersonal/personal problems.

Constraints are external factors that directly or indirectly limit the range of the command team's actions or the degrees of freedom of action. Although each of the conditions possesses aspects that can constrain the team in one way or another, we focus here on those related to the broader mission framework within which the team is functioning. Environmental, political, cultural, media-related, and temporal-spatial factors were identified as constraints that are particularly relevant for commanders to consider in contemporary military operations. Environmental factors encompass issues such as weather and terrain, locally prevalent diseases, and availability of water at all stages of the operation. Political factors that can limit the team include local and military legal issues, approval requirements for actions, oversight from numerous and potentially conflicting stakeholders, and adherence to national criteria, such as ethical codes of conduct. Cultural factors that may impede effectiveness may derive from the locale of the operation and include local religion and language or may derive from working with multinational and multicultural coalition forces in the conduct of an operation and include language limitations, conflicting national policies of coalition partners, and differing approaches to the conduct of routine functions within a military organization. Media-related factors include local and international perceptions of the mission and interpretation of actions in fulfillment of the mission. Finally, temporal-spatial factors reflect to the management of potential actions within specific time and space boundaries. In complex, modern military operations, temporal-spatial factors often are a critical element for success.

An obvious and critical aspect that distinguishes military command teams from more conventional teams (e.g., sports teams, project teams) is the broader implications of their success or failure. These stakes form the basis of the mission and as such are intertwined with the desired end state or end goals, and they underlie the constraints, uncertainties, and stresses encountered in a mission. For present purposes, stakes refers to the immediate, intermediate, or long-term consequences of team effectiveness. The most immediate consequence of action is the potential for casualties—either within coalition forces, by enemy or friendly fire, or in terms of the harming or killing of innocent civilians. In the intermediate term, military operations have an impact nationally (domestic); in terms of the broader costs of success or failure, military operations can have an impact both politically and economically. In the longer term, military operations may have a significant global impact in terms of international politics, goodwill, and economic power.

Task

The task component is important in the model of command team effectiveness because it describes the core characteristics of the work to be done. This component emphasizes only those aspects that have implications for the processes and the outcomes of the work, which have been clustered into task complexity, workload, goal clarity, and goal stability.

Task complexity is a multifeatured concept that includes, for example, having to deal with rapidly evolving situations, cognitive complexity, and interacting parts that have to be combined. In addition, a task can be complex if the work contains multiple and concurrent tasks, uncertainty, changing plans, compressed work procedures, and high workload (e.g., Xiao, Hunter, Mackenzie, Jefferies, & Horst, 1996). A number of the aforementioned features of complexity (e.g., uncertainty, changing plans, workload) are covered by other aspects of the task component or other components in the conditions part in the model. Here, we focus on task difficulty, number of subtasks, subtask interdependency, and subtask interference. Task difficulty refers to the cognitive or physical demands of the task and the degree of skill required to execute the task. In the case of the command team, this feature refers to each of the subtasks that the team members have to perform on behalf of the team. Number of subtasks refers to the number of different subtasks that the team members have to perform, including whether they have to be performed sequentially or in parallel. It is obvious that if many subtasks have to be combined, the task of the team is more complex than when there is only one task or a well-balanced series of tasks in which team members are involved. Subtask interdependency refers to the degree to which subtasks are related to another. The interdependence can take several forms, including sequential, pooled, and intensive (Saavedra, Earley, & Van Dyne, 1993). Subtask interference refers to the potential influence that the execution of one subtask may have on the successful execution of another subtask. For example, interference may occur when two team members have to use the same resources to perform separate subtasks.

Workload is related to the external demands arising from the present situation (Shanahan, 2001). It is an important characteristic to consider in a command team environment, since the workload in a command team can be very high. A number of features have to be considered regarding workload, including several related to the well-known National Aeronautics and Space Administration Task Load Index (NASA-TLX) (e.g., Hart & Staveland, 1988). Included as aspects of workload within the CTEF model are physical workload, cognitive workload, emotional workload, and time pressure. Physical and cognitive workload and time pressure are aspects of workload common to a wide variety of team task environments. Emotional workload represents the emotional component of performance, which may be exacerbated, for example, when the team is presented with a morally untenable situation or is required to announce significant casualties as a result of military action.

Goal clarity for a command team can be defined as the degree to which the team members know and understand the objectives and priorities. This concept is therefore strongly related to the concept of *commander's intent*. Goal clarity is crucial for sensemaking or sensegiving to the tasks implied in the mission. There is a large body of literature on the impact of goal clarity on performance and hence on effectiveness (e.g., goal-setting theory; Locke & Latham, 1990).

Goal stability is defined as the degree to which the goals to be reached remain the same over time. When goals are stable, the team can manage its activities in a predictive way. On the contrary, suddenly changing goals or gradually shifting goals need particular attention from the team members to reorient themselves and to adapt to the new situation.

Organization

The organization, as a broader framework within which the team operates, can have a positive or a negative influence on the performance of the team and hence its effectiveness. Many of the existing models of team effectiveness refer to one or more aspects of the organization as a context variable that have a direct or an indirect impact on team effectiveness. The organization component of the CTEF model encompasses four aspects: (1) congruity of the team's mission and organizational goals; (2) clarity of the command structure; (3) autonomy of the team; and (4) organizational support.

Congruity of the team's mission and the organizational goal refers to the degree to which the team's goals fit with the organization's goals. The team goals may be at variance with the organizational goals when the team chooses so deliberately or when the goals are unclear or ambiguous. Such a situation may occur, for example, in peace support operations where military and humanitarian objectives have to be pursued simultaneously.

Clarity of command structure refers to the extent to which it may be unclear who is authorized to give orders to the team. For example, in a matrix structure—as opposed to the classic staff-and-line structure—command teams are confronted with different responsibilities in the horizontal chain of command, and in the vertical one they have different authorities to report to and may face problems with prioritizing regarding one or the other chain of command.

Autonomy refers to the degree to which the team is given the freedom to make decisions about its conditions, its processes, and the way to reach its goals. It is obvious that, in operational settings where troops are widely dispersed over the area of responsibility and where the situation can evolve quickly, autonomy may be a crucial variable for team effectiveness (Mylle, Callaert, Sips, & Bouwen, 2001, 2002).

Organizational support enables the team to perform its tasks through a number of mechanisms, including personnel recognition, maintenance of a supportive climate, and provision for material support. Of particular relevance here is the notion of a supportive climate. This aspect relates strongly to the concept of psychological safety (Edmondson, 2004). In an atmosphere in which mistakes are not allowed, persons and teams will not be willing to take risks. Material support implies that teams receive the means that are necessary and sufficient to fulfill the assigned mission in an efficient and effective way, not only before but also during the mission.

Leader

Despite recent exploration of "leaderless teams" (e.g., Kickul & Neuman, 2000), there is a long-standing body of research that demonstrates the positive impact an effective leader can have on team performance (e.g., Hogan, Curphy, & Hogan, 1994; Judge, Piccolo, & Ilies, 2004; Kureca, Austin, Johnson, & Mendoza, 1982). The leader shapes team members' understanding of the task (McCann & Pigeau, 2000; Weick, 1993), directs and influences member task behavior, and mediates resource and information flow with the larger organization. The leader's influence may be realized through direct influence on the team product or indirectly through facilitation of best-possible performance of team members, individually and collectively.

There are many types of leaders, and many models of leadership have been proposed (see Northouse, 2004). It is possible to distinguish among assigned leaders and emergent leaders. It is possible to distinguish between leaders who are primarily focused on directing the task performance of team members and those who focus on facilitating the social interactions among team members. In addressing the leaders of command teams, we have chosen to address the assigned leader: the person who is designated by legitimate authority as having immediate responsibility for the performance and outcome of individual team members and of the team as a whole. This assigned leader will need to fulfill the interpersonal aspects of the leader's role as well as the task-oriented elements of the leader's role.

We focus on leaders' capabilities, not on questions of their style or approach to fulfilling the role. Following Hersey and Blanchard (1982, 1993) and Bass, Avolio, Jung, and Berson (2003), we see style of leadership as a matter of choice, and the interpersonal abilities involved in effective leadership can be seen as the mechanism for making style choices. The aspects of the leader considered in this framework, then, are leader skills, knowledge, and the match between the leader's personal goals and the organizational goals. With respect to the leader's skills, we are concerned both with the leader's abilities as they relate to the military task at hand and with the leader's abilities as leader of the team. These skills include tactical, technical, interpersonal, and cognitive skills. The requisite leader knowledge encompasses all of the knowledge, wisdom, and experience, which the leader can bring to bear in accomplishing the mission. This includes knowledge of the task itself as well as means to accomplish the task, knowledge of how to guide effective teams as well as knowledge about the particular members of this team, and knowledge of the organizational context within which the team is operating.

It is not necessary for team leaders to know all, or even most, of the critical elements needed to get the job done, but they must have sufficient understanding to be able to effectively guide others in the technical details of the task.

Little research directly addresses the issue of the congruence of the team leader's personal goals and those of the larger organization. One slim thread of research (Pilisuk & Halpin, 1967) has identified a tendency for members of an organization to be subject to an implicit socialization process that brings members' belief structures, values, and goals in line with that of the organization at large. There is work in organizational commitment (e.g., Gustafson & Mumford, 1995; Schneider, 1987; Schneider, Goldstein, & Smith, 1995) that addresses the likelihood that persons will leave an organization if there is too large a mismatch of personal to organizational goals. It can be expected that a close match of personal to organizational goals will permit more effective team outcomes due to increased leader motivation, to increased leader understanding of the assigned mission, and, in common terms, through increased "buy-in" by the leader.

Team Members

The literature strongly indicates that the competencies of an individual or team member will have significant bearing on the effectiveness of a team;

research has shown that this finding is evident in both military and civilian teams (McIntyre & Salas, 1995; Thordsen, Klein, & Kyne, 1994). Team member input characteristics have been defined as a cluster of input variables that have a significant bearing on the team process. Many of the existing models of team effectiveness place a great emphasis on the importance that team members have on overall team effectiveness (Rasker et al., 2001; Tannenbaum et al., 1992) and include team member skills, knowledge, and goal congruity with the organization as critical features. Team member skills are the requisite abilities held by individual team members, which enable them to complete their tasks within the team setting. The requisite skills identified as most critical to team effectiveness include tactical, technical, cognitive, and interpersonal skills. Team member knowledge refers to the requisite information, wisdom, and experience held by individual team members, which enable them to complete their task within the team setting. Research has shown that the performance of the team proportionally increases in relation to the individual level of task knowledge among its team members (Bouchard, 1972). The requisite knowledge identified as the most critical to team effectiveness includes task knowledge, team knowledge, and organizational knowledge. Whereas a considerable amount of research has looked at individual skills and knowledge, comparatively little research has been conducted to examine the similarity of personal goals (i.e., the aim of an individual toward which his or her endeavor is directed) to organizational goals and its subsequent impact on team effectiveness. Furthermore, most models of team effectiveness do not explicitly refer to the influence of matching personal goals to those of the organization. However, the influence of personal goals is alluded to through the use of the term "individual motivation" (Tannenbaum et al., 1992). Greater congruence between personal goals and organizational goals may lead to a greater sense of a "common" goal among the team; hence, the team members will be more interdependent and will experience less conflict.

Team

The aspects of the team component are team composition, team size, team architecture, team maturity, and match of team goals to organizational goals. Team composition refers to the mix of people on the team according to certain criteria, such as skills, traits, and seniority. Operationally, team composition includes the mix of skills, demographics, and personality characteristics present in the team. Team composition also addresses team member longevity within the team. It is important to have a proper balance of these characteristics within the team to execute the task. For example, command and control teams require individuals who have uniformly high abilities in their respective duties. Their functions are both highly specialized and interdependent; hence, the entire team can suffer if one team member does not have the requisite skills for the task and no one is able to back it up (Paris, Salas, & Cannon-Bowers, 1999). The mix of personality characteristics determines how individuals interact with other team members and how they perform. Quality of interaction is critical for teams that require more coordination, such as command and control teams (Klimoski & Jones, 1995; Paris, Salas, & Cannon-Bowers, 1999).

Team size refers to the number of individuals in the team. The core question is to know if the team is sufficiently staffed, but not grossly overstaffed, to accomplish the task within the given constraints. Team size limits the manner in which the team can be organized and how members can interact as related to the nature of the roles and the tasks to be performed. It is important to stress that team effectiveness is not a linear function of the team size. Among others, adding more people to a team heightens coordination needs and does not necessarily increase the team's productivity due to opportunities for social loafing (Gladstein, 1984; Kidd, 1961; Latané, Williams, & Harkins, 1979; Paris et al., 1999; Steiner, 1972; Sundstrom, De Meuse, & Futrell, 1990). As a rule, teams should be staffed to the smallest number needed to do the work (Hackman, 1987; Sundstrom et al., 1990).

Team architecture refers to the organization and distribution of personnel, subtasks, and roles and how they are related to each other. It includes features such as decision authority, chain of command, procedural requirements, and constraints for managing and decision making. It includes team member responses to demands imposed by team structure. Apart from a more formal architecture provided by the organization, the architecture may be determined by the degree of perceived status or power differences among team members. Architecture also determines how team members respond to a high degree of interdependence among team members' responsibilities.

Team maturity refers to the extent to which team members have worked together and have developed as an intact team (Swezey & Salas, 1992). Team maturity is manifested in the degree to which the team can improve in the absence of a trainer, can dynamically adapt its behaviors to changing conditions, and can foresee one another's needs, thereby depending less on overt communication to perform effectively. Team maturity embodies team experience, shared knowledge and expectations, attitudes, and shared commitment to the team goals (Bowers, Braun, & Morgan, 1997; Morgan, Salas, & Glickman, 1994).

Team goals are accepted quantitative or qualitative results, achievements, performance outcomes, or measures of effectiveness toward which team members are willing to work. They should be consistent with mission objectives, outcome measures, and interests of stakeholders. They vary in terms of specificity, difficulty, and feasibility. Important is the degree to which team goals are clear and understandable, the degree to which there is awareness of these goals, and both acceptance and commitment to them. A central question is if and to what extent the team's goals are aligned with those of the organization.

Processes

Task-Focused Behaviors

This component is broken down into six aspects: managing information, assessing the situation, making decisions, planning, directing and controlling, and liaising with other command teams. Managing information is the team's way of handling information or knowledge. A team's effectiveness is tied to its ability to acquire the lacking information and to manage, process, and exchange the information it possesses.

Situation assessment embodies three primary dimensions. The first is the team's awareness of the state of the system within which it is operating, and its shared perception of the environmental elements (with emphasis on the temporal and spatial dimensions) within its problem space. Second is the team's evaluation of the state of the system, and its interpretation of the meaning of elements and their implications for action. Third is the team's prediction of future events, based on its understanding of the current situation. In short, it involves perceiving, recognizing, and anticipating environmental elements or events. *Situation assessment* is the process of actively seeking to understand and evaluate the meaning of situational elements by searching for additional information or sensemaking with other persons and team members.

Team decision making includes defining the problem space, integrating differing perspectives and opinions of team members, identifying or creating options for action, estimating consequences, and formulating orders and subsequently monitoring the effects. Command and control teams frequently have very little time to make decisions and, as a result, tend to engage in satisfying behaviors where a quick, viable option may be preferred to an optimal solution that may take too long to implement.

Planning is the process of formulating the actions that are necessary for attaining the team goal, determining the time needed for each of these actions, and comparing the latter with time available. Planning enables a team, for example, to respond more effectively to stressors such as unexpected contingencies, high workload, time pressure, or task/role ambiguity. Specifically, planning encompasses anticipating future tasks and events, their demands, and potential contingencies; scheduling actions and specifying resources with respect to personnel; distributing material resources;

and defining strategies to accomplish the mission, including developing operational policies and procedures and assessing their effectiveness.

Directing and controlling represents the cluster of processes that occur between planning and attaining the goal. Three specific processes are distinguished: organizing, managing, and monitoring progress. Organizing refers to how the team will implement the plan. It is the process of systematically structuring, sequencing, or coordinating team actions to ensure efficiency in achieving a specified goal before the action starts. Managing is the process of governing, guiding, or steering the team toward successful accomplishment of goals during the course of action. Managing includes adapting procedures, setting priorities, and communicating them to team members; dynamically adjusting resources and schedules; managing expectations of stakeholders and team members. Monitoring progress means gauging or assessing advancement toward milestones, goals, and objectives.

Liaising with other command teams refers to the process of interacting with other command teams for the purpose of building alliances, engaging in cross-functional activities, conducting promotional activities, and collaborating across boundaries. A team can benefit from such coordination through strengthening of their internal support basis, which may facilitate goal achievement. It can profile for potential alliances by assessing capabilities and characteristics of individuals who can support or contribute to the achievement of team goals. It can promote relations and team image and can convince others of the organization's or team's point of view. It can help the team keep current with developments in the environment. Finally, it can facilitate cross-team planning for tasks that will require capabilities or resources specific to certain teams. These types of activities are also referred to in the literature as boundary management or boundary-spanning activities.

Team-Focused Behaviors

This component is broken down into six aspects: providing and maintaining vision, maintaining common intent, interacting within the team, motivating, adapting to changes, and providing team maintenance. Providing and maintaining vision is the process of generating and preserving direction and purpose for the team. This is often a function of the team leader, who strives to energize the team to perform in accordance with the team mission. Leaders may even encourage visionary thinking or inspire team members to exceed standards or to transcend the status quo.

While maintaining vision keeps the team focused on its higher purpose or mission, maintaining common intent specifically operates to preserve a shared sense or common mental picture of desired goals and objectives and how to reach them. Unless leaders can ensure a clear, accurate, and common understanding of those goals, the team's effectiveness may be compromised. Leaders need to communicate how team member roles and team strategies will be used to carry out a plan for achieving team goals and to communicate priorities for the team as well as limits or constraints on goal-directed actions. Through these activities leaders can help the team to overcome obstacles and to act adequately in the absence of the leader.

Though team interactions involve many different behaviors, three of these are thought to be critical for team effectiveness: communicating, coordinating, and providing feedback. Communicating refers to aspects of openness, style, and expression of feelings and thoughts. These communications are directed specifically at modifying teamwork aspects. Team-related communications exploit opportunities that influence team interactions, organization, and functioning. Team effectiveness is bolstered by positive communications (e.g., those that encourage, guide, or correct team behavior). Negative communications (e.g., those that stimulate conflict, pessimism, destructive criticism), on the other hand, can threaten team cohesion. Team communications that bolster team interactions, commitment, and sustainability serve to enhance team cohesion and effectiveness, and to mitigate the effects of stress. Coordinating means acting in a harmonious, complementary, supportive manner to achieve goals. Coordinating involves synchronizing team members' activities such that they reduce role conflicts and redundancies and ensures that members are able to tap each other's unique resources to work efficiently. Providing feedback encompasses offering advice to one another about how to improve performance. This advice can vary in intent, degree to which the feedback is tailored to the situation, whether feedback is solicited or received, source, credibility, and degree of objectivity and specificity of the feedback.

Motivating is the process of influencing the direction, intensity, and persistence of team members' behaviors using external contingencies or by inspiring team members to develop intrinsic interest in task- or team-related work. Motivating can result in team-level efficacy or esprit de corps as a result of positive past performance and adequate feedback. Motivating the team extrinsically and intrinsically are the two features for this aspect of team-focused behaviors.

Adapting is the process by which team members change their behavior and relationship with other team members according to the changes in the environment or in the team. Operationally, it requires recognition of cues that trigger needed behaviors important for optimizing the team's performance. These behaviors are: Monitoring in which team members observe and assess their own and each other's performance, Correcting (self and others) in which team members offer feedback or guidance to improve their team members' performance; and Backing Up in which team members support one another with compensatory behaviors, such as assuming duties, offering coaching, or assistance.

Providing team maintenance refers to the actions that keep team members together. It includes providing social support, regulating emotions, maintaining cohesion, and managing conflict. Providing social support refers to behaviors that buffer against stress. Team members may demonstrate *intramember reinforcement* behaviors or may offer encouragement to one another. Behaviors that provide social support tend to increase bonding and loyalty toward fellow team members. Regulating emotions implies influencing emotions or maintaining emotional balance among team members. For example, team members might prevent excessive communication of negative emotions. Developing and maintaining cohesion happens through promoting unity, solidarity, or esprit de corps among team members. Managing conflict refers to handling conflict, such that maladaptive discord or friction is resolved or, if impossible, reduced as much as possible.

Outcomes

Task Outcomes

Task outcomes provide important indications of what the team really achieved. A distinction is made between end goals—what the team has finally accomplished—and intermediate goals as steps toward the end goals. The task outcomes can be evaluated from the perspective of a number of stakeholders. The most important stakeholder is the one that the team is working for—often the commander who assigned the mission. However, a variety of other stakeholders may also have expectations about what has to be achieved to be effective in the long run. These stakeholders have to be identified as clearly as possible since they may impact the perceptions of team effectiveness. Such stakeholders can include the local authorities, the local population of the region in which the operation takes place, the subordinates of the team members, or the soldiers outside the team.

The most important question is this: To what degree did the team achieve the goals that were set out by the stakeholders? A problem with this measure, of course, is that if the goals are too difficult, then the team can never be successful; conversely, if the goals are set too easy, then the team will never fail. Because of this reason, achievement of the goals cannot be the only measure of effectiveness. With respect to the achievement of the goals, evaluation may take place after the team has finished its work or during the process on the basis of intermediate goals.

Further, stakeholders may have—explicitly or implicitly—set a number of criteria, which the team should satisfy. The criteria may include timeliness, efficiency, flexibility, robustness, risk and adequacy of plans. In any operation a number of stakeholders may be identified that influence the decisions or the actions of the team. These stakeholders and their interests should be identified to satisfy them as much as possible. This will guarantee better commitment with what the team is trying to accomplish. The work of the team should also stay within those rules or limits that are set for the operation. For example, in a peace support operation, the team must conform to the rules of engagement and other policies set by theater and national command authorities.

Team Outcomes

Team outcomes refer to the improvement of the team as a result of the team processes. Often, the team outcomes are not the reason why the team has been formed; rather, they are emergent properties of the team. These team outcomes are in most of the cases desirable results of a team's actions to reach the goal. For example, a team will be more satisfied if it has achieved its mission; a team that has been working together for some time may have grown more cohesive. These outcomes will feed back into the initial conditions—more specifically, into the people components— and subsequently will improve its continued processes and effectiveness.

In the present work, we expand the scope of the team outcome component to include a number of aspects that have been shown to either impact team effectiveness directly, or emerge as a consequence of effective team functioning. In addition, these aspects appear to hold particular significance within military team contexts; this has been confirmed through our interviews with military officers, representative of our target groups.

Recent work by Adams and Webb (2003) reviewed the critical role that trust plays in military teams. Two broad theoretical views of trust were identified: one in which trust is based on long experiences with an individual (i.e., person based); and the other based on recognition of features in an individual previously associated with trust (i.e., category based). A definition presented in a recent paper by Costa, Roe, and Taillieu (2001) highlights the nature of trust as a psychological state that manifests itself in the behaviors toward others.

Manning (1991) described morale as the enthusiasm and persistence with which a member of a group engages in the prescribed activities of that group. In this sense morale is a concept at the level of the individual, which can be influenced by both individual variables (e.g., having a goal, a role, and self-confidence) and group variables (e.g., common experiences).

It is generally accepted that team cohesion is strongly related to team performance. Indeed, in a now famous quote from the classic Festinger,

Schachter, and Back (1950, p. 164), cohesion is referred to as "the 'total field of forces,' which act on members to remain in the group." Research has shown that, when a team is communicating well within the process stage, the cohesion level among team members increases (Shaw, 1981).

According to Bandura (1986), collective efficacy refers to the ability of the team to perform effectively given a specific set of task demands. Cannon-Bowers, Tannenbaum, Salas, and Volpe (1995) concluded from their review that collective efficacy has a facilitating effect on team effectiveness (see also Shea & Guzzo, 1987). The consensus of work in this area appears to support a motivational basis for the effect of collective efficacy on team performance. For example, team members who have high confidence in the team (i.e., believe that the team is up to the task) will be motivated to perform well and thus will increase the likelihood of a successful outcome.

Shared vision refers to the team having a shared common perception on how to behave in the future in a similar setting—combining both explicit intent, based on the commander's statements and orders, and implicit intent, which is based on underlying intentions assumed throughout the orders that are founded on military, cultural, and political expectations (Pigeau & McCann, 1998). Research has indicated that a shared understanding of the commander's intent will enable team members to fulfill the leader's intentions better, thus improving team performance (Molloy, Blendell, Catchpole, & Pascual, 2002).

According to McIntyre and Salas (1995), mutual respect is one of the critical "principles" regulating team effectiveness. It refers to the fact that team members try to understand each other despite their differences. This applies as much with respect to the leader–team member relationship as it does among team members themselves.

Feedback

The CTEF model specifies three feedback loops. The feedback loops represent iterative development, adjustment, and learning processes, which follow (more or less) formal reviews of the progress of the team against the outcomes. Note that intrinsic feedback processes may be present within the team- and task-processes as a natural element in performing tasks and providing feedback when working together. The feedback loops specify more explicitly the reviewing activity. The specified feedback loops are: Process Adjustment Loop, which addresses the required interventions in the management or performance in the task and team processes; Conditions Adjustment Loop, which addresses the changes needed in the structural basis of the processes, either in personnel, organization, or mission and task factors; Organizational Learning Loop, which addresses the evaluation of all components of the effectivess in light of the successes and failures in the mission; for the commander and team's own learning cycle, and the advice to the organization and follow up commanders.

Conclusion

The concept of military command as a team activity is gaining in recognition, precisely because modern operations are so dynamic and complex. Given the importance of teamwork, it is necessary to be able to monitor and improve aspects that can make teamwork successful. The team effectiveness models reviewed all seek to capture the most critical elements of effectiveness. We believe that the CTEF model captures the best of it and includes additional elements critical in a command environment.

An integral model of effectiveness, with a number of variables listed, is virtually impossible to validate in terms of interrelated effects. On the other hand, research should move up a level away from isolated effects. Our vision is that the team effectiveness model will be developed further by applying it in practice (e.g., operations, training scenarios, field trials), quasi-experimental setups, and conventional experiments; by measuring the levels of the variables and the achievement of intermediate goals; by analyzing causes of suboptimal results; and by measuring the effects of feedback on the processes. Based on the model, we also developed a draft version of a concise instrument that can be used to evaluate the effectiveness of a command team and that we plan to apply in our further study. The model and instrument should be used by military commanders as a self-diagnostic measure of their command teams and also to educate themselves on the various team-related factors underlying performance that they may not naturally think of when they are monitoring and evaluating the performance of their teams.

References

Adams, B. & Webb, R. (2003). *Trust development in small teams*. DRDC-Toronto Technical Research Report CR-2003-016.

Bandura, A. (1986). *Social foundations of thought and action*. Englewood Cliffs, NJ: Prentice-Hall.

Bass, B. M., Avolio, B. J., Jung, D. I., & Berson, Y. (2003). Predicting unit performance by assessing transformational and transactional leadership. *Journal of Applied Psychology, 88*, 207–218.

Blendell, C., Henderson, S. M., Molloy, J. J., & Pascual, R. G. (2001). Team performance shaping factors in IPME (Integrated Performance Modeling Environment). Unpublished DERA Report. DERA, Fort Halstead, UK.

Bouchard, T. J., Jr. (1972). Training, motivation and personality as determinants of
the effectiveness of brainstorming groups and individuals. *Journal of Applied
Psychology, 49,* 387– 392.

Bowers, C. A., Braun, C. C., & Morgan, B. B., Jr. (1997). Team workload: Its meaning and measurement. In M. T. Brannick, E. Salas, & C. Prince (Eds.), *Team
performance and assessment measurement: Theory, methods, and applications* (pp.
63–84). Mahwah, NJ: Erlbaum.

Cannon-Bowers, J. A., Tannenbaum, S. I., Salas, E., & Volpe, C. E. (1995). Defining
competencies and establishing team training requirements. In R. A. Guzzo,
E. Salas, & Associates (Eds.), *Team effectiveness and decision making in organizations.* San Francisco, CA: Jossey-Bass Publishers.

Collins, B. E. & Guetzkow, H. (1964). *A social psychology of group processes for decision-making.* New York: Wiley.

Costa, A. C., Roe, R. A., & Taillieu, T. (2001). Trust within teams: The relation with
performance effectiveness. *European Journal of Work and Organizational Psychology, 10*(3), 225–244.

Driskell, J. E., Salas, E., & Hogan, R. (1987). *A taxonomy for composing effective naval
teams.* Naval Training Systems Center, Human Factors Division (Code 712),
Orlando, FL.

Edmondson, A. (2004). Psychological safety, trust and learning: A group-level
lens. In R. Kramer & K. Cook (Eds.), *Trust and distrust in organizations: Dilemmas and approaches,* (pp. 239–272). New York: Russell Sage.

Endsley, M. R. & Jones, W. M. (2001). A model of inter- and intrastream situational awareness: Implications for design, training, and measurement. In
M. McNeese, E. Salas, & M. Endsley (Eds.), *New trends in cooperative activities: Understanding system dynamics in complex environments* (pp. 46–67). Santa
Monica, CA: Human Factors & Ergonomics Society.

Essens, P. J. M. D., Vogelaar, A. L. W., Tanercan, E. C., & Winslow, D. J. (2001). *The
human in command: Peace support operations.* Amsterdam: Mets & Schilt.

Essens, P. J. M. D., Vogelaar, A. L. W., Mylle, J. J. C., Blendell, C., Paris, C., Halpin, S.
M., et al. (2005). *Military command team effectiveness: Model and instrument for
assessment and improvement.* NATO RTO HFM-087 TP/59, Paris, France.

Festinger, L., Schachter, S., & Back, K. (1950). *Social pressures in informal groups: A
study of human factors in housing.* New York: Harper Collins.

Gladstein, D. L. (1984). Groups in context: A model of task group effectiveness.
Administrative Science Quarterly, 29, 499–517.

Gustafson, S. B. & Mumford, M. D. (1995). Personal style and person-environment
fit: A pattern approach. *Journal of Vocational Behavior, 46,* 163–188.

Hackman, J. R. (1983). *A normative model of work team effectiveness.* Technical Report
2, Yale University, New Haven, CT.

Hackman, J. R. (1987). The design of work teams. In J. W. Lorsch (Ed.), *Handbook of
organizational behavior* (pp. 315–342). Englewood Cliffs, NJ: Prentice-Hall.

Hart, S.G. & Staveland, L.E. (1988). Development of NASA-TLX (Task Load Index):
Results of empirical and theoretical research. In P.A. Hancock & N. Mesh-
kati (Eds.), *Human mental workload* (pp. 139–183). North-Holland, The Netherlands: Elsevier Science.

Henderson, S. & Walkinshaw, O. (2002). *Command team assessment: Principles, guidance and observations.* Unpublished report, QinetiQ, Fort Halstead.

Hersey, P. & Blanchard, K. H. (1982). Grid principles and situationalism: Both! A response to Blake & Mouton. *Group and Organization Studies, 7,* 207–210.

Hersey, P. & Blanchard, K. H. (1993). *Management of organizational behavior: Utilizing human resources* (6th ed.). Upper Saddle River, NJ: Prentice-Hall.

Hogan, R., Curphy, G. J., & Hogan, J. (1994). What we know about leadership: Effectiveness and personality. *American Psychologist, 49,* 493.

Ilgen, D. R., Hollenbeck, J. R., Johnson, M. D., & Jundt, D.K. (2005). Teams in organizations: From input-process-output models to IMOI models. *Annual Review of Psychology, 56,* 517–543.

Judge, T. A., Piccolo, R. F., & Ilies, R. (2004). The forgotten ones? The validity of consideration and initiating structure in leadership research. *Journal of Applied Psychology, 89,* 36–51.

Kickul, J. & Neuman, G. (2000). Emergent leadership behaviors: The function of personality and cognitive ability in determining teamwork performance and KSAs. *Journal of Business and Psychology, 15,* 27–51.

Kidd, J. S. (1961). A comparison of one-, two-, and three-man work units under various conditions of workload. *Journal of Applied Psychology, 45,* 195–200.

Klimoski, R. & Jones, R. G. (1995). Staffing for effective group decision making: Key issues in matching people and teams. In R. A. Guzzo, E. Salas, & Associates (Eds.). *Team effectiveness and decision making in organizations* (pp. 219–332). San Francisco, CA: Jossey-Bass Publishers.

Kureca, P. M., Austin, J. M., Johnson, W., & Mendoza, J. L. (1982). Full and errant coaching effects on the assigned role leaderless group discussion performance. *Personnel Psychology, 35,* 805–812.

Latané, B., Williams, K., & Harkins, S. (1979). Many hands make light the work: The causes and consequences of social loafing. *Journal of Personality and Social Psychology, 37,* 823–832.

Locke, E. A. & Latham, G. P. (1990). *A theory of goal setting and task performance.* Englewood Cliffs, NJ: Prentice Hall.

Manning, F. J. (1991). Morale, cohesion, and esprit de corps. In R. Gal & D. Mangelsdorff (Eds.), *Handbook of military psychology* (pp. 453–470). Chichester, England: John Wiley & Sons.

McCann, C. & Pigeau, R. (2000). Redefining command and control. In C. McCann & R. Pigeau (Eds.), *The human in command: Exploring the modern military experience* (pp.163–184). New York: Kluwer Academic/Plenum Publishers.

McIntyre, R. M. & Salas, E. (1995). Measuring and managing for team performance: Emerging principles from complex environments. In R. A. Guzzo, E. Salas, & Associates (Eds.), *Team effectiveness and decision-making in organizations* (pp. 9–45). San Francisco, CA: Jossey-Bass.

Molloy, J. J., Blendell, C., Catchpole, L. J., & Pascual, R. G. (2002). *Command intent support approaches.* London: QinetiQ Publication.

Morgan, B. B. Jr., Salas, E., & Glickman, A. S. (1994). An analysis of team evolution and maturation. *Journal of General Psychology, 120,* 277–291.

Mylle, J., Callaert, J., Sips, K., & Bouwen, R. (2001). *Perceived team effectiveness in peace support operations: A cross-sectional analysis in a Belgian task force.* Proceedings of the 43th Annual Conference of the International Military Testing Association, Canbarra, Australia.

Mylle, J., Callaert, J., Sips, K., & Bouwen, R. (2002). *Does experience change perceived team effectiveness in peace support operations?* Proceedings of the 44th Annual Conference of the International Military Testing Association, Ottawa, Canada.

Northouse, P. G. (2004). *Leadership theory and practice* (3d ed.). Thousand Oaks, CA: Sage Publications.

Paris, C. R., Salas, E., & Cannon-Bowers, J. A. (1999). Human performance in multi-operator systems. In P. A. Hancock (Ed.), *Handbook of perception and cognition series* (2d ed., pp. 329–386). San Diego, CA: Academic Press.

Pigeau, R. & McCann, C. (1998). *Re-defining command and control.* Toronto: Defence and Civil Institute of Environmental Medicine.

Pilisuk, M. & Halpin, S. M. (1967) *Vocational commitment to roles in a defense oriented social system.* Krannert Graduate School Research Report 4, Purdue University, West Lafayette, IN.

Rasker, P., van Vliet, T., van den Broek, H., & Essens, P. (2001). *Team effectiveness factors: A literature review,* TNO Technical Report TM-01-B007, Soesterberg, The Netherlands.

Saavedra, R., Earley, P. C., & Van Dyne, L. (1993). Complex interdependence in task-performing groups. *Journal of Applied Psychology, 78,* 61–72.

Salas, E., Dickinson, T., Converse, S. A., & Tannenbaum, S. I. (1992). Toward an understanding of team performance and training. In R. W. Swezey & E. Salas (Eds.), *Teams: Their training and performance* (pp. 219–245). Norwood, NJ: Ablex.

Schneider, B. (1987). E = f(P,B): The road to a radical approach to person-environment fit. *Journal of Vocational Behavior, 31,* 353–361.

Schneider, B., Goldstein, H. W., & Smith, D. B. (1995). The ASA framework: An update. *Personnel Psychology, 48,* 747–773.

Shanahan, P. (2001). *Mapping team performance shaping factors.* Fort Halstead: QinetiQ.

Shaw, M. E. (1981). *Group dynamics: The psychology of small group behavior* (3rd ed.). New York: McGraw Hill.

Shea, G. P. & Guzzo, R. A. (1987). Group effectiveness: What really matters? *Sloan Management Review, 3,* 25–31.

Steiner, I. D. (1972). *Group processes and productivity.* New York: Academic Press.

Sundstrom E., De Meuse, K. P., & Futrell, D. (1990). Work teams: Applications and effectiveness. *American Psychologist, 45,* 120–133.

Swezey, R.W. & Salas, E. (1992). Guidelines for use in team-training development. In R.W. Swezey & E. Salas (Eds.), *Teams: Their training and performance* (pp. 219–246). Norwood, NJ: Ablex.

Tannenbaum, S. I., Beard, R. L., & Salas, E. (1992). Team building and its influence on team effectiveness: An examination of conceptual and empirical developments. In K. Kelley (Ed.), *Issues, theory, and research in industrial/organizational psychology* (pp. 117–153). New York: Elsevier Science.

Thordsen, M. L., Klein, G., & Kyne, M. (1994). *A model of advanced team performance.* Fairborn, OH: Klein Associates.

Weick, K. E. (1993). The collapse of sensemaking in organizations: The Mann Gulch disaster. *Administrative Science Quarterly, 38,* 628–652.

Xiao, Y., Hunter, W. A., Mackenzie, C. F., Jefferies, N. J., & Horst, R. L. (1996). Task complexity in emergency medical care and its implications for team coordination. *Human Factors, 38,* 636–645.

12

The Incorporation of Time in Team Research: Past, Current, and Future

Susan Mohammed, Katherine Hamilton, and Audrey Lim

Judging from the increased reliance on teams in the workplace as well as the considerable theoretical and methodological progress being made in research, "it is *the time* for teams" (Harrison, Mohammed, McGrath, Florey, & Vanderstoep, 2003, p. 634, italics added). Yet team research has not given *time* the attention it deserves, as evidenced by virtually every major review of the team literature pointing to the need for more research on temporal issues in groups (e.g., Argote & McGrath, 1993; Cohen & Bailey, 1997; Ilgen, Hollenbeck, Johnson, & Jundt, 2005; Kozlowski & Bell, 2003; Mathieu, Maynard, Rapp & Gibson, 2008). For example, McGrath and Argote (2001) stated that one of the "major limitations of earlier work on groups, by scholars with both basic and applied interests is that groups have been studied as relatively static entities" (pp. 621–622). Even the popular input–process–output (IPO) framework that underlies much of the research on teams has frequently been criticized as being static, although it clearly implies a temporal progression as teams move from inputs to processes to outcomes (e.g., Ilgen et al., 2005; Marks, Mathieu, & Zaccaro, 2001). Furthermore, time has been referred to as "perhaps the most neglected critical issue" in team research (Kozlowski & Bell, 2003, p. 364). Given that time in groups has been simultaneously regarded as ubiquitous, fundamental, and often ignored, it is worth considering how to reverse the "vicious cycle of neglect of temporal effects in substantive, conceptual, and methodological domains" (Kelly & McGrath, 1988, p. 86).

Rather than merely considering time as a backdrop against which events occur or simplistically assuming that study results are time free (Bluedorn & Denhardt, 1988), Ancona and colleagues have advocated adopting a "temporal lens" that focuses on when behaviors arise as well as how quickly they occur and in what cycles (e.g., Ancona & Chong, 1999; Ancona, Goodman, Lawrence, & Tushman, 2001). With the goal of sharpening the temporal lens used in conducting team studies, this chapter reviews relevant past and current work to consider how future team research can more seriously and explicitly incorporate temporal dynamics. Through reviewing, integrating, and expanding on existing work, we endeavor to stimulate deliberate and thoughtful consideration of the role of time in various team phenomena to advance the study of temporal concerns in group studies. Toward this aim, the latter part of the chapter offers suggestions of specific avenues for deeper integration of temporal issues using a multilevel framework. Throughout the chapter, the terms *group* and *team* are used interchangeably (e.g., Kozlowski & Bell, 2003).

Teams and Time: An Organizing Framework

Although the numerous criticisms regarding the lack of attention given to temporal matters in teams are well founded, this is not to say that time in teams has gone unstudied. Most notably, Joseph McGrath and colleagues have integrated temporal dynamics into a number of general group-based theories, including the theory of time, interaction, and performance (McGrath, 1991) and the theory of groups as complex systems (Arrow, McGrath, & Berdahl, 2000). In general, empirical work on time and teams has not kept pace with theoretical developments, leading one of the most recent reviews of the team literature to conclude that "...while the importance of dynamic conditions experienced over time are accepted by all, the empirical work is only beginning to consider the implications of time in research designs" (Ilgen et al., 2005, p. 536). Nevertheless, there is an emerging body of research focusing on temporal dynamics in teams; many of these studies are summarized and integrated in the content of this chapter.

The treatment of time in the team literature can be organized into four categories. First, some studies are longitudinal in nature, measuring well-known input or process constructs at multiple points in time. For example, Jehn and Mannix (2001) measured task, process, and relationship conflict over three time periods, whereas Maznevski and Chudoba (2000) qualitatively examined three global virtual teams over 21 months. Rather than adopt a longitudinal approach, a second category of team studies incorporates explicitly time-oriented constructs such as temporal planning (e.g., Janicik & Bartel, 2003) and time urgency (e.g., Mohammed & Angell, 2004) in cross-sectional research designs. Integrating the first two categories, some phenomena are both inherently temporal in nature and require longitudinal measurement to assess appropriately. Therefore, a third grouping focuses on constructs such as member socialization (e.g., Chen, 2005) and group development (e.g., Gersick, 1988). Fourth, time can be considered part of the general context, such as time pressure (e.g., Gevers, van

Eerde, & Rutte, 2001) and perceptions of time famine (Perlow, 1999). This four-part temporal organizing framework is used herein to review existing theoretical and empirical work on time and teams as well as to discuss possibilities for future work. Each is considered in turn in the following sections.

Teams over Time: A Longitudinal Approach

Because members, tasks, and technology rarely remain constant over a group's life span, continuous calls for the need to measure processes and performance over time have dominated discussions of temporal dynamics in the team literature. For example, the constraints of one-hour laboratory studies are often contrasted with the dynamic nature of "real-world" team processes, group development, and changes over time (Arrow et al., 2000; McGrath & Argote, 2001). Similarly, the challenge noted by Kozlowski and Bell (2003) for addressing time in field research is extending beyond static representations to sampling over time. To illustrate, Jehn and Mannix (2001) discovered different patterns of results between high- and low-performing groups regarding task, relationship, and process conflict across three time periods that would not have been possible with a cross-sectional design. Some of the concerns with cross-sectional studies stem from the potential for Type I and Type II temporal errors, in which the conclusions from short-lived teams would not hold up over the longer term, and the conclusions from longer-term teams would not occur in short-lived teams, respectively (McGrath, Arrow, Gruenfeld, Hollingshead, & O'Connor, 1993). For example, Harrison, Price, Gavin, and Florey (2002) found that the effects of surface-level diversity diminished over time but that the effects of deep-level diversity strengthened as group tenure increased.

Given the constant refrain for more longitudinal designs in conceptual and review papers (e.g., Cohen & Bailey, 1997; Kozlowski & Bell, 2003; McGrath & Argote, 2001) as well as the empirical demonstration that observing teams over time is critical to uncovering and interpreting team effects, it is worth investigating whether team researchers are, in fact, heeding the calls to move beyond static input–output designs. To assess the extent to which time is incorporated into empirical team studies, we content coded articles from 1990 to 2004 in three highly regarded applied psychology journals (Extejt & Smith, 1990; Johnson & Podsakoff, 1994): *Journal of Applied Psychology* (*JAP*), *Personnel Psychology* (*PP*), and *Organizational Behavior and Decision Processes* (*OBHDP*). Time-based coding categories included one-shot teams (e.g., a single survey administration or experimental data collected at one time period), measurement of *different* variables over time, and measurement of the *same* variables over time. The latter two categories included two or more survey administrations, groups returning to the laboratory for multiple sessions, or experiments where respondents were asked to complete measures over time. Although the measurement of *different* variables over time separates criteria from predictors to avoid common method bias (e.g., Podsakoff, MacKenzie, Lee, & Podsakoff, 2003), it is the measurement of the *same* variables over time that is considered truly longitudinal in nature. Only studies that had two or more measurements for at least one *team-level* variable were coded as longitudinal.

As Table 12.1 depicts, one-shot studies dominated team research across a 14-year time span for three top psychology journals (63.4%), with a much smaller percentage of studies (14.7%) measuring different variables over time. Only 51 of 232 empirical studies (22%) met the longitudinal criteria for team-level variables. Given the repeated calls for empirical research to measure teams over time (e.g., Cohen & Bailey, 1997; Kozlowski & Bell, 2003) and methodological chapters delineating analysis techniques for measuring collective data longitudinally (e.g., McGrath & Altermatt, 2001), it is worth considering why the percentage of studies incorporating multiple measurements of the same team-level variables is so low. One obvious reason is due to the formidable logistical obstacles encountered in doing longitudinal team research. As difficult as it can be to gain organizational access for cross-sectional studies, cooperation may not be forthcoming to allow group members to be surveyed at multiple points in time. Member attrition also poses considerable challenges to team-level analyses, because a majority of members need to respond to justify aggregation to the group level. In addition, although laboratory researchers can attest to the difficulty of getting enough students assembled at the same time and in the same place to randomly assign one-shot groups, convincing intact groups to return over multiple weeks is especially burdensome (although it has been done successfully; see Harrison et al., 2003; Hollenbeck et al., 1995; McGrath, 1993). Furthermore, participant fatigue is a significant factor to consider in studies that measure multiple iterations of performance in a simulation that lasts several hours. With the struggle to achieve an adequate group sample size, cross-sectional team research is often already fraught with difficulties, and the addition of a longitudinal design component may prove implausible in many contexts.

Unfortunately, the methodological difficulties with conducting longitudinal research do not end with the challenge to obtain repeated measurements of important team phenomena at multiple points in time but extend to determining the appropriate time intervals for measurement. Mitchell and James (2001) advocated for being more precise with the timing of measurement as well as with the frequency and stability of measurement,

TABLE 12.1

Time-Based Coding for Empirical Team Studies from 1990 to 2004

Content Categories	Journal of Applied Psychology		Personnel Psychology		Organizational Behavior and Human Decision Processes		Total across All Three Journals	
	Frequency	Percentage	Frequency	Percentage	Frequency	Percentage	Frequency	Percentage
Article Categories								
Empirical team articles[a]	79		18		93		190	
Empirical team studies	100		22		110		232	
Time-Based Categories								
One-shot teams	48	48.0	11	50.0	88	80.0	147	63.4
Measurement of *different* team variables over time	27	27.0	3	13.6	4	3.6	34	14.7
Longitudinal: Measurement of the *same* team variables over time	25	25.0	8	36.4	18	16.4	51	22.0

Note: Since several articles consisted of multiple studies, percentages are based on the number of empirical team studies as opposed to the number of empirical team articles.

[a] Empirical team articles excluded studies that utilized imaginary groups (e.g., Jackson & LePine, 2003; Kristoff-Brown, Jansen, & Colbert, 2002).

especially for dependent variables. The critical issue of when to measure has received substantially less attention in team studies than the other choice points of what to measure, how to measure, and how often. Unfortunately, the timing of longitudinal measurement may be somewhat arbitrary or understandably based on the convenience of data collection. For example, in studies involving student project teams, dependent measures are commonly collected at the beginning, middle, and end of the semester (e.g., Harrison et al., 2002; Jehn & Mannix, 2001), but it is not entirely clear whether measurement is properly aligned with when critical team processes are occurring. To illustrate, some groups may start working on their final projects late in the semester, making midsemester measurements of conflict, coordination, and communication less meaningful than when the level of interaction is higher. Therefore, it is not enough to collect measures at regular intervals, but "particular types of measures should be gathered at appropriate times... —all based on the knowledge garnered from a time-sensitive team task analysis" (Marks et al., 2001, p. 371).

Qualitative studies can inform survey-based research of when critical temporal milestones are likely to occur in group development, allowing for more precise matching between measurement and the occurrence of relevant team phenomena. Indeed, Gersick's (1988) observation of every meeting of eight groups revealed that each group showed a distinctive pattern of interaction styles, performance strategies, and external relationships. The finding that groups did not make task progress based on a standard sequence of activities led to the punctuated equilibrium model (Gersick, 1989). Discovering a different temporal pattern than that of face-to-face teams, case-study research concluded that effective global virtual teams developed a temporal rhythm in which face-to-face meetings were interspersed with less intensive, shorter, media-based communication (Maznevski & Chudoba, 2000). Therefore, one value of qualitative studies is that the idiosyncratic temporal cycles and rhythms of groups can be captured and utilized to inform theory.

Because time has been empirically demonstrated to have a profound effect on group functioning (e.g., Gersick, 1988, 1989; Harrison et al., 2002, 2003), researchers should continue to aggressively seek opportunities to conduct longitudinal work. Nevertheless, given the methodological and logistical difficulties of studying teams over time, relying on longitudinal measurement as the primary mechanism by which to address temporal issues is unlikely to spark a rapid proliferation of time-based team research. Although the need for longitudinal designs of group processes and performance has dominated discussions on time and teams thus far, this is only one component of what should be a more comprehensive incorporation of temporal issues into the group literature. Fortunately, however, there are multiple ways to examine temporal factors in teams, including time as part of variable content and temporal context. These are discussed in the following sections.

Time as Part of Variable Content: Team Temporal Constructs

According to Zaheer, Albert, and Zaheer (1999), "Virtually any concept, process, or event that involves human action must address the issue of time scale, because human action always occurs in time and, therefore, has a time scale or scales associated with it" (p. 739). As different time scales can lead to very different interpretations of phenomena, it is important to explicitly specify temporal reference points in the conceptualization and operationalization of variables. Although many popular team constructs have not directly included a temporal referent, a number of researchers are beginning to overtly incorporate a temporal perspective. For example, Janicik and Bartel (2003) measured temporal planning (i.e., discussions about temporal issues concerning how long tasks will take and when particular actions will occur), and Gevers, Rutte, and van Eerde (2004) assessed temporal reminders (i.e., mechanisms by which group members remind each other of important temporal aspects of the task). In addition, temporal norms (i.e., informal rules adopted by groups to regulate responses to temporal issues) were found to mediate the relationship between temporal planning and task performance (Janicik & Bartel, 2003). Whereas time is implicitly included as an aspect of coordination that is not part of other group processes such as cooperation and communication, Montoya-Weiss, Massey, and Song (2001) explicitly included time by defining a temporal coordination mechanism as a "process structure imposed to intervene and direct the pattern, timing, and content of communication in a group" (p. 1252). Although not measured empirically, the notion of shared cognitions on time has been introduced as the extent to which group members hold similar views about the temporal demands that they face (Bartel & Milliken, 2004; Gevers et al., 2004). Furthermore, temporal reflexivity (i.e., the extent to which team members evaluate and communicate adjustments in plans to meet temporal milestones; Gevers et al., 2004) and temporal leadership (leader coordination of internal team change and external deadlines; Ancona et al., 2001) have been suggested as fruitful avenues for future time-related research.

By more explicitly specifying temporal reference points in the conceptualization and measurement of team constructs, this genre of team studies adopts a temporal lens with cross-sectional research (e.g., Janicik & Bartel, 2003). Although not replacing the acute need for longitudinal designs, this category of research is logistically attractive and therefore likely to contribute to more rapid growth of time-based team studies in the short term. It is important to rethink the operationalization of classic team variables because "one must always consider the possibility that a difference in time scale could lead to a difference in the meaning and relationships among phenomena and that a theory that works at one time scale may not work at another" (Zaheer et al., 1999, p. 739). Highlighted below are popular topics in team research that arguably can be enriched by adopting a temporal perspective, including collective efficacy, team mental models, and conflict.

Collective Efficacy

Defined as a group's shared sense of competence to organize and execute action, collective efficacy is conceptualized as a task-specific construct (Bandura, 1997). Magnitude and strength ratings assess the confidence by which groups can succeed at several gradations of task difficulty (Bandura, 1997; Gibson, Randel, & Earley, 2000). However, in some contexts, the critical issue may not be whether group members feel that they can do the task but in what time frame. Given enough time, most members may express confidence that their group can succeed, but few teams have unlimited time in which to complete their work. Because time-pressured environments are increasingly commonplace, it may be moot for group members to be 100% confident that they can complete a task in three months when they only have six weeks. Likert-type collective efficacy scales have also neglected time. Items often ask how confident participants are that their teams can perform particular tasks, but without specifying "when," interpretation is difficult, as confidence levels may vary widely from the short term to the long term.

Gibson et al. (2000) experimented with time-based group efficacy on a sample of students performing a multiparty negotiation by asking members to estimate how certain they were that the group could reach a decision in a specified number of minutes (e.g., 30–44, 45–59, 60–74). Although an exception in the collective efficacy literature, such a measure could be adapted to a wide variety of applied team contexts. The inclusion of a time frame would increase measurement precision and allow for a more fine-tuned assessment as to when time constraints start eroding a team's collective sense of competence. Given the beneficial effects of collective efficacy on performance (e.g., Gully, Incalcaterra, Joshi, & Beaubien, 2002), temporally based collective efficacy measures could prove useful in diagnosing when group members perceive the rate of performance to be challenging versus impossible to achieve. Therefore, in addition to being task-specific, measures of collective efficacy should be time specific, especially in contexts where time is a vital strategic element.

Team Mental Models

Defined as an organized understanding of relevant knowledge that is shared by team members, the general thesis of the team mental model literature is that team effectiveness will improve if members have an adequate shared understanding of relevant team dimensions (e.g., Mohammed & Dumville, 2001). From its inception, the construct of a team mental model was designed to account for the fluid, implicit coordination frequently observed in effective teams, with the "blind pass" in basketball being commonly offered as an illustration (e.g., Cannon-Bowers, Salas, & Converse, 1993). Since coordination has a temporal element, issues of timing are inherent in the broad conceptualization of a team mental model. However, in specifying the content of team mental models, the emphasis has been placed on task procedures and team-interaction patterns (e.g., Mathieu, Heffner, Goodwin, Salas, & Cannon-Bowers, 2000). Nevertheless, it is possible for a group to be on the same page with regard to what to do and with whom but to fail to perform adequately because of the lack of attention given to when.

Not only has time been downplayed in the conceptualization of team mental models, but measurement techniques have been temporally deficient as well. In common team mental model assessment tools, content is elicited by means of relatedness judgments, which are then submitted to Pathfinder (e.g., Marks, Sabella, Burke, & Zaccaro, 2002), multidimensional scaling (e.g., Rentsch & Klimoski, 2001), or UCINET (e.g., Mathieu et al., 2000) to determine the relationships between elements in an individual's mind. Although relatedness could be due to several factors, including co-occurrence in time or causation, respondents use their own internal standards and are not generally asked to specify their definition of similarity (Mohammed, Klimoski, & Rentsch, 2000). Therefore, time is not explicitly incorporated into these measures of team mental models. Although similarity ratings are sometimes collected over time (e.g., Mathieu et al., 2000), greater temporal precision could be achieved by including a time referent in the measure itself.

Another team mental model measurement technique used in the literature has been team-interaction concept maps, in which members select prelabeled concepts that best depict their actions as well as those of their teammates during a task and place them in the appropriate rows on a concept map (e.g., Marks et al., 2002; Marks, Zaccaro, & Mathieu, 2000). Although time has not been traditionally incorporated into this technique, temporal referents could easily be added to concept mapping to increase measurement precision. Clearly, future research could be sharpened conceptually and operationally by explicitly addressing team mental models as shared, organized mental representations of who is going to do what (taskwork), with whom (teamwork), and when.

Process Conflict

Although most research has focused on relationship and task conflict (e.g., De Dreu & Weingart, 2003), process conflict refers to differences in how task accomplishment will be carried out, including who should do what and how much responsibility members should receive (Jehn & Mannix, 2001). Despite the fact that it has been the least examined, process conflict has the greatest potential to incorporate time-related effects. Whereas process conflict has focused on disagreements regarding "how task accomplishment will proceed" (ibid., p. 239), the construct could easily be expanded to also reflect disagreements regarding when task accomplishment will proceed. In a qualitative study of six work units, Jehn (1997) concluded that "high levels of process conflict interfered with performance by allowing group members to work at cross-purposes, by creating inconsistencies in task roles in the group, and generating time-management problems that sometimes resulted in failure to meet deadlines" (p. 548). Failure to meet deadlines not only may result from disagreements about who should do what but also may be an outgrowth of differences in opinion regarding when work should be accomplished. Although the three-item process conflict scale only references disagreements about task responsibilities, resource allocation, and task delegation (Shah & Jehn, 1993), the measure could easily be expanded to capture controversies related to when tasks should be accomplished and in what order.

Teams over Time: Team Temporal Constructs

Integrating the first two categories from the temporal organizing framework, some phenomena are both quintessentially time oriented and require longitudinal measurement to assess appropriately. The majority of existing work linking time to teams falls in this category. Group socialization, group development models, and familiarity incorporate time as a feature of team membership. Specifically, Moreland and Levine's (1982) model described the socialization process by which newcomers, through their interactions with old-timers, become full group members. More recently, a model of newcomer role performance in the context of work teams was proposed, and results of a study of high-tech project teams supported predictions regarding motivational and interpersonal processes as proximal predictors of newcomer effectiveness (Chen & Klimoski, 2003). A follow-up study modeled newcomer performance longitudinally and found that newcomer performance improved over time and was related to subsequent empowerment and intentions to quit (Chen, 2005). Whereas socialization examines the relationship between a person and a team over time, models of group development temporally track the psychosocial dynamics (e.g., forming, storming, norming, performing, adjourning) that characterize the group as a whole (e.g., Tuckman & Jensen, 1977). Even assuming constancy in membership and task demands, teams evolve continuously over time. Focusing on specific stages of development, some research has been devoted to the formation of groups (e.g., Moreland, 1987), but work on group termination is less common.

Time is also the medium for teams developing member familiarity (e.g., Harrison et al., 2003; Okhuysen, 2001). Given that existing research has shown that familiarity exerts significant influences on team processes and performance (e.g., Gruenfeld, Mannix, Williams, & Neale, 1996; Hollenbeck et al., 1995; Okhuysen, 2001; Shah & Jehn, 1993), we content coded articles from 1990 to 2004 in *JAP*, *PP*, and *OBHDP* with regard to their treatment of familiarity. Coding categories included manipulations of familiarity (teams composed based on whether participants previously knew or did not know each other), ad hoc teams (created for the purpose of research), and preexisting teams (together before the research study started). For both the ad hoc and preexisting teams, we created subcategories to reflect if experiments reported checking whether team members actually knew each other prior to group formation and whether team tenure data was recorded, respectively. As Table 12.2 depicts, the majority of empirical studies across the three journals involve ad hoc teams (78%), with only a small percentage stating that they assessed actual member familiarity (7.3%). Because participants may sign up for experiments with friends or be in classroom teams with previous work partners, researchers should check to ensure that intended ad hoc teams are composed of members with zero history. Interestingly, more studies using preexisting teams failed to mention how long the teams have been together (11.6%) than to report team tenure data (8.2%). Organizational tenure seems to be a more standard descriptive variable, even for team-based studies. Given that familiarity facilitates interpersonal attraction and cohesiveness as well as has implications for performance (e.g., Gruenfeld et al., 1996; Hollenbeck et al., 1995; Okhuysen, 2001), future research should give more attention to measuring and reporting the amount of contact that group members have had with one another.

In addition to time as a feature of group membership, time is also a feature of task continuity. According to the punctuated equilibrium model, groups experience inertia until the midpoint of the allotted time when they undergo a major transition that results in a reevaluation of their progress and significant changes in strategy (Gersick, 1988, 1989). Because of its focus on temporal features of task completion under a deadline, a number of researchers have categorized punctuated equilibrium as a task progress model instead of a group development model (Okhuysen & Waller, 2002; Seers & Woodruff, 1997). Recent work has challenged the

TABLE 12.2

Team Member Familiarity Coding for Empirical Team Studies from 1990 to 2004

Content Categories	Journal of Applied Psychology		Personnel Psychology		Organizational Behavior and Human Decision Processes		Total across All Three Journals	
	Frequency	Percentage	Frequency	Percentage	Frequency	Percentage	Frequency	Percentage
Article Categories								
Empirical team articles[a]	79		18		93		190	
Empirical team studies	100		22		110		232	
Familiarity Categories								
Manipulated Familiarity	2	2.0	2	9.1	1	0.91	5	2.2
Ad hoc teams	67	67.0	9	40.9	105	95.5	181	78.0
No mention of whether team members knew each other before	63	63.0	8	36.4	93	84.5	164	70.7
Checking for member familiarity	4	4.0	1	4.5	12	10.9	17	7.3
Preexisting teams	31	31.0	11	50.0	4	3.6	46	19.8
No mention of how long teams were together	19	19.0	6	27.3	2	1.8	27	11.6
Team tenure data reported	12	12.0	5	22.7	2	1.8	19	8.2

Note: Since several articles consisted of multiple studies, percentages are based on the number of empirical team studies as opposed to the number of empirical team articles.

[a] Empirical team articles excluded studies that utilized imaginary groups (e.g., Jackson & LePine, 2003; Kristoff-Brown, Jansen, & Colbert, 2002).

punctuated equilibrium model by comparing it with alternative models (e.g., Arrow, 1997; Chang, Bordia, & Duck, 2003; Seers & Woodruff, 1997) and has refined the conditions under which midpoint transitions emerge (e.g., Okhuysen & Waller, 2002).

As a feature of task continuity, some of the most promising work on time and teams is being done on entrainment, "the adjustment of the pace or cycle of an activity to match or synchronize with that of another activity" (Ancona & Chong, 1996, p. 258). Derived from the concept of circadian rhythm where bodily cycles entrain to light–dark cycles, social entrainment theory (McGrath & Kelly, 1986) states that routines internal to the team become synchronized with pacers external to the team. A number of studies have shown that groups persist in the pace they establish to meet deadlines on initial trials, even if time limits are later changed (e.g., Harrison et al., 2003; Kelly, 1988; Kelly, Futoran, & McGrath, 1990).

The work relating to time as a feature of team membership and task continuity indicates that group processes and performance are characterized by many forms of temporal patterning and that these affect group activity in numerous ways. Clearly, researchers should be cautious about interpreting their findings without considering task progress, social entrainment, team member familiarity, and the developmental levels of the teams they are studying.

Time as Part of the General Context: Team Temporal Environment

In addition to a longitudinal approach, team temporal constructs, and the integration of the two, time can also be considered part of the general environment. Clearly, teams do not operate in a vacuum, and the group, organizational, and societal context imposes temporal demands. In addition to the need for research on temporal dynamics, a constant refrain mentioned by practically every major review of the team literature is the failure to fully account for contextual influences impinging on groups (e.g., Cohen & Bailey, 1997; Kozlowski & Bell, 2003; Mathieu et al., 2008; McGrath & Argote, 2001). Although there are several noteworthy exemplars that examine how teams interact with their larger environment (e.g., Ancona & Caldwell, 1992; Marks, DeChurch, Mathieu, Panzer, & Alonso, 2005), most of the research is intrateam in nature. This section explores several aspects of temporal context, including deadlines, time pressure, and the organizational as well as the cultural environment.

Deadlines

Virtually all teams have some sort of implicit or explicit time constraint, and deadlines are a significant component of a group's temporal context. Nevertheless, the length of time needed to complete tasks is typically ignored as a criterion variable in recent empirical research on teams. Although timeliness is included in the conceptualization of team effectiveness (Hackman, 1990), quality and quantity are measured far more frequently (e.g., Austin, 2003; Chen & Klimoski, 2003; DeShon, Kozlowski, Schmidt, Milner, & Wiechmann, 2004). For example, in their meta-analysis of cognitive ability and team performance, Devine and Philips (2001) were unable to conduct separate analyses for accuracy/quality, speed, and quantity because of the limited number of studies that reported multiple criteria. A more recent meta-analysis on the relationship between cohesion and performance partitioned the dependent variable by effectiveness versus efficiency measures (Beal, Cohen, Burke, & McLendon, 2003), but the timeliness of work completion was not explicitly considered.

The lack of attention to timeliness as a criterion variable in the empirical research stands in stark contrast to the dominant conception in modern work organizations of time as a valuable, scarce resource, necessitating the need to carefully manage scarce temporal resources (McGrath & Rotchford, 1983). Increasingly, the timely completion of work is regarded as an important measure of project success (Freeman & Beele, 1992) as well as a persistent problem (e.g., Gupta & Wilemon, 1990; Lientz & Rea, 2001). For example, 56% of 91 project team managers indicated that deadlines were often missed or exceeded (Tukel & Rom, 1998). Pointing to the consequences of missed deadlines, Vesey (1991) showed that high-technology products (within budget) that were six months late in entering the market earned 33% less over a five-year period than they would have if on time. Indeed, speed is especially critical in teams operating in high-velocity industries, which experience higher rates of new product introductions, shorter process life cycles, and greater degrees of obsolescence than low-velocity industries (Eisenhardt & Tabrizi, 1995). For teams where time is a competitive asset, high-quantity and high-quality outputs completed past stringent deadlines will not qualify as successful performance. For example, in contexts such as seasonal retail promotions and emergency medical crises, unless the product or service can be delivered on time, its quality will not matter (Beersma et al., 2003).

Clearly, the importance and weighting of criteria will vary considerably across team and task types (Hackman, 1990). Speed and accuracy have been found to be distinct aspects of a task, and a recent study of student teams performing a networked computer simulation found evidence for a speed–accuracy trade-off (Beersma et al., 2003). Nevertheless, there are plenty of organizational examples where both speed and accuracy are required, including air traffic controllers and nuclear power plant operators attempting to avoid an accident as well as police officers deciding whether situations warrant the use of force. In addition, the weighting of dimensions will depend on group development and task cycle. For example, speed may be emphasized more toward the latter stages of a product development team's work cycle when the focus is on launching the product before competitors, whereas quality may be emphasized more toward the beginning stages when the focus is on the formation of a marketable product (Beersma et al., 2003). Therefore, the importance of precision with regard to the timing of measurement as opposed to arbitrary assessment periods is again emphasized (e.g., Marks et al., 2001; Mitchell & James, 2001).

Although research has traditionally neglected the study of time limits, recent studies have been giving greater attention to this topic. For example, Labianca, Moon, and Watt (2005) found that student teams that began their tasks at atypical times (e.g., 3:52) transitioned from the planning phase to the action phase later in group life and ultimately performed more poorly than teams with prototypical starting times (e.g., 3:45). In addition, although most previous research has focused on stable deadlines, Waller, Zeller-Bruhn, and Giambatista (2002) found that changed deadlines increased the salience of time resources, regardless of the direction of the deadline change. In addition, when deadlines moved further away, attention to time influenced task activity less than when deadlines were stable (ibid.).

Time Pressure

Although deadlines are environmental stimuli that are characterized by a set duration of clock time to complete a task, they are also perceived and interpreted by group members. Whereas time constraints exist whenever there is a deadline, time pressure results from the perception that available time is insufficient and that the violation of time limits has undesirable consequences (Rastegary & Landy, 1993; Svenson & Benson, 1993). Time pressure is not necessarily negative, as too little time pressure may result in boredom and lack of focus whereas too much may result in excessive stress that leads to procrastination (Rastegary & Landy, 1993). The Attentional Focus Model (AFM) identifies the situations under which time pressure is expected to enhance or reduce group performance as a function of members' attentional focus and information-processing strategies (Karau & Kelly, 2004). Empirical studies of this model reveal that groups under time pressure work at a faster rate of performance, focus on a reduced but task-relevant set of cues, employ more heuristic processing, and engage in more self-censorship of information (ibid.). In addition to the time pressure–performance relationship, it is also important to consider the antecedents that affect how time pressure is perceived.

For example, in a study of 22 student groups examined over 13 weeks, Gevers et al. (2001) found that group potency affected the influence of time pressure on project progress. Specifically, high time pressure negatively affected the performance of low-potency groups in that they did not make timely progress in the earlier orientation phase and were unable to recover from the work backlog in the later execution phase.

Clearly, temporal context should be measured both objectively (e.g., whether deadlines are met, the time frame in which work is accomplished) and subjectively (e.g., workload intensity, perceptions of time pressure). It would be useful to assess the extent to which members perceive that they do not have enough time, have just enough time, or have more than enough time for team tasks. Schriber and Gutek (1987) advocated measuring time allocation, which is the extent to which employees perceive that there is sufficient time for tasks (e.g., schedules are not too tight, tasks do not take longer than planned, and time is not a constraint to achieving goals).

Organizational Temporal Context

The organizational environment in which externally imposed deadlines and time pressure perceptions are embedded should also be considered. The temporal perspective adopted by organizations can affect perceptions by outsiders and insiders as well as how the organization approaches decision making and strategic planning. Schriber and Guteck (1987) identified 13 dimensions of organizational culture, including schedules and deadlines, punctuality, future orientation, time boundaries between work and nonwork, quality versus speed, synchronization and coordination, awareness of time use, and work pace. More recently, Blount and Janicik (2001) proposed that the temporal information generated by organizations includes explicit schedules and deadlines, implicit paces and rhythms, and sociotemporal norms. Employees' perceptions of the organization's temporal agenda provide cues for marking time, communicate to members how they should spend their time, allow individuals to plan their time, and create meaning by linking personal schedules with broader company goals (ibid.). Illustrating the importance of temporal environment, Perlow (1999) concluded that an intervention that created planned times when software engineers could work alone and engage in interactive activities was not sustainable over time because the engineering culture perpetuated a vicious work cycle of crisis mentality and rewards based on individual heroics. Therefore, individual-level change needs to be couched within a sociology of work time where the social and temporal context perpetuate each other (Perlow, 1999).

Within the organizational environment, the intergroup temporal context must also be considered. For example, within the same firm, engineering and product marketing teams have different time orientations (Schriber & Gutek,

1987). Many employees now work on several group projects simultaneously, which may induce different norms about deadlines and result in competing demands on their time. In addition, a team's stakeholders (e.g., customers, suppliers, competing work teams) also impose temporal demands for speedy delivery of products or services, which Bartel and Milliken (2004) called time compression. Diverse temporal norms between various constituencies can result in significant misunderstanding if not carefully managed.

Cultural Temporal Context

Unfortunately, team research has given little attention to the broader cultural context in which individuals, groups, and organizations are embedded. Nevertheless, some of the most significant nonlanguage difficulties in cross-cultural interactions are those arising from temporal differences (Bluedorn, Kaufman, & Lane, 1992). Indeed, Hofstede (2001) identified long-term versus short-term orientation as a characteristic of national culture, which refers to members expecting either immediate or delayed gratification of their material, social, and emotional needs. Cultures with a short-term orientation (e.g., United States, Russia) focus on the past and present, whereas cultures with a long-term orientation (e.g., Japan, China) are not nearly as concerned with immediate benefit as they are with persistence (ibid.). In comparison with other societies, most Western countries are regarded as monochronic in that they place more emphasis on tasks than relationships and tend to end meetings before their purpose has been accomplished to comply with predetermined schedules (Hall, 1983). In contrast, polychronic countries stress involvement with people and completion of interactions rather than adherence to schedules (Onken, 1999). In addition, the definition of what constitutes acceptable punctuality clearly varies from culture to culture (Levine, 1988). Whereas North America and northern Europe subscribe to clock time in which events follow prespecified schedules and time is tightly allocated, Latin America and southern Europe subscribe to event time in which schedules are fluid and meetings take as long as they take (Blount & Janicik, 2001). Therefore, perceptions of how much margin there is around deadlines will be affected by cultural differences.

Teams and Time: A Multilevel Perspective

Based on our review of the existing work on time and teams, we conclude that a comprehensive incorporation of temporal issues into the group literature necessitates a multilevel perspective. In listing questions regarding time-related phenomena that remain unanswered, Goodman, Lawrence, Ancona, and Tushman (2001) asked, "How do we think about time in relation to the unit of analysis?" as well as, "How do we think about time in a multilevel context?" (p. 509). Furthermore, in their comprehensive review of the team literature, Kozlowski and Bell (2003) recommended that future research "should explicitly address the implications of time for team phenomena" and "must be cognizant of and consistent with the principles of multilevel theory, data, and analyses" (p. 364). Because both micro- and macroperspectives have limitations, a multilevel perspective permits an expanded understanding of phenomena that unfold across levels in organizations (Kozlowski & Klein, 2000). As such, an integrated conceptualization of the role of time in team functioning should address individual difference, team-level, and contextual influences as well as their combined effects.

From a multilevel perspective, a more comprehensive incorporation of temporal issues in the team literature begins with the individual. Despite the fact that deadlines may be given to work groups and time pressure is a contextual variable that affects the group as a whole, individuals perceive temporal factors in different ways (e.g., Bluedorn, 2002; Zimbardo & Boyd, 1999). Indeed, temporal orientation has been recognized as one of the fundamental parameters of individual differences (Bluedorn & Denhardt, 1988). Three temporal individual differences that have been discussed in the psychology and organizational behavior literatures are time urgency, time perspective, and polychronicity. Time urgency relates to the need to have control over deadlines as well as the feeling of being driven and chronically hurried (e.g., Conte, Mathieu, & Landy, 1998). Time perspective serves as a cognitive temporal bias toward being past, present, or future oriented (e.g., Zimbardo & Boyd, 1999), whereas polychronicity refers to the preference to work on several tasks at one time (e.g., Bluedorn, 2002). Together, time urgency, time perspective, and polychronicity combine to describe a type of temporal personality that results in differences between individuals in the way that the timing of typical events is perceived.

The research on time urgency and time perspective has mostly been conducted at the individual level of analysis, and polychronicity has been conceptualized both as an individual difference as well as a cultural variable. However, little empirical work has investigated how these temporal constructs impact group-level functioning. Another way to incorporate time into this area of research is to consider time urgency, time perspective, and polychronicity as temporal team composition variables by examining the configurations of these individual differences within the group. Multilevel theorists have developed various frameworks to explain how lower-level properties combine to form collective phenomena, and the most popular is to aggregate to the group level by mean or sum (e.g., Kozlowski & Klein, 2000). For example, Waller, Conte, Gibson, and Carpenter (2001) predicted that under conditions of time pressure, teams composed of individuals who are lower in time urgency will have difficulty meeting deadlines and teams composed of individuals higher in time urgency will be successful in meeting deadlines. In addition, they postulated that teams with more future time perspective members would have less difficulty planning for meeting long-term deadlines, whereas teams with more present time perspective members would have less difficulty meeting short-term deadlines (ibid.).

Nevertheless, more interesting team-based phenomena may occur, not from examining how mean-aggregated time urgency, time perspective, or polychronicity impact group outcomes but from examining the variability of individual differences within a team. Individuals with different temporal personalities are likely to work in proximity on similar teams, which may be a source of misunderstanding because of their contrasting approaches to time management. For example, individuals with future time perspectives may perceive team members with present time perspectives as undisciplined, whereas individuals with present time perspectives may perceive team members with future time perspectives as uptight and demanding (Waller et al., 2001). In addition, because time-urgent individuals are chronically hurried and non-time-urgent individuals underestimate the passage of time, the mix of time-urgent and non-time-urgent individuals within a team may generate dysfunctional conflict. Providing some support for this hypothesis on a sample of business student teams working on industry-sponsored projects, Mohammed and Angell (2004) examined the impact of intragroup time-urgency variability on relationship conflict (tension, animosity, and annoyance among individuals) and found a moderated relationship with team processes. Specifically, when the occurrence of effective team processes (leadership, cooperation, communication) was more frequent within the team, higher time-urgency diversity produced lower relationship conflict than when the occurrence of effective team processes was less frequent. Also examining time urgency, Jansen and Kristof-Brown (2005) found that employees whose hurriedness did not match that of their coworkers were less satisfied with their work environment and less likely to engage in helping behavior.

Although a few studies have begun to integrate temporal individual differences into the study of team composition (e.g., Mohammed & Angell, 2004; Waller, Giambatista, & Zellmer-Bruhn, 1999), many promising avenues for further work have not yet been empirically explored. For example, a mix of temporal individual differences within teams also has the potential to be beneficial under certain circumstances. Although high variability on polychronicity in the group may lead to increased conflict and impaired communication in the short run, a mix of monochrons and polychrons may prove to be advantageous in the long run. Whereas a monochronic orientation is beneficial from the standpoint of focus and greater depth of involvement, a polychronic orientation is beneficial from the standpoint of flexibility and cross-fertilization or integration of ideas across tasks (Bluedorn, 2002). Therefore, for complex tasks that require both flexibility and focus, a balance of monochrons and polychrons in the team may be optimal. In dynamic environments and uncertain tasks where inherent tensions define performance, temporal heterogeneity within teams may be most effective.

From an applied perspective, the challenge for teams is to synergistically leverage temporal differences while minimizing the process losses that may be incurred. Groups should develop an awareness of their own temporal approach and actively manage temporal diversity to achieve temporal synchronization and high performance levels. How teams resolve the temporal asynchrony that individual differences introduce may prove critical to optimal functioning and performance. Therefore, attention should be given to the skills needed to effectively mediate interpersonal disagreements based on time-based individual differences, especially when they hinder team goal-setting behaviors and accurate task perceptions.

In addition to the bottom-up perspective used to discuss temporal individual differences, Kozlowski and Klein (2000) also advocated a top-down perspective in that "organization factors are contexts for individual perceptions, attitudes, and behaviors and need to be explicitly incorporated into meaningful models of organizational behavior" (p. 10). Although emergent phenomena have their origins in lower levels, the process is clearly constrained by higher-level contextual factors (ibid.). For example, cultural orientation shapes the beliefs, preferences, and values of group members toward time. Therefore, variability in temporal individual differences may be exacerbated in cross-cultural or globally dispersed teams. Indeed, Bluedorn et al. (1992) speculated that "when a relatively monochronic North American interacts with a more polychronic Latin American, misinterpretations and misattributes of behavior, if not friction and conflict, are likely to occur unless some attention has been paid to identifying and learning such differences in temporal behavior and norms" (p. 25).

In addition to examining within-team differences regarding the orientation to time, the fit between individuals and organizations as well as between groups and organizations should also be investigated. To illustrate, a non-time-urgent individual in a highly time-urgent organization may experience low satisfaction, commitment, and productivity. Moreover, the temporal norms of specific work groups (quality over speed) may be out of sync with organizational temporal norms (speed over quality), creating the potential for conflicting goals and misunderstandings.

Adopting a multilevel perspective, future work could examine how various configurations of temporal individual differences affect time-referenced emergent states and team processes such as collective efficacy, team mental models, and conflict. In addition to completion times and whether deadlines are met, other dimensions of temporality should be assessed, including interruptions (disruptions in task progress), sequence (order in which activities occur), pace (rate at which activities can be accomplished), temporal location (points in time in which tasks take place), cycles (periodic regularity in which work is completed repeatedly), and autonomy of time use (freedom in setting schedules for work completion) (Lee, 1999; Schriber & Guteck, 1987). Because individual differences in temporal perspectives will be more salient when cooperation and coordination among group members is critical, the moderating role of team interdependence should be considered. Furthermore, a time-pressured environment may exacerbate the conflict caused by heterogeneity on time urgency or time perspective within the team. However, temporal leadership, temporal planning, or temporal reflexivity may serve as mechanisms to diffuse the destructive conflict resulting from diversity on temporal individual differences. Therefore, it would be important to examine interactions among temporal composition, team processes, task characteristics, and temporal context in deriving specific hypotheses.

Conclusion

Despite the difficulty of disputing that "humans exist in time, that every human life is time bound, and that time is ubiquitous in every known culture" (Zimbardo & Boyd, 1999, p. 1284), time has often been neglected in team research (e.g., Kozlowski & Bell, 2003) and is rarely considered in either single-level or multilevel models of organizational behavior (Kozlowski & Klein, 2000). Therefore, the purpose of the current chapter was to review past and current work to consider how future team research can more explicitly and intentionally integrate temporal dynamics by adopting a multilevel perspective. We believe that an increased concern with temporal matters is of extreme importance for future research on teams. Although several group constructs are eminently temporal, time remains implicit in the measurement of many basic team concepts, highlighting the need for time to be placed at the forefront instead of the periphery.

Because the need for longitudinal studies has dominated previous discussions of temporal dynamics and is only one component of a thorough incorporation of temporal issues into the team literature, emphasis was placed on the need to more explicitly specify temporal reference points in the conceptualization and measurement of many popular group constructs and to consider the broader temporal context. An expanded conceptualization of the role of time in team functioning should address temporal individual differences, team-level processes and outcomes, and contextual influences as well as their combined effects. Therefore, by adopting a multilevel perspective, we hope to spark a more systematic and comprehensive approach to integrating temporal issues team studies.

In their recent review, Ilgen et al. (2005) pointed out that the team literature has progressed from generic questions of *what* predicts team effectiveness to more complex questions regarding *why* certain groups are more effective than others. However, from the standpoint of the current paper, the next wave of research must address the question of *when* groups are more and less effective. Eisenhardt (2004) stated that "the next few years should see much deeper understanding of group processes, better shaping of constructs and measures, compelling methods, and an attack on the controversies and confusion surrounding how groups intersect time" (p. 281). In adopting a temporal lens (Ancona et al., 2001) that goes beyond the call for longitudinal research, the current chapter contributes to this aggressive research agenda by revealing several new opportunities for future team research using a multilevel framework.

Acknowledgments

We thank David Harrison for his helpful comments on earlier drafts.

References

Ancona, D. G. & Caldwell, D. F. (1992). Bridging the boundary: External activity and performance in organizational teams. *Administrative Science Quarterly, 37,* 634–665.

Ancona, D. & Chong, C. L., (1996). Entrainment: Pace, cycle, and rhythm in organizational behavior. In L. L. Cummings & B. M. Staw (Eds.), *Research in organizational behavior: An annual series of analytical essays and critical reviews, 18* (pp. 251–384). New York: Elsevier Science/JAI.

Ancona, D. & Chong, C. L. (1999). Cycles and synchrony: The temporal role of context in team behavior. *Research on Managing Groups and Teams, 2,* 33–48.

Ancona, D. G., Goodman, P. S., Lawrence, B. S., & Tushman, M. L. (2001). Time: A new research lens. *Academy of Management Review, 26,* 645–663.

Argote, L. & McGrath, J. E. (1993). Group processes in organizations: Continuity and change. In C. I. Cooper & I. T. Robertson (Eds.), *International review of industrial and organizational psychology, 8* (pp. 333–389). New York: John Wiley & Sons, Ltd.

Arrow, H. (1997). Stability, bistability, and instability in small group influence patterns. *Journal of Personality and Social Psychology, 72,* 75–85.

Arrow, H., McGrath, J. E., & Berdahl, J. L. (2000). *Small groups as complex systems: Formation, coordination, development, and adaptation.* Thousand Oaks, CA: Sage.

Austin, J. R. (2003). Transactive memory in organizational groups: The effects of content, consensus, specialization, and accuracy on group performance. *Journal of Applied Psychology, 88,* 866–878.

Bandura, A. (1997). *Self-efficacy: The exercise of control.* New York: Freeman.

Bartel, C. A. & Milliken, F. J. (2004). Perceptions of time in work groups: Do members develop shared cognitions about their temporal demands? In S. Blount (Ed.), *Research on managing groups and teams: Time in groups* (Vol. 6, pp. 87–109). New York: Elsevier.

Beal, D. J., Cohen, R. R., Burke, M. J., & McLendon, C. L. (2003). Cohesion and performance in groups: A meta-analytic clarification of construct relations. *Journal of Applied Psychology, 88,* 989–1004.

Beersma, B., Hollenbeck, J. R., Humphrey, S. E., Moon, H., Conlon, D. E., & Ilgen, D. R. (2003). Cooperation, competition, and team performance: Toward a contingency approach. *Academy of Management Journal, 46,* 572–590.

Blount, S. & Janicik, G. A. (2001). When plans change: Examining how people evaluate timing changes in work organizations. *Academy of Management Review, 26,* 566–585.

Bluedorn, A. C. (2002). *The human organization of time: Temporal realities and experience.* Stanford, CA: Stanford University Press.

Bluedorn, A. C. & Denhardt, R. B. (1988). Time and organizations. *Journal of Management, 14,* 299–320.

Bluedorn, A. C., Kaufman, C. F., & Lane, P. M. (1992). How many things do you like to do at once? An introduction to monochronic and polychronic time. *Academy of Management Executive, 6,* 17–26.

Cannon-Bowers, J. A., Salas, E., & Converse, S. (1993). Shared mental models in expert team decision making. In N. J. Castellan (Ed.), *Individual and group decision making* (pp. 221–246). Hillsdale, NJ: Lawrence Erlbaum Associates.

Chang, A., Bordia, P., & Duck, J. (2003). Punctuated equilibrium and linear progression: Toward a new understanding of group development. *Academy of Management Journal, 46,* 106–117.

Chen, G. (2005). Newcomer adaptation in teams: Multilevel antecedents and outcomes. *Academy of Management Journal, 48,* 101–116.

Chen, G. & Klimoski, R. J. (2003).The impact of expectations on newcomer performance in teams as mediated by work characteristics, social exchanges, and empowerment. *Academy of Management Journal, 46,* 591–607.

Cohen, S. G. & Bailey, D. E. (1997). What makes teams work: Group effectiveness research from the shop floor to the executive suite? *Journal of Management, 23,* 239–290.

Conte, J. M., Mathieu, J. E., & Landy, F. J. (1998). The nomological and predictive validity of time urgency. *Journal of Organizational Behavior, 19,* 1–13.

De Dreu, C. K. W. & Weingart, L. R. (2003). Task versus relationship conflict, team performance, and team member satisfaction: A meta-analysis. *Journal of Applied Psychology, 88,* 741–749.

DeShon, R. P., Kozlowski, S. W. J., Schmidt, A. M., Milner, K. R., & Wiechmann, D. (2004). A multiple-goal, multilevel model of feedback effects on the regulation of individual and team performance. *Journal of Applied Psychology, 89,* 1035–1056.

Devine, D. J. & Philips, J. L. (2001). Do smarter teams do better: A meta-analysis of cognitive ability and team performance? *Small Group Research, 32,* 507–532.

Eisenhardt, K. & Tabrizi, B. N. (1995). Accelerating adaptive processes: product innovation in the global computer industry. *Administrative Science Quarterly, 40,* 84–110.

Eisenhardt, K. M. (2004). Five issues where groups meet time. In S. Blount (Ed.), *Time in groups: Research on managing groups and teams* (Vol. 6), pp. 267–283. New York: Elsevier.

Extejt, M. M. & Smith, J. E. (1990). The behavioral sciences and management: An evaluation of relevant journals. *Journal of Management, 16,* 539–551.

Freeman, M. & Beele, P. (1992). Measuring project success. *Project Management Journal, 23,* 8–17.

Gersick, C. J. G. (1988). Time and transition in work teams: Toward a new model of group development. *Academy of Management Journal, 31,* 9–41.

Gersick, C. J. G. (1989). Marking time: Predictable transitions in task groups. *Academy of Management Journal, 32,* 274–309.

Gevers, J. M., van Eerde, W., & Rutte, C. G. (2001). Time pressure, potency, and progress in project groups. *European Journal of Work and Organizational Psychology, 10,* 205–221.

Gevers, J. M., Rutte, C. G., & van Eerde, W. (2004). How project teams achieve coordinated action: A model of shared cognitions on time. In S. Blount (Ed.), *Research on managing groups and teams: Time in groups* (Vol. 6, pp. 67–85). New York: Elsevier.

Gibson, C. B., Randel, A. E., & Earley, P. C. (2000). Understanding group efficacy: An empirical test of multiple assessment methods. *Group and Organization Management, 25,* 67–97.

Goodman, P. S., Lawrence, B. S., Ancona, D. G., & Tushman, M. L. (2001). Introduction (to special issue on time). *Academy of Management Review, 26,* 507–511.

Gruenfeld, D. H., Mannix, E. A., Williams, K. Y., & Neale, M. A. (1996). Group composition and decision making: How member familiarity and information distribution affect process and performance. *Organizational Behavior & Human Decision Process, 67,* 1–15.

Gully, S. M., Incalcaterra, K. A., Joshi, A., & Beaubien, J. M. (2002). A meta-analysis of team-efficacy, potency, and performance: Interdependence and level of analysis as moderators of observed relationships. *Journal of Applied Psychology, 87,* 819–832.

Gupta, A. K. & Wilemon, D. L. (1990). Accelerating the development of technology-based products. *California Management Review, 32,* 24–44.

Hackman, J. R. (1990). *Groups that work and those that don't.* San Francisco: Jossey-Bass.

Hall, E. (1983). *The dance of life: The other dimension of time.* New York: Anchor Press.

Harrison, D. A., Mohammed, S., McGrath, J. E., Florey, A. T., & Vanderstoep, S. W. (2003). Time matters in team performance: Effects of member familiarity, entrainment, and task discontinuity on speed and quality. *Personnel Psychology, 56,* 633–669.

Harrison, D. A., Price, K. H., Gavin, J. H., & Florey, A. (2002). Time, teams, and task performance: Changing effects of surface- and deep- level diversity on group functioning. *Academy of Management Journal, 45,* 1029–1045.

Hofstede, G. (2001). *Culture's consequences: Comparing values, behaviors, institutions, and organizations across nations.* Thousand Oaks, CA: Sage.

Hollenbeck, J. R., Ilgen, D. R., Sego, D. J., Hedlund, J., Major, D. A., & Phillips, J. (1995). Multilevel theory of team decision making: Decision performance in teams incorporating distributed expertise. *Journal of Applied Psychology, 80,* 292–316.

Ilgen, D. R., Hollenbeck, J. R., Johnson, M., & Jundt, D. (2005). Teams in organizations: From input-process-output models to IMOI models. *Annual Review of Psychology, 56,* 517–543.

Jackson, C. L. & LePine, J. A. (2003). Peer response to a team's weakest link: A test and extension of LePine and Van Dyne's model. *Journal of Applied Psychology, 88*(3), 459–475.

Janicik, G. A. & Bartel, C. A. (2003). Talking about time: Effects of temporal planning and time awareness norms on group coordination and performance. *Group Dynamics: Theory, Research, and Practice, 7,* 122–134.

Jansen, K. J. & Kristof-Brown, A. L. (2005). Marching to the beat of a different drummer: Examining the impact of pacing congruence. *Organizational Behavior and Human Decision Processes, 97,* 93–105.

Jehn, K. A. (1997). A qualitative analysis of conflict types and dimensions in organizational groups. *Administrative Science Quarterly, 42,* 530–557.

Jehn, K. A. & Mannix, E. A. (2001). The dynamic nature of conflict: A longitudinal study of intragroup conflict and group performance. *Academy of Management Journal, 44,* 238–251.

Johnson, J. L. & Podsakoff, P. M. (1994). Journal influence in the field of management: An analysis using Salancik's index in a dependency network. *Academy of Management Journal, 37,* 1392–1407.

Karau, S. J. & Kelly, J. R. (2004). Time pressure and team performance: An attentional focus integration. In S. Blount (Ed.), *Research on managing groups and teams: Time in groups* (Vol. 6, pp. 185–212). New York: Elsevier JAI.

Kelly, J. R. (1988). Entrainment in individual and group performance. In J. E. McGrath (Ed.), *The social psychology of time: New perspectives, Vol. 91* (pp. 89–110), Newbury Park, CA: Sage.

Kelly, J. R., Futoran, G. C., & McGrath, J. E. (1990). Capacity and capability: Seven studies of entrainment of task performance rates. *Small Group Research, 21,* 283–314.

Kelly, J. R. & McGrath, J. E. (1988). *On time and method.* Newbury Park, CA: Sage.

Kozlowski, S. W. J. & Bell, B. S. (2003). Work groups and teams in organizations. In W. C. Borman, D. R. Ilgen, & R. J. Klimoski (Eds.), *Handbook of psychology (Vol. 12):Industrial and organizational psychology* (pp. 333–375). New York: Wiley.

Kozlowski, S. W. J. & Klein, K. J. (2000). A multilevel approach to theory and research in organizations: Contextual, temporal, and emergent processes. In K. J. Klein & S. W. J. Kozlowski (Eds.), *Multilevel theory, research, and methods in organizations: Foundations, extensions, and new directions* (pp. 3–90). San Francisco, CA: Jossey-Bass.

Kristof-Brown, A. L., Jansen, K. J., & Colbert, A. E. (2002). A policy-capturing study of the simultaneous effects of fit with jobs, groups, and organizations. *Journal of Applied Psychology, 87*(5), 985–993.

Labianca, G., Moon, H., & Watt, I. (2005). When is an hour not 60 minutes? Deadlines, temporal schemata, and individual and task group performance. *Academy of Management Journal, 48*, 677–694.

Lee, H. (1999). Time and information technology: Monochronicity, polychronicity and temporal symmetry. *European Journal of Information Systems, 8*, 16–26.

Levine, R. V. (1988). The pace of life across cultures. In J. E. McGrath (Ed.), *The social psychology of time* (pp. 39–59). Newbury Park, CA: Sage Publications.

Lientz, B. P. & Rea, K. P. (2001). *Breakthrough technology project management*. London: Academic Press.

Marks, M. A., DeChurch, L. A., Mathieu, J. E., Panzer, F. J., & Alonso, A. (2005). Teamwork in multiteam systems. *Journal of Applied Psychology, 90*, 964–971.

Marks, M. A., Mathieu, J. E., & Zaccaro, S. J. (2001). A temporally based framework and taxonomy of team processes. *Academy of Management Review, 26*, 356–376.

Marks, M. A., Sabella, M. J., Burke, C. S., & Zaccaro, S. J. (2002). The impact of cross-training on team effectiveness. *Journal of Applied Psychology, 87*, 3–13.

Marks, M. A., Zaccaro, S. J., & Mathieu, J. E. (2000). Performance implications of leader briefings and team-interaction training for team adaptation to novel environments. *Journal of Applied Psychology, 85*, 971–986.

Mathieu, J. E., Heffner, T. S., Goodwin, G. F., Salas, E., & Cannon-Bowers, J. A. (2000). The influence of shared mental models on team process and performance. *Journal of Applied Psychology, 85*, 273–283.

Mathieu, J. M., Maynard, T., Rapp, T., & Gilson, L. (2008). Team effectiveness 1997–2007: A review of recent advancements and a glimpse into the future. *Journal of Management, 34*, 410–476.

Maznevski, M. L. & Chudoba, K. M. (2000). Bridging space over time: Global virtual team dynamics and effectiveness. *Organization Science, 11*, 473–492.

McGrath, J. E. (1991). Time, interaction, and performance (TIP): A theory of groups. *Small Group Research, 22*, 147–174.

McGrath, J. E. (1993). The JEMCO workshop: Description of a longitudinal study. *Small Group Research, 24*, 285–306.

McGrath, J. E. & Altermatt, T. W. (2001). Observation and analysis of group interaction over time: Some methodological and strategic choices. In M. A. Hogg & R. S. Tindale (Eds.), *Blackwell handbook of social psychology: Group processes* (Vol. 3, pp. 525–556). Oxford, England: Blackwell.

McGrath, J. E. & Argote, L. (2001). Group processes in organizational contexts. In M.A. Hogg & R. S. Tindale (Eds.), *Blackwell handbook of social psychology: Group processes* (Vol. 3, pp. 603–627). Oxford, England: Blackwell.

McGrath, J. E., Arrow, H., Gruenfeld, D. H., Hollingshead, A. B., & O'Connor, K. M. (1993). Groups, tasks, and technology: The effects of experience and change. *Small Group Research, 24*, 406–420.

McGrath, J. E. & Kelly, J. R. (1986). *Time and human interaction*. New York: Guilford.

McGrath, J. E. & Rotchford, N. L. (1983). Time and behavior in organizations. *Research in Organizational Behavior, 5*, 57–101.

Mitchell, T. R. & James, L. R. (2001). Building better theory: Time and the specification of when things happen. *Academy of Management Review, 26*, 530–547.

Mohammed, S. & Angell, L. (2004). Surface- and deep-level diversity in workgroups: Examining the moderating effects of team orientation and team process on relationship conflict. *Journal of Organizational Behavior, 25,* 1015–1039.

Mohammed, S. & Dumville, B. (2001). Team mental models in a team knowledge framework: Expanding theory and measurement across disciplinary boundaries. *Journal of Organizational Behavior, 22,* 89–106.

Mohammed, S., Klimoski, R., & Rentsch, J. R. (2000). The measurement of team mental models: We have no shared schema. *Organizational Research Methods, 3,* 123–165.

Montoya-Weiss, M. M., Massey, A. P., & Song, M. (2001). Getting it together: Temporal coordination and conflict management in global virtual teams. *Academy of Management Journal, 44,* 1251–1262.

Moreland, R. L. (1987). The formation of small groups. In C. Hendrick (Ed.), Review of personality and social psychology: Group processes (Vol. 8, pp. 80–110). Newbury Park, CA: Sage.

Moreland, R. L. & Levine, J. M. (1982). Socialization in small groups: Temporal changes in individual-group relations. In L. Berkowitz (Ed.), *Advances in experimental social psychology* (Vol. 15, pp. 137–192). New York: Academic Press.

Okhuysen, G. A. (2001). Structuring change: Familiarity and formal interventions in problem-solving groups. *Academy of Management Journal, 44,* 794–808.

Okhuysen, G. A. & Waller, M. J. (2002). Focusing on midpoint transitions: An analysis of boundary conditions. *Academy of Management Journal, 45,* 1056–1065.

Onken, M. H. (1999). Temporal elements of organizational culture and impact on firm performance. *Journal of Managerial Psychology, 14,* 231–243.

Perlow, L. A. (1999). The time famine: Toward a sociology of work time. *Administrative Science Quarterly, 44,* 57–81.

Podsakoff, P. M., MacKenzie, S. B., Lee, J., & Podsakoff, N. P. (2003). Common method biases in behavioral research: A critical review of the literature and recommended remedies. *Journal of Applied Psychology, 88,* 879–903.

Rastegary, H. & Landy, F. J. (1993). The interactions among time urgency, uncertainty, and time pressure. In O. Svenson and A. J. Maule (Eds.), *Time pressure and stress in human judgment and decision-making* (pp. 217–240). New York: Plenum Press.

Rentsch, J. R. & Klimoski, R. J. (2001). Why do 'great minds' think alike? Antecedents of team member schema agreement. *Journal of Organizational Behavior, 22,* 107–120.

Schriber, J. B. & Gutek, B. A. (1987). Some time dimensions of work: Measurement of an underlying aspect of organization culture. *Journal of Applied Psychology, 72,* 642–650.

Seers, A. & Woodruff, S. (1997). Temporal pacing in task forces: Group development or deadline pressure? *Journal of Management, 23,* 169–187.

Shah, P. & Jehn, K. (1993). Do friends perform better than acquaintances? The interaction of friendship, conflict, and task. *Group Decision and Negotiation, 2,* 149–166.

Svenson, O. & Benson, L., III (1993). Framing and time pressure in decision making. In O. Svenson & A. J. Maule (Eds.), *Time pressure and stress in human judgment and decision making* (pp. 133–144). New York: Plenum.

Tuckman, B. W. & Jensen, M. A. C. (1977). Stages of small-group development revisited. *Group and Organization Studies, 2,* 419–427.

Tukel, O. I. & Rom, W. O. (1998). Analysis of the characteristics of projects in diverse industries. *Journal of Operations Management, 16*, 43–61.

Vesey, J. T. (1991). The new competitors: They think in terms of speed to market. *Academy of Management Executive, 5*, 23–33.

Waller, M. J., Conte, J. M., Gibson, C. B., & Carpenter, M. A. (2001). The effect of individual perceptions of deadlines on team performance. *Academy of Management Review, 26*, 586–600.

Waller, M. J., Giambatista, R. C., & Zellmer-Bruhn, M. E. (1999). The effects of individual time urgency on group polychronicity. *Journal of Managerial Psychology, 14*, 244–256.

Waller, M. J., Zellmer-Bruhn, M. E., & Giambatista, R. C. (2002). Watching the clock: Group pacing behavior under dynamic deadlines. *Academy of Management Journal, 45*, 1046–1055.

Zaheer, S., Albert, S., & Zaheer, A. (1999). Time scales and organizational theory. *Academy of Management Review, 24*, 725–741.

Zimbardo, P. G. & Boyd, J. N. (1999). Putting time in perspective: A valid, reliable individual-differences metric. *Journal of Personality and Social Psychology, 77*, 1271–1288.

Section III

Measurement Tools

13

Measuring Teams in Action: Automated Performance Measurement and Feedback in Simulation-Based Training

David Dorsey, Steven Russell,
Charles Keil, Gwendolyn Campbell,
Wendi Van Buskirk, and Peter Schuck

Anyone who has ever watched a high-performance team in action can appreciate the extent to which teams can communicate, coordinate, and integrate dynamically to achieve results. This is true across domains—be it a sports team, military unit, business team, or medical unit. However, such seamless performance does not happen instantaneously. Teams form, develop, and change over time (often over substantial periods of time). Thus, organizations that rely on teams continue to search for performance measurement and training technologies that can give teams an edge in developing and reaching optimal performance.

This pursuit is aided by a rich and steadily growing domain of instructional technologies (Seels & Richey, 1994). From blackboards to virtual reality simulators, educational and training specialists continue to develop new tools and technologies for instruction. However, many of these technologies have been developed and evaluated only within the confines of traditional academic settings and only in the context of training individual technical skills. Thus, current and future research must continue to focus on developing technology-enabled interventions that can be used to train teams (and teamwork skills) in the context of dynamic, real-world environments.

An important platform for such research is the use of virtual and simulation-based training systems (Salas, Stagl, & Burke, 2004). Various industries and sectors of the economy, such as the military, have steadily increased investment in such systems, based on the view that such systems offer safer, more cost-effective means to train team skills relevant to operating in dangerous and complex environments. However, before the promise of simulation-based team training can be realized, a number of challenges must be addressed. First, researchers and practitioners must continue to move beyond a technology-centric view of training. That is, technologies, in and of themselves, are not training interventions—they serve merely as vehicles for interventions (Dorsey, Campbell, & Russell, in press; Salas & Cannon-Bowers, 2001). Some researchers have recognized this challenge and have developed training models that tie an explicit focus on learning objectives and interventions to the use of simulation/scenario-based systems (e.g., the Event-Based Approach to Training; ibid.).

Second, simulation-based systems place a substantial burden on human instructors as they attempt to gather objective performance information to assess and diagnose performance (Bolton, Dorsey, & Campbell, 2004). This challenge is amplified when training interventions move beyond the level of individual teams to address "teams of teams," as is the case with multitier, distributed team systems (Weil, Hussain, Diedrich, Ferguson, & MacMillan, 2004). In addition, the realistic nature of performance within dynamic team training systems actually complicates measurement. In contrast to traditional or "static" assessment approaches, the stimuli or assessment content of higher-fidelity simulations may not be fully known a priori (Gunnar et al., 2000). Instead, each new simulation/scenario run generates a unique set of stimulus-response combinations. A scenario designed originally to elicit examples of technical performance may turn into an exercise in team-supporting behavior if one team member fails to meet his or her role requirements. Thus, a performance standard (or set of criteria) is required that can facilitate evaluating performance against a changing environmental landscape. Traditionally, this challenge is handled by using "over the shoulder" performance raters or evaluators. However, in distributed team systems, capturing all relevant examples of performance via human observation can be difficult, especially if the purpose of such observation is to provide contiguous or immediate feedback.

To summarize, the challenge of "measuring and training teams in action" is a multifaceted endeavor that raises issues such as (1) what types of technologies enable effective measurement and training, (2) what types of embedded interventions enable effective learning, and (3) to what extent previous research in more static, academic, and individual skill domains can be generalized. Given this broad statement of challenges, there are two goals associated with this chapter. First, a program of research being pursued by the chapter authors is described, which focuses on specific automated strategies for measurement and instruction in team-oriented virtual and simulation-based environments. In describing this program, related research in the areas of automated assessment, performance measurement, and feedback generation and delivery is highlighted (especially as they relate to team performance). Second, unresolved research questions that are ripe for further investigation are delineated.

Foundations

Model-Based Feedback

Currently, a program of applied research is being pursued by the authors that is focused on two technical and methodological challenges:

1. Measuring teamwork performance during simulation-based training exercises via automated collection and analysis of team performance patterns.
2. Providing a basis for automated, tailored feedback about teamwork skills.

This program draws on various interdisciplinary research threads, including feedback and learning theories and techniques, computational modeling, and simulation-based training principles. These threads are incorporated in a central, driving concept that has been labeled *model-based feedback* (Bolton, Buff, & Campbell, 2003). Here, *model* refers to a computational human behavior representation (HBR) that has been constructed for use in training. Such models can be rooted in a variety of computer-based (e.g., simulation, expert systems, cognitive modeling architectures) and mathematical (e.g., matrix algebra, network analysis, discrete and continuous equations) formalisms (Carley, 1995). A simple and concrete example of model-based feedback is provided by Campbell, Buff, and Bolton (2006). These authors calculated linear regression equations to describe how both trainees and referent experts made tactical decisions regarding whether a track on a radar screen was friendly or hostile, using cues such as speed, altitude, a voluntary identification signal (IFF), and a radar signal (EWS). Subsequently, qualitative feedback was provided based on whether the trainee weighted cues in a manner similar to the experts. For example, if a trainee failed to weight "speed" as a significant cue, feedback such as the following was provided:

> The expert also takes speed into consideration when trying to identify the intent of unknown tracks. In particular, according to the expert, faster tracks are more likely to be hostile.

The models used in Intelligent Tutoring Systems (ITS) to represent expert and student knowledge are another example of HBRs. Many of these models are used to diagnose trainee deficiencies and to generate instructional materials. Typically, ITS rely on symbolic, rule-based approaches for model building, such as those found in cognitive modeling architectures (e.g., Adaptive Control of Thought-Rational [ACT-R], COGNET/iGEN, and Soar; Bolton et al., 2003). Because ITS models often represent what a student or trainee should be doing, given a current state of the problem or the environment, they offer an intriguing remedy for the problem of dynamic performance assessment described earlier (i.e., changing assessment stimuli).

The modeling approaches used in our research diverge somewhat from those used in ITS. Specifically, rather than using existing cognitive architectures, we have investigated the use of mathematical and statistical models as a basis for capturing and understanding team-related performance patterns to assess performance and generate tailored feedback. As elaborated as follows, the impetus for the investigation of quantitative models stems from the possibility that such models might be easier to construct, more parsimonious, and possibly equally effective approaches to model development, when behavior is being modeled at a high, coarse level of granularity (e.g., representing basic procedural task performance; Beck & Woolf, 2000a, 2000b). Such applications of computational models stand in contrast to efforts to model behavior (or cognition) at a "micro" level (Gray & Boehm-Davis, 2000), which is often a stated goal in using cognitive modeling architectures such as ACT-R.

Mathematical models are potentially viable tools to facilitate automated or semiautomated performance assessment and feedback generation for a variety of reasons. First, much of the teamwork behavior of current interest involves decision making (e.g., deciding when to back up a teammate, deciding when and how to pass information to a teammate). Correspondingly, there is a rich history of psychological research on modeling decision making using mathematical and statistical models. This stream of research dates back to Brunswik's (1955) foundational work on the "lens model." Second, mathematical models of judgment have been used historically not only as methods to describe judgment but also as methods to diagnose underlying reasoning strategies (Brehmer, 1981). Third, because teams can be viewed as complex, adaptive systems (Ilgen, Hollenbeck, Johnson, & Jundt, 2005), a wealth of interdisciplinary mathematical tools designed for studying dynamic systems may be relevant. Such tools include differential equations, finite-automata, logic and graphical models, machine learning algorithms, and sequential decision processes (Singh, James, & Rudary, 2004).

Considering these various types of modeling tools, an important and unresolved question is what level of model complexity—which can be conceptualized in a number of ways (e.g., number of free parameters, number of lines of code, amount of knowledge engineering or task analysis required)—or features of models are necessary to support dynamic performance assessment and intelligent feedback and instruction, in domains such as team training? The answer to this question has not been fully investigated. In fact, there have been very few direct comparisons of modeling approaches for generating model-based feedback. An exception to this dearth of research is work by Bolton, Holness, Buff, and Campbell (2001). Bolton and colleagues demonstrated that several mathematical modeling techniques were effective at reliably extracting patterns from a set of performance data. Moreover, Bolton et al. (2003) went further and demonstrated that these techniques were as effective as more complex cognitive architecture models at generating useful instruction for individual taskwork skills. Such research is in alignment with general findings from more than 30 years of decision-making research, which has shown that more complex models are not always better at approximating outcomes of interest (Dawes, 1979; Gigerenzer, 2004).

While it is not currently known what types or levels of models are necessary or sufficient for applications such as automated team performance measurement and feedback generation, model efficacy will likely be context and task dependent. Thus, a general principle of quantitative modeling is typically followed, which states that "all models are wrong" (MacCallum, 1998) and that model choice should be based on balancing validity, parsimony, and usefulness. Moreover, for use in training applications, models must demonstrate "diagnostic validity" over and above predictive validity—that is, models are only useful to the extent that they can help generate feedback that improves performance.

Despite the type of model used, the first step in any modeling effort is to clearly define the phenomenon or domain of interest. Thus, in the following section, we turn to various definitions of teamwork.

Definition of Teamwork

Team performance can be conceptualized at multiple levels, including the level of individual taskwork and the level of team interactions (e.g., Kozlowski & Bell, 2002). Moreover, there is a host of taxonomies of teamwork skills available in the literature (Salas et al., 2004). Thus, for any given research effort, an operational definition of teamwork is required. For example, for the research program described in this chapter, the initial focus is on the teamwork skill of *supporting behavior*. Supporting behavior is demonstrated through either correcting performance errors or backing up teammates. This is one of four dimensions of teamwork in the Team Dimensional Training taxonomy (Smith-Jentsch, Johnston, & Payne, 1998). This taxonomy has been supported empirically and is particularly relevant to the types of military teams of current interest in our research (ibid.).

Once a particular taxonomy of teamwork skills has been defined, there are still several significant challenges associated with extending modeling to the study of teamwork. First, empirical models typically require a large number of data points to detect reliable patterns. Teamwork behaviors, such as error correction or backup behaviors, generally occur at a much lower base rate than taskwork actions. Second, many elements of teamwork occur using natural language. This imposes the requirement that spoken interactions among teammates be captured and represented in a format that can be used in modeling efforts. Moreover, effective teamwork requires shifts in attention from a focus on one's own taskwork to effectively monitoring others and the team environment to coordinate, support others, and generally act as a team (Kozlowski, Gully, Nason, & Smith, 1999). Thus, modeling efforts must directly reflect a type of dynamic utility estimation that involves knowing when to attend to one's own technical tasks versus supporting a teammate.

It is important to emphasize that supporting behavior is only one dimension of effective team performance. Potentially, the idea of creating a computational human performance model to guide dynamic performance assessment and feedback generation is generalizable to other team performance dimensions. For example, Yin, Miller, Ioerger, Yen, and Volz (2000) discussed the modeling of team characteristics such as the sharing of responsibilities and team communication patterns, using a combination of agent- and state-based modeling formalisms.

Leveraging Ideas from the Feedback Literature

In complex team systems, human instructors "in the loop" are faced with the difficult challenge of tracking relevant trainee actions. To assist instructors, a great deal of applied research is being directed toward measurement mechanisms that can be embedded in automated team training systems (Johnston, Freeman, & Serfaty, 2003). In considering such systems, some amount of *backward design* (Wiggins & McTighe, 1998) is warranted. Specifically, when the type of feedback that would help improve performance is known, then the appropriate mechanisms for generating such feedback can be developed, including using various types of computational models. The following sections review various types and models of feedback.

Types of Feedback

In its most basic form, *descriptive feedback* simply lets trainees know "what happened" (Cannon-Bowers & Salas, 1997; Kozlowski et al., 1999). For example, students may be told, "You solved 17 out of 20 problems correctly." However, without being able to interpret feedback relative to a standard, feedback has little impact on performance (e.g., Kluger & DeNisi, 1996). Thus, *evaluative feedback* provides feedback relative to some type of performance standard, which allows a trainee to cognitively process feedback and decide on a course of action.

Even if trainees receive evaluative feedback and decide to attempt to improve their performance, they may not have the knowledge required.

This gap is filled by *process feedback* (e.g., Atkins, Wood, & Rutgers, 2002). The most obvious type of process feedback is to simply tell trainees what process they should follow and reinforce such procedures with repeated practice (e.g., Ericsson, Krampe, & Tesch-Römer, 1993). However, although such guidance might lead to short-term improvements, long-term results are not assured. Thus, additional interventions such as discovery training have been developed. Discovery training is an inductive method of instruction, where students must explore and experiment to infer and learn strategies for effective performance. Following this model, feedback is most useful if it allows trainees to infer the underlying principles of performance (Kirlik, Fisk, Walker, & Rothrock, 1998).

Various models for getting trainees to explore or discover aspects of performance have been developed. For example, *scaffolding* can be used to gradually lead trainees toward understanding through a series of hints during performance (e.g., Aleven & Koedinger, 2002). This process reflects an effort to encourage trainees to be active, engaging in a learning process rather than passively accepting instruction. A number of researchers have argued that encouraging various types of self-regulation is a key function of feedback (e.g., Kozlowski et al., 1999).

The use of facilitated or active reflection has been shown to be effective in training teams. For example, in the Guided Team Self-Correction (GTSC) process (Smith-Jentsch, Zeisig, Acton, & McPherson, 1998), the instructor's primary role is to facilitate a process of *group reflection* on completion of a scenario. Such reflection is intended to target specific dimensions of effective teamwork. While an instructor might provide observations, the focus of this type of training intervention is for team members to gain insight into their own team processes and performance. Great strides have been made in automating processes such as cueing, scaffolding, and encouraging reflection (Aleven & Koedinger, 2002; Cohen, Freeman, & Thompson, 1998; Cohen & Thompson, 2001).

Intelligent Tutoring Systems

ITS architectures generally include the following components: generative feedback, student modeling, expert modeling, instructional modeling, mixed-initiative dialogues, and self-improvement (Woolf, Beck, Eliot, & Stern, 2001). Of most direct relevance to our research are the concepts of expert modeling, generative feedback, and mixed initiative dialogues.

The term *expert model* corresponds to components within an ITS that encode and approximate expert-level knowledge or performance. Principally, such models serve as a performance standard, against which student performance can be evaluated. Expert models can range from *black-box* models (Anderson, 1988), which match student answers against a known, stored criterion, to more advanced cognitive tutors, which can explain their reasoning (McArthur, Lewis, & Bishay, 1993).

The ITS concept of generative feedback encompasses various capabilities to generate and deliver appropriate instructional guidance, including elements like problems, hints, and suggestions, based on student performance (Woolf et al., 2001). More advanced ITS solutions go beyond just providing "canned" responses; instead, they generate unique content dynamically.

The ITS concept of mixed-initiative corresponds to mechanisms for students to learn via a conversational dialogue with the ITS. While there are many topics that could be explored in such dialogues, Schank and Neaman (2001) articulated a model of learning that centers on the necessity of exploring failures. In Schank and Neaman's model, students are motivated to perform at a level where failure is likely and then are given mechanisms to explore failures via a question-and-answer process and access to expert responses. For our purposes, this corresponds conceptually to providing paths for trainees to explore critical behaviors that were not performed.

Feedback and Sequencing in Dynamic Decision-Making Environments

Some of the previously reviewed instructional strategies provide a fairly continuous stream of feedback to trainees. This is consistent with well-accepted principles that feedback should be provided contiguous to performance (Goldstein & Ford, 2002; Kozlowski et al., 1999). However, some research has shown that feedback given too frequently, or in "real time," can be detrimental, distracting trainees from concentrating on performance (Kluger & DeNisi, 1996). This facet of feedback is of particular concern in scenario-based, team training environments, where the demand on trainees' limited cognitive resources must be monitored and controlled. In general, both the nature and timing of feedback are more difficult to optimize in dynamic decision environments (Diehl & Sterman, 1995). This may account for the finding that feedback has not generally proven to be effective in improving performance in dynamic decision-making environments (Gonzalez, 2005). Recent research suggests that *feedforward*, which allowed learners to watch and consider the performance of experts, was more effective than other forms of feedback, even when individuals were not consciously aware of the heuristics that the expert used (ibid.).

Another critical, unresolved factor in training teams in dynamic environments is how feedback and training content should be sequenced. For example, Adaptive Guidance (AG; Bell & Kozlowski, 2002) training includes the provision of feedback regarding current progress toward task mastery (self-evaluation), suggestions for what to study based on progress (self-monitoring), and interpretation of trainee progress to build self-efficacy (self-reactions). Bell and Kozlowski emphasized that learning objectives within AG must be sequenced from very basic to complex to maximize training effectiveness and to build self-efficacy during early learning trials, when negative discrepancies are likely to exist between goals and performance. AG is an extension of *advisement* research, which shows that guiding trainees through computer-based instruction is more effective than extending complete control of the training environment to either the trainee or a computer program (Tennyson, 1980; Tennyson & Buttrey, 1980).

However, the issue of providing feedback in dynamic environments is still an open question. For example, Gibson (2003) asked participants to engage in a dynamic, one-on-one negotiation task with simulated opponents. In some conditions, participants interacted with opponents that were programmed to consistently use a complex negotiation strategy. In other conditions, participants interacted with opponents that progressively used more complex negotiation strategies (similar to Bell and Kozlowski's "sequencing" idea). Subsequently, Gibson found that during a final "transfer" task, participants who had learned by interacting with the consistently complex opponents performed better than participants who had learned with a series of "evolving" opponents.

Bringing It All Together: A Proposed Technical Approach

In the previous sections, a broad overview of various research areas that have influenced the current program of research has been provided. These include learning theories and techniques, computational modeling, and simulation-based training principles. In the following sections, a specific technical approach is described, which features a method of automated performance measurement and feedback generation that is targeted toward the training of teamwork skills.

Task Domain

In our research, we are currently using an artificial domain that is modeled loosely after the U.S. Navy Air Defense Warfare (ADW) mission. To protect the security interests of Navy ADW teams, all technical details associated with actual tactics and operational capabilities were changed. Moreover, to facilitate collecting data with diverse types of participants (e.g., college students), the mission was simplified, team size was decreased, and system interfaces were dramatically modified. Also, to elicit teamwork behavior, the assignment of responsibilities to team members was modified.

The resulting domain requires a two-person command-and-control team for the following purposes:

1. To collect data and determine the identity of unknown aircraft in the airspace around their simulated "ship."
2. To evaluate the level of threat that each of these aircraft poses.
3. To interact with these aircraft according to strictly defined rules of engagement (ROE).

Although studies using two-person teams are currently being conducted under this program of research, a three-person version of this tactical team has been created as well.

The team leader is referred to as an antiair warfare commander (AAWC). The primary supporting team member is the air intercept controller (AIC). The AAWC is responsible for making the final decisions regarding an aircraft's identity and level of threat. There are several sources of information available to help make these decisions. The AAWC can access some of this information directly through his or her own workstation. Other types of information must be accessed through a request to the other team member. The AAWC is also responsible for any necessary weapons engagements. The team has a small number of simulated Navy pilots flying aircraft in the airspace around their ship, and the AIC is responsible for monitoring, allocating, and protecting these friendly air assets, called defensive counter air (DCA).

Coordination is required for each of the teammates to perform the task. As one example, the AAWC is responsible for obtaining certain types of information about unknown aircraft to make identifications. One source of information on these unknown aircraft is the character readout (CRO) display, which logs general flight characteristics. A second method for obtaining information is to request that the AIC obtain a visual identification (VID) by vectoring a DCA.

In addition to the previously described coordination activities, team members may support each other through specific backup and error correction actions. Some of these teamwork behaviors occur through the system, via keystrokes, whereas other teamwork actions are executed verbally. A speech recognition system is currently undergoing development to capture such actions as part of the automated performance measurement system.

As is hopefully evident from the preceding descriptions, team roles are distinct from one another, yet the successful completion of a scenario requires coordination and cooperation. In addition, the criticality of any particular action clearly depends on the current status of the environment. For example, identifying an unknown aircraft that has appeared at the far boundary of the radar screen (an AAWC task) is likely to be less critical than sending a warning to a hostile aircraft that has moved within 50 nautical miles (NM) of your ship. However, identifying an unknown aircraft that has suddenly popped up on the radar within 30 NM of the ship is likely to be more important than giving that same warning. Experience to date suggests that when paired with appropriately designed scenarios, there are times in this task domain when teamwork actions may be more critical than taskwork actions (and vice versa). Thus, this domain satisfies a key assumption underlying this research effort, which is that action criticalities must be assessed in context.

The task domain just described has been instantiated in a suite of software programs called the Team Aegis Simulation Platform (TASP; Bhandarkar, Thiruvengada, Rothrock, Campbell, & Bolton, 2004). The data collection and recording capabilities of this test bed are extensive. System data, including the characteristics of all simulated entities in the environment, are updated and recorded at 6 second intervals. Multimodal performance data, including speech, are automatically time stamped and recorded during a scenario run. Data are stored at multiple levels of analysis. At the lowest level, all raw keystrokes and mouse movements are stored. Simultaneously, these actions are aggregated into unit tasks, such as issuing a warning to a hostile aircraft that flies too close to the ship.

Finally, a performance measurement system is embedded in the test bed. This performance assessment system employs the *windows of opportunity* (WOOP) paradigm that has been used successfully to assess taskwork performance in previous research (Rothrock, 2001). This paradigm has been extended to include teamwork assessment by noting opportunities to provide backup and error correction to teammates. Thus, the data collection capabilities of this test bed satisfy two additional requirements of this research—that all relevant system and environment cues and all trainee actions can be captured.

Conceptual Approach to Model Development

An initial modeling strategy that is being evaluated is based on the idea of estimating context sensitive and action criticalities and of using that information to assess a trainee's performance. That is, what should the operator be doing in a given time period, given the state of the scenario/simulation environment? This type of modeling strategy requires capturing expert judgments of action criticality, based on environmental and system cues. As such, this modeling approach follows an extensive literature of modeling decision making, based on cue to decision variable mappings (e.g., Campbell et al., 2006; Dorsey & Coovert, 2003; Rothrock & Kirlik, 2003). The actual procedures used to develop "cue profiles" and to elicit expert judgments concerning relevant actions are described in a following section.

Note that the most direct extension of the individual taskwork modeling that has been done in previous research (e.g., Campbell et al., 2006) would involve building separate models for each teamwork behavior and to use those models to identify the cues that initiate that particular type of behavior for an individual. However, this approach suffers from the problem mentioned earlier of insufficient data. For example, in a scenario of moderate length, there is no way to expose a trainee to all possible combinations of contexts that might or might not induce a particular type of backup action.

To resolve this issue, the modeling challenge was reformulated. The proposed solution was to shift the focus to a broader perspective and view working within a team as a multitasking situation. Specifically, each teammate must determine when to engage in taskwork versus teamwork behaviors, and these two classes of behavior will often compete for attention. From this perspective, the objective of modeling becomes selecting the most important action from a competing set of possibilities. An advantage of this approach is that each action taken becomes a data point reflecting that person's strategy of choosing among multiple candidate actions. Thus, the low base rate problem is to some extent minimized.

This shift in modeling strategies required a mathematical or computational model that was capable of dynamically capturing the relative criticality of each major action (either for teamwork or taskwork) at each time, t, in a scenario. Developing this type of model required a way to capture and link expert judgments of criticality to environmental and system cues. A subject matter expert (SME) panel process was used to gather such judgments, as is discussed in a later section.

Figure 13.1 presents a conceptual overview of our proposed modeling approach. As shown in this figure, a computational model would be developed, based on a set of "weights," that would effectively create a multivariate mapping, predicting the criticality of various actions from system input variables. As suggested already, using a multivariate model would allow examination of multiple, viable actions within a given time window. That is, more than one action might be viable (i.e., critical), based on the cues available in the environment. Consequently, trainees could be evaluated based on whether they chose one of the more critical actions that were "afforded" by the environment. An initial mathematical formalism that was chosen to operationally define this conceptual model is elaborated on in the next section.

Mathematical Formalism and Modeling Properties

Having developed a conceptual approach to modeling, relevant literature was reviewed to identify specific mathematical or statistical techniques that could be used to operationalize and implement the modeling

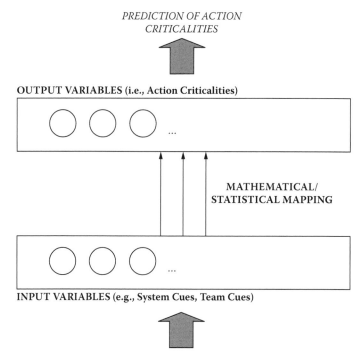

PREDICTION OF ACTION
CRITICALITIES

OUTPUT VARIABLES (i.e., Action Criticalities)

MATHEMATICAL/
STATISTICAL MAPPING

INPUT VARIABLES (e.g., System Cues, Team Cues)

FIGURE 13.1
Conceptual diagram of computational model.

strategy. Both traditional multivariate statistical models and alternative approaches such as machine learning algorithms were reviewed. Examples of models found in the literature include various connectionist models (e.g., Gibson, Fichman, & Plaut, 1997), canonical correlation models (e.g., Shafto, Degani, & Kirlik, 1997), various types of Markov models (e.g., Liu & Salvucci, 2001), and models based on Bayesian networks (e.g., Mulgund & Zacharias, 1996).

Despite finding a variety of potential modeling approaches, it was unclear whether there was sufficient working knowledge of the domain to resort to purely empirical methods. Specifically, computational models can be thought of in terms of black-box versus *white-box* models, according to how much a priori information is used (Lindskog, 1997). A black-box model consists of empirically identified relationships, without reference to a priori information. In contrast, a white-box model is often an analytical model, where all necessary information is specified a priori. Consequently, it was decided to start modeling efforts with a white-box, analytical model, based on a linear, matrix algebra formalism and devised to capture the basic system dynamics between cues in the environment and expert actions. In our view, such a model afforded a compact, transparent representation of the dynamic modeling problem, which would allow the testing of general modeling ideas prior to engaging in more advanced, empirical modeling efforts. An overview of this approach is outlined in the following section.

Mathematical Formalism

Through work with SMEs, a set of cue profiles mapped to a closed set of operator tasks/actions was defined. This set of operator actions contains both taskwork and teamwork (supporting behavior) actions. The cues are binary (present/absent), and a cue profile is associated with each action, such that when the profile is present, a particular action is "afforded" by the environment and is appropriate. Thus, at each time period, t, in a scenario, the presence or absence of all possible cues can be summarized as a vector of binary values,

$$C = [c_1 \quad c_2 \quad \ldots \quad c_j]$$

This vector represents the current state of the "problem space."

Likewise, the set of appropriate behaviors at any point in time, t, can also be summarized in a vector of values,

$$B = [b_1 \quad b_2 \quad \ldots \quad b_k]$$

Because the vector of cues **C** determines the appropriateness of behaviors in vector **B**, it is possible to develop a matrix that summarizes the relationship between the cues and behaviors. This matrix, called a linear transformation matrix, **T**, consists of a set of weights that directly links the cues to the behaviors. Using matrix algebra, the cue matrix, **C**, is multiplied by the linear transformation matrix, **T**, to yield a vector of values ranging from 0 to 1, **B**:

$$[c_1 \cdots c_j] * \begin{bmatrix} t_{1,1} & \cdots & t_{1,k} \\ \vdots & & \vdots \\ t_{j,1} & \cdots & t_{j,k} \end{bmatrix} = [b_1 \cdots b_k]$$

Another way of thinking about this operation is as follows. To understand what operator actions should be viable options or choices at each time, t, the cues currently in the environment, **C**, are multiplied by a matrix of weights, **T**, to arrive at what actions were "instantiated" for a given time period (the weight matrix essentially aggregates how many cues were present for each action, resulting in **B**, a vector of behaviors/actions). Each element in **B** takes on a value in the interval [0,1], where 0 means that none of the cues were present and 1 means that all of the cues were present. Values between 0 and 1 mean that some subset of cues was present for a given action. Based on SME input, initial models will be noncompensatory, meaning that if any cue is missing for a given action, experts would not take that action. Subsequently, the values in the behavior vector will be dichotomized (using a nonlinear "thresholding" operation), with all values less than 1 being truncated to 0.

Within the behavior vector **B**, the relative importance or criticality of the behaviors will vary at a given point of time. In other words, during the course of a TASP scenario, one plausible behavior may be more critical than another plausible behavior. Thus, the final step in determining operator actions involves assigning the relative importance/criticality to each behavior. This involves multiplying the vector of appropriate behaviors, **B**, by a diagonal matrix of the associated importance/criticality weights, **I**, that were assigned a priori by experts:

$$[b_1 \ ... \ b_k] \Rightarrow Dichotomize \ [b_1 \ ... \ b_k]$$

$$[b_1 \cdots b_k] * \begin{bmatrix} i_{1,1} & 0 & 0 \\ 0 & \ddots & 0 \\ 0 & 0 & i_{k,k} \end{bmatrix} = [e_1 \cdots e_k]$$

This multistep map yields a final vector, **E**, which represents "expected actions." Specifically, the elements with the highest values in **E** correspond to the most important/critical behaviors, given the current state of the scenario and simulation environment, as summarized in the original cue vector, **C**.

Concurrently, we plan to capture, at each time period, t, whether a trainee engaged in a critical action, according to the model. That is, did the trainee engage in one of the elements/actions in **E** that equals (max (**E**))? If not, the missed opportunities would be tracked to populate a database of possible instructional events. Moreover, outcome or output matrices can be constructed. For example, one type of output matrix is a matrix specifying the set of expected actions across all time periods. Consequently, it may be possible to "decompose" such a matrix using mathematical techniques to derive specific, quantitative measures of scenario difficulty or complexity.

A few properties of the modeling approach previously described are noteworthy. First, this approach is closely aligned to various models for predictive representations of state (e.g., Markov models; Singh et al., 2004). In fact, the current modeling approach can be conceived as a Markov process, in that the probability of actions is only dependent on the current environmental state. Conceptually (and possibly in practice), the importance/criticality values attached to operator actions can be thought of as transition probabilities (i.e., the more important the action, given the current state, the higher the probability of engaging in that action). Second, from a decision analysis point of view, the current approach can be thought of as calculating a type of utility (Busemeyer & Johnson, 2004), using a matrix-based system of linear equations. The criticality values in this modeling approach can be thought of as utility values (i.e., more critical actions are likely to have a higher "payoff"). This approach features something like a real-time utility estimation, in the sense that actions "compete" for the operator's attention, and the utility associated with actions is a deterministic function of the criticality ratings provided a priori by SMEs.

SME Procedures

As with any type of model development, some type of task analysis or knowledge engineering is required to capture critical information for model development. As such, a brief, high-level overview of the SME procedures used for model development is provided. These activities are discussed in terms of developing the AIC model, although the steps would be the same for other roles in this task domain.

Based on a review of fundamental rules of engagement and additional background materials, a preliminary matrix of actions and associated cue profiles relevant to the AIC role was developed. During a subsequent meeting, SMEs reviewed and edited the preliminary matrix, expanding the number of cues and actions.

Next, SMEs sorted the various AIC actions into high, moderate, and low criticality categories, based largely on rules of engagement and expert strategies. Additional distinctions were made within categories to further rank order the actions in terms of relative criticality (resulting in six levels of criticality). Where SMEs believed that the criticality of an action would vary based on environmental conditions, additional action/cue profiles were created to account for these distinctions. After several rounds of revision by SMEs, the action-to-cue profile matrix was integrated with the mathematical model development, using the approach previously discussed. To provide the reader with a concrete idea of how this modeling approach operates, Appendix A presents a practical example using the model of the AIC operator role.

Generating Model-Based Feedback

Based on the type of computational model contemplated herein, global assessments of the extent to which an individual trainee selected the most critical taskwork and teamwork actions within the context of a given scenario can be produced. The model can also be used to identify specific instances

Average criticality rating* of SUPPORTING OPPORTUNITIES:
Taken: 1.5
Missed: 3.0

Average criticality ratings of TASKWORK OPPORTUNITIES:
Taken: 4.5
Missed: 2.0

*Scale: 5–Highly Critical to 1–Not Critical

FIGURE 13.2
Example of summary-level performance information derived from modeling.

during a training scenario when the trainee made a poor action selection. This serves as the gateway to providing tailored, event-based feedback.

If the outlined computational approach is successful, then this technique can serve as the internal reasoning of an instructional agent. This agent can be embedded into the TASP test bed to act as a kind of "measurement engine" to predict on a dynamic basis the relative importance/criticality of various operator actions using algorithms from the computational model. Based on these estimated criticalities, various performance scores can be derived from trainees' performance. For example, the average criticality of actions/opportunities taken by a trainee can be contrasted with actions/ opportunities missed or not taken. This information can be reported to the trainee or instructor as performance measures, as shown in Figure 13.2. These model-based performance metrics can be used to indicate whether a given trainee is attending to the most critical actions and opportunities across the entire scenario. Such measures could be aggregated to various levels, possibly providing scores for various types of supporting behavior or taskwork actions. In addition, it may be possible to empirically validate such scores against evaluations from expert human raters.

The metrics provided by this modeling strategy can also be used to generate event-based feedback. Specifically, opportunities or actions that can be characterized as the most critical, based on the estimated criticalities derived from the computational model, could be presented to the trainee in a debriefing module to facilitate exploring or discovering why these critical opportunities were missed. A relatively small number of such critical opportunities could be presented in feedback (e.g., the three most critical missed actions), so that the trainee is not overwhelmed with information. Because the action criticalities are estimated dynamically within a given scenario run, it is probable that different trainees would have different actions/opportunities flagged. Thus, the feedback mechanism is adaptive—each time focusing on the types of opportunities the trainee missed during the last training exercise. As envisioned, information regarding the nature of the missed action/opportunity, when it occurred,

---

Below are the two most critical actions you missed during the last scenario. Click on the name of the action to learn more about it and then answer the assessment questions for each action.

1. Supporting Opportunity #1

   Help AIC vector DCA away from WEZ
   Estimated Criticality = 4.5
   Scenario time occurred = 10.5 minutes

   Assessment:

   1. If you did not recognize this opportunity or thought it was not important, click here.
   2. If you recognized this opportunity but did not know how to respond, click here.

2. Supporting Opportunity #2

   Provide AIC backup regarding DCA refueling
   Estimated Criticality = 4.2
   Scenario time occurred = 14.5 minutes

   Assessment:

   • If you did not recognize this opportunity or thought it was not important, click here.
   • If you recognized this opportunity but did not know how to respond, click here.

FIGURE 13.3
Example of event-based feedback derived from modeling.

and its estimated criticality would be presented for each missed action, as demonstrated in Figure 13.3.

Furthermore, for each of the "critical" missed actions provided to the trainee as feedback, a dialogue could ensue to help students diagnose why they did not respond to the opportunity or take the appropriate action. For example, Figure 13.3 introduces some diagnostic questions that could be posed to trainees to aid in the diagnosis. Each question or subset of questions corresponds to specific missed opportunities or actions. Depending on trainees' responses, they would receive different instructional information addressing either why certain actions were important (i.e., why to help) or how they should respond to the specific opportunity (i.e., how to help). Note that the idea of exploring specific instances of failure within a simulation environment is consistent with the idea of event- and scenario-based training, where "the scenario is the curriculum" (Salas, 2001, p. 26).

As a default, the type of feedback mechanism described here selects feedback based on the most critical actions missed during the exercise run. It is hypothesized that this type of mechanism will be effective, as the most basic feedback (i.e., the most critical actions) should be generated first. Subsequently, as trainees improve their performance, more subtle (and possibly strategic or teamwork-oriented) types of feedback will be generated, due to the fact that trainees will have "mastered the basics." As such, this type of feedback mechanism shares similarities with Bell and Kozlowski's AG feedback mechanism. However, rather than relying on an a priori prioritization of instructional material, instruction and feedback is generated adaptively, based on the needs of individual trainees. Note that exploration of the exact format of the feedback is still being conducted. As such, additional elements such as positive feedback, indicators of progress, or other feedback facets that facilitate self-regulatory processes (Kozlowski et al., 1999) may need to be incorporated.

Model Validation and Training Effectiveness Research

Because the instructional strategy outlined herein is multifaceted, containing aspects of computational modeling, providing tailored feedback, and facilitating the exploration of feedback, various types of validation and training effectiveness research are warranted.

Model Validation

The computational modeling approach proposed will require empirical validation to establish the degree to which the estimates of action criticality generated by the model match expert judgments regarding the priority and importance of actions. Currently, a validation plan is being developed. The plan will likely involve comparisons to direct SME judgments, as well as evaluations of model sensitivity to differences in the expertise of teams/trainees and differences in scenario difficulty. This type of validation primarily indicates internal validity—that is, that the model reasonably represents an expert perspective of action importance and that subsequent feedback (based on the trainee's actual actions) is in line with expected "instructional events." However, models must also not be "brittle"; they must maintain some degree of generalizability or external validity when applied to novel situations/inputs, different from those used during model development. To test this, models will be evaluated across different "teams" (i.e., different trainee role players) and scenarios.

Training Effectiveness

A laboratory-based training effectiveness study will follow validation efforts to assess the ability of the model-based feedback approach to support the instructional goal of improving team performance. Specifically, a set of teams will complete a series of scenarios to collect performance data. Between scenario runs, the teams will receive either model-based feedback, an alternative type of feedback currently employed by the U.S. Navy, or some combination of feedback types. Performance on a final set of scenarios will be compared to draw conclusions about the effectiveness of the feedback strategies. Following recent trends in team research, dependent variables will likely include affective, cognitive, and behavioral outcomes (at both individual and team levels; Chen, Thomas, & Wallace, 2005). Behavioral measures will tap both taskwork and teamwork (i.e., supporting behavior) constructs.

Summary and Future Research Needs

This chapter highlighted research designed to address two major challenges in developing effective teams. First, the challenge of measuring teamwork performance during action was addressed by exploring the use of tools such as a sophisticated team training test bed and concurrent assessment of performance against a computational representation or model of performance. A second challenge, the improvement of teamwork performance, was addressed by considering the use of model-based feedback, tailored to the needs of individual team members. Such feedback can be delivered in a manner that prompts exploratory or discovering learning. The research described in this chapter builds on prior work investigating intelligent tutoring systems (e.g., Woolf et al., 2001), performance in dynamic decision-making environments (e.g., Gonzalez, 2005), and model-based feedback (e.g., Bolton et al., 2003). In the final section, a number of research needs and areas for further exploration are put forth.

Earlier in this chapter, we described our work as drawing from various interdisciplinary research threads. Fortunately, this means that the number of potential directions for future research is both manifold and diverse. Hopefully, the research presented here will be of interest and use to scientists and practitioners in the areas of training and development, performance measurement, instructional design principles, computational modeling, and other areas. The following is a mere subset of potential directions, loosely categorized by the research challenges of (1) measuring teamwork performance, (2) improving teamwork performance, and (3) studying team formation and development.

Future Research Needs: Measuring Teamwork Performance

We have found that a number of research directions can be formulated simply by observing experts interact with a simulation. For instance, the nature of TASP's dynamic scenarios is such that teammates sometimes develop informal strategies to achieve success (e.g., visually "splitting" the screen so that each teammate is responsible for monitoring one half of the environment). Whether the proposed measurement approach is sensitive enough to detect teammate strategies, over and above basic performance criteria, represents one interesting area of exploration. Further, while the focus of much of the research discussed here has been at the individual level (training individuals to be better team members), one might ask whether models of performance can be developed at the team level, such that at any time during a scenario, the expected actions of all teammates are known. We believe that such a metamodel can be constructed. If possible, such a model would suggest new avenues for both team performance measurement and feedback research.

Woolf et al. (2001) hinted at a different research direction, pointing out various advantages to using mathematical and data-driven models in intelligent tutoring applications. Potential advantages include the ability to adapt models to individual students and the possibility of developing predictive "student models" that can be used to estimate parameters such as the probability that a trainee will miss the next item/action. Incorporating data-driven models in the present context opens up exciting possibilities, such as the use of item-response theory (IRT) models as a principled way to establish a trainee's ability, within the scope of intelligent tutoring (Beck & Woolf, 2000b; Mangos, 2004). The extent to which performance measurement capabilities can accommodate advanced measurement theories such as IRT could pave the way for additional innovative research. In general, the entire area of "authentic" assessment and automated scoring of assessment instruments is a burgeoning research area (Drasgow, Luecht, & Bennett, 2005).

Another area for research would involve using dynamic performance measurement models to improve scenario design within team simulation-based training systems. As suggested earlier, output from computational models may prove useful in constructing precise, quantitative estimates of scenario complexity or difficulty.

Future Research Needs: Improving Teamwork Performance

One immediate research need would be met by additional "training effectiveness" comparisons between "coarse-grained" model-based feedback such as the kind described here and more "fine-grained" model-based feedback that may be possible under cognitive architectures like ACT-R, COGNET/iGEN, and Soar. The broader level of modeling outlined in this chapter is hypothesized to be appropriate for generating feedback at the level of procedural behaviors or tasks. Fortunately, the proposed method of performance measurement lends itself to multiple modeling techniques. In addition, basic analytical models such as the modeling approach outlined here are extensible—new directions for extending such models include using machine learning or statistical algorithms to establish more complex cue to action weights or translating criticality values into transition probabilities (in something like a Markov or Bayesian formalism) to build a stochastic representation.

Another application of model-based feedback would be the development of a "rational agent" (Dal Forno & Merlone, 2002). That is, an intelligent agent acting on the basis of the modeling approach would assume a fully accessible environment that is sufficient to understand the current state and to choose from a fixed set of actions accordingly. This agent could interact intelligently with trainees as a "synthetic" teammate capable of providing the same types of "cueing" and "scaffolding" feedback as more traditional training vehicles.

Another research direction worth mentioning is the potential application of the proposed modeling approach to create training-oriented situational judgment tests (SJTs; Fritzsche, Stagl, Salas, & Burke, 2006). Historically, SJTs have been used as an employee selection tool, requiring job applicants to identify effective and ineffective solutions to problems that can surface in the workplace. However, by establishing links between cues in the environment and plausible operator actions, we have assembled a virtual "item pool" for a training-oriented SJTs. Specifically, trainees could view either video or still images of the TASP environment, select a most effective behavior, and receive a score that is based on a comparison with SME behaviors. Where trainees deviate from the expert model, a feedback intervention would be invoked. This type of SJT intervention would work well as a precursor to more costly, high-fidelity simulator training. Specifically, by "knowing what students know" (National Research Council, 2001), using low fidelity SJT-type measures, basic gaps in declarative and procedural knowledge could be addressed prior to training in higher-fidelity learning environments. Such a practice may facilitate more efficient training, as trainees take advantage of richer, higher-fidelity learning environments to hone more advanced, strategic skills rather than spending time trying to learn the basics. The practice of matching the fidelity of learning and assessment tools to stages of development may be a promising area for future research.

Future Research Needs: Studying Team Formation and Development

Before teams can be trained and reach adequate levels of performance, they must be designed and formed to create a basic team structure. Thus, an intriguing area for future research is the concept of *model-based team design,* looking at the role that computational models can play in understanding and guiding the design, formation, and development of team structures. Levchuk, Chopra, Levchuk, and Paley (2005) presented a fascinating example of research and development in this area. These authors demonstrated how a quantitative Team Optimal Design (TOD) methodology could be used to design maximally efficient team configurations in a command and control aircraft setting. This was accomplished by developing "functional process flows," based on SME input, and developing model-based representations of work functions, task responsibilities, and specified information flow constraints. More research and development of this type is needed to ascertain the value that computational models can play in maximizing team performance, before teams are even formed.

Hopefully, the research highlighted in this chapter was interesting and informative. In the spirit of this chapter, the authors welcome you to assess our performance and provide feedback using the model of your choice.

Acknowledgments

We would like to thank our funding sponsors Susan Chipman, Ray Perez, and Harold Hawkins of the Office of Naval Research for supporting this work. In addition, we would like to thank Ling Rothrock and his graduate students at The Pennsylvania State University, who built the team training test bed used for this research. We also thank Amy Bolton for her guidance and contributions and Allison McCreary and Cheryl Johnson for their valuable SME input.

References

Aleven, V. A. W. M. M. & Koedinger, K. R. (2002). An effective metacognitive strategy: Learning by doing and explaining with a computer-based cognitive tutor. *Cognitive Science, 26,* 147–179.

Anderson, J. R. (1988). The expert module. In M. Polson & J. Richardson (Eds.), *Handbook of intelligent training systems* (pp. 21–53). Hillsdale, NJ: Erlbaum.

Atkins, P. W. B., Wood, R. E., & Rutgers, P. J. (2002). The effects of feedback format on dynamic decision making. *Organizational Behavior and Human Decision Processes, 88,* 587–604.

Beck, J. & Woolf, B. (2000a). High-level student modeling with machine learning. In G. Gauthier, C. Frasson, & K. VanLehn (Eds.), *Proceedings of fifth International Conference on Intelligent Tutoring Systems* (pp. 584–593). New York: Springer Verlag.

Beck, J. E. & Woolf, B. F. (2000b). Reasoning from data rather than theory. In J. Etheredge & B. Manaris (Eds.), *Proceedings of the 13th International Florida Artificial Intelligence Research Symposium Conference* (pp. 34–39). Menlow Park, CA: AAAI Press.

Bell, B. S. & Kozlowski, S. W. J. (2002). Adaptive guidance: Enhancing self-regulation, knowledge, and performance in technology-based training. *Personnel Psychology, 55,* 267–306.

Bhandarkar, D., Thiruvengada, H., Rothrock, L., Campbell, G., & Bolton, A. (2004). *TASP: A toolkit to analyze team performance in a complex task environment.* Presented at the IIE 13th Industrial Engineering Research Conference, May 15–19, Houston, TX.

Bolton, A. E., Buff, W. L., & Campbell, G. E. (2003). Faster, cheaper, and "just as good"? A comparison of the instructional effectiveness of three HBRs that vary in development requirements. In *Proceedings of the 12th Conference on Behavior Representation in Modeling and Simulation* [CD-ROM].

Bolton, A. E., Dorsey, D. W., & Campbell, G. E. (2004). Application of time-sensitive computational models to training within a scenario-based team training system. In *Proceedings of the 13th Conference on Behavior Representation in Modeling and Simulation* [CD-ROM].

Bolton, A. E., Holness, D. O., Buff, W. L., & Campbell, G. E. (2001). An application of mathematical modeling in training systems: Is it a viable alternative to cognitive modeling? In *Proceedings of 10th Conference on Computer Generated Forces and Behavioral Representation* (pp. 497–505). Norfolk, VA: SISO, Inc.

Brehmer, B. (1981). Models of diagnostic judgments. In J. Rasmussen & W. B. Rouse (Eds.), *Human detection and diagnosis of systems failures,* (pp. 231–239). New York: Plenum.

Brunswik, E. (1955). Representative design and probabilistic theory in functional psychology. *Psychological Review, 62,* 193–217.

Busemeyer, J. R. & Johnson, J. G. (2004). Computational models of decision making. In D. Koehler & N. Harvey (Eds.), *Handbook of judgment and decision making.* Malden, MA: Blackwell Publishing Co.

Campbell, G. E., Buff, W. L., & Bolton, A. E. (2006). Viewing training through a fuzzy lens. In A. Kirlik (Ed.), *Adaptation in human-technology interaction: Methods, models, and measures* (pp. 286–311). New York: Oxford University Press.

Cannon-Bowers, J. & Salas, E. (1997). A framework for developing team performance measures in training. In M. Brannick, E. Salas, and C. Prince (Eds.), *Team performance assessment and measurement: Theory, research, and applications* (pp. 45–62). Mahwah, NJ: Lawrence Erlbaum Associates.

Carley, K. (1995). Computational and mathematical organization theory: Perspective and directions. *Computational and Mathematical Organization Theory, 1*(1), 39–56.

Chen, G., Thomas, B. A., & Wallace, J. C. (2005). A multilevel examination of the relationships among training outcomes, mediating regulatory processes, and adaptive performance. *Journal of Applied Psychology, 90,* 827–841.

Cohen, M. S., Freeman, J. T., & Thompson, B. (1998). Critical thinking skills in tactical decision making: A model and training strategy. In J. A. Cannon-Bowers & E. Salas (Eds.), *Making decisions under stress: Implications for individual and team training* (pp. 155–189). Washington, DC: American Psychological Association.

Cohen, M. & Thompson, B. (2001). Training teams to take initiative: Critical thinking in novel situations. In E. Salas (Ed.), *Advances in cognitive engineering and human performance research* (Vol. 1, pp. 251–291). Greenwich, CT: JAI Press.

Dal Forno, A. & Merlone, U. (2002). A multi-agent simulation platform for modeling perfectly rational and bounded-rational agents in organizations. *Journal of Artificial Societies and Social Simulations, 5*(2). Retrieved from http://jasss.soc.surrey.ac.uk/5/2/3.html.

Dawes, R. M. (1979). The robust beauty of improper linear models in decision making. *American Psychologist, 34,* 571–582.

Diehl, E. & Sterman, J. D. (1995). Effects of feedback complexity on dynamic decision making. *Organizational Behavior and Human Decision Processes, 62*(2), 198–215.

Dorsey, D., Campbell, G., & Russell, S. (in press). Adapting the instructional science paradigm to encompass training in virtual environments. Special Issue on "Optimizing Virtual Training Systems." *Theoretical Issues in Ergonomic Science.*

Dorsey, D. W. & Coovert, M. D. (2003). Mathematical modeling of decision making: A soft and fuzzy approach to capturing hard decisions. *Human Factors, 45*(1), 117–35.

Drasgow, F., Luecht, R., & Bennett, R. (2005). Technology and testing. In R. L. Brennan (Ed.), *Educational measurement* (4th ed., pp. 471–515). Westport, CT: American Council on Education and Praeger Publishers.

Ericsson, K. A., Krampe, R. Th., & Tesch-Römer, C. (1993). The role of deliberate practice in the acquisition of expert performance. *Psychological Review, 100,* 363–406.

Fritzsche, B. A., Stagl, K. C., Salas, E., & Burke, C. S. (2006). Enhancing the design, delivery and evaluation of scenario based training: Can SJTs contribute? In J. A. Weekley & R. E. Ployhart (Eds.), *Situational judgment tests* (pp. 301–318). Mahwah, NJ: Lawrence Erlbaum Associates.

Gibson, F. P. (2003). Supporting learning in evolving dynamic environments. *Computational and Mathematical Organization Theory, 9*(4), 305–326.

Gibson, F. P., Fichman, M., & Plaut, D. C. (1997). Learning in dynamic decision tasks: Computational model and empirical evidence. *Organizational Behavior and Human Decision Processes, 71*(1), 1–35.

Gigerenzer, G. (2004). Fast and frugal heuristics: The tools of bounded rationality. In D. Koehler & N. Harvey (Eds.), *Blackwell handbook of judgment and decision making* (pp. 62–88). Oxford, England: Blackwell.

Goldstein, I. & Ford, J. K. (2002). *Training in organizations: Needs assessment, development, and evaluation.* Belmont, CA: Wadsworth Group.

Gonzalez, C. (2005). Decision support for real-time, dynamic decision-making tasks. *Organizational Behavior and Human Decision Processes, 96,* 142–154.

Gray, W. D. & Boehm-Davis, D. A. (2000). Milliseconds matter: An introduction to microstrategies and to their use in describing and predicting interactive behavior. *Journal of Experimental Psychology: Applied, 6*(4), 322–335.

Gunnar, S., Chernyshenko, O., Baumann, M., Sniezek, J., Bulitko, V., Borton, S., et al. (2000). *A new approach to scoring dynamic decision making performance on high fidelity simulators: Reliability and validity issues*. Paper presented at the 15th Annual Conference for the Society for Industrial and Organizational Psychology, New Orleans, LA.

Ilgen, D. R., Hollenbeck, J. R., Johnson, M., & Jundt, D. (2005). Teams in organizations: From input-process-output models to IMOI models. *Annual Review of Psychology, 56*, 517–543.

Johnston, J. H., Freeman, J., and Serfaty, D. (2003). Performance measurement for diagnosing and debriefing distributed command and control teams. In *Proceedings of the 8th International command and control research and technology symposium*. National Defense University Washington, DC, June 17–19, 2003.

Kirlik, A., Fisk, A. D., Walker, N., & Rothrock, L. (1998). Feedback augmentation and part-task practice in training dynamic decision-making skills. In J. A. Cannon-Bowers & E. Salas (Eds.), *Making decisions under stress: Implications for individual and team training* (pp. 91–113). Washington, DC: American Psychological Association.

Kluger, A. & DeNisi, A. (1996). The effects of feedback interventions on performance: A historical review, a meta-analysis, and a preliminary feedback intervention theory. *Psychological Bulletin, 119*, 254–284.

Kozlowski, S. W. J. & Bell, B. S. (2002). Work groups and teams in organizations. In W. C. Borman, D. R. Ilgen, & R. J. Klimoski (Eds.), *Comprehensive handbook of psychology (Vol. 12): Industrial and organizational psychology*. New York: Wiley.

Kozlowski, S. W. J., Gully, S. M., Nason, E. R., & Smith, E. M. (1999). Developing adaptive teams: A theory of compilation and performance across levels and time. In D. R. Ilgen & E. D. Pulakos (Eds.), *The changing nature of work performance: Implications for staffing, personnel actions, and development* (pp. 240–292). San Francisco, CA: Jossey-Bass.

Kozlowski, S. W. J., Toney, R. J., Mullins, M. E., Weissbein, D. A., Brown, K. A., & Bell, B. A. (1999). Developing adaptability: A theory for the design of integrated-embedded training systems. In E. Salas (Ed.), *Human/technology interaction in complex systems* (Vol. 10). Greenwich, CT: JAI Press.

Levchuk, G. M., Chopra, K., Levchuk, Y., and Paley, M. (2005). *Model-based organization manning, strategy, and structure design via team optimal design (TOD) methodology*. Proceedings of the 10th International Command and Control Research and Technology Symposium, McLean, VA.

Lindskog, P. (1997). Fuzzy identification from a grey box modeling point of view. In *Fuzzy model identification: Selected approaches* (pp. 3–50). London: Springer-Verlag.

Liu, A. & Salvucci, D. (2001). *Modeling and prediction of human driver behavior*. Proceedings of the 9th International Conference on Human-Computer Interaction, New Orleans, LA.

MacCallum, R. (1998). Commentary on quantitative methods in I/O research. *Industrial-Organizational Psychologist, 35*, 19–30.

Mangos, P. (2004). *A psychometric framework for intelligent scenario generation*. Paper presented at the 48th Annual Conference of the Human Factors and Ergonomics Society. New Orleans, LA.

McArthur, D., Lewis, M., & Bishay, M. (1993). *The roles of artificial intelligence in education: Current progress and future prospects,* RAND DRU-472-NSF. Retrieved from http://www.rand.org/hot/mcarthur/Papers/role.html.

Mulgund, S. S. & Zacharias, G. L. (1996). A situation-driven adaptive pilot/vehicle interface. *In Proceedings of the Third annual symposium on human interaction with complex systems* (pp. 193–198).

National Research Council (2001). *Knowing what students know: The science and design of educational assessment.* Washington, DC: National Academy Press.

Rothrock, L. (2001). Using time windows to evaluate operator performance. *International Journal of Cognitive Ergonomics, 5*(2), 95–119.

Rothrock, L. & Kirlik, A. (2003). Inferring rule-based strategies in dynamic judgment tasks: Toward a noncompensatory formulation of the lens model. *IEEE Transactions on Systems, Man, and Cybernetics: Part A. Systems and Humans, 33*(1), 58–72.

Salas, E. (2001). *Training crews for high performance: Myths, reality, and what works!* Paper presented at the Situation Assessment and Decision-Making Conference, Human Factors Group of the Royal Aeronautical Society, London, England.

Salas, E. & Cannon-Bowers, J. A. (2001). The science of training: A decade of progress. *Annual Review of Psychology, 52,* 471–499.

Salas, E., Stagl, K. C., & Burke, C. S. (2004). 25 years of team effectiveness in organizations: Research themes and emerging needs. In C. L. Cooper & I. T. Robertson (Eds.), *International Review of Industrial and Organizational Psychology* (pp. 47–91). New York: John Wiley & Sons.

Seels, B. & Richey, R. (1994). *Instructional technology: The definition and domains of the field.* Washington, DC: Association for Educational Communications and Technology.

Shafto, M., Degani, A., & Kirlik, A. (1997). Canonical correlation analysis of data on human-automation interaction. *Proceedings of the 41st annual meeting of the Human Factors and Ergonomics Society.* Albuquerque, NM: Human Factors Society.

Shank, R., & Neaman, A. (2001). Motivation and failure in educational systems design. In K. Forbus and P. Feltovich (Eds.), *Smart Machines in Education* (pgs. 37–69). AAAI Press/The MIT Press, Cambridge, MA.

Singh, S., James, M. R., & Rudary, M. R. (2004). *Predictive state representations: a new theory for modeling dynamical systems.* Proceedings of the 20th Conference on Uncertainty in Artificial Intelligence, Banff, Canada.

Smith-Jentsch, K. A., Johnston, J. H., & Payne, S. (1998). Measuring team-related expertise in complex environments. In J. Cannon-Bowers & E. Salas (Eds.), *Making decisions under stress: Implications for individual and team training* (pp. 61–87). Washington, DC: American Psychological Association.

Smith-Jentsch, K., Zeisig, R., Acton, B., & McPherson, J. A. (1998). Team dimensional training: A strategy for guided team self-correction. In J. A. Cannon-Bowers & E. Salas (Eds.), *Making decisions under stress: Implications for individual and team training* (pp. 271–297). Washington, DC: American Psychological Association.

Tennyson, R. D. (1980). Instructional control strategies and content structure as design variables in concept acquisition using computer-based instruction. *Journal of Educational Psychology, 72,* 525–532.

Tennyson, R. D. & Buttrey, T. (1980). Advisement and management strategies as design variables in computer-assisted instruction. *Educational Communication and Technology Journal, 28,* 169–176.

Weil, S. A., Hussain, T., Diedrich, F., Ferguson, W., & MacMillan, J. (2004). *Assessing distributed team performance in DARWARS training: Challenges and methods.* Proceedings of the 2004 Interservice/Industry Training, Simulation, and Education Conference (I/ITSEC).

Wiggins, G. & McTighe, J. (1998). *Understanding by design.* Alexandria, VA: Association for Supervision and Curriculum Development.

Woolf, B. P., Beck, J., Eliot, C., & Stern, M. (2001). Growth and maturity of intelligent tutoring systems. In K.D. Forbus & J. Feltovich (Eds.), *Smart machines in education.* Cambridge, MA: MIT Press.

Yin, J., Miller, M. S., Ioerger, T. R., Yen, J., & Volz, R. A. (2000). A knowledge-based approach for designing intelligent team training systems. In *Proceedings of the Fourth International Conference on Autonomous Agents* (pp. 427–434), New York: ACM Press.

Appendix A. Demonstration of Mathematical Modeling Approach

The following example demonstrates the process by which the AIC model identifies expected actions during a TASP scenario. Figure 13.4 below displays a typical screen shot as viewed by the AIC position. From the north, an unknown track approaches at approximately 65 NM from ownship. Assume that the AAWC notices this and requests that the AIC identify this track. Also note that the DCA closest to the unknown track has sufficient fuel (98%) to carry out this order.

Consider the cue profiles for two possible actions, "Assign Primary ID" and "Vector DCA for VID of unknown track." There are four necessary cues to instantiate the action "Assign Primary ID." Each of these cues is given a weight of .25 in the linear transformation matrix **T**, and all other cues would have a weight of 0 for this particular cue profile. Thus, if all cues are present and multiplied by the transformation matrix, the associated element in the behavior vector **B** will be 1, meaning the action is instantiated.

With respect to the "vectoring" action, this action is instantiated by four cues as well. Each of the four cues would be associated with a weight of .25 in the weight matrix for the same reasons previously discussed. If there were only three cues in the profile, each would be weighted .33 (if two cues were necessary, weights would be .5, and so forth).

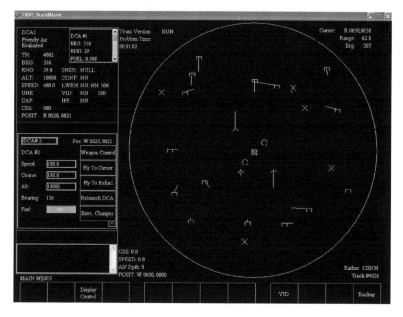

FIGURE 13.4
Example AIC Position Screenshot.

The following table illustrates an abbreviated **C** vector for this point in time, where 1 = cue is present and 0 = cue is not present. Actual matrices used to determine expected AIC actions will be much larger than those shown in this example.

AAWC orders AIC to vector DCA for VID	DCA has enough fuel to reach target	Aircraft at 50 NM or less	Track Primary ID missing	Have VID	Unknown track visible on radar
1	1	0	1	0	1

The next table illustrates an abbreviated **T** matrix for these two cue profiles:

	Assign Primary ID	Vector DCA for VID of unknown track
AAWC orders AIC to vector DCA for VID	0	.25
DCA has enough fuel to reach target	0	.25
Aircraft at 50 NM or less	.25	0
Track Primary ID missing	.25	.25
Have VID	.25	0
Unknown track visible on Radar	.25	.25

Multiplying the **C** and **T** matrices results in the following **B** matrix:

$$B = [0.5 \quad 1.0]$$

In this matrix, "Vector DCA for VID of unknown track" has been fully instantiated, whereas "Assign primary ID" has not. In a noncompensatory model, all elements in this **B** matrix that are less than 1 would be recoded to 0. In a compensatory model, the matrix is left as is (i.e., actions can be partially instantiated).

Continuing with the example as a noncompensatory model, the final step involves multiplying the **B** matrix (consisting of 0's and 1's only) by a diagonal importance matrix **I** that contains criticality information from SMEs:

$$I = \begin{bmatrix} 4 & 0 \\ 0 & 3 \end{bmatrix}$$

The resulting "expected behaviors" matrix **E** would look like the following:

$$E = [0.0 \quad 3.0]$$

Thus, "Vector DCA" would be an expected AIC action during this time-frame (value of 3.0), but "Assign Primary ID" would not (value of 0.0). Note that it is possible for the AIC model to recommend several actions of the same criticality during a given time period.

14

Assessing Team Processes in Complex Environments: Challenges in Transitioning Research to Practice

Kelley J. Krokos, David P. Baker, Alexander Alonso, and Rachel Day

Introduction

Much of today's work is performed by teams. An integral part of ensuring the success of these teams in the complex environments in which they work is assessing their performance. Specifically, assessment is a critical component of determining readiness and providing feedback after training. The objective of this chapter is to identify the challenges currently facing practitioners in their efforts to assess team performance and to provide guidance regarding management of these challenges. Particular attention is paid to the difficulty in transitioning research into practice, a problem that often stems from a lack of research to inform the assessment process. We begin with an overview of the structure and functioning of teams and the current state of team performance measurement. Then, research is presented that investigates specific deficiencies regarding the assessment of team performance. Finally, based on the review and the research results, guiding principles regarding how best to assess team performance in complex environments are provided.

Team Performance in Complex Environments

On September 17, 2004, the U.S. Coast Guard made the largest single drug seizure in its history when Coast Guard and U.S. Navy forces discovered more than 30,000 pounds of cocaine in a sealed ballast tank aboard the fishing vessel *Lina Maria* near the Galapagos Islands (Rhynard, 2004). The tactical law enforcement team aboard the USS *Curts* seized the drugs and took the crew members into custody. Just seven days later, a second Coast Guard/Navy team aboard the USS *Crommelin* intercepted the fishing vessel *San Jose*, the sister ship to the *Lina Maria*, and upon boarding discovered and seized an additional 26,250 pounds of cocaine that was found in the fish hold. In addition to being record-setting drug interdiction successes, a distinguishing feature of these seizures is the multiagency nature of the missions. Team members from the Coast Guard, the Navy, the Drug Enforcement Agency (DEA), the Federal Bureau of Investigation (FBI), the U.S. Immigration and Customs Enforcement, and the Joint Interagency Task Force South worked together as a cohesive interagency team to gather the intelligence regarding the potential transport of cocaine aboard the vessels, to locate both vessels, to seize those vessels and their cargo, and to take their crew members into custody. Large-scale drug interdiction missions such as these create complex environments that are dynamic, fast paced, ill structured, and hazardous. For organizations and their work teams to be successful within these complex environments, individuals working on these teams must have highly specialized skills and be able to work together synergistically.

Aviation, medicine, and nuclear power industries are also characterized by complex daily operating environments, due in large part to the requirement that teams of specialists work together to solve difficult problems in a time-sensitive manner and the extreme consequence of error if they are unable to work together effectively. For example, patient care is an interdependent process carried out by teams of individuals with advanced technical training who have varying roles and decision-making responsibilities. To be successful, physicians, nurses, pharmacists, technicians, and other health-care professionals must coordinate their activities to make safe and efficient patient care a priority. Given the importance of effective work teams to success in myriad industries and situations, an understanding of the fundamental nature of teams is required.

Overview of Teams

What Is a Team?

There is general consensus that a team consists of two or more individuals who have specific roles, perform interdependent tasks, are adaptable, and share a common goal (Salas, Dickinson, Converse, & Tannenbaum, 1992). Teams also share mutual accountability. That is, they hold the team, rather than specific individuals, accountable for success or failure (Knox & Simpson, 2004). For example, health-care workers perform interdependent tasks (e.g., removing a patient's appendix) and function in specific roles (e.g., surgeon, anesthesiologist, surgical assistant) while sharing the common goal of providing safe care to patients.

What Do Teams Do?

The work that teams perform is composed of both individual contributions (taskwork) and collective contributions (teamwork). Taskwork and teamwork are distinct, but both are required for teams to be effective in complex environments (Morgan, Glickman, Woodward, Blaiwes, & Salas, 1986). Morgan, Salas, and Glickman (1994) described taskwork as the individual responsibilities of team members that involve understanding the nature of the task, how to interact with equipment, and how to follow proper policies and procedures. Taskwork activities have also been referred to as operational or technical skills (Davis, Gaddy, & Turney, 1985). For example, members of combat-information center (CIC) teams utilize radar equipment to determine a contact's speed, location, direction, and intent.

While taskwork represents the specific steps and strategies associated with a particular job, teamwork refers to the steps or processes that team members use to coordinate their actions (e.g., Cannon-Bowers, Tannenbaum, Salas, & Volpe, 1995; Smith-Jentsch, Johnston, & Payne, 1998). Extensive research on teamwork during the past 20 years (Howard, Gaba, Fish, Yang, & Sarnquist, 1992; Helmreich & Foushee, 1993; McIntyre, Salas, & Glickman, 1989) suggests that teamwork is defined by a set of interrelated knowledge, skills, and abilities (KSAs) that facilitate coordinated, adaptive performance (Salas, Bowers, & Cannon-Bowers, 1995; Baker, Gustafson, Beaubien, Salas, & Barach, 2003). In a review of teamwork processes, Cannon-Bowers et al. (1995) found more than 130 different labels used to describe teamwork processes or skills. After sorting these skills based on their similarities, eight major teamwork dimensions emerged: adaptability, shared situational awareness, performance monitoring and feedback, leadership/team management, interpersonal relations, coordination, communication, and decision making.

Despite these findings, when teamwork is measured through observations or some other metric, ratings are often collapsed into a single overall teamwork score due to high intercorrelations among the teamwork skills measured (Marks, Sabella, Burke, & Zaccaro, 2002; Marks, Zaccaro, & Mathieu, 2000; Mathieu, Heffner, Goodwin, Salas, & Cannon-Bowers, 2000). Such findings have prompted researchers to conclude that it may be too difficult to measure more than four distinct teamwork processes at any given time (e.g., Brannick, Prince, Salas, & Prince, 1993; Brannick, Roach, & Salas, 1993). Smith-Jentsch, Zeisig, Acton, and McPherson (1998) reported that subject matter experts (SMEs) could reliably discriminate between only four higher-level teamwork dimensions: leadership, communication delivery, information exchange, and supporting behavior.

More recently, Salas, Sims, and Burke (2005) identified the "Big Five" of teamwork to include team leadership, mutual performance monitoring, backup behavior, adaptability, and team orientation. In addition, three support mechanisms were identified: (1) mutual trust, (2) closed-loop communication, and (3) shared mental models. Together, these processes are proposed to yield improved team effectiveness and efficiency.

Alonso and colleagues (2006) later identified a model of teamwork skills that are trainable at the individual level. Skills included team leadership, mutual support, situation monitoring, and communication, all of which when learned and honed by team members would result in performance-based, knowledge-based, and attitudinal outcomes. For example, shared mental models were viewed as a result of monitoring and backup behaviors. This new framework of trainable team skills and teamwork outcomes is presented in Figure 14.1.

The circle in Figure 14.1 includes skills that are proposed to be trainable: leadership, situation monitoring (mutual performance monitoring), mutual support (backup behavior), and communication. Performance outcomes, knowledge outcomes, and attitudinal outcomes are depicted in the corners and are proposed to result from proficiency on the central skills. Collectively, this research suggests that the four team skills described in

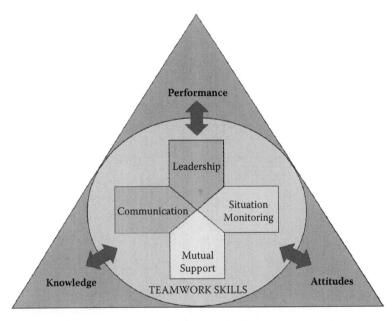

FIGURE 14.1
The TeamSkills triangle.

the following sections are measurable and most likely account for and best describe the fundamental components of teamwork.

Leadership

A clearly designated team leader may help facilitate problem solving, may provide performance expectations, may direct and coordinate activities, and may motivate fellow team members (Cannon-Bowers et al., 1995). The leader also clarifies team member roles and evaluates performance that affects team functioning (Barach & Weingart, 2004).

Mutual Performance Monitoring

Team members continually engage in mutual performance monitoring. That is, they develop common understandings of their surroundings and apply strategies to accurately monitor their own and other team members' performance. These strategies allow team members to identify mistakes or lapses in other team members' actions and provide feedback to facilitate self-correction (McIntyre & Salas, 1995).

Backup Behavior (Mutual Support)

Teams operate at an optimal level and error is reduced when members engage in support or backup behaviors during periods of high workload. Support may take the form of suggestions, cautioning advice, or feedback. Likewise, team members balance workload by offering task assistance or filling in for each other when necessary. These backup behaviors provide another set of eyes for error detection (Roberts, 1990b; Wilson, Burke, Priest & Salas, 2005). For example, air traffic controllers are normally assigned in groups of two so that each can act as a check on the other and can act more quickly upon problems that arise (Roberts, 1990a). To provide mutual support, team members must anticipate their fellow team members' needs through accurate knowledge of their responsibilities.

Communication

To contribute to effective teamwork, communication must include following up to ensure the message was received and clarifying with the sender that the message received is the same as the intended message. This process is known as closed-loop communication (McIntyre & Salas, 1995). According to Salas et al. (2005), "Communication is especially important as the environment increases in complexity, as it not only distributes needed information to other team members but also facilitates the continuous updating of the team's shared mental model" (p. 567).

Measuring Team Performance

Why Is Measuring Team Performance Important?

Effective teamwork is required to conduct work in complex environments and to enhance safety. To capitalize on the unique efficiencies of teams, it must be determined what a team does well, where its performance is deficient, and how each team member contributes to each deficiency. When measured, these issues shed light on the team's effectiveness, which in turn, can be used to assess readiness and to identify areas of weakness that may be addressed through feedback and training.

Traditional Approaches to Team Performance Measurement

Although the need for accurate team performance measurement is clear, two critical questions must be addressed by researchers and practitioners when measuring team performance. The first question deals with how to measure team performance, and the second major question concerns what to measure. The answers to these questions will determine the level of diagnosticity and usefulness of team performance measures.

How to Measure Team Performance

The *how* of performance measurement is composed of two issues: (1) the identification of whom or what does the assessing; and (2) how the performance data are quantified and recorded. First, performance may be assessed by a human observer or observers who are either external to the task or who are participants in the task, or may be captured automatically by the simulator or equipment being used (Baker & Salas, 1992, 1997).

Second, performance data may be quantified and recorded via a variety of measurement formats: (1) checklists; (2) frequency counts; (3) distance and discrepancy (D&D) scales; and (4) rating scales including behaviorally anchored ratings scales (BARS; Smith & Kendall, 1963) and behavioral observation scales (BOS).

Checklists have been employed in instances where the emphasis was placed on assessing whether key processes or behaviors were demonstrated in specific instances (e.g., Fowlkes, Lane, Salas, Franz, & Oser, 1994). For example, a checklist can be used to tell if a team member communicated vital information at the appropriate moment. A checklist typically consists of behaviors that have dichotomous responses such as yes/no, right/wrong, or performed action versus failed to perform action.

Frequency scales have generally been employed in instances where quantity (e.g., number of times that a behavior, action, or error occurs) is important. For instance, frequency scales have been used to assess the number of times that effective communication behaviors were exhibited (e.g., Stout, Cannon-Bowers, Salas, & Milanovich, 1999) and the number of accidents that occurred on the job (e.g., Goodman & Garber, 1988). Frequency counts can be generated by incumbents via self-report or by raters external to the task or can be generated automatically.

In contrast, D&D scales provide a numerical index of how actual performance on the task may have differed from ideal performance on the same task. For example, D&D scales have been used to compare what was actually covered in a meeting with what was scheduled to be covered or to compare how long it took a team to perform a task with the target amount of time to complete the task.

Finally, rating scales are utilized where the emphasis is on quality rather than quantity. For example, rating scales have been used to measure the accuracy of decisions (e.g., Hollenbeck, Ilgen, Tuttle, & Sego, 1995) as well as the use of critical teamwork processes (e.g., Marks et al., 2000). Rating scale judgments are often behaviorally anchored and include a corresponding numeric value (e.g., Rate the efficiency of the fire team's quarter deck exercise on a scale of 1 to 5, where 1 = very efficient and 5 = very inefficient).

What to Measure

A more fundamental question with regard to the measurement of team performance is what should be measured. Individual taskwork and teamwork KSAs have previously been discussed as important contributors to effective teamwork. However, a significant consideration is whether to measure the process, the outcome, or both, and at which level (i.e., individual, team, or multiteam level). Current approaches range from focusing on individual taskwork contributors to teamwork to focusing on the KSAs that comprise teamwork to focusing on objective events-based outcomes such as error reduction (Smith-Jentsch, Johnston & Payne, 1998). Despite the myriad accepted practices for measuring team performance, each has met with limitations when applied to real-world complex situations.

Individual skills-based performance measures are indicators of performance that focus on individual processes and outcomes. Individual processes measurement involves gauging competency on individual skills such as detecting a signal for a radar team operator or communicating external systems information for a copilot. Individual outcomes measurement includes taking into account the number of errors made by team members when performing individual tasks that contribute to overall team success. Traditionally, individual skills-based performance has been measured using behavioral observations and ratings scales designed to capture the degree to which team members are competent at tasks that are directly related to team performance. Checklists have also been used as a means of tracking individual processes and outcomes performance. For example, in the case of an emergency medical technicians team, supervisors (i.e., observers or performance appraisers) are often sent on ride-along observations to gauge training needs. These supervisors assess individual process and outcome by recording the communication and clinical errors made by each team member. This record is then used to assess the team's competence when performing tasks and to provide feedback for improvement.

Teamwork performance measures are indicators of performance that focus on processes and outcomes of teamwork. Process indicators capture the interactions among team members that are proposed to lead to desired outcomes such as targets destroyed for a tactical flight crew. As previously discussed, Alonso et al. (in press) proposed that the four team skills presented in the Team Skills Triangle (Figure 14.1) should serve as the foundation for process measurement. Measurement of team processes has typically relied heavily on rating scales and outcomes-based measures. However, some researchers (e.g., Marks, DeChurch, Mathieu, Panzer, & Alonso, 2005) have expanded on the measurement of these processes by incorporating self-report measures of team orientation and collective efficacy. Others have focused on self-report measures of team performance via measures of shared cognition and perceived conflict management styles like avoidant and adaptive styles (Amason & Schweiger, 1997; Sternberg & Dobson, 1987).

Teamwork outcome indicators focus on information about critical events throughout the performance episode and team responses to these events. Measurement formats used include rating scales and checklists that rely heavily on the observations and ratings of trained experts. For example, Marks et al. (2005) employed checklists as a means of identifying flight team performance outcomes during simulated flight. Outcome measures included targets destroyed and flight team survival without damage. An aggregate score was computed based on these outcome data, and teams were ranked. Similarly, Beaubien and Alonso (2004) proposed using similar measures for surgical team performance by assessing the number of errors made during critical moments in surgical procedures and the amount of time surgical teams spent working on surgical procedures. For this effort, a surgical simulator modeling complex surgical practices was used.

Because they rely heavily on human observers, traditional measurement methods raise concerns about unreliability and accuracy (Baker & Salas, 1992, 1997). For example, the use of checklists or rating scales can be difficult to incorporate in complex performance situations, as raters must devote considerable attention to capture processes, performance decisions, and actions simultaneously. The task is cognitively taxing even when observing the simplest of tasks and is likely to fail as the degree of complexity and realism increases. In addition, the need for multiple raters presents a problem in that rater training is required to ensure that all raters use the same standards and frame-of-reference during observations.

Without this similar frame-of-reference, interrater reliability is jeopardized (Baker & Dismukes, 2002). Furthermore, the use of multiple raters is often not feasible in many complex team environments due to limited space and safety concerns associated with having observers in environments such as cockpits, command-and-control centers, and operating rooms. Finally, there is the possibility of the Hawthorne effect (i.e., changes in team performance resulting from the observation process).

Many of these potential disadvantages of human observers can be mitigated by training raters to ensure a collective frame of reference and proper control in simulated settings to limit obtrusiveness of observers. In addition, automation can alleviate some of the difficulties associated with human observers by directly capturing indicators of performance. For example, high-fidelity aircraft simulators can precisely measure aircrew performance outcomes such as deviations from approach and landing profiles when conducting a single-engine landing. However, drawbacks of automated measurement include the potential need for auxiliary backup sources of observation, the need for further interpretation or coding by raters, and the cost to develop and collect the automated data. Self-report measures may also reduce or eliminate the need for multiple external observers. However, they may be limited by unreliability and may be limited in applicability to specific team performance-relevant constructs.

Finally, although traditional measurement formats, when used individually, generally fail to capture the complex and multilevel nature of teamwork, these formats can be quite useful if they are used for triangulation of performance by contributor and dimension. That is, the best use of these measures occurs when they are employed in combination with one another to provide the most complete measurement of inputs, processes, and outcomes in the team performance episode, as highlighted in the following sections.

Other Approaches to Team Performance Measurement

To provide a more complete picture of teamwork performance, some researchers have employed a combination of traditional performance assessment methods. Smith-Jentsch, Johnston, et al. (1998) delineated a complex model for measuring team performance at multiple levels while incorporating the use of BARS, checklists, and objective computerized data capture. The model delineates two kinds of performance (processes and outcomes) that take place at two distinct levels (individual and team). Individual processes included cognitive processes and individual task skills and were measured using BOS and checklists. Team processes included supporting behaviors, information exchange, communication, and team leadership and were measured using BARS and checklists. Individual performance outcomes included latency and accuracy while team outcomes included mission effectiveness and aggregate latency and accuracy. The authors proposed that the combination of process and outcomes (or event-based measures) were both important because the former were needed to identify training needs and the latter were necessary to tell which processes are crucial for optimal performance. During a series of studies, teams were asked to make tactical decisions under stress using a naval warfare simulation. Teams were assessed throughout an entire war exercise for all relevant processes and outcomes. A computerized data collection effort of team performance was devised to validate outcome and process findings collected via raters using BOS or checklists.

Lessons learned from these studies and others conducted under the Tactical Decision Making Under Stress (TADMUS) project have far-reaching implications for team training and team performance measurement. Smith-Jentsch, Johnston, et al. (1998) identified a series of performance measurement standards for teams based upon their TADMUS work:

1. Define performance dimensions and levels clearly before embarking on measurement.
2. Use events-based measurement that focuses on specific behavioral manifestations rather than generalized construct definitions.
3. Use events-based measurement for uncovering the link between process and performance.
4. Focus team performance measures on information-exchange processes and opportunities for supporting behaviors.

Recently, efforts have been made by other researchers (e.g., Johnston, Vincenzi, Radtke, Salter, & Freeman, 2004) to develop systems to aid raters of team performance in complex high-fidelity simulated training exercises. These researchers devised a simulation involving naval air strike exercises where two E2C aircraft mission stations were linked through a local area network. Each station was run by a naval flight officer (NFO) who was responsible for monitoring the airspace, compiling information from two radar officers, and communicating with other aircraft. In this scenario, the two radar officers within each E2C simulator were confederates. Then, two two-person teams of evaluators tracked team processes of the confederates and performance between the two aircraft. One team of evaluators was alerted visually of critical decision points and asked to rate accuracy and timeliness of communications along with leadership and supporting behaviors of the NFO confederates within each simulator. The other was alerted visually of critical decision points and was asked to rate accuracy and timeliness of communications along with information exchange and communication. Results of the initial debriefing, distributed, simulation-based exercise (DDSBE) study indicate that the use of an automated alert system helped improve reliability between team members. Visual prompting also made it possible for raters to observe more critical decision points while enabling them to identify which processes and skills are deficient and to target more detailed debriefings for feedback.

Summary

What Is Known about Team Performance Measurement

This overview suggests that much has been learned about teams and the measurement of their performance (see Table 14.1 for a summary). First, the components of team performance have largely been identified. That is, team performance is proposed to be composed of both individual taskwork and teamwork. Consensus is beginning to emerge regarding the critical KSAs required for effective teamwork including team leadership, mutual performance monitoring, backup behaviors, and communication.

In addition to understanding the components of teamwork, much is known regarding how to measure team performance. That is, team performance can be captured by human observers who are external or internal to the measurement process or via automated data collection equipment. Performance can be quantified and recorded via different measurement formats including checklists, frequency counts, D&D scales, and rating

TABLE 14.1

Summary of Team Performance Measurement Variables

Components of Team Performance (Work Types)

    Individual procedural taskwork

    Individual nonprocedural taskwork

    Teamwork

        Team leadership

        Mutual performance monitoring

        Backup behaviors

        Communication

Performance Targets (What to Measure)

    Individual, team, or multiteam level processes

    Individual, team, or multiteam level outcomes

Measurement Instrument Formats

    Checklist

    Frequency scale

    D&D scale

    Rating scale

scales. With regard to the target to be measured, both process and outcome are important, and these may occur at the individual, team, or multiteam level.

Finally, this overview also suggests that team performance measurement is most effective under conditions in which measurement (1) employs a combination of measurement formats; (2) is based on a clearly defined theory of multilevel team processes and outcomes and attempts to capture the multiple contributors to effective teamwork; (3) employs multiple raters who have been trained using frame-of-reference and behavioral observation training; and (4) maximizes technological advances and automated data collection methods to reduce the cognitive load on raters.

What Is Unknown about Team Performance Measurement

One of the greatest weaknesses regarding team performance measurement is that many practitioners argue that performance measurement research is not necessarily relevant to the practice of performance appraisal (Bernardin, Hagan, Kane, & Villanova, 1998). That is, despite advances in identifying relevant team-related variables, there exists little practical guidance when it comes to how to combine the variables for use in real-world team performance settings. For example, little or no guidance exists to inform practitioners as to which type of measurement format would be most effective in measuring team performance under specific conditions. That is, it is not known whether the purpose of a training event (e.g., diagnosis of the root causes of a performance problem, providing feedback, evaluation of readiness) may influence whether a checklist, frequency count, D&D scale, or rating scale would be most appropriate.

To address these deficiencies, the current research strives to further define the domain of team performance measurement and to expand the generalizability of lessons learned to a wider array of complex environments with multiple types of teams. This research is described next.

Current Research

It is unknown which measurement format is appropriate under which organizational circumstances. This deficiency was highlighted during a recent project conducted for the Navy (see Baker, Krokos, & Holtzman, 2004). The project goal was to develop a tool to assist instructors in providing more specific and useful feedback to trainees during posttraining debriefing sessions. To build a valid job aid, it was necessary to address these deficiencies. Consequently, a series of studies was conducted to determine the appropriate metrics for measuring human performance in military settings. This research is described in more detail in the following sections.

Identifying the Variables of Interest

A literature review was conducted to identify the variables relevant when measuring performance in the military environment (see Costar, Baker, & Calderon, 2003). The first variable to be considered was performance criteria (i.e., what might be useful to measure about the multitude of individual and teamwork behaviors that may be possible in any given situation). Six performance criteria for assessing taskwork or teamwork behaviors in the naval context were identified:

1. Accuracy: the precision in which tasks are performed.
2. Timeliness: how quickly tasks are performed.
3. Safety: the degree to which tasks are performed in a way that does not unduly jeopardize human and capital resources.
4. Productivity: the rate at which actions are performed or tasks are accomplished within a given situation.
5. Efficiency: the ratio of resources required to those expended to accomplish a task.
6. Effect: the degree to which the desired result was achieved.

Next, we identified the four measurement instrument formats that could be used to measure performance: checklist, frequency scale, D&D scale, and rating scale. In addition to performance criterion and measurement format, which are directly related to the performance of the individual or team, performance takes place in a variety of organizational settings that may influence how or why performance could or should be measured. Consequently, after identifying performance criteria and measurement formats, additional variables that may influence performance measurement were identified.

The first variable identified was level of analysis. That is, depending on the situation, it may be important to select a measurement format based on whether individual, team, or multiteam performance is being measured.

Next, three work types were identified: procedural taskwork, nonprocedural taskwork, and teamwork. Finally, as the research was being conducted in a military context, we identified three purposes for training: diagnosis of the root causes of a performance problem; feedback; and evaluation of proficiency or readiness.

Once the variables of interest were identified, research was conducted to determine which of the four measurement formats should be used under particular conditions. It was proposed that if SMEs agreed on when and how to use the measurement formats, then these rules could be used to inform the development of a job aid for training instructors.

Study 1: Survey of Performance Measurement Experts

In Study 1, data were collected from a group of performance measurement experts via survey. The goal was to determine if these SMEs would demonstrate a pattern in their preferences regarding the assignment of measurement format to work type, criteria, and training purpose. In addition to choosing the most appropriate measurement format for the six high-level performance criteria (accuracy, timeliness, productivity, efficiency, safety, and effects) and three work types (procedural task-work, nonprocedural taskwork, and teamwork), SMEs were also asked to assign a measurement format based on the purpose of training (diagnosis, feedback, proficiency/readiness) within the confines of a contextualized scenario.

Participants were 15 psychologists with either a master's or Ph.D. in industrial and organizational psychology. All participants have a background in training, performance measurement, or team performance. Experience ranged from a minimum of 5 years to a maximum of 25 years.

Each participant was given a packet with four sections: background, hypothetical scenario, definitions, and response survey. The background section briefly described the purpose of the study. To ensure that all SMEs shared a common frame of reference, a one-paragraph vignette describing a hypothetical training scenario was provided. Finally, all SMEs were provided with definitions of the variables. After the SMEs familiarized themselves with the materials, they were asked to select one of the four measurement formats (checklist, frequency, D&D, or rating scale) that they felt was the most appropriate for the six performance criteria (accuracy, timeliness, productivity, efficiency, safety, and effects), three work types, and the three purposes for training.

Responses for each criterion, process, and purpose were tabulated and tested with the χ^2 test (Table 14.2). Of the 12 categories, 9 had significant χ^2-values, which suggests high agreement among SMEs in terms of which formats they believed were most appropriate for these nine categories. However, a close examination of Table 14.2 reveals that the rating scale format was judged to be the most appropriate for six of the nine. Disproportionately few SMEs indicated that checklist, frequency count, or D&D were appropriate measurement formats. There are four notable exceptions to the trend of overreliance on the rating scale format. For the accuracy criterion, SMEs recommended using checklists and D&D formats. For timeliness, the D&D format was recommended. For measuring procedural

TABLE 14.2

Study 1 Results: Frequencies by Measurement Format and χ^2 Tests

	Measurement Format				
	Checklist	Frequency Count	D&D	Rating Scale	χ^2
Performance Criteria					
Accuracy	6[a]	0	7[a]	2	8.73*
Timeliness	1	0	14[a]	0	37.53**
Productivity	5	5	1	4	2.87
Efficiency	1	2	4	8	7.67
Safety	3	2	0	10[a]	15.13*
Effects	5	0	0	10[a]	18.33**
Work Type					
Procedural taskwork	15[a]	0	0	0	45.00**
Nonprocedural taskwork	7[a]	0	1	7[a]	11.40*
Teamwork	3	1	0	11[a]	19.93**
Evaluation Purpose					
Diagnose	5	0	4	6	5.53
Feedback	1	0	3	11[a]	19.93**
Proficiency/ready	0	0	2	13[a]	31.13**

Note: $* p < .05, ** p < .001.$
[a] Most appropriate rating format.

taskwork, the checklist format was recommended, but checklists and rating scales were recommended to measure nonprocedural taskwork.

Taken together, these results suggest that SMEs reached moderate agreement regarding which measurement format to use in measuring different facets of training evaluation. However, there appears to be an overreliance on the rating scale format. This is problematic in that while rating scales can be applied to most situations, they may not be the best measurement format for all situations. For example, rating scales are not the most appropriate format for the proficiency/readiness evaluation dimension. When assessing proficiency and readiness from training, one wants to know if a person is or is not proficient and ready; it is not valuable to know how relatively proficient/ready a person is as a result of training. Rating scales, however, provide only relative information and not absolute; this format does not provide a yes or no answer. For this reason, checklists would be more appropriate when assessing proficiency and readiness, especially when clear performance standards exist, because checklists provide yes or no information regarding a person's ability. In addition to the inappropriate nature of rating scales for some purposes, a rigorous process is required for rating scales to be properly developed.

Study 2: Investigate Contextualized Interaction and Level of Analysis

Participants for Study 2 were nine performance measurement experts. All had a Ph.D. in industrial and organizational psychology. Several had expertise in teamwork and training evaluations. In addition, some had experience working for military clients.

Three focus groups, consisting of three participants each, were conducted. To investigate the impact of level of analysis, each group of SMEs was assigned a different level of analysis. For example, one group examined measurement formats at the individual level of analysis, another group focused on the team level, and a final group made assignments at the multiteam level. Each session began with an introduction and overview of definitions and examples[1] of seven performance criteria (completion, accuracy, timeliness, productivity, efficiency, safety, and effects[2]), three work types (procedural taskwork, nonprocedural taskwork, and teamwork), two purposes for training (diagnosis and certification/proficiency[3]), and four measurement formats (checklist, frequency, D&D, and rating scale). After this introduction, participants were given a performance measurement scenario, which consisted of a hypothetical project to develop a certification exam for the American Sailing Association. Participants were given an example from the scenario for each work type and performance criterion at the appropriate level of analysis. Then they were asked to write their preferred measurement format for each work type and criterion measure on a spreadsheet considering the analysis level assigned to the group. Participants completed this activity for both training purposes. Then each participant read his or her response aloud. The group discussed the results to consensus regarding a measurement method for each work type and criterion. By determining the method through consensus, participants were able to raise any issues about the format for a condition, to discuss their concerns, and to use their combined knowledge and backgrounds to collaboratively determine an appropriate format.

With regard to format by performance criteria, the results suggest that SMEs agreed with little or no discussion regarding many of the criteria (Table 14.3). However, there was some initial disagreement among the groups for some of the criteria. Interestingly, the disagreements were almost invariably due to incoherence or inconsistency in the criterion labels, definitions, examples, the interaction of the three, or the inherent assumptions in the definitions.

For example, several participants initially disagreed about which format was best to use for measuring safety (frequency or rating scale). Although they ultimately reached consensus on the frequency scale, the discussions

TABLE 14.3

Measurement Format by Performance Criterion and Work Type

Work Type	Performance Criterion					
	Completion	Accuracy	Quantity	Productivity	Efficiency	Results
Procedural taskwork	Checklist	Numeric scale with a standard	Numeric scale with or without standard	Numeric scale with a standard	Numeric scale with a standard	Rating scale
Nonprocedural taskwork	Checklist	Numeric scale with a standard	Numeric scale with or without standard	Numeric scale with a standard	Numeric scale with a standard	Rating scale
Teamwork	Checklist	Numeric scale with a standard	Numeric scale with or without standard	Numeric scale with a standard	Numeric scale with a standard	Rating scale

revealed that the disagreements were not attributable to process, level of analysis, or purpose of training, but rather lack of clarity regarding the criterion variable. It was felt that safety did not capture something uniquely measurable and, consequently, that the appropriate measurement format would depend on how the user defined safety and what data might be available to capture these behaviors. Safety was ultimately deleted as a performance criterion variable.

Similarly, the timeliness criterion was discussed at length. Early discussions suggested that duration was more appropriate than timeliness, which suggests comparison to a standard (i.e., being on time versus being late). Ultimately, it was determined that duration was only one type of quantity that might be important and that a more global label, quantity, was more appropriate. This ultimately led to a renaming of the scale from frequency, which also reflects only one type of quantity, to numeric. Similarly, the D&D scale, which refers to a specific quantity (distance), was eliminated in favor of adding a performance standard numeric scale.

Finally, some of the performance criteria definitions assume that the underlying behavior of interest can actually be measured, which may not be an appropriate assumption. The SMEs suggested that additional information might be necessary to provide a measurement format. It was proposed that whether the behavior can be seen or heard and can be quantified in numeric terms and whether the rater is interested in examining the root causes of the behavior should be considered. Because these issues would be addressed prior to actually measuring performance, they were determined not to be related to which measurement format should be selected. While these issues regarding performance criteria generated some initial confusion, the resulting discussions revealed important concepts and resolution of the issues led to better agreement of which format was appropriate.

With regard to the other variables being considered, the results suggest that the level of analysis (individual, team, and multiteam) and work type (procedural taskwork, nonprocedural taskwork, and teamwork) were virtually negligible in their impact on the assignment process and in general need not be considered when selecting a measurement format. The results also suggest that training purpose is unimportant when selecting a measurement format. That is, all three focus groups selected the same measurement formats for diagnosis and certification/proficiency. However, the groups did note that the use of the performance data would likely vary by training purpose. For example, instructors would probably use a standard against which to compare performance for certification/proficiency purposes, but for diagnostic purposes, a standard may not be necessary.

Conclusion

The results of this research, which are based on SMEs, suggest that, contrary to the conclusion by Smith-Jentsch et al. (1995) that level of analysis is an important factor, training purpose and level of analysis are not crucial to the selection of a measurement format. Performance criteria appear to be key drivers in determining the appropriate measurement format. Second, SMEs relied heavily on the definitions and examples during the assignment process. In fact, the definitions were the primary factor driving the measurement format selected. This suggests that performance criteria must be defined in clear and concise ways, and that any examples provided must clearly match the definition of the criterion in order to be useful. Third, although team performance measurement often relies on rating scales, this research suggests that their almost exclusive use for measuring team performance is not justified.

These three discoveries informed the rest of the project. Specifically, based on the results of this research, logic rules were developed that indicate which measurement format should be used under which conditions. These rules were embedded into a software tool for use as a job aid by training instructors, thus effectively transitioning research into practice.

Guiding Principles

Effective measurement of team performance is a challenging endeavor. However, team performance measurement can and should be a goal-directed process. Following are principles that are derived from the overview and the current research that will assist researchers and practitioners in transitioning research into practice. Principle 1, Principle 2, and Principle 3 address what to measure with regard to team performance. Principle 4, Principle 5, and Principle 6 address how to measure it.

Principle 1: Capture the Multiple Contributors to Teamwork Effectiveness

The work that teams perform is composed of both individual and collective contributions. Consequently, to be able to provide specific feedback, individual, team, and if appropriate, multiteam level contributions should be assessed. In addition, processes, which capture moment to moment interaction, and outcomes, which capture the result of teamwork behaviors, are both important in describing team performance; both should be captured if possible. Similarly, observable behaviors are critically important, but when possible, cognitive behaviors and strategies (e.g., decision making) and attitudes (Cannon-Bowers & Salas, 1997) should also be captured.

Principle 2: Measure Specific Facets of Performance

Researchers and practitioners should avoid using holistic or overall teamwork ratings when assessing teamwork. Instead, raters should be asked to measure specific processes and outcomes associated with known contributors to effective teamwork such as leadership, communication, and support (Smith-Jentsch, Zeisig, et al., 1998).

Principle 3: Clearly Define Performance Criteria

Once the performance behaviors of interest have been identified, researchers and practitioners must identify the criteria that are important with regard to each behavior or set of behaviors, such as efficiency or productivity. These performance criteria must be clearly described if raters are to be consistent in their assessments. To help clarify performance criteria, examples should be provided that clearly match each criterion's definition (Baker et al., 2004).

Principle 4: Train Raters to a Common Frame of Reference to Maximize Rater Reliability

The use of human observers should be managed to maximize the reliability and accuracy of their ratings. First, raters should be trained using frame of reference and behavioral observation training (Baker & Dismukes, 2002). Where possible, technological advances and automated data collection methods should be maximized to reduce the cognitive load on raters.

Principle 5: Select Measurement Format
Based on Performance Criteria

Regardless of measurement purpose (e.g., evaluation of readiness, use in administrative decisions, diagnosis), the selection of measurement format should be dependent on the performance criterion being measured. For example, a numeric scale with a performance standard may be better suited for measuring accuracy than a checklist (Baker et al., 2004). However, when feasible, several measurement formats (e.g., checklists, rating scales) should be used in conjunction with one another to provide the most comprehensive measurement of inputs, processes, and outcomes in team performance.

Principle 6: Consider Measurement Purpose and Practicality

Principles 1 through 5 provide guidance on what and how to measure regarding team performance. However, measurement purpose and practicality should also guide all aspects of teamwork assessment. For example, with regard to purpose, consideration should be given to gathering information that assesses, diagnoses, and remediates skill deficiency (Cannon-Bowers & Salas, 1997). Practicality lies in considering the burdens placed on participants, raters, developers, and the organization when building research methodology.

Future Directions

Although the research described here made strides in identifying effective means for measuring team performance, additional issues remain to be addressed.

Validation of Measurement Formats and Combinations

One area that has yet to be addressed is the construct validation of measurement formats or combinations thereof. For example, little is known about how effective numeric scales with performance standards are for measuring accuracy of taskwork when compared with checklist formats attempting to measure the same dimension. This contention can also be extrapolated to the level of evaluation purpose. That is, a comparison could be conducted of all processes and performance criteria by all measurement formats under differing evaluation conditions. The end result would be three multitrait, multimethod matrices, each representing a given evaluation dimension. These results would provide empirical evidence of the impact of performance criteria and measurement format.

Validation of Measurement Formats across Populations

Still another area is the validation of findings for preferred measurement formats for given evaluation purposes and performance criteria. Further evidence that the recommendations of performance measurement SMEs are valid in the eyes of those who perform the actual measurement is needed. In addition, these SMEs should address other facets of the measurement formats such as (1) ease of development and use; (2) cognitive burden; and (3) appropriateness of the format given the work being performed by those being evaluated.

Contextualization of Performance Measurement

The final area that remains untapped is the contextualization of performance measurement to specific team environments and teams. For instance, general recommendations have been made about preferred performance measurement formats and dimensions for military action teams, but very few recommendations have been made about these same topics for teams operating in other military environments (e.g., military health-care settings, command and control) or nonmilitary teams working in nuclear power plants, hospitals, or paramilitary settings (e.g., SWAT teams). These teams all operate in high-complexity environments but they vary greatly in the nature of the work conducted, the degree to which their tasks are interdependent, and the degree of cross-functionality. Consequently, additional research needs to be conducted with these different types of teams to evaluate the lessons learned from this initial study to these new environments and to examine the possibility of the development of a general framework for use for all types of teams.

Transitioning Research into Practice

We began this chapter with the goal of highlighting the difficulty of transitioning what is known from research into practice. It was proposed that this problem often stems from a lack of research that truly informs the assessment process. The research presented here exemplifies this problem; the job aid developed for Navy instructors required knowledge of which measurement format to use based on the performance criteria being measured. However, no such guidance existed in the literature.

The current research demonstrated how researchers and practitioners alike can begin to fill such gaps in our science to produce evidence-based tools. For this effort, we began by specifying what was known from the research literature and incorporating this information into the job aid. For example, we embedded four teamwork processes validated by Smith-Jentsch et al. (1998) into the tool in such a way that they cannot be modified by the user. Then we conducted studies by systematically collecting information from performance measurement experts to identify measurement formats that are appropriate for specific performance criteria. Once this information was identified, we built the rules that dictate certain actions in the tool. For example, once the user selects a performance criterion to assess, the job aid automatically recommends a measurement format. Additional guidance was embedded as follows. First, the sequence of events is controlled in that users must build the behaviors of interest before they select performance criteria for that behavior. Second, a tutorial was embedded that provides guidance regarding team performance related issues that may be unfamiliar to instructors, such as information regarding process versus outcome, how to prioritize which behaviors should be measured, and queries that help the instructor build the behavioral anchors for BARS, standards for numeric entry formats, and content and order for checklists. Finally, drop-down boxes and help buttons were included to provide additional information in a less intrusive way. By embedding what was known from the literature and what was discovered during our investigations, it was possible to build a job aid that is appropriate for field use, that maximizes the likelihood that users will build an effective performance measure, and that minimizes the burden on the user.

In summary, this chapter reflects what we believe is a significant challenge for social science researchers: making our research findings relevant. We hope that this chapter will stimulate future efforts to transition research finding into practical and useful tools, particularly in the area of teamwork, which is now recognized as a critical component of most jobs. As Baker and Salas (1997) pointed out 10 years ago, there has been much progress in the area of team performance measure, but there is still much to be learned. Significant research, development, and transitions need to continue.

Endnotes

1. Prior to Study 2, inconsistencies were discovered in the outcome definitions and examples that were presented to SMEs in Study 1. For example, accuracy was defined as the precision with which a task is performed. However, the example involved identifying whether a bomb hit the target. The definition implies a standard, but the example identifies a result. These inconsistencies were remedied in the definitions list presented to SMEs in Study 2.

2. It was determined prior to Study 2 that an additional outcome, completion, was necessary. This was due to the procedural nature of naval aviation tasks, and the existence of a measurement format (checklist) designed specifically to capture completion.

3. Note that this differs somewhat from Study 1, which examined three training purposes. It was decided that combining diagnosis and feedback was appropriate due to the nature of the relationship between them. That is, diagnosis requires a level of detail that would be appropriate for providing feedback. It was felt that querying SMEs on these two dimensions independently would result in redundant data.

References

Alonso, A., Baker, D. P., Day, R., Holtzman, A. K., King, H., Toomey, L., et al. (2006). Reducing medical error in the military health system: How can team training help? *Human Resources Management Review 16*(3), 396–415.

Amason, A. C. & Schweiger, D. M. (1997). The effects of conflict on strategic decision making effectiveness and organizational performance. In C. K. W. De Dreu & E. Van de Vliert (Eds.), *Using conflict in organizations* (pp. 101–115). Thousand Oaks, CA: Sage.

Arvey, R. D. & Murphy, K. R. (1998). Performance evaluation in work settings. *Annual Review of Psychology, 49*, 141–168.

Baker, D. P. & Dismukes, R. K. (2002). Training pilot instructors to assess aircrew performance: Theory, research and practice. *International Journal of Aviation Psychology, 12*, 203–222.

Baker, D. P., Gustafson, S., Beaubien, J. M., Salas, E., & Barach, P. (2003). *Medical teamwork and patient safety: The evidence-based relation*. Washington, DC: American Institutes for Research.

Baker, D. P., Krokos, K. J., & Holtzman, A. K. (2004). *An authoring tool for rapid development of human performance measures: Aviation validation study results*. Scientific and Technical Report presented to NAVAIR, Orlando, FL.

Baker, D. P. & Salas, E. (1992). Principles for measuring teamwork skills. *Human Factors, 34*, 469–475.

Baker, D. P. & Salas, E. (1997). Principles for measuring teamwork: A summary and look toward the future. In M. T. Brannick, E. Salas, & C. Prince (Eds.). *Assessment and measurement of team performance: Theory, methods, and applications* (pp. 331–355). Mahwah, NJ: Lawrence Erlbaum.

Barach, P. & Weingart, M. (2004). Trauma team performance. In W. Wilson, C. Grande, & D. Hoyt (Eds.), *Trauma: Resuscitation, anesthesia, surgery, & critical care*. New York: Dekker, Inc.

Beaubien, J. M. & Alonso, A. (2004). *Developing a teamwork-based measure of surgical team performance*. White paper submitted to the Agency for Healthcare Research and Quality.

Bernardin, H. J., Hagan, C. M., Kane, J. S., & Villanova, P. (1998). Effective performance management: A focus on precision, customers, and situational constraints. In J. W. Smither (Ed.), *Performance appraisal: State of the art in practice* (pp. 3–48). San Francisco, CA: Jossey-Bass, Inc.

Brannick, M. T., Prince, A., Salas, E., & Prince, C. (1993, April). *Impact of raters and events on team performance measurement.* Paper presented at the Eighth Annual Conference of the Society for Industrial and Organizational Psychology, San Francisco, CA.

Brannick, M. T., Roach, R. M., & Salas, E. (1993). Understanding team performance: A multimethod study. *Human Performance, 6*(4), 287–308.

Bretz, R. D., Jr., Milkovich, G. T., & Read, W. (1992). The current state of performance appraisal research and practice: Concerns, directions, and implications. *Journal of Management, 18*, 321–352.

Cannon-Bowers, J. A. & Salas, E. (1997). A framework for developing team performance measures in training. In M. T. Brannick, E. Salas, & C. Prince (Eds.), *Team performance assessment and measurement: Theory, methods, and applications.* Mahwah, NJ: Erlbaum.

Cannon-Bowers, J. A. & Salas, E. (1998). *Making decisions under stress: Implications for individual and team training.* Washington, DC: American Psychological Association.

Cannon-Bowers, J. A., Tannenbaum, S. I., Salas, E., & Volpe, C. E. (1995). Defining competencies and establishing team training requirements. In R. A. Guzzo, E. Salas, & Associates (Eds.), *Team effectiveness and decision-making in organizations* (pp. 333–380). San Francisco, CA: Jossey-Bass.

Costar, D. M., Baker, D. P., & Calderon, R. (2003). *Scenario-based training: Understanding the requirements for human performance measurement.* Technical report submitted to NAVAIR, Orlando, FL.

Davis, L. T., Gaddy, C. D., & Turney, J. R. (1985). *An approach to team skills training of nuclear power plant control room crews* (NUREG/CR-4258GP-R-123022). Columbia, MD: General Physics Corporation.

DeChurch, L. A. & Marks, M. A. (2003). *Teams leading teams: Examining the role of leadership in multi-team systems.* Unpublished doctoral dissertation.

Fowlkes, J. E., Lane, N. E., Salas, E., Franz, T., & Oser, R. (1994). Improving the measurement of team performance: The targets methodology. *Military Psychology, 6*, 47–61.

Goodman, P. S. & Garber, S. (1988). Absenteeism and accidents in a dangerous environment: Empirical analysis of underground coal mines. *Journal of Applied Psychology, 73*, 81–86.

Helmreich, R. L. & Foushee, H. C. (1993). Why crew resource management? Empirical and theoretical bases of human factors training in aviation. In E. L. Weiner, B. G. Kanki, & R. L. Helmreich (Eds.), *Cockpit resource management* (pp. 3–45). San Diego, CA: Academic Press.

Hollenbeck, J. R., Ilgen, D. R., Tuttle, D. B., & Sego, D. J. (1995). Team performance on monitoring tasks: An examination of decision errors in contexts requiring sustained attention. *Journal of Applied Psychology, 80*(6), 685–696.

Howard, S. K., Gaba, D. M., Fish, K. J., Yang, G., & Sarnquist, F. H. (1992). Anesthesia crisis resource management training: Teaching anesthesiologists to handle critical incidents. *Aviation, Space, and Environmental Medicine, 63*, 763–770.

Johnston, J. H., Vincenzi, D. A., Radtke, P. H., Salter, W., & Freeman, J. (2004). *A human systems integration method for validating team performance assessment within a simulation-based training system.* Unpublished manuscript.

Knox, G. E. & Simpson, K. R. (2004). Teamwork: The fundamental building block of high-reliability organizations and patient safety. In B. J. Youngberg & M. J. Hatlie (Eds.), *Patient safety handbook* (pp. 379–415). Boston: Jones and Bartlett.

Landy, F. J. & Farr, J. L. (1980). Performance rating. *Psychological Bulletin, 87,* 72–107.

Marks, M. A., DeChurch, L. A., Mathieu, J. E., Panzer, F. J., & Alonso, A. (2005). Teamwork in multiteam systems. *Journal of Applied Psychology, 90,* 964–971.

Marks, M. A., Mathieu, J. E., & Zaccaro, S. J. (2001). A temporally based framework and taxonomy of team processes. *Academy of Management Review, 26,* 356–376.

Marks, M. A., Sabella, M. J., Burke, C. S., & Zaccaro, S. J. (2002). The impact of cross-training on team effectiveness. *Journal of Applied Psychology, 87*(1), 3–13.

Marks, M. A., Zaccaro, S. J., & Mathieu, J. E. (2000). Performance implications of leader briefings and team-interaction training for team adaptation to novel environments. *Journal of Applied Psychology, 85*(6), 971–986.

McIntyre, R. M. & Salas, E. (1995). Measuring and managing for team performance: Emerging principles from complex environments. In R.A. Guzzo, E. Salas, & Associates (Eds.), *Team effectiveness and decision making in organizations* (pp. 9–45). San Francisco, CA: Jossey-Bass.

McIntyre, R. M., Salas, E., & Glickman, A. S. (1989). *Team research in the 80s: Lessons learned.* Orlando, FL: Naval Training Systems Center.

Mathieu, J. E., Heffner, T. S., Goodwin, G. F., Salas, E., & Cannon-Bowers, J. A. (2000). The influence of shared mental models on team process and performance. *Journal of Applied Psychology, 85*(2), 273–283.

Morgan, B. B., Glickman, A. S., Woodward, E. A., Blaiwes, A. S., & Salas, E. (1986). *Measurement of team behaviors in a Navy environment* (Rep. No. Tech. Report NTSC TR-86-014). Orlando, FL: Naval Training Systems Center.

Morgan, B. B., Jr., Salas, E., & Glickman, A. S. (1994). An analysis of team evolution and maturation. *Journal of General Psychology, 120,* 277–291.

Murphy, K. & Cleveland, J. (1995). *Understanding performance appraisal: Social, organizational, and goal-based perspectives.* Thousand Oaks, CA: Sage.

Panzer, F. J., Fernandez De Cueto, J. E., DeChurch, L. A., Alonso, A., Marks, M. A., Reichard, R., et al. (2003, April). *Diversity in action teams.* Paper presented at the 18th annual meeting of the Society for Industrial and Organizational Psychology, Orlando, FL.

Roberts, K. H. (1990a, Summer). Managing high reliability organizations. *California Management Review,* 101–113.

Roberts, K. H. (1990b). Some characteristics of high reliability organizations. *Organization Science, 1,* 160–177.

Rhynard, P. (2004, November). CG breaks cocaine seizure record. *Coast Guard,* 6.

Salas, E., Bowers, C. A., & Cannon-Bowers, J. A. (1995). Military team research: 10 years of progress. *Military Psychology, 7,* 55–75.

Salas, E., Dickinson, T. L., Converse, S. A., & Tannenbaum, S. I., (1992). Toward an understanding of team performance and training. In R. W. Swezey & E. Salas (Eds.), *Teams: Their training and performance* (pp. 3–29). Norwood, NJ: Ablex.

Salas, E., Sims, D. E., & Burke, S. C. (2005). Is there a "Big Five" in teamwork? *Small Group Research, 36*(5), 555–599.

Smith, P. C. & Kendall, L. M. (1963). Retranslation of expectations: An approach to the construction of unambiguous anchors for rating scales. *Journal of Applied Psychology, 47,* 149–155.

Smither, J. W. (1998). Lessons learned: Research implications for performance appraisal and management practice. In J. W. Smither (Ed.), *Performance appraisal: State of the art in practice* (pp. 537–547). San Francisco, CA: Jossey-Bass, Inc.

Smith-Jentsch, K. A., Campbell, G. E., Milanovich, D. M., & Reynolds, A. M. (2001). Measuring teamwork mental models to support training needs assessment, development, and evaluation: Two empirical studies. *Journal of Organizational Behavior, 22,* 179–194.

Smith-Jentsch, K. A., Johnston, J. H., & Payne, S. C. (1998). Measuring team-related expertise in complex environments. In J. A. Cannon-Bowers & E. Salas (Eds.), *Making decisions under stress: Implications for individual and team training* (pp. 61–87). Washington, DC: American Psychological Association.

Smith-Jentsch, K. A., Zeisig, R. L., Acton, B., & McPherson, J. A. (1998). Team dimensional training: A strategy for guided team self-correction. In J. A. Cannon-Bowers, & E. Salas (Eds.), *Making decisions under stress: Implications for individual and team training* (pp. 61–87). Washington, DC: American Psychological Association.

Smith-Jentsch, K. A., Zeisig, R. L., Acton, B., & McPherson, J. A. (1998). Team dimensional training. In J. A. Cannon-Bowers & E. Salas (Eds.), *Making decisions under stress: Implications for individual and team training* (pp. 271–297). Washington, DC: APA Press.

Squires, P. & Adler, S. (1998). Linking appraisals to individual development and training. In J. W. Smither (Ed.), *Performance appraisal: State of the art in practice* (pp. 445–495). San Francisco, CA: Jossey-Bass, Inc.

Sternberg, R. J. & Dobson, D. M. (1987). Resolving interpersonal conflicts: An analysis of stylistic consistency. *Journal of Personality and Social Psychology, 52,* 794–812.

Stout, R. J., Cannon-Bowers, J. A., Salas, E., & Milanovich, D. M. (1999). Planning, shared understanding, and coordinated performance: An empirical link is established. *Human Factors, 41*(1), 61–71.

Sundstrom, E., De Meuse, K. P., & Futrell, D. (1990). Work teams: Applications and effectiveness. *American Psychologist, 45,* 120–133.

Wilson, K. A., Burke, C. S., Priest, H. A., & Salas, E. (2005). Promoting health care safety through training high reliability teams. *Quality & Safety in Health Care, 14,* 303–309.

Zaccaro, S. J., Rittman, A., & Marks, M. A. (2001). Team leadership. *Leadership Quarterly, 12,* 451–483.

Section IV

Methodological Tools and Developments

15

Automated Communication Analysis of Teams

Peter W. Foltz and Melanie J. Martin

With the advent of advanced communication technology, individuals are better able to work as teams in complex and geographically distributed situations. Teams provide effective means to solve problems in these complex task environments. In such domains as military, civil emergency response, business planning, and medicine, tasks can often exceed the capacity of individual performance. This necessitates that individuals work in teams, with each individual providing some part of the overall solution. One critical difference between problem solving as an individual and in teams is that team members must communicate with each other, providing information that can permit a more effective solution than any one individual working alone. This communication can be a rich indicator of teamwork, coordination, learning, knowledge, collaboration, situation awareness, stress, and workload. Therefore, analysis of such communication can be used to generate measures of team performance and can provide a better understanding of team processes.

While such an analysis can provide useful characterizations of team performance and processes, communication analysis can be very time consuming, often requiring large amounts of tedious hand-coding of the data. Even when the analyses are performed, it can still be hard to relate the results to models of performance in a way that may be generalized to other teams and domains. Thus, what is required are ways of quickly analyzing communication and automatically deriving models of performance. This chapter focuses on automated approaches to characterizing team performance through team communication data. It examines a number of methods that analyze both the pattern of interactions as well as the content of what is said by team members. The chapter takes a multidisciplinary approach, incorporating methods from computational linguistics, machine learning, artificial intelligence, as well as engineering psychology approaches to modeling teams. Highly effective measures of team performance can be derived using this approach, and these measures can be used for both improving the modeling of teams and within applications for team training and monitoring.

Does Communication Predict Performance?

Communication is a very rich source of data on team interactions. When tasks are performed by individuals, it is difficult to measure what a person is thinking. In contrast, tasks that require team members to communicate with each other force the team members to transmit information that, in turn, reveals parts of their cognitive states. These states can include information about individual and common knowledge, situation awareness, degree of uncertainty present, and plans and strategies. Viewed in this manner, team communication may provide something akin to a verbal protocol analysis (e.g., Ericsson & Simon, 1984). Unlike many other measures taken during team tasks (e.g., tests of knowledge, situation awareness; see Cooke, Salas, Cannon-Bowers, & Stout, 2000), it is not invasive and is a natural byproduct of team interaction.

Subjectively, by listening to teams performing tasks and with reasonable accuracy, how well a team is performing can be characterized. Illustrating this is the fact that subject matter experts (SMEs) often monitor teams by purely listening to their communication. For example, in military situations, commanders may listen to radio communication and, based on its content, flow, and speed, may be able to assess their unit's performance. Communication serves as a noninvasive, yet important, proxy for measuring cognition reflected in both team process and performance.

A wide range of studies have shown that hand-coded analyses of communication in teams can predict performance (see Harris & Sherblom, 2002 for a review). These studies have looked at the frequency, patterns, and content of communication. The frequency of types of communications has often been quantified to measure performance. Bowers, Jentsch, Salas, and Braun (1998) analyzed communication sequences of aircrews in flight simulation experiments with a goal of providing better team training and of reducing crew-generated errors. They developed a tag set to annotate the team discourse, and the results of their manual analyses showed promise for further automated investigation of team communication patterns. For example, they found that by examining individual statements, poorer-performing teams had a higher proportion of nontask-related communications. An analysis of the communication patterns, revealed significant differences between successful and unsuccessful crews; generally good teams were more likely to follow statements of uncertainty, fact, planning, or action with acknowledgments or responses (Bowers et al., 1998; see also Oser, Prince, Morgan, & Simpson, 1991).

In another study of communication patterns, Xiao, Seagull, Mackenzie, Ziegert, and Klein (2003) asked experts to annotate videotapes of surgical teams doing trauma resuscitations for initiator and target team members. These communication diagrams were then analyzed for particular patterns. Using this technique, they were able to quantitatively differentiate high versus low task urgency, high versus low team experience, and leadership.

Computing the frequency of communication has also been used to characterize performance, although with varied results. In some research, high-performing teams communicate with higher overall frequency than low-performing teams (Mosier & Chidester, 1991; Orasanu, 1990), but in other cases, this finding has not been supported (e.g., Thornton, 1992). Communication frequency can be affected by such factors as the level of team workload, task difficulty, and team and individual expertise. In some studies frequency is reduced with high workload (Kleinman & Serfaty, 1989; Oser et al., 1991), whereas in other studies it is increased with high workload (e.g., Stout, 1995). Although not all findings are consistent, taken as a whole, results suggest that the manual analysis of communication (based on the frequency, pattern, and content) may be useful in characterizing aspects of team performance.

Automatically Analyzing Communication

While manual analysis of communication can prove useful, it can be quite expensive and time consuming. A single team, such as a team in a command and control center, could generate many hours of data in a typical one-day task. Despite the large volume of communication generated during team tasks, very small amounts of the data are typically collected or analyzed because the amount of communication can easily exceed the capacities of the people who need to study it. Emmert and Barker (1989, p. 244) cited an example of a study requiring 28 hours of transcription and encoding for each hour of communication. Automating the study of communication has the potential to permit such analyses to be done in near real time. The claim made in this chapter is that by applying computational approaches to modeling language, methods to model team communication can be derived that provide an automated and highly accurate approach for generating team performance measures.

Building Communication Models

The remainder of the chapter lays out an approach to automated analysis of communication using a range of cross-disciplinary modeling methods. With the description of each method, the chapter also details studies that test the approach in a number of domains. Finally, a description is given of the utility of this approach to improving modeling of teams as well as developing applications for team monitoring and training.

There are two primary approaches to developing models of human performance. The first, which we call a *theory-driven approach*, is to start with a cognitive, social, or communication theory that posits something about task communication. The researcher then decides the key factors to examine and devises an approach to test these factors. After running an experiment, the experimenter concludes how well the model accounts for the factors. The second approach is a *model-building approach*, which we use in this chapter. In this approach, we start with a set of human-derived or objective performance measures for teams. Human-derived measures are ratings of team performance by SMEs, often including intuitive or holistic ratings of communication, situation awareness critical events, team errors, or classifications of utterances that are indicative of performance (e.g., uncertainty vs. planning). Objective performance measures can include time on task, objectives completed, resource utilization, kills, or communication failures. Given that a set of communication outputs from the team and some performance measures exist, machine-learning techniques are then used to infer the relationship between the performance measures and the communication data. Essentially, the system is discovering relationships between communication and performance. The theory-driven and model-driven approaches differ in that the latter does not initially posit a particular relationship between communication and performance but instead tries to find out if, and the degree to which, such a relationship exists. The validity of the relationship can then be tested on new or held-out data.

Of course, to find these relationships one must have capable computational models that can perform this inferential step. These computational models must accurately measure features in communication that would relate to measures of team cognition. To create such a model, recent advances in the fields of computational cognitive models (e.g., latent semantic analysis, or LSA; Landauer, Foltz, & Laham, 1998); computational linguistics (e.g., Jurafsky & Martin, 2000); social network analysis (see Carley & Prietula, 2001, and Chapter 16 in this volume); machine-learning techniques that employ hill climbing, clustering, classification, and generalization methods; and automated speech recognition can be leveraged. By combining these techniques and applying them to team communication and performance data, predictive models of performance can be derived.

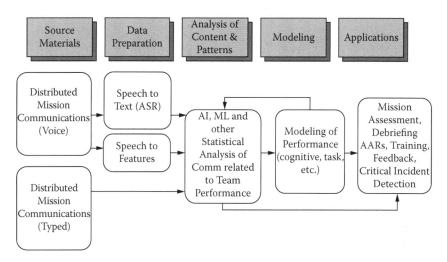

FIGURE 15.1
Communications analysis pipeline.

The goal is a communication analysis system that can turn communication into performance metrics. Figure 15.1 shows the outline of such a system. A communication analysis pipeline should be able to take input from voice data (or written chat or e-mail). Speech is automatically converted to text, which is then analyzed through computational linguistics and machine-learning statistical processes. The output can then be incorporated with other cognitive and task models of performance. In addition, the final output can provide indications of performance that can be used within training, feedback, or monitoring of teams.

Automated Communication Analysis Methods

To perform automated communication analysis, we need to distinguish the types of communication that can be analyzed. Communication data can be separated into two distinct types. First, pattern data describe the physical pattern of interactions among team members. This type of data includes who talks to who, when, and how much. Second, content focuses on what was actually said, including the content of the whole team's discourse, individual utterances, and the classification of these utterances. The remainder of the chapter covers these approaches with an emphasis on the analysis of content.

Pattern of Communication

The pattern of communication provides information about the type and duration of interactions among team members. This information can be turned into such measures as the duration of communication among team members, a characterization of the patterns of interactions, or frequency counts of team members' contributions. Analyses of the network of dynamic patterns can provide information about the social networks within the team (see Monge and Contractor, 2003, and Chapter 16 in this volume on social network analysis).

Interaction pattern data are often readily available from team tasks. These data can be obtained by, for example, recording the time and duration of communication events such as microphones, telephone calls, e-mail, or instant message use. This makes collection and analysis relatively straightforward and can permit a range of measures addressing team quality and performance, situation awareness, social structure, and adaptability of the team network.

The communication patterns can be related to social theories of communication and analyzed as a complex networked system. Such analyses can be used to measure the communication patterns over time by using lag sequential or Markov chains, time series modeling, Fourier analysis (Watt & VanLear, 1996, p. 12), or related methods that reveal the changes in the communication patterns over time (Sanderson & Fisher, 1994). The patterns can also be linked to social theories, thereby providing characterization of how well a set of communication patterns matches particular expected social patterns. Communication patterns can be analyzed as frequency counts of the categories or as a series of events (called *interaction analysis*; see Emmert, 1989 for discussion and Poole, Holmes, Watson, & DeSanctis, 1993 for an example) or by using lag sequential analysis, which examines sequences of communication patterns over different time lags. For example, in a simulated unmanned air vehicle (UAV) environment with three team members, Kiekel, Cooke, Foltz, Gorman, and Martin (2002) analyzed turn-taking sequences and dominance of team members using a communications log (CommLog) that records the quantity of communication: who is speaking to whom and the duration of the speech. Using procedural networks (ProNet; Cooke, Neville, & Rowe, 1996), which perform an automated sequential analysis using the Pathfinder (Schvaneveldt, 1990) network modeling tool, they were able to derive network path-length variables to measure a team's consistency and turn-taking behavior. These variables correlated with team performance, particularly in the skill acquisition phase of team training (Kiekel et al., 2002), and successfully identified communication glitches, where the communication channel between two team members fails during a mission (Kiekel, Gorman, & Cooke, 2004).

Kiekel et al. (2002) also developed Clustering Hypothesized Underlying Models in Sequence (CHUMS), a clustering method to determine pattern shifts in sequences of data of who talked with whom. This measure of the stability of team communications correlated with team performance during the skill acquisition phase and with situation awareness after skills had been acquired. This measure was also used to study the effects of a communication glitch on colocated and distributed teams.

Taking a different approach, but also using a simulated military framework, Carley and colleagues (Carley, Moon, Schneider, & Shigiltchoff, 2005; Moon, Carley, Schneider, & Shigiltchoff, 2005) analyzed a large amount of interaction data from America's Army, an on-line multiparty first-person-shooter game. Two types of team communication analysis were conducted on this data: (1) who talks after whom (all communications are from an individual to the whole team); and (2) type of communication. The two types of communication considered were "normal" and "in report." In-report communication occurs when a player presses a special "hot" key that broadcasts his or her location to other team members, whereas normal communication consists of the selection of predefined phrases or typed messages to broadcast to the team. Their work is automated, first creating a relational database to organize, mine, and then perform statistical analyses. Results indicated that high-frequency in-reporting was essential for winning games. Among findings for who talked after whom, a communication structure with a high sequential edge count and high network level can reduce the damage a team received (Carley et al., 2005).

In subsequent work Moon, Carley, Schneider, and Shigiltchoff (2005) used the same data with location information added to the log records, a who-was-close-to-whom social network was created. Results suggested that dense networks with two subgroups performed best. In communication network analysis, two dominant communication networks—star-shaped and long-chained—were found. Long-chained networks minimized the need for excess communication and were better (e.g., higher-performing teams communicated more than poor-performing teams; Moon et al., 2005). Some of the tools used in the work by Moon et al. (2005) just discussed have been applied to studying team situation awareness and mental models of teams during a simulated task of planning to rescue personnel from an island in the midst of war (Weil, Carley, Diesner, Freeman, & Cooke, 2006).

Analysis of the Content of Communication

While analysis of patterns of interaction among team members provides information about *who* is talking and *when* information was passed, it does not provide information on *what* information was passed. By focusing on the communication content, one can monitor the exact words used to determine an individual's and a team's level of knowledge, situation awareness, errors in process, and workload and potentially to predict future performance problems. Thus, analysis of the content of the communication provides a much greater wealth of information about the performance of the team than pattern-based analysis alone.

Nevertheless, content analyses of verbal interactions have been hindered by a lack of effective tools. While some methods described earlier rely on tedious hand-coding of verbal interactions, automated analyses through computational linguistic and knowledge representation techniques provide the promise of real-time assessment of teams' and users' mental and performance states. A number of artificial intelligence, statistical, and machine-learning techniques have been applied to discourse modeling, generally for the purpose of improving speech recognition and dialogue systems. However, few have focused directly on just the content of a team's discourse.

In the remainder of this chapter, several computational approaches to content analysis are described, with a focus primarily on the approach of using latent semantic analysis, a cognitive discourse modeling technique. LSA is a fully automatic corpus-based statistical modeling method for extracting and inferring relations of expected contextual usage of words in discourse (Landauer et al., 1998). In LSA a training text is represented as a matrix, where each row represents a unique word in the text and each column represents a text passage or other unit of context. The entries in this matrix are the (possibly weighted) frequency of the word in the context. A singular value decomposition (SVD) of the matrix results in a 100–500 dimensional "semantic space," where the original words and passages are represented as vectors. One effect of the creation of the semantic space is that semantically similar words in the corpus are represented close to each other in the semantic space. The meaning of any passage is the average of the vectors of the words in the passage (Landauer, Laham, Rehder, & Schreiner, 1997). Words, utterances, and whole documents can then be compared with each other by computing the cosine between the vectors representing any two texts. This provides a measure of the semantic similarity of those two texts, even if they do not contain words in common. LSA has been used for a wide range of applications and for simulating knowledge representation, discourse, and psycholinguistic phenomena. Additional details are not covered here, but information on the theory behind LSA and its application can be found in papers about information retrieval (Deerwester, Dumais, Furnas, Landauer, & Harshman, 1990), automated essay scoring (Landauer Laham, & Foltz, 2000), and automated text analysis (Foltz, 1996, 2007).

To apply LSA to communication analysis, we generate predictive models to measure the free-form verbal interactions among team members. Because LSA can measure and compare the semantic information in these verbal interactions, it can be used to characterize the quality and quantity of information expressed. LSA analysis can be used to determine the semantic content of any utterance made by a team member as well as to measure the semantic similarity of an entire team's communication to another team.

There are two primary approaches to which the LSA-based content analysis has been applied. The first approach is to generate predictive models of performance. These models predict such measures as SME ratings of situation awareness, solution quality, planning, and objective measures of performance. The second approach is to tag (annotate) the communication for features that are predictive of performance. For example, one might want to identify all utterances where a team member does planning or expresses uncertainty (e.g., Bowers et al., 1998). In both cases we use the model-building approach. The computer generates variables from computational analyses of the communication and then uses these variables to predict objective or subjective measures of performance. The following section describes these two approaches.

Generating Predictive Models of Performance

Generating a predictive model of performance is based on the notion that team performance is reflected in the team's communication. The goal of creating such a model is to train an algorithm to extract features from the communication predictive of the team's performance. In a sense, the system learns to mimic the ability of humans to observe the communication of teams and generate a score for the team. A wide range of potential scores of performance or team process can be used to evaluate team performance and process: ratings of team performance by SMEs; holistic ratings of communication; situation awareness; identification of critical events; team errors; and objective performance measures such as time on task, number of objectives completed, kills, or communication failures. The system must infer the relationship between given scores and automatically extracted communication features.

The communication features used are a series of LSA-based measures as well as other computational linguistic features, including syntactic features and statistical features of the language (see Jurafsky & Martin, 2000 for examples of typical features used in computational linguistics). The features include measures that examine how semantically similar a team transcript is to other transcripts of known quality, measures of the semantic coherence of one team member's utterance to the next, the overall cohesiveness of the dialogue, characterizations of the quantity and quality of information provided by team members, and measures of the types of words chosen by the team members. Hill-climbing methods (e.g., step-wise regression, random forests, support vector machines) are then used to select a subset of the features that best predict performance variables (see Witten & Eibe, 1999). Typically, the derived model has three to five features that together best predict the team performance score. The quality of the model is then tested by using cross-validation or hold-out procedures in which the model is derived on a subset of the data and tested on the remaining data. Additional details of the measures and technical information on this approach applied to military and simulated military team communication can be found in Foltz, Martin, Abdelali, Rosenstein, and Oberbreckling (2006), Gorman, Foltz, Kiekel, Martin, and Cooke (2003), and Kiekel et al. (2002).

Predictive models have been built using a number of team communication data sets and for a number of different performance measures within those data sets. Table 15.1 shows a summary of results of using derived models to predict different team performance measures across a number of data sets. For each one, every transcript was associated with one or more objective performance scores or SME ratings for the team's mission. Each of the models was developed to be specific to that particular data set and performance measure.

The data sets are as follows:

1. CERTT-UAV: Typed transcripts of teams of three people who performed UAV missions in a synthetic task environment with an objective measure of their overall team performance (see Gorman et al., 2003).

2. Tactical Decision Making Under Stress (TADMUS): Typed transcripts collected at the Surface Warfare Officer's School (SWOS) (see Johnston, Poirer, & Smith-Jentsch, 1998). In the scenario, a ship's air defense warfare (ADW) team performed the detect-to-engage (DTE) sequence on aircraft in the vicinity of the battle group and reported it to the tactical action officer and bridge. Associated with the transcripts were a series of SME-rated performance measures.

3. Air Force Research Laboratory (AFRL) F16: Automatic speech recognition generated transcripts of teams of four F-16s and an airborne warning and control system (AWACS) controller in AFRL Mesa's Distributed Mission Training Simulator with SME ratings of a range of team performance variables.

4. Office of Naval Research (ONR) noncombatant evacuation operation (NEO): Typed transcripts from teams of undergraduates who performed planning for a simulated noncombatant extraction operation with SME ratings of overall team performance.

TABLE 15.1

Predictions of Performance for Different Team Data Sets

Data Source	Number of Transcripts	Team Performance Measure	Objective/ Subjective	Corr. to Measure
CERTT-UAV AF1	67	Composite score of objective measures	O	0.76
CERTT-UAV AF3	85	Composite score of objective measures	O	0.72
Navy TADMUS	64	Leadership	S	0.73
Navy TADMUS	64	Completeness of reports	S	0.63
Navy TADMUS	64	Providing/requesting backup	S	0.62
Navy TADMUS	64	Error correction	S	0.57
Navy TADMUS	64	Information exchange	S	0.50
AFRL F-16 DMT	229	Planning operations	S	0.58
AFRL F-16 DMT	229	Situation awareness	S	0.54
AFRL F-16 DMT	229	Overall engagement quality	S	0.44
AFRL F-16 DMT	229	Number of prior missions in simulator	O	0.67
ONR NEO	16	Rating of overall team performance	O	0.90
ARL SASO	480	Aggregate score for correct team actions	O	0.61

5. Army Research Laboratory (ARL) stability and support operations (SASO): Typed transcripts from undergraduates who performed intelligence decision making during simulated stability and support operations.

The correlations presented are Pearson correlations using a hold-out procedure in which each team transcript score is predicted by deriving a model based on all remaining transcripts. This approach provides a conservative estimate of prediction ability and generalizability.

Overall, the results from Table 15.1 show that the technique can predict many different objective and SME-rated metrics of team performance. These metrics include quality of communication, leadership, information passing, providing and requesting assistance, error correction, planning, situation awareness, and engagement quality. These metrics are aspects not only of communication but also of general cognition, knowledge, and skills involved in performing team tasks. Although predicted performance varied across domains, all were highly significant and, as such, suggest ways to improve performance in those areas. Human interrater reliability was not assessed for any of the subjective measures; however, the correlations presented in Table 15.1 are likely close to the level of agreement among humans. For example, a prior study on similar AFRL human subject ratings data found SME agreement (using alpha) of 0.42 (see Krusmark, Schreiber, & Bennett, 2004). Thus, it is likely that the computer-based methods were correlating at near the maximum level of human–human intercorrelation.

The results show that by measuring language variables from a team's transcript as a whole, one can accurately characterize the quality of the team. While the models used LSA as a critical component for measuring content in the discourse and it accounted for the largest amount of variance, additional language variables significantly improved the predictions. These variables included the complexity of language, the frequency of usage, and the choice of words.

While these studies all focus on spoken or written speech acts, it should be noted that communication does not just have to represent actual speech acts. Communication can be any information shared among team members, such as documents. Hill, Dong, and Agogino (2002) studied levels of shared understanding and team cohesiveness in engineering design teams by applying LSA to design documents generated in the collaborative design process (e.g., mission statements, concept selection rationale, prototype description, test plans, design evaluation). Assessments generated by their automated methods had about 80% agreement with the assessments of human experts.

Automated Discourse Annotation of Content

As described already, analyzing networks based on who speaks to whom and the content of a team's whole transcript can provide a large amount of information about team processes, situation awareness, and performance. However, a more complete picture requires that we also analyze the content of the individual utterances or dialogue acts within the team communication dialogue. This provides refined information about what any individual or group of individuals are saying at any point in time. For instance, one would want to know when an individual is planning versus expressing uncertainty, since this provides information about the individual's situation awareness and their performance as a team member contributing to the overall team performance. Similarly, if a particular person has passed information to his or her commander, or if a leader has sent the appropriate commands at the appropriate time, this may enable real-time performance evaluation during training and monitoring of teams.

Most analysis of discourse content at the utterance level has required hand annotation of the discourse (e.g., Bowers et al., 1998). Manual annotation is expensive and time-consuming and can introduce subjectivity or bias. To remedy the situation, extensive recent work in the computational linguistics community has been performed to develop automatic annotation techniques using primarily statistical and machine learning tools. Essentially, the problem of annotating is a problem of classification. A computer or human annotator needs to examine a part of the communication and assign it to a particular category. This work is now surveyed to give the reader an idea of the range of methods that can be applied.

Classifiers

Dialogue act annotation or tagging can be viewed as a classification problem: Given a finite set of tags and a set of features (attributes) of the dialogue act (utterance), the goal is to assign the correct (or most probable) tag to the utterance guided by the values of the features. Viewed this way, the problem is well suited to supervised machine-learning approaches to build a classifier. Machine learning in this context is generally supervised because the classifier needs to learn to tag the dialogue acts based on some amount of manually tagged data.

To better comprehend the classifier, it is noted that the set of possible tags is predefined and may be specific to the discourse genre being tagged. For example, a tag set for annotating military mission transcripts may be smaller than would be necessary for unrestricted general conversations. A key element in building a classifier is finding a good set of features that can be efficiently and automatically extracted from the dialogue. Features generally contain information about the syntax, semantics, or context of the utterance. Each utterance can be represented by a vector containing the values for each feature on that utterance. The vector can then be used by the classifier to assign an appropriate tag to the utterance.

LSA-Based Classifiers

LSA lends itself well as a feature for classifiers because it provides information about the semantic content of any utterance. Martin and Foltz (2004) and Foltz et al. (2006) used LSA to classify utterances from the CERTT-UAV corpus using the Bowers et al. (1998) tag set. In their classifier, the main features were the semantic similarity between a given utterance and utterances whose tags are known, augmented with some additional syntactic features. The semantic similarity between utterances is measured by the cosine of the angle between the vectors representing the utterances in the LSA semantic space. The concept behind the approach is that if a subset of the utterances was already tagged by a human, the computer could then learn to tag in the same way by comparing a new utterance to utterances that had already been tagged. The results showed that the system could tag within 15% of the accuracy of human taggers, as measured by human–human agreement versus Human–computer agreement (see Foltz et al., 2006). In addition, the system was able to tag an hour of team discourse in under a minute, whereas it took human taggers about 45 minutes per hour of dialogue. A similar approach was taken by Serafin and Di Eugenio (2004) to classify dialogue acts in tutoring conversations.

Additional Tagging Methods

Many of the other methods that have been applied to discourse annotation or dialogue act tagging have been successfully used in part-of-speech tagging, where context features play a larger role. Prominent among these methods are decision trees, Markov chains (n-gram models), and hidden Markov models (HMMs).

A decision-tree classifier is constructed by recursively partitioning the training data (an already classified set of utterances) based on statistical features extracted from the utterances. At each step the feature is selected that most reduces the uncertainty about the class in each partition of the data. Once the decision tree is constructed, it can be used to assign the most probable class to a new utterance, based on its features. In relatively early work, studies by Mast, Niemann, Nöth, and Schukat-Talamazzini (1996) and Core (1998) used decision trees in dialogue act classification and concluded that n-gram or HMMs seemed more promising.

N-grams or Markov chains estimate the probability of a given tag under the assumption that the probability of the tag depends only on the previous n-tags (local context) and that it is stable over time. A Markov chain can be represented as a state diagram, where the states are tags and the edges are transitions between the states; when a probability is assigned to each edge, we have a Markov model. An HMM has an additional layer of broader categories or hidden relationships learned by the classifier. Promising results in the area of dialogue act tagging were obtained by Chu-Carroll (1998), Stolcke et al. (2000), and Venkataraman, Stolcke, and Shirberg (2002). For example, Stolcke et al. was able to predict the tags assigned to discourse within 15% of the accuracy of trained human annotators in conversational speech.

As automatic dialogue act tagging continues to grow as a research area, the range of tag sets, corpora, and methodologies has grown. In more recent work, Clark and Popescu-Belis (2004) explored the use of multilayered maximum entropy classifiers on multiparty meeting corpora. Their work includes the definition of a new tag set and discussion of some issues of tag-set design, including theoretical soundness, empirical validation, and mapping to existing tag sets. Also working in the area of multiparty meetings and using a maximum entropy classifier, Ang, Liu, and Shirberg (2005) found that both the segmentation of spoken dialogue and classification of dialogue acts are difficult for a fully automatic system in this domain. Challenges include system performance degradation due to word recognition errors, multiple speakers with frequent overlap, and interruption. Ji and Bilmes (2005), who also worked in this area, provided a full analysis of how graphical models—in particular generative and conditional dynamic Bayesian networks—can be adapted to dialogue act tagging.

In the area of e-mail dialogue act classification, Carvahlo and Cohen (2005) developed a dependency-network-based collective classification algorithm using maximum entropy classifiers that provides modest but statistically significant improvement in some cases. Also providing a new approach, combining natural language processing (NLP) analysis with information retrieval (IR) techniques, Feng, Shaw, Kim, and Hovy (2006) were able to detect conversation focus in threaded discussions.

Overall, the area of dialogue act tagging is an emerging area of proven usefulness in many settings, including automated tutoring systems and information retrieval. Work discussed herein shows reasonable success with LSA-based methods and HMMs. Improved results will aid in our ability to understand team communication and, hence, processes, mental models, situation awareness, and performance. Thus, although this area is growing quite quickly in computational linguistics, the techniques are quite applicable to those who want to apply them to team analyses.

Conclusions

Communication represents a rich resource for monitoring and assessing teams. It provides a natural form of data that reveals cognitive and social aspects of individual and team functioning. Recent research has started to examine the role of communication in team cognition, both from the point of view of understanding how communication affects teams and how communication can reveal the functioning of the teams. However, until recently, the large amounts of transcript data and the difficulty in having reliable coding have limited researchers from performing effective analyses of team discourse. Team performance measurement requires understanding theories and techniques from a range of fields. Most typically these fields have included human factors, cognitive psychology, educational measurement, and communications. This chapter posits that more attention to computational language fields can further improve measurement of team process and performance. With the advances in artificial intelligence, computational cognitive modeling, and computational linguistics, as well as sufficiently fast computers, it has become possible to perform automated analyses of team discourse.

The methods described in this chapter primarily took a model-driven approach, deriving the team performance model from collected data rather than generating a theory-based model and then testing against the data. Both approaches are valid ways of performing team analysis; however, the model-driven approach lends itself well to applying computational linguistic and machine-learning techniques to large amounts of team communication data. The two approaches can still be used on the same data and may help support each other.

There is a range of different types of communication that can be analyzed in teams, including analysis of patterns, communication content of the team as a whole, and individual utterances. Within each of those, a range of computational techniques can be applied. Therefore, before applying such analyses, team researchers will need to determine what aspects of communication they want to measure and what performance metrics they want to derive from the analysis. For example, a pattern analysis may be more suitable for addressing questions of social structure within a team, whereas automatically deriving team performance scores from the content may be more suitable for analysis of team and individual situation awareness. Nevertheless, these methods can be combined. One can use the methods together to examine the pattern of the flow of content. For instance, to trace a commander's intent, one could use content-based tagging to identify utterances associated with the commander's intent and then could use pattern analysis to measure how that particular information has moved through the network of team members. Indeed, a hybrid approach in which multiple automated measures are used can help provide converging evidence, higher reliability, and novel methods of tracing content across teams.

The methods described in this chapter can yield information on how communication can be turned into metrics that are valid, reliable, and useful to the assessment and understanding of team performance and cognition. The measures can address both individual- and group-level performance and can provide metrics to quantify aspects such as the quality of team planning, decision making, performance, communication, and process. The metrics can further be used to identify sources of failures and successes within teams, which can be used for both monitoring and feedback to teams. Thus, such metrics are necessary prerequisites to the development of team training programs and the design of technologies that facilitate team performance. In particular, application domains that are communications intensive and that require a high degree of team coordination can especially benefit from such streamlined methods for assessing team communication.

A number of applications have been developed to perform automated analyses. Foltz, Laham, and Derr (2003) and Foltz et al. (2006) showed that they could take audio communication from F-16 pilots in simulators, convert it through automated speech recognition, and produce overall team performance predictions in almost real time. In an application focusing more on monitoring teams of learners, LaVoie et al. (in press), Lochbaum, Streeter, and Psotka (2002), and Streeter, Lochbaum, and LaVoie (2007) developed and tested a collaborative learning environment called knowledge post. The application consisted of an off-the-shelf threaded discussion group that has been substantially augmented with LSA-based functionality to evaluate and support individual and team contributions. Tests on the system at the Army War College and the U.S. Air Force Academy showed that it was able to automatically notify the instructor when discussion went off-topic, to insert expert comments and library article interjections into the discussion in appropriate places by automatically monitoring the discussion activity, and to enhance the overall quality of the discussion and consequent learning level of the participants when compared to more standard threaded discussion applications. Thus, the team analysis pipeline shown in Figure 15.1 can be completed. The techniques described in this chapter can be implemented within tools to automatically monitor teams and have effective measures and feedback.

This approach suggests a range of potential applications for assessing teams. These applications can include systems to detect critical incidents, to monitor for poor performance, to generate automated after-action reviews, to detect workload, and to provide feedback to teams and individuals on such aspects as communication and process quality, knowledge, and situation awareness failures. While helping provide new applications, the approach also helps inform theories and models of team cognition and communication. This opens new frontiers in research in which we can improve our modeling of teams through applying computational modeling. As we are better able to analyze the wealth of communication data generated by teams, we will be better able to understand and develop better theories of how teams perform.

Acknowledgments

This research was has benefited from collaboration work with the team members from Pearson Knowledge Technologies (Robert Oberbreckling, Mark Rosenstein, Noelle LaVoie, and Marcia Derr), the Cognitive Engineering Research on Team Tasks (CERTT) laboratory (Nancy Cooke, Preston Kiekel, Jamie Gorman, and Susan Smith); the Computing Research Laboratory at New Mexico State (Ahmed Abdelali and David Farwell); and from data provided by Joan Johnston at the Naval Air Systems Command (NAVAIR), Norm Warner at the Office of Naval Research (ONR), and Winston Bennett at the Air Force Research Laboratory (AFRL). This work was supported by the ONR, the Defense Advanced Research Projects Agency (DARPA), Army Research Laboratory, and AFRL.

References

Ang, J., Liu, Y., & Shriberg, E. (2005). Automatic dialog act segmentation and classification in multiparty meetings. In *Proceedings of the International Conference of Acoustics, Speech, and Signal Processing* (Vol. 1, pp. 1061–1064). Philadelphia.

Bowers, C. A., Jentsch, F., Salas, E., & Braun, C. C. (1998). Analyzing communication sequences for team training needs assessment. *Human Factors, 40*, 672–679.

Carley, K. M. & Prietula, M. (Eds.). (2001). *Computational organization theory*. Hillsdale, NJ: Lawrence Erlbaum Associates.

Carley, K. M., Moon, I., Schneider, M., & Shigiltchoff, O. (2005*). Detailed analysis of factors affecting team success and failure in the America's Army game.* Technical Report CMU-ISRI-05-120. Pittsburgh, PA: CASOS, Carnegie Mellon University.

Carvalho, V. & Cohen, W. W. (2005). On the collective classification of e-mail "speech acts." In *Proceedings of the 28th Annual International ACM SIGIR Conference on Research and Development in Information Retrieval*, 345–352. New York, NY: ACM Press.

Chu-Carroll, J. (1998). A statistical model for discourse act recognition in dialogue interactions. In J. Chu-Charroll & N. Green (Eds.), *Applying machine learning to discourse processing. Papers from the 1998 AAAI spring symposium.* Technical Report SS-98-01 (pp. 12–17). Menlo Park, CA: AAAI Press.

Clark, A. & Popescu-Belis, A. (2004). Multi-level dialogue act tags. *Proceedings of SIGDIAL '04 5th SIGDIAL workshop on discourse and dialog*, 163–170. East Strandsburg, PA: Association of Computational Linguistics.

Cooke, N. J., Neville, K. J., & Rowe, A. L. (1996). Procedural network representations of sequential data. *Human-Computer Interaction, 11*, 29–68.

Cooke, N. J., Salas, E., Cannon-Bowers, J. A., & Stout, R. (2000). Measuring team knowledge. *Human Factors, 42*, 151–173.

Core, M. (1998). Analyzing and predicting patterns of DAMSL utterance tags. In J. Chu-Charroll & N. Green (Eds.), *Applying machine learning to discourse processing. Papers from the 1998 AAAI spring symposium.* Technical Report SS-98-01 (pp. 18–24). Menlo Park, CA: AAAI Press.

Deerwester, S., Dumais, S. T., Furnas, G. W., Landauer, T.K., & Harshman, R. A. (1990). Indexing by latent semantic analysis. *Journal of the American Society for Information Science, 41*, 391–407.

Emmert, V. J. (1989). Interaction analysis. In P. Emmert & L. L. Barker (Eds.), *Measurement of communication behavior* (pp. 218–248). White Plains, NY: Longman, Inc.

Emmert, P. & Barker, L. L. (1989). *Measurement of communication behavior.* White Plains, NY: Longman, Inc.

Ericsson, K. A. & Simon, H. A. (1984). *Protocol analysis.* Cambridge, MA: MIT Press.

Feng, D., Shaw, E., Kim, J., & Hovy, E. (2006). Learning to detect conversation focus of threaded discussions. In *Proceedings of the 2006 Human Language Technology Conference of the North American Chapter of the Association for Computational Linguistics*, 208–215. East Standsburg, PA: Association for Computational Linguistics.

Foltz, P. W. (1996). Latent semantic analysis for text-based research. *Behavior Research Methods, Instruments, and Computer, 28*, 197–202.

Foltz, P. W. (2007). Discourse coherence and LSA. In T. K Landauer, W. Kintsch, D. McNamara, & S. Dennis (Eds.), *Handbook of latent semantic analysis*. Mahwah, NJ: Lawrence Erlbaum Publishing.

Foltz, P. W., Laham, R. D., & Derr, M. (2003). Automated speech recognition for modeling team performance. In *Proceedings of the 47th Annual Human Factors and Ergonomic Society Meeting*, 673–677. Santa Monica, CA: HFES.

Foltz, P. W., Martin, M. J., Abdelali, A., Rosenstein, M. B., & Oberbreckling, R. J. (2006). Automated team discourse modeling: Test of performance and generalization. *Proceedings of the 28th Annual Cognitive Science Conference*, 1317–1322. Mahwah, NJ: Lawrence Erlbaum Associates.

Gorman, J. C., Foltz, P. W., Kiekel, P. A., Martin, M. J., & Cooke, N. J. (2003). Evaluation of latent semantic analysis-based measures of communications content. *Proceedings of the 47th annual human factors and ergonomic society meeting*, 424–428. Santa Monica, CA: HFES.

Harris, T. E. & Sherblom, J. C. (2002). *Small group and team communication*. New York: Allyn & Bacon.

Hill, A. W., Dong, A., & Agogino, A. M. (2002). Towards computational tools for supporting the reflective team. In J. Gero (Ed.), *Artificial intelligence in design* (pp.305–325). Dordrecht, The Netherlands: Kluwer Academic Publishers.

Ji, G. & Bilmes, J. (2005). Dialog act tagging using graphical models. *Proceedings of the International Conference of Acoustics, Speech, and Signal Processing* (pp. 33–36). Piscataway, NJ: IEEE.

Johnston, J. H., Poirier, J., & Smith-Jentsch, K. A. (1998) Decision making under stress: Creating a research methodology. In J. A. Cannon-Bowers & E. Salas (Eds.), *Making decisions under stress: Implications for individuals and teams* (pp. 39–59). Washington, DC: APA.

Jurafsky, D. & Martin, J. H. (2000). *Speech and language processing: An introduction to natural language processing, computational linguistics, and speech recognition*. Upper Saddle River, NJ: Prentice-Hall.

Kiekel, P. A., Cooke, N. J., Foltz, P. W., Gorman, J., & Martin, M. J. (2002). Some promising results of communication-based automatic measures of team cognition. *Proceedings of the Human Factors and Ergonomics Society 46th annual meeting*, 298–302. Santa Monica, CA: HFES.

Kiekel, P., Gorman, J., & Cooke, N. (2004). Measuring speech flow of co-located and distributed command and control teams during a communication channel glitch. *Proceedings of the Human Factors and Ergonomics Society 48th annual meeting*, 683–687.

Kleinman, D. L. & Serfaty, D. (1989). Team performance assessment in distributed decision making. In R. Gilson, J. P. Kincaid, & B. Godiez (Eds.), *Proceedings of the Interactive Networked Simulation for Training Conference* (pp. 22–27). Orlando, FL: Institute for Simulation and Training.

Krusmark, M., Schreiber, B., & Bennett, W. (2004). *The effectiveness of a traditional gradesheet for measuring air combat team performance in simulated distributed mission operations.* AFRL-HE-AZ-TR-2004-0090. Air Force Research Laboratory, Warfighter Readiness Research Division.

Landauer, T., Laham, D., Rehder, B., & Schreiner, M. (1997). How well can passage meaning be derived without using word order? A comparison of latent semantic analysis and humans. In M. G. Shafto & P. Langley (Eds.), *Proceedings of the 19th annual meeting of the Cognitive Science Society* (pp. 412–417). Mahwah, NJ: Erlbaum.

Landauer, T. K., Foltz, P. W., & Laham, D. (1998). An introduction to latent semantic analysis. *Discourse Processes, 25,* 259–284.

Landauer, T., Laham, D., & Foltz, P. (2002). The intelligent essay assessor. *IEEE Intelligent Systems 15*(5), 27–31. Piscataway, NJ: IEEE.

LaVoie, N., Streeter, L., Lochbaum, K., Boyce, L., Krupnick, C., & Psotka, J. (in press). Automating expertise in collaborative learning environments. *International Journal of Computer-Supported Collaborative Learning.*

Lochbaum, K., Streeter, L., & Psotka, J. (2002). *Exploiting technology to harness the power of peers.* Paper presented at the Interservice/Industry Training, Simulation and Education Conference. Arlington, VA: NTSA.

Martin, M. J. & Foltz, P. W. (2004). Automated team discourse annotation and performance prediction using LSA. In *Proceedings of the Human Language Technology and North American Association for Computational Linguistics Conference (HLT/NAACL),* Boston, MA.

Mast, M., Niemann, H., Nöth, E., & Schukat-Talamazzini, E. G. (1996). Automatic classification of dialog acts with semantic classification trees and polygrams. In S. Wermter, E. Riloff, & G. Scheler (Eds.), *Connectionist, statistical, and symbolic approaches to learning for natural language processing.* Heidelberg: Springer.

Monge, P. R. & Contractor, N. S. (2003). *Theories of communication networks.* Oxford, England: Oxford University Press.

Moon, I., Carley, K. M., Schneider, M., & Shigiltchoff, O., (2005). Detailed analysis of team movement and communication affecting team performance in the America s Army Game. Technical Report CMU-ISRI-05-129, Carnegie Mellon University.

Mosier, K. L. & Chidester, T. R. (1991). Situation assessment and situation awareness in a team setting. In Y. Quéinnec & F. Daniellou (Eds.), *Designing for everyone: Proceedings of the 11th Congress of the International Ergonomics Association* (pp. 798–800). London: Taylor & Francis.

Orasanu, J. (1990). *Shared mental models and crew performance* (Report CSLTR-46). Princeton, NJ: Princeton University.

Oser, R. L., Prince, C., Morgan, B. B., Jr., & Simpson, S. (1991). *An analysis of aircrew communication patterns and content* (NTSC Tech. Rep. 90-009). Orlando, FL: Naval Training Systems Center.

Poole, M.S., Holmes, M., Watson, R., & DeSanctis, G. (1993). Group decision support systems and group communication: A comparison of decision making in computer-supported and nonsupported groups. *Communication Research, 20,* 176–213.

Sanderson, P. M. & Fisher, C. (1994). Exploratory sequential data analysis: Foundations. *Human-Computer Interaction, 9,* 251–317.

Serafin, R. & Di Eugenio, B. (2004). *FLSA: Extending latent semantic analysis with features for dialogue act classification.* In *Proceedings of the 42nd annual meeting of the Association for Computational Linguistics,* 692–699. East Strandsburg, PA: Association for Computational Linguistics.

Schvaneveldt, R. W. (1990). *Pathfinder associative networks: Studies in knowledge organization.* Norwood, NJ: Ablex.

Stolcke, A., Ries, K., Coccaro, N., Shriberg, E., Bates, R., Jurafsky, D., et al. (2000). Dialogue act modeling for automatic tagging and recognition of conversational speech. *Computational Linguistics, 26,* 339–373.

Stout, R. J. (1995). Planning effects on communication strategies: A shared mental model perspective. In *Proceedings of the Human Factors Society 39th annual meeting,* 1278–1282.

Streeter, L. A., Lochbaum, K. E., & LaVoie, N. (2007). Automated tools for collaborative learning environments. In T. K. Landauer, W. Kintsch, D. McNamara & S. Dennis. (Eds.) *LSA: A Road to Meaning,* (pp. 279–292). Mahwah, NJ: Lawrence Earlbaum Associates.

Thornton, R. C. (1992). *The effects of automation and task difficulty on crew coordination, workload, and performance.* Unpublished doctoral dissertation, Old Dominion University, Norfolk, VA.

Venkataraman, A., Stolcke, A., & Shirberg, E. (2002). Automatic dialog act labeling with minimal supervision. In *Proceedings of the 9th Australian International Conference on Speech Science and Technology,* 70–73. Canberra City, Australia: ASSTA.

Watt, J. H. & VanLear, A. C. (1996). *Dynamic patterns in communication processes.* Thousand Oaks, CA: Sage Publications.

Weil, S. A., Carley, K. M., Diesner, J., Freeman, J., & Cooke, N. J. (2006). *Measuring situational awareness through analysis of communications: A preliminary exercise.* The Command and Control Research and Technology Symposium, San Diego, CA.

Witten, I. A. & Eibe, F. (1999). *Data mining: Practical machine learning tools and techniques with Java implementations.* New York: Morgan Kaufmann.

Xiao, Y., Seagull, F. J., Mackenzie, C. F., Ziegert, J. C., & Klein, K. J. (2003). Team communication patterns as measures of team processes: Exploring the effects of task urgency and shared team experience. In *Proceedings of the Human Factors and Ergonomics Society 47th annual meeting,* Santa Monica, CA, 1502–1506.

16

Social Network Analysis: Understanding the Role of Context in Small Groups and Organizations

Andrew J. Slaughter, Janie Yu, and Laura M. Koehly

As organizations enter a modern competitive environment, they have turned to the increased use of teams to help meet their needs for increased adaptation, productivity, and performance (Hollenbeck et al., 1995; Kozlowski & Bell, 2003). With teams becoming a more critical part of the foundation of work in organizations, there are increased pressures for team researchers to identify the key variables and processes that explain how teams and their constituent members interact with one another and how their interaction facilitates or hinders the development of valued outcomes such as enhanced flexibility, performance, and learning.

The study of teams and work groups can be approached in a variety of ways, but over the last several years there has been an increasing consensus that models of teamwork and team outcomes must take into account the fact that teams are complex, dynamic creatures. McGrath, Arrow, and Berdahl (2000) argued that instead of treating work groups as though they were homogenous or unitary, it must be recognized that teams are complex entities with internal and external patterns of relationships, behaviors, cognitions, and affiliations.

These patterns of interactions and sets of dependencies have significant impact for individuals, teams, and the organizations in which they are embedded. They represent the ways individuals and groups connect to one another; how information, affect, and resources flow between them; and how group processes emerge and evolve over the lifespan of a team. Social network analysis provides a unique family of tools to explore these sorts of complex systems. At its most powerful, social network analysis provides a kind of "x-ray" into the social life of a group, quantifies and explains important features of relationships, and connects them to constructs and outcomes of interest.

In organizational studies, the use of network analysis has seen a resurgence (Borgatti & Foster, 2003). Network-based research has already shown how social structure affects a wide variety of variables such as communication (Rice, 1994), leadership (Brass & Krackhardt, 1999; Mullen, Johnson, & Salas, 1991; Pastor, Meindl & Mayo, 2002), information diffusion and social influence (Leenders, 2002; Valente, 1995), turnover (Feeley & Barnett, 1997), satisfaction (Kilduff & Krackhardt, 1994), and team performance and viability (Balkundi & Harrison, 2006). However, team research has largely failed to take advantage of social network analysis in the same way as other areas.

The purpose of the chapter is twofold: (1) to familiarize the reader with basic terminology and some common structural characteristics; and (2) to provide some examples of "structural" research questions and analyses. First, basic assumptions and goals of the social network perspective will be presented. Second, we will review some of the terminology and concepts common to social network research. Next, we introduce and describe several of the structural characteristics and measures frequently encountered in the network literature. Finally, we discuss some of the various issues involved in data analysis, mention some of the statistical procedures and software packages that may be used to analyze network data, and provide some examples using two hypothetical networks.

The Network Perspective

Traditional research in psychology has focused on the attributes of individuals (i.e., nodes) while ignoring significant aspects of relationships—particularly the structure of relationships within a group. Most importantly, these linkages (i.e., ties), and the patterns of linkages, hold meaning that can significantly add to the understanding of teams. These connections are assumed to be important features of the team and the team members that display them and thus should be accounted for in team research. Social network procedures allow researchers to quantify and delineate interactional–relational patterns that naturally occur in teams.

Of primary importance to the social network perspective is the premise that individuals' behaviors and outcomes are significantly affected by how that individual is tied into the larger web of social connections. This web of connection can be seen as a depiction of the social structure that can be defined as the interpersonal environment within which individual observations, perceptions, and decisions are made (Koehly & Shivy, 1998). Others have noted that the social structure serves as a source of external influence on the attitudes (Erickson, 1997), behaviors, interactions, and information to which an individual is exposed (Wasserman & Galaskiewicz, 1994) and places limits on the frequency, affective intensity, and duration of interpersonal interactions among members.

The social network approach provides the theoretical framework for studying the patterning of interpersonal relationships and social interaction. The social network perspective is grounded in structural theories, which hypothesize that behaviors and attitudes shape—and are in turn shaped—by the social structure. A fundamental aspect to the development of network methods is that the unit of analysis is not the individual but is an entity consisting of a collection of individuals and the relations among them. The network perspective can encompass theories, models, and applications that are expressed in terms of relational concepts or processes (Wasserman & Faust, 1994).

Across disciplines, there are shared principles that distinguish the social network approach from other research approaches. According to Wasserman and Faust (1994), the four core principles common to social network research are as follows:

1. Actors and their actions are necessarily interdependent rather than independent.
2. Relational linkages or ties between actors serve as channels for the transfer of resources.
3. The structure of the social environment can constrain or provide opportunities for individual action.
4. Network models conceptualize structure as enduring patterns of relationships among actors.

Wasserman and Galaskiewicz (1994) offered an outline of the core tenets of the social network paradigm, and Wellman (1988) provided a description of the fundamental principles that unify network approaches across disciplines. Examples of research that is grounded in the social network perspective can be found in *Connections*, *Social Networks*, and the *Journal of Social Structure*. Additional resources can be found on the International Network for Social Network Analysis website (http://www.insna.org).

Social Network Analysis

Social network analysis represents a collection of techniques for identifying, describing, and explaining various kinds of structures among individuals, groups, and organizations. It is a set of tools used to help account for the relationships or interactions of individuals who interact within a given social context. Specially, network methods can be used to describe the often complex web of ties between people in a group. These relations can be examined at many different levels, revealing information about the network as a whole as well as about individual actors within the network.

Network analysis differs significantly from the types of analyses commonly used in the social sciences. The commonly used models and statistical analyses focus on individual people, teams, and organizations as largely independent bundles of attributes, where the focus is usually on the attributes and the relationships between them. To the extent that the data may have dependencies, techniques such as hierarchical linear models (HLMs) are available; however, these often depend on being able to properly identify and specify relevant dependencies ahead of time. Network analysis, on the other hand, treats people as connected, *interdependent* actors. The focus is on the ties rather than individuals or their attributes, and much of the data is inherently nonindependent in nonobvious ways. For this kind of analysis, even techniques such as HLMs may be insufficient due to the highly complex dependencies that results from random chance, structural forces, highly permeable boundaries, and nonnested structures.

What Is a Social Network?

A social network consists of a set of actors (or nodes) and the relations (or ties) between these actors (Wasserman & Faust, 1994). Actors may be individuals, groups, organizations, or entire communities, and relations may span across or within levels of analysis. These relational variables are defined and measured at the dyadic level and can include a wide variety of social and physical ties, each of which may have a number of different basic properties (Monge & Contractor, 2003; Wasserman & Faust, 1994).

One such property is the *type* of relational tie. Common team-related ties might include the following: (1) workflow; (2) formal ties, such as who is superior to whom in the organizational hierarchy; and (3) interpersonal communication, such as the type and frequency of communication. For example, two associates from the same sales team would likely have a workflow tie; a sales associate and his or her manager would have a formal tie (the sales associate reports to the sales manager); and both sales associates might have communication ties of different types, both with one another and their manager.

Another property of ties is *directionality*. Directional relationships represent ties that are sent or received. Thus, a directional measure of advice-seeking might ask people to name team members they go to for advice. Nondirectional relations represent ties that are shared between individuals. For example, it would probably not make sense to treat a "works with" relation as a directional relation—either two people work together, or they do not. Finally, in multirelational networks, one can consider *multiplex* ties, which represent a "bundle" of relations such that a dyad shares more than one relational tie (e.g., X and Y are friends and trust each other).

Types of Networks

Several different types of networks can be examined using social network analysis. These provide alternative approaches to the study of social structure and will be more or less appropriate depending on the research questions being investigated. For example, not all forms of networks obtain measurements among all possible dyads for a given set of actors. Wasserman and Faust (1994) referred to these as *special dyadic designs*, of which the most widely used is the *ego-centered* network, where individuals (termed *ego*) report on their relationships with others (termed *alters*) and sometimes provide their perceptions of relationships between alters. This provides a small "slice" of the social structure as seen by particular actors and has been widely used in studies of social capital and social support.

The most common type of network is referred to as a *complete network*, where relational ties are measured among all members of a bounded group. For example, the complete trust network of a top-management team would involve mapping the trust relations between each member of the management team. This type of network provides a tremendous amount of information about the social structure of the set of actors. Because of its flexibility, it is probably the most widely studied type of social network, for which the greatest range of descriptive and analytic techniques has been developed.

Recently, researchers have begun to take interest in a third type of network, *sociocognitive networks*, or *cognitive social structures* (CSSs). Sociocognitive networks (Krackhardt, 1987a) represent a superset of complete networks—rather than just assessing the actual reported relationship between each dyad in the network, information is collected on the perceptions or beliefs held by each actor about all other possible dyadic relationships in the network. Such data allow researchers to study the complex interactions among actor attributes, social structure, and the accuracy or similarity of social cognitions—the latter of which is a core concept of the literature on team member schemas (McNeese & Rentsch, 2001; Rentsch & Hall, 1994; Rentsch & Woehr, 2004)—and also to examine the analyses possible using complete networks.

Data Collection

Collecting network data presents a number of unique challenges. For complete networks, high response rates from group members are important because it is not clear what the effects of missing data may be. Complete network data can be difficult to collect—for example, for large networks measures may take researchers more time to create and participants may take more time to complete. A number of different methods are used to collect information on the social relationships among actors, each with his or her own strengths and weaknesses. Four primary data collection techniques are questionnaire, interview, observational, and archival methods.

Sociometric questionnaires are by far the most prevalent data collection method in social network analysis. Such questionnaires involve asking each member of the target network of interest to identify others with whom they have a certain kind of social tie or relationship. Other data collection methods such as interviews and observation are used less frequently than questionnaires, but they may be desirable in situations where questionnaires are not feasible or provide inadequate response rates or when more "objective" networks are desired. Archival data may be obtained by examining coattendance at meetings, coauthorship of an article, or e-mail exchanges.

Data Representation

In traditional actor-oriented analyses, data are usually stored in a rectangular case x variable array. However, for relational data, data are typically represented using a *sociomatrix*, in which the entries of the matrix denote various relational ties. An *adjacency* matrix is a sociomatrix for a dichotomous relation. The adjacency matrix is the most common type of sociomatrix and the one most frequently used in the analytical procedures described in this chapter. A typical adjacency matrix X is a square $g \times g$ matrix, where g is the number of persons in the group; in this matrix, rows usually correspond to senders and columns to receivers. For nondirectional ties, the adjacency matrix is symmetric (like a correlation matrix). For directed ties, entries in the matrix denote relationships or nominations sent from actors in the rows to actors in the columns of the matrix. In this case, the matrix X is not necessarily symmetric.

The basic sociomatrix can also be transformed and manipulated in various ways, allowing us to create data sets that reverse directions of the relations (e.g., telling us who is communicated *with*) or even combine individual networks into a single multirelational network, allowing researchers to look at multiplexity. This latter transformation can be particularly useful, allowing researchers to examine hypotheses involving bundles of several ties simultaneously. These sorts of operations are easily accessible in most available network analysis software.

To visually represent networks, researchers often use graphs. In these graphs, individual actors are represented by nodes, whereas the ties between them are represented by lines in the case of nondirected data and arcs (lines with arrows) in the case of directed data. Current software for network analysis gives researchers a wide range of options for graphing networks that can aid the interpretation of network data. For example, different line weights may be used to signify relationship strength, different node colors, sizes, or shapes may be used to signify actor characteristics like gender, tenure, or position in the network (e.g., how central an actor is to the network).

To help understand the basics of sociometric notation and graph visualization, let us examine two hypothetical teams: a 10-member planning team and a 17-member emergency response team composed of three smaller teams working together (i.e., a multiteam system). For the first network, assume we were interested in advice-seeking among members of the planning committee, using items such as, "Which team members do you find yourself going to for advice?" For the second network, assume we were interested in the communication relationships among members of the emergency response team, using an item like, "Please list all people with whom you communicate frequently." Items such as these will result in dichotomous, directed networks, as shown in the Figure 16.1 matrices. If we had been interested in valued relationships, we could have used an item such as, "List the number of times in the past week you have sought advice from the following people," which would have given a sociomatrix with frequencies in the cells instead of 0s and 1s.

To better visualize the data, two graphical representations, shown in Figure 16.2 and Figure 16.3, were constructed from the sociomatrices in Figure 16.1. Graphs such as these are sometimes used as part of case studies to help identify potential problems with the group such as communication bottlenecks and problems with team cohesiveness. The use of arrows indicates the direction of the tie: For example, in Figure 16.2, the planning team appears to have a fairly centralized structure, with some people having many ties and some having very few ties. Figure 16.3 shows the emergency response team; in this example, node shapes identify members of the component teams to aid in visualization of communication in the emergency response team.

Social Structure

Of course, the primary interest of many people who study teams and small groups is to be able to quantitatively describe theoretically important

	A	B	C	D	E	F	G	H	I	J
A	0	0	0	0	0	0	0	1	0	0
B	1	0	1	0	0	1	0	0	0	0
C	1	1	0	0	0	1	0	0	0	1
D	1	0	0	0	1	0	1	0	0	0
E	1	0	0	1	0	0	0	0	1	0
F	0	1	1	0	0	0	0	0	0	0
G	1	0	0	1	0	0	0	0	0	0
H	1	0	0	0	0	0	0	0	0	0
I	0	0	0	0	1	0	0	0	0	0
J	0	0	1	0	0	0	0	0	0	0

	A	B	C	D	E	F	G	H	I	J	K	L	M	N	O	P	Q
A	0	1	0	0	0	0	0	0	0	0	0	0	0	0	0	0	0
B	1	0	0	1	0	0	0	0	0	0	0	0	0	0	0	0	0
C	1	1	0	1	0	0	0	0	0	0	1	1	0	0	0	0	0
D	0	1	0	0	0	0	0	0	0	0	0	0	0	0	0	0	0
E	0	0	0	0	0	1	1	0	0	1	1	0	0	0	0	0	0
F	0	0	0	0	1	0	1	0	0	0	0	0	0	0	0	0	0
G	0	0	0	0	1	1	0	1	0	1	0	0	0	0	0	0	0
H	0	0	0	0	0	0	1	0	1	0	0	0	0	0	0	0	0
I	0	0	0	0	0	0	0	1	0	1	1	0	0	0	0	0	0
J	0	0	1	0	1	0	0	0	1	0	1	0	1	0	0	1	1
K	0	0	1	0	1	1	0	0	1	1	0	0	0	0	0	1	1
L	0	0	0	0	0	0	0	0	0	0	0	0	1	0	0	0	0
M	0	0	0	0	0	0	0	0	0	0	0	1	0	0	0	0	0
N	0	0	0	0	0	0	0	0	0	0	0	0	0	0	1	0	0
O	0	0	0	0	0	0	0	0	0	0	0	0	0	1	0	0	0
P	0	0	0	0	0	0	0	0	0	0	1	1	1	1	1	0	0
Q	0	0	0	0	0	0	0	0	0	1	1	0	1	1	1	0	0

FIGURE 16.1
Sociomatrixes for the planning team (left) and emergency response team (right).

properties of social groups and use that information to test hypotheses of interest. Social network analysis provides a number of different measures that can be used for this purpose. With the advent of increasingly sophisticated computer software, the use of social network measures has become more accessible. In this section, we review some basic network properties and structural measures and discuss how they might be used to address theoretical issues of interest to team research. Examples of the different measures and analyses using our two example networks are also presented in the section on data analysis.

A bewildering array of measures that describe a variety of structural properties at different levels of analysis is available. Some authors describe five common levels of analysis (Monge & Contractor, 2003; Wasserman & Faust, 1994). The lowest level of analysis is the *individual*. At this level, measures are mainly used to describe the positions of the individual actors in the social structure, such as the degree to which they are deeply embedded or share similar roles with others in the network. The next level of analysis is the *dyad*. At this level, there are measures that describe ties that exist between pairs of individuals—for example, whether or not social relationships are reciprocated or how important certain ties are for connecting the network.

At the triadic level of analysis, researchers may be interested in the ways small clusters of individuals form or how dyadic relationships are affected by third parties. This can include effects like balance (e.g., Are my friends' friends also *my* friends?) or the extent to which shared relationships between two people affect their ties to a third (e.g., Do friends

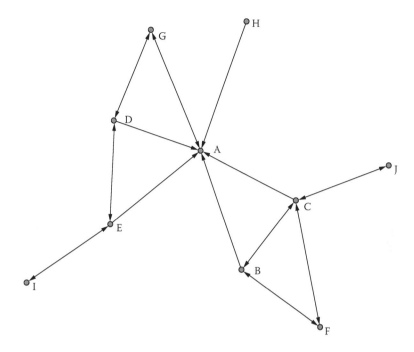

FIGURE 16.2
Planning team advice-seeking network.

tend to go to the same people for advice?). At the subgroup level of analysis, researchers may be interested in identifying various types of cohesive subgroups such as cliques and the differences within and between them. Finally, at the global level of analysis, researchers are interested in describing relational patterns across the overall network, including properties such as the extent to which a network is weakly or strongly connected. Table 16.1 describes a few of the properties of interest that can be measured at different levels of analysis.

Centrality and Prestige

One of the most basic relational properties of individuals in a network is the extent to which those individuals are embedded in the existing social structure—that is, the extent to which they are tied to others in the network. The most common way of defining this is through measures of centrality. Centrality indices provide a way of quantifying the extent to which a given individual is connected to the rest of the network and is often interpreted as a measure of structural importance. Prestige indices can be constructed only for directional relations and can focus on the

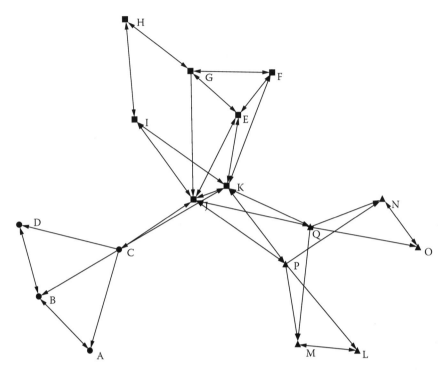

FIGURE 16.3
Emergency response team: Communication. Team membership is indicated by different node shape.

actor as the recipient of relational ties. Thus, prestige indices represent the popularity of an individual actor. For directed relations, centrality indices focus on the actors as senders of relational ties. Past research has found strong links to leader emergence (Mullen, Johnson, & Salas, 1991) and performance (Balkundi & Harrison, 2006), among other outcomes. There are many centrality and prestige indices in the literature; the commonly encountered measures are presented next.

Degree Centrality and Prestige

One of the most simple and frequently used measures of structural importance is the number of ties an individual has, which is known as *degree centrality.* For nondirectional relations, degree centrality provides an index of the number of direct network partners for each individual in the network. For directional relations, ties can be partitioned into incoming or outgoing ties, representing *indegree* and *outdegree,* respectively. Indegree has been referred to as an index of prestige (Wasserman & Faust, 1994) and is sometimes interpreted as the "popularity" of a given

TABLE 16.1

Examples of Common Structural Features of Interest

Individual location, importance (centrality)
Roles (structural, regular equivalence)
Homophily
Reciprocity, direct exchange
Generalized exchange
Multiplexity
Type and degree of hierarchy (core-periphery structures, centralization)
Intergroup versus intragroup connectivity
Network redundancy, efficiency
Balance, imbalance
Role interlocking
Activity, popularity
Strong/weak clustering, distribution of clusters
Size, type, and distribution of cohesive subgroups
Size, diameter of network
Density
Interdependencies across individuals, tasks, and resources
Cognitive/perceptual interdependencies

actor. Outdegree is less frequently used than indegree centrality but may still provide an important measure of individual activity. In communication research, some authors have used indegree and outdegree to describe whether a given node acts as "wells" (i.e., where communication originates) or "sinks" (i.e., where communication is received) (Monge & Contractor, 2003). In the context of information exchange, good team members should exhibit a high degree of in and out communication. Poor team members, however, will be sinks, or those who receive and hold information to themselves.

Closeness Centrality and Proximity Prestige

Another frequently used measure of centrality is *closeness* centrality (Lin, 1976; Sabidussi, 1966). In many settings, the distance between actors may represent important features of communication or interaction. For example, actors who are very far away from others in the communication network will tend to be the last to receive information. Closeness centrality quantifies this feature—it provides an index of actors' average distances to others in the network. Thus, actors for whom it requires very few "hops" through the network to reach all other actors will have a high closeness centrality. Closeness centrality is sometimes interpreted as a measure of access to information or other resources. For directional relations, closeness centrality focuses on the distance from a given actor to others in the network, whereas *proximity prestige* represents the closeness of other network members to a given actor (Lin, 1976).

Betweenness Centrality

Betweenness centrality is the third type of centrality that frequently appears in the literature (Freeman, 1977; Stephenson & Zelen, 1989). Network members are rarely directly related to everyone in their network. For information or work to move from one individual to another, it must often pass through a number of intermediaries or facilitators. In many settings, being the intermediary (or broker) is said to provide a measure of control or power. Betweenness centrality provides an index of the extent to which a given individual falls along the shortest paths (or *geodesics*) connecting pairs of other actors.[1] In the case of a multiteam system, for example, boundary spanners may control the shortest paths between members of different teams, giving them increased influence over the system as a whole.

Status or Rank Prestige

A fourth major type of centrality is sometimes referred to as *status* or *rank prestige* (Bonacich, 1987; Katz, 1953). Although most types of centrality and prestige are based on an individual's position in the network, rank prestige also takes into account the position of individuals to which a given actor is tied. For example, in some situations, characteristics such as status or prestige may be a function of characteristics of the actors to whom an individual is tied—having a relationship to a prestigious actor may itself improve an actor's prestige.

Relational Equivalence

Many researchers are interested less in the exact relational positions of individuals per se than the characteristics and outcomes associated with particular roles. Roles may be defined in many ways, but social network analysis explicitly defines them in terms of social relationships. For example, in a team, the role of leaders may involve instructing others: specifically, telling other team members what to do but not being instructed themselves. For their role, leaders' lieutenants (if any) may be expected to both give and take instructions, whereas subordinates may be expected to only take instruction and never give it. In this case, studying the similarities in each actor's relationships could identify each of these three roles and which individuals fill them.

One of the strictest definitions is *structural equivalence* (Lorrain & White, 1971). Two actors are said to be structurally equivalent if and only if they have the same ties to the same sets of other actors. So, if person *A* is friends with persons *B*, *C*, and *D* but not *E*, then person *F* must also be friends with *B*, *C*, *D*, and not *E* for actors *A* and *F* to be structurally equivalent. A much less stringent definition of equivalence is *regular equivalence* (Borgatti & Everett, 1989; Doreian, 1987). Regularly equivalent individuals do not need to have the same patterns of ties to the exact same people; they merely need to have the same patterns of ties to people in similar roles. For example, a product development team may have members who tend to produce ideas, members who tend to transmit those ideas to others, and members who receive the ideas. Members who create ideas may not send them to the same individuals, but they may all tend to send them to those who retransmit the ideas. This type of regular equivalence is often used to identify groups who comprise different role sets in the network.

Subgroup Analyses

Not all researchers are interested in the structural characteristics of individuals—some seek to identify and explain structural features at a higher level of analysis. By studying units such as dyads, triads, and higher-level groupings, it is possible to identify and explain relational dependencies across the network at a *local* level.

Dyads

One of the most basic units of analysis in social network analysis is the *dyad*, or pair. At this level of analysis, researchers may be interested in the degree to which relationships between individuals are reciprocated (*mutual* dyads), not reciprocated (*asymmetric* dyads), or not formed at all (*null* dyads). In the case of multirelational networks, researchers may be interested in dyadic relationships like the tendency to "exchange" one type of tie for another, or the tendency to send or receive several different ties at once. Dyadic analyses may involve simple tests of the extent to which certain types of dyadic patterns are observed or may involve more complex questions such as whether one type of tie predicts another, how individual attributes affect tie formation between pairs of individuals, or how shared ties affect individual outcomes using specialized loglinear models or exponential random graph models (ERGMs).

Triads

Another basic unit of analysis in social network analysis is the triad, a set of three actors. At a general level, the numbers of strongly connected triads in a network is sometimes seen as evidence of clustering, but many specific triadic configurations are associated with important structural tendencies. Some structural tendencies that can be examined at the triadic level are given as follows with examples:

- Transitivity/balance: My leader's leader is also *my* leader.
- Generalized exchange/cyclicity: What goes around comes around—I give work to one person, who gives it to a second, who passes it back to me.
- Role interlocking: When I get praise (or criticism), I pass it on to someone else.

In team research, triadic analyses offer the opportunity to address a variety of different questions. At a basic level, researchers may be interested in studying whether or not there are significant levels of transitivity, generalized exchange, or other relevant triadic structures in the teams they study and the extent to which teams in different settings display these characteristics. Other research could examine the extent to which such aspects of triadic structures are associated with individual attributes—for example, whether team members with certain levels of experience tend to hold certain positions in the local network, such as critical role interlock positions.

Cliques and Subgroups

Oftentimes, researchers may be interested in slightly larger subgroups that stand apart from the rest of the group in some way, investigating questions about the formation, distribution, and composition of cohesive subgroups. There are a huge number of different ways of defining cohesive subgroups, and using various definitions will provide very different pictures of the extent of subgrouping in the data. The strictest definition of a cohesive subgroup is the *clique* proper. A clique is defined as a subgroup that is completely connected—every clique member is directly connected to every other clique member (Luce & Perry, 1949; Harary, Norman, & Cartwright, 1965). In practice, such strictly defined cliques may be very rare. Other definitions of subgroups (for example, *n-cliques* and *k-cores*) allow for more relaxed and inclusive definitions (see Alba, 1973; Seidman, 1983).

Group-Level Indices

At the global network level, it is often necessary to characterize aspects of the overall graph structure rather than focusing on various "local" structures like dyads and triads. Researchers may be interested in the extent to which a network displays hierarchical tendencies or whether information is equally likely to flow quickly across different networks. Although measures are available that capture many different aspects of a network's overall structure, the most frequently encountered measures include *density* and *centralization.*[2]

Density

In most networks, not every actor will be connected to every other actor. Relationship type and team context all affect the extent to which individuals will realize potential ties with other actors. Density provides a measure of the proportion of possible ties to the number of potential ties in the network and is sometimes used as an index of group cohesion. A high density means that any two actors are likely to be connected, whereas a low density means the network is relatively sparse, with few connections between actors. It is possible to test densities statistically, answering questions such as whether two networks have similar densities or whether a network's density differs from some expected level.

Centralization

Another basic property of graphs is the extent to which the social structure appears to be dominated by a few central actors. Centralization measures the extent to which the graph as a whole appears to be highly centralized. This is usually measured in terms of the dispersion of actor-level centralities: Networks with large variability in actor centrality will have a high degree of centralization, whereas networks with substantial similarities in actor centrality will have low levels of centralization. The various indexes of centralization are typically standardized to range from 0 (low centralization) to 1 (high centralization).

Data Analysis

Applications of Network Data

At a purely descriptive level, social network analysis may be used to identify nested and cross-classified groups (both formal and informal) at many different levels of analysis simultaneously; it can provide new ways of quantifying and comparing aspects of group processes like communication, cohesion, leadership, and workflow. It can also provide valuable individual-level data, indicating how and where individual actors are tied to others in the network and what their roles are.

These data can be usefully interpreted in their own right, but perhaps more useful to team and small-group researchers the data can then be used as predictors and outcomes in more traditional analyses—for example, using certain types of informal cliques as a level of analysis in HLMs; identifying the independent effects of team training on communication density, centralization, and clustering; or studying the effect of different types and levels of informal hierarchy on team adaptability.

At an inferential level, there are a variety of more specialized techniques for the analysis of social networks. These allow for research questions that may be difficult—and in some cases, impossible—to test using more traditional methods of analysis. For hypotheses involving a dyadic level of analysis, the quadratic assignment procedure (QAP; Krackhardt, 1987b, 1988) is an easily accessible technique that allows for research questions such as whether individuals' similarity (e.g., same race/ethnic origin, same sex) affects trust relations over and above the effect of reciprocated communication ties or whether individuals who communicate with one another tend to perform similarly on the job. QAP is a permutation test that accounts for the inherent dependencies within social network data. An empirical distribution of all possible alternative outcomes (e.g., the correlation between communication relations and similarity in job performance) is generated by permuting the rows and columns of the observed network data. The observed outcome (e.g., correlation) is then compared with this empirical distribution of alternative outcomes to obtain an index of statistical significance for the referent statistic.

Advanced Methods and Models

Some of the most recent analytical developments are in the form of *exponential random graph models* (Besag, 1974), which allow for the modeling of complex patterns of dependencies at different levels of analysis. Exponential random graph models define the probability of an observed network as a function of different structural characteristics such as density, reciprocity, or cliquing; these models allow for simple research questions, such as whether there are homophily effects in networks (e.g., McPherson, Smith-Lovin, & Cook, 2001), or more complex research questions like whether the tendency toward various hierarchy-related structures differ across groups that use different strategies to complete a team task. Other constraints can be defined due to social settings (Pattison & Robins, 2002), allowing for a more ecologically valid approach to modeling multiteam systems. For example, each team could define a separate setting, allowing for overlapping setting structures through those members who transfer resources between teams.

For large networks, direct estimation of random graph model parameters can be difficult. In the past, indirect procedures using pseudo likelihood estimation have been used; this method has the advantage of not being overly complex and can be implemented using any standard statistical package (Anderson, Wasserman, & Crouch, 1999). However, the pseudo-likelihood approach provides biased standard errors and heuristic methods of model fit. Current methods of estimation typically involve Markov Chain Monte Carlo (MCMC) procedures and are implemented in a number of network analysis software packages. Complex models (e.g., that incorporate setting structures) are not easily accommodated by available statistical software.

Multirelational Models

It is likely that network processes involve different types of relational ties; thus, interesting relational hypotheses may include more than a single relation. Multirelational networks are obtained when relational measurements of different types are obtained among members of the network. Thus, one might measure respect, advice seeking, and friendship among a set of team members. It may be of interest to examine whether group members are more likely to seek advice from their friends or those they respect. A more complex hypothesis might examine whether friends tend to respect the same people. Exponential random graph models have been extended to multirelational networks (Koehly & Pattison, 2005; Pattison & Wasserman, 1999), allowing one to examine hypotheses involving more than a single relation.

Longitudinal and Dynamic Models

In team research, there have been several calls to recognize the dynamic, temporal nature of teams (e.g., McGrath et al., 2000). The use of dynamic models for network analysis provides a statistical framework to examine how, for example, informal leaders emerge in groups over time. Robins and Pattison (2001) extended ERGMs to longitudinal networks, focusing on two discrete time points. However, recent work by Snijders (2005) allows network evolution to be modeled while assuming continuous time.

Cognitive Social Structures

Sociocognitive network approaches hold great promise for small group research. These networks are obtained when multiple observers provide their cognitive representation of the social structure among group members. Cognitive social structures (CSSs) (Krackhardt, 1987a) represent the most commonly studied type of sociocognitive network. Theoretical questions that might be of interest include questions about consensus, bias, or individual differences in perceptions of social structure. Consensus refers to the agreement or congruence between two or more perceivers' cognitive structures—for instance, whether team members share the same cognitive map of the groups' social relationships, similar to a shared mental model. Questions of bias examine how individuals' perceptions differ from some criterion or target network. These perceptual biases may be due to actor attributes (e.g., personality) or network location. ERGMs for multiple raters (Koehly & Pattison, 2005; Koehly, Yu, & Slaughter, 2008; Yu, Slaughter, & Koehly, 2004) provide a statistical framework for investigating these structural hypotheses for sociocognitive networks.

Software

Huisman and van Duijn (2005) provided an overview of software available for social network analysis. They presented a review of available visualization software as well as software for descriptive and statistical analysis of network data. Three available software packages that allow for most of the basic analyses presented here—in addition to many others—are UCINET, Pajek, and the SNA package for R (a library of routines for network analysis and visualization). Regarding the random graph models previously presented, there are two specialized software packages: MultiNet and StOCNET.

MultiNet can be used to estimate simple random graph models for single relations. The program can integrate nodal attributes in the analysis, allowing for examination of blockstructures defined by actor attributes and of structural characteristics including density, reciprocity, in-stars, out-stars, transitivity, and cycles. MultiNet uses a maximum pseudo-likelihood approach to parameter estimation. StOCNET (through the SIENA module) allows ERGMs to be fitted for single relations as well as network evolution models, estimating parameters using an MCMC approach. For more complex models, such as those that specify setting structures, there is no available statistical software, meaning interested users will need to program their own models. Appendix A in Koehly and Pattison (2005) provides SPSS code to set up the data for pseudo-likelihood estimation in the multiple-relations case.

Examples

Now let us return to the two earlier team examples: (1) the 10-member planning team advice network shown in Figure 16.1; and (2) the

17-member emergency response team communication network shown in Figure 16.2. Table 16.2 provides a list of some various measures of centrality for each network, along with measures of overall graph density and centralization.

For the 10-member planning team, the results indicate that the observed density is significantly lower than 0.5, which we might expect if relationships were random, and that there is a moderate level of centralization that differs depending on the type of centrality. There is an indegree centralization score of 0.48, which indicates that the observed distribution of indegree scores is about 48% of the maximum possible value for a network of this size, indicating a fairly high level of centralization in the graph. The outdegree centralization score of 0.23 suggests that there is much less variation in individual outdegrees.

Thus, individuals in this production team appear to vary substantially in the extent to which their advice is sought but not in the extent to which they seek advice. This is most clearly seen in the high indegree score of actor *A,* who represents a potentially powerful *cutpoint*—removing this person from the network would completely disconnect the existing advice network. There is also substantial variation in the extent to which actors are close to others in the network and are connected to central individuals, but there is less variation in the extent to which a given actor is likely to fall on a path between others in the network.

To explore the local structural characteristics of the team, SIENA was used to implement a random graph approach to study the advice network for several important dyadic and triadic structures—reciprocity, popularity, activity, transitivity, and cyclicity (i.e., generalized exchange)—conditioned on density. The results of the analysis in Table 16.3 show that reciprocity, transitivity, and cyclicity all appear to play a significant role in explaining the observed structure.

The positive reciprocity parameter suggests that there is a tendency for individuals to go to one another for advice. The significant transitivity parameter suggests that individuals tend to form balanced, partially ordered clusters of advice relationships—that is, if the person I go to for advice goes to someone else for advice, I am likely to seek advice from that person as well. The significant, negative cyclicity parameter indicates substantial bias against generalized exchange in advice-seeking relations in this network; thus, in the case of advice seeking in this team, what goes around *doesn't* tend to come around.

Turning to our analysis of the 17-member emergency response team, we see some substantially similar patterns. The density of communication relations is only 0.19, meaning that only 19% of the possible communication relationships between individuals are being reported—a very sparse network! The centrality and centralization scores in Table 16.2 show that the network clearly has two actors who dominate the communication

TABLE 16.2

Centrality, Centralization, and Density for Planning and Emergency Response Teams

Planning Team

Centrality	Actor										Centrality Index
	A	B	C	D	E	F	G	H	I	J	
Indegree	6	2	3	2	2	2	2	0	1	1	.48
Outdegree	1	3	4	3	3	2	2	1	1	1	.23
Betweenness	.27	.03	.15	.19	.14	.00	.23	.00	.00	.00	.20
Closeness[a]	.15	.11	.12	.10	.10	.08	.09	.09	.07	.08	.58
Eigenvector	.57	.36	.39	.35	.31	.23	.28	.17	.09	.12	.46

Network density = 0.23, $p < .001$

Emergency Response Team

Centrality	Actor																	Centrality Index
	A	B	C	D	E	F	G	H	I	J	K	L	M	N	O	P	Q	
Indegree	2	3	2	2	4	3	3	2	3	7	6	2	3	3	2	2	2	.27
Outdegree	1	2	5	1	4	2	4	2	3	6	7	1	1	1	1	5	5	.27
Betweenness	.00	.01	.14	.00	.07	.01	.06	.01	.07	.26	.19	.00	.01	.01	.00	.08	.08	.17
Closeness[b]	.00	.00	.10	.00	.10	.07	.10	.07	.09	.13	.13	.00	.00	.00	.00	.10	.10	.44
Eigenvector	.08	.09	.26	.08	.31	.22	.24	.10	.23	.46	.46	.10	.15	.15	.10	.29	.29	.35

Network density = .19, $p < .001$

[a] Closeness centrality and centralization scores are based on a non-directional, symmetrized matrix.

[b] Tests of density compare observed network to a baseline density of .50.

TABLE 16.3

Dyadic and Triadic Random Graph Analysis Example

Planning Team		
Model Parameter	Value	S.E.
Reciprocity	4.75*	1.35
Activity	–0.58	0.51
Popularity	0.20	0.27
Transitivity	0.93*	0.42
Cyclicity	–1.97*	0.95
Emergency Response Team		
Model Parameter	Value	S.E.
Reciprocity	4.39*	0.84
Activity	0.22	0.13
Popularity	–0.20	0.22
Transitivity	0.48*	0.22
Cyclicity	–1.41	0.61
Team membership	2.71*	0.77

* $p < .05$.

network, J and K; they send and receive the most communication. J has the highest betweenness centrality, indicating that this individual is a boundary spanner, connecting the three teams within the multiteam system. However, the overall level of centralization in the network is rather low, largely due to the sparse, evenly spread communication between other team members.

At the dyadic and triadic levels of analysis, Table 16.3 shows that the communication network displays significant tendencies toward reciprocity and transitivity and away from generalized exchange. The analysis also shows a significant homophily effect—common team membership is a significant predictor of communication ties. Additionally, there appears to be a marginally significant ($p < .10$) activity effect, suggesting that there may be some individual differences in the tendency to initiate communication relations with multiple partners after taking into account other structural factors.

Conclusion

In team research, many key variables involve interpersonal and inter-group processes or team-level characteristics. The analysis of these variables using more traditional methods such as hierarchical modeling often requires various aggregation procedures, assumptions about nesting, or a priori group specifications, usually based on formal relationships. The network approach provides the tools for small-group research to move beyond many of these limitations in ways that can supplement existing analyses or allow for entirely new ones. These techniques permit researchers to describe the intricate array of ties that bind individuals and teams and provide a way to measure and define the social context—for example, by identifying informal boundaries and describing ways various formal and emergent relationships are intertwined.

The methods of social network analysis could help researchers further explore a number of current topics in team research. For example, various theories of group development posit stages through which teams and workgroups progress (Hare, 1976; Poole, 1983; Tuckman, 1965). Network analysis could be used to identify structural patterns associated with different stages in team development. Do multiplexity and reciprocity tend to occur early in team development or later? How stable are emergent role sets across different networks and stages of team development? Do we see similar core-periphery patterns emerge across production teams and management teams? Across task and affective networks?

Another area where network methods could prove useful is the study of multiteam systems (Mathieu, Marks, & Zaccaro, 2002). Although it is easy to identify formal team boundaries, network analysis can be used to identify informal social boundaries, to quantify various aspects of their permeability, or to identify characteristics associated with taking on boundary-spanning roles across multiple networks. It can also be used in other ways—for instance, team members whose teams have strong norms toward reciprocity and generalized exchange may come into conflict with those whose teams have norms against reciprocity and toward hierarchy. By identifying structural tendencies present in different teams, potential conflicts can be identified before they occur.

A third area where network concepts have the potential for a major impact is in the study of cognitive social structures (Krackhardt, 1987a) with shared cognitions and team mental models (Cannon-Bowers, Salas, & Converse, 1993; Klimoski & Mohammed, 1994). Recent work on team mental models (e.g., Espinosa et al., 2002; Mohammed, Klimoski, & Rentsch, 2000; Graham, Schneider, Bauer, & Bessiere, 2004) has discussed ways network methods and tools can be used to elicit, measure, and quantify perceptions of formal and informal ties, knowledge, or skill within a team; these data may then be used to address questions about the extent to which individuals share accurate or similar perceptions.

However, in many ways, the application of advanced social network methods to the study of team member perceptions is still relatively undeveloped. As a wider variety of network methods is applied to team member cognitions, researchers will be better able to study the effects of individual differences on the tendency to perceive certain types of relational patterns between actors or how shared ties, roles, or clique memberships affect accuracy and congruency. More complex questions can also be addressed, such as whether individual positions (e.g., highly central team members, being relatively isolated, being involved in an unbalanced triad) affect perceptions of the team structure, conditional on individual differences in tie perceptions and overall rates of tie formation across different networks.

Network analysis provides a common framework and language for the analysis of relational ties of all sorts and has gained popularity across a wide range of disciplines. It also provides a way to identify and quantify complex relational patterns simultaneously across many different levels of analysis. Thus, network analysis provides an opportunity to increase the ecological validity of team research by better capturing the complexity of the social environment and also gives additional opportunities for researchers interested in cross-disciplinary research. Just as importantly, it presents new constructs, new ways of operationalizing old constructs (e.g., cohesion), and methods for analyzing their relationship that are able to handle this highly complex data.

Acknowledgments

This research was supported in part by the Intramural Research Program of the National Human Genome Research Institute at the National Institutes of Health.

Endnotes

1. Another type of centrality, called information centrality, relaxes the assumption of shortest paths and provides an index of the extent to which an individual lies on many paths across the network.

2. Another measure worth mentioning is connectivity, the extent to which a network is cohesive and resistant to being broken into unconnected components by the removal of a few ties or actors.

References

Alba, R. D. (1973). A graph-theoretic definition of a sociometric clique. *Journal of Mathematical Sociology, 3*, 113–126.

Anderson, C. J., Wasserman, S., & Crouch, B. (1999). A p^* primer: Logit models for social networks. *Social Networks, 21*, 37–66.

Balkundi, P. & Harrison, D. A. (2006). Ties, leaders, and time in teams: Strong inference about network structure's effect on team viability and performance. *Academy of Management Journal, 49*, 305–326.

Besag, J. E. (1974). Spatial interaction and the statistical analysis of lattice systems. *Journal of the Royal Statistical Society, Series B, 36*, 96–127.

Bonacich, P. (1987). Power and centrality: A family of measures. *American Journal of Sociology, 92*, 1170–1182.

Bondonio, D. (1998). Predictors of accuracy in perceiving informal social networks. *Social Networks, 20*, 301–330.

Borgatti, S. P. & Everett, M. G. (1989). The class of regular equivalences: Algebraic structure and computation. *Social Networks, 11*, 65–88.

Borgatti, S. P. & Foster, P. C. (2003). The network paradigm in organizational research: A review and typology. *Journal of Management, 29*(6), 991–1013.

Brass, D. & Krackhardt, D. (1999). The social capital of twenty-first century leaders. In J.G. Hunt & R.L. Phillips (Eds.), *Out of the box leadership: Challenges for the 21st century army* (pp. 179–194).

Cannon-Bowers, J. A., Salas, E., & Converse, S. A. (1993). Shared mental models in expert team decision making. In N. J. Castellan (Ed.), *Individual and group decision making: Current issues* (pp. 221–246). Hillsdale, NJ: Erlbaum.

Doreian, P. (1987). Measuring regular equivalence in symmetric structures. *Social Networks, 9*, 89–107.

Erickson, B. H. (1997). The relational basis of attitudes. In W. Berkowitz (Ed.), *Social structures: A network approach. Contemporary studies in sociology* (Vol. 15, pp. 99–129). Greenwich, CT: JAI Press.

Espinosa, J. A., Carley, K., Kraut, R. E., Slaughter, S. A., Lerch, F. J., & Fussell, S. (2002). *The effect of task knowledge similarity and distribution on asynchronous team coordination and performance: Empirical evidence from decision teams.* Second Information Systems Cognitive Research Exchange (IS CoRE) workshop, Barcelona, Spain.

Feeley, T. H. & Barnett, G. A. (1997). Predicting employee turnover from communication networks. *Human Communication Research, 23*(3), 370–387.

Freeman, L. (1977). A set of measures of centrality based on betweenness. *Sociometry, 40*, 35–41.

Graham, J., Schneider, M., Bauer, A., & Bessiere, K. (2004). Shared mental models in military command and control organizations: Effect of social network distance. *Human Factors and Ergonomics Society Annual Meeting Proceedings, 48,* 509–512.

Harary, F., Norman, R. Z., & Cartwright, D. (1965). *Structural modes: An introduction to the theory of directed graphs.* New York, NY: John Wiley & Sons.

Hare, A. (1976). *Handbook of small group research.* (2d ed.). New York: Free Press.

Hollenbeck, J. R., Ilgen, D. R., Sego, D. J., Hedlund, J., Major, D. A., & Phillips, J. (1995). Multilevel theory of team decision making: Decision performance in teams incorporating distributed expertise. *Journal of Applied Psychology, 80,* 292–316.

Huisman, M. & van Duijn, M. A. J. (2005). Software for social network analysis. In P. Carrington, J. Scott, & S. Wasserman (Eds.), *Models and methods in social network analysis* (pp. 270–316). New York: Cambridge University Press.

Katz, L. (1953). A new status index derived from sociometric analysis. *Psychometrika, 18,* 39–43.

Kilduff, M. & Krackhardt, D. (1994). Bringing the individual back in: A structural analysis of the internal market for reputation in organizations. *Academy of Management Journal, 37*(1), 87–108.

Klimoski, R. & Mohammed, S. (1994). Team mental model: Construct or metaphor? *Journal of Management, 20,* 403–437.

Koehly, L. M. & Pattison, P. (2005). Random graph models for social networks: Multiple relations or multiple raters. In P. Carrington, J. Scott, & S. Wasserman (Eds.), *Models and methods in social network analysis* (pp. 162–191). New York: Cambridge University Press.

Koehly, L. M. & Shivy, V. A. (1998). Social network modeling: A new methodology for counseling researchers. *Journal of Counseling Psychology, 45,* 3–17.

Koehly, L. M., Yu, J., & Slaughter, A. J. (2008). *Perceptual congruence of an organization's social structure among organizational members with common attributes.* Manuscript under review.

Kozlowski, S. W. J. & Bell, B. S. (2003). Work groups and teams in organizations. In W. C. Borman, D. R. Ilgen, & R. J. Kilmoski (Eds.), *Handbook of psychology: Industrial and organizational psychology* (Vol. 12, pp. 333–375). London: Wiley.

Krackhardt, D. (1987a). Cognitive social structures. *Social Networks, 9,* 109–134.

Krackhardt, D. (1987b). QAP partialling as a test of spuriousness. *Social Networks, 9,* 171–186.

Krackhardt, D. (1988). Predicting with networks: Nonparametric multiple regression analysis of dyadic data. *Social Networks, 10,* 359–381.

Leenders, R. (2002). Modeling social influence through network autocorrelation: Constructing the weight matrix. *Social Networks, 24,* 21–47.

Lin, N. (1976). *Foundations of social research.* New York: McGraw-Hill.

Lorrain, F. & White, H. C. (1971). Structural equivalence of individuals in social networks. *Journal of Mathematical Sociology, 1,* 49–80.

Luce, R. D. & Perry, A. D. (1949). A method of matrix analysis of group structure. *Psychometrika, 14,* 95–116.

Mathieu, J. E., Marks, M. A., & Zaccaro, S. J. (2002). Multiteam systems. In N. Anderson, D. S. Ones, H. K. Sinangil, & C. Viswesvaran (Eds.), *Handbook of industrial, work, and organizational psychology* (Vol. 2, pp. 289–313). Thousand Oaks, CA: Sage Publications.

McGrath, J. E., Arrow, H., & Berdahl, J. L. (2000). The study of groups: Past present and future. *Personality and Social Psychology Review, 4*(1), 95–105.

McNeese, M. D. & Rentsch, J. R. (2001). Identifying the social and cognitive requirements of teamwork using collaborative task analysis. In M. McNesse, S. Edurado, & E. Mica (Eds.), *New trends in cooperative activities: Understanding system dynamics in complex environments* (pp. 96–113). Santa Monica, CA: Human Factors and Ergonomics Society.

McPherson, M., Smith-Lovin, L., & Cook, J. M. (2001). Birds of a feather: Homophily in social networks. *Annual Review of Sociology, 27,* 415–444.

Mohammed, S., Klimoski, R., & Rentsch, J. (2000). The measurement of team mental models: We have no schema. *Organizational Research Methods, 3*(2), 123–165.

Monge, P. R. & Contractor, N. (2003). *Theories of communication networks.* New York: Oxford University Press.

Mullen, B., Johnson, C., & Salas, E. (1991). Effects of communication network structure: Components of positional centrality. *Social Networks, 13*(2), 169–185.

Pastor, J., Meindl, J. R., & Mayo, M. C. (2002). A network effects models of charisma attributions. *Academy of Management Journal, 45*(2), 410–420.

Pattison, P. (1994). Social cognition in context: Some applications of social network analysis. In S. Wasserman & J. Galaskiewicz (Eds.), *Advances in social network analysis: Research from the social and behavioral sciences* (pp. 79–109). Thousand Oaks, CA: Sage Publications, Inc.

Pattison, P. & Robins, G. (2002). Neighborhood-based models for social networks. *Sociological Methodology, 32,* 301–337.

Pattison, P. & Wasserman, S. (1999). Logit Models and Logistic Regressions for Social Networks: II. Multivariate Relations. *British Journal of Mathematical & Statistical Psychology, 52,* 169–193.

Poole, M. S. (1983). Decision development in small groups III: A multiple sequence model of group decision development. *Communication Monographs, 50*(4), 321–341.

Poole, M. & Roth, M. (1989). Decision development in small groups. *Human Communication Research, 15,* 549–589.

Rentsch, J. R. & Hall, R. J. (1994). Members of great teams think alike: A model of team effectiveness and schema similarity among team members. In M. M. Beyerlein & D. A. Johnson (Eds.), *Advances in interdisciplinary studies of work teams: Vol. 1. Series on self-managed work teams* (pp. 223–262). Greenwich, CT: JAI.

Rentsch, J. R. & Woehr, D. J. (2004). Quantifying congruence in cognition: Social relations modeling and team member schema similarity. In S. Eduardo & F. M. Stephen (Eds.), *Team cognition: Understanding the factors that drive process and performance.* Washington, DC: American Psychological Association.

Robins, G. & Pattison, P. (2001). Random graph models for temporal processes in social networks. *Journal of Mathematical Sociology, 25,* 5–41.

Rice, R. E. (1994). Network analysis and computer-mediated communication systems. In S. Wasserman and J. Galaskiewicz (Eds.), *Advances in social network analysis: Research from the social and behavioral sciences* (pp. 167–203). Thousand Oaks, CA: Sage Publications, Inc.

Sabidussi, G. (1966). The centrality index of a graph. *Psychometrika, 31,* 581–603.

Seidman, S. B. (1983). Network structure and minimum degree. *Social Networks, 5,* 97–107.

Snijders, T. A. B. (2005). Models for longitudinal network data. In P. Carrington, J. Scott, & S. Wasserman (Eds.), *Models and methods in social network analysis* (pp. 215–247). New York: Cambridge University Press.

Stephenson, K. & Zelen, M. (1989). Rethinking centrality: Methods and applications. *Social Networks, 11*, 1–37.

Tuckman, B. (1965). Developmental sequences in small groups. *Psychological Bulletin, 63*, 384–399.

Valente, T. W. (1995). *Network models of the diffusion of innovations.* Cresskill, NJ: Hampton Press.

Wasserman, S. & Faust, K. (1994). *Structural analysis in the social sciences.* New York: Cambridge University Press.

Wasserman, S. & Galaskiewicz, J. (Eds.). (1994). *Advances in social network analysis: Research from the social and behavioral sciences.* Thousand Oaks, CA: Sage Publications, Inc.

Wellman, B. (1988). Structural analysis: From method and metaphor to theory and substance. In B. Wellman & S. Berkowitz (Eds.), *Social structures: A network approach* (pp. 19–61). Cambridge, England: Cambridge University Press.

Yu, J., Slaughter, A. J., & Koehly, L. M. (2004, April). *Perceptual congruence of an organization's social structure.* Paper presented at the annual meeting of the Society for Industrial and Organizational Psychology, Los Angeles, CA.

17

Computational Representations and Methods for Modeling Teams

Wayne Zachary, Benjamin Bell, and Joan Ryder

Introduction

The study of team effectiveness has historically relied largely on experimental and naturalistic data from empirical human teams, typically analyzed and summarized by mathematical and statistical analysis methods. Computational modeling, in contrast, has been much less frequently employed. This low use of modeling is particularly noticeable in comparison with the life or physical sciences or even with other branches of behavioral science such as cognitive science or linguistics. In these latter areas, computational modeling is routinely used as a core scientific method for managing complexity, for comparing and testing theories, and for dealing with problems and limitations to empirical observation and experimental control. Such issues apply to team performance and effectiveness research, suggesting that the broader use of computational modeling would be both appropriate and highly beneficial to the field. The existing body of work on computational modeling of teams, although small, can form a foundation for more widespread use of this approach. This chapter provides an overview of the use of computational models in team effectiveness, focusing on the differences among the various types of models and the various purposes that computational models of teams may serve.

General reviews of the use of modeling for individual and team behaviors are provided elsewhere (cf. Pew & Mavor, 1998; Zachary, Campbell, Laughery, Glenn, & Cannon-Bowers, 2001). However, four key propositions about modeling are keys to the remainder of this chapter:

1. *A model has an intended use or purpose.* Models are constructed so that they can serve a specific purpose (e.g., to render a theory testable) or to answer a specific question (e.g., What should the design be for a new team?). The way the model is developed and

the information it generates or elucidates are always based on the purpose behind the model.

2. *A model is a simplifying representation.* Models seek to recreate or predict some aspects of real-world phenomena through some representation of those phenomena. Given that the focus of this chapter is on computational models, the representation is typically expressed based in symbols and operations on those symbols. Even more important than being representations, however, is the fact that models are developed deliberately to represent only some of the aspects of the phenomena being modeled and thus are deliberately simplifications of what they are trying to represent.

3. *Model simplifications are based on assumptions.* Deliberate choices must therefore be made about which aspects are to be included and which are to be left out. For those aspects to be included, additional choices must be made about what representation will be used and how that representation will simplify that aspect of the phenomena. These deliberate choices are typically expressed as explicit assumptions that underlie the model (e.g., that model assumes that communication is instantaneous and completely understood in all cases). Such explicit assumptions tell the model user (or the reader here) what simplifications have been made (e.g., that communication delays and communication errors have been assumed away).

4. *Model assumptions are framed in the subjunctive.* The assumptions incorporated into a model are not inherently hypotheses about the phenomena being modeled, as, for example, experimental hypotheses are. Rather, they express the notion that the phenomenon is being represented *as if* it were built or operated in that way. For example, the maker of road maps may represent the land surface as if it were a two-dimensional plane but does not actually think that the world is in fact flat. Explicit model assumptions provide guidance to the model builder, model user, and model analyst about how to interpret the outputs of the model or the limits of its power.

Framework for Computational Models of Teams

Virtually all models of teams can be derived from a very simple foundation, which is pictured in Figure 17.1. In its simplest form, teams consist of people and the relationships between and among these people. The individuals in the team can be generically termed *nodes* because different models represent individuals at varying levels of abstraction, ranging from specific individuals to categories of people or even generally (i.e., any person). Similarly, the relationships that interconnect the nodes can be generically termed *links* because different models represent different aspects of these relationships, ranging from highly structural (e.g., who communicates with whom) to organizational (e.g., who reports to whom) to procedural (e.g., what work or information passes through or along a given relationship).

This simple definition of a team as being composed of links and nodes allows for a surprisingly large number of ways to modeling teams based on different stances toward this foundational representation and different elaborations of the basic concept. Several distinctions underlie most of the variation in team modeling approaches:

- *Team-centric versus individual-centric stances*: A team-centric stance views and represents the team as a whole, whereas an individual-centric stance views and represents the team in terms of the individual nodes that comprise it.

- *Process-oriented versus structure-oriented stance*: A process-oriented stance views the team in terms of its dynamics and the work or other processes in which the team or its constituent nodes engage. Based on the stance taken, models will focus on either (1) the events and processes that occur within the team or between the team and its environment over time (i.e., process-oriented stance) or (2) the static organization and pattern of composition of components, whether concrete or abstract, within the nodes and links that make up the team (i.e., structure-oriented stance). Further elaboration of the concept of link can be made, given a structure-oriented stance. The links can be viewed, for example, as representing either *formal* or *informal* interconnections between the people in the team.

- *Behavioral versus cognitive stance*: A behavioral stance considers only the specific observable actions that a team or the node in it can or do undertake, without regard to any internal information processing (i.e., cognition) involved in generating or interpreting those behaviors. A cognitive stance, in contrast, considers the knowledge or reasoning processes that are involved in generating the behavior of the team of nodes within it. A cognitive stance can be further elaborated to differentiate, for example, *rationality-situated* or *socially situated* reasoning. Cognition can be represented in terms of pure rationality, which considers only the task/goal to be accomplished and the constraints posed by the environment, or it can be represented in terms of social intelligence, which considers only the human social relationship aspect of the links within the team and the individual characteristics of the nodes themselves in terms of, for example, motives or personality.

Different approaches to team modeling arise when different stances are taken toward (and different concept elaborations made regarding) the basic representation in Figure 17.1. These reflect different combinations of assumptions about teams in general (or about specific teams) as well as the purpose for which the model is being created. The stance taken and assumptions made can, in turn, reflect underlying specific aspects of psychological or organizational theory.

A specific computational model allows its assumptions (and underlying theory) to be tested and explored through computational simulations or mathematical analysis. This is particularly important in complex systems such as human teams, where emergent phenomena abound and effects and implications of (theoretically-based) assumptions are almost impossible to control for experimentally. Model-based predictions can be compared with empirical team data to partition the observed variability in terms of the specific assumptions made.

Other uses of computational models are also possible (and described next). These include designing teams, improving team performance through use of computational team models as embedded decision support, and even developing realistic synthetic teams for use in simulation-based team training.

Four specific major classes of computational models of teams are briefly discussed next in terms of their differing stances, underlying assumptions, and computational representations. At least one case study is provided for each class of model. These case studies, all taken from the authors' team modeling laboratory, reflect the range of purposes that team models can serve.

Team Modeling Using Social Network Representations

One of the simplest ways of modeling teams is to focus exclusively on the structure of relationships between and among the members of the team using a diagram similar to that given in Figure 17.1. In this representation, usually called a social network representation, the cognitive processes within individuals in the team are virtually ignored, and the effects of the pattern of relationships becomes of primary importance. This makes it a team-centric representation, although it is also possible to use it to analyze the view of the team from the perspective of any individual within it.

A social network representation (see Borgatti, 1994; Borgatti & Foster, 2003; Hanneman, 2001) is constructed as a mathematical graph consisting of a set of nodes, which represent the individuals in the team, and a set of links between the nodes, which represent relationships between nodes. Links in the graph can be directional, representing asymmetrical

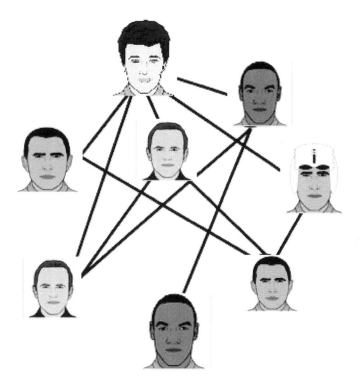

FIGURE 17.1
Foundation for team modeling.

relationships (*a* supervises *b* but not vice versa), or can be bi-directional, representing symmetrical relationships (*a* and *b* have a communication channel between them). The links can also be quantified to represent characteristics of the links (e.g., the amount of information that could or that does flow across a communication channel between two nodes). Because the mathematical graph can be easily formalized in matrix terms (and other formalizations as well), a rich body of mathematical methods has been developed over the last 50 years to analyze and abstract properties of network models, especially structural characteristics such as component structures (e.g., subgroups, cliques). As noted in the first case study, the effect of the relationships on team processes can also be modeled with social network representations. Generally, however, the social network approach is structure focused rather than process focused.

The simplicity of the social network model is enabled by a very strong assumption underlying it. This approach to modeling teams assumes that one can predict or identify features or characteristics of a team by examining only the relationships among the people on the team *as if* the characteristics of the individual people—their knowledge, reasoning processes, personalities, emotions, culture—had no effect.

Conceptually, social network models are simple to construct, although the amount of data required can often be daunting. These representations are created in a two- or sometimes three-step process as follows:

1. Bound the team or group being modeled, and identify all the individuals involved, making them nodes for the network.

2. Identify the relationships to be included in the model, and for each pair of nodes (and each relationship, if multiple relationships are being represented) determine whether that relationship exists between those two nodes; add it as a link in the model.

3. (Sometimes) determine characteristics of the relationships to be included in the model, and, for each link in the model, quantify or annotate the link to reflect the characteristics of the relationship between those two individuals.

From this complete model, appropriate methods for analysis need to be defined and applied to the data that make up the social network representation of the team being modeled. Two case studies are given next to demonstrate different kinds of social network models and the different ways the models can be used.

Case Study 1: Information Flow in an Athletic Team

Purpose

Whereas many teams are kept in existence by powerful institutions or social forces, there are also many other teams that are more ephemeral and come into existence and later break up and cease to exist. The process of fission in ephemeral teams is important but poorly understood, because the opportunity seldom arises in which to collect detailed data on it. One such ephemeral team was being researched for other reasons when it became embroiled in a controversy and separated into two smaller groups that eventually became competitive with each other. The social network data were gathered into a model of the team, focusing on the flow of information through the team. This model was used to test a hypothesis that information flow through the team was constrained by the network structure and led to a "bottleneck" that structurally separated the two subgroups, which eventually split apart.

The Team Modeled

The team modeled was a nonvarsity university athletic team (specifically a martial arts team) that trained together and took part in regional competitions. Because it was nonvarsity, the team had no institutions that required it to stay together (or even exist); rather, it was a purely voluntary team. When a controversy arose about the costs for the coach/instructor (which the team members bore out of pocket), the team eventually split into two separate teams, each with a different coach/instructor.

Modeling Technology Used

The 34 individuals in the original team were represented as nodes in a social network model, with the links between the nodes representing the existence of a social relationship outside the context of the team. Additionally, each link was quantified to indicate the communication bandwidth of that relationship.

What's in the Model

The resulting social network was fairly sparse, in that less than 10% of the possible links were actually present. The relationships that did exist, however, varied greatly in their quality, ranging from dyads that interacted in only a very limited context outside the team (e.g., eating lunch together) to other dyads that interacted in a very broad range of contexts. Ultimately, the number of contexts in which each dyad interacted was used as an indicator of the breadth of the relationship, and that breadth was used as a measure of that relationship's potential for information flow.

Model Results and Significance

The resulting quantified network was analyzed to determine if the network structure limited the flow of information through it and, if so, if there was a unique partition of the network that represented this limitation (see Zachary, 1977). This was a test of a theory-based hypothesis that informal communication among group members was the mechanism by which team cohesion was either maintained or lost and that such a structural bottleneck to information flow would eventually lead to the two subgroups on either side of it becoming more cohesive than the team as a whole and fission would follow. The mathematical analysis supported this hypothesis, demonstrating that a unique information flow bottleneck existed in the network, and that predicted the location of the team fission precisely.

Case Study 2: Dynamic Structure in Ad Hoc Military Teams

Purpose

Under the concepts of network-centric warfare (see Alberts, Garstka, & Stein, 2002; Alberts & Hayes, 2003), understanding of battlespace is shared throughout the force through advanced information technology, decreasing the so-called fog of war. This same information technology enables enhanced collaboration and adaptation by all parts of the force, decreasing the "friction" that delays and confounds the translation of commander's intent into distributed action. In practice, network-centric warfare allows units that are widely distributed both geographically and organizationally to come together on short notice to achieve specific operational goals, creating ad hoc organizations that can morph and change through time. Gaining awareness of such ad hoc structures and of their changes is thus a new challenge that has been created by network-centric warfare. One way to create this awareness is to develop dynamic models of these structures using social network representations and to use these representations to help commanders visualize and understand the structures of these ad hoc teams.

The Team Modeled

The Command Post of the Future (CPOF) is an advanced computer workstation designed to meet the needs of modern network-centric warfare. It embodies advanced technology for collaboration, both synchronous and asynchronous, for both colocated and geographically distributed teams. Although it does not directly track the formation or activities of ad hoc teams as just described, CPOF does provide a powerful logging and data recording facility. These data contain information on interactions (both structural and semantic) between and among units involved in current operations, as well as other units interacting for other reasons. Thus, the model addresses the problem of extracting the current ad hoc operational teams and visualizing these for commanders.

Modeling Technology Used

The principal focus of this project for the military is to understand the various risks to successful achievement of organization/team goals. The analysis tool selected for this purpose is the Organizational Risk Analyzer (ORA) developed by Kathleen Carley and colleagues at Carnegie Mellon University (CMU) (Carley, Ren, & Krackhardt, 2000). ORA provides analyses not just of the standard types of organizational and communication links between individuals but also various kinds of links between individuals and other significant entities in military command and control such as geographic locations, events, tasks, and resources. Analysis results then serve to identify significant risks to any of the entities that are controllable such as personnel, tasks, resources, and communications. A variety of statistical and graph theoretic analyses is used to identify weak links, critical links, network substructures, and imbalances that can point to risks to team performance.

What's in the Model

The raw data from using CPOF include the large volume of data generated by interaction of military users with one another and with tactical information through the CPOF system. Data are available to identify all user interactions that involve creation and alteration of tactical information in CPOF, as well as all e-mail and even voice-over-Internet Protocol (VOIP) communications. Through the analysis of all these data in combination, it is possible to identify not only who is communicating with whom but also who is likely to be most knowledgeable about which resources, geographic locations, or events. It is also possible to use semantic analysis tools in conjunction with social network analysis (SNA) to analyze the content of e-mail (and even VOIP) communications, but it is not necessary to extend the analyses beyond the basic graphical network data to identify important patterns.

Model Results and Significance

Candidate users indicated that many of the SNA results are valuable elements of situation awareness (SA) for the CPOF users and the commander who oversees CPOF operations. This complete package of SNA analyses is being organized via an SA-aiding user interface to provide ready access to all of the major domains of command and control information: personnel, intelligence, operations, logistics, and communications. Analyses of results from this interface, called C2Insight, are provided as overlays on a tactical map, as standard timeline graphs, or as simple tabular or text data, including the possibility of user-defined alert thresholds to trigger the display of data indicative of specific problems.

Team Modeling Using Individual Cognitive Representations

A very different way of modeling teams focuses on the internal cognitive processes of the individuals that comprise the team rather than on the relationships between those individuals. Approached in this way, the links in Figure 17.1 virtually disappear, and the information representation and manipulation processes inside the individuals grow to primary importance. The knowledge, skills, and abilities of each individual in the team are modeled in substantial detail so that each individual's behaviors can be predicted in a context-sensitive manner with the behaviors of each individual in the team becoming a part of the context for generating behavior for each other individual in the team. Thus, team processes are presumed to emerge from the interactions among these separate but interacting individual cognitive processes, making this an individual-centric and process-focused representation. Put differently, this approach allows one to model and predict team behavior *as if* only individual knowledge and rational cognition were involved.

The main technology for modeling teams in this manner is that of architecture-based cognitive modeling (see comparative reviews in Gluck & Pew, 2005; Pew & Mavor, 1998; Ritter, et al., 2000). This technology involves computational architectures that are designed to mimic the structure and organization of human cognition based on specific cognitive theories. As noted in Pew and Mavor (1998, Figure 3.1), most of these cognitive architectures follow a general scheme that can be traced back to Broadbent (1958) and that divides human information processing into four interconnected components: (1) sensation and perception; (2) memory; (3) cognition; and (4) motor behavior. Memory is further divided into working memory, which provides access to a small amount of (currently) activated information for processing by sensation/perception and cognition, and long-term memory, which provides access to persistent declarative and procedural knowledge and to more transient knowledge that is constructed to support situational reasoning. This transient knowledge includes awareness of the current situation and instances of contextualized procedural knowledge in the form of situational task knowledge. Generally, architecture-based cognitive models are developed in four steps:

1. Selecting a specific existing general cognitive architecture.
2. Gathering procedural, declarative, and situational knowledge that would be needed by a person to function in a specific domain or situation.
3. Formalizing that knowledge in a form that can be used by the selected cognitive architecture and integrating the two (knowledge + architecture) into an executable cognitive model.
4. Executing the model as part of a simulated (or real) problem environment, complete with situational representations that allow the environment to respond realistically to the model's actions and to generate appropriate sensory inputs to the model.

As previously noted, a team can be modeled in this manner by including, within the knowledge of the executable cognitive model, the knowledge needed to generate and perceive/respond to team behaviors and execution of models of other team members within the problem environment.

Case Study 3: Team Interaction Analysis with Reusable Agents (TIARA)

Purpose

The TIARA study (Bell & Scolaro, 2003) was a research effort to create a set of individual cognitive models that could interact with each other in a simulated problem environment and aggregately represent the behaviors of a human team under stressful conditions. The long-term goal was to create a synthetic team that could serve a range of applied uses, including the following:

- A low-cost test bed for analysis of team responses to various kinds of stress and to various stress-mitigation strategies.
- Synthetic teams and teammates that could take the place of human role players in team training simulations.

The key to unlocking team support technologies is better understanding of team interactions, particularly under conditions of inherent task complexity, high workload, rapid operational tempo, or environmental (e.g., noise, vibration) and physiological (fatigue, anxiety) stressors.

The Team Modeled

TIARA modeled a military team that works on command and control (C2) tasks in naval aviation, specifically a three-person team that works on an E-2C aircraft. This team works together to build and maintain awareness of the tactical airspace situation and to control friendly aircraft as needed in that airspace. More than just a simple air traffic control responsibility, the E-2C C2 team must support various teams of fighter aircraft in achieving its mission goals, must ensure that fratricide (friendly aircraft shooting down friendly aircraft under the "fog of war") is prevented, and must integrate information from multiple sensor and off-platform human sources (e.g., from ships, from intelligence aircraft) into the situational picture and C2 processes.

There are three roles in the team: the combat information center officer (CICO); the air control officer (ACO); and the radar operator (RO). The CICO is the team lead, interacting primarily with the RO and ACO, giving them advice, giving them information about activity outside the focus of their attention, and taking over part of their workload under peak-load situations. The ACO is primarily responsible for communications with entities under control of the E-2C C2 team and sharing specific information within the on-board team. The CICO may closely supervise the ACO as part of the ACO's routine progression to CICO responsibilities in the future. The RO, as one might expect, monitors the radar systems and shares information from the radar with the rest of the on-board team.

Modeling Technology Used

Each of the three team roles was modeled using the COGNET/iGEN cognitive architecture (see Zachary, Ryder, et al., 2005 for a detailed description).

This architecture was developed specifically to support modeling of cognitive processes that involve complex work that unfolds across minutes or even hours of time, with an attendant loss of detail at very fine-grained processing levels. Five kinds of knowledge are used to build a COGNET/iGEN model:

1. *Declarative knowledge*: A hierarchical multifaceted representation of both transitory information (e.g., current SA, plans under development or execution) and long-term information (e.g., problem-domain ontologies).

2. *Procedural knowledge*: Complex chunks of procedural knowledge used to generate either instances of specific general tasks customized to the current situation understanding or of interpretation/reasoning activities to integrate perceived information into current SA or plans.

3. *Perceptual knowledge*: Rules to govern how internal (symbolic) information is created and placed in memory in response to sensation of different stimuli via the sensory channels.

4. *Action knowledge*: Procedures determining how to create instances of physical actions (manual or verbal) in the environment.

5. *Metacognitive knowledge*: Rules and patterns determining how to contextually prioritize the use of various chunks of procedural knowledge and declarative information on the current state of reasoning (and methods for deliberately modifying it).

A model with all five kinds of information, fully specified and formalized, is then executed via a software engine that is interconnected to a real or simulated problem environment.

What's in the Model

The model of each role was built to contain two broad types of knowledge, both involving all five COGNET/iGEN knowledge types. *Taskwork* knowledge allowed the model to perform its designated work task involving understanding the external tactical situation, interacting with its workstation equipment, and using mission objectives to dynamically develop and execute local and context-sensitive actions and plans. *Teamwork* knowledge allowed the model to develop situation awareness of the team itself (as well as the external situation), to form expectations of what other team members would and should do, and to communicate within the team in the ways that a good teammate would. The teamwork knowledge was based on Smith-Jentsch, Zeisig, Acton, and McPherson's (1998) four dimensions of teamwork: timely backup behaviors, proactive information exchange, adherence to communication protocols, and visible leadership. Details of the cognitive models used in TIARA are discussed in Zachary, Ryder, et al. (2005).

A general limitation of cognitive models is that they do not show substantial variability as a result of skill level or situational stress unless such factors are explicitly incorporated into the models, either as more elaborated knowledge (to provide additional skill) or as performance parameters that vary or moderate behavior as a result of specific stressors. Of particular interest in TIARA was the ability to commit errors with regard to accuracy (i.e., doing the task incorrectly or only partially correctly) and efficiency (i.e., doing the task correctly but in a less efficient manner). This was accomplished by modifying the knowledge needed to accomplish certain tasks to make the application of that knowledge sensitive to the stress perceived by the model (as represented in an internal model measure of overall current workload) and to a model parameter that represented operator skill level (more highly skilled operators were set to be less responsive to stress and to make fewer baseline errors).

Model Results and Significance

The TIARA models were then executed jointly in a test bed that simulated the work environment of the E-2C aircraft and a realistic tactical mission simulated by the Navy's Joint Semi-Automated Force (JSAF) mission simulation program. The simulation environment was implemented to monitor behavior of the operators (whether human or synthetic) on a range of team performance measures based on Smith-Jentsch's et al.'s (1998) four dimensions. A series of simulations using scenarios with varying workload and different combinations of operator skill level show the following main qualitative characteristics of the synthetic team:

1. Workload increases perceived levels of stress.
2. Increases in workload increase communications activity.
3. Performance is inversely related to workload.
4. Being more proactive increases subjective workload.
5. Increases in workload are accompanied by increased need for coordination.
6. Resilience to stressors is correlated with skill.
7. The ability to modulate coordination in response to stress is correlated with skill.

From a validity perspective, these results have face validity in that they seem equally plausible statements about human teams.

The measures used in the TIARA test bed were taken from a large prior research program on human decision making under stress (see Cannon-Bowers & Salas, 1998). This allowed us to see if the TIARA synthetic team could replicate and thus predict the behavior of human teams as measured in that prior program and thus achieve a degree of predictive validity as well. Of particular relevance here are characteristics 5 through 7 as previously listed. Importantly, these were also found to be main characteristics of human teams in the Cannon-Bowers and Salas (ibid.) study. Thus, this approach to modeling team performance was shown to be capable of predicting key aspects of team behavior using only representations of individual cognition.

Team Modeling Using Group Cognitive Representations

Models such as TIARA demonstrate that it is possible to model and generate a surprisingly cohesive and productive team simply by modeling each individual's ability to generate behaviors that support teamwork, based solely on the individual's relationship to the overall problem situation. The individual agents in the TIARA model do not reason about the relationships that comprised the team because these are not an explicit part of the individual cognitive models. Rather, knowledge about such relationships is implicitly represented only as part of the solution logic of the individual model, making individual cognitive models an almost completely complementary representation to social network models of teams.

Team or group cognitive representations are intermediate between these two extremes. This type of model includes both an explicit representation of the reasoning processes inside the nodes of Figure 17.1 and an explicit representation of the roles and relationships that comprise the team or organizational structure that connects the individual nodes. Such models allow, among other things, analyses of the impact of team structure on cognition and vice versa. They also provide a basis for the design of teams and teamwork, as demonstrated in the next case study.

The team or group cognitive models include two interconnected aspects. The first is a *cognitive work model* of the cognitive processing that is needed to accomplish the work of the team or purposive goal of the organization. The second is a *team/organizational design model* of the team role structure, which partitions the cognitive processing and assigns it to specific individuals. Once the cognitive processes have been so partitioned and assigned, the team resembles a TIARA team, and its behavior can be simulated against various environmental or work scenarios. This allows the interplay between the cognitive work and the team/organizational design to be analyzed and characterized. In terms of Figure 17.1, the cognitive work model provides a representation of the processing that occurs within all of the nodes, and the team/organizational design provides a representation of the sets of links and relationships that make up the team. Thus, team processes are assumed to emerge from the interactions among individual cognitive processes and team structure. Another noteworthy assumption is that the individuals follow the team structure and role precisely and only think and behave in a rational manner (i.e., have no emotions, personalities, or personal "agendas"). This last assumption is revisited in the next model type discussed.

The technology for modeling teams in this manner is a superset of the cognitive modeling technology used to build individual cognitive representations. The same general four steps described for individual cognitive model development must be followed but should be generalized to deal with the team-based aspect of the cognitive work model. Additional steps are needed to create the team/organizational model and to create a specific instance of the team/cognitive model (i.e., one in which the cognitive work knowledge is partitioned and assigned to specific individuals, or models, in the team). As noted in the following case study, this instantiation step may involve the addition of communication and perception knowledge needed to enable the interaction among team members and the interaction between individuals and the problem environment (e.g., work displays). The general sequence of building a group cognition model of a team is as follows:

1. Selecting a general cognitive simulation tool that supports this paradigm.

2. Gathering the procedural, declarative, and situational knowledge that needs to be used somewhere within the team for the team as a whole to function in the specific work domain or situation.

3. Formalizing that knowledge in a representation that can be partitioned and allocated to various individual roles within the team and simulated using a set of individual-level executable cognitive models.

4. Developing specific models of the roles and relationships that make up the team or organization that is performing the cognitive work.

5. Creating a team model instance by partitioning the cognitive work knowledge according to the team relationships and by adding perceptual/communicational knowledge necessary to enable the team members to communicate needed information about their work processes, to engage in teamwork behaviors, and to perceive information from other environmental sources.

6. Executing the model instance as part of a simulated (or real) problem environment, TIARA-style.

Because of the tandem representations, team cognitive models are more complex than individual cognitive models performing teamwork; as a result, research into this area is at an earlier stage than either of the two types of models discussed previously.

Case Study 4: Organizations as Networks of Cognitive Tasks (ORGNET)

Purpose

ORGNET (Ryder, Iordanov, Le Mentec, Barba, & Eilbert, 2002; Weiland & Eilbert, 2000; Zachary, Weiland, & Le Mentec, 1997) is a modeling tool created to facilitate the model-based design of teams based on the allocation of cognitive work to roles in the team, and its use follows the sequence outlined in the previous section. An ORGNET model starts with an analysis of the cognitive work that must be accomplished by the team. That team-level cognitive representation is then simulated as if a single "agent" were performing the work of the whole team, but in a way that is unrestricted by performance limitations such as memory or fatigue. However, the aggregate agent-level execution assumes that only one work task can be performed at a time. Running a team-level model gives a view of how the performance of work tasks, the use of knowledge, and the information flow between and among work tasks are interrelated in different work scenarios.

A team to perform the work is then defined using data from these team-cognition simulations and a set of design principles derived from team and organizational theory. The team design is represented as a series of interacting roles or jobs. The cognitive work in the team-level cognitive model is then assigned to specific roles in the team, resulting in a computational model of the team based on these specific role definitions and cognitive work assignments. This individual-level model is then exercised to simulate the team's behavior under different work scenarios, using a set of measures of both individual and team performance. The team design is then evaluated using visualizations of the measures and is iteratively refined or optimized using formal optimization algorithms.

The Team Modeled

ORGNET was used to create a set of designs for a team on board a new Navy ship, specifically a team responsible for managing the defense of the ship against airborne threats, a function called air defense warfare (ADW). The overall function of the ADW team is to identify and monitor aircraft based on sensor data (typically radar) within the ship's area of operation and to defend the ship using the ship's weapons if the aircraft become threatening or attack. Because ORGNET is design focused, the models built did not reflect any empirical team but rather a range of hypothetical ADW team designs. The design goals of this ship were to reduce manning, so the objective of the ORGNET ADW-team model was to find a minimally sized team that could robustly perform the function over a broad range of anticipated situations or scenarios. On conventional Navy warships, ADW teams range from as few as three to as many as seven roles. The focus in this model was to see if it was possible to design a team of only two persons to perform the task.

Modeling Technology Used

ORGNET uses a combination of several technologies. The core is an individual cognitive architecture similar to that used in TIARA. Specifically, ORGNET uses a variant of the COGNET/iGEN architecture that is generalized in three ways. The first generalization allows the architecture to perform without the inherent limits of an individual human when a team-level or aggregate-level model is being executed but to operate with these same limits when an individual-level or disaggregate model is being executed. Both aggregate and disaggregate ORGNET models use a COGNET/iGEN-based representation to represent the cognitive work required by the team. As with TIARA, this representation consists of an explicit model of cognitive task knowledge, declarative knowledge, perceptual knowledge, and metacognitive or control knowledge.

The second generalization allows the cognitive work representation to be automatically decomposed and translated into individual-level models based on the assignment of specific cognitive tasks to individual roles in a team. This second generalization involves a separate technology that automates most of the construction of individual-level representation for the disaggregate ORGNET model. Specifically, it:

1. Allows the team modeler to assign a set of cognitive tasks (i.e., high level chunks of procedural knowledge) to a role by a single action or gesture (e.g., "drag and drop" on the screen).

2. Automatically analyzes the rest of the cognitive work representation to determine which portions of declarative, perceptual, and metacognitive knowledge need to be assigned to the individual level model of that role or individual.

3. Completes the rest of the executable cognitive model for each individual role based on the results of that analysis.

The third generalization of the basic cognitive architecture involves adding measurement instrumentation to it, thus allowing the modeler to analyze the team design using the model. ORGNET instruments the cognitive architecture as follows:

- *Information flow* measures amount and type of information that must be communicated (either externally between individuals or internally within a single individual's own cognitive processes) to accomplish each pair of cognitive tasks in the cognitive work model.
- *Dynamic information flow* measures volume of information, relative to a specific simulated scenario, that must be communicated (either externally between individuals or internally within a single individual's own cognitive processes) to accomplish each pair of cognitive tasks in the cognitive work model.
- *Static shared information bandwidth* measures the maximum possible information flow between each pair of cognitive tasks from the cognitive work model without regard to any scenario.
- *Workflow* measures the frequency, concurrence, and difficulty of task sequences relative to a specific problem scenario.
- *Dynamic cognitive complexity* measures the total number of cognitive operations required by each task relative to a specific problem scenario.

What's in the Model

The cognitive work model provided the main content of the model. The cognitive work required to accomplish the ADW function was modeled as nine high-level cognitive tasks:

- *Discard noise*: Filter out extraneous noise as sensor errors rather than real tracks.
- *Evaluate track*: Check noise frequency parameter of the track, and determine the possible compatible aircraft.
- *Identify track*: For possible aircraft, check altitude and speed of track against aircraft parameters to identify track as friendly, enemy, commercial, or unknown.
- *Confirm track*: Contact the pilot to confirm track identity (for friendly and commercial).
- *Issue alert*: To organization that uses identified aircraft, for unknown or enemy tracks.
- *Monitor commercial tracks*: Periodically examine the behavior of commercial aircraft tracks for anomalous behavior (e.g., leaving commercial air corridors).

- *Monitor friendly tracks*: Periodically examine the behavior of friendly aircraft tracks for anomalous behavior (e.g., leaving designated patrol areas).

- *Monitor enemy tracks*: Periodically examine the behavior of enemy aircraft tracks for anomalous behavior (e.g., suddenly moving toward a ship or some other friendly target).

- *Monitor unidentified tracks*: Periodically examine the behavior of unidentified tracks for additional information that can lead to their correct identification and classification.

Each cognitive task was represented in multiple levels of detail as needed to capture the procedural reasoning needed to complete all possible instances of the task.

The declarative knowledge needed by this set of cognitive tasks was represented as two types of declarative knowledge ontology: (1) geospatial information (e.g., tracks and their characteristics, geopolitical boundaries); and (2) track classification information (e.g., known aircraft types and characteristics, military organizations, sensor characteristics).

Alternative designs for an ADW team were expressed as different assignments of the various cognitive tasks to different roles to create model instances.

Finally, a set of problem scenarios was created to represent different work conditions. Examples were routine monitoring of air traffic in a commercial space (e.g., as off the U.S. coast), high-intensity warfare (e.g., a military engagement involving an air strike on the Navy ship), and low-intensity warfare (e.g., observing a low-level military engagement between two combatants to which the United States is neutral). These scenarios were designed to test each team model under different conditions so that the overall effectiveness could be assessed.

Model Results and Significance

Various ADW team designs were created and simulated against different scenarios, as was the aggregate ADW team cognitive model. The different measures showed substantial variation across the scenarios as well as among the different team designs. No single design emerged as superior in all scenarios or on all measures. Although this might seem discouraging, it nonetheless points to the significance of this type of model.

Human factors practitioners and systems engineers are frequently called on to design work teams as part of the development of hardware/systems designs. Except by conducting human-in-the loop experiments, these professionals have very little in the way of analytical tools to compare and assess the implications of a given team design that, once committed to, can constrain system performance and lock in training and staffing costs for years—sometimes even decades. Team cognition models such as the ADW team model allow the teams to be designed, analyzed, and compared with theoretically based, quantitative measures. If, as was the case here, no single design emerges as superior in all cases, it provides a basis for explicit design decisions. For example, the team can be designed to maximize performance under specific conditions, and performance or training aides can be added to improve performance under conditions in which the chosen team design would be expected to lead to suboptimal performance.

Team Modeling Using Social Intelligence Representations

Both individual and team cognition models allow one to model and predict team behavior as if the organizational structure were always followed precisely and people always acted out of rational cognition alone. Although this might be a reasonable assumption for modeling, experience with real people suggests that this assumption is not always correct. People may *generally* behave in a rational way that pursues the team goals and objectives, but they also intrude their personalities, emotions, and personal motives into the overall process as well. For example, a person may *not* fully support a perceived rival in the team for power or influence in key situations, or shy persons or persons from cultures conscious of social hierarchy may avoid noting problems or suggesting solutions if they fear embarrassment for themselves or their superiors. The kinds of information processing underlying such behavior is different from the purely rational cognition so intensively analyzed and modeled with the cognitive architectures previously described. Rather than the purposive rationality aspect of intelligence, it reflects the social dimension of intelligence.

The implications of the various aspects of social intelligence on group and team behavior have been extensively studied by social psychology for more than half a century and have consistently shown that factors such as personality, affect, and culture play a huge role in the way empirical teams operate. Until recently, however, this research on social intelligence in teams has approached the subject from an analytical perspective that is essentially qualitative. This has changed in the last half decade, with the development of computational representations that explicitly consider that social intelligence. These social intelligence representations, like the group cognitive representations already discussed, model both the information processing inside the individual nodes in Figure 17.1 as well as the relationships that interrelate these nodes. However, unlike models such as ORGNET, the social intelligence representations consider the interpersonal aspects of those relationships as well as the formal team/work aspects and also take into account the impacts of the personality and culture of the individuals represented by the nodes as well as their work-directed purposive rational cognitive processes. The main purpose of these models is to allow the effects of these social intelligence factors to be partitioned from and compared with the effect of team/organizational structure and rational cognition.

The dynamics and individual variability of personality and affect are typically represented using subsymbolic models of information processing (Gratch & Marsella, 2004; Velasquez, 1997; Weaver, Silverman, Shin, & Dubois, 2001). These are models that operate not by constructive processes that operate on symbolic information (as do the various cognitive architectures) but rather by models of neurobiological structures and processes. In many social intelligence models, such as the Personality-Affect-Culture (PAC) model discussed next, the subsymbolic representations are integrated with aspects of symbolic processing schemes so that they connect with cognitive constructs such as SA and context. Additional socially oriented forms of knowledge are incorporated into social intelligence representations, but the forms of that knowledge differ widely from model to model. Generally, the knowledge helps form the bridge between subsymbolic constructs such as need, motives, or emotions and actions in a specific behavioral context based on those actions.

The overall assumption underlying this class of models is that it is possible to predict the effects of social intelligence on team-situated behavior *as if* team structure and rational intelligence were not involved.

Case Study 5: Personality-Affect-Culture

Purpose

Computer simulations have long been used to provide training and mission rehearsal for complex work tasks. To a large extent, however, simulation has focused on individually based work (e.g., flying aircraft, shooting weapons, and operating heavy and complex machinery) where the behavior of other people does not have to be simulated. Where the roles of other people (i.e., teammates) need to be included, human role players are frequently used behind the scenes to dynamically generate the appropriate behavior. Where computer models of teammates are used, they either have been created with very scripted behaviors showing little adaptability or have been built using cognitive architectures that generate more complex adaptive team behaviors but only at the work-focused rational cognitive level. Thus, the effects of personality, culture, or other aspects of social intelligence are missing and ignored. Conversely, work situations where such factors are crucial have largely been outside the ability of computer simulation technology to address. PAC (Read, Miller, Monroe, et al., 2006) is a social-intelligence-based model that was created to solve this problem by providing computational models of teammates in virtual environments that could exhibit realistic interpersonal variability on social-intelligence dimensions for training and mission rehearsal simulations that required this kind of variability.

The Team Modeled

PAC was used to model a set of characters in a variant of a cultural-familiarization training game called VECTOR (Deaton et al., 2005). VECTOR is aimed at teaching military personnel to interact appropriately with members of other cultures in the context of military operations such as peacekeeping, disaster relief, or counterinsurgency. The characters modeled are members of a Kurdish Arabic community and members of a U.S. military patrol trying to gain information on recent acts of sabotage. The groups of local characters involved in interactions—typically in shops or offices—have to deal with the patrol team based on their social expectation about how such interactions should proceed as well on their individual personalities and those of the members of the patrol team. For example, a shopkeeper highly motivated by fear for personal safety should react to an information request from the patrol differently from a shopkeeper highly motivated by the potential for material (i.e., business) gain, just as patrol leaders acting aggressively should engender responses differently from patrol leaders acting patiently or even fearfully.

Modeling Technology Used

Personality is defined as enduring tendencies to think, feel, and behave in consistent ways. In PAC, these tendencies are generated from the construct of "motives," which represent pervasive but diffuse intentions for behavioral outcomes, particularly in a social space. PAC maps the many traits that make up the five dimensions of personality in psychology (see McCrae & Costa, 1999) into specific constellations of motives. An interconnected set of component models generates the activation and control of motives in a dynamic behavioral context. Motive strength is influenced by a subsymbolic activation process that is itself controlled by a hierarchy of subsymbolic processes. These govern motive strength dynamics (via competing "approach" and "avoidance" processes) and motive influence on behavior (in terms of narrower vs. broader motive focus). Importantly, each motive and each control process has preset parameters that represent specific individual predispositions. By identifying individual by type, expressed as combinations of personality traits, a personality-specific individual model is created by setting the corresponding presets prior to model execution.

Emotions (e.g., fear, happiness) are activated through an appraisal process that relates the agent's situational understanding to the agent's currently activated motives. Personality and emotion models in PAC are linked to, and driven by, the individual's internal understanding of the situation and by knowledge structures that are presumed to be shared across the individuals in the team. This knowledge takes the form of generative narrative story structures, which (1) indicate alternative possible pathways through a type of interaction, and (2) provide affordances for activation (or suppression) of specific motives during an instance of the story narrative.

For example, a story of a team meeting may involve states or steps in which some individual stands up and provides a plan to the team. Such a step affords an opportunity for an assertive person to pursue a motive for gaining status, whereas the complementary states in the story structure (e.g., sit by while someone else stands up) would afford opportunity for a shy person to pursue the motive for avoiding public interaction. Thus, with the same knowledge, different individuals (models) would behave differently because they had different personalities.

The narrative structures are presumed to be pervasively shared within a culture or subculture. When individuals from different cultures interact, additional behavioral variability will be created by the fact that they will be viewing the interactions through different story lenses and thus perceiving different motive affordances.

What's in the Model

The model consisted of two parts: the knowledge component and the character/individual component. The character component consists of parameter values representing the personality of each character involved (whether on the patrol team or the local community group). These consisted of the baseline strength of the approach/avoidance/motive-focus control systems and the baseline activation strength for each general motive. These parameters could be changed in each simulation of the model, allowing different combinations of personalities to be simulated within the teams.

The knowledge component consisted of narrative story structures that defined the space of evolutions that could occur during different types of interaction. This story space consisted of recognized starting and ending points to possible story threads as well as different pathways among intermediate transactions (called plot units) in the story. Each plot unit and transition between plot units includes implications for motive dynamics, either requiring a certain level of activation for a given motive or implying a certain degree of change for a given motive. Different personalities among the people involved in a simulation will lead to different story evolutions unfolding and often to very divergent outcomes. One character may be a human player (e.g., the patrol leader), who then must learn to recognize and adapt to the personalities with whom he or she is interacting to create a desired outcome.

In a variation of this model, the story spaces differ to some degree between the two teams representing cultural differences—so the community members share Arabic cultural expectations about how interactions will unfold, whereas the patrol team will share American cultural expectations. These differences in social knowledge can interact with personality variability and further contribute to varied outcomes of the model execution.

Model Results and Significance

A series of simulations reported in Read, Miller, Rosoff, et al. (2006), Zachary, Le Mentec, Miller, Read, & Thomas-Meyers (2005) showed that even within a specific simulation scenario, the full gamut of possible behaviors (as defined by the space of variation allowed by the interaction structure) can and will occur simply by varying the personality and emotional presets for the various individuals modeled. This result is significant because it is a simple version of a long-sought after characteristic of team/interpersonal models—creating variability in team processes without changing relationships or work knowledge, only individual social intelligence parameters. Such a capability allows team variability on social intelligence to be modeled, simulated, or analyzed based on only a single, knowledge acquisition and engineering process.

Conclusions

Models of teams and team effectiveness are varied in their technological basis as well as in their underlying assumptions. Although modeling is a relatively new approach in this field, it has proven to be a useful fulcrum with which to provide leverage for both theoretical and applied pursuits. In closing, several conclusions can be offered on the value and use of computational models in team effectiveness research:

1. *Models are not "right" or "wrong" in and of themselves.* They only serve as crucibles with which to assess and explore the assumptions built into them. Consider the contrasting assumptions of two of the case studies, TIARA and PAC. One (TIARA) varies the knowledge across individuals and focuses only on purposive

rationality. The other (PAC) keeps knowledge constant and focuses only on social-intelligence factors of motive and personality that vary across individuals. Neither contains any representation of social organization or structure of the team. Yet both lead to variability in behavior that is both meaningful and realistic. They provide complementary views of teams and team effectiveness that partition out certain factors *as if* they had no effect.

2. *Models allow observation and controlled manipulation of organizational states otherwise unamenable to empirical investigation.* It is not possible to eliminate personality or emotion in the empirical world, but models such as TIARA (and, in fact, most cognitively based models) provide a means to explore such situations. It is also not possible (for both ethical and methodological reasons) to measure and control empirically emotional effects such as fear or motivation factors, but models such as PAC offer the opportunity to do so. Modeling (as with ORGNET) also makes it possible to design a team to work within a sociotechnical system that has not yet been built and to test that team's ability to complete the work required. In allowing hypothetical situations to be observed, manipulated, and analyzed in detail, models provide a way around many problems of observation and experimentation that have been persistent roadblocks for the team effectiveness research.

3. *Models can be powerful vehicles for expression and elaboration of theory.* All the models discussed herein demonstrate how theories about team behavior, structure, and effectiveness can be formalized and expressed in computational terms, such that subsidiary and deeper processes and structure become visible, discoverable, and ultimately expressible in formal and testable terms. Modeling also adds power to the expression of theoretical propositions by tying them to frameworks that support their dynamic simulation and scientific visualization.

4. *Modeling technology and representations can and should be theory agnostic but customizable to test and apply different theories or hypotheses.* Models are not theories but can be expressions of theories. This is where their power lies. Each of the cases considered here could have employed alternative theoretical or analytical approaches. ORGNET could have employed alternative knowledge representation theories, C2Insight could have employed different SNA analytical methods; TIARA could have used different cognitive architectures; PAC could have employed different theories of personality. Too little advantage has perhaps been taken of such possibilities—it is important that in the future the power of "agnostic" models be used more to compare and contrast theories

in a controlled manner as well as to compare and contrast underlying assumptions.

Computational modeling of individual performance has a long and rich tradition in behavioral science. Team/organizational models have thus far been "the road less traveled," but increasing research in this area is clearly showing the power of this approach. This field has only begun to be plowed, and the best harvests are certainly yet to come.

Acknowledgments

The authors acknowledge and appreciate the comments and suggestions made by Floyd Glenn on the manuscript, the contributions by Roger Chapman to earlier drafts that did not survive to the final version, and the thoughts, encouragement, and patience of Eduardo Salas and Shawn Burke. We also thank CHI Systems and OSI Geospatial for supporting the completion of the manuscript and Christine Volk for her support in manuscript preparation.

References

Alberts, D. S., Garstka, J. J., & Stein, F. P. (2002). *Network-centric warfare: Developing and leveraging information superiority* (2d ed.). Washington, DC: CCRP.

Alberts, D. S. & Hayes, R. E. (2003). *Power to the edge: Command and control in the information age.* Washington, DC: CCRP.

Bell, B. & Scolaro, J. (2003, May). A research testbed for studying team interaction, errors and stress. *Proceedings of the 2003 Conference on Behavior Representation in Modeling and Simulation (BRIMS)*, Scottsdale, AZ.

Borgatti, S. P. (1994). A quorum of graph theoretic concepts. *Connections, 17*(1), 47–49.

Borgatti, S. P. & Foster, P. (2003). The network paradigm in organizational research: A review and typology. *Journal of Management, 29*(6), 991–1013.

Broadbent, D. E. (1958). *Perception and communication.* New York: Pergamon.

Cannon-Bowers, J. A. & Salas, E. (1998). *Individual and team decision making under stress: Theoretical underpinnings.* In J. A. Cannon-Bowers & E. Salas (Eds.), Making decisions under stress: Implications for individual and team training. Washington, DC: American Psychological Association.

Carley, K. M., Ren, Y., & Krackhardt, D. (2000, June 26–28). Measuring and modeling change in C3I architecture. *Proceedings of the 2000 Command and Control Research and Technology Symposium.* Naval Postgraduate School, Monterey, CA, Evidence Based Research, Vienna, VA.

Deaton, J., Barba, C., Santarelli, T., Rosenzweig, L., Souders, V., McCollum, C., et al. (2005). Virtual environment cultural training for operational readiness (VECTOR). *Virtual Reality, 8*(3), 156–167.

Gluck, K. & Pew, R. (Eds.). (2005). *Modeling human behavior with integrated cognitive architectures: Comparison, evaluation, and validation.* Mahwah, NJ: Erlbaum.

Gratch, J. & Marsella, S. (2004). A domain-independent framework for modeling emotion. *Journal of Cognitive Systems Research, 5*(4), 269–306.

Hannemann, R. A. (2001). Introduction to social network methods. Online textbook, Department of Sociology, University of California. Retrieved from http://www.researchmethods.org/NETTEXT.pdf.

McCrae, R. R. & Costa, P. T., Jr. (1999). A five-factor theory of personality. In L. A. Pervin & O. P. John (Eds.), *Handbook of personality: Theory and research* (2d ed., pp. 139–153). New York: Guilford Press.

Pew, R. & Mavor, A. (eds.) (1998). *Modeling human and organizational behavior: Application to military simulations.* Washington, DC: National Academy Press.

Read, S., Miller, L., Rosoff, A., Eilbert, J., Iordanov, V., Le Mentec, J., et al. (2006) Integrating emotional dynamics into the PAC cognitive architecture. In *Proceedings of the 15th Conference on Behavior Representation in Modeling and Simulation* (pp. 189–198). Orlando: Institute for Simulation & Training.

Read, S., Miller, L., Monroe, A., Zachary, W., Le Mentec J.-C., & Iordanov, V. (2006). A neurobiologically-based model of personality in an intelligent agent. In *Proceedings of Intelligent Virtual Agents 2006* (pp. 316–328). New York: Springer.

Ritter, F. E., Avraamides, M., & Council, I. G. (2002). An approach for accurately modeling the effects of behavior moderators. In *Proceedings of the 11th Computer Generated Forces Conference* (pp. 29–40) 02-CGF-002. Orlando: University of Central Florida.

Ritter, F. E., Shadbolt, N. R., Elliman, D., Young, R., Gobet, F., & Baxter, G. D. (2001). *Techniques for modeling human performance in synthetic environments: A supplementary review. (State-of-the-art-report).* Wright-Patterson Air Force Base, OH: Human Systems Information Analysis Center.

Ryder, J., Iordanov, V., Le Mentec, J.-C., Barba, C., & Eilbert, J. (2002). *ORGNET/PRO: A methodology and program for redesigning organizations,* Technical Report 011010.8805. Ft. Washington, PA: CHI Systems.

Smith-Jentsch, K. A., Zeisig, R. L., Acton, B., & McPherson, J. A. (1998). Team dimensional training. In J. A. Cannon-Bowers & E. Salas (Eds.), *Making decisions under stress: Implications for individual and team training.* Washington, DC: American Psychological Association.

Velasquez, J. (1997). Modeling emotions and other motivations in synthetic agents. In *Proceedings of the 1997 National Conference on Artificial Intelligence (AAAI97)* (pp. 10–15). Providence, RI.

Weaver, R., Silverman, B. G., Shin, H., & Dubois, R. (2001). Performance moderator functions for modeling adversary organizations in asymmetric conflicts. In *Proceedings of the 2001 Conference on Behavioral Representation* (pp. 39–44). Norfolk, VA.

Weiland, M. & Eilbert, J. L. (2000). Using cognitive models in the design and evaluation of team structure. In *Proceedings of the Cognitive Science Society*, Philadelphia, PA.

Zachary, W., Ryder, J., Stokes, J., Glenn, F., Le Mentec, J.-C., & Santarelli, T. (2005). A COGNET/iGEN cognitive model that mimics human performance and learning in a simulated work environment. In K. A. Gluck & R. W. Pew (Eds.), *Modeling human behavior with integrated cognitive architectures: Comparison, evaluation, and validation* (pp. 113–175). Mahwah, NJ: Erlbaum.

Zachary, W., Campbell, G., Laughery, R., Glenn, F., & Cannon-Bowers, J. (2001). The application of human modeling technology to the design, evaluation, and operation of complex systems. In E. Salas (Ed.), *Advances in human performance and cognitive engineering research* (pp. 201–250). Amsterdam, The Netherlands: Elsevier.

Zachary, W., LeMentec, J.-C., Miller, L., Read, S., & Thomas-Meyers, G. (2005, June). *Human behavioral representations with realistic personality and cultural characteristics.* Paper presented at the 10th International Command and Control Research and Technology Symposium, Department of Defense, McLean, VA.

Zachary, W., Weiland, M., & Le Mentec, J.-C. (1997). Allocating cognitive and decision-making functions from cognitive models of team requirements. In *Proceedings of the First International Conference on Revisiting the Allocation of Functions Issue (ALLFN '97)*. Galway, Ireland: National University Ireland.

Zachary, W. (1977). An information-flow model for conflict and fission in small groups. *Journal of Anthropological Research, 33*, 452–73.

Section V

Commentaries and Summary: A Look Ahead

18

Measuring Team-Related Cognition: The Devil Is in the Details

Kimberly A. Smith-Jentsch

The notion that team performance is affected by members' cognitive representations of their tasks, roles, teammates, and equipment underlies much of the team research conducted since the 1990s. Moreover, empirical studies have demonstrated general support for this notion. Recent theories regarding team cognition (many described in this volume) delve into complexities such as when, how, and for whom specific dimensions of team cognition should be most important. In this commentary, I highlight several measurement and design issues that I feel are important for future researchers to address so that our empirical research on team cognition can keep pace with our theories. In this regard, the devil is truly in the details. The manner in which team cognition is measured from study to study varies in myriad ways, and these differences are too often glossed over or oversimplified.

I separate my arguments into three major sections. The first discusses the manner in which measurement details influence our ability to *describe* the phenomena we are interested in studying. The second section discusses details associated with *evaluating* levels of cognitive convergence and accuracy. The third and final section discusses measurement details that affect our ability to *diagnose* meaningful linkages between team cognition and performance.

Describing Team Cognition

A critical step in the advancement of theories and practical recommendations regarding team cognition is to achieve greater specificity in the way that we describe and differentiate the many facets we study. In this section, I highlight three challenges for future research in this regard: to achieve clarity and parsimony with respect to the manner in which facets of team cognition are operationally defined (i.e., content of our measures) (challenge 1); to measure and test for configurations of team cognition (i.e., interactions between various types and forms) (challenge 2); and to specify the impact of various methods for eliciting team cognition (i.e., measurement strategies) (challenge 3).

Challenge 1: Achieve Clarity and Parsimony with Respect to the Manner in which Facets of Team Cognition Are Operationally Defined

In their commentary on theories of team performance, Laurie Weingart and Matthew Cronin (Chapter 19 in this volume) make a compelling argument for the need to achieve parsimony with respect to the constructs and the models proposed to explain team performance. I echo this plea and focus my attention more specifically on the manner in which researchers translate abstract definitions of constructs into the content or stimuli employed in their measures. My review of the literature on team cognition suggests that researchers often use the same terms and definitions to describe their constructs of interest, yet the manner in which those constructs are operationally defined from study to study is quite different—and not simply in superficial ways. For instance, many researchers have focused on mental models of team interactions. Cannon-Bowers, Converse, and Salas (1993) described these as cognitive representations reflecting the interdependent role responsibilities and communication patterns associated with various positions on a team.

However, the stimuli used to measure team interaction models have varied substantially across studies; even those published in the same journal. Mathieu, Heffner, Goodwin, Salas, and Cannon-Bowers (2000), for instance, operationally defined team interaction models using task-generic dimensions of teamwork (e.g., communication, coordination) whereas Marks, Zaccaro, and Mathieu (2000) focused on the sequencing of task-specific actions (e.g., shoot target) and Smith-Jentsch, Mathieu, and Kraiger (2005) investigated interdependencies among position-specific goals (e.g., minimize takeoff delays). Each of these measures theoretically falls within the umbrella of team interaction models as defined by Cannon-Bowers et al. (1993); however, each may also be distinct enough so as to yield systematically different results. Yet, too often, when authors summarize the findings from such studies and attempt to reconcile mixed findings, they fail to consider the possible impact of differences in operational definitions. Conversely, authors also frequently fail to incorporate relevant findings from studies that employed highly similar measures but simply labeled them differently. The terms teammate knowledge consensus (Austin, 2003), teammate mental models (Smith-Jentsch, Kraiger, Cannon-Bowers, & Salas, 2006), and teammate schemas (Rentsch, Heffner & Duffy, 1994), for example, have each been operationally defined in very similar ways to describe team members' understanding of one another's strengths, weaknesses, habits, and preferences.

In sum, when interpreting findings from prior studies, researchers must look beyond the labels used by various researchers to describe their constructs of interest and must instead carefully consider how those constructs were operationally defined. Moreover, when reporting one's own research, authors should explicitly note how their particular operational definitions may have influenced study results and how those definitions match up with prior research using similar or different terminology. The failure to do so will ultimately slow our collective progress toward the goal of validating a multidimensional model of team cognition.

Challenge 2: Describe Configurations of Team Cognition

Joan Rentsch, Lisa Delise, and Scott Hutchison (Chapter 9 in this volume) differentiate and discuss cognitive similarity in terms of the content domain (e.g., task, teammates, equipment, interaction patterns), the form of similarity (e.g., accuracy, teammate convergence), and the form of cognition (e.g., schema, mental model). More specifically, these authors advance the notion that we need to consider the manner in which these dimensions of cognitive similarity combine to form "configurations" that predict important team outcomes. This means that multiple facets of team cognition must be measured in the same study and that interactions among those facets are tested in addition to simple main effects. A relatively small number of studies have done this to date.

Notably, researchers have begun to examine interactions between cognitive accuracy and cognitive congruence while holding the content domain constant. Edwards, Day, Arthur, and Bell (2006) argued that team cognition is accurate if it mirrors the "true state of the world" (p. 728). Two studies have found that accuracy strengthened the positive relationship between cognitive similarity among teammates and performance (Austin, 2003; Mathieu, Heffner, Goodwin, Cannon-Bowers, & Salas, 2005), whereas another found the reverse to be true (Marks et al., 2000). Additional research is clearly needed to specify under what conditions cognitive similarity makes cognitive quality more or less important.

Researchers have also begun to measure multiple *types* of team cognition that differ in content within the same study (e.g., Lim & Klein, 2006; Mathieu et al., 2000; Marks et al., 2000; Smith-Jentsch et al., 2005). However, only one of these has investigated interactions between the different content types. In this study, Smith-Jentsch et al. (2005) found that cognitive similarity regarding positional goal interdependencies interacted with cognitive similarity regarding cue-strategy associations to predict safety and efficiency for air traffic control teams. Specifically, similarity with respect to mental models of positional goal interdependencies was positively associated with these team outcomes when cue-strategy associations were highly similar but was negatively associated with team outcomes when cue-strategy associations were dissimilar. As a result, neither type of mental model exerted main effects on performance. These findings suggest that untested interactions between different types of cognitive similarity may explain the lack of main effects found in some prior studies.

Rentsch et al. (Chapter 9 in this volume) noted that another dimension on which cognitive similarity can be evaluated has to do with the degree to which team members accurately perceive their level of accuracy or congruence with teammates. For instance, do individuals recognize that they hold a highly dissimilar mental model of teamwork from their teammates? Perceived congruence and accuracy may be very different from actual congruence or accuracy. However, despite the fact that perceptions of reality are generally believed to have a stronger effect on individuals' behavior, perceived congruence, and accuracy of team-related cognition are seldom measured. In a notable exception, Hoeft (2006) found that perceptions of teammate similarity interacted with actual teammate similarity to predict communication processes. Specifically, team communication increased when a mismatch existed (perceptions did not reflect reality). It was suggested that as teammates gained experience working together, some began to suspect that their perceptions of cognitive similarity were not accurate and attempted to resolve that discrepancy through overt communication with their partners. These findings highlight the need to incorporate measures of team members' perceived similarity into our research and to test interactions between these measures and more typical measures of actual similarity.

Finally, it is important to note that certain configurations of team cognition may exist in the field but not in the laboratory. In this situation, a researcher will fail to detect an interaction that truly exists (i.e., a false negative). For instance, as I mentioned earlier, my colleagues and I found that groups of air traffic controllers with highly consistent team interaction mental models but inconsistent task mental models had the worst safety and efficiency records. This particular configuration of task and team mental model convergence is unlikely to be prevalent in a lab study of ad hoc team members who start out as unfamiliar with one another as they are with their experimental task. However, experimental manipulations can be used to achieve such combinations. For instance, Hoeft (2006) experimentally manipulated actual and perceived similarity of task mental models through training (actual similarity) and instructions that led participants to believe they either did or did not receive the same training (perceived similarity).

One must also be wary when interpreting interactions found in the lab that depict configurations of cognitive convergence that likely do not exist for longer-term teams in the field and thus have little external validity. For instance, extremely low task-knowledge accuracy may never exist alongside extremely high team-interaction accuracy in the field if a minimum level of task-knowledge accuracy is necessary to perform a task safely.

In sum, the fact that cognitive similarity among teammates relates positively to team performance in some studies and not others (e.g., Cooke, Salas, Kiekel, & Bell, 2003; Cooke et al., 2004) may be explained by measuring additional forms (e.g., accuracy) or content areas (i.e., both task and team) and testing interactions between these measures. Moreover, investigating interactions between dimensions of cognitive similarity may help to uncover those situations whereby cognitive similarity is actually a bad thing. This is a critical step in advancing theories of team cognition and a necessary one to specify meaningful training and staffing recommendations for operational teams.

Challenge 3: Specify the Impact of Knowledge Elicitation Methods

A number of different methods for eliciting team-related cognition have been employed in prior research. However, little empirical evidence exists to suggest how these different methods may affect the results obtained by researchers in this area (Mohammed & Dumville, 2001). Card sorting, concept mapping, and pairwise comparison ratings, for instance, have each been used to assess knowledge regarding team interactions. Even within these methods, there are nontrivial differences across studies with respect to the instructions provided to participants. In terms of concept mapping, one study may have participants place experimenter-generated terms into slots within a preexisting structure (e.g., Marks et al., 2000), whereas another study may ask participants to generate their own terms and free-draw their own structure (e.g., Rentsch, Heffner, & Duffy, 1994). In terms of pairwise comparison ratings, participants may be asked to rate the similarity of concepts or the relatedness of concepts.

A comparison of knowledge elicitation methods in terms of their predictive validity is hindered by the fact that, across studies, knowledge elicitation method (e.g., pairwise comparisons) tends to be confounded with the particular type of mental model studied (e.g., teamwork mental models), the specific manner in which that construct was operationalized (i.e., stimuli used), and very often the type of team task employed in the primary studies (e.g., flight simulation, group problem-solving task). I hope to see more studies in which multiple methods of eliciting team-related cognition are directly compared (holding content constant) so that we may better understand the way such choices are likely to affect our data. Moreover, at a minimum, when integrating one's results within the existing literature, researchers should explicitly address the manner in which their methods are similar or different from those employed by others and to discuss how this may explain similarities and differences in the results obtained. These steps are necessary to achieve the goal of specifying which methods are most appropriate for eliciting different types of team-related cognition.

Evaluating Team-Related Cognition

In this next section, I turn my attention to the manner in which team-related cognition is evaluated. Specifically, the following sections describe additional challenges for researchers of team cognition associated with identifying valid referents for evaluating accuracy (challenge 4); specifying the impact of alternative similarity indices (e.g., agreement or consistency) (challenge 5); and determining when various strategies for aggregation or compilation of data to the team level of analysis are appropriate (challenge 6).

Challenge 4: Identify Valid Referents for Evaluating Accuracy

Whereas numerous empirical studies have measured cognitive similarity among teammates, far fewer have measured the quality or accuracy of team member cognitions. This is likely due to the challenges involved in identifying an expert referent from which to evaluate quality/accuracy. Before I describe three approaches to doing so, let us consider the consequences of identifying incorrect or deficient referents for cognitive accuracy. Most obviously, if we score the accuracy or quality of team cognition against an invalid referent, we will underestimate the relationship between cognitive accuracy and performance. Less obvious is the idea that we may also overestimate the importance of teammate similarity. Consider, for example, that if a single accurate mental model exists, those with highly accurate mental models will also have highly similar mental models. Thus, if only similarity is measured and not accuracy, a researcher may falsely conclude that teammate similarity facilitates performance when in fact it is really cognitive accuracy. Even if one is able to identify and measure a valid high-quality referent, it may represent only one of multiple distinct but equally valid cognitive representations held by team members. In this case, it may be that teams that score low on similarity to one's prespecified "expert" referent but high on teammate similarity tend to share the same alternative (and unmeasured by you) high quality model. Once again, this would cause the relationship between cognitive quality and performance to appear weaker than it is and also the relationship between teammate similarity and performance to appear stronger than it really is.

The most typical method of defining a referent from which to judge cognitive accuracy or quality is to identify a group of experts based on their prior experience, to measure their knowledge, and to score participants' accuracy against that knowledge. A potential problem with this method is that the "experts," who are identified a priori, may not, in fact, hold high-quality knowledge of the type in which you are interested. In this regard, my colleagues and I (Smith-Jentsch, Campbell, Milanovich, & Reynolds, 2001; Smith-Jentsch, Zeisig, Cannon-Bowers, & Salas, 1997) found that those with greater experience in a particular team task domain in general (i.e., time in Navy service, years as a Federal Aviation Administration [FAA] air traffic controller) did not have significantly different beliefs about or knowledge regarding teamwork requirements from those with lesser team task experience. However, certain types of team task experiences were associated with team-related knowledge (i.e., time as an on-the-job training instructor, military rank). Thus, the a priori identification of those holding expert knowledge is not always as straightforward as it may seem.

Another approach to evaluating accurate/high-quality team cognition is to model expert team performance directly and use that model as a referent. Some of the techniques for automated performance assessment and computational modeling described in this volume should be helpful in this regard (David Dorsey et al., Chapter 13 in this volume; Wayne Zachary, Benjamin Bell, & Joan Ryder, Chapter 17 in this volume). This process is complicated by the fact that mathematical models of team behavior may predict performance effectiveness and still not accurately reflect the cognitive representations that members of effective teams hold (Campbell, Buff, Bolton, & Holness, 2001). Thus, cognitive accuracy scored against a mathematically derived model of "expert performance" may not predict performance, even though one's hypothesis that mental model accuracy predicts performance is in fact correct. Ultimately, if one has empirically captured at least one of the high-quality representations of team cognition held by effective teams, manipulations designed to lead teams to hold those representations should also improve team performance.

My colleagues and I followed this logic in our attempt to define an expert mental model of teamwork for Navy command and control teams (Smith-Jentsch, Cannon-Bowers, Tannenbaum, & Salas, 2008). Behavioral ratings of teamwork were collected from a large sample of teams and submitted to a factor analysis. Results indicated that 11 component behaviors clustered within four higher-order dimensions and that each of these dimensions explained unique variance in team performance. In a subsequent study, we found that higher-ranking personnel tended to hold mental models of teamwork that were more similar to this mathematically derived model than did lower-ranking personnel. Finally, teams debriefed using this model as an organizing framework increased team performance and mental model accuracy (using the expert model as a referent) mediated this relationship.

In sum, inaccurate or deficient expert knowledge referents can lead a researcher to underestimate the relationship between teammate knowledge accuracy and performance or to overestimate the relationship between teammate knowledge similarity and performance. I have highlighted three approaches to identifying referents for judging cognitive accuracy/quality as well as their associated strengths and weaknesses. Of course, the effectiveness of all three methods is dependent on issues I have discussed earlier in terms of operationally defining the content of interest (i.e., measurement stimuli) and selecting an appropriate knowledge elicitation method. In other words, even if one correctly identifies a group of experts a priori, he or she will still end up with an invalid referent for cognitive accuracy if the terms or methods used do not enable him or her to detect meaningful differences in the way those experts represent their knowledge.

Challenge 5: Specify the Impact of Cognitive Similarity Indices

The two most commonly used indices for judging cognitive similarity (either among teammates or between individuals and an expert model) are agreement indices and consistency indices. Agreement indices reflect absolute differences between members' ratings (e.g., distance scores, percentage of exact agreements) without regard to the direction of those differences (teammate A responded 1 point higher than teammate B or vice versa), whereas consistency indices reflect correlations between such ratings. Many of the methods used to elicit team-related knowledge could be scored in both ways. Typically, however, researchers tend to report only one of the two. As a result, we know little about the impact of utilizing agreement versus consistency indices when measuring cognitive similarity. It is possible and perhaps likely, that the relative validity of the two types of indices is dependent on the specific cognitive content (e.g., task or teamwork knowledge) being measured or the knowledge elicitation method (e.g., paired comparisons, card sorting) employed. Moreover, task characteristics may determine in part when it is most important for teammates to have consistent mental models and when it is most important for them to be in close or exact agreement.

Utilizing the wrong index in a given context may lead one to a false negative conclusion regarding the relation between teammate similarity and performance. For instance, my colleagues and I conducted a study in which we measured the mental model similarity of air traffic controllers and tested our hypotheses by scoring the data using both an agreement and a consistency index (Smith-Jentsch et al., 2005). We found that task and team interaction mental models interacted to predict two separate outcome variables (i.e., safety, efficiency) when the consistency index was used. No significant main or interactive effects were found, however, when the agreement index was used. We noted that when interpreting these findings, one must consider both the nature of the measures we used and the nature of the decision-making task.

Our cue-strategy association measure asked controllers to rate the likelihood (0%–100%) that a series of possible strategies would be effective at solving a particular problem scenario. None of the strategies had the potential to make the situation worse, and many of them could be attempted simultaneously. Generally speaking, controller teams will strive to exhaust all possible means of preventing an accident right to the end. Thus, teams whose members consistently rated the relative likelihood that each strategy would be successful would have been "in sync" with respect to which strategy to try first, second, and so on. If, for example, two different teams rated strategy A as being the most likely to succeed but one of the teams was in exact agreement as to the probability of success and the other was not, both teams would nonetheless attempt strategy A first. Thus, in this case, it was less important that teammates agreed on probabilities for success than it was that they consistently differentiated strategies with respect to their relative probabilities of success. However, in a context whereby teams can only attempt one strategy at a time and must determine how long to persist before abandoning one strategy for another or when strategies carry with them the potential to make matters worse, teammate agreement on probabilities for success might be more predictive of performance than the consistency of relative probability ratings.

In sum, the relationship between team cognition and performance is likely to vary as a function of the manner in which cognitive convergence or similarity is indexed. Such differences should be considered in light of the particular type of team cognition measured and the characteristics of one's team task. Additional research is needed to better understand how and when consistency or agreement indices better explain important differences in team cognition. A comparison across published studies to date is hindered by the fact that indexing method and knowledge elicitation method tend to be confounded. Whenever possible, researchers should index their data in both ways and should compare the results.

Challenge 6: Specify the Impact of Aggregation/Compilation Methods

The typical method of aggregating measures of cognitive similarity to the team level of analysis involves averaging or summing either the accuracy of individual members (team-level accuracy) or the similarity among all possible dyads within the team (team-level similarity). Using such methods, team members' inputs are equally weighted. However, as Nancy Cooke, Jamie Gorman, and Leah Rowe (Chapter 6 in this volume) point out, this ignores important sources of heterogeneity among team members in terms of both their place in the social structure as well as their individual differences. In other words, certain team members are likely to have a stronger impact on the team's processes and outcomes than others, and this should be taken into account. Similar arguments have been made regarding the aggregation of team composition variables such as personality and cognitive ability.

For instance, Barrick, Stewart, Neubert, and Mount (1998) described three alternatives to averaging or summing individual-level composition variables to form a team-level score. These included computing the minimum, maximum, or variance of the individual scores within the team. With respect to the minimum and maximum score, the authors noted that individual team members with extreme scores could have an inordinate effect on their team's performance. Thus, the minimum (e.g., weakest link) or maximum (e.g., strongest link) score may be a better predictor of the team's performance than would be the team's mean on a particular variable. Barrick et al. found, for example, that higher-performing teams were less likely to have extremely disagreeable or introverted members (i.e., higher minimum scores on agreeableness and extraversion). Similarly, one might expect that under certain circumstances, a team's performance may be most associated with the mental model accuracy of its weakest member (i.e., minimum score). Or, alternatively, the task mental model accuracy of a team's strongest member (i.e., maximum score) may be most predictive of the team's problem-solving performance as long as all team members hold highly accurate mental models of their teammates' relative expertise (a cognitive configuration).

A third method of aggregating team composition variables involves calculating the variance among teammates. Barrick et al. (1998) found that teams whose members varied greatly on team member conscientiousness exhibited less effective team performance. Although measures of variance are standard for computing cognitive similarity among teammates, they are not typically used to measure team-level cognitive accuracy. In other words, studies typically average team members' cognitive accuracy rather than examining possible relationships between the variability of team members' accuracy and team performance.

Finally, aggregation approaches might consider team members' position within the team's social network. Social network analysis methods described by Andrew Slaughter, Janie Yu, and Laura Koehly (Chapter 16 in this volume) hold great promise in this regard. For instance, the cognitive accuracy of members identified as being central within a team's network or in a higher position of prestige might be a better predictor of team performance than a simple average of all teammates' cognitive accuracy. Moreover, team members' average level of cognitive congruence with adjacent members may be more indicative of team processes than the average congruence among all members of the team. One might expect a team containing two subgroups or cliques whose members hold highly similar mental models to one another but highly dissimilar mental models with members of the other subgroup or clique to perform differently from a team where all members hold moderately similar mental models. These two teams may nonetheless receive similar scores for teammate similarity using a simple averaging approach.

In sum, the manner in which data from measures of team cognition are aggregated or compiled to form team-level scores has the potential to substantially affect the results of one's study. Theoretically, we may underestimate relationships or misinterpret relationships between team cognition and performance if we continue to use gross measures (averages) rather than exploring the possibility that the cognitive accuracy of certain members or the cognitive similarity of certain subgroups or dyads within a team may disproportionately affect performance outcomes. Future studies should investigate the relative prediction of scores aggregated in multiple ways so that we can begin to understand the conditions under which different aggregation methods are most appropriate. At a minimum, future researchers should clearly articulate the manner in which their data were indexed and aggregated and discuss the manner in which these choices may have affected their results.

Diagnosing Root Causes of Team Performance

Ultimately, our interest in team cognition is to help explain the performance problems of ineffective teams (and the superior performance of effective teams). In other words, we do not simply wish to predict which teams will succeed and which will not but also to explain how and why so that we can intervene appropriately. In this final section of my commentary, I argue that to achieve this we must face challenges associated with validating multidimensional measures of teamwork processes (challenge 7) and specifying the manner in which time and experience moderates relationships between team cognition and performance (challenge 8). The failure to do so makes our findings not only less interesting theoretically but also less useful from a practical perspective.

Challenge 7: Validate Multidimensional Measures of Teamwork Processes

Although teamwork is generally described as being multidimensional, studies measuring teamwork and linking it to team-related cognition most often employ global teamwork process measures rather than multiple measures of teamwork facets to test their hypotheses. This is typically done after attempting to measure multiple distinct facets and finding that those measures are too highly correlated to be examined separately. As a result, little is known about which specific facets of team cognition are related to which specific facets of teamwork and what the relative strength of those relationships is. This sort of understanding is critical if, for example, measures of team cognition are to be used to diagnose specific training needs. The issues I have raised earlier in this chapter regarding the description and evaluation of team cognition apply equally well to measures of teamwork process. The terms and operational definitions used to measure various dimensions of teamwork vary from study to study as do the rating scales, sources of ratings, indexing, and aggregation techniques. If our goal is to specify linkages between specific components of team cognition and specific teamwork processes, future research must employ multidimensional measures of teamwork that demonstrate both convergent and discriminant validity.

Kelley Krokos, David Baker, Alexander Alonso, and Rachel Day (Chapter 14 in this volume) report that practitioners have somewhat consistent preferences for particular scale formats based on the content they are measuring. However, these authors note that little is known about the manner in which scale formats affect the construct validity of teamwork ratings. Lessons can likely be drawn from the literature on assessment center ratings of individual performance. This literature demonstrates, for instance, that construct validity is improved when only five or so dimensions are rated at once, when construct definitions are highly distinctive, when those definitions are behaviorally based, and when component ratings are combined mathematically rather than subjectively (Lievens, 1998; Lievens & Conway, 2001).

My review of the existing literature with respect to teamwork process measures suggests that the definitions of teamwork dimensions used are often not distinct. Moreover, these definitions often include a mixture of behavioral, cognitive, attitudinal, and outcome-based criteria. Finally, the definitions employed often require the rater to make inferences as to team member intentions rather than to describe observable or audible behaviors.

I hope to see researchers strive for more distinct measures of teamwork process and to compare the validities obtained when various formats are used. For instance, my colleagues and I tested the notion that teamwork dimension ratings would demonstrate better discriminant validity when compiled mathematically rather than subjectively (Smith-Jentsch, Johnston, & Payne, 1998). We had raters evaluate the same four dimensions of teamwork in two ways. The first involved a subjective rating at the dimension level (using a Likert scale), and the second asked them to provide frequency counts of component behaviors that were later summed to the dimension level. The subjectively compiled dimension-level ratings demonstrated poor discriminant validity (average interdimension correlation .59), whereas the composite dimension ratings were far less correlated (average interdimension correlation .15). Moreover, the discriminant validity of subjectively compiled dimension ratings was negatively affected by raters' prior knowledge of team performance outcomes, but this was not true for the mathematically compiled scores.

In sum, our ability to provide diagnostic guidelines about when and how antecedents such as team cognition will impact team performance is dependent on the use of multidimensional measures of teamwork process that demonstrate both convergent and discriminant validity. Future researchers should strive for distinct definitions of teamwork dimensions; should ensure that those definitions are behavioral in nature and are not confounded with attitudinal, cognitive, and outcome-based criteria; and should limit themselves to a reasonable number of dimensions (e.g., five). Moreover, future studies should directly compare the effects of scale format on the construct and predictive validity of teamwork process ratings.

Challenge 8: Specify the Manner in which Time Moderates Relationships between Team Cognition and Performance

Susan Mohammed, Katherine Hamilton, and Audrey Lim (Chapter 12 in this volume) report that only 22% of the studies on teams published in the *Journal of Applied Psychology, Personnel Psychology,* and *Organizational Behavior and Decision Processes* between 1990 and 2004 incorporated repeated measures of the same variables over time. These authors note that cross-sectional team studies can suffer either "Type I or Type II temporal errors, in which conclusions from short-lived teams would not hold up over a longer period of time and the conclusions from longer-term teams would not occur in short-term teams, respectively" (p. 317). For instance, results from two prior studies indicated that mental model similarity was a stronger predictor of performance than was mental model accuracy using a short-term laboratory task (i.e., Marks et al., 2000; Mathieu et al., 2005). However, when Edwards et al. (2006) compared the predictive validities of task mental model accuracy and similarity over time in a field setting, they found no differences after two days of training and better prediction for accuracy than for similarity after four days of training.

Over time, team members gain experience with their tasks and teammates and, as a result, become more familiar with them. When ad hoc teams are asked to perform an unfamiliar laboratory team task, teammates' knowledge about one another and about their task develops in tandem, whereas in field settings team members can be very experienced with respect to a particular task yet unfamiliar with their current team members. Thus, correlations between teammate knowledge similarity and task knowledge similarity are likely to be inflated in lab studies. This unrealistically high shared variance could lead one to underestimate the unique contribution of each to the prediction of team performance. On the other hand, if one but not the other is measured in a particular study (e.g., team but not task) and the two are highly correlated with each other due to the confounding variable of time, the relationship between the component measured and performance will be overestimated. In sum, future research on team performance, and specifically its relation to team cognition, should incorporate multiple measures of the same constructs over time and should directly measure and control for task and team familiarity and experience.

Where Do We Go from Here?

In this section I close with several prescriptions for future research in this area. Some of these pertain to the design of new studies, whereas others could be accomplished by reanalyzing data from preexisting studies; still others have more to do with the way we describe our methods and interpret our findings.

Next Steps: Describing Team Cognition

With respect to the next steps in describing team cognition, more studies are needed in which measures of multiple facets of team cognition using the same method are collected and the resulting similarity scores are factor analyzed. This type of work is needed to validate and extend existing theoretical frameworks describing dimensions of the team cognition construct (e.g., Cannon-Bowers et al., 1994). Moreover, such studies should employ multiple operational definitions of the same theoretical dimension (e.g., multiple ways of defining team interaction models) and should examine possible subdimensions. Future studies are also needed in which multiple methods (e.g., concept mapping, paired comparison ratings) for measuring the same content are compared—a metric bake-off of sorts—to determine their relative validity. The most appropriate knowledge elicitation methods may well vary depending on the type of team cognition measured, and this should be explored as well. It is important to note that elicitation method and content tend to be confounded within existing studies. Thus, one would have to be careful when interpreting results from a meta-analytic comparison of primary studies to date.

A much needed direction for future research is to go beyond examining the main effects of multiple types and forms of team cognition and to test interactions among these so we can begin to understand important configurations. Careful attention should be paid to the external validity of configurations studied in the lab. In this regard, field and laboratory research should build on one another. Experimental manipulations may be used to ensure that configurations observed in the field are represented in laboratory research.

Finally, future authors need to be much more specific about the types of team cognition they are studying, noting the manner in which their operational definitions and elicitation methods differ from those used by others. Additionally, when synthesizing others' prior work, authors should focus more on the manner in which constructs have been measured and less on superficial similarities and differences in the terminology used.

Next Steps: Evaluating Team Cognition

In terms of evaluating team cognition, I hope to see many more studies conducted in which accuracy is considered together with teammate similarity. Moreover, I hope that researchers will be more likely to explore the possibility that multiple "expert" or high-quality referents exist. This is necessary to truly parse the relative contribution of teammate similarity and cognitive quality. Existing data from prior studies can always be rescored against new expert referents to determine whether this changes study results. Similarly, existing data from prior studies of team cognition can be used to examine the impact of indexing convergence in terms of agreement or consistency as well as alternative strategies for aggregating that data to the team level of analysis. Ultimately, we need to better understand the task characteristics that determine when a particular method of indexing and aggregating data is most appropriate. As with comparisons of content and elicitation method across existing studies, comparisons of indexing methods must deal with the issue of confounds (e.g., of index and content) across studies.

Next Steps: Diagnosing Team Performance Problems

My final set of recommendations for future research should help us to diagnose with greater specificity the underlying causes of team coordination breakdowns and triumphs. A key advance in this regard would be for researchers to determine the effects of rating format and of operational definitions on the convergent and discriminant validity of the scores obtained. Once construct valid teamwork measures are developed, researchers can then hypothesize and test for differential relationships between specific components of team cognition and specific dimensions of teamwork.

Finally, future studies are needed in which time and experience are tested as moderators of the relationships between team cognition and performance. In cross-sectional studies, this means measuring time-related variables (e.g., job tenure), whereas true and quasi-experiments could employ repeated measures of team cognition and of performance dimensions. As I mentioned earlier, task characteristics are likely to further moderate these relationships. I hope to see future studies in which task characteristics are manipulated to explore possible interactions. Additionally, I hope to see researchers employ a greater variety of team task types across studies so that eventually we may meta-analytically examine task characteristics as a moderator. At a minimum, authors of primary studies should clearly articulate key features of their tasks and address the manner in which differences in task characteristics across studies may explain inconsistent findings.

Closing Remarks

In this commentary, I have argued that to progress to the next stage of theory development and testing, research on team cognition must pay closer attention to measurement and design details and the manner in which these can bias our results or keep us from answering the questions that interest us most. These questions have now matured from, "Does team cognition matter?" to "How and when do various configurations of team cognition affect performance?" and "How does this vary by task type?" I have detailed what I see as key challenges before us with respect to answering such questions and have offered some directions for future research in this area. The results from such research should assist us in refining our theories as well as developing tools and recommendations that practitioners can use to enhance team cognition and ultimately team performance.

Acknowledgments

Supported by the Office of Naval Research (ONR) through the Multidisciplinary University Research Initiative (MURI) "Cognition and Collaboration in Network Centric Operations: Understanding & Measuring Macrocognition in Teams" (Contract N000140610446) to the University of Central Florida (UCF). The opinions expressed in this paper are those of the author and do not necessarily correspond with those of UCF, the Department of Defense, Department of the Navy, or the ONR.

References

Austin, J. R. (2003). Transactive memory in organizational groups: The effects of content, consensus, specializations, and accuracy on group performance. *Journal of Applied Psychology, 88*, 866–878.

Barrick, M. R., Stewart, G. L., Neubert, M. J., & Mount, M. K. (1998). Relating member ability and personality to work-team processes and team effectiveness. *Journal of Applied Psychology, 83*(3), 377–391.

Campbell, G. E., Buff, W. L., Bolton, A. E., & Holness, D. O. (2001). The application of mathematical techniques for modeling decision-making: Lessons learned from a preliminary study. In E. M. Altman, A. Cleermans, C. D. Schunn, & W. D. Gray (Eds.), *Proceedings of the Fourth International Conference on Cognitive Modeling* (pp. 49–54). Mahwah, NJ: Lawrence Erlbaum.

Cannon-Bowers, J. A., Salas, E., & Converse, S. A. (1993). Shared mental models in expert team decision making. In N. J. Castellan, Jr. (Ed.), *Current issues in individual and group decision making* (pp. 221–246). Hillsdale, NJ: Lawrence Erlbaum.

Cooke, N. J., Kiekel, P. A., Salas, E., Stout, R., Bowers, C., & Cannon-Bowers, J. (2003). Measuring team knowledge: A window to the cognitive underpinnings of team performance. *Group Dynamics: Theory, Research and Practice, 7*, 179–190.

Cooke, N. J., Salas, E., Kiekel, P., & Bell, B. (2004). Advances in measuring team cognition. In E. Salas & S. M. Fiore (Eds.), *Team cognition: Understanding the factors that drive process and performance.* Washington, DC: American Psychological Association.

Edwards, B. D., Day, E. A., Arthur, W., & Bell, S. T. (2006). Relationships among team ability composition, team mental models, and team performance. *Journal of Applied Psychology, 91*(3), 727–736.

Hoeft, R. (2006). *Investigating the mechanisms that drive implicit coordination in teams.* Unpublished doctoral dissertation. University of Central Florida, Orlando.

Lievens, F. (1998). Factors which improve the construct validity of assessment centers: a review. *International Journal of Selection Assessment, 6*, 141–152.

Lievens, F. & Conway, J. M. (2001). Dimension and exercise variance in assessment center scores: A large-scale evaluation of multitrait–multimethod studies. *Journal of Applied Psychology 86*, 1202–1222.

Lim, B. & Klein, K. J. (2006). Team mental models and team performance: A field study of the effects of team mental model similarity and accuracy. *Journal of Organizational Behavior, 27*, 403– 418.

Marks, M., Zaccaro, S., & Mathieu, J. (2000). Performance implications of leader briefings and team-interaction training for team adaptation to novel environments. *Journal of Applied Psychology, 85*(6), 971–986.

Mathieu, J. E., Heffner, T. S., Goodwin, G. F., Cannon-Bowers, J. A., & Salas, E. (2005). Scaling the quality of teammates' mental models: Equifinality and normative comparisons. *Journal of Organizational Behavior, 26*, 37–56.

Mathieu, J. E., Heffner, T. S., Goodwin, G. F., Salas, E., & Cannon-Bowers, J. A. (2000). The influence of shared mental models on team process and performance. *Journal of Applied Psychology, 85*, 273–383.

Mohammed, S. & Dumville, B. C. (2001). Team mental models in a team knowledge framework: expanding theory and measurement across disciplinary boundaries. *Journal of Organizational Behavior, 22,* 89–106.

Rentsch, J., Heffner, T., & Duffy, L. (1994). What you know is what you get from experience: Team experience related to teamwork schemas. *Group & Organization Management, 19,* 450–474.

Smith-Jentsch, K. A., Campbell, G., Milanovich, D. M., & Reynolds, A. M. (2001). Measuring teamwork mental models to support training needs assessment, development, and evaluation: Two empirical studies. *Journal of Organizational Behavior, 22,* 179–194.

Smith-Jentsch, K. A., Cannon-Bowers, J. A., Tannenbaum, S. I., & Salas, E. (2008). Guided team self-correction: Impacts on team mental models, behavior, and effectiveness. *Small Group Research, 39*(3), 303–327.

Smith-Jentsch, K. A., Johnston, J. H., & Payne, S. C. (1998). Measuring team-related expertise in complex environments. In J. A. Cannon-Bowers & E. Salas (Eds.), *Decision making under stress: Implications for individual and team training* (pp. 61–87). Washington, DC: American Psychological Association.

Smith-Jentsch, K. A., Kraiger, K., Cannon-Bowers, J. A., & Salas, E. (2006). *Can familiarity breed backup? Interactive effects of team efficacy and shared teammate knowledge.* Paper presented at the Annual Meeting of the Academy of Management, Atlanta, GA.

Smith-Jentsch, K. A., Mathieu, J. E., & Kraiger, K. (2005). Investigating linear and interactive effects of shared mental models on safety and efficiency in a field setting. *Journal of Applied Psychology, 90,* 523–535.

Smith-Jentsch, K. A., Zeisig, R. L., Cannon-Bowers, J. A., & Salas, E. (1997, April 27–May 1). Defining and training tower cab teamwork. *International Symposium on Aviation Psychology, 9th, Proceedings, 1,* 201–206.

19

Teams Research in the 21st Century: A Case for Theory Consolidation

Laurie R. Weingart and Matthew A. Cronin

In 1973 Allen Newell wrote, "You Can't Play 20 Questions with Nature and Win," a commentary on a set of papers given at the eighth annual Carnegie Symposium on Cognition. In this paper he asked what the science of psychology should look like in 20 years. Newell expressed concern that although the papers in the symposium were all well executed and interesting, he doubted that they would move a broader understanding of human psychology forward in any substantial way:

> What I wanted was for these excellent pieces of the experimental mosaic to add up to the psychology that we all wished to foresee. They didn't, not because of any lack of excellence locally, but because most of them seemed part of a pattern of psychological activity that didn't seem to cumulate. (ibid., p. 293)

Richard Moreland and John Levine (Chapter 2 in this volume) pose a similar question about what a science of groups should look like. In the same vein, we wonder how such a science will cumulate?

It is clear from reading the chapters in this book that the study of groups has made a number of important advances. For example, Peter Essens, Ad Vogelaar, Jacques Mylle, Carol Blendell, Carol Paris, Stanley Halpin, and Joseph Baranski (Chapter 11 in this volume) consider the critical knowledge and processes inherent in the classic Input–Process–Outcome (IPO) framework of teams (Hackman, 1987) in the context of military teams. Amy Edmondson and Kathryn Roloff (Chapter 7 in this volume) provide a complementary approach by examining how the interpersonal phenomenon of psychological safety affects teams. Leslie DeChurch and John Mathieu (Chapter 10 in this volume) consider a higher level of analysis with multiteam systems, broadening our understanding of teams in context. Separately, each chapter provides an important contribution to the literature. But jointly, how much do they serve to clarify and unify the field? We argue in our commentary that the time has come for researchers to bear in mind a set of broader questions about group phenomena while they are examining their specific research questions. For example, how does one's own perspective fit together with those of other researchers? Does a study serve to link bodies of knowledge within and across disciplines? Does the elaboration of theory organize our understanding of how groups work so that the added complexity is "worth it"? Do we have a shared sense of what we hold to be well-established knowledge about groups? Is our science cumulating, and if not, how can we contribute to its accumulation?

Scientific disciplines grow and mature. In early stages of our science, general models of teams were developed to gain an overall view of their functioning and performance (e.g., System for Multiple Level Observation of Groups [SYMLOG] as a way to map group processes; IPO as general model of team performance). When these theories were not nuanced enough to predict outcomes in specific types of teams or to understand specific group phenomena, narrower, midrange theories were developed. Yet this need to differentiate and accommodate ever narrower distinctions has resulted in the proliferation of theories about groups and teams. This is exacerbated by the fact that in the past 20 years, teams are emerging in unique contexts while facing new organizational arrangements and technological advances. We believe that the time to start consolidating those theories is upon us. Our vision is that group research can represent a body of knowledge that is interdisciplinary, novel, and rooted in the scholarship of the disciplines from which it borrows. We first discuss why the time has come for consolidation and then offer some suggestions for how to do that.

As the number of researchers and published studies on group phenomena has grown, so have constructs proliferated. As noted in Kelley Krokos, David Barker, Alexander Alonso, and Rachel Day (Chapter 14 in this volume), Cannon-Bowers, Tannenbaum, Salas, & Volpe (1995) identified 130 different names for group processes or skills. Although some have tried to pare down this list (Salas, Sims, & Burke, 2005), the focus in the literature is on the naming of new phenomena or creation of finer means of classification. For example, Joan Rentsch, Lisa Delise, and Scott Hutchison (Chapter 9 in this volume) discuss the notion of cognitive similarity and describe three dimensions of cognitive similarity: form of similarity, form of cognition, and content domain, each of which has multiple subtypes. Essens et al. (Chapter 11 in this volume) identify six conditions that are key to military team effectiveness (mission framework, task, organization, leader, team structure, and team member characteristics), each with multiple subtypes. While interesting and relevant within a specific context, the continual identification of new effects and naming new phenomena is not a sustainable practice. Even with an organizing framework, the combinatoric possibilities of how constructs influence each other quickly grow beyond what can reasonably be called parsimonious or cognitively manageable.

Exacerbating the confusion created by construct proliferation is that the "new" phenomena are not always new. New constructs are often closely related to existing constructs in other fields or even within the same field. For example, constructs related to people's a priori beliefs about what needs to be done to achieve an objective have been researched extensively in the teams literature under the heading of "mental models." Yet this same construct has a history in cognitive psychology (albeit by a different name—problem representation; see Hayes & Simon, 1974). Though researchers in the mental model tradition might prefer not to define their construct exactly as a "problem representation," by not relating to this literature they miss the opportunity to capitalize on a well-respected and substantial body of prior work. At the same time, these "new" constructs are likely to be inconsistently defined, used, or measured because of their shorter history. As a result, when group research proceeds using a new construct that has not yet achieved consistency in measurement or definition, the task of reconciling and integrating those streams of research becomes quite daunting (see a discussion of this point with regard to shared mental model research by Mohammed, Klimoski, & Rentsch, 2000). Without the integration of findings, no knowledge can accumulate.

The need for clarification and parsimony holds true at the level of theory as well, and again the answer, we believe, is integration. Just as construct development benefits from links to prior literatures, theory development can benefit from links to related theories. This is true in terms of content domains (e.g., psychology, sociology) but also across theories of differing scope: grand (or general) theories, middle-range theories, and domain-specific theories. While there is a history of debate regarding the efficacy of the alternatives types of theories, we argue (as have others before us) that theories of different scope should interrelate via nesting. That is, related grand, middle-range, and domain-specific theories need to fit together in a meaningful structure; this is the purpose of theory. Ultimately, related theories must work together if we are to have a cumulative science. For example, the goal of more general theories like those presented in this volume by Krokos et al. (Chapter 14); Nancy Cooke, Jamie Gorman, and Leah Rowe (Chapter 6); and Rentsch et al. (Chapter 9) should be to provide a framework within which more specific theories of teams can provide more detailed knowledge. At the same time, Essens et al. (Chapter 11) pose a domain-specific theory related to performance in military teams that must be connectable to middle-range and general theories of teams.

The previously raised issues lead us to the conclusion that the time has come to consolidate and organize the knowledge we have produced. We therefore offer three suggestions to teams' scholars to help consolidate our knowledge:

1. Consider the way your theory fits with other proximal theories. Proximal theories can be at the same level of analysis but in related domains (e.g., problem solving should be related to both decision making and learning) or can be about the same phenomenon at levels above and below the group level of analysis (e.g., group learning needs to fit with individual and organizational learning). Theory can then serve its purpose as an organizing framework for broader sets of ideas and findings that will serve to bridge disciplines rather than being simply the back story for a single study.

2. Maintain the integrity of concepts across studies, disciplines, and levels of analysis. This will serve to leverage disciplinary research already executed as a foundation on which emergent[1] group properties can be built and will increase consistency in the measurement and use of concepts in empirical research. It will also build bridges across disciplines of research.

3. Use classification systems to integrate rather than just differentiate. This should help reduce and manage the constructs in use to describe teams.

We discuss each of these suggestions next, presenting a "checklist" that scholars can use to focus on issues of theory consolidation when developing their own theories.

Paths to Theory Consolidation

Hierarchically Arranged Theory

Our first suggestion is to position new theory within the hierarchy of other more general and specific theories of related phenomena. In line with Merton (1968) and Pinder and Moore (1979), we support the view that midrange theories of teams need to relate to more general theories of teams, resulting in an hierarchical arrangement of theories (Figure 19.1).

To be specific about our definitions, general (or grand) theories of teams are designed to capture similarities of phenomena across team types and to offer theoretic parsimony but often result in predictive inaccuracy (Pinder & Moore, 1979). In contrast, midrange theories attempt to explain only a subset of team phenomena. They tend to be moderately abstract and more precise than general theories and to include constructs that are measurable. According to Merton (1968), midrange theories have fewer concepts and variables within their structure, are presented in a more testable

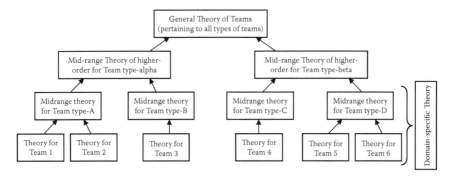

FIGURE 19.1
Hierarchically arranged midrange and general theory. (Adapted from Pinder, C. C. & Moore, L. F. (1979). The resurrection of taxonomy to aid the development of middle range theories of organizational behavior. *Administrative Science Quarterly, 24*(1), 99–118. With permission.)

form, have a more limited scope, and have a stronger relationship with research and practice. Different midrange theories will make different assumptions about teams, will consider different parameters to be important, and thus may lead to different prescriptions. Pinder and Moore (1979) observed that midrange theories are constructed in multiple ways—either by dealing with a specific phenomenon, by limiting the sample by sorting teams into categories (developing taxonomies or typologies), or by combining the two approaches in some way. We label theories that limit both the phenomena explained and the team type *domain-specific theories* (e.g., Essens, Chapter 11 in this volume).

Pinder and Moore (1979) noted that higher-order theories can be developed in two ways, ultimately reducing the total number of paradigms in a field. They can be based on the detection of similarities of phenomena and relationships across groups or via a valid synthesis of domain-specific and midrange theories. Hackman (2003) was more explicit about this practice in his discussion of *bracketing*. He argued that by clearly connecting one's focal phenomenon to broader and more specific theory, one can gain new insights into the operation of the phenomenon as a whole because most occur at multiple levels. Yet in bracketing this way, one is forced to maintain consistency and connectedness to the proximal theories that are relevant to a particular phenomenon. Similarly, Moreland and Levine (Chapter 2 in this volume) implicitly advocate a hierarchical ordering of theory when they note that an effective way to build bridges across disciplines is to develop midrange theories and then to extend them to explain other related phenomena. They provide the useful example of how the midrange social-identity/self-categorization theories, which were social psychological theories that applied to collections of groups, were reexamined in the *intragroup* context by various researchers, bringing new insights into the study of groups.

We believe that any theory can and should be connected into an integrated hierarchy of theory. That is, general theories should encompass multiple midrange theories, which in turn should encompass many domain-specific theories, and as one moves across levels of analyses the theories may address emergent properties particular to that level but will all be fundamentally consistent with each other. A nonteam example is the job characteristics theory (Hackman, 1983), which is a midrange theory that is an articulation of expectancy theory (Vroom, 1964) in a particular domain. Job characteristics theory maps its constructs (e.g., autonomy, task significance) onto the components of expectancy theory (i.e., valence, instrumentality, expectancy). The midrange theory (job characteristics theory) adds specificity to the components and relationships of the grand theory (expectancy theory). This serves to make the grand theory more predictive, while at the same time the grand theory can broaden the meaning of the components of the midrange theory (e.g., task significance is a valence), which enriches the concepts and links them to other midrange theories.

While general theories are the top of the organizing hierarchy, general theories can still be refined by linking multiple general theories together (rather than pitting them against each other). For example, Cooke et al. (Chapter 6 in this volume) discusses a general theory about how knowledge is partially embedded in the environment, and in discussing this, the authors take issue with information processing theory for making the locus of cognitive processing entirely within the individual. We are sympathetic to this critique, yet we believe that Cooke et al.'s theory could be better integrated with rather than pitted against information processing. Cooke et al. explicitly contrast "ecological versus information processing" and subsequently discuss the different perspective each side would take and their fundamental incompatibilities:

> These two perspectives formulate entirely different questions (not to mention levels of analysis) of team cognition.... Each approach may be capable of good or harm; nevertheless, between these alternatives the scientist must choose, and theories (and thus measures) will obtain at a like scaling. In short, the scientist must choose between analyzing the elements (information processing) or the flow (ecological perspective). (p. 171)

We do not believe that the two approaches are necessarily incompatible, so rather than advocating a "one or the other" perspective on these grand theories, we support efforts to integrate them into a "grander" theory of how environmentally embedded information and interpersonal interaction shape the way that information is processed.

In addition to clarifying regions of a grand theory, a good midrange theory should also be able to accommodate relevant, domain-specific theories. For example, it is possible to use representational gap theory (Cronin & Weingart, 2007) to accommodate Essens et al.'s (Chapter 11 in this volume) specific theory about command team effectiveness in military environments. Essens et al. state, "Our premise is that to be potentially effective, commanders must understand (1) what conditions they start with, particularly mission demands and individual and team capabilities; (2) what the end goals, intermediate goals, and criteria are; and (3) what they can direct and control in task and team" (p. 288). These parameters can be mapped onto the components of a joint cognitive representation (composed of team members' goals, assumptions, elements, and operators about the task at hand) (Cronin & Weingart, 2007). For example, mission demands reflect team members' assumptions about the nature of the task; distal and proximal goals within the mission demands reflect the team's goal hierarchy; aspects of the mission that people can direct and control are the elements; and individual and team capabilities (and the resultant task- and team-focused behaviors) comprise the operators that team members can employ to improve the current situation, in service of the goals. If we were to recast Essens et al.'s domain-specific theory into the language of our midrange theory of representational gaps, we could provide a consistent language across these streams of research. In addition, Essens et al.'s theory could be linked to similar phenomena in other types of teams via the midrange theory. For example, we could determine which group processes are common between Essens et al.'s command and control teams and cross-functional teams examined in other team research (e.g., Lovelace, Shapiro, & Weingart, 2001; Weingart, Cronin, Houser, Cagan, & Vogel, 2005).

While it is not new to claim that a science cumulates when theories fit together (more or less), we go further by saying that to make this happen, researchers must explicitly consider how their theories connect to other theories. Research on groups whose members work on subcomponents of the task shows that individuals have a tendency not to consider how their work will be integrated when working on specialized parts of a problem (Heath & Staudenmayer, 2000). Thus, it should not be surprising that individual researchers might not be mindful of how their theory fits with others. In light of the difficulty of relating one's work to the work of others, the next section provides a more concrete and fundamental suggestion for how to move forward on theory consolidation—simply to explicitly borrow concepts from core academic disciplines.

Use and Maintain the Integrity of Concepts from Other Sources

For a science to cumulate, researchers must build on extant theory and research when doing their own. Especially with regard to team research, relevant theories can be found both in one's own academic discipline and in others. This section discusses the merits of borrowing from related academic disciplines and from other levels of aggregation, capitalizing on the fact that group phenomena lie among individual, multigroup, and organizational dynamics.

Borrowing from Related Academic Disciplines

The study of groups is inherently interdisciplinary. This is why Moreland and Levine (Chapter 2 in this volume) offer suggestions about how to build bridges among pockets of researchers in different disciplines working on group phenomena. One of the hopes we have is that the study of groups would use the insight from the various disciplines on which it draws rather than wasting time rediscovering knowledge that has a long history in other domains. To that end, we suggest that one critical piece of this puzzle is to use well-researched concepts from the various core disciplines and to maintain the integrity of those concepts. While this may seem obvious, in practice people can sometimes either reinvent the wheel or define terms in such a way that disconnects the new findings from a large existing body of knowledge.

Consider the example of group learning. Learning is a construct with a long history in psychology. Yet in studying group learning, much of the insight about learning from the psychology literature seems to have been overlooked. For example, fundamental to the study of learning in psychology is that learning is not performance (Tolman, 1932). However, the literature on group learning often treats the two as the same (Wilson, Goodman, & Cronin, 2007). Moreover, whereas individual-level learning requires storage and retrieval processes to occur, most group-learning research focuses on sharing processes (transference of knowledge between group members) while mostly overlooking storage and retrieval processes. When the study of group learning is only concerned with sharing knowledge (which is an emergent property of group-level learning; see Wilson et al., 2007), it is not able to draw on what we know about learning from more than a century of research on learning in individuals.

When we do not attend to existing discipline-based research on group-level constructs we can find ourselves with limited conceptualizations. Continuing with the example of learning, by conflating group learning with performance we inadvertently imply that learning is always good and will always have a positive influence on performance (Wilson et al., 2007). This substantially limits our understanding of what group learning is. Group performance can improve without learning (e.g., when a product development team is able to reduce time to market because a supplier delivers a key component early), and groups often learn the wrong things

(Levitt & March, 1988) probably through the same processes used to learn the right things.

Consistency across Levels of Analysis

Considering multiple levels of analysis when developing theory allows for consistency of constructs across levels and increases efficiency and parsimony in construct development. Aggregating up a level of analysis often results in emergent properties of a construct, so researchers must identify which properties of multilevel constructs are similar across levels and which are different. Thus, a particular construct should not fundamentally change when moving up a level of analysis, but properties may be added to it, or its impact may be altered. To return to the group-learning example, learning may acquire additional features (e.g., the need to be shared) as one moves from the individual to the group level, but what is true about learning at one level should not be contradicted at another (e.g., if learning is not performance at the individual level, it should not be performance at the group level).

DeChurch and Mathieu (Chapter 10 in this volume) provide a nice example of looking to other levels of analysis in their discussion of multiteam systems. They look to the literature on teams when identifying factors important to the design of multiteam systems (i.e., size, heterogeneity, and distribution); they consider the research on organizational design to motivate distinctions among three forms of functional interdependence. As they continue to develop and test their theory, we suggest that DeChurch and Mathieu pursue a deeper understanding of why extant team findings may be qualitatively different in multiteam systems. For example, what makes the effect of increasing size different in a multiteam system (MTS) versus a regular team? Does leadership take on a different quality in an MTS because there is no single boss to whom one is ultimately answerable? Does heterogeneity take on a different quality because of the subgroup identities potentially nested in an MTS? A concept may or may not change as one moves across levels of analysis; if it does not, then we are able to generalize findings from a lower level of analysis without the need for extensive empirical work. If it does, then being explicit about what is different guides how the construct should be studied at the new level.

In addition to articulating how constructs' properties change across levels, researchers need to be sensitive to properties that emerge at higher levels of analysis. For example, the "boundary spanner" might be an emergent, necessary role in an MTS^2, whereas this role would not be necessary to a traditional team. The converse is that one should identify what is not a property at a lower level of analysis, such as when comparing a group with an individual. An example of this can be drawn from the literature on group learning. At the individual level, learning resides within a person. However at the group level, an emergent property is tied to the notion that whatever is learned must be shared among group members (Wilson et al., 2007); the sharing process is not something that occurs in an individual. Similarly, a joint representation (i.e., the teams' conceptualization of what the problem is) can have inconsistencies within it; but an individual representation cannot (Cronin & Weingart, 2007). In sum, the ways constructs operate at one level provide clues to how they will operate and how they might be studied at another level. At the same time, finding the emergent properties as constructs across levels helps clarify what is truly different at the group level.

Thus far, we have made the case for borrowing from other disciplines and levels of analysis as a way to develop a cumulative science and not reinvent the wheel. These strategies will move us toward a more well-integrated science, but explicit organizing mechanisms are also needed. The next section considers the use of classification systems as a means of clarifying and simplifying complex sets of phenomena.

Classifications that Clarify and Simplify

Classification systems encompass both taxonomies (which are derived empirically) and typologies (which are created a priori) (Doty & Glick, 1994). For example, in the late 1960s and early 1970s researchers struggled with ways to classify organizations (McKelvey, 1978) in an attempt to identify the meaningful characteristics on which organizations could vary. These characteristics would help pinpoint the important factors for organizational functioning and would help limit inappropriate generalizations between different kinds of organizations. Developing such classification systems was not a trivial matter, and papers were written simply on how to make good classification systems (McKelvey, 1975, 1978).

Group researchers would do well to consider this advice. In particular, we would suggest that at this stage in the development of the field of groups research, classification schemes are needed more to consolidate than differentiate. Note that consolidation focuses on how phenomena are the same but in doing so also reaffirms what is meaningfully different. The end result is a method to simplify a complex field of phenomena and a guide so that people do not make inappropriate generalizations or meaningless distinctions.

An excellent example of this kind of clarifying typology is the recent typology of diversity proposed by Harrison and Klein (2007). Their typology arrays diversity along three dimensions: separation, variety, and disparity. Separation is the difference among people on a single bipolar attribute (e.g., religiousness), implying a difference in degree (more or less religious). Variety is the difference among people in terms of the categories represented (e.g., nationality), implying categorical differences (English,

French, Japanese). Disparity is the difference among people in terms of a desired or valued attribute (e.g., power), implying differences in rankings (high vs. low status).

For the cost of these three new constructs, this typology brings substantial organization to the research on diversity and its effects. First, Harrison and Klein's (2007) typology provides a consistent means to compare relative levels of diversity across the different kinds of attributes used to characterize teams as diverse (e.g., age, ethnicity, functional background, group membership). Moreover, the taxonomy conveys a set of three general, underlying features of diversity attributes (e.g., variety, whether from age, ethnicity, or functional background, will relate to the same notions of difference). Second, the distinctions also speak to how we might most appropriately measure diversity across the various types of diversity. Separation can be studied using variance, variety using dispersion indices, and disparity using rank. Third, because these dimensions were extracted from prior empirical research on diversity, one can get a sense of what is important about each type of diversity as well as what the particular type of diversity is likely to affect. For example, since separation is about contrasting positions on an attribute, this kind of diversity is likely to influence disagreement or conflict, whereas disparity, which is really about resource allocation, will be related to issues of power and fairness. Finally, and perhaps most important of all, a simplifying taxonomy of this type allows us to think more systematically about what actually matters in terms of team diversity. When diversity is simply anything that can be used to differentiate people on a team, then the list is practically infinite, and many differences will be surface features that have no lasting impact (Harrison, Price, & Bell, 1998). In saying which attributes are *not* meaningfully different, Harrison and Klein's (2007) work reduces the number of distinctions that need to be tested to a more manageable amount and points us toward research questions that are more likely to show meaningful differences that build on prior work. For those who are interested in but not studying diversity, it provides an elegant but precise way to think about diversity.

It would seem that the more common tendency when building classification systems is to try to capture all the complexity in a system. However, this often leads to a proliferation of constructs and needs to be tempered by the degree to which the new constructs clarify a phenomenon. This is just as true in the groups literature as in other fields. For example, the notion of what "shared" means in terms of a team mind was discussed by Rentsch et al. (Chapter 9 in this volume). They differentiate three dimensions of cognitive similarity and then explore the multiple subtypes and regions of this three-dimensional space using examples from prior team research. The three dimensions do a nice job of capturing potential distinguishing factors of cognitive similarity. However, we would argue that the distinctions among the three dimensions matter only inasmuch as they are shown to differentially affect an outcome of interest. In this way the choice of dimensions on which to distinguish cognitive similarity could be better motivated. In addition, because of the multiple potential categories identified within each dimension, the typology can quickly become unwieldy. Just crossing the categories identified in their table of sample types of cognitive similarity (p. 242, this volume) would result in 189 possible types. And, as Rentsch et al. point out, "The possible cognitive content domains are infinite" (p. 241). Therefore, we challenge Rentsch et al. to allow empirical results to aid in both motivating the choice of dimensions and in limiting the set of categories addressed.

While we believe consolidation needs to happen, we also caution against overgeneralizations. McKelvey (1978) addressed the issue of overgeneralization with regard to organizational forms and argued using the biological metaphor that certain expectations are not appropriate for both mammals and reptiles (while others are). Nonetheless, we feel that at this point in the development of research on teams, we need to take a more concerted effort toward consolidation by being very explicit about the evidence for anything that is claimed to distinguish a team. For example, Essens et al. (Chapter 11 in this volume) make the assumption that military teams in complex situations and facing life-or-death decisions are different from other teams. While the intuition seems reasonable, it lacks the precision needed to judge what exactly makes this kind of team unique. Does "complex" mean that the situation is ill structured (Galotti, 1989), has no right answer (such as in a judgmental task; Laughlin & Hollingshead, 1995), is multistep, or is some combination of these? These distinctions are well defined and have a history in related disciplines, providing guidelines to determine what generalizations to or from other types of teams are appropriate. Pushing further, what is it about life-or-death decisions that matters? If the extremity of the consequence changes the nature of a team, then the operation of a military team engaged in a simulation (vs. a real-world battle) may not be generalizable.

Overall, a good classification will highlight the distinctions that matter (as well as the ones that do not). The important distinctions will provide direction for future research while limiting overgeneralization of findings. To figure out what distinctions matter is nontrivial but should probably be decided with an eye toward the general, not the particular.

In Closing

When writing a commentary on a collection of papers, a central task is to find linkages across or commonalities among the papers. As we attempted that task, we quickly realized that there were many implicit or potential theoretical links that were not exploited within the chapters. While this may not be surprising given the breadth of chapters presented in this volume, we found it to be somewhat disconcerting. Upon further reflection we realized it was very representative of the state of the "field" of groups research today, and it provided an excellent opportunity to consider how the field might be consolidated.

In considering how to consolidate theory and research on groups and teams, we made three basic points. First, theories need to fit within the broader landscape of existing related theories. Second, the integrity of concepts must be maintained across studies. And third, classifications systems should be used to integrate, not just to differentiate. In making these goals concrete for researchers, our points can be reframed as a series of questions that researchers need to be considering while developing their next theory or motivating their next empirical paper (Table 19.1). We hope other researchers find these questions useful in guiding their theory building and development of research questions.

Endnotes

1. Emergent properties are present at a certain level of aggregation but not at the levels below them; Hackman (2003) gave the example of "odor"—which is a property of molecules but not atoms.
2. We thank Michelle Marks for this example.

TABLE 19.1

Questions for Researchers to Ask Themselves When Developing Theory

1. Relatedness to other theories:
    a. Scope (grand, midrange and domain specific theories)
        i.   Does my theory fit within a grander theory?
        ii. If my theory is a grand theory, does it link to and integrate with other grand theories?
        iii. Does my theory help organize theories that are more specific in scope?
    b. Level of analysis (within one's topic area)
        i. Can I see how my group level theory connects to organization level theories?
        ii. Can I see how my group level theory connects to individual level theories?
    c. Interdisciplinarity
        i. Have I researched my idea in the literatures of other disciplines?
        ii. Have I tried to make connections to theories from other disciplines?
2. Conceptual integrity
    a. Am I using related literatures to identify useful existing constructs? Have I cast a wide net?
    b. Am I using the construct as intended?
    c. Do my extensions build on rather than fundamentally change that construct?
    d. Have I explicitly identified any emergent properties that do (if going up a level) or do not (if going down a level) exist at my level of analysis?
3. Classification systems
    a. Does my classification system integrate existing theories?
    b. If I am introducing a new construct, do we really need it? What is the value of the distinction?
    c. Is there evidence that the features I'm distinguishing matter?
    d. Have I tried to be as parsimonious as possible in articulating my classifications?

References

Cannon-Bowers, J. A., Tannenbaum, S. I., Salas, E., & Volpe, C. E. (1995). Defining competencies and establishing team training requirements. In R. A. Guzzo & E. Salas (Eds.), *Team effectiveness and decision making in organizations* (pp.333–380). San Francisco, CA: Jossey-Bass.

Cronin, M. A. & Weingart, L. R. (2007). Representational gaps, information processing and conflict in functionally diverse teams. *Academy of Management Review, 32*, 761–773.

Doty, D. H. & Glick, W. H. (1994). Typologies as a unique form of theory building: Toward improved understanding and modeling. *Academy of Management Review, 19,* 230–251.

Galotti, K. M. (1989). Approaches to studying formal and everyday reasoning. *Psychological Bulletin, 105,* 331–351.

Hackman, J. R. (1983). Designing work for individuals and groups. *Perspectives on behavior in organizations.* New York: McGraw-Hill.

Hackman, J. R. (1987). The design of work teams. In J. W. Lorsch (Ed.), *Handbook of organizational behavior* (pp. 315–339). Englewood Cliffs, NJ: Prentice-Hall Inc.

Hackman, J. R. (2003). Learning more by crossing levels: Evidence from airplanes, hospital, and orchestras. *Journal of Organizational Behavior, 24,* 905–922.

Harrison, D. A., Price, K. H., & Bell, M. P. (1998). Beyond relational demography: Time and the effects of surface- and deep-level diversity on work group cohesion. *Academy of Management Journal, 41,* 96–107.

Harrison, D. A. & Klein, K. J. (2007). What's the difference? Diversity constructs as separation, variety, or disparity in organizations. *Academy of Management Review, 32,* 1199–1228.

Hayes, J. R. & Simon, H. A. (1974). Understanding written problem instructions. In L. W. Gregg (Ed.), *Knowledge and cognition* (pp. 167–200). Hillsdale, NJ: Lawrence Erlbaum.

Heath, C. & Staudenmayer, N. (2000). Coordination neglect: How lay theories of organizing complicate coordination in organization. *Research in Organizational Behavior, 22,*153–191.

Laughlin, P. R. & Hollingshead, A. B. (1995). A theory of collective induction. *Organizational Behavior & Human Decision Processes, 61*(1), 94–107.

Levitt, B. & March, J. G. (1988). Organizational learning. *Annual Review of Sociology, 14,* 319–340.

Lovelace, K., Shapiro, D., & Weingart, L. R. (2001). Maximizing cross-functional new product teams innovativeness and constraint adherence: A conflict communications perspective. *Academy of Management Journal, 44*(4), 779–783.

McKelvey, B. (1975). Guidelines for the empirical classification of organizations. *Administrative Science Quarterly, 20,* 509–525.

McKelvey, B. (1978). Organizational systematics: Taxonomic lessons from biology. *Management Science, 24,* 1428–1440.

Merton, R. K. (1968). *Social theory and social structure.* New York: Free Press.

Mohammed, S., Klimoski, R., & Rentsch, J. R. (2000). The measurement of team mental models: We have no shared schema. *Organizational Research Methods, 3,* 123–165.

Newell, A. (1973). You can't play 20 questions with nature and win: Projective comments on the papers of this symposium. In W. G. Chase (Ed.), *Visual information processing* (pp. 441–486). New York: Academic Press.

Pinter, C. C. & Moore, L. F. (1979). The resurrection of taxonomy to aid the development of middle range theories of organizational behavior. *Administrative Science Quarterly,24*(1), 99–118.

Salas, E., Sims, D. E., & Burke, S. C. (2005). Is there a "Big Five" in teamwork? *Small Group Research, 36,* 555–599.

Tolman, E. C. (1932). *Purposive behavior in animals and man.* New York: Appelton-Century-Crofts.

Vroom, V. H. (1964). *Work and motivation.* Oxford, England: Wiley.

Weingart, L. R., Cronin, M. A., Houser, C. J. S., Cagan, J., & Vogel, C. (2005). Functional diversity and conflict in cross-functional product development team: Considering perceptual gaps and task characteristics. In L. L. Neider & C. A. Schriesheim (Eds.), *Understanding teams*. Greenwich, CT: Information Age Publishing.

Wilson, J. M., Goodman, P., & Cronin, M. A. (2007). Group learning. *Academy of Management Review*, 32, 1041–1059.

20

Ten Critical Research Questions: The Need for New and Deeper Explorations

Eduardo Salas and Jessica L. Wildman

The chapters in this volume have discussed some of the most recent, state-of-the-science thinking in teams, and, clearly, team effectiveness research has progressed in leaps and bounds over the last decade. Much has been learned and applied to the composition, management, and direction of teams in organizations, but the journey is never complete. As the world continually changes and adapts, the functioning of teams in organizations also changes and new areas of research interest emerge. In this final chapter, we submit 10 critical questions in team research that we believe still remain unanswered and are in need of deeper exploration. Although these 10 questions clearly do not encompass the full extent of research avenues left to explore, they function as a point of departure to stimulate new undertakings in what we believe to be the most critical concepts for future team research.

As is the case for any research agenda put forth in social science, there are many ways to interpret these research questions. The spirit of the questions submitted here is one that offers a direction of exploration where precise propositions and hypotheses can be derived. Moreover, as has been noted in prior work, all teams are not created equal, and the research questions that follow are most relevant to teams where there is high task interdependence.

Question 1: What (and How) Do Teams Think, Feel, and Do "in the Wild"?

Work teams are embedded in organizations and influenced by myriad factors. Hence, there is a need to know more about teams performing in their natural context—the what, how, and why of teams "in the wild."

Although laboratory research has a solid place in our science and has provided much valuable insight regarding team dynamics, it may not be capturing the full set of complex processes engaged by teams in the wild. Laboratory research tightly controls team processes to increase the chances that a true causal relationship is being observed, but the real world, as we know, is not a tightly controlled laboratory setting. In natural settings, teams often perform a multitude of processes and tasks simultaneously in response to the competing demands placed on them. This creates a host of complex operations within the team, and often this complexity is reduced in laboratory settings. In addition to the extensive laboratory research taking place, we need to observe and record teams in action to discern what processes might not be captured in controlled experimental conditions and how complex factors function within operational teams.

The good news is that in the last decade, we have seen a notable interest in team-based field research. This is gratifying. Field research is difficult, labor intense, and expensive (Guzzo & Dickson, 1996; Salas, Stagl, & Burke, 2004). Researchers find it difficult to gain access to teams in the field or are unwilling to spend the extra time and expenses necessary to deal with the messiness of conducting field studies and observations. However, there are several published field studies that demonstrate the advantages of studying teams in natural settings (e.g., Espinosa, DeLone, & Lee, 2006; Espinosa, Slaughter, Kraut, & Herbsleb, 2007; Halfhill, Nielsen, Sundstrom, & Weilbaecher, 2005; Lewis, 2003; Lim & Klein, 2006). One particularly striking example is Gersick's (1988) punctuated equilibrium model of group development, discovered through the observation of eight naturally occurring project teams over their entire lifespan. This now well-accepted, field-driven theory had an immense impact on organizational science in that it demonstrated that real-world team development did not fit any of the existing theoretical models. In another published naturalistic field study, Banker, Field, Schroeder, and Sinha (1996) observed high-performance work teams over a period of several months. The extensive detailed data they collected allowed them to gain insight regarding the evolution and functioning of the teams over time.

Clearly, field research has the potential to illuminate new, complex, and often unexpected knowledge about teams in organizations. As teams in organizations change and adapt in response to a changing world, there remains a continual need to observe them in action. To really understand the way teams function in organizations and how simultaneous team processes interact to influence team outcomes, there is a need to gather more direct observational data of teams performing in the wild. Increased data from field studies, in balance with continuing laboratory research, will paint a more complete picture of team dynamics and inform theoretical work that leads to new avenues for empirical research.

Question 2: Teamwork Processes: What Exactly Are They and How Do They Work?

A recent review of the team literature concluded that more than 130 models and frameworks of team performance or some component thereof have been developed over the past few decades (Salas, Stagl, Burke, & Goodwin, 2007). One of the most critical conclusions reached in team research is that teams engage in a set of processes, commonly referred to as *teamwork*, that are unique and separate from individual-level or taskwork processes (i.e., a team's interactions with tasks, tools, machines, and systems; Bowers, Braun, & Morgan, 1997, as cited in Marks, Mathieu, & Zaccaro, 2001). Researchers have long been attempting to explain what teamwork comprises. Generally, research has concluded that teamwork refers to the set of interrelated thoughts, actions, and feelings that each team member engages in, that are needed to function as a team, and that combine to facilitate coordinated, adaptive performance (e.g., Marks et al., 2001; Morgan, Glickman, Woodard, Blaiwes, & Salas, 1986; Salas, Sims, & Klein, 2004). What is included in this "set of thoughts, actions, and feelings," however, is less agreed on. Despite the fact that the term *teamwork* is a frequently investigated and seemingly understood concept in organizations and organizational research, the definition remains elusive and disjointed.

While numerous typologies exist that describe a finite set of teamwork processes (e.g., Campion, Medsker, & Higgs, 1993; Dickinson & McIntyre, 1997; Gladstein, 1984; Hackman, 1987; Naylor & Dickson, 1969), they all tend to emphasize different aspects of teamwork. For example, an early taxonomy developed by Fleishman and Zaccaro (1992) focused on task accomplishment with a concern for member interconnectedness. This taxonomy listed a set of teamwork behaviors such as load balancing and general activity pacing. Marks et al. (2001) later presented a temporally based taxonomy of team processes that emphasized the role of time on team functioning. Critical processes in this taxonomy included transition processes such as mission analysis and goal specification, action processes such as systems monitoring and coordination, and interpersonal processes such as conflict management and motivation. Salas, Sims, and Burke (2005) proposed that the set of processes comprising teamwork could be boiled down to the "Big Five" core processes: team leadership, mutual performance monitoring, backup behavior, adaptability, and team orientation. The most recent conceptualizations of teamwork have ranged in focus from team adaptation processes (Burke, Stagl, Salas, Pierce, & Kendall, 2006), to a three-dimensional model of teamwork (Yeh, Smith, Jennings, & Castro, 2006), to implicit coordination processes (Rico, Sanchez-Manzanares, Gil, & Gibson, 2008).

Despite the several taxonomies and frameworks that have been developed, team effectiveness researchers have yet to agree on a unified, comprehensive definition of critical teamwork processes. McGlynn, Sutton, Sprague, Demski, and Pierce (1997) made an early attempt at a unified teamwork definition by synthesizing elements of other's research (e.g., Fleishman & Quaintance, 1984; Salas, Dickinson, Converse, & Tannenbaum, 1992) into one taxonomy of team functions, and Salas and colleagues (2007) more recently developed an integrated framework of team effectiveness that included a set of team processes. Still, there is a need in team research to further this work and to develop a single (if possible) and current working definition of teamwork that integrates as much of the existing knowledge regarding team processes as possible, including the most contemporary theories. Rather than being simply task based, temporally based, or knowledge based, the science of teams needs a model of teamwork that accounts for all (or most) known variables. By integrating past teamwork research into a more comprehensive taxonomy, future research on team processes will be more universally applicable and knowledge will be accumulated—generating a more robust science.

Question 3: What (and How) Do Teams "Think, Feel, and Do" Differently across Time?

Teams are not static entities existing outside of temporal influences. The processes teams engage in are never instantaneous—all team functioning occurs over time. While the role of time may vary for different types of teams, factors such as deadlines, schedule synchronization, and coordination efforts still impact team functioning for all teams in some way (Marks et al., 2001). Theoretical work has begun to describe the possible influences of time on team functioning, including Chapter 12 in this volume by Susan Mohammed, Katherine Hamilton, and Audrey Lim. For example, McGrath (1991) presented the time, interaction, and performance (TIP) theory of groups, which included propositions regarding generic temporal problems and the impact of time on group performance. McGrath (2000) later discussed temporal structure and patterning in groups, emphasizing entrainment processes. Another theory of team functioning originally proposed by Kozlowski, Gully, Nason, and Smith (1999) and repeated in Chapter 5 in this volume by Steve Kozlowski, Daniel Watola, Jaclyn Nowakowski, Brian Kim, and Isabel Botero conceptualized team development as a process that proceeds across levels and time. They also specify content, processes, and outcomes that are relevant at different times throughout the developmental phases.

Marks and colleagues (2001) presented a temporally based framework of teamwork processes similarly proposing that different team processes are critical at different temporal phases of task execution. Specifically, they suggested that team performance can be conceptualized as a series of Input–Process–Output episodes and that these episodes occur cyclically throughout alternating phases of action and transition. Harrison, Mohammed, McGrath, Florey, and Vanderstoep (2003) further emphasized the integral role of time in team functioning by empirically demonstrating that long-term teams work faster and create better products than short-term teams because they are become more familiar with each other as time passes. Hackman and Wageman (2005) suggested that the effectiveness of team coaching interventions depends heavily on the timing of the effort because team readiness varies across the team's lifespan. The most recently developed temporal research examines the phenomenon of team adaptation, in which teams adjust and change their functioning across time in response to dynamic environmental cues (Burke, Stagl, et al., 2006).

Despite these recent theoretical movements toward an understanding of time and team process and performance, there has only been a small amount of empirical research directly examining these theorized effects. Some research has looked at specific temporally based team phenomenon, such as team adaptation (LePine, 2003, 2005). Other recent research has attempted to capture the temporal aspect of team performance by utilizing a longitudinal research design (e.g., Harrison et al., 2003; Pearce, Gallagher, & Ensley, 2002; Tasa, Taggar, & Seijts, 2007). Keller (2006) examined transformational leadership and initiating structure as longitudinal predictors of team performance. Another recent longitudinal team study examined how affective states in teams are linked across time (Ilies, Wagner, & Morgeson, 2007).

Although these particular examples do investigate team-level phenomenon over time, they look solely at team performance rather than at how specific team processes differ or change over a team's lifespan. There is a strong need to empirically examine the theorized influences of time on team processes in addition to performance, considering much is unclear or disjointed in this area. For example, Levesque, Wilson, and Wholey (2001) found that over time, role differentiation increases in teams, leading to a decrease in interaction and a subsequent decrease in shared mental models. Conversely, McComb (2007) presented a framework describing the process of mental model convergence and provided preliminary empirical evidence that team mental models converge over time. Other researchers have begun to respond to this more recent mental model convergence framework and propose the next steps in the field (e.g., Cannon-Bowers, 2007; Rentsch & Small, 2007).

Currently, there is no coherent, integrated, and robust understanding of how team functioning differs across time. More thorough, well-designed, longitudinal research is necessary to uncover the patterns of team dynamics over time and to develop a more comprehensive understanding of the temporal aspects of team functioning. Along with creating a more robust understanding of teams and the impact of time on team processes, longitudinal research provides another advantage for research. Several empirical studies examining various team-level phenomena have expressed the need for future longitudinal research to uncover the causal links between the relationships of interest (e.g., Drach-Zahavy & Somech, 2001; Pearce & Sims, 2002). We know cross-sectional research has its limitations, so by measuring variables over time, the causality of the relationship can be determined. Thus, more and better longitudinal team studies are necessary to improve our understanding of how team processes and performance differ over time—a big challenge, but with big payoff for our science.

Question 4: What's the Environment Got to Do with Teams?

Teams don't perform in a vacuum. They perform in context rich environments, full of external cues and extraneous environmental factors that can have significant impacts on team functioning. Chapter 11 by Peter Essens, Ad Vogelaar, Jacques Mylle, Carol Blendell, Carol Paris, Stanley Halpin, and Joseph Baranski presented a framework for team functioning in complex settings and proposed that contextual variables such as situational uncertainty, stress potential, and situational constraints can have a significant impact on team functioning. A review of the team classification literature presented seven underlying contextual dimensions critical to the classification of teams: (1) fundamental work cycle, (2) physical ability requirements, (3) temporal duration, (4) task structure, (5) active resistance, (6) hardware dependence, and (7) health risk (Devine, 2002). Though most of the existing team effectiveness frameworks describe contextual variables as critical inputs to team functioning (e.g., Campion et al., 1993; Gladstein, 1984; Hackman, 1987; Sundstrom, De Meuse, & Futrell, 1990), there is only a small amount of empirical work investigating the nature of these relationships (e.g., Cannon-Bowers & Salas, 1998; Driskell, Salas, & Johnston, 1999). One recent field study concluded that job and organizational characteristics such as opportunity for personal growth have a considerable impact on team performance variables, supporting the importance of understanding the contextual influences on team dynamics (Thamhain, 2004).

Not only is the environment clearly an integral factor in team dynamics, but context also varies widely across teams and organizations. Not all teams operate in the same environment, meaning not all teams perform the same processes or function in the same way. For example, military combat teams often perform in extremely physically stressful environments, whereas strategic command and control teams perform in an environment with much less immediate physical stress but may encounter high levels of cognitive stress. The differing impact of heat, noise, or other contextual factors may cause these teams to engage in extremely different sets of processes. For example, Gorman, Cooke, and Winner (2006) theorized that team situation awareness differs for teams in a decentralized command and control setting. Because teams always function within a specific environment, we cannot fully understand the functioning of various teams without understanding how the surrounding context impact processes and performance. Thus, it is integral that researchers examine the differing impact of environmental context on team functioning. More research is needed to examine how environmental factors such as situational uncertainty or stress level impact team processes and performance and how teams functioning within varying conditions differ. These are just a few of the contextual questions that merit further exploration.

Question 5: How Do Team Cognitive Processes Integratively Influence Team Functioning?

One of the most recent areas of interest in team research involves the role of higher level cognitive processes in team functioning (Salas & Fiore, 2004). Substantial research, including a couple chapters in this book, specifically focuses on concepts within team cognition (e.g., Cannon & Edmondson, 2001; Ensley & Pearce, 2001; Rentsch & Klimoski, 2001). Chapter 9 in this volume, by Joan Rentsch, Lisa Delise, and Scott Hutchison, focuses on the lens of schema theory to gain an understanding of team cognition. Gibson (2001) presented a framework for collective cognition with four phases: accumulation, interaction, examination, and accommodation. Ensley and Pearce (2001) developed a group cognition model suggesting that cognitive and affective conflict are the group processes through which strategic shared cognition may relate to organizational performance. Chapter 6 in this volume by Nancy Cooke, Jamie Gorman, and Leah Rowe examines the role of shared mental models within teams. A large amount of other team cognition research has also emphasized the importance of shared mental models in successful team performance (Bierhals, Schuster, Kohler, & Badke-Schaub, 2007; Cannon-Bowers, Salas, & Converse, 1993; Salas & Fiore, 2004). For example, there has been research suggesting that shared mental models facilitate team coordination and are positively related to team process and performance (e.g., Marks, Zaccaro, & Mathieu, 2000; Mathieu, Heffner, Goodwin, Salas, & Cannon-Bowers, 2000; Minionis, Zaccaro, & Perez, 1995). Other research has examined the measurement of shared mental models (Smith-Jentsch, Campbell, Milanovich, & Reynolds, 2001). Transactive memory systems are another of the more recent developments in team cognition research. A transactive memory system can be defined as a group-level collective system for encoding, storing, and retrieving information that is distributed across group members (Wegner, 1995). Restated, a transactive memory system is a shared awareness of who knows what. Although research on this concept is still relatively new, preliminary studies have shown that transactive memory systems may mediate the effects of group training on task performance (Liang, Moreland, & Argote, 1995; Moreland, 1999).

Based on the previous examples, there is clearly a growing and improving literature on team cognition. While this collection of information is very valuable to scientists and practitioners interested in team cognition, there is a remaining need to integrate this cognitive research. Mohammed and Dumville (2001) began this endeavor by presenting an integrated team knowledge framework based on the existing shared mental model, transactive memory, and information-sharing literature. Yet researchers need to continue exploring the dynamic interrelationships between these team-level cognitive constructs. For example, through what mechanisms do all of the team cognitive structures influence subsequent processes and performance? We need to better delineate the boundaries of the constructs subsumed under team cognition as well as to continue examining the ways that these constructs interact and how they influence functioning in teams.

Question 6: Where They Come from: What Role Does Culture Play in Team Functioning?

As organizations continue to globalize, more and more teams composed of members from multiple national and cultural backgrounds are appearing, and the management of multicultural teams is becoming a hot topic in mainstream literature (e.g., Brett, Behfar, & Kern, 2006; Holland, 2007). Culture is the acquired knowledge people use to interpret experience and generate social behavior (Sutton, Pierce, Burke, & Salas, 2006). This knowledge can stem from an individual's national origin, organizational background, or even regional influences. Cultural knowledge forms values, creates attitudes, and influences behavior. Cross-cultural theory has suggested that there are differences in the way individuals influenced by different cultures tend to think and behave (e.g., Gibson & Zellmer-Bruhn,

2002; Schwartz, 1999; Triandis, 1989; Witkin & Berry, 1975). For example, Hofstede (1980) distinguished between individualistic and collectivistic cultures. Team members from an individualistic culture tend not to take disagreement with their ideas personally, whereas individuals from a collectivistic culture seek group harmony and may consider disagreement improper behavior. Another theory of culture postulates that cultures differ in regards to time orientation (Hall & Hall, 1990). In this theory, cultures with a monochronic time orientation consider things one at a time and adhere strictly to schedules, whereas cultures with a polychronic time orientation believe plans are constantly changing and thus that schedules are only general guidelines.

Theoretically, it follows that team functioning would be significantly influenced by the cultural makeup of the team. Chapter 8 in this volume by Shawn Burke, Heather Priest, Samuel Wooten, Deborah DiazGranados, and Eduardo Salas begins to address this issue by examining the phenomenon of team adaptation in a multicultural setting. Other literature has also begun to theoretically discuss the probable effects of culture on teams (e.g., Mateev & Milter, 2004). Most recently, Sutton and colleagues (2006) presented several propositions regarding the impact of cultural differences on team dynamics. For example, they speculated that team members with monochronic time orientations may fail to grasp the context of verbal communication that is presented over time since they tend to isolate events. This could potentially lead to poor understanding within the team and could be detrimental to performance. As another example, a team made up of only individualistic members may differ dramatically from a team of only collectivistic members in regards to process. A culturally diverse team presents even more opportunities for cultural impact. Burke and colleagues also made several propositions regarding the impact of interteam cultural diversity on team leadership processes (Burke, Hess, & Salas, 2006; Burke, Priest, Upshaw, Salas, & Pierce, in press; Salas, Burke, Wilson-Donnelly, & Fowlkes, 2004). These theorized differences in culture have the potential to affect what processes the team engages in, what processes are most critical, and what strategies are most effective for improving team function.

While researchers such as Sutton and colleagues (2006) and Burke, Hess and Salas (2005) have proposed possible implications of culture on teamwork, the small amount of empirical work directly examining the influence of culture on team-level functioning only begins to scratch the surface (e.g., Alavi & McCormick, 2007; Salk & Brannen, 2000). In one recent study, it was found that culture, specifically individualism and power distance, moderated the relationship between directive leadership and group organizational citizenship behaviors across teams from different cultures (Euwema, Wendt, & van Emmerik, 2007). Other research has examined intercultural diversity in a virtual or distributed setting (e.g.,

Connaughton & Shuffler, 2007; Hardin, Fuller, & Davison, 2007; Symons & Stenzel, 2007). There is a remaining need for more empirical work examining the impact of cultural diversity on team processes and performance. Particularly, we need more research focusing on teams of mixed cultural diversity examining how and why cultural diversity influences team processes in collocated teams in addition to the existing research on virtual or distributed teams. Not only is cultural team research needed to expand the state of the art; it is also becoming an ever more critical topic as the prevalence of multicultural teams in organizations increases.

Question 7: So We Know Team Composition Matters ... but How and Why?

Teams are made up of individuals, and as such, individual differences inevitably impact team functioning. Individuals differ on many terms, including factors such as personality, general mental ability, and values. These individual differences can have a significant impact on both team process and performance. For example, a recent meta-analysis summarized the relationships between several team composition variables and team performance (Bell, 2007). Specifically, Bell concluded that several team composition factors (e.g., preference for teamwork, openness to experience, and general mental ability) were significantly related to team performance outcomes. LePine (2003) found that teams with members with higher cognitive ability, achievement, and openness and with lower dependability were more able to adapt their role structure when faced with unforeseen changes in the task context, and this led to higher team performance. A following study by LePine (2005) again found that team member cognitive ability was associated with team adaptation.

Although there is a considerable amount of extant research examining the relationships between team composition variables and team performance, there are limitations to the existing research. Specifically, Bell's (2007) meta-analysis suggested that several moderators appear to be simultaneously affecting the relationships between team composition variables and subsequent team performance but that these relationships are not yet clear. Edwards, Day, Arthur, and Bell (2006) conducted a study that begins to explore the potential moderators between team composition variables and team performance, finding that teams with high mental ability composition had higher team performance and that this relationship was partially mediated through the accuracy of team mental models. More research examining other proposed moderators is needed if the role of team composition in team functioning is to be fully understood. There is also a lack of research examining what specific teamwork processes team composition variables impact. Driskell, Goodwin, Salas, and O'Shea (2006) presented a theoretical framework linking team personality traits to specific teamwork dimensions. This piece could potentially serve as a starting point for future empirical work investigating the relationships between team personality composition and teamwork processes. Additionally, there is a need for research investigating some of the more underrepresented team composition factors such as collectivism, preference for teamwork, and emotional intelligence (Bell, 2007). More well-designed research looking at the relationships surrounding team composition and team dynamics would contribute greatly to the science.

Question 8: How Can Simulation and Agent-Based Capabilities Contribute to Team Research?

In an era of rapid technological advancement, more and more research has turned to computer simulation, virtual reality, and other recently developed technology as testing tools. Computer technology has infiltrated all arenas of research and embodies several advantages that lend themselves to team research applications. Marks (2000) described several advantages of computer simulations for team research including the ability to script scenarios, immense data-handling capabilities, the ability to test hard-to-study environments, and the ability to perform studies with distributed participants. The dynamic nature of simulations also provides a powerful method for studying the complex functioning of teams and allows for the control and manipulation of problem variables, for large sets of scenarios to be generated quickly, and for the testing and development of new theories (Nogueira & Raz, 2006). Despite these advantages, simulations and other technological test beds have just recently entered the team research arena.

Some of the most commonly used existing team-based simulation test beds include Distributed Dynamic Decision-making (DDD; Kleinman & Serfaty, 1989; MacMillan, Entin, Hess, & Paley, 2004; Song & Kleinman, 1994), Team Interactive Decision Exercise for Teams Incorporating Distributed Expertise (TIDE2; Brannick, Salas, & Prince, 1997), and Decision Making Evaluation Facility for Tactical Teams (DEFTT; Cannon-Bowers & Salas, 1998). These test beds are usually utilized in military oriented research and are accordingly best suited for command and control team research. There is a need to examine what aspects of these test beds could be useful in other types of team research or what limitations must be overcome to expand these existing test beds to research in other team environments. Along the same lines, the development of better team research simulations and test beds is a promising area for future research. Based on the numerous advantages of computer simulation technology, it would be beneficial for researchers to develop and validate simulations specifically designed to examine team processes and performance for various types of teams across a variety of contexts.

One particular type of simulation known as agent-based simulation, in which computer programmed intelligent agents are used to serve in roles that normally would be performed by other human beings, has shown initial promise for use within teams (Nogueira & Raz, 2006). Specifically, work has begun to examine the utility of agent-based technology in a military team context (Heinze et al., 2002; Lewis, Sycara, & Payne, 2003). Agent-based simulations present a very promising advantage for team research because they can potentially reduce the effort and cost of team research and thus allow more significant contributions to the scientific community. For example, team research could use agent-based capabilities to simulate the other team members in a team, effectively allowing team research to be conducted using one participant per simulation. More research is needed to investigate the utility of agent-based capabilities in team research and take advantage of this technology.

Question 9: "Teams of Teams": What's Different about Multiteam Systems?

Chapter 10 in this volume by Leslie DeChurch and John Mathieu introduces the concept of multiteam systems (MTSs) and the core features that may impact the processes and performance of these units. A fairly new concept within team research, an MTS is defined as a set of "two or more teams that interface directly and interdependently ... towards the accomplishment of collective goals" (Marks, DeChurch, Mathieu, Panzer, & Alonso, 2005, p. 964). As the prevalence of teams increases within organizations around the world, these "teams of teams" are quickly becoming the next step in organizational structuring. MTSs are fairly unique arrangements that encompass processes beyond what is apparent at the team level of analysis. Preliminary research has shown that MTSs interact not only at a within-team level but also at a cross-team level (Marks et al., 2005).

While initial researchers have assumed that team-level processes are homologous at the MTS level of inquiry, this may not necessarily be the case. MTSs are complex structures made up of multiple teams aligning goals and actions both vertically and horizontally. This complexity of interaction and coordination may require MTSs to engage in different teamwork processes beyond that of individual teams. Due to the infancy of this topic, existing research has only begun to scratch the surface of this phenomenon. Mathieu, Cobb, Marks, Zaccaro, and Marsch (2004) utilized a PC-based flight simulation known as the Multiteam Air Campaign Effectiveness Simulation (ACES) as a research platform for studying the dynamics of MTSs. Using this platform, DeChurch and Marks (2006) examined the role of leadership in multiteam systems and found that functional leadership is positively related to MTS performance. Besides this, very little else is known regarding MTSs and the unique aspects regarding their processes and performance. This is one of the most untouched avenues for potential team research, and it presents an unparalleled opportunity for furthering the state of science. As the prevalence of MTSs in organizations continues to increase, there is a definite need for more research examining the unique dynamics of multiteam systems.

Question 10: How Can We More Accurately Measure Team-Level Phenomenon?

The science of team measurement has undergone significant growth in the recent years. There have been published volumes devoted to the subject (e.g., Brannick et al., 1997), and numerous tools for the assessment and measurement of team performance have been developed and validated (e.g. Brannick, Prince, Prince, & Salas, 1995; Cooke et al., 2003; Fowlkes, Lane, Salas, Franz, & Oser, 1994; Prince, Ellis, Brannick, & Salas, 2007). Even Chapter 13 by David Dorsey, Steven Russell, Charles Keil, Gwendolyn Campbell, Wendi Van Buskirk, and Peter Schuck and Chapter 14 by Kelley Krokos, David Baker, Alexander Alonso, and Rachel Day in this volume discuss the issue of team measurement. However, the quest for more effective measurement can never be complete. As in any other area of research, due to the ever changing nature of the world and knowledge, there will always be a need for improved team measurement techniques. Baker and Salas (1997) suggested that there are still numerous questions unanswered involving what to measure, when to measure, and how to measure team-level phenomenon.

One area of measurement that merits special attention is that of measuring teams in field settings. Salas, Burke, and Fowlkes (2006) posited that although there has been much learned regarding effective team performance measurement systems over the past few decades, much of this knowledge has not been extended into a field context. What we know about team measurement has primarily taken place in a laboratory setting. Measurement of teams in a lab setting may not necessarily transfer to measurement of teams in the field considering real-world teams exist in complex, context-rich environments. For example, teams in the field may be distributed, multicultural, under an extremely heavy workload, or exposed to any other number of unique situations that make measurement of the team challenging. Considering that not all teams are created equal, the underlying nature and requirements of each particular team dictate the relative importance of the various teamwork dimensions (McIntyre & Salas, 1995). This, in turn, should dictate the development of appropriate measurement tools. It would be advantageous for team researchers to have unobtrusive, real-time, practical measures of team process and performance for use in the field since many existing technologies do not meet these requirements. In such tools, it is important that both team process and team outcomes are captured. The creation of team-level measures should also consider several factors including measurement purpose, included stimuli, targeted competencies, nature of stimuli, and cost concerns (McIntyre & Salas, 1995). There is a need for scientists to focus research efforts on the development of more context-friendly, effective team process and performance measures.

Another area within team research that calls for improved measurement is that of team cognition. For example, shared mental models literature has made numerous calls over the years for research focusing on improved measurement techniques (e.g., Converse, Cannon-Bowers, & Salas, 1991; Klimoski & Mohammed, 1994). Mohammed, Klimoski, and Rentsch (2000) attempted to answer this call by providing a set of measurement standards for group cognition along with evaluating a set of techniques for measuring team mental models. There has also been little research devoted to the development of effective measurement techniques of transactive memory systems (e.g., Lewis, 2003) given the infancy of the topic, and most empirical work looking at transactive memory systems has used some sort of recall measures (Hollingshead, 2001; Moreland, 1999).

Cooke and colleagues have contributed substantially to the literature regarding team cognition measurement, examining the measurement of team knowledge and team situation awareness (e.g., Cooke, Kiekel, & Helm, 2001; Cooke & Salas, 2000; Cooke, Salas, Kiekel, & Bell, 2004; Cooke, Stout & Salas, 2001; Kiekel & Cooke, 2005). However, this type of research needs to be continued, integrated, and extended into other areas, especially within the newer concepts such as transactive memory. More research is needed to investigate the appropriateness of current measures of team cognition as well as to explore new, more effective possibilities. The journey to improve team measurement can never be complete.

Concluding Remarks

The science of teams has generated robust knowledge and understanding about team functioning. The science is now multidisciplinary, theoretically rich, empirically rooted, and seeking deeper insight about team performance. All is well. But, of course, more is needed, and the science must continue to create knowledge that is cumulative, robust, and applicable to teams, groups, and collectives. This chapter (and hopefully this volume) will motivate more, better, deeper, and dynamic research.

References

Alavi, S. & McCormick, J. (2007). Measurement of vertical and horizontal idiocentrism and allocentrism in small groups. *Small Group Research, 38,* 556–564.

Baker, D. P. & Salas, E. (1997). Principles for measuring teamwork: A summary and look toward the future. In M. T. Brannick, E. Salas, & C. Prince (Eds.), *Team performance assessment and measurement: Theory, methods, and applications* (pp.331–356). Mahwah, NJ: Lawrence Erlbaum Associates.

Banker, R. D., Field, J. M., Schroeder, R. G., & Sinha, K. K. (1996). Impact of work teams on manufacturing performance: A longitudinal study. *Academy of Management Journal, 39,* 867–890.

Bell, S. T. (2007). Deep-level composition variables as predictors of team performance: A meta-analysis. *Journal of Applied Psychology, 92,* 595–615.

Bierhals, R., Schuster, I., Kohler, P., & Badke-Schaub, P. (2007). Shared mental models—linking team cognition and performance. *CoDesign, 3,* 75–94.

Bowers, C. A., Braun, C. C., & Morgan, B. B. (1997). Team workload: Its meaning and measurement. In M. T. Brannick, E. Salas, & C. Prince (Eds.), *Team performance assessment and measurement: Theory, methods, and applications* (pp. 85–108). Mahwah, NJ: Lawrence Erlbaum Associates Publishers.

Brannick, M. T., Prince, A., Prince, C., & Salas, E. (1995). The measurement of team process. *Human Factors, 37,* 641–651.

Brannick, M. T., Salas, E., & Prince, C. (1997). *Team performance assessment and measurement: theory, methods, and applications.* Mahwah, NJ: Lawrence Erlbaum Associates.

Brett, J., Behfar, K., & Kern, M. C. (2006). Managing multicultural teams. *Harvard Business Review, 84,* 84–91.

Burke, C. S., Hess, K., & Salas, E. (2006). Building the adaptive capacity to lead multicultural teams. In C. S. Burke, L. Pierce, & E. Salas (Eds.), *Advances in human performance and cognitive engineering research* (pp. 175–211). Oxford, England: Elsevier Science.

Burke, C. S., Priest, H. A., Upshaw, C. L., Salas, E., & Pierce, L. (in press). A sense-making approach to understanding multicultural teams: An initial framework. In D. I. Stone & E. F. Stone-Romero (Eds.), *Cultural diversity and human resource practices*. Mahwah, NJ: Lawrence Erlbaum Associates.

Burke, C. S., Stagl, K. C., Salas, E., Pierce, L., & Kendall, D. L. (2006). Understanding team adaptation: A conceptual analysis and model. *Journal of Applied Psychology, 91*, 1189–1207.

Campion, M. A., Medsker, G. J., & Higgs, A. C. (1993). Relations between work group characteristics and effectiveness: Implications for designing effective work groups. *Personnel Psychology, 46*, 823–850.

Cannon, M. D. & Edmondson, A. C. (2001). Confronting failure: Antecedents and consequences of shared beliefs about failure of organizational work groups. *Journal of Organizational Behavior, 22*, 161–177.

Cannon-Bowers, J. A. (2007). Fostering mental model convergence through training. In F. Dansereau & F. Yammarino (Eds.), *Multi-level issues in organizations and time* (pp. 149–157). San Diego, CA: Elsevier.

Cannon-Bowers, J. A. & Salas, E. (1998). *Making decisions under stress: implications for individual and team learning*. Washington, DC: American Psychological Association.

Cannon-Bowers, J., Salas, E., & Converse, S. (1993). Shared mental models in expert team decision making. In N. J. Castellan, Jr. (Ed.), *Individual and group decision making: Current issues* (pp. 221–246). Hillsdale, NJ: Lawrence Erlbaum Associates.

Connaughton, S. & Shuffler, M. (2007). Multinational and multicultural distributed teams. *Small Group Research, 38*, 387–412.

Converse, S. A., Cannon-Bowers, J. A., & Salas, E. (1991). Team member shared mental models: A theory and some methodological issues. In *Proceedings of the 35th Annual Human Factors Meeting* (pp. 1417–1421). San Francisco, CA.

Cooke, N., Kiekel, P. A., & Helm, E. (2001). Measuring team knowledge during skill acquisition of a complex task. *International Journal of Cognitive Ergonomics, 5*, 297–315.

Cooke, N. J., Kiekel, P. A., Salas, E., Stout, R., Bowers, C., & Cannon-Bowers, J. (2003). Measuring team knowledge: A window to the cognitive underpinnings of team performance. *Group Dynamics: Theory, Research, and Practice, 7*, 179–199.

Cooke, N. A. & Salas, E. (2000). Measuring team knowledge. *Human Factors, 42*, 151.

Cooke, N. A., Salas, E., Kiekel, P. A., & Bell, B. (2004). Advances in measuring team cognition. In E. Salas & S. M. Fiore (Eds.), *Team cognition: Understanding the factors that drive process and performance* (pp. 83–106). Washington, DC: American Psychological Association.

Cooke, N. A., Stout, R., & Salas, E. (2001). A knowledge elicitation approach to the measurement of team situation awareness. In M. McNeese, E. Salas, & M. Endsley (Eds.), *New trends in cooperative activities: Understanding system dynamics in complex environments* (pp. 114–139). Santa Monica, CA: Human Factors and Ergonomics Society.

DeChurch, L. A. & Marks, M. A. (2006). Leadership in multiteam systems. *Journal of Applied Psychology, 91*, 311–329.

Devine, D. (2002). A review and integration of classification systems relevant to teams in organizations. *Group Dynamics: Theory, Research, and Practice, 6*, 291–310.

Dickinson, T. L. & McIntyre, R. M. (1997). A conceptual framework for teamwork measurement. In M. T. Brannick, E. Salas, & C. Prince (Eds.), *Team performance assessment and measurement: Theory, methods, and applications* (pp. 19–43). Mahwah, NJ: Lawrence Erlbaum Associates Publishers.

Drach-Zahavy, A. & Somech, A. (2001). Understanding team innovation: The role of team processes and structures. *Group Dynamics: Theory, Research, and Practice, 5,* 111–123.

Driskell, J. E., Goodwin, G. F., Salas, E., & O'Shea, P. G. (2006). What makes a good team player? Personality and team effectiveness. *Group Dynamics: Theory, Research, and Practice, 10,* 249–271.

Driskell, J. E., Salas, E., & Johnston, J. H. (1999). Does stress lead to a loss of team perspective? *Group Dynamics, 3,* 291–302.

Edwards, B. D., Day, E. A., Arthur, W., & Bell, S. T. (2006). Relationships among team ability composition, team mental models, and team performance. *Journal of Applied Psychology, 91,* 727–736.

Ensley, M. D. & Pearce, C. L. (2001). Shared cognition in top management teams: Implications for new venture performance. *Journal of Organizational Behavior, 22,* 145–160.

Espinosa, J. A., DeLone, W., & Lee, G. (2006). Global boundaries, task processes and IS project success: A field study. *Information Technology & People, 19,* 345–370.

Espinosa, J. A., Slaughter, S. A., Kraut, R. E., & Herbsleb, J. D. (2007). Team knowledge and coordination in geographically distributed software development. *Journal of Management Information Systems, 24,* 135–169.

Euwema, M. C., Wendt, H., & van Emmerik, H. (2007). Leadership styles and group organizational citizenship behavior across cultures. *Journal of Organizational Behavior, 28,* 1035–1057.

Fleishman, E. A. & Quaintance, M. K. (1984). *Taxonomies of human performance: The description of human tasks.* Orlando FL: Academic Press.

Fleishman, E. A. & Zaccaro, S. J. (1992). Toward a taxonomy of team performance functions. In R. W. Swezey & E. Salas (Eds.), *Teams: Their training and performance* (pp. 31–56). Westport, CT: Albex Publishing.

Fowlkes, J. E., Lane, N. E., Salas, E., Franz, T., & Oser, R. (1994). Improving the measurement of team performance: The targets methodology. *Military Psychology, 6,* 47–61.

Gersick, C. J. G. (1988). Time and transition in work teams: Toward a new model of group development. *Academy of Management Journal, 31,* 9–41.

Gibson, C. B. (2001). From knowledge accumulation to accommodation: Cycles of collective cognition in work groups. *Journal of Organizational Behavior, 22,* 121–134.

Gibson, C. B. & Zellmer-Bruhn, M. E. (2002). Minding your metaphors: Applying the concept of teamwork metaphors to the management of teams in multicultural contexts. *Organizational Dynamics, 31,* 101–116.

Gladstein, D. L. (1984). Groups in context: A model of task group effectiveness. *Administrative Science Quarterly, 29,* 499–517.

Gorman, J. C., Cooke, N. J., & Winner, J. L. (2006). Measuring team situation awareness in decentralized command and control environments. *Ergonomics, 49,* 1312–1325.

Guzzo, R. A. & Dickson, M. W. (1996). Teams in organizations: Recent research on performance and effectiveness. *Annual Review of Psychology, 47*, 307–338.

Hackman, J. R. (1987). The design of work teams. In J. Lorsch (Ed.), *Handbook of organizational behavior* (pp. 315–342). Englewood Cliffs, NJ: Prentice-Hall.

Hackman, J. R. & Wageman, R. (2005). A theory of team coaching. *Academy of Management Review, 30*(2), 269–287.

Halfhill, T., Nielsen, T. M., Sundstrom, E., & Weilbaecher, A. (2005). Group personality composition and performance in military service teams. *Military Psychology, 17*, 41–54.

Hall, E. T. & Hall, M. R. (1990). *Understanding cultural differences: Germans, French, and Americans.* Garden City, NY: Intercultural Press.

Hardin, A., Fuller, M., & Davison, R. (2007). I know I can, but can we? Culture and efficacy beliefs in global virtual teams. *Small Group Research, 38*, 130–155.

Harrison, D. A., Mohammed, S., McGrath, J. E., Florey, A. T., & Vanderstoep, S. W. (2003). Time matters in team performance: Effects of member familiarity, entrainment, and task discontinuity on speed and quality. *Personnel Psychology, 56*, 633–669.

Heinze, C., Goss, S., Josefsson, T., Bennett, K., Waugh, S., Lloyd, I., et al. (2002). Interchanging agents and humans in military simulation. *Artificial Intelligence Magazine, 23*, 37–47.

Hofstede, G. (1980). Culture and organizations. *International Studies of Management & Organization, 10*(4), 15–41.

Holland, K. (2007, April 22). How diversity makes a team click. *New York Times, 156*, 16–16.

Hollingshead, A. (2001). Cognitive interdependence and convergent expectations in transactive memory. *Journal of Personality and Social Psychology, 81*, 1080–1089.

Ilies, R., Wagner, D. T., & Morgeson, F. P. (2007). Explaining affective linkages in teams: Individual differences in susceptibility to contagion and individualism-collectivism. *Journal of Applied Psychology, 92*, 1140–1148.

Keller, R. T. (2006). Transformational leadership, initiating structure, and substitutes for leadership: A longitudinal study of research and development project team performance. *Journal of Applied Psychology, 91*, 202–210.

Kiekel, P. A. & Cooke, N. J. (2005). Human factors aspects of team cognition. In R. W. Proctor & K. L. Vu (Eds.), *Handbook of human factors in web design* (pp. 90–103). Mahwah, NJ: Lawrence Erlbaum Associates Publishers.

Kleinman, D. L. & Serfaty, D. (1989). Team performance assessment in distributed decision making. In R. Gilson, J. P. Kincaid, & B. Godiez (Eds.), *Proceedings: Interactive Networked Simulation for Training Conference* (pp. 22–27). Orlando, FL: Institute for Simulation and Training.

Klimoski, R. & Mohammed, S. (1994). Team mental model: Construct or metaphor? *Journal of Management, 20*, 403–437.

Kozlowski, S. W. J., Gully, S. M., Nason, E. R., & Smith, E. M. (1999). Developing adaptive teams: A theory of compilation and performance across levels and time. In D. R. Ilgen & E. D. Pulakos (Eds.), *The changing nature of performance: Implications for staffing, motivation, and development* (pp. 240–292). San Francisco, CA: Jossey-Bass.

LePine, J. A. (2003). Team adaptation and postchange performance: Effects of team composition in terms of members' cognitive ability and personality. *Journal of Applied Psychology, 88*, 27–39.

LePine, J. A. (2005). Adaptation of teams in response to unforeseen change: Effects of goal difficulty and team composition in terms of cognitive ability and goal orientation. *Journal of Applied Psychology, 90*, 1153–1167.

Levesque, L. L., Wilson, J. M., & Wholey, D. R. (2001). Cognitive divergence and shared mental models in software development project teams. *Journal of Organizational Behavior, 22*, 135–144.

Lewis, K. (2003). Measuring transactive memory systems in the field: Scale development and validation. *Journal of Applied Psychology, 88*, 587–604.

Lewis, M., Sycara, K., & Payne, T. (2003). Agent roles in human teams. In *AAMAS-03 Workshop on Humans and Multi-Agent Systems*, Melbourne, Australia, July 14.

Liang, D. W., Moreland, R., & Argote, L. (1995). Group versus individual training and group performance: The mediating factor of transactive memory. *Personality and Social Psychology Bulletin, 21*, 384–393.

Lim, B. & Klein, K. J. (2006). Team mental models and team performance: A field study of the effects of team mental model similarity and accuracy. *Journal of Organizational Behavior, 27*, 403–418.

MacMillan, J., Entin, E. B., Hess, K. P., & Paley, M. J. (2004). Measuring performance in a scaled-world: Lessons learned from the Distributed Dynamic Decision-making (DDD) synthetic team task. In E. Salas (Ed.), *Scaled worlds: Developments, validation, and applications* (pp. 154–180). Burlington, VT: Ashgate.

Marks, M. A. (2000). A critical analysis of computer simulations for conducting team research. *Small Group Research, 31*, 653–675.

Marks, M. A., DeChurch, L. A., Mathieu, J. E., Panzer, F. J., & Alonso, A. (2005). Teamwork in multiteam systems. *Journal of Applied Psychology, 90*, 964–971.

Marks, M. A., Mathieu, J. E., & Zaccaro, S. J. (2001). A temporally based framework and taxonomy of team processes. *Academy of Management Review, 26*, 356–376.

Marks, M. A., Zaccaro, S. J., & Mathieu, J. E. (2000). Performance implicatons of leader briefings and team-interaction training for team adaptation to novel environments. *Journal of Organizational Behavior, 22*, 89–106.

Mateev, A. V. & Milter, R. G. (2004). The value of intercultural competence for performance of multicultural teams. *Team Performance Management, 10*, 104–111.

Mathieu, J. E., Cobb, M. G., Marks, M. A., Zaccaro, S. J., & Marsch, S. (2004). Multiteam ACES: A low-fidelity platform for studying multiteam systems. In E. Salas (Ed.), *Scaled worlds: Developments, validation, and applications* (pp. 297–315). Burlington, VT: Ashgate.

Mathieu, J. E., Heffner, T. S., Goodwin, G. F., Salas, E., & Cannon-Bowers, J. A. (2000). The influence of shared mental models on team process and performance. *Journal of Applied Psychology, 85*, 273–283.

McComb, S. A. (2007). Mental model convergence: The shift from being from being an individual to be a team member. In F. Dansereau & F. Yammarino, (Eds.), *Multi-level issues in organizations and time* (pp. 95–147). San Diego, CA: Elsevier.

McGlynn, R. P., Sutton, J. L., Sprague, V. L., Demski, R. M., and Pierce, L. G. (1997). *Development of a team performance task battery to evaluate the command and control vehicle (C2V) crew.* U.S. Army Research Laboratory, Aberdeen Proving Ground, MD (Contract DAAL01-96-P-0875).

McGrath, J. E. (1991). Time, interaction, and performance (TIP): A theory of groups. *Small Group Research, 22,* 147–174.

McGrath, J. E. (2000). Time matters in groups. In J. Galegher, R. E. Kraut, & C. Egido (Eds.), *Intellectual teamwork* (pp. 23–61). Hillsdale, NJ: Lawrence Erlbaum Associates.

McIntyre, R. M. & Salas, E. (1995). Measuring and managing for team performance: Emerging principles from complex environments. In R. Guzzo & E. Salas (Eds.), *Team effectiveness and decision making in organizations* (pp. 149–203). San Francisco, CA: Jossey-Bass.

Minionis, D. P., Zaccaro, S. J., & Perez, R. (1995). Shared mental models, team coordination, and team performance. In J. Mathieu (Chair), *Mental models and team effectiveness: Three empirical tests.* Symposium presented to the 10th annual conference of the Society for Industrial/Organizational Psychology, Orlando, FL.

Mohammed, S. & Dunville, B. C. (2001). Team mental models in a team knowledge framework: Expanding theory and measurement across disciplinary boundaries. *Journal of Organizational Behavior, 22,* 89–106.

Mohammed, S., Klimoski, R., & Rentsch, J. R (2000). The measurement of team mental models: We have no shared schema. *Organizational Research Methods, 3*(2), 123–165.

Moreland, R. (1999). Transactive memory: Learning who knows what in work groups and organizations. In L. L. Thompson, J. M. Levine, & D. M. Messick (Eds.), *Shared cognition in organizations: The management of knowledge.* Mahwah, NJ: Lawrence Erlbaum Associates Publishers.

Morgan, B. B., Jr., Glickman, A. S., Woodard, E. A., Blaiwes, A. S., & Salas, E. (1986). *Measurement of team behaviors in a Navy environment* (Technical Report 86-014). Orlando, FL: Naval Training Systems Center.

Naylor, J. C. & Dickson, T. L. (1969). Task structure, work structure, and team performance. *Journal of Applied Psychology, 53,* 167–177.

Nogueira, J. C. & Raz, T. (2006). Structure and flexibility of project teams under turbulent environments: An application of agent-based simulation. *Project Management Journal, 37*(2), 5–10.

Pearce, C. L., Gallagher, C. A., & Ensley, M. D. (2002). Confidence at the group level of analysis: A longitudinal investigation of the relationship between potency and team effectiveness. *Journal of Occupational and Organizational Psychology, 75,* 115–119.

Pearce, C. L. & Sims, H. P. (2002). Vertical versus shared leadership as predictors of the effectiveness of change management teams: An examination of aversive, directive, transactional, transformational, and empowering leader behaviors. *Group Dynamics: Theory, Research, and Practice, 6,* 172–197.

Prince, C., Ellis, E., Brannick, M. T., & Salas, E. (2007). Measurement of team situation awareness in low experience level aviators. *International Journal of Aviation Psychology, 17,* 41–57.

Rentsch, J. R. & Klimoski, R. J. (2001). Why do 'great minds' think alike?: Antecedents of team member schema agreement. *Journal of Organizational Behavior, 22,* 107–120.

Rentsch, J. R. & Small, E. E. (2007). Understanding team cognition: The shift to cognitive similarity configurations. In F. Dansereau & F. Yammarino (Eds.), *Multilevel issues in organizations and time* (pp. 159–174). San Diego, CA: Elsevier.

Rico, R., Sanchez-Manzanares, M., Gil, R., & Gibson, C. (2008). Team implicit coordination processes: a team knowledge-based approach. *Academy of Management Review, 33,* 163–194.

Salas, E., Burke, C. S., & Fowlkes, J. E. (2006). Measuring team performance "in the wild": Challenges and tips. In W. Bennett, C. Lance, & D. Woehr (Eds.), *Performance measurement: Current perspectives and future challenges.* Mahwah, NJ: Lawrence Erlbaum Associates.

Salas, E., Burke, C. S., Wilson-Donnelly, K. A., & Fowlkes, J. E. (2004). Promoting effective leadership within multi-cultural teams: An event-based approach. In D. Day, S. J. Zaccaro, & S. M. Halpin (Eds.), *Leader development for transforming organizations: Growing leaders for tomorrow* (pp. 293–323). Mahwah, NJ: Lawrence Erlbaum Associates, Inc.

Salas, E., Dickinson, T. L., Converse, S. A., & Tannenbaum, S. I. (1992). Toward an understanding of team performance and training. In R. J. Swezey & E. Salas (Eds.), *Teams: Their training and performance* (pp. 3–29). Norwood, NJ: Ablex.

Salas, E. & Fiore, S. M. (2004). *Team cognition: Understanding the factors that drive process and performance.* Washington, DC: American Psychological Association.

Salas, E., Sims, D. E., & Burke, C. S. (2005). Is there "big five" in teamwork? *Small Group Research, 36*(5), 555–599.

Salas, E., Sims, D. E., & Klein, C. (2004). Cooperation at work. In C. D. Speilberger (Ed.), *Encyclopedia of applied psychology* (Vol. 1, pp. 497–505). San Diego, CA: Academic Press.

Salas, E., Stagl, K., & Burke, C. S. (2004). 25 years of team effectiveness in organizations: Research themes and emerging needs. In C. L. Cooper & I. T. Robertson (Eds.), *International review of industrial and organizational psychology* (Vol. 19, pp. 47–91). New York: John Wiley & Sons.

Salas, E., Stagl, K. C., Burke, C. S., & Goodwin, G. F. (2007). Fostering team effectiveness in organizations: Toward an integrative theoretical framework of team performance. In J. W. Shuart, W. Spaulding, & J. Poland, (Eds.), *Modeling complex systems: Motivation, cognition and social processes, Nebraska Symposium on Motivation, 51* (pp. 185–243) Lincoln: University of Nebraska Press.

Salk, J. E. & Brannen, M. Y. (2000). National culture, networks, and individual influence in a multinational management team. *Academy of Management Journal, 43,* 191–202.

Schwartz, S. H. (1999). A theory of cultural values and some implications for work. *Applied Psychology: An International Review, 48,* 23–47.

Song, A. A. & Kleinman, D. L. (1994). A distributed simulation system for team decisionmaking. In *Proceedings of the Fifth Annual Conference on AI and Planning in High Autonomy Systems,* 129–135.

Smith-Jentsch, K. A., Campbell, G. E., Milanovich, D. M., & Reynolds, A. M. (2001). Measuring teamwork mental models to support training needs assessment, development, and evaluation: Two empirical studies. *Journal of Organizational Behavior, 22,* 179–194.

Sundstrom, E., de Meuse, K. P., & Futrell, D. (1990). Work teams: Applications and effectiveness. *American Psychologist, 45,* 120–133.

Sutton, J. L., Pierce, L., Burke, C. S., & Salas, E. (2006). Cultural adaptability. In C. S. Burke, L. Pierce, & E. Salas (Eds.), *Advances in human performance and cognitive engineering research* (pp. 143–173). Oxford, England: Elsevier Science.

Symons, J. & Stenzel, C. (2007). Virtually borderless: an examination of culture in virtual teaming. *Journal of General Management, 32,* 1–17.

Tasa, K., Taggar, S., & Seijts, G. H. (2007). The development of collective efficacy in teams: A multilevel and longitudinal perspective. *Journal of Applied Psychology, 92,* 17–27.

Thamhain, H. J. (2004). Team leadership effectiveness in technology-based project environments. *Project Management Journal, 35*(4), 35–46.

Triandis, H. C. (1989). The self and social behavior in different cultural contexts. *Psychological Review, 96,* 506–520.

Witkin, H. A. & Berry, J. W. (1975). Psychological differentiation in cross-cultural perspective. *Journal of Cross-Cultural Psychology, 6,* 4–87.

Wegner, D. M. (1995). A computer network model of human transactive memory. *Social Cognition, 13,* 319–339.

Yeh, E., Smith, C., Jennings, C., & Castro, N. (2006). Team building: A 3-dimensional teamwork model. *Team Performance Management, 12*(5/6), 192–197.

Author Index

Subject Index

E

F